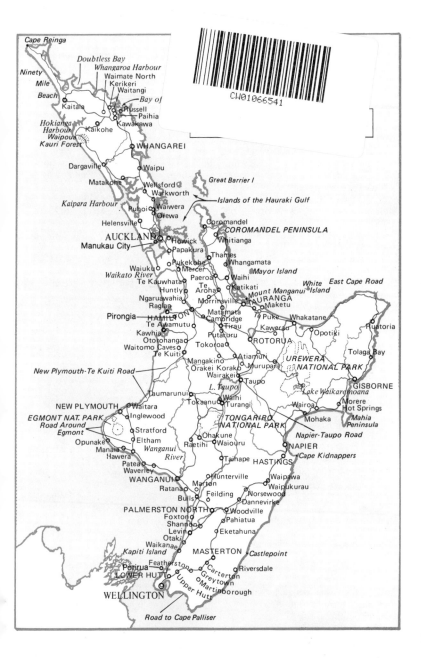

Where a place is without an individual entry, or a person or an event is discussed in greater detail elsewhere, the reference may be given (*see pp. xx*), (*see △ Katikati*), referring the reader to an entry in the Alphabetical Section, or (*see index*).

Starring system: Places and things to see and do have been graded thus:
★★★: worth a journey ★★: worth a detour
★: interesting no star: see if possible
These are necessarily subjective assessments, and serve only to guide travellers who are unfamiliar with an area as to the relative strengths of competing claims for their attention.

Accommodation: Because of the constantly changing nature of New Zealand's tourist and accommodation industry, details of hotels, motels and camping grounds have not been included. Readers are referred to the annual publications of the New Zealand Automobile Association.

Visitor Centres: Where a place has a Visitor or Information Centre, its address and telephone number are given. These offices generally provide free information on what there is to see and do, will attempt to answer queries of any description and will frequently assist in locating and booking accommodation and in arranging local tours.

OVERSEAS VISITORS

THIS BOOK is as much for New Zealanders travelling within their own country as it is for overseas visitors. It suffices here to note that the country is slightly larger than the United Kingdom, about the size of Italy or half of that of France. Its area equals that of the state of Colorado. The population totals some 3.4 million, of which some 322,000 are Maori and about 125,000 Pacific Islanders.

The country lies in the temperate zone of the South Pacific about 2,250 kilometres south-east of Australia. The "four main centres", Auckland, Wellington, Christchurch and Dunedin, are evenly spaced along the country's 1,600-kilometre length.

Information on such matters as visas, currency, health requirements, travel and up-to-the-minute details of package tours (including special interest and adventure tours) is available free of charge from travel offices within New Zealand and from New Zealand Tourism Board offices at:

Sydney: Level 8, 35 Pitt St, NSW 2000; tel. (02) 247-3111; fax (02) 241-1136

Melbourne: Level 19, Como Office Tower, 644 Chapel St, PO Box 414, South Yarra, Victoria 3141; tel. (03) 823-6283; fax (03) 823-6276

Brisbane: Level 11, 145 Eagle St, Brisbane, Queensland 4000; tel. (07) 831-8315; fax (07) 831-5337

Los Angeles: 501 Santa Monica Blv #300, Santa Monica, CA 90401; tel. 1-800-388-5494

New York: 780 3rd Avenue, Suite 1904, New York, NY 10017-2024; tel. (0212) 832-8482; fax (0212) 832-7602

Chicago: 1111 North Dearbord St, Suite 2705, Chicago, Illinois 60610; tel. (0312) 440-1345; fax (0312) 440-3808

Vancouver: Suite 1200, 888 Dunsmuir St., Vancouver BC V6C 3K4; tel. (0604) 684-2117; fax (0604) 684-1265

London: New Zealand House, Haymarket, SW1Y 4TQ; tel. (0171) 973-0363; fax (0171) 839-8929

Frankfurt: Friedrichstrasse 10-12, 60323 Frankfurt am Main, Germany; tel. (069) 971-211(0); fax (069) 971-21113

Singapore: 391 Orchard Rd, #15-01 Ngee Ann City, 15th fl., Tower A, Singapore 0923; tel. (65) 738-5844; fax (65) 235-2550

Tokyo: NZ Embassy Annex, 2nd Floor, Toho Twin Tower Building, 1-5-2 Yurakucho Chiyoda-ku, Tokyo 100; tel. (03) 3508-9981; fax (03) 3501-2326

Osaka: Meiji Seimei Sakaisuji Homachi Building, 2nd floor, 1-7-15 Minami Honmachi, Chuo ku, Osaka-shi 541; tel. (06) 268-8335; fax (06) 268-8412

Seoul: Room 1608, Sunwha Building, 5-2 Sunwha-dong, Chung-ku, Seoul; tel. (02) 777-9282; fax (02) 777-9285

Taipei: Room 1512, 25F International Trade Building, 333 Keelung Road, Section 1, Taipei 10548; tel. (062) 757-9514; fax (062) 757-6114

Hong Kong: 3414 Connaught Centre, Connaught Rd, Central Hong Kong; tel. (852) 526-0141

Head Office: PO Box 95, Wellington, New Zealand

Published by Reed Books, a division of Reed Publishing (NZ) Ltd, 39 Rawene Road, Birkenhead, Auckland. Associated companies, branches and representatives throughout the world.

ISBN 0 7900 0436 4

First published 1973
Second impression 1973
Revised edition 1975
Third edition revised 1977–78
Fourth edition revised 1979–80
Fifth edition fully revised 1984
Reprinted with revisions 1986, 1987
Sixth edition fully revised 1990
Seventh edition revised 1991, 1992
Eighth edition fully revised 1993
Ninth edition fully revised 1996, Reprinted 1997

Printed in Singapore by KHL Printing Co Ltd.

Mobil
New Zealand
Travel Guide

North Island

Diana and Jeremy Pope
with illustrations by Karen Beck

REED

Contents

Acknowledgements

We are greatly indebted to a large number of individuals, government departments, historical societies, Visitor Information Centres, and staff of the Alexander Turnbull Library and of the New Zealand Historic Places Trust, both in respect of preparing the original *Guide* and of subsequent revisions. Special thanks are due to staff of the Department of Conservation across the country. The late Norman Forest spent many hours in helping to design the original format.

Particular thanks are extended, among others, to Susan Brierley, Alison Southby, Chris Lipscombe, Jenny Smith and the indefatigable Hugh Rennie. We are also indebted to Pat Adams, Sheila Williams, Lesley and Laurie Powell, Darea Sherratt, Rodney Lewington, Jill Tasker, Keith Legg, Alex Armour, Nick Miles, Adam Pope, A.M. Isdale, Alison Rothschild, Aran Ebbett, Barry and Margaret Exton, Betty Tasker, Bob Walker, Brian Cotter, Bruce Young, C.F. Kingston, Cam Sycamore, Cecil Badley, Cheryl Lee, Claire Melrose, D.N. Campbell, D.R. Williams D.W. Cimino, David Hoskins, Dianne Chester, Doreen McLeod, Elaine Tapsell, Gail Troughton, George Livingston Baker, Gerald Weekes, Geraldine Martell, Gill Fish, Gillian Munro, Glenys Mullooly, Graham Dearsly, Helen Watson, Hilda McDonnell. Ian Rockel, J. Lundy, J.F. Mandeno, Jack Lee, Jackie McGill, Jan Seabrook, Jane Flavell, Jocelyn Brown, John Ombler, Joy M. Plowright, Julie Lander, K.A.Challenger, Lisa Pittar, M.D. Sterling, M.J. Gardiner, Major R.P. Withers, Margaret Cooper, Margaret Davy, Mel Trounson, Michelle Terry, Mrs D.L. Moroney, Mrs Mary Small, Nick Davies, Noela Stevens, P.L. Dimond, Pamela Ryder, Pip Winiata, R.E. Lambert, Rev. G. Dempsey, Roger Mulvay, Lee-Anne Edwards, Stephen Edson, Tony Kirby, Turi Ducommun and Vivian Morris.

To each of these, and many more, the authors are extremely grateful.

The authors are also appreciative of the assistance given by the Department of Statistics. The publishers would like to thank the Department of Survey and Land Information for permission to reproduce the maps, under map licence L&S 1978/12.

Diana and Jeremy Pope, 1995

INTRODUCTION

THE MAORI GENESIS

IN POLYNESIAN MYTHOLOGY, people, the elements and every aspect of nature are descended from the one primal pair, the Sky Father and the Earth Mother. It was for this reason that the ancient Maori identified themselves so closely with nature. Before felling a tree (so slaying a child of Tane Mahuta, god of the forest) they would placate the spirits; searching for food they would not speak of their purpose for fear that the prey might hear and make good its escape.

In the beginning there was only the darkness, Te Ponui, Te Poroa (the Great Night, the Long Night). At last, in the void of empty space, a glow appeared, the moon and the sun sprang forth and the heavens were made light. Then did Rangi (the Sky Father) live with Papa (the Earth Mother), but as the two clung together their offspring lived in darkness. The Sky lay upon the Earth, and light had not yet come between them.

Their children were vexed that they could not see, and argued among themselves as to how night and day might be made manifest. The fierce Tumatauenga (god of war) urged that they kill their parents, but Tane Mahuta (god of the forests) counselled that they separate their father Rangi from their mother Papa and in that way achieve their object. Tane's wisdom prevailed, and in turn each of the children struggled mightily to prise the Sky from the Earth. Rongo (god of cultivated food) and Tangaroa (god of the sea) did all they could, and the belligerent Tumatauenga cut and hacked. But to no avail. Finally it was Tane Mahuta who by thrusting with his mighty feet gradually lifted the anguished Rangi away from the agonised Papa. So was night distinguished from day.

Heartbroken, Rangi shed an immense quantity of tears, so much so that the oceans were formed. Tawhiri (god of wind and storm), who had opposed his brothers in the venture, was fearful that Papa would become too beautiful, and followed his father to the realm above. From there he swept down in fury to lash the trees of Tane Mahuta until, uprooted, they fell in disarray. Tawhiri then turned his rage on Tangaroa (god of the sea) who sought refuge in the depths of the ocean. But as Tangaroa fled his many grandchildren were confused, and while the fish made for the seas with him, the lizards and reptiles hid among rocks and the battered forests. It was then for Tangaroa to feel anger. His grandchildren had deserted him and were sheltering in the forests. So it is that to this day the sea is eating into the land, slowly eroding it and hoping that in time the forests will fall and Tangaroa will be reunited with his offspring.

The creation of woman: When the participants lay exhausted and peace at last descended, Tane Mahuta fashioned from clay the body of a woman, and breathed life into her nostrils. She became Hine-hauone ("the Earth-formed Maid") and bore Tane Mahuta a daughter, Hine-titama ("the Dawn Maid") who in time also bore daughters to Tane.

But Hine-titama had been unaware of her father's identity, and when she found he was the Tane she thought was her husband, she was overwhelmed with shame. She left the world of light, Te Ao, and moved to Te Po, the world below, where she became known as Hinenui-te-Po ("Great Hine the Night").

The children of Tane were plentiful, and increased and multiplied, for death held no dominion over them.

THE MAUI CYCLE

The birth of Maui: Maui, fifth of his parents' sons, was born so premature, so frail and so underdeveloped that he could not possibly have survived. So his mother, Taranga, wrapped the foetus in a knot of her hair and threw it into the sea—hence Maui's full name of Maui-tikitiki-a-Taranga ("Maui, the topknot of Taranga"). For certain he would have died, but the gods intervened and Rangi, the Sky Father, nursed him through infancy.

As a grown child, Maui returned to confront his bewildered mother and to amaze his family with feats of magic.

The snaring of the sun: Not surprisingly, Maui's four brothers were jealous of the favouritism shown him by their mother Taranga, but when he offered to slow down the sun so that the days would be longer and they would all have more time to find food, they agreed to help.

Carrying the enchanted jawbone of his grandmother, Maui led his brothers eastwards, to the edge of the pit from which the sun rises each morning. There, as it rose, the brothers snared the sun with huge plaited flax ropes. As they held it still, Maui with the enchanted jawbone cruelly smashed the sun's face time and time again, until it was so feeble that it could but creep across the sky—and continues so to do to this very day.

The Fish of Maui: Maui's brothers, weary of seeing their younger brother catch fish by the kitful when they could barely hook enough to feed their families, usually tried to leave him behind when they went fishing. But their wives complained to Maui of a lack of fish, so he promised them a catch so large they would be unable to finish it before it went bad.

To make good his boast Maui carefully prepared a special fishhook which he pointed with a chip from the magic jawbone, and then hid under the flooring mats of his brothers' fishing canoe.

At dawn the brothers silently set sail, thinking they had managed to leave their brother behind, and only when they were well out to sea did Maui emerge. The brothers were furious, but it was too late to turn back. After they had fished in vain, Maui suggested that they sail until well out of sight of land, where they would catch as many fish as the canoe could carry. The dispirited brothers were easily persuaded, and Maui's prediction came true. But even when the canoe was so overladen with fish that it was taking on water and the brothers were ready to set sail for home, Maui produced his own hook and line and against their protests insisted on throwing it out. For bait, he struck his nose until it bled and smeared the hook with his own blood. As Maui began to chant a spell "for the drawing up of the world" the line went taut. Though the canoe lurched over and was close to sinking, Maui grimly hauled all the harder and his terrified brothers bailed the more furiously.

At last Maui's catch was dragged to the surface and they all gazed in wonder. For Maui's hook had caught in the gable of the whare runanga (meeting house) of Tonganui (Great South) and with it had come the vast wedge of land now called the North Island of New Zealand, called by the Maori Te Ika a Maui, "the Fish of Maui".

Such an immense fish was indeed tapu (sacred) and Maui hastily returned to his island home for a tohunga (priest) to lift the tapu. Though he bade them wait till he return before they cut up the fish, Maui's brothers began to scale and eat the fish as soon as he was gone — a sacrilege that angered the gods and caused the fish to writhe and lash about. For this reason much of the North Island is mountainous; had Maui's counsel been followed the whole island today would have been level.

In mythology the feat of Maui in providing land ranks only after the separation of Earth and Sky in the story of creation. According to some tribes not only is the North Island the "Fish of Maui" but the South Island is the canoe from which the gigantic catch was made and Stewart Island its anchor-stone. Maui's fishhook is Cape Kidnappers in Hawke's Bay, once known as Te Matau a Maui, "Maui's fishhook".

Throughout Polynesia the Maui myths are recounted and the claim is made by other islands that Maui fished them from the deep. This supports the theory that Maui may have been an early voyager, a creator-discoverer, who seemed to fish up new land as it slowly appeared above the horizon.

Maui tries to conquer death: Maui's final feat was to try to win immortality for mankind. Had not Maui tamed the sun? Could he not also tame the night of death? With an expedition, Maui set out to the west, to the place where Hinenui-te-Po, the goddess of death, lay asleep. To accomplish his aim, Maui was to enter her womb, travel through her body and emerge from her mouth. If he succeeded death would never have dominion over humans. With the bird who went with him Maui discussed the plans for his most daring feat, for which he would take on the form of a caterpillar, his magic jawbone making such transformation possible. But the sight of Maui as a caterpillar inching his way over Hine's thigh as she lay sleeping was altogether too much for the little tiwakawaka (fantail), who could not restrain a chirrup of delight. With a start Hine awoke, realised the plan and crushed the helpless Maui between her thighs.

So died Maui-tikitiki-a-Taranga, and so death remained in the world for ever more.

THE COMING OF THE POLYNESIAN

Origin of the Polynesian: Linguistic and archaeological evidence has established that Polynesia was peopled from Asia. As the population there expanded, people probably filtered east across the Malayan and Indonesian archipelagos and Melanesia. This movement became increasingly isolated from its cultural origins; the culture it carried began to develop independently and recognisably differing cultures ultimately emerged. By about the time the movement reached Tonga and Samoa, perhaps 4,000 years ago, the "Polynesian" culture may be said to have emerged.

Thor Heyerdahl has argued that the population movement from Asia in fact took place in a northerly direction, then swept east across the Bering Strait and finally reached the Pacific proper by way of the Americas. Central to this thesis is the presence throughout Polynesia of the kumara, a sweet potato native to South America, the distribution of which remains something of a puzzle. The kumara grows from a tuber and so could not have been borne by birds; nor, is it clear, could the plant have survived being carried by sea currents across the ocean from South America to East Polynesia. It must have been carried by Man. Moreover, not only is the plant found throughout Polynesia, but it is also known by its South American name. Although Heyerdahl's celebrated *Kon-Tiki* expedition (1947) established that it was possible for Polynesia to have been peopled by way of the Americas, his theory has failed to win general acceptance.

"Hawaiki": In time the Marquesas and later the Society Islands evolved as early centres of Polynesian culture. On one of the Society group, Rai'atea (west of Tahiti), Polynesian culture found its highest form. Many believe that it was this revered cultural centre that was "Hawaiki", a place much venerated in tradition as the "homeland" of the Maori people, for it is plain that Maori culture derives from East Polynesia.

The concept of "Hawaiki", of a "homeland" from which the forbears of each migratory group had come, is found throughout Polynesia and is applied to differing areas both within and without the region. It may simply have been a general way of describing the area from which the last movement had been made in the course of the settlement of the island groups throughout Polynesia.

To some Maori tribes "Hawaiki" is a reference to the Cook Islands, possibly because their ancestors came to New Zealand from the Society Islands by way of the Cook group. Maori in the Chatham Islands have even referred to the South Island of New Zealand in this way.

It was on the base of Polynesian culture that the intricacies of Maori culture were structured. Indeed, throughout Polynesia there are common elements in language, legend and place names. The myth of the separation of Earth and Sky is generally constant, and the Maui cycle is common throughout the region.

The coming of Kupe: According to popular tradition (whose authenticity is at the very least questionable) it was the Polynesian voyager Kupe (*fl c.* 950 A.D.) who discovered New Zealand, a land he named Aotearoa (usually translated as "land of the long white cloud"). In one of a variety of conflicting legends it is said that in "Hawaiki" Kupe had murdered the carver Hoturapa and made off not only with Hoturapa's canoe, but also with his wife. Hoturapa's relatives sought vengeance and pursued the guilty pair who, in the course of a lengthy voyage, lived for some time in Aotearoa and named several of its features. Curiously, only some tribes have any traditions of Kupe at all. Those who do generally say that Kupe found the "Fish of Maui" uninhabited and eventually returned to "Hawaiki" to give the sailing instructions that, according to popular belief, were followed by migrating canoes four centuries later.

Kupe Memorial, Taipa, Doubtless Bay.

Toi and Whatonga: If Kupe encountered no tangata whenua ("people of the land"), according to popular tradition the next Polynesian voyagers said to have reached Aotearoa most certainly did. Whatonga (*c.* 1130-90?), so one version runs, was competing in canoe races off "Hawaiki" when, in a sudden storm, his canoe was blown out to sea. His grandfather, Toi (*fl. c.* 1150), despaired of his ever returning and so set out to find him. In the meantime Whatonga is said to have returned to "Hawaiki", to have found Toi gone and in turn to have set out to look for him. The story concludes with the pair being reunited at Whakatane (Bay of Plenty) in *c.* 1150.

Those on Toi's canoe intermarried with local tangata whenua and settled at Whakatane to form the genesis of today's Ngati Awa and Te Ati Awa tribes. Those with Whatonga made their homes on the Mahia Peninsula.

Chronology doubted: The Kupe-Toi-Whatonga chronology is based in present-day tradition and, with the "Fleet" myth, is viewed with scepticism by most historians. Some genealogies establish Kupe in the fourteenth century and so would have him living in Aotearoa well after settlement had been established. Toi is placed anywhere from 29 to 42 generations ago, and some conclude that not only were there two Kupe but there were also two Toi—Toi kai rakau, a native-born origin ancestor, and Toi te huatahi, an "Hawaikian" who never came to New Zealand.

Some early students of the Maori distorted and even at times destroyed material that did not accord with their theories. The works of these historians have passed not just into European folklore but have been "fed back" into Maori tradition. This is not to discount the value of Maori tradition as prehistory, but to query the status accorded some tradition as authentic Maori tradition.

Migration from East Polynesia: Tradition continues that two centuries after the expedition of Toi and Whatonga, the Society Islands had become so overpopulated that food shortages and war were inducing a number of Polynesians to migrate. In Maori tradition a number of canoes made the journey to New Zealand, among them the *Arawa, Tainui, Aotea, Mataatua, Tokomaru, Takitimu, Horouta, Tohora, Mamari, Ngatokimatawhaorua, Mahuhu* and *Kurahaupo*. It is from these canoes, which some believe arrived in the fourteenth century, that most Maori claim their descent.

Early New Zealand historians gave rise to the concept of an organised "fleet" setting sail for New Zealand, but this view has been completely discredited and is without foundation in Maori tradition.

Conversely, it has even been suggested that a single canoe with perhaps 30 occupants, of which half were women, could, with an annual increase of only one per cent, account for a population in 1769 of the dimensions described by Cook. According to this theory a single canoe might have landed in Northland from "Hawaiki". Over the generations the "ancestral" canoes of Maori tradition might have set sail not from the Society Islands but from a Northland "Hawaiki", and not to voyage across the Pacific but to skirt the New Zealand coastline.

That at least one canoe arrived from East Polynesia, either directly or indirectly, is beyond dispute (and if one could arrive, why not two?). *Why* it came remains a matter of controversy. Did each canoe which came deliberately set sail for New Zealand? Or did they come by chance over a span of up to three centuries, being blown off course while travelling between groups of islands?

Those who support the theory that migration throughout Polynesia was deliberate rather than accidental claim an extraordinary navigational ability for the Polynesians which would have enabled them to sail vast distances to reach minute destinations. Cook noted that "the sun is their guide by day and the stars at night . . . (in a storm) they are then bewildered, frequently miss their intended port and are never heard of more."

This suggests that the peopling of the farther islands of Polynesia such as New Zealand and Hawaii may have been accidental rather than deliberate—or the product of "drift voyages" which took place when whole groups were forced to abandon their home islands and simply set sail for wherever the elements bore them. However, there is a considerable body of opinion and evidence to the contrary and the topic remains one of controversy. Maori tradition with its history of ancestral canoes generally opposes the theory of accidental settlement.

Wherever their starting point, some of the ancestral canoes are said to have travelled in pairs for the greater part of the journey, and may have been single-hulled canoes joined together. This would have given greater stability for an ocean voyage, with the hulls separating for the hazardous business of making landfall, and would explain how the *Tainui* and *Arawa* could have arrived at the same place (Whangaparaoa, East Cape) at so nearly the same time that the tribes could argue as to which had arrived first. It would also account for the *Aotea* canoe's being close by to rescue those in the *Kurahaupo* when it was wrecked en route.

Once arrived, the canoe passengers soon intermarried with the tangata whenua. Although the tangata whenua (who had their own tribal groups) were ultimately absorbed, they remain important in the folklore of a number of tribes. These derive status and prestige from their descent from particular ancestral canoes but attribute their land rights to "origin ancestors" among the tangata whenua.

The presumed arrival of these later Polynesians is generally taken as marking the end of the Archaic era and the beginning of the Early Period of the Classic Maori era, although the two periods obviously overlap to a considerable degree. Of all the cultural innovations the new arrivals would have brought with them, the most far-reaching were tropical plants, pre-eminently the kumara (sweet potato). Hitherto the tangata whenua had lived a very much hand-to-mouth existence, dependent on wild plants and birdlife for survival. From this time on horticulture began to be practised (or at least to be practised on a scale not known before), slowly banishing many of the uncertainties of the past and stabilising the area where a particular hapu (sub-tribe) would live.

Tangata whenua: The term simply means "the people of the land", i.e. the people already living in a particular place. Here it is used to refer to those Polynesians already established in a part of New Zealand when others arrived there. Today a Maori going to live in a city may use the same term to describe collectively the Maori already living there.

The expression is not a synonym for "Archaic Maori" (or "Moa Hunter") but may have that meaning where the context so requires.

MAORI CULTURE PERIODS

Archaic Maori: Before the arrivals from "Hawaiki", the Archaic Maori (or Moa Hunter) thrived during what may be called the Archaic Phase of New Zealand Eastern Polynesian culture. Just where they came from with their simple culture, and when, remains more of a mystery than the doubt that surrounds the later arrivals from East Polynesia, but the Archaic Maori clearly originated in Polynesia (not, as some have suggested, in Melanesia) and was established here at least by 750 A.D. Little of their traditions survived down to European times.

They found the moa and other flightless birds, now extinct, both plentiful and easy prey. And with an abundance of food and a small population, war may have been virtually unknown—unless they used wooden weapons which have since perished. But as the number of moa dwindled, the Archaic Maori was forced to turn to fishing, fowling and tool-making (from such hard stones as obsidian), and perhaps even in a small way to experiment with horticulture.

Although the Archaic Maori is popularly called a "Moa Hunter", the expression, with its economic overtones, is misleading as there were areas of the country populated by people from East Polynesia who would have never encountered the bird.

Archaeological evidence points clearly to the Archaic Maori population as concentrated in the South Island. This is to be expected as the moa (a flightless, emu-like bird of which there were several species, some about three metres in height) grazed on open grasslands of which the South Island had great areas. A large number of "campsites", as Archaic Maori settlements are known, have been found, principally along the east coast of the South Island and on the North Island's west coast around Taranaki.

Classic Maori: Systematic horitculture dates from the introduction of food plants such as taro, uhi (yam), hue (gourd) and, most importantly, kumara—a variety of sweet potato and the only tropical plant really to flourish in New Zealand's cooler conditions. In tradition Kupe, when eventually he returned to "Hawaiki", reportedly summarised the New Zealand climate when he said that he preferred a warm breast to a cold one. However, it is likely that the climate was significantly warmer then than now. The kumara is a tropical plant and is not grown easily in New Zealand. It is probable that when the kumara was introduced, the climate permitted traditional cultivation techniques to be used and that, as it gradually cooled, these were adapted to the changing conditions. Evidence from a variety of sources points to a brief cool period in the mid-fifteenth century, and to a more sustained deterioration from the seventeenth to nineteenth centuries.

For protein the Maori remained dependent on fish, bird-life and the occasional Maori rat, and it seems that the practice of cannibalism may have had its origin in this lack of meat—although in later times it was to assume a religious rather than a dietary character.

With systematic horticulture evolved the Classic Maori culture, with stabilised pa (fortified villages) replacing nomadic "campsites" and with less permanent kainga (unfortified villages) generally sited close by the kumara grounds. In favourable areas, successful and intensive horticulture enabled experts to devote progressively more time to their specialities and progressively less to manual labour, and so saw arts such as carving and the making of ornaments flourish as never before and usher in the Classic Maori period.

However, it is clear that the two cultural periods overlapped to a considerable extent. It is now believed that the kumara may have been introduced at a very much earlier date than was thought hitherto, and that the significant breakthrough came not with its introduction but with the development of effective storage methods, in particular the rua (underground pit). The kumara is highly susceptible to frost. It was when the technique of lifting the tuber in the autumn and storing it through the winter, both for food supply and for the next season's planting, was developed that cultivation would have become possible over a much wider area of the country.

By the time the European arrived, less than 5 per cent of the Maori population was living in the South Island, and in the North distribution was concentrated in the northern reaches—presumably because it was in this warmer area that the Classic Maori culture based on tropical horticulture could best thrive.

Although some aspects of Maori culture were universal, there was significant regional variation not only in arts, crafts and language, but also in the way of life dictated by environmental and political factors. In some districts societies lived in open, unprotected villages in an atmosphere of tranquillity: in others the threat of imminent invasion provoked a preoccupation with the maintenance of strongly fortified pa.

CLASSIC MAORI SOCIETY

Social organisation: The iwi (tribe) was the largest political unit within Classic Maori society, although an affinity with other tribes which shared descent from the same canoe frequently gave rise to military allegiances. However, the main unit was not the iwi but the hapu (sub-tribe), a highly localised group of perhaps 500 people of common descent made up of several inter-related whanau (extended family groups) bound together by a common ancestor who might have lived perhaps 10 generations earlier.

The hapu was a fully autonomous and independent grouping, a self-sufficient economic unit which cultivated its own land and caught fish and snared birds from within its own boundaries. A village settlement might have comprised a single or perhaps several hapu.

An ariki (chief) was the leader of a hapu and attained his rank from the common belief that vested in him was the mana (prestige) of his predecessors. If he were not an effective political leader he might retain his religious role while vesting political leadership in a more suitable relative. Whenever an important decision affecting the hapu was to be made, a public meeting would be held on the marae (square) in front of the whare runanga (meeting house). The various kaumatua (family leaders) might all speak, but the ariki spoke first and last, and his decision, which would reflect the opinions expressed, was final.

The word hapu literally means "pregnancy", emphasising the concept of kinship, and iwi, "bones", the pre-occupation with relationships and lines of descent. But while the hapu would combine to battle with external enemies as a tribal unit, fighting between hapu within the same iwi was by no means exceptional.

The tohunga: Within the hapu each member did the job for which he or she was best suited, and rank depended not on the accumulation of goods but on the extent to which a person provided them for others. A tohunga was a "specialist" (e.g., a woodcarver was a tohunga whakairo rakau) but few were engaged full-time on their special skill. When not so occupied they would join in the ordinary everyday work of the tribe from which even the ariki was not exempt. Quite apart from the considerable pleasure the Maori gained from their work, its desirability was underscored by "public condemnation of idleness and public recognition of useful achievement".

Part of a tohunga's expertise lay in his knowledge of the rituals connected with his craft, and so each tohunga was to some degree also a priest. Today the term tohunga is used loosely to refer only to the most important of the various ranks of tohunga, high priests trained in the most sacred lore of the whare wananga (house of learning). These were entrusted with intimate details of tribal history too tapu for the remainder of the tribe to know, and were also versed in the innermost secrets of Io, the one God, the Supreme Being. Their proximity to the gods was believed to give them supernatural powers and their knowledge of ritual was essential to the wellbeing of their people. As high priests they were natural leaders and advisers in tribal councils, and exercised great power.

Curiously absent were large religious constructions. Maori religion left little material trace, and the small tuahu (altar) does not compete with the massive shrines of Easter Island and Tahiti – factors which suggest that religious developments there post-dated contact with New Zealand.

Tapu and noa: The dual concept of tapu (sacred) and noa (free from tapu) regulated every facet of Maori life. Tapu was a positive force, associated with life, immortality, masculine objects and women of the highest rank. Noa was its antithesis, a negative force associated with death and feminine objects.

Tapu was in one sense a religious or superstitious restriction, and all who violated it were doomed to be overcome at least by misfortune, at worst by death. To remove tapu, for example from a newly completed meeting house, a tohunga would have to perform an appropriate ceremony and the tapu might in the case of a house be neutralised by a woman of rank entering. Odd numbers could be noa and even numbers tapu. If a mistake were made and an even number of rafters erected in a meeting house, the tapu of the house would be so powerful it could never be removed and so the house could never be used by women.

Tapu emanated from the gods and with only the atua (gods) shielding humans from the forces of evil it was not to be taken lightly. All objects under construction were tapu, and it would be a breach of tapu to eat cooked food indoors (cooked food and the human head were surrounded by innumerable tapu). A tohunga under tapu would have to be fed by another with food skewered to the end of a stick.

More than mere superstition, tapu served a practical function. A fishing ground might be placed under tapu as a conservation measure to allow depleted fish to multiply; a tapu river area might denote an otherwise dangerous crossing; a variety of tapu regulated matters of public health.

Without its former rigidity, tapu persists to this day in certain situations, but observation is rapidly being reduced to the level of etiquette. Certainly the belief that all sickness was caused by the sufferer's breach of tapu has long perished, and the Tohunga Suppression Act of 1907 was repealed in 1963. However, in certain respects (e.g., in the case of traditional tribal burial grounds and traditionally venerated objects), observation of tapu is universal.

Utu and mana: In utu and mana the Maori were carrying in their culture the seeds of self-destruction. No slight to one's mana (prestige) could be ignored, however trivial, and to offend one person was to affront an entire hapu. Retribution (utu) was called for in every instance and was often exacted to a degree out of all proportion to the original insult. As a consequence war played an essential part in Classic Maori life, but was a seasonal activity restricted to times of year when the kumara plantations did not require attention.

It was essential for the tribe's mana to be preserved at all costs. For mana was derived from the gods, and without it the tribe would win no battles, could grow no crops and was doomed to perish.

Cunning was as much admired as physical courage, and on countless occasions friendship would be feigned and feasts be in progress before guests would rise up to strike down their unsuspecting hosts, or vice-versa. All was fair, and the unwary got only what they deserved. But common, too, were examples in set battle where food would be provided for beleaguered defenders by rival warriors anxious to determine on equal terms which side was the superior—a practice the Maori found to their surprise was not followed by the Pakeha soldiers. Such chivalry did not extend to the treatment of prisoners, women and children, and those spared by victorious war parties might be kept as slaves only until required as food.

While the hapu who had exacted utu could feel that mana was restored, they had of necessity given rise to a grudge against themselves. Occasionally a hapu were forced by circumstance to wait generations before they were in a position to exact retribution. Wait they might, forget they would never. The fighting was endless.

This state of affairs could survive while fighting was hand-to-hand and the numbers lost in combat relatively small. But the introduction by traders of firearms and of European concepts of conquest and kingship changed the dimension of the slaughter and made possible devastation to an unprecedented degree. While the traders enriched their Sydney bank accounts as a roaring trade developed in flax and preserved heads, the Maori decimated their own. From perhaps 250,000 in Cook's time the Maori population had by 1854 slumped to 60,000, albeit a decline accelerated by disease and ill-health induced by changed living conditions. In 1872 novelist Anthony Trollope could fairly write: "There is scope for poetry in their past history. There is room for philanthropy as to their present condition. But in regard to their future—there is hardly a place for hope." By the end of the nineteenth century the Maori, then numbering barely 40,000, appeared doomed. Only the strenuous and dedicated efforts of people such as Ngata, Buck, Pomare, Heke and more recently Ratana *(for all, see index)* saw the Maori as a people survive.

Ownership: The earliest students of Maori society concluded that the Maori community operated a primitive form of "communism", without any individual property rights. This is now known to be an oversimplification, for although property rights were limited they were nevertheless of importance and were zealously guarded. Everyone had their own spears, ornaments, bird-snares and garments; in some cases ownership of standing trees was passed down from father to son. Slaves taken in battle were the absolute property of the chief who had captured them. Food was only occasionally placed in the communal storehouse, as more often the whanau would keep the produce of its own labours. Even when the whole hapu embarked on a joint expedition (e.g., the building of a large eel weir or fishing with giant seine nets) the catch was divided by the chief among the whanau, the larger shares generally going to those with the hardest workers—those with the "wet skins".

Within the territorial boundaries of the iwi the hapu had their own areas, and in turn parts of these were divided among the various whanau.

Land was Papa, the Earth Mother from whom the Maori was descended, and there was no concept of land alienation other than by conquest. Even then the conquering tribe had to establish a relationship with the land by occupying it before ownership was achieved. Despite this, if in time the vanquished could return and rekindle their fires of occupation, the earlier relationship was revived and ancestral atua re-established.

Today land titles split among large numbers of Maori owners are a legacy of communalism and such fragmentary ownership places difficulties in the path of the land's being put to good use. The Department of Maori Affairs invests heavily to bring such land into production and to constitute Maori incorporations to vest control of the lands in committees of manageable proportions.

Trade: The widespread use of greenstone (found only on the South Island's west coast) and of obsidian (predominantly from Mayor Island) illustrates the extent to which trading was carried on both between iwi and hapu. This grew out of the custom of homai o homai, "a gift for a gift".

An iwi or a hapu on a friendly visit would take with them a variety of presents, usually chosen with a view to supplying what their hosts would most appreciate. Seaside visitors would carry fish inland, inland dwellers would supply potted birds and rats. Hapu with celebrated artisans would give articles such as carvings and garments. There was no element of barter, but custom required that in time the hospitality be reciprocated and further that the original gift be not merely matched but surpassed by the original recipients. In this way limited resources were widely spread and the practice of increasing the generosity of the gifts ensured that trade was continually expanding.

It was for visits such as these, and also to guard against possible food shortages, that the ariki would stock their large storehouses to capacity, for the handing over of gifts was followed by feasting, games and entertainments.

The pa and the kainga: Pa (forts), formerly spelt pah, were built on suitable ridges and in easily defended strategic positions where sea, river or swamp formed a natural barrier on at least one side. To complete the defences trenches were dug, earth ramparts thrown up and the whole site was fenced with palisades. Inside were thatched houses built of raupo, rua (food-storage pits) and a pahu, a wooden gong that was sounded in times of emergency to summon those living in outlying kainga.

Reconstructed kainga, Kerikeri Basin.

The kainga was an unfortified village of a temporary nature and with few or no wood carvings. It was usually sited close to the kumara plantations.

The word pa has come to be applied to any collection of Maori-occupied houses, generally in the vicinity of a meeting house.

MAORI ARTS, CRAFTS AND CUSTOMS

Meeting house: The traditional carved whare runanga (meeting house) is seen throughout the North Island. Built of wood, they are in the main of fairly recent origin, though they tend to perpetuate the style and symbolism of older houses on the same sites and frequently contain interior carvings of an age much greater than the houses themselves. The building of large meeting houses appears to have been a nineteenth-century development, although their central concepts reflect a continuity with earlier, if less substantial, buildings.

The meeting house faces the marae, the focal point of the pa. It is on this open square that public gatherings are still held on matters of moment and it is traditionally regarded as the spiritual centre of the tribal unit to whom it belongs. Visitors should, where possible, ask permission locally before entering a meeting house, and should walk around a marae rather than across it.

The concept of the meeting house is symbolic of a single person, usually a tribal ancestor. His head is represented by the koruru (mask) immediately below the tekoteko (gable figure) at the apex above the porch. The maihi (barge-boards), usually tipped with "fingers" (raparapa), represent his arms, the interior his belly, the lengthy ridge-pole his spine and the rafters the cages of his ribs. The individual carvings, too, are heavy with symbolism and may depict a variety of tribal ancestors, mythical figures and occasionally gods, each intimately related to the tribe. In this way the carvings served as a visual aid for the handing down of tribal history for a people with no written language.

The pare (carved lintel) over the door was of vital ritualistic importance as it served to neutralise the tapu of men who entered, usually by depicting a noa feminine subject. The fully carved interior is a comparatively recent innovation made the more feasible by the iron tools of the Pakeha which replaced the slower stone chisels of tradition. Although Cook on his first voyage noted a fully carved interior at Tolaga Bay, and in the Urewera and Arawa districts there were pre-European houses with carved figures on all poupou (wall panels), these were then the exception rather than the rule. Between the poupou are usually tukutuku panels woven in geometric designs from flax and reeds. The poutokomanawa (posts which support the ridge-pole) frequently depict the captains of ancestral canoes who "welcome" those who enter. Painted patterns, frequently scrolls similar to the uncurling fern frond, embellish the rafters. Interlocking and rhythmic, these traditional designs have modern appeal and were originally executed in black (soot mixed with shark oil), red (ochre and shark oil) and white (natural wood colour). These patterns, also used to decorate canoes, have been given symbolic names but these are open to doubt as they may have been

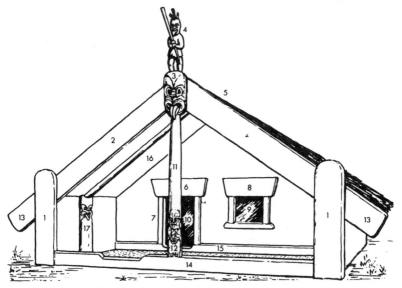

Names of parts of a Maori meeting house

1. Ama *or* amo
2. Maihi, mahihi
3. Koruru
4. Tekoteko
5. Parata, maui
6. Pare
7. Whaka-wae, waewae
8. Korupe
9. Matapihi, pihanga
10. Tatau
11. Pou-koukou-aro, pou-tou-aroaro
12. Tekoteko-aro
13. Raparapa
14. Paepae-kai-awa
15. Paepae
16. Heke
17. Poupou

(Drawing from *The Art of Maori Carving,* by Dr. S.M. Mead, A.H. & A.W. Reed Ltd., Wgtn, 1961)

prompted by the appearance of the designs rather than be descriptive of the motivating force behind them.

A dining hall is often close by the meeting house as traditionally it is a breach of tapu to eat in a whare runanga. However, modern meeting houses frequently include dining areas and ancillary rooms alien to the whare runanga, earning them the more appropriate description of "community hall".

Ceremony on the marae: The marae, the area in front of the meeting house, is in Maoritanga of much greater importance than the house itself. It is here that the Maori gathers to celebrate and to mourn, to discuss tribal or family matters, and to honour distinguished visitors.

It is when important guests are being received that the marae assumes an atmosphere of age-old ritual, yet one relevant to the present even as it perpetuates the past. The visitors (manuhiri) wait outside the marae until being called upon to enter by the home people (tangata whenua). The call (karanga) is usually made by one or more women who, in high-pitched voice, invite the visitors by name to enter and be welcomed (or, in the case of a funeral, to mourn).

If the guests are of high rank, the karanga is preceded by the challenge (wero), perhaps the most spectacular of all Maori ceremonies. Deriving from the need in former times to ascertain the intentions of visitors, the cry first goes up from a sentry for his people to be alert. Then, when the visitors are at the gates, he warns again, "He taua! He taua!" ("A war party!"). A warrior then dances out towards the visitors, places an object such as a stick on the ground before them, and taunts them with war-like gestures from his taiaha (spear). The leader of the visitors then picks up the object, indicating that they come in peace, whereupon the challenger turns his back on them and leads them onto the marae.

After the call of welcome, a powhiri (dance of welcome) may take place, followed by a pause for mourning. Even when guests have come to celebrate, respect is paid to the dead.

Welcome in speech and in song follows, and it is only after the replies to the speeches of welcome have been delivered that the gap between visitors and hosts finally closes and the first physical contact takes place – the visitors are invited to cross the marae to be greeted in person, both hand-to-hand (hariru) and nose-to-nose (hongi), and with words of welcome, "Tena koe".

Contrary to popular belief, the hongi does not involve a rubbing of noses, but a touching, either bridge to bridge or, occasionally, first one side and then the other. Nor is it a perfunctory ritual: Samuel Marsden recounted occasions on which people would "remain in this position for at least half an hour; during which time they sob and howl in the most doleful manner". The hongi remains today a greeting charged with emotion, and on occasions of sorrow it still assumes a special poignancy.

The ceremony completed, informality reigns; the visitors' baggage is collected and food is served. If visitors are staying overnight they may sleep in the meeting house, bedding down communally on mattresses, wrapped in blankets and, inevitably, debating long into the night.

Maori carving: The most common figures found in Maori carving are the human figure and the manaia (a bird-like, beaked figure). The most usual surface design is the spiral, used either on its own or incorporated in figures to accentuate the joints and points of movement. Secondary motifs include the marakihau (a mermaid figure whose tubular tongue could suck up whole canoes), the pakake (whale) and the moko (lizard). Phallic imagery abounds, symbolic of virility in war and a desire to see the tribal lineage perpetuated.

Theories differ as to why the Maori distorted the human figure as much as they did, though the head was probably magnified as it was the most tapu part of the body. To explain both the three-fingered hand and the slanted eyes the theory has been advanced that they are derived from a customary imposition of bird-like features on the human figure in various parts of the Pacific.

Tiki is a term applied to carved human figures generally, and the significance of the well-known charm (strictly a hei-tiki) has also been lost. The supposition that it might be a fertility charm representing the human embryo seems unlikely as early European visitors saw men as well as women wearing them, and no man of rank would have worn such a noa object.

Ancestral figures are usually depicted in warlike posture, with mere (club) in hand, eyes bulging and tongue defiantly out-thrust, a gesture which also provided protection from evil forces.

The preferred wood for carving was, and still is, totara, a wood both durable yet comparatively soft. Paua shell is still used, as it was traditionally, to depict a figure's eyes.

Today most carvings have been painted a uniform red, a colour sacred throughout Polynesia as symbolic of mana and the power of the gods. However, traditionally only selected carvings were coloured, and then with red ochre mixed with shark oil, a substance that wore off high spots so enhancing the fine lines of the carving.

Unfortunately many of the older carvings, too, have been disfigured by the application of a thick and even coat of oil-based paint, a misguided act that has even occurred in New Zealand's museums.

Carving was by no means confined to the meeting house. Superb examples of the carver's skill are seen in the intricate canoe prows found in museums throughout the country, and virtually every prized possession was decorated. These included treasure boxes, paddles, bailers, musical instruments, chests for burying bones, god-sticks, storehouses, gateways to pa and stockade images.

Two varieties of greenstone found only on the west coast of the South Island, pounamu (nephrite—a hard jade) and tangiwai (bowenite—a translucent softer stone), were highly prized for the making of tools and jewellery. This work was extremely time-consuming, for using traditional implements it might have taken as long as six months of full-time work to fashion a single hei-tiki to perfection.

Carvers in different areas tended to have their own distinctive styles, but great carvers were often also great travellers and so their work was by no means confined to their tribal locality. Generally carving received a setback with the arrival of the missionaries, who were appalled by the carvers' uninhibited approach both to the naked form and to the sex act.

There is a tendency today to think of Maori art as stagnating after the arrival of the colonists. However, the Europeans' metal tools made carving very much faster, and with speed came an inevitable lowering of standards. The European, too, favoured the more ornate form of carving with an elaborate working of the entire surface area, and the art form may have developed to accommodate this interest. Most surviving carvings were executed with iron tools in the post-European period. Vivid examples of the development of folk-art and wall paintings are to be seen in the Rongopai meeting house near Gisborne.

With the resurgence of the Maori came renewed cultural pride, and more carved meeting houses have been erected in the past 50 years than in any other period.

Maori carving differs from that of tropical Polynesia but there seems little doubt that the basic patterns would have come with the later arrivals from East Polynesia.

Maori music: Traditional Maori songs were described by some early European voyagers as "dreary monotones". They included a variety of chants and a large number of waiata (songs) both of lament (waiata tangi) and of love (waiata aroha). Waiata melodies moved within a very limited range, perhaps as little as a fourth, and the singer slid from one note to the next, an interval often less than a semi-tone. The ability to sing in this complex manner has almost disappeared.

The familiar "Maori" songs, such as "Pokarekare ana" and "Haere ra" ("Now is the hour"), date from European times. Tunes are frequently plagiarised and the "traditional" harmonies are more-or-less based on the Victorian hymnal. The Maori words, however, can show great originality and in poetic terms far surpass those they displace.

Classic Maori instruments were of the flute and trumpet variety, fashioned from stone, whalebone, wood and even human bone. Drums were unknown, rhythm being supplied by foot stomping, the slapping of both chest and thighs with the hands and occasionally the tapping of a resonant piece of wood with a stick.

Haka: The word haka, commonly applied only to the spirited Maori war dance, correctly extends to all forms of rhythmic posture dancing. Traditionally the art form derives from the marriage of Hine-raumati (the Summer Maid) with Ra (the Sun), and their child, Tanerore, whose appearance on warm summer days was manifest by the quivering atmosphere. It is this quivering which pervades all forms of Maori dancing, from the peruperu (war dance) to the gentle poi dance (a dance performed only by women in which raupo balls on the end of strings are swirled in time with music).

The peruperu was performed by warriors with taiaha (long clubs) in hand. Their leader held a quivering mere (short greenstone club) and to his shouts of command the warriors would reply in chorus, stamping their feet in unison and moving their quivering hands through a series of gestures as they rolled their eyes and contorted their faces. All the while the performance was anxiously watched for omens of good or ill.

Pre-eminent among haka choruses (and one often used by touring All Black rugby teams) is that associated with Te Rauparaha (*pp.*115-16) as he hid in a kumara pit while his enemies hunted for him. As discovery seemed certain he breathed "Ka mate! Ka mate!" ("It is death! Death!"), and as the searchers moved away he sighed, "Ka ora! Ka ora!" ("It is life! Life!"). When all was safe he emerged and expressed thanks to the hairy chief Te Wharerangi who had shielded him:

"Ka mate! Ka mate!	"It is death! It is death!
Ka ora! Ka ora!	It is life! It is life!
Tenei te tangata puhuruhuru,	This is the hairy person
Nana nei i tiki mei	
I whakawhiti re ra!	Who caused the sun to shine!

17

Upane! Upane!	One upward step! Another upward step!
Upane! Kaupane!	One last upward step! The step forth!
Whiti te ra!"	Into the sun that shines!"

The peruperu has been adopted by a number of schools and some sporting groups, and is occasionally performed at school rugby matches.

Weapons: The Maori stone-age culture was based first on obsidian and later, from about 1,000 years ago, on greenstone (pounamu and tangiwai). The shift in emphasis came when quantities of these fine-grained rocks were found on the South Island's west coast.

In the Archaic Maori period, warfare seems to have been unknown. The population was small and food was plentiful. But the later Polynesian arrivals brought with them the short club (patu) made of wood, bone or stone, and the long-handled club, the taiaha and tewhatewha. Most highly prized of all, and cherished for generations, was the mere, a patu pounamu (greenstone club). So fabled was the occasional individual mere that a prisoner-of-war might actually ask to be killed by it—a request granted only if the prisoner were considered worthy of the honour.

Tattooing: Although some younger Maori are reviving the practice in modern form, the traditional Maori art of tattooing (moko) has long ceased. In Classic Maori society the male was liberally embellished, the fully tattooed flourishing decorated cheeks, chin, nose and forehead as well as buttocks and thighs. Tattooing was a sign of status and far from simply decorating the face, the Maori of rank did not acquire his "real" face until he had been tattooed. Indeed, personal tattoo patterns were often remembered rather than facial characteristics.

After death the mummified heads of one's own tribe were affectionately preserved and the heads of chiefs of other tribes were similarly kept, but as objects to be both insulted and humiliated. Pakipaki (preserved, not shrunken heads) are occasionally seen in museums and for a time in the early 1800s they were keenly sought after by traders as curios which commanded high prices in Europe.

Tattooing was a painful process, conducted with uhi (serrated chisel) and mallet, soot being rubbed into the open wound to provide colouring. The Maori differed from other Polynesian tattooing in that designs were actually cut and not just pricked into the flesh.

Rock drawings: Drawings on rocks are found in various parts of the North Island but more particularly in the South Canterbury and North Otago regions of the South. These are either painted with red ochre or scratched out with sharp stones. There is no certain way of dating these drawings but the appearance of huts and ships in some makes it plain that some at least post-date the arrival of the European. Subjects vary, but common are birds, canoes and apparently mythical figures.

THE EUROPEAN DISCOVERERS

Abel Tasman: Europe had for long been fascinated by the speculation that there must exist in the South Pacific a great unknown continent, *Terra australis incognita*, to "balance" the land masses of the Northern Hemisphere. It was to discover this continent, though for the purpose of trade rather than to further scientific knowledge, that in 1642 the Dutch East India Company dispatched Abel Janszoon Tasman (1603-59) from Batavia (now Djakarta) as commander of two small ships, the *Heemskerck* and the *Zeehaen*. So confident was the enterprise of success that Tasman's orders were detailed even to cover the possibility of encountering civilised races. Such people, he was told, were to be deceived—"[make] them believe that you are by no means eager for precious metals, so as to leave them ignorant of the value of the same; and if they should offer you gold or silver in exchange for your articles, you will pretend to hold the same in slight regard, showing them copper, pewter, or lead, and giving them an impression as if the minerals last mentioned were by us set greater value on".

Tasman first sailed south-west, to Mauritius, before turning east, eventually to reach the island now called Tasmania but which Tasman himself named "Van Diemen's Land", after the Governor-General of the Dutch East Indies who had directed the voyage. From there he crossed the Tasman Sea, and on 13 December 1642 he became the first known European voyager to sight New Zealand when land in the vicinity of Hokitika was seen. It is consistent with the vagueness which clouds New Zealand's early history that even the identity of her European discoverer should be open to question. Some suspect that Portuguese and Spanish expeditions may have preceded Tasman, basing their theories on old maps, a curious bell found by the missionary Colenso, and the finding of an old Spanish helmet in Wellington's harbour some years ago. Historians generally discount these possibilities.

Tasman followed the west coast of the South Island northwards before anchoring in the shelter of Golden Bay. There he experienced his only encounter with the Maori. As a cockboat travelled between Tasman's two ships it was intercepted by a canoe and in a brief clash four sailors died. Curiously, Tasman chose not to exact reprisals, a decision out of keeping with the times as later French explorers were to illustrate. Instead, disillusioned, Tasman named the area "Murderers' Bay" and put back to sea. Foul weather frustrated his attempt to enter Cook Strait, which he tentatively plotted as a bay. Had the weather been kinder the possibility of the new land being the great southern continent would have been exploded then and there. As it was, Tasman was left to skirt the North Island's west coast before finally leaving the inhospitable shores of the country he had discovered but not set foot upon.

He named his discovery "Staten Landt", both to honour the States-General of the United Netherlands and because he thought it could be connected with the Staten Landt discovered off the tip of South America some 26 years earlier (a name still applied to a small island there). His masters regarded the voyage as fruitless. Although he went on to discover islands in the Fiji and Tonga groups, Tasman had found no riches and had displayed somewhat less enterprise in exploring his discoveries than his masters would have wished.

Two years later Tasman explored the northern Australian coastline before the Dutch East India Company finally abandoned its attempt to find the unknown continent in favour of developing an island trade.

Only two of Tasman's New Zealand place names survive—Cape Maria Van Diemen, near Cape Reinga (named for the Governor-General's wife), and Three Kings, the islands off the tip of North Cape where he spent the Feast of the Epiphany. But Tasman had added a tantalising new mapline to an otherwise empty area, and suspicion lingered that he had in fact discovered *Terra australis incognita*.

The naming of "New Zealand": Tasman's name of "Staten Landt" did not long survive, for within a year Hendrik Brouwer had proved that the original Staten Landt was an island. Australia had been designated "Compagnis Niev Nederland" (Company's New Netherland) by the Dutch East India Company's map-makers, and "Nieuw Holland" (New Holland) became the usual Dutch name for the Australian continent. By the mid-seventeenth century the name "Nieuw Zeeland" had begun to be applied to New Zealand (doubtless bestowed by analogy to "Nieuw Holland", as Zeeland is a Dutch maritime province) and eventually the English equivalent emerged. It is still not known just who actually "named" New Zealand.

James Cook (1728-79): If Tasman's motives had been mercenary, the purpose of Captain James Cook's voyages to New Zealand was almost wholly scientific. Initially he was sent in 1768 on the bark *Endeavour* (368 tons) to Tahiti (discovered by Wallis the year before), there to observe the transit of the sun by the planet Venus— a rare phenomenon whose sightings from various parts of the world enabled astronomers for the first time to calculate accurately the distance between the earth and the sun. His mission fulfilled, the tall, rather obstinate Yorkshireman opened his "secret additional instructions" and sailed south-west in search of the unknown continent which, if discovered, was to be explored and, if uninhabited, was to be annexed for Britain. Cook, of course, encountered no such continent and, in terms of his instructions, continued on to "fall in with the Eastern side of the Land discover'd by Tasman and now called New Zealand", there to make charts, to "observe the Nature of the Soil", to collect specimens and to observe the "Genius, Temper, Disposition and Number of the Natives". He was also ordered "with the Consent of the Natives to take possession of Convenient Situations in the Country in the Name of the King of Great Britain; or if [he found] the Country uninhabited take Possession for His Majesty by setting up Proper Marks and Inscriptions, as first discoverers and possessors".

All this the diligent Cook most meticulously accomplished. Landfall was made on 9 October 1769 at Gisborne, where misunderstandings quickly led to bloodshed. Without the food and water he needed, Cook left "Poverty Bay" (so called "because it afforded us no one thing we wanted") and it was not until he reached Mercury Bay on the Coromandel Peninsula that he departed from his instructions inasmuch as without the consent of any Maori he displayed the English Colours and "took formal possession of the place in the name of His Majesty".

North to the tip of the North Island he sailed and there only a storm averted what would have been the coincidence of all time. For in the gale and off the coast of a country ignored by Europe for over a century, the French explorer de Surville passed close by as he sailed in search of refuge for his ailing crew. In the fury of the storm neither was aware of the other's presence.

In the main Cook found the "Indians" both friendly and helpful as he circumnavigated both islands and plotted them to such a degree of accuracy that it was left for subsequent explorers merely to provide missing detail and to correct the occasional lapse—such as his assumptions that Stewart Island was part of the mainland and Banks Peninsula an island. All this is the more remarkable in that he was without the newly invented chronometer which was to bring to navigation a degree of accuracy it had never before known.

After the accounts of Cook's first voyage were published, New Zealand was known to the world. Not only had Cook methodically charted the coastline, but the botanists Banks and Solander had also observed its flora and fauna, artists had sketched its peoples, and both Banks and Cook had recorded the first details of Maori custom. During his second and third voyages Cook again visited New Zealand, making his base at Ship Cove in Queen Charlotte Sound (across Cook Strait from Wellington). His voyages of discovery in the Pacific ranged as far north as Alaska and above the Arctic circle, and as far south as Antarctica. By the end of his second voyage the concept of *Terra australis incognita* had evaporated.

It was in the Pacific that Cook died. The strain of lengthy voyages in tiny crowded ships and of coping with the problems that daily beset those who venture into the unknown finally took their toll. Cook's increasingly testy temper saw him in a moment of crisis shoot an innocent Polynesian, and Hawaiians stoned and stabbed to death the man they had adored as a god.

French explorers: During an ill-fated voyage in search of a fabulously rich island believed to lie in the direction of Peru, Jean Francois Marie de Surville (1717-70) was forced to sail south to the land discovered by Tasman in order to get food and rest for his scurvy-stricken crew. At Doubtless Bay, after 14 days of amity during which the hard-pressed French had made gifts of pigs, poultry and grain which they could ill-afford, an incident involving a dinghy which broke loose during a storm ended tragically. De Surville set out to retrieve it but the Maori, possibly believing it to be theirs by reason of muru (the plundering of a person who suffered a misfortune), hid it from him. Relations had previously been amicable but now the enraged de Surville burned huts and other property and captured a chief, Ranginui. He sailed for South America taking Ranginui, who soon died of scurvy. Not long afterwards de Surville himself was drowned when a boat in which he was attempting to get ashore capsized in the surf.

Just over two years later, in 1772, the explorer Marion du Fresne (1714-72), with the *Mascarin* and the *Marquis de Castries,* called at the Bay of Islands. He knew nothing of de Surville's visit and Cook's account of his first voyage had not then been published. As Marion du Fresne had only Tasman's charts and journals he was justified in concluding that he had rediscovered the country. Accordingly, it was claimed for France by Marion du Fresne's officers. Marion du Fresne himself, and about 25 of his men, after five weeks of most friendly relations which had culminated in a ceremony interpreted by du Fresne as being his own elevation to chiefly rank, were unaccountably murdered at Assassination Cove. The killings were apparently premeditated and probably resulted from some inadvertent and inevitable breaches of tapu. Utu for de Surville's outrages has been suggested as a motive, but this has generally been dismissed: it was a different tribe who had suffered at de Surville's hands, and one with which the tribes at the Bay of Islands had frequently been at war. Marion du Fresne's remaining crew exacted their own utu, burning three villages and killing numerous Maori before departing.

Scientific interest in the Pacific and popular interest in its "noble savages" grew rapidly. Vancouver, who had sailed under Cook and whose charts of the north-west American coastline rank in excellence with those of his mentor, spent some time in 1791 at Dusky Sound and improved Cook's chart of that region. Visits by D'Entrecasteaux and the Spaniard Malaspina foreshadowed the sealers who in turn proved the existence of Foveaux Strait. Further French expeditions came to New Zealand: Duperrey (1824), Laplace (1831), Cécille and Dupetit-Thouars (both 1838). But of them all, Jules Sebastien César Dumont d'Urville (1790-1842) in 1827 performed the most notable work.

Dumont d'Urville, who had sailed as Duperrey's second-in-command three years earlier, on the *Astrolabe* both sought out and explored the areas Cook had left as doubtful, and replaced many of Cook's names with those of the Maori—"[For] there will come a time when such names will be the only vestiges of the tongue spoken by the primitive inhabitants." Dumont d'Urville's sympathy and his ear for language flavoured his published accounts of the country and its people as had none other before him, but when in 1840 he visited New Zealand for the last time he found that the "noble savage" had been debased and he could well deplore the activities of the British at the Bay of Islands.

EXPLOITATION

Sealers, whalers, timber traders: In the wake of the scientific voyagers came the commercial exploiters, and by the 1790s sealers were streaming in to hound the fur seals round the New Zealand coast to the point of extinction in three frantic decades. Hunting seals for their fur and oil was lucrative but by no means easy work. Parties were left ashore in the wildest of settings; some were abandoned, some were forgotten, some were not rescued for years. And for all the hazards, it seems that the big money was not made by those who experienced sealing at first hand.

By the turn of the century whalers were calling spasmodically at the Bay of Islands. As the sperm whaling trade expanded the area became a provisioning and refitting base where Maori crewmen might be recruited, and in the late 1820s this gave birth to the first centre of European settlement in New Zealand, Kororareka (now known as Russell). Escaped and time-expired convicts from the Australian penal settlements, brutal whalers and adventurers of every description combined to earn for Kororareka the reputation of being the "Hell-hole of the Pacific". The whaling trade dropped sharply in 1841 when port and customs duties began to be levied, and it later dwindled further as whales became scarce and new whaling grounds opened elsewhere.

While sealers and whalers plundered the coasts, timber traders were felling Northland's massive kauri trees as quickly as they could ship the timber out. The British Navy, too, found the kauri ideal for masts and spars, and by 1810 kauri was sought after in Sydney by shipbuilders. Timber-milling settlements sprang up around the coast of Northland, principally on Hokianga Harbour. Although the trees were virtually irreplaceable (the kauri takes up to 800 years to reach maturity) the timber lasted longer than the seals and the whales. By 1853 kauri timber exports accounted for 31 per cent of the country's total exports, but five years later had slumped to a mere 4 per cent. Only since World War II, with vast areas of exotic *Pinus radiata* planted during the Depression years of the 1930s coming into maturity, has forestry regained a major export role. The kauri was ravished and major stands survive only at Waipoua (north of Dargaville) and in the rugged Coromandel Ranges.

The country's natural assets had been exploited mercilessly. No less so were the Maori themselves.

Flax and firearms: Maori society reeled under the impact of the traders. Not only did the traders bring firearms that were to alter drastically the Maori way of life but with them too came contagious diseases to which the Maori had no resistance. Influenza alone wiped out thousands, and for generations the Maori were to be plagued by incessant epidemics. To prepare and dress the flax the traders sought so eagerly, the Maori found it more practicable to live by the flax swamps. There, in unhealthy surroundings, they drove themselves relentlessly and lowered their resistance to the new diseases still further as they meticulously prepared and dressed a full ton of flax to earn a solitary musket. Their diet, too, was reduced to increase the quantities of pig and vegetables for trading.

Traders also brought pigs, dogs and rats. The pigs, too precious in terms of trade to kill, uprooted precious kumara plantations, and the dogs and rats devastated a birdlife with no experience and no fear of such animals.

The pattern of Maori life was totally disrupted, but the musket was to prove even more devastating.

INTER-TRIBAL WARS

TRADITIONALLY, rival groups had joined battle at the slightest pretext. Life was cheap, the doctrine of utu (revenge) uncompromising and for the communal Maori to insult one was to insult all. But to exact utu was only to offend those who had given offence; they were then honour-bound to exact utu in return. To and fro the clashes took place.

As long as the season for fighting was comparatively brief (what little time could be spared away from the kumara plantations) and as long as only a few hundred were engaging in hand-to-hand fighting on more or less equal terms, the toll in lives was no more than the societies could bear. But with the muskets came imbalances in power and a new dimension to the slaughter. And with the musket, too, came the European concept of domination, of one supreme king to whom all owed allegiance. The pattern was irrevocably changed.

The Northland tribe of Ngapuhi, in whose territory were the initial trading centres at the Bay of Islands, were the first to acquire firearms in any number and they lost no opportunity to try out their new weapons on their traditionally armed neighbours. Their chief, Hongi Hika (*c.* 1780-1828), in 1820 had travelled to England and there as an "equal" met George IV. In Sydney, on his way home, he used the presents London society had showered on him to barter for muskets, and he returned to his tribe resolved to emulate the king he had met. In a series of devastating raids as far south as Wellington, the Ngapuhi swept all before them.

It was clear to the other tribes that they too must possess muskets—even though the musket was really only indirectly the cause of the slaughter that followed. At first the Maori had little idea of how to maintain their new weapons, were frequently short of powder, and even when they had serviceable weapons were often bad shots. It has been noted that the psychological, almost supernatural, effect of a volley was so overwhelming to those without guns that they frequently fled, and that in the retreat far more died by the traditional mere than were ever killed by musketfire.

Judge Maning recorded in a Native Land Court judgement: "No human flesh and blood, however hardened, could endure much longer the excitement, privations, danger and unrest ... War had attained its most terrible and forbidden aspect; neither age nor sex was spared; agriculture was neglected; the highest duty of man was to slay and devour his neighbour." In a period of bloodshed almost without parallel, over 60,000 are estimated to have died as each tribe and every hapu recalled age-old insults and set out to avenge them.

Revenge was not the only impulse. Ngati Toa, a tribe from Kawhia, unleashed another series of battles during the same period in their quest for new territory to settle. Under threat from their Waikato neighbours, they migrated south to the Kapiti region and, thanks to the combined ferocity and diplomacy of their leader Te Rauparaha (*c.* 1768-1849), within a few years were the most powerful force in the lower half of the North Island and much of the South.

Holding sway over such vast territory, Te Rauparaha perhaps came closest to the European concept of domination. Indeed, later Europeans were to dub him "the Maori Napoleon" and despite European incursions he was a force to be reckoned with right up to his death in mid-century. The influence of other great warrior chiefs lasted even longer: Tamati Waka Nene (*c.* 1780-1870) became one of the greatest Maori allies the Pakeha ever had, while Potatau Te Wherowhero (*c.* 1800-60) became the first Maori King and thus the focus of opposition to European land settlement during the 1850s.

These inter-tribal battles are not to be confused with the Land Wars with the Pakeha settlers that were to follow, even though a tribe might take sides for or against the Pakeha as much to settle old scores with other participating tribes as to resolve the land struggles with the settlers.

MISSIONARIES

THE BRUTALITY and persecution displayed by the Rev. Samuel Marsden (1765-1838) as a Magistrate in New South Wales contrast with his role in New Zealand's history as the zealous and dedicated missionary responsible for the introduction of Christianity. In New South Wales Marsden had met a number of Maori who had crossed the Tasman as members of ships' crews, and through this accident of "Divine Providence" he became interested in establishing missions in New Zealand. At his own suggestion the London-based Church Missionary Society (an offshoot of the Church of England) in 1808 directed him to establish the country's first mission stations. The enterprise was delayed by general fear engendered by the burning of the *Boyd (p.* **308**) at Whangaroa Harbour, and it was in 1814 that he led the first of a series of parties across the Tasman to set up missions at the Bay of Islands. There the sensitive missionaries lived under the aegis of the Ngapuhi chief Hongi Hika and periodically shuttered their windows to shelter their families from the sight of cannibal rites. Not for 11 years were the first converts to Christianity made, as the missionaries were determined not to baptise a Maori before he or she had a thorough understanding of the faith.

Progress was slow, but by the time the Treaty of Waitangi was signed in 1840 mission stations of three denominations were scattered over much of the northern North Island.

The Anglican missionaries, the first in the field, formed the largest and most effective evangelical organisation in the country. The Wesleyans followed in 1823, when a short-lived mission was established at Whangaroa Harbour and was later re-established at Hokianga Harbour. At first the two denominations co-operated in their common endeavour, but they eventually fell out when both sought to establish stations in the same region, the well-populated Waikato. The coming of Catholicism in 1838 served to re-unite the Protestants. It was then that Bishop Pompallier (*p.* **205**) was appointed Catholic Bishop of Western Oceania and came to live first at Kororareka and later at Auckland. When Pompallier arrived there were scarcely any Catholics in the country, and the established missionaries stirred up considerable hostility and were not above assuring the wondering Maori that Pompallier himself had finally seen the light and had become a convert to their creed.

The missionaries, many of whom made epic expeditions across the length and breadth of the land, played a key role in trying to protect the Maori from exploitation at the hands of Pakeha trader and settler alike while they taught them the skills they were to need to face an uncertain future. More than this, the missionaries, through their protests both in London and in Sydney against the outrageous activities of European adventurers in a land without law, were largely responsible for New South Wales legislation being extended to New Zealand in 1817 and for Busby's being appointed British Resident in 1832. Finally, albeit with reluctance, they urged Britain to assume sovereignty over the country for the Maori's own protection, and used their considerable influence to persuade the Maori to sign the Treaty of Waitangi in 1840.

The missionaries at times confused their creed with their devotion to European culture, and this urge to "civilise" saw extravagant demands being made on Maori culture, which all too rapidly accelerated the Maori's identity crisis and the demise of much that was beneficial in their tradition. Objection was taken to everything from their manner of dress to the sexual symbolism of their carvings, and by way of repentance for the latter much fine artwork was destroyed. Measured in terms of numbers of converts the missionaries hardly achieved a success commensurate with their efforts. However, by schooling the Maori in European modes of agriculture they laid the foundation for their rapid assimilation into the economy the settlers were to bring with them. Most of the early settlements were dependent on the diligent and successful Maori farmers, and it was they who became the country's first exporters with shipments of produce to Australia.

As the missionaries gained respect, so grew their mana and they were able to have slaves freed, cannibalism abandoned and at times even to avert war. For their part the Maori were both bewildered and bemused as missionaries of differing denominations argued as to whose was the superior atua (god) and at least once even put the missionaries to a form of trial by ordeal (see *p.* **244**). When approaching a village and asked which god they worshipped, the shrewder missionary would ensure an hospitable reception by answering, "The one true God!"

In the fury of the inter-tribal wars, the Maori became progressively more receptive to the concept of a God of peace, and by the 1840s in many villages prayers were said daily. But in the north, British sovereignty had brought customs duties and a drop in income for Hone Heke's Ngapuhi. Soon war had flared to cripple missionary endeavour (missionaries often acted as spies for the settlers), and almost half a century was to pass before Maori and Pakeha were to come to terms.

ANNEXATION BY BRITAIN

Law and disorder: Sealers, whalers, flax and timber traders all came hard on the heels of Cook, interested only in exploiting the new land and its people. A few became Pakeha-Maori and lived as members of a tribe, but quite a number settled at Kororareka (now Russell) where they introduced the Maori to liquor, to prostitution and to diseases to which the Maori had no resistance.

From time to time news of atrocities perpetrated by Europeans in New Zealand filtered back to New South Wales and Britain. None more so than in 1820 when Captain John Stewart on the brig *Elizabeth* ferried Te Rauparaha and a war party from Kapiti Island to Akaroa. Stewart enticed a rival chief to board his ship where, with a number of his followers, he was kidnapped, tortured and slain. The Governor of New South Wales felt impotent at his inability to punish the predominantly British perpetrators of such outrages, and Kororareka was a continual scandal to the large number of humanitarians in Britain.

In 1817 New South Wales legislation and in 1823 the jurisdiction of its courts were extended to New Zealand, but delays in investigating offences and the difficulties in ferrying often reluctant witnesses across the Tasman to give their evidence rendered the gestures empty if well intentioned. Authority was given but law was unenforceable.

Pressures for annexation: Extremists in Britain felt that natives of countries such as New Zealand could be protected only if the Europeans' contaminating influences were kept away, but as nothing could be done to prevent what was taking place in New Zealand it became apparent that sooner or later Britain would have to step in. Historians generally ascribe Britain's motives for eventually annexing the country to the agitation of British humanitarians, who then had a large and powerful following both within and without the Government. But it has also been suggested that far from being a magnanimous gesture of goodwill, Britain's principal concern may have been to prevent France, her European rival, from acquiring a toehold comparatively close to her Australian colonies. Added to these factors was the growing pressure to colonise the country which was coming from the New Zealand Company and its influential adherents. The French do not at any stage appear to have any more than flirted with the idea of annexing New Zealand, and if there was a "race for New Zealand" it may be seen as taking place not between the British and the French but rather between the British Government and the New Zealand Company.

The suggestion that annexation was prompted primarily by humanitarian considerations is deeply embedded in the country's folklore, but has been challenged by some historians. They argue that Busby, for personal reasons, was sending distorted despatches in the hope of enhancing his own position. The missionaries, too, probably over-reacted, for reasons both of paternalism and religious conviction. By contrast, growing numbers of pioneers were prepared to bring their families with them, an action which seems hardly consistent with the country's being in the grip of anarchy. Perhaps the menace from which the country most needed protection was the threat of uncontrolled settlement from Britain.

The British Government, extended by commitments to an already vast Empire, was reluctant to commit herself to further responsibilities. Indeed, although Cook had claimed the country for Britain in 1769 and was under orders so to do, the British had since then studiously excluded New Zealand from published lists of her territories.

British Resident: Hesitantly, in 1832, James Busby (1801-71) was sent from New South Wales to be "British Resident", to protect the Maori from the British adventurer and to protect those British who wished to live and trade in peace—and in that order. But even had a better-suited man been sent he would have accomplished nothing. Busby, a "man-o'war without guns", had nothing more potent than moral persuasion with which to enforce his dictates on an incorrigible collection of reprobates, and the exercise was one of futility.

Ensconced in his residence at Waitangi at the Bay of Islands, Busby's only achievement came in 1835 when he induced 35 chiefs to proclaim themselves the "United Tribes of New Zealand", an action taken when it was learned that the deluded and self-styled "Sovereign Chief" Baron de Thierry was on his way from Britain to found his "kingdom". The son of French emigré parents, he claimed to have purchased much of the Hokianga district through Thomas Kendall (the country's first resident missionary) and dreamed of establishing a Utopia on the shores of the harbour there. The "United Tribes" declaration was ridiculed in New South Wales as "a paper pellet fired off at Baron de Thierry", but was taken more seriously in London.

At the same time increasing numbers of speculators were crossing the Tasman to "buy" vast areas of land for ludicrous sums. One Australian syndicate claimed to have purchased the entire South Island, with Stewart Island thrown in, all for a few hundred pounds. As the situation developed, so grew the clamour for official British action.

THE TREATY OF WAITANGI

ACTION finally came in 1839 when the unwilling Captain William Hobson, RN (1793-1842) (*pp.* **43-44**) was despatched from London under orders to negotiate with the chiefs for the transfer of sovereignty to the British Crown with "the free and intelligent consent of the natives". Thereafter he was to declare himself Lieutenant-Governor and be subject to the over-riding authority of the Governor of New South Wales. New Zealand was to be a dependency of that Australian colony for a year, until it was established as a separate colony.

Hobson muddled his orders—prematurely declaring himself Lieutenant-Governor—but with the help of Busby and the missionaries drafted the Treaty of Waitangi and persuaded an assembly of chiefs to sign it at Busby's residence on 6 February 1840.

The "Treaty" was consistent with the British fiction of regarding the Maori as a fully sovereign people. It assigned sovereignty to Britain and in exchange guaranteed the Maori peaceful possession of their lands and granted them "all the Rights and Privileges of British Subjects". The Crown was granted the exclusive right to buy such land as the Maori might in future wish to sell. Few chiefs could have understood what was involved. The Maori had no concept of sovereignty and at least one chief later explained that his Queen had sent him a blanket and he had signed only to acknowledge its safe receipt. Indeed, in the course of drafting the Treaty the word "kawanatanga" was invented by the missionaries to describe sovereignty—"Governor" was first transliterated into "kawana", and then "kawanatanga" was coined to mean "governorship" or "sovereignty". As a legal agreement it must be regarded as being at best dubious.

As a glance at the texts below will show, there were considerable disparities between the two versions, including, in Article Two, references to fishing and other rights, as "the exclusive right of Preemption", which do not appear in the Maori text, and to rights of "chieftainship" (or Maori sovereignty), which do not appear in the English version. These differences have engendered considerable controversy in recent times.

More fundamentally, the Treaty could satisfy no one. The Maori was forced to sell land only to the Government, who paid pitiful sums in return; the settler could buy, at vastly inflated prices, only from the Government. Both Maori and settler believed they had been harshly done by. Nor did the Maori find themselves with "all the Rights and Privileges of British Subjects"—most conspicuously they were denied the vote on the pretext that they did not own land, and this despite the Royal guarantee of "full exclusive and undisturbed possession". Further, the concept that lay behind Article Two, that in more populous regions special districts would be declared in which Maori custom would enjoy the force of law, was never realised as Sir George Grey was hostile to any suggestion that the "barbaric" customs of the native should anywhere prevail over the "civilised" code of the settler.

Thus the Treaty, while securing apparent legitimacy for the annexation by Britain, miscarried in its most important respect by failing to unify the races. It has remained a contentious issue in Maori circles ever since, and although "Waitangi Day" (6 February) is celebrated as the country's national day, the Treaty has never been accorded the force of law.

The Treaty concluded, leisurely inquiries then began into the land claims of Europeans, and those unable to show that value had been given and free consent obtained either had their claims markedly reduced or totally disallowed. However it was not land but the imposition of customs duties that first sparked violence between Maori and settler.

The duties dissuaded passing ships from putting in to the Bay of Islands and the disgruntled Ngapuhi under Hone Heke, irate at the loss in trade, felled the Union Jack-bedecked flagstaff at Kororareka on no fewer than four occasions before they finally attacked and sacked the township. Battle honours were even after a number of engagements with British troops, and when Governor Sir George Grey arrived to take up his post he hurried to the north and personally supervised the troops who overwhelmed Ruapekapeka pa to end the "War in the North". The New Zealand Company settlements at Nelson (in the South Island), Wanganui and Wellington saw the first skirmishes of the Land Wars, but in the south, too, Grey acted with decision and the Wellington uprising was firmly put down.

The English text: "Her Majesty Victoria Queen of the United Kingdom of Great Britain and Ireland regarding with Her Royal Favour the Native Chiefs and Tribes of New Zealand and anxious to protect their just Rights and Property and to secure to them the enjoyment of Peace and Good Order has deemed it necessary in consequence of the great number of Her Majesty's Subjects who have already settled in New Zealand and the rapid extension of Emigration both from Europe and Australia which is still in progress to constitute and appoint a functionary properly authorised to treat with the Aborigines of New Zealand for the recognition of Her Majesty's Sovereign authority over the whole or any part of those islands—Her Majesty therefore being desirous to establish a settled form of Civil Government with a view to avert the evil consequences which must result from the absence of the necessary Laws and Institutions alike to the native population and to Her subjects has been graciously pleased to empower and to authorise me William Hobson a Captain in Her Majesty's Royal Navy Consul and Lieutenant Governor of such parts of New Zealand as may be or hereafter shall be ceded to Her Majesty to invite the confederated and independent Chiefs of New Zealand to concur in the following Articles and Conditions.

Article The First

The Chiefs of the Confederation of the United Tribes of New Zealand and the separate and independent Chiefs who have not become members of the Confederation cede to Her Majesty the Queen of England absolutely and without reservation all the rights and powers of Sovereignty which the said Confederation or Individual Chiefs respectively exercise or possess, or may be supposed to exercise or to possess over their respective Territories as the sole Sovereigns thereof.

Article The Second

Her Majesty the Queen of England confirms and guarantees to the Chiefs and Tribes of New Zealand and to the respective families and individuals thereof the full exclusive and undisturbed possession of their Lands and Estates Forests Fisheries and other properties which they may collectively or individually possess so long as it is their wish and desire to retain the same in their possession; but the Chiefs of the United Tribes and the individual Chiefs yield to Her Majesty the exclusive right of Preemption over such lands as the proprietors thereof may be disposed to alienate at such prices as may be agreed upon between the respective Proprietors and persons appointed by Her Majesty to treat with them in that behalf.

Article The Third

In consideration thereof Her Majesty the Queen of England extends to the Natives of New Zealand Her royal protection and imparts to them all the Rights and Privileges of British Subjects.

W.HOBSON Lieutenant Governor.

Now therefore We the Chiefs of the Confederation of the United Tribes of New Zealand being assembled in Congress at Victoria in Waitangi and We the Separate and Independent Chiefs of New Zealand claiming authority over the Tribes and Territories which are specified after our respective names, having been made fully to understand the Provisions of the foregoing Treaty, accept and enter into the same in the full spirit and meaning thereof: in witness of which we have attached our signatures or marks at the places and the dates respectively specified.
Done at Waitangi this Sixth day of February in the year of Our Lord One thousand eight hundred and forty.
(Here follow signatures, dates, etc.)"

The Maori text: "Ko Wikitoria te Kuini o Ingarani i tana mahara atawai ki nga Rangatira me nga Hapu o Nu Tirani i tana hiahia hoki kia tohungia ki a ratou o ratou rangatiratanga me to ratou wenua. a kia mau tonu hoki te Rongo ki a ratou me te Atanoho hoki kua wakaaro ia he mea tika kea tukua mai tetahi Rangatira—hei kai

wakarite ki nga Tangata maori o Nu Tirani—kia wakaaetia e nga Rangatira maori
te kawanatanga o te Kuini ki nga wahikatoa o te wenua nei me nga motu—na te
mea hoki he tokomaha ke nga tangata o tona Iwi Kua noho ki tenei wenua, a e haere
mai nei.

Na ko te Kuini e hiahia ana kia wakaritea te Kawanatanga kia kana ai nga kino e
puta mai ki te tangata Maori ki te Pakeha e noho ture kore ana.

Na. kua pai te Kuini kia tukua a hau a Wiremu Hopihona he Kapitana i te Roiara
Nawi hei Kawana mo nga wahi katoa o Nu Tirani e tukua aianei. amua atu ke te
Kuini. e mea atu ana ia ki nga Rangatira o te wakaminenga o nga hapu o Nu Tirani
me era Rangatira atu enei ture ka korerotia nei.

Ko te Tuatahi

Ko nga Rangatira o te wakaminenga me nga Rangatira katoa hoki ki hai i uru ki
taua waka-minenga ka tuku rawa atu ki te Kuini o Ingarani ake tonu atu—te
Kawanatanga katoa o o ratou wenua.

Ko te Tuarua

Ko te Kuini o Ingarani ka wakarite ka wakaae ki nga Rangatira ki nga hapu—ki
nga tangata katoa o Nu Tirani te tino rangatiratanga o o ratou wenua o ratou kainga
me o ratou taonga katoa. Otiia ko nga Rangatira o te wakaminenga me nga Rangatira
katoa atu ka tuku ki te Kuini te hokonga o era wahi wenua e pai ai te tangata nona
te Wenua—ki te ritenga o te utu e wakaritea ai e ratou ko te kai hoko e meatia nei
e te Kuini hei kai hoko mona.

Ko te Tuatoru

Hei wakaritenga mai hoki tenei mo te wakaaetanga ki te Kawanatanga o te Kuini—
Ka tiakina e te Kuini o Ingarani nga tangata maori katoa o Nu Tirani ka tukua ki a
ratou nga tikanga katoa rite tahi ki ana mea ki nga tangata o Ingarani.

(Signed) W. Hobson
Consul & Lieutenant Governor.

Na ko matou ko nga Rangatira o te Wakaminenga o nga hapu o Nu Tirani ka
huihui nei ki Waitangi ko matou hoki ko nga Rangatira o Nu Tirani ka kite nei i te
ritenga o enei kupu. ka tangohia ka wakaaetia katoatia e matou. koia ka tohungia ai
o matou ingoa o matou tohu.

Ka meatia tenei ki Waitangi i te ono o nga ra o Pepueri i te tau kotahi mano, e
waru rau e wa te kau o to tatou Ariki."

The Maori text translated: "Here's Victoria, Queen of England, in her gracious
remembrance towards the chiefs and tribes of New Zealand, and in her desire that
the chieftainships and their lands should be secured to them and that obedience also
should be held by them, and the peaceful state also; has considered it as a just thing,
to send here some chief to be a person to arrange with the native men of New
Zealand, that the Governorship of the Queen may be assented to by the native chiefs
in all places of the land, and of the islands. Because too many together are the men
of her tribe who have sat down in this land and are coming hither.

Now it is the Queen who desires that the Governorship may be arranged that evils
may not come to the native men, to the white who dwells lawless. There! Now the
Queen has been good that I should be sent, William Hobson, a captain of the Royal
Navy, a Governor for all the places in New Zealand that are yielded now or hereafter
to the Queen. She says to the Chiefs of the Assemblage (Confederation) of the tribes
of New Zealand, and other chiefs besides, these laws which shall be spoken now.

Here's the first: Here's the chief of the Assemblage, and all the chiefs also who
have not joined the Assemblage mentioned, cede to the utmost to the Queen of
England for ever continually to the utmost the whole Governorship of their lands.

Here's the second: Here's the Queen of England arranges and confirms to the
chiefs, to all the men of New Zealand the entire chieftainship of their lands, their
villages, and all their property.

But here's the chiefs of the Assemblage, and all the chiefs besides, yield to the
Queen the buying of those places of land where the man whose land it is shall be
good to the arrangement of the payment which the buyer shall arrange to them, who
is told by the Queen to buy for her.

Here's the third: This, too, is an arrangement in return for the assent of the
Governorship of the Queen. The Queen of England will protect all the native men
of New Zealand. She yields to them all the rights, one and the same as her doings
to the men of England.

(Signed) W. Hobson
Consul & Lieutenant Governor.

Now here's we: Here's the chiefs of the Assemblage of the tribes of New Zealand who are congregated at Waitangi. Here's we too. Here's the chiefs of New Zealand, who see the meaning of these words, we accept, we entirely agree to all. Truly we do mark our names and marks.

This is done at Waitangi on the six of the days in February, in the year one thousand eight hundred and four tens of our Lord.''

THE PATTERN OF EUROPEAN SETTLEMENT

The New Zealand Company: Once the Treaty of Waitangi was signed the way was clear for organised settlement to begin. Indeed, as far as the New Zealand Company was concerned it had already begun.

The Company has its origins in the "Wakefield Scheme" of colonisation, conceived by Edward Gibbon Wakefield (1796-1862) (*p. 282*) at a time when colonisation was at its zenith. The scheme had the overall conservative aim of preserving the existing social and economic structure by transporting a cross-section of English society, excluding only its lowest level. In essence the scheme called for the Company to acquire large blocks of cheap land. This was then to be sold at a "sufficient price"; a price low enough to encourage wealthy migrants yet high enough to prevent labourers from immediately becoming landowners. The difference in price was then to be used to ship labourers to the colony to provide the landowners with the labour they needed and to maintain a proper balance between capital and labour.

In London in 1837 a "New Zealand Association" was formed, but its altruistic plans for a second "East India"-type of company (with the Association systematically colonising the country and governing its own territories) were rejected by the British Government. The following year the Association gave way to the "New Zealand Company" which, as a profit-making enterprise, promptly defied British policy by dispatching Colonel William Wakefield on the *Tory* to buy land for settlement at Wellington and elsewhere. Opposition to the move came from humanitarians within the British Government who were anxious to protect the Maori from exploitation and hopeful of concluding a formal treaty with the "natives" before any organised settlement got under way. For although the New Zealand Company claimed that only its initiative forced the British to annex New Zealand ahead of the French and so save the country for the Empire, in fact the British Government had already decided to annex New Zealand, but in its own time.

Knowing the Government's intentions, and eager to obtain cheap land before the Crown, by treaty, acquired the sole right to purchase land from the Maori, the New Zealand Company in London hastily recruited settlers, "sold" land and dispatched its first passenger ships, all before Colonel William Wakefield aboard the *Tory* had even arrived in New Zealand, let alone purchased any land. Further, the Company had foreseen the future commercial importance of Wellington and had expected its "settlement" there to be chosen as the country's capital—a hope that was not realised until 1865 as Governor Hobson with good reason preferred the hitherto deserted site of Auckland. The so-called "race for New Zealand" was, therefore, not between the British and the French, with the Company urging the British on, but rather between the would-be exploiters of the New Zealand Company and the humanitarians within the British Government.

About the time that the Company's first settlers were reaching Wellington, Governor Hobson and his accompanying civil servants were moving from Sydney to the Bay of Islands to conclude the Treaty of Waitangi, so setting the scene for a 30-year struggle between the two groups.

The "New Zealand bubble" bursts: Far from inducing only sturdy and mildly heroic stock to migrate to New Zealand, the New Zealand Company's advertising was calculated to persuade "men of refinement" that they "might emigrate without any material disturbance of their habits"—and predictably enough, when such "gentlemen" encountered grim reality many lost little time in moving on to more established settlements in Australia, Canada and the USA. Further, instead of achieving large-scale and orderly "planned settlements", the Company succeeded best in encouraging absentee landowning and wild speculation.

The role of absentee landowners has been widely misinterpreted, for rather than undermining the venture the Company depended on them for success. An ingenious lottery system was devised to attract their participation which overcame the "first come first served" dangers of the best sites selling swiftly but the less choice hanging fire, and actually saw the 1,000 "land orders" for Wellington's original land sale, each costing £101, sell out in London in a single month.

Although in formative years absentee landowners effectively denied economic stability to the Company's settlements, at Wellington, Nelson, Wanganui and New Plymouth it was really only their participation that enabled the settlements to be founded at all. To encourage landowners to emigrate to New Zealand, the Company gave them a 75 per cent rebate on their purchase money to meet the cost of fares.

Thus the more landowners there were who claimed the rebate, the less surplus money there was available for the Company to send out labourers. It was therefore in the Company's best interests to have a large proportion of absentee landowners—those who never claimed the 75 per cent rebate.

In England, at the time the first "land orders" were being sold, colonial land was believed to rise rapidly in value and speculators moved in to give birth to a frenzy of land jobbing. But while speculators were anxious to be in on the ground floor, this could only last for the first land sale for each settlement. Enthusiasm was hard to raise for subsequent land development, by which time colonial land had lost its appeal as a quick means to a fortune. It was on this rock that the New Zealand Company foundered, and in 1850 its remaining New Zealand land (437,000 hectares) was taken over by the British Government for £268,000. This sum, to the rage of the settlers, became a first charge on the future land revenue of New Zealand—rage, as settlers, even those who owed nothing to the efforts of the Company, found themselves forced to indemnify shareholders who had already profited on their investment. Secondary reasons for the Company's failure, and those most commonly given, were disputes over land titles, difficult terrain which was slow to survey, and the neglect of wool which alone could have been profitably exported.

The New Zealand Company's hostility to the Treaty of Waitangi and its lack of benevolence towards the Maori aroused the ire of British humanitarians en masse. It had been impractical in the extreme when it came to organising the settlers, and its London directors had tended to prefer the interests of shareholders and landowners in England to those of the settlers in the infant colony. Yet it is to the Company's credit that from May 1839 to January 1843 it dispatched no fewer than 57 ships and nearly 19,000 migrants who otherwise would probably have emigrated to North America.

Other organised immigration: Wakefield was not the first to plan settlements for New Zealand. An earlier New Zealand Company had as early as 1827 made an abortive attempt to settle land at Hokianga, and 10 years later the errant knight Baron de Thierry arrived in the same area with a riff-raff of followers, in his fantasy believing he might establish himself as "Sovereign Chief of New Zealand".

Later efforts were to meet with greater success. The New Zealand Company established settlements at Wellington (1840), Wanganui (1840), Nelson (1841) and New Plymouth (1841). The Canterbury Association, an offshoot of the New Zealand Company, established Christchurch (1850) and the Free Church of Scotland, another exponent of the "Wakefield Scheme", founded Dunedin (1848). Of the "four main centres", only Hobson's choice for capital, Auckland, was not a "Wakefield settlement".

The philosophy of the promoters of "Wakefield Schemes" was basically conservative: to transplant existing British society—even if in practice those transplanted rebelled at the notion. In sharp contrast were the apostles of change and a number of nonconformist groups who saw in the new land an opportunity to realise their ideals. Among the visionaries were George Vesey Stewart (Katikati 1875 and Te Puke 1880), the Rev. Norman McLeod (Waipu 1853) and William Brame (Albertland, on Kaipara Harbour, 1863). There were also bands of compatriots, such as the Bohemians who came to Puhoi (1863) and the Scandinavians who were brought to build roads and founded such settlements as Dannevirke and Norsewood (1872). Other organising corporations included the French colonising company of Nanto-Bordelaise (Akaroa 1840) and the Manchester Corporation which, though styled as a charity, actually returned handsome profits to its "benefactors" at the same time as it settled parts of the Manawatu in the 1870s (e.g., Feilding).

In later years, too, handfuls of disaffected radicals were to make their way to New Zealand, to compound the country's dichotomy of ultra-conservative and vigorous reformer. These included such men as Joseph Masters, founder of the Small Farm Association and responsible for settlement in the Wairarapa (e.g., Masterton, Greytown) and Samuel Parnell, who in 1840 insisted on working an eight-hour day and before he died noted that "the chord struck at Petone fifty years ago is vibrating round the world".

Settlements, too, grew up at random on harbours (e.g., Napier, Gisborne), on navigable rivers (e.g., Dargaville), and at other strategic points, often where there was already a Maori village.

On the collapse of the New Zealand Company, provincial governments assumed the mantle of coloniser and encouraged migrants with free passages, land grants and guaranteed employment on roadworks while they broke in their new land. Earlier, Governor Hobson had forseen the problem of finding labour for road-building and in 1839 had actually suggested that New Zealand, at least in part, be declared a penal settlement—a cure that would certainly have been worse than the ill.

The Land Wars brought the military settlers, the soldiers offered land and free passage in exchange for service. To accommodate them when the fighting was over, a number of military settlements were founded, principally in the Waikato (e.g., Hamilton).

28

Gold discoveries, fostered by rewards tended by hopeful provincial governments, drew large numbers from the Californian and Australian goldfields, many of whom stayed on after the gold had petered out. Indeed, in 1863 alone some 35,000 fortune-seekers flocked into the country, a number which exceeded the country's entire European population of only nine years earlier. Gold also attracted many Chinese, whose meticulous approach to their task quickly earned them the ire of other miners, and few remained.

With Vogel's policy in the 1870s of massive overseas borrowings and free-spending on public works came a further flood of assisted migrants, and as they forged new railways through virgin bush fresh townships were established (e.g., Taihape, Te Kuiti). By the end of the century kauri gum had lured Dalmatians, among others, to Northland.

New Zealand is thus seen to have been peopled in a myriad of ways, and it was random immigration that in the final analysis provided the bulk of the country's European population, the New Zealand Company by comparison providing a "mere trickle". The migrants, if disenchanted by the rigours of the industrial revolution, were generally enterprising if of lower class, and brought with them the wish for a better life in a classless society, or at least a society with only a middle class.

For many years, central government consistently supported immigration from Europe, principally from Britain and particularly in the post-World War II period. More recently, however, immigration has been largely restricted to those with skills in short supply on the local labour market.

Over the last 50 years, as pressure of population has increased in the Pacific Islands, New Zealand has also witnessed the arrival of large numbers of Polynesian immigrants, and Auckland has come to have the largest Islander population of any Polynesian centre.

THE LAND WARS

The Maori and land: The early European arrivals, fresh from countries seemingly overpopulated and intensively farmed, could not readily comprehend the use the Maori made of their land. Burial grounds and kumara fields they could, but hunting, fishing and tapu areas appeared to be lying idle and as such seemed to be "waste lands". Nor could they understand the concept of Maori land tenure whereby land was vested not in an individual or even a chief but in a whole hapu whose unanimous agreement would be needed to dispose of it but to whom the very act of voluntary disposal was both alien and an anathema. Traditionally land changed hands only by conquest followed by occupation, and land was Papa, the Earth Mother with whom the Maori enjoyed an intimate relationship on which their spiritual wellbeing as well as their material culture was founded.

It is plain that the early land deals were regarded by the Maori "sellers" as more in the nature of a lease, transferring rights of occupation and enjoyment rather than as a transfer of any substance. Indeed the Treaty of Waitangi was explained by one chief as transferring the "shadow of the land" to Queen Victoria: "The substance of the land remains with us." But within a year he was bemoaning that "the substance of the land goes to the Europeans, the shadow only will be our portion."

The Treaty gave the Crown the sole right to buy land from the Maori, so that as the European population grew and as the Maori became progressively less willing to sell, confrontation between the Crown and the Maori was inevitable. The concept of the New Zealand colony had been born in Britain of humanitarian principles but, with typically rapacious settlers, it was in practice quickly degenerating, for the aspirations of the Maori and those of the settlers were quite incompatible.

Fighting first flared in 1843 near the New Zealand Company settlement at Nelson when in the "Wairau Affray" militant settlers rashly sought to claim the fertile Wairau plains long before their disputed title was investigated by the Lands Commissioner. Further fighting broke out in Northland in 1845—"Heke's War", the War in the North, prompted by customs duties. The following year saw clashes at Wellington, where ancestral land was "sold" by another tribe to the New Zealand Company, and in 1847 skirmishes took place at Wanganui after land had been occupied which the Maori claimed never to have sold. However, it was not until 1860 that the North Island as a whole was plunged into war.

Portents of War: To problems posed by a complex concept of land ownership and compounded by poor administration, and economic and population pressures on the part of the settlers, was added in 1858 the spectre of the Maori King Movement (*pp.* **159-60**). The King Movement had its genesis in attempts to form "land leagues" to resist the sale of Maori land and in the fact that little was being done for the Maori by the Government—even though it sold Maori land for 20 times what was paid for it and the Maori provided about half of its taxation revenue. The Maori were being ineptly governed by the Pakeha, they were denied the vote, and if sound administration was wanted they would have to provide it for themselves. The movement, although dedicated to the retention of Maori-owned land, politically had much to offer had its possibilities been realised, for the country's constitution actually provided for Maori areas of local government where custom would have the force of law. The settlers chose rather to regard the movement as an act of rebellion, though Queen Victoria was included in the movement's prayers and its leaders, at least initially, planned only for peace with the Pakeha.

Until 1852 the country had been under direct rule from Britain, but with the bestowing of self-government the Maori's position had become the more invidious. Although the Governor formally retained control of native affairs as a matter affecting Imperial interests, he was nonetheless dependent on the legislature to pass what laws he needed. The two could not find common ground on matters of native policy, and at a time when constructive action was needed either to counter or encourage the Maori King Movement, nothing was done. The executive and the legislature were deadlocked. Governor Gore Browne, largely ignorant of Maori custom, virtually delegated his responsibilities to Donald McLean, who was convinced that the Maori King Movement would collapse like other so-called "land leagues" before it. More than this, the Maori saw McLean, both Secretary for Native Affairs and Chief Land Purchase Officer, as living proof that the Governor's policy towards the Maori was simply dedicated to the acquisition of their land.

The settlers, hemmed in by surrounding Maori-owned land, had practised a more-or-less subsistence form of agriculture and in the mid-1850s were crippled by a slump in farm export prices. Moreoever, crop farming was not suited to the conditions of the time, and before the settlers could break out into pastoral farming much larger areas of land were needed. From their point of view, a way had to be found to open up the vast tracts of Maori land. In some respects the land shortage was apparent rather than real, for speculators had bought up large areas without the slightest intention of farming them, and rather than meet the high prices demanded by the speculators, the settlers urged the Government to acquire more Maori land and make it available cheaply. In 1858 the number of settlers for the first time surpassed that of the Maori, and two years later the undercurrent of mutual resentment reached flashpoint. The Government then chose to enforce a patently defective "purchase" by marching troops on to the Waitara Block (near New Plymouth) and dispossessed its rightful Te Ati Awa owners (*pp. 263-64*).

Conflict: From the Waitara, war engulfed Taranaki and fighting spread across the central regions of the North Island. But the Maori people were themselves divided. The tribes that comprised the Waikato-based Maori King Movement were largely descended from the *Tainui* canoe, and although Taranaki and Waikato tribes were able to forget past histories of bitter conflict, a number of other tribes grasped the opportunity to level old scores by joining the Government to fight against their traditional enemies.

The Waikato was invaded from the north (*p. 91*). A series of battles along the river forced the Kingites south until, in its finest hour, the movement was vanquished at Orakau in 1864 to the cry of "Peace shall never be made! Never! Never!" Would-be reinforcements from the East Cape were intercepted at Rotoiti as they made their way inland and in the same month, in the Bay of Plenty, the supporters of the Maori King scored a notable victory at Gate Pa before being overwhelmed at Te Ranga (*p. 217*).

At once a new challenge arose: Hauhauism (*p. 167*), a revivalist religion whose rituals its detractors maintained induced "true believers" to think they had immunity from Pakeha bullets. Certainly the fighting that resulted was the fiercest of all the campaigns. Fighting once more enflamed Taranaki and spread to the East Cape "like fire in the fern". Before the Hauhau movement was spent, Te Kooti (*pp. 234-35*) escaped from captivity on the Chatham Islands to conduct a brilliant guerrilla campaign from his Urewera sanctuary until, with the participants exhausted, fighting petered out in 1872.

But Te Kooti had slipped through to the safety of the "King Country", the rugged inland area where dwelt the Maori King and his many followers and into which the Pakeha ventured at their peril. It was not until peace was made in 1881 that the threat of further conflict subsided.

Had the Maori participants chosen to fight a purely guerrilla campaign (Te Kooti, for example, was only really worsted when he sought a confrontation) they might well have succeeded in deterring further settlement if not in expelling the Pakeha completely. But the Maori lacked any form of unifying nationalism, for not until the land question arose did they have any common bond beyond a loose "canoe-type" of inter-tribal allegiance. Tradition, too, died hard. The gallant Maori were generally keen to determine which side had the better fighters, an anxiety that led them to fight set battles which, with artillery ranged against them, they could rarely win. Not that they were unable to defeat both Imperial and Colonial forces on a number of celebrated occasions (e.g., at Ohaeawai, Puketakauere, Gate Pa and Te Ngutu-o-te-manu—*for all see index*).

To "punish" so-called "rebel" tribes, the Government arbitrarily confiscated vast areas of ancestral land, a form of justice dispensed unevenly and with more weight being given to the fertility of the land involved than to the relative hostility of each tribe. Some was given to "friendly" tribes as a reward for their "loyalty"; some was allocated to military settlers lured to New Zealand to fight by the promise of land grants; some was sold to recoup part of the cost of the wars.

Note: Individual battles, campaigns and local wars are more particularly described under appropriate entries in the Alphabetical Section.

Resentment lingers: The end of hostilities did not mean the end of resistance, and at Parihaka (*p.* **77**) the chiefs Te Whiti and Tohu led a campaign of civil disobedience. Surveyors were obstructed, roads blocked with fences, and cleared land ploughed up. Jubilant Maori were led off to gaols soon crowded to capacity while those still at Parihaka rejected all things European and saved for a "Day of Reckoning" when the Pakeha would voluntarily leave the country.

But the "Day of Reckoning" dawned on 5 November 1881, a day of infamy when armed troops marched into the defenceless Parihaka to arrest the unresisting chiefs, to forcibly disperse the unarmed and peaceful population of several thousand, and to destroy the village.

Active and passive resistance had failed, but it was many years before the smouldering resentment subsided. The prophet Rua Kenana (*pp.* **240-41**) urged his followers to boycott military service during World War I, but before that war had ended, a battalion had been formed that was exclusively Maori, the forbear of the "Maori Battalion" that fought with considerable distinction in World War II.

Land unlocked: The Land Wars achieved the Government's purpose, and choice areas of fertile land in places such as the Waikato, Taranaki and the Bay of Plenty were acquired by the settlers. Yet in the last analysis it was the abolition of the Crown right of pre-emption in 1862 which in the long run unlocked the remaining Maori land. Land Courts individualised Maori land ownership as they were required to name at first no more than 10 persons and then only one person as the owner of each block. Their unity destroyed, these individuals became easy prey for unscrupulous land agents who plied them with alcohol and money and for traders who let Maori landowners run well into debt before offering them the choice of sale or gaol.

Under Crown pre-emption the Maori had sold some 2.8 million hectares; by the wars' end another 1.2 million hectares had been confiscated, and between 1865 and 1892 a further 2.8 million hectares were sold. They were left with about 4.4 million hectares, a quarter of which was leased to settlers and the remainder of which was so rugged and then of little use. Today, only about 5 percent of the country's land remains in Maori (i.e. communal) ownership. This, then, is the legacy of contemporary New Zealand and still the source of seething discontent.

TOWARDS A MULTI-CULTURAL SOCIETY

THOSE VISITING in the 1990s might be forgiven for thinking that the country was in a state of uproar over its colonial past. On the one hand, Maori activists periodically occupy symbolic sites, and on the other, Pakeha New Zealand seems determined to impose solutions rather than negotiate them. A bitterness on the part of the Maori for reasons of deprivation seems matched by a resentment by Pakeha for apparent Maori preferment. In the media, journalists and politicians alike are experiencing a "feeding frenzy" on matters Maori — and not always to the enlightenment of those listening.

The modern resurgence of Maoritanga followed a prolonged period of decline provoked by the massive post-World War II shift of Maori population to the cities, during which the rural-based tribal authority effectively collapsed. As their people dispersed to the cities, both to serve new industries and in response to increasingly mechanised farming techniques, traditional forms of control proved progressively less effective. Government policies now stress the country's biculturalism.

Whereas forty years ago, the Maori language was seldom heard, today it covers the airwaves and a cluster of Maori language publications (often with some articles in English) serve as valuable points of access to contemporary Maori debate. In earlier times Maori children were beaten at school, and at times at home, for using their own language, but in recent years schools have embraced the language and there are over 40 state schools where classes are only conducted in Maori.

At the same time the Pakeha have ceased claiming for their country the title of "the best race relations in the world", and Maori increasingly point to shockingly disproportionate rates of conviction and imprisonment and marked degrees of economic deprivation as illustrating the fact that there is still some considerable distance to be travelled.

It was the Fourth Labour Government who, in 1984, began the moves to confront honestly and fairly the legacies of the colonial past. Through the Waitangi Tribunal it accorded a long overdue importance to the spirit of the Treaty of Waitangi, and the law courts also recognised for the first time the Treaty's special place in a society without a written constitution. The shifts in resources implicit in these developments, particularly returns of land to Maori ownership and recognition of Maori rights to fishing beds, have disconcerted some elements of a Pakeha population previously comfortable in its dominant role. Much of New Zealand society remains in a stage of uneasy transition in which perceptions of the Treaty are slowly moving from its being an ambivalent symbol of colonial oppression to forming the cornerstone of bicultural good faith. But if some of European society is in turmoil, so, too, is much of Maoridom. Leaders are still traditional, they have no democratic credentials and they are increasingly challenged by younger radicals.

Ironically for the Pakeha nationalists, the Maori claims on contentious land in state ownership have effectively frozen state land sales and thereby partially checked sales of land to foreigners.

About 93 percent of the Maori population lives in the North Island. Four of the seats in Parliament have been reserved for Maori Members, although Maori could opt instead to vote on the General rather than the Maori roll. A feature in recent years has been the small but growing number of Maori and even Samoan who have been elected from the General electoral roll, signs that a multi-cultural society is, indeed, emerging.

The definition of "Maori" has become increasingly less distinct with the high rate of intermarriage over the generations. There are now very few Maori of full blood, and innumerable Pakeha with Maori ancestors. Although the Electoral Act of necessity has defined "Maori" in terms of ancestry, in practice the distinction has moved from being one of lineage to one of personal cultural identity.

CONSTITUTION

Constitution: New Zealand, like Britain, has an "unwritten constitution". The operation of Cabinet (the basic organ of government) is ruled by convention rather than by statute, and theoretically not even the adult franchise, the secret ballot or the life of Parliament is immune from change by a simple majority vote in the House of Representatives. The New Zealand Parliament (though now without an upper house) in its trappings has zealously modelled itself on the British House of Commons, from the formal "Opening of Parliament" and "Speech from the Throne" to the extent of naming its Members' restaurant "Bellamy's"—an institution which persists in Wellington if not still at Westminster. The Governor-General, as the Queen's representative, performs the ceremonial function of the Monarch. A Bill of Rights was enacted in 1990.

In operation, Parliament has differed markedly from the House of Commons, with the Government's "Caucus" (i.e., total membership) playing a much more prominent role and being involved in decision-making often so as to pre-empt any serious debate on the floor of the house. This will change under proportional representation modelled on the German system, being introduced at the next election. Parliament presently comprises 97 elected representatives, four of whom represent the Maori people.

Direct rule: Constitutional government dates from 1840. Before then jurisdiction over New Zealand had been exercised in a vague way by the Governor of New South Wales. For a year after the Treaty of Waitangi was signed in 1840, New Zealand was a dependency of New South Wales, but once the country was constituted a separate colony in 1841 it was administered through a resident Governor by the Colonial Secretary in London.

The colony's first five years were fraught with indecision. Governor Hobson was a sick man and soon died, and his successor, FitzRoy, proved no more capable. It was when Grey was sent, in 1845, fresh from his successes in South Australia, that administration became more decisive, helped, too, by the British Treasury's being less skinflint with Grey than it had been with his predecessors. In the interval of peace following the Land Wars, agitation for representative government grew to see the colony divided into two provinces—New Ulster (the northern half of the North Island) and New Munster (the remainder).

Provincial government: Before the two provinces were properly established, the New Zealand Constitution Act of 1852 was passed by the British Parliament. Self-government was granted to a Governor (appointed by London), a Legislative Council (an upper house, its Members appointed by the Governor) and a House of Representatives (an elected lower house). This did not mean that New Zealand became a fully sovereign power. For many years after 1852 the British Crown could and did disallow New Zealand legislation, even after the Governor had given his formal assent to it.

In addition to a central government, the country (then with a European population of only about 31,000) was divided into no fewer than six provinces—Auckland, New Plymouth, Wellington, Nelson, Canterbury and Otago—each self-governing to a degree and each keeping the proceeds of land sales. By 1873 four further provinces had been added (Hawke's Bay, Marlborough, Southland and Westland), but three years later the free-spending Sir Julius Vogel, an ardent "Centralist", led a successful assault on this quasi-federal system. In its stead the country acquired an omnipotent national Parliament augmented by the "confused multitude" of boards and councils that still fulfil the needs of local government.

Although it did not specifically say so, the Constitution Act was treated as denying the Maori the vote. Only individual landowners were enfranchised, and the settler conveniently argued that this did not embrace the Maori form of communal land ownership. In 1867 representation was extended to the Maori, but for a time Maori Members of Parliament were drawn only from those chiefs who had supported the Crown in the Land Wars.

Responsible government: Theoretically, self-government had come with the Constitution Act of 1852, when Governor Gore Browne was instructed by the Colonial Office to appoint Ministers to advise him. But the realm of Maori affairs remained a prerogative of the Governor and it was not until Parliament acquired control of this field and finally, in 1891, of the exercise of the Royal prerogative of mercy, that the status of responsible government can be said to have been fully attained. Moreover, it was as late as 1947 that the country acquired the final legal powers to amend its own constitution and to pass laws inconsistent with British legislation that applied to New Zealand. The Legislative Council was promptly voted out of existence, and since then the one elected "lower" house has governed as "Parliament".

PARTY POLITICS

FROM THE TIME of self-government the country was ruled by a succession of cliques which combined from time to time to form a series of Ministries—indeed in the first 30 years of self-government there were no fewer than 24 changes of Premier.

For the two decades before 1890, what is now known as the "Continuous Ministry", an essentially conservative combination, held sway. Although there were no political parties, there were still frequent changes of Premier as allegiances shifted on the many divisive issues of the day—provincialism versus centralism, overseas borrowing versus "self-reliance"—but these involved no real change in government. Power was firmly in the hands of those dedicated to the social and economic *status quo.*

This state of affairs ended abruptly in 1890, by which time the factions had narrowed down to two major groups, and the Liberal Party (an amalgam of Liberal and Labour) was triumphant. This was largely the result of the growth of trade unions and reaction against the depression of the 1880s. The conservatives held on tenaciously and used their superior numbers in the appointed Legislative Council to block virtually all the Liberals' legislation, and before any significant reforms could be made the Liberals had to weather a constitutional confrontation with the Governor. In the last resort they appealed to London, and the Governor was directed that he was constitutionally bound by the advice of his Ministers and so had to grant Ballance's request for the appointment of Liberal supporters to the upper chamber.

The Liberals held power until 1912, first under Ballance and later under Seddon, and displayed a crusading spirit by introducing the world's first Old Age Pension and by being the first Government to extend the vote to women. With tax measures the Liberals accelerated the break-up of large land holdings, and in 1894 introduced the world's first form of compulsory state arbitration for industrial disputes. Their success in blending capitalism with socialism earned for New Zealand the contemporary description of being the "birthplace of the twentieth century". After Seddon's death in 1906 the Liberals slowly lost touch with the public; the small farmers became dissatisfied and the Labour movement began its defection to form its own independent party. Indeed, today both the major parties, National and Labour, lay claim to being Seddon's political heirs.

Massey's Reform Party came to power in 1912, but was overtaken by World War I, during which the country was ruled by a coalition Cabinet. On Massey's death in 1925, Coates assumed the leadership and became the first New Zealand-born Prime Minister. But Coates, who subsequently won a spectacular election victory, could not with deeds match his publicists' extravagant promises. The Reform Party claimed to be "true Liberals" but really had its basis in a rural conservatism opposed to the rising tide of socialism. During its period in office the organisation of farming and the marketing of its produce were welded into the efficient entity it is today.

In 1928 the Reform Party gave way to the Liberal Party's successor, the United Party, under Sir Joseph Ward, which was returned to power with unfulfilled promises of lavish borrowing and generous spending. Three years later the Great Depression saw the United and Reform parties form a coalition that ruled until Labour, under Savage, dramatically won office in 1935 and ushered in the Welfare State.

From 1949-72, except for the short-lived Second Labour Government (1957-60) of Sir Walter Nash, the National Party held power, principally under Sir Sidney Holland and Sir Keith Holyoake. In 1972 the late Norman Kirk swept Labour back into power, but the Third Labour Government inevitably suffered as a result of world economic crises and was defeated in the elections of 1975.

In recent years there has been a remarkable reversal in the respective stands of the two major parties. First National, originally formed "to oppose interference by State in business and State control of industry", under Sir Robert Muldoon, between 1975-84, developed one of the most centrally-controlled and over-protected economies in the Western world. Then, after the electorate turned against the Muldoon style of interventionism in 1984, the incoming Labour government, in an even more surprising reversal, embarked on a wholesale restructuring of the economy, shedding subsidies and protectionism in an unabashed attempt to return the economy to the realities of the marketplace. Labour, under David Lange, pressed ahead with plans to revitalise the social welfare state on the basis of a competitive and successful economy, attracting international attention for its non-nuclear policy, with legislation banning visits even by its allies' nuclear-powered ships. In 1987 the electorate returned Labour to power, but grew disenchanted with its economic restructuring as the party distanced itself from its traditional grassroots, and swept National back into power in 1990. In a final act of disillusionment, the electorate opted in 1993 to reject the Westminster style of government altogether, in favour of German-styled proportional representation (MMP). The political scene is presently highly volatile.

The social laboratory: New Zealand enjoys the reputation of being an adventurous social innovator, most recently in restructuring its economy. This stems from three major turning points in New Zealand political life — the election of a Liberal Government in 1890, of the First Labour Government almost half a century later and the rejection of Muldoon protectionism in 1985. In the 1890s the country led the world in three major areas — extending the vote to women, introducing compulsory State arbitration in industrial disputes, and establishing the first Old Age Pension in the face of vigorous opponents who claimed that the security the pension would give would undermine the moral fibre of the nation and so "destroy our civilisation".

Although the scope of the pension scheme was steadily widened over the years, it was not until the election of the First Labour Government and the passage of its Social Security Act of 1938 that the country again took the initiative, with a scheme which not only promised subsistence for those who could not provide for themselves, but also introduced an income-related comprehensive health scheme.

In 1962 New Zealand acquired the first "Ombudsman" outside Scandinavia, a Parliamentary Commissioner who investigates citizens' complaints against officialdom and an institution which has since swept the English-speaking world. Subsequently, New Zealand became the first country to impose a form of "absolute liability" for most personal injuries. The welfare state foundered with the collapse of Muldoon's economic policies, and his vote-buying un-funded superannuation which the country simply could not sustain.

Foreign policy: Until 1919 New Zealand's international policies were dictated by Imperial Britain, but even once emancipation was achieved New Zealand for two decades saw herself as the dutiful daughter and in 1939 declared war on Germany almost as a reflex action. A division of loyalties came in 1942 when Britain under siege vainly tried to fulfil its guarantees against Japanese aggression and it was left for the United States to preserve New Zealand's integrity at a time when New Zealand's own forces were predominantly committed to the struggle in Europe.

Since then, although a member of the (British) Commonwealth, dependence on the USA was the cornerstone of New Zealand's international relations until Washington's objections to the non-nuclear policy severely strained relations between the two countries. Relations with France have been marred by differences over nuclear testing in the Pacific and the intolerable attack on the Greenpeace vessel, *Rainbow Warrior*, in Auckland Harbour. New Zealand was a keen advocate of the League of Nations and, traditionally conscious of her own smallness, has solidly supported the United Nations and served on the Security Council (1993-94).

ECONOMIC GROWTH

Plunder: Before 1840, Europeans had generally come to New Zealand simply to exploit the new land, to plunder it of all that could readily be taken—seals, whales, flax. Timber remained the one staple export, but resources of kauri were finite, and in time were exhausted.

Agriculture: New Zealand's great tradition of agricultural exports dates from missionary times, when the Maori was taught European agricultural techniques and before long was supplying visiting ships, and even markets in Australia.

For the settlers who came from 1840 onwards there were uncertain years of subsistence farming before gold was discovered in Victoria, Australia. With men from the world over flocking there by the thousands, a booming market developed for New Zealand foods. As the Australian goldfields declined, wool came to the fore and the country's pastoral economy evolved, stimulated by the development of the Corriedale, a Romney-Lincoln crossbred with the dual virtues of long fleece and prime carcass.

Gold rushes: New Zealand had the first of her own gold rushes in the early 1860s, and the influx of fortune-seekers saw the European population almost double in three hectic years. Gold stimulated the economy as never before, and in 1863 accounted for 70 per cent of total exports.

Refrigeration: Gold in turn dwindled and after a decade of gloom the advent of refrigeration saw in 1882 the first of an endless stream of frozen meat leave Dunedin's port for London.

Refrigeration gave both sheep and dairy farming a new viability and set the pattern for today's grasslands economy. Indeed, in the late 1950s the country's exports comprised

PATTERNS OF TRADE
PRINCIPAL EXPORTS

Period	News-print and wood pulp	Butter	Cheese	Casein	Meats	Wool	Total exports of New Zealand produce	Exports of pastoral produce	
								Value	% of total
	tons (000)					1b (m)	NZ $ million		
1910	—	17.8	22.6	—	132.7	204.4	43.9	35.0	79.8
1920	—	15.6	61.1	1.3	231.5	162.3	91.2	83.1	91.2
1930	—	94.2	90.6	2.9	201.8	197.2	88.4	82.7	93.6
1940	—	131.1	101.7	1.2	348.8	300.3	145.9	138.1	94.6
1950	—	138.3	99.9	5.5	338.0	294.0	364.7	348.8	95.6
1960	119.6	157.1	79.4	28.2	466.7	522.4	599.8	561.6	93.6
1970	200.4	194.8	89.2	61.0	648.8	668.7	1,064.8	873.7	82.1
1980	701.2	213.0	69.2	63.4	423.7	579.5	5,830	3000	*61.5
1990	570.4	217.3	90.4	56.1	648.4	†209.1	14,588.9	4,579.2	31.3

* Does not include forest products.   † million tonnes.

EXPORTS BY PRINCIPAL COUNTRIES OF DESTINATION			IMPORTS BY PRINCIPAL COUNTRIES OF ORIGIN		
	1968	1991		1968	1991
Country	NZ $ million		Country	NZ $ million	
Australia	57.4	2937.7	Australia	131.2	2876.8
Belgium	11.4	166.4	Belgium	3.3	80.8
Britain	344.1	1024.2	Britain	196.1	992.8
Canada	9.7	232.1	Canada	31.9	244.7
China	5.7	186.1	China	3.1	194.6
Fiji	5.7	195.2	France	5.3	314.3
France	26.3	167.8	Germany	22.3	645.4
Germany	20.7	372.1	Hong Kong	13.6	171.8
Hong Kong	2.6	241.0	Italy	9.2	330.9
Iran	0.2	114.5	Japan	56.8	2101.6
Italy	15.3	252.7	Korea	0.2	228.8
Japan	68.2	2603.5	Malaysia	5.6	130.3
Korea	0.9	719.2	Netherlands	6.9	157.1
Malaysia	6.7	394.5	Singapore	2.2	205.0
Netherlands	10.9	157.2	Sweden	8.4	522.5
Peru	4.0	37.4	Switzerland	6.5	174.4
Philippines	5.8	115.7	Taiwan	0.1	357.2
Singapore	6.0	226.5	USA	74.3	2412.6
Taiwan	1.0	316.3			
USA	129.2	2063.6			
USSR	5.8	182.3			
Total all countries	780.1	15,850.4	Total all countries	624.1	14,051.0

NB. Goods may be re-exported from foreign countries and so these figures can be misleading, e.g., normally a proportion of wool exported to Britain is subsequently re-exported to the Continent.

When in a national park, please respect the "minimum impact code" to ensure that the least harm is caused to the environment.

a higher proportion of grassland products than ever before. There are now more than 25 times as many animals as people, a ratio probably not exceeded in any other country; some dairy farms carry more than two cows to the hectare and good sheep country supports 25 sheep to the hectare the year round.

Manufacturing: Manufacturing, which has flourished in the past two decades, had previously really served only to substitute domestic production for items the country could not otherwise have afforded. Today Auckland, as the principal industrial centre, dominates the New Zealand domestic economy.

The need to export finished products has shown itself throughout the primary industries. Most wool is still exported in its greasy state, but carpet manufacture is expanding, and various yarns are produced in addition to the traditional woollen blanket. The dairy industry has diversified its basic milk product into varieties of cheese, milk powder, ghee, casein, frozen cream, butter oil and the protein milk biscuit. In the same way the meat industry is now pre-cutting and packaging meat, and selecting special cuts for different markets rather than simply exporting whole carcasses for butchering on arrival at their destination.

However, New Zealand, which for nearly three-quarters of a century based her economy on the supply of grassland products to mother Britain, has re-orientated her economy as she faced a Britain wooed by Europe and the rundown of her traditional access to British markets. Coincidentally there has been an upsurge of trading with the Middle East and Japan, and Japanese companies are exploiting a variety of New Zealand's raw materials, among them ironsands, coal and timber. The discovery of natural gas and oil condensate in the Taranaki represents the beginning of what is hoped will be a series of discoveries in the continuing quest for significant mineral deposits which will lessen the country's dependence on imported fuels.

Thanks to the efficiency of her farmers and their willingness to co-operate with each other, New Zealand has realised the impossible dream in achieving relative affluence without effluence, and a standard of living that ranks with that of industrialised countries. But her existence is nonetheless hazardous as she depends on the continued willingness of other countries to accept her cheap food, a trading area of sensitivity in many countries which, for emotional, political and certainly not economic reasons, tend to protect their small and comparatively inefficient farmers.

Many manufacturing export industries are associated with farming, such as quick-frozen vegetables, sausage casings, casein, butter, cheese, dried milk and frozen meat. Other products processed from indigenous raw materials and also exported include leathers, scoured wool, wool tops and yarns, woollen fabrics, carpets, rugs and blankets, wood pulp, newsprint and sawn timber.

As a consequence of the radical economic restructuring and free market reforms in recent years, many manufacturing industries previously protected by subsidies and trade barriers, have gone out of business, resulting in high unemployment.

New Zealand and the EC: Britain's entry into the European Community in 1973 had a traumatic impact on both the country's pattern of trade and its psyche. For a century Britain had been the country's principal market for food exports as well as, for much of the population, its cultural "home". At a stroke the country which had settled the colony, and for whose freedom New Zealand servicemen had sustained appalling losses in two world wars, had retreated behind a protectionist barrier designed to sustain uneconomic Continental farming units.

The challenge for New Zealand was to try to buy time in which to develop new markets while at the same time having to contend with the EC itself periodically dumping its artificially induced surpluses on the international market. As the percentage of New Zealand's exports to Britain slumped from over 50 per cent in 1960 to 14 per cent in 1981, New Zealand cheese disappeared from the shelves of British supermarkets, the price of its butter soared as the result of EC tariffs (designed to divert a share of the New Zealand butter price to the less-efficient European producer), and the first of what was to become an annual round of negotiations was embarked upon to endeavour to sustain dwindling quotas for butter and lamb at the highest possible levels. Subsequently the EC and New Zealand, as the two largest suppliers of dairy products to the international market, in recent times achieved a set of understandings designed to safeguard the dairy market, maintain prices and smooth out fluctuations.

Britain's move into Europe, coupled with restrictions on New Zealanders' rights of entry there, have forced the country to look beyond its traditional relationship with Britain and towards a cultural reappraisal of its place in the world. This has brought a new awareness of its role as a nation of the South Pacific and not as a far-flung appendage to Europe.

Energy: The country has traditionally tapped plentiful sources of coal and hydroelectric power. Subsequently, geothermal resources were utilised to generate electricity, but the search for oil remained elusive. More recently, enormous finds of natural gas and condensate have been made in the Taranaki region, both onshore and offshore, giving rise to a number of major, energy-based industrial projects. *These are described under △ New Plymouth.*

THE NATURAL ENVIRONMENT

Continental drift: According to the theory of "continental drift", there was once the single continent of "Gondwanaland" into which the major land masses fitted like the pieces of a global jigsaw. According to this theory, the continent subsequently fragmented and its various segments were carried apart, rather like icebergs, by the spreading of the sea floor.

Precisely where New Zealand would have fitted is uncertain, but it is theorised that between 300 and 135 million years ago its land mass may have lain near the margins of the Gondwanaland continent, for some New Zealand fossils from the late Cretaceous period suggest that links with Gondwanaland existed at least up to that time.

New Zealand as a land mass is certainly geologically very young and forms part of what is described as the "circum-Pacific mobile belt", a belt which arcs north through Japan and down the west coast of the Americas and in which mountain building, volcanic activity and earthquakes are still taking place.

Just as the country itself is young, so too is its rich alpine vegetation, which developed late in time when the country's mountains had been uplifted and its climate begun to cool. Possibly this vegetation originated in Antarctica and preserves those plants that could cross the ocean, whether windblown or carried by birds, before the Antarctic's climate became too cold to continue to support vegetation.

A varied topography: The outstanding feature of the country's topography is the wide variety of land forms that are contained within a relatively small area. The "drowned river valleys" of Northland result from the rise in sea levels which occurred with the melting of Pleistocene ice, but the peninsula itself is a part of one of the main "wrinkles" in the earth's crust—a wrinkle which resurfaces in the islands of New Caledonia. A second "wrinkle" runs from the central Volcanic Plateau of the North Island to resurface in first the Kermadec and then the Tongan island groups. The two meet in the central plateau, and contribute to its volcanic features. These volcanoes showered ash over much of the North Island and buried vast tracts of forest, while lava flows dammed river valleys and so formed the lakes of the Rotorua district.

The south-eastern region of the North Island is a continuation of the Alpine Fault, the fault which created the 650-kilometre-long ranges of the Southern Alps.

A further feature of the country's structure is a number of major earthquake fault lines, tears in the earth's crust, many of which are still active.

A unique flora: New Zealand has been separated from other land masses for so long that it constitutes a distinctive botanical region; of its flowering indigenous species, as many as three-quarters are unique.

It is plain that the country must have been isolated before the appearance of mammals, as birds occupy the position adopted by mammals in other ecologies, and only in the absence of mammals could the several species of fearless, flightless and slow-moving birds have survived to evolve. These range from the now-extinct moa, which grazed on open grasslands, to the kiwi which still sniff for grubs in the bush.

A state of flux: It is incorrect to suppose that before the arrival of the European the country's flora was to any degree stable. As world-wide climatic changes occurred, the pattern of distribution varied—as temperatures dropped, sub-tropical plants were forced either to coastal areas (where, with the eventual melting of the ice, they were destined to be flooded) or to the north. Between glacial periods plants were able to recolonise both higher land and land to the south.

In a slowly changing environment species dwindled or died out completely as new species developed in a continuing evolutionary process that has, of course, not ended. The last glacial period occurred as comparatively recently as 12,000 to 15,000 years ago.

With the Polynesian migrant, too, came change. For although they are popularly supposed to have made little impact on the country's vegetation, in fact they burned forests repeatedly and indiscriminately, and also checked regeneration of vast areas such as that already denuded by the Taupo eruption of *c.* 135 A.D.

But greater change by far came with the European settlers.

"Acclimatisation madness": The Pakeha found abundant bird life but encountered only four types of mammal: the rat, the Maori dog (both brought by Polynesian migrants), and two species of native bat. Had the colonists but paused to think, they must surely have realised that a land without mammals was quite the worst place to introduce them.

But in a rash of acclimatisation madness, by World War I over 50 species of wild animals had been introduced, some 35 of which are now a permanent feature. From hares and rabbits, through stoats and weasels to thar, chamois, mountain goat and a variety of deer, animals were liberated in what has been described as being "one of the most bizarre ecological disasters in the history of man's tampering with nature". Even the country's three main species of frog were introduced, from Australia.

The animals were brought as much out of nostalgia as to provide sport, to control pests (not infrequently, pests already themselves introduced!) and for their pelts (e.g., the opossum). Oddly enough, against the heavy toll exacted must be offset the rescue from extinction of the Parma wallaby, a species thought to be extinct in its Australian homeland at a time when, it transpired, the Parma wallaby was being slaughtered indiscriminately on Kawau Island.

Acclimatisation by Europeans dates right back to Cook, who introduced, along with the flourishing potato, a domestic pig which went wild and is today hunted as the "Captain Cooker". He even unsuccessfully freed the country's first sheep.

As settlement grew, so too did the belief that the New Zealand flora and fauna would in time be replaced by their European counterparts. Introduced animals wiped out species of native birds and greatly affected the vegetation and so the soil—even the economic welfare of the country was imperilled, rendering campaigns necessary to cull if not eradicate the deer, rabbit and opossum.

The effect on a flora which had evolved in the absence of browsing animals was devastating. Rabbit, goat, pig and deer attacked trees from the ground up, and as if to spare no quarter the tree-climbing opossum was liberated, which attacked the higher branches. The effect on native birdlife was even more disastrous, and today a number of species face the same fate of extinction that many others have already met.

But, if indeed there has been acclimatisation "madness" in ecological terms, in an economic sense the acclimatisation of the sheep, cow and a variety of grasses has made possible today's grasslands economy and the high standard of living it supports. The fast-growing timber industry, too, is principally based not on native woods but on the exotic pine.

The recent introduction of deer farming has provoked an onslaught on deer in the wild, with helicopters and tranquilliser guns being employed to capture breeding stock. As a result, the population of deer in the wild has plummeted, and an unexpected gain has been the re-emergence on the mountainsides of plant species long believed to have become extinct.

Flora today: The countryside today presents a scene of delightful confusion. Native as well as European birds flit between contrasting exotic and indigenous trees. But while the species are integrated to a degree, vigilance is needed if slowly regenerating stands of native forest are to be preserved.

Native forest areas for the most part may be walked through freely, a situation that did not prevail before the coming of acclimatised game, when tangled creeper and dense ground cover made the going heavy.

The indigenous flora remains remarkable by any standards. Included are the world's largest buttercup (*Ranunculus lyallii,* the mountain lily); forget-me-not with leaves as large as rhubarb *(Myosotis hortensia);* a speedwell 12 metres high; the pigmy pine, the pine-tree family's smallest known member *(Dacrydium laxifolium);* tree-like daisies; arborescent lilies; plants of the carrot family with bayonet-like leaves *(Aciphylla aurea);* mosses more than 60 centimetres tall (*Dawsonia superba*—giant moss), and the strange anomaly, the "vegetable sheep" *(Raoulia exima).*

With the exception of the beech forests, the evergreen native forest is extremely varied and contains a variety of tree types. Few of these indigenous species are deciduous, brilliance of bloom is rare, and seasonal changes have a subtlety not immediately apparent to the casual observer. Beauty lies as much in the dense and gloomy forest canopy as in the profusion of fern which underlies it.

National Parks: The country's system of national parks dates from 1887, when Te Heuheu Tukino IV (Horonuku) and his Tuwharetoa gave the nucleus of the Tongariro National Park to the nation to preserve the integrity of a venerated tribal area. Other national parks in the North Island are the Urewera National Park, Egmont National Park and the recently-created Whanganui National Park.

The policy of the National Parks and Reserves Authority is to "preserve in perpetuity as National Parks, for the benefit and enjoyment of the public, areas of New Zealand that contain scenery of such distinctive quality or natural features so beautiful or unique that their preservation is in the national interest."

HUNTING, SHOOTING AND FISHING

NEW ZEALAND is a paradise for sports enthusiasts, with a variety of game birds, deer and some splendid trout, salmon and big-game fishing waters.

Deer were once abundant and hunted as noxious animals, but commercial hunting using helicopters now requires that shooters enter more remote and more rugged country to find animals of trophy class. Even there they may find competition from commercial hunters, both aerial and on foot. Tourist Board offices can arrange the services of professional guides.

Most native birds are protected by law, as are the rare native frog, native bat, native snail and tuatara. Most introduced birds may be hunted, but some game birds are protected outside a short open season.

Details of licences to shoot game birds and to fish, along with details of relevant regulations and game distribution, are available from sports shops and Department of Conservation offices.

Most areas have brown and rainbow trout in nearby streams and lakes, but except for Rotorua and Taupo the season is limited, from about October through to April. Some areas are set aside for fly-fishing, but most waters are open to both types of angling. Salmon fishing is confined to the South Island.

Generally, no licence is needed to hunt introduced wild mammals, but permits are required to shoot in National Parks, forestry parks and scenic reserves. *Department of Conservation offices in main centres and in forestry areas provide permits and details of hut locations and can suggest good hunting areas.*

Charters may be arranged in the main big-game fishing areas, off the east coast of Northland *(principally from △ Russell)* and the Bay of Plenty *(principally from △ Tauranga and △ Mayor Island).* A number of world-record catches have been made. The season extends from about December through to May.

A BRIEF MAORI VOCABULARY

THE MAORI LANGUAGE belongs to the Polynesian sub-family of languages, a fact which enabled Captain Cook's Tahitian interpreter, Tupaia, to translate for him on his initial voyage of discovery to New Zealand in 1769.

The language was first reduced to writing by the early missionaries, but they simply used English letters to represent Polynesian sounds and only comparatively recently have appropriate techniques been evolved to establish the significant sound contrasts in the Maori language. These are not yet in common use.

The alphabet is restricted to 15 letters—h, k, m, n, p, r, t, w, a, e, i, o, u, wh and ng. Every syllable ends in a vowel, and the quantity of the vowel may vary, so changing the meaning of a word. Such subtle differences are beyond the capacity of most Pakeha.

In general:
A is pronounced as in "rather"
E is pronounced as in "ten"
I is pronounced as in the "ee" in "seen"
O is pronounced as in the "oa" in "board"
U is pronounced as in the "oo" in "bloom".

When two vowels come together each is given its proper sound: e.g., Aotea is pronounced "A-o-te-a". (Longer Maori names are occasionally hyphenated to assist with pronunciation.)

WH is usually pronounced as f, although the correct sound has been likened to an f but without the top teeth touching the lower lip. NG is pronounced as in "singing". Words which commonly form part of Maori place names are as follows:

AHI	fire	ONE	mud, sand or beach
AO	cloud	PA	fortified village
ARA	path or road	PAE	ridge, or resting place
ATA	shadow	PAPA	broad, flat, or ground covered with vegetation
ATUA	god		
AWA	river, channel, gully, valley	PO	night
HAKA	dance	PUKE	hill
HAU	wind	PUNA	spring of water
HUA	fruit, egg	RANGI	sky
IKA	fish	RAU	hundred, many or leaf
ITI	small	RIKI	small or few
KAI	food, or eat	ROA	long or high
KINO	bad	ROTO	lake
MA	white or clear	RUA	cave, hollow or two
MA (short for manga) tributary or stream		TAHI	one, single
MANGA	tributary or stream	TAI	sea, coast or tide
MANU	bird	TAPU	forbidden or sacred
MATA	headland (also many other meanings)	TE	the
		TEA	white or clear
MAUNGA	mountain	WAI	water
MOANA	sea, lake	WAKA	canoe
MOTU	island	WHANGA	bay, inlet, stretch of water
MURI	end	WHARE	house
MUTU	ended, finished	WHATA	raised platform for storing food
NUI	big, or plenty of		
O	of, or the place of	WHENUA	land or country

The standard reference Maori dictionary, *A Dictionary of the Maori Language* by H.W. Williams, had its origins in a dictionary and grammar compiled by the missionary,

Bishop William Williams *(see index)* and issued by the Mission Press at Paihia in 1844.

Members of the Williams family saw the work through its first five editions and three reprints, and the dictionary now bears as author the name of Bishop Herbert W. Williams, William's grandson. The latest edition, the seventh, was published in 1971, and reprinted in 1975.

NOTES ON PLACE NAMES

THE EARLIEST PLACE NAMES were supposedly bestowed by Kupe in *c.* 950 A.D. when he named such features as Hokianga.

As migrants arrived they brought with them place names from other parts of Polynesia (e.g., Mt Hikurangi, Maketu) and, as they settled, tended to name places after events and legendary happenings (e.g., Katikati-o-Tamatekapua, "the place where Tamatekapua ate his food slowly"). These in time were contracted (e.g., to Katikati), but one surviving example of a name which still records events at length is that of a Hawke's Bay hill styled Taumatawhakatangihangakoauauotamateapokaiwhenuakitanatahu, "the place where Tamatea, the man with the big knees, who slid, climbed and swallowed mountains, known as 'landeater', played his flute to his loved one". In an even more expansive version this is claimed as the world's longest place name.

The first European voyagers left their own names (e.g., Tasman Sea, Cook Strait, D'Urville Island), those of their patrons (Cape Maria van Diemen, Mt Egmont) and, less commonly, those prompted by events of the moment (Cape Kidnappers, Cape Runaway) and by flights of fancy (Mayor Island and the Aldermen Islands).

Many of the names given by the voyagers and the subsequent explorers did not survive, as Maori usage perpetuated the names they had sought to displace. The settlers in turn bestowed names—of heroes (e.g., Nelson, Wellington), outstanding figures of the day (Auckland), of promoters of settlement (Hutt River), of events of the day (Napier, Havelock, and other figures of the Indian Mutiny) and of their own number (Featherston, Masterton, Foxton). The new arrivals, too, carelessly corrupted a number of names—Pito-one became Petone; Te Nganaire became "The Nunneries".

No note can overlook the quaintly named North Canterbury district of Nonoti. Not, as it might appear, a Maori name but an appellation laughingly given when a politician was invited to name a new railway station. "No, not I," he modestly declined.

NEW ZEALAND HISTORIC PLACES TRUST

THE TRAVELLER will in both town and country encounter the Trust's bronze plaques and descriptive noticeboards which mark sites of Maori and European significance.

The role of the Trust is to preserve such physical links with the past as still remain, and today it maintains buildings, both European and Maori, and assists in the preservation of sites of historical and archaeological importance. Its recent work in restoring marae around the country has been of special significance.

Always underfunded and challenged by the urgency of much of its work, the Trust relies to a great extent on its associate members whose annual subscriptions entitle them to free entry to Trust properties and to copies of various Trust publications. Membership application forms are available from the Secretary, New Zealand Historic Places Trust, Private Bag, Wellington.

CITIES, TOWNS AND LOCALITIES OF PARTICULAR INTEREST ARRANGED IN ALPHABETICAL ORDER

When looking for a place name, first look in the index at the back of the book

The symbol △ indicates a place with its own entry elsewhere in this Alphabetical Section.

Volcanic Plateau   Map 8 Pop. 223   **ATIAMURI**
44 km SW of Rotorua; 40 km N of Taupo.

ATIAMURI, a tiny hydro town, is set in vast pine plantations close to the banks of Lake Atiamuri on the Waikato River. The hydro-electric power station (1958) stands in a former river gorge, immediately below the dam. The lake itself extends some 5 kilometres up stream. Nearby, the curious thumb of Mt Pohaturoa (520 m) rises a sheer 245 metres above the river.

Atiamuri may mean "turned back" (as Tia, older brother of the captain of the *Arawa* canoe, "turned back" here after encountering the since-flooded Atiamuri Falls on the river), or it may be a contraction of the tribal name of Ngati-a-Muri.

MT POHATUROA

The upthrust of Pohaturoa ("tall rock") features prominently in both Arawa and Ngati Raukawa tradition, for it served as a lookout post during the inter-tribal conflicts and was the scene of many a prolonged siege. One such siege took place several centuries ago when invading Ngati Raukawa relentlessly forced Ngati Kahupungapunga (possibly a surviving Moahunter tribe) to retreat to this their final stronghold. Lack of food finally forced the defenders to abandon their refuge, but only five escaped with their lives. The cause of the conflict is said to have been the murder of a Ngati Raukawa woman who had been given in marriage to a chief of Ngati Kahupungapunga.

Early paintings show the rock and its surrounds as almost completely devoid of cover. The omnipresent pine trees date from 1927 and have been a source of controversy as an unwarranted intrusion upon the tapu (sanctity) of the rock.

The rock overlooks a lake formed by the Atiamuri hydro-electric power station.

★★★ AUCKLAND

Auckland   Map 4   Pop. 1,002,700 (combined urban areas)

655 km N of Wellington via Taumarunui; 668 km via Western Lake Taupo (faster route). Visitor Centre, Aotea Sq, 299 Queen St; also at Queen Elizabeth Sq, 1 Queen St; tel. (09) 366-6888, fax (09) 366-6893. International Airport Information Centre, Mangere; tel. (09) 275-7467 (especially good for accommodation on arrival). Department of Conservation Regional Office, cnr Karangahape Rd and Liverpool St; tel. (09) 307-9279. Regional Parks Information Centres, Ferry Building, Quay St; tel. (09) 366-2166 and Arataki Visitor Centre (Waitakere Ranges), Scenic Drive, Titirangi; tel. (09) 817-7134.

Auckland Metro, a monthly magazine, is highly recommended as a handy source for details of things to see and do in and about Auckland.

THE COUNTRY'S LARGEST metropolis and one of the world's most stunning cities is flung over a narrow isthmus, characterised by numerous pa-sculptured volcanic cones and the many reaches of the city's twin harbours to east and west. Guarding the entrance to Waitemata Harbour is Rangitoto Island, whose sweeping cone and broad skirts seemingly form a backdrop to every view.

The weekday bustle of New Zealand's major industrial centre contrasts with its summer weekend serenity, when hundreds of yachts cruise on sheltered harbours and among the scattered islands of the △ Hauraki Gulf. This is the home of New Zealand yachting and of many of the world's top yachtsmen — and presently, too, of the prestigious America's Cup (up for challenge in 1999-2000).

Employment and educational opportunities have attracted many Pacific Islanders to the city, and they, as well as a large Maori community and a more recent influx

from South East Asia, give Auckland a vibrance and cosmopolitan flavour along with the cultural contrasts of larger cities.

The city was named by Governor Hobson in 1840 after his former commander, Lord Auckland (1784-1849), then Viceroy of India and a hero of the time. The following year came disaster and Lord Auckland's ignominious recall, reflected in the naming of a central street "Khyber Pass" after the British reverse there. "Mount Eden" preserves Lord Auckland's family name. His statue, a gift from Calcutta when the Government of West Bengal was quitting itself of colonial relics, stands opposite the Town Hall (*Grey's Ave*).

Annual events: Auckland's industrial Easter Show incorporates the largest of the country's Agricultural and Pastoral shows. The Anniversary Day regatta (*about 29 January*), the largest one-day yachting event in the world, dates from boat races held on the day in 1840 when Auckland was declared capital — a status it was to enjoy for only 25 years. The "Round the Bays" fun run (*March*), a demonstration of the country's passion for jogging, is joined by about 80,000 runners. Chinese New Year is celebrated as energetically on the water as off it.

SOME HISTORY

"The spouse of a hundred lovers": According to tradition, a number of Polynesians from "Hawaiki" settled here after the migration of about six centuries ago. The Tamaki isthmus, the narrow neck of land where the Tamaki River and the Manukau Harbour combine to all but sever the North Island, was peopled by descendants of Marama-Kikohura, wife of Hoturoa, captain of the *Tainui* canoe. It is said that the canoe was hauled across the isthmus to Otahuhu only with much difficulty, as Marama-Kikohura had committed adultery with a slave and so rendered canoe-hauling chants ineffective. When the canoe reached Manukau Harbour it sailed on, leaving the disgraced Marama-Kikohura and others behind to establish the Nga-Marama tribe.

As time went by the fertile isthmus of Tamaki-makau-rau ("the spouse contested by a hundred lovers"), was coveted by a number of tribes, and after a series of invasions, Kiwi Tamaki (*c.* 1720-50) held sway during the district's most prosperous years. From his massive pa on One Tree Hill (*see below*) he dominated an area in which virtually every volcanic cone was fortified. The era came to an end with a funeral feast on Kaipara Harbour at which Tamaki slew several fellow guests. He was rewarded when his hosts invaded the isthmus to slay the hot-headed Tamaki, sack his mighty pa and enslave many of his followers.

Criss-crossed by Ngapuhi war parties from Northland, and its population decimated by successive epidemics, the isthmus was all but deserted when it was chosen in 1840 as the site for the colony's permanent capital.

A colonial capital: From whaling times the administrative centre had been at △ Russell, but after the signing of the Treaty of Waitangi in 1840, Governor Hobson decided to move the "capital" south to a more central position. Several sites were considered before Auckland was finally chosen—factors in its favour included fertile soil, a good port on Waitemata Harbour, and the network of internal waterways formed by the Kaipara and Manukau Harbours and the Waikato and Waipa Rivers.

In September 1840 the land was purchased for £55 in gold and the usual assortment of blankets, trousers, shirts and waistcoats, some pots, axes, tobacco and pipes, and a single bag each of sugar and flour. Officials then came from the Bay of Islands formally to proclaim the site as capital: "The flag was run up, the whole assembly gave three cheers . . . Her Majesty's health was then most rapturously drunk."

The town was laid out by Felton Mathew, allotments sold and quaint wooden houses, stores and shops built. On what is now Albert Park the Albert Barracks were constructed overlooking the town and harbour, and these accommodated nearly 1,000 men not only for internal defence but also to keep a wary eye on Britain's European rivals. Soon the town had "parsons without churches and magistrates without courts, but scrambled through [its] divinity and [its] law somehow or other".

Unlike the other three main centres, Auckland was not a "planned settlement" and so there were no organised migrants arriving regularly. There was an influx of officials, traders and labourers from the Bay of Islands, and not until 1842 did the first immigrant ships arrive direct, with some 500 Scots on board.

The first Governor: Captain William Hobson (1793-1842), New Zealand's first Governor (second if one includes the year Hobson, as Lieutenant-Governor, was subject to the over-riding authority of the Governor of New South Wales), is one of the country's more enigmatic figures.

Before he was ten, Hobson had gone to sea, and rose steadily until in 1834, through the influence of Lord Auckland, he gained command of HMS *Rattlesnake*. Two years later while he and his crew were assisting in laying out the town of Melbourne, they were despatched across the Tasman after Busby had sent for help to protect the British population at the Bay of Islands from anticipated tribal hostilities.

Hobson had been hoping to gain command of a flagship and was dismayed when on the basis of this brief visit he was directed to return to New Zealand, there to negotiate with the Maori and so acquire sovereignty for Britain. Late in 1839 he sailed for New Zealand, pausing at Sydney to confer with Governor Gipps and continuing on to the Bay of Islands where he swiftly concluded the Treaty of Waitangi (*pp.* **24, 262**). Barely a month after his arrival Hobson was crippled by a paralytic stroke which forced him to abandon plans for a series of Waitangi-type meetings throughout the country, leaving it for troops and for missionaries to collect the signatures of Maori elsewhere.

From the time of his stroke his administration seemed bedevilled. A dying man with no real sense of mission, Hobson received little support from any quarter. The settlers who preceded him generally resented his efforts to break up their speculative land holdings; the New Zealand Company, outraged by his choice of Auckland as "capital" and infuriated by tardy investigations into land purchases, subjected him to the most scurrilous of attacks; the Colonial Office denied him both the troops and the finance he desperately needed, and the civil servants with whom he was provided were incompetent if not corrupt. As a stern naval disciplinarian he could not even begin to cope with tribes who repudiated the Treaty of Waitangi and rejected his authority. The situation was beyond the control of an ailing man who had once been the most able of officers, and only death forestalled shameful recall.

If the unhappy state of affairs seemed due to Hobson, it was for his successor, FitzRoy, to show that fault lay with the Colonial Office and its unrealistic approach to the problems New Zealand presented. *(Hobson lies buried in a cemetery in Symonds St, on the Khyber Pass Rd side of Grafton Bridge.)*

Decline and revival: As the settlement grew, its settlers came to envy the rich, Maori-owned land to the south, and it was only a matter of time before Auckland became embroiled in the Land Wars. Conflict had engulfed Taranaki in 1860, when many Waikato Maori had forgotten old differences and gone to the aid of the tribes fighting there. In Auckland the entire adult male population had been enlisted for service by 1864. Imperial troops arrived and Auckland became "a very gay and jolly place to live . . . what with naval and military reviews, regattas, cricket and football and race meetings". A distinctive chain of "Fencible" settlements (*pp.* **107-08**) was established across the isthmus to protect the town from a feared invasion from the south by Waikato tribes. Skirmishes took place in outlying areas to the south, but the attack never came. Instead Governor Grey carried the war into the Waikato.

With the end of the conflict came depression, and migrants arrived to find not opportunity but unemployment waiting. The Otago gold rushes drew fortune-seekers south; in 1865 Auckland lost the role of capital to the New Zealand Company settlement at Wellington (and with the title went many public servants); finally most of the Imperial troops and their families were recalled to Britain.

Increased activity on the △ Thames goldfields and intense agricultural development aided Auckland's recovery and she entered the twentieth century on the crest of a wave which has carried her to her present position, where, still growing faster than any other urban area in New Zealand, she dominates the country both industrially and through sheer weight of numbers. The continued "drift to the north", motivated by the city's attractive setting, balmy climate and proximity to markets, poses a threat to centres further south and is periodically the subject of calls for Government action.

"The Father of Auckland": If Hobson was the city's founder, the title of its "father" firmly rests with Sir John Logan Campbell (1817-1912), one of Auckland's two European residents when the site was chosen for the country's first capital. With his partner William Brown, Campbell prospered as the city grew, and as Mayor he lived to greet the Duke and Duchess of Cornwall (later George V and Queen Mary) in the course of their 1901 Tour.

Campbell arrived in New Zealand from Edinburgh as a young doctor of 21 and purchased land at the first Auckland land sale. He preferred to busy himself in the arts of agriculture and commerce rather than to practise medicine—though he was universally referred to as "Dr Campbell". Monuments to his foresight are the many companies he helped to found, among them the New Zealand Shipping Company, the Bank of New Zealand, the New Zealand Insurance Company and the Auckland Savings Bank.

Sir John chose the occasion of the Royal Visit to give the major portion of his One Tree Hill estate to the people of New Zealand, and to name it "Cornwall Park" after his royal guests. Within the park now stands Auckland's oldest surviving building (1841), a cottage built by Sir John and his partner.

Campbell explained his preference for business when he wrote to his father at the conclusion of a more-than-profitable transaction: "What a botheration lot of pulses one would require to feel—tongues to look at and prescriptions to write before the fees would come up to the above sum, and as for a poor devil of a dentist, he would require to slay at least 310 teeth . . ." But if this seems a mercenary approach, it was not borne out in practice, for Sir John went on to become one of Auckland's greatest benefactors and the "Sir John Logan Campbell Trust" (with assets worth nearly $1.2 million) is only one of several charities well endowed by his benevolence.

Sir John lies buried on the crest of One Tree Hill where, towering beside his grave, an obelisk rises to mark his "admiration for the achievements and character of the great Maori people". Nearby, in Manukau Road, is a statue of his patriarchal figure, erected in his lifetime. His story is entertainingly told in his autobiography, *Poenamo—Sketches of the Early Days of New Zealand.*

Harbour Bridge: Regular transport across Waitemata Harbour dates back over a century, when with open boats an intrepid company inaugurated a cross-harbour ferry to link with the isolated North Shore. In time vehicular ferries were plying to and fro, and as early as 1929 the Waitemata Harbour Transit Commission heard evidence on the need for a harbour bridge. A later scheme for a tunnel was rejected, but it was a controversial 30 years before in 1959 the present bridge closed the gap between the city and its northern suburbs. The rate of traffic increase—trebling in a bare ten years—far exceeded all forecasts, and with the addition of what became known as the "Nippon clip-ons" (after the Japanese contractors), the bridge was widened to its present eight lanes.

The bridge, a steel structure, is 1,020.5 metres long, and its 244-metre navigation span rises 43 metres above high-water mark.

The vision of a bridge across the Waitemata extends back into the mists of mythology, when tribes of fabled patupaiarehe (fair-skinned fairies) were said to have peopled the Tamaki isthmus. One of these tribes was peaceloving and longed to reach the tranquillity of the North Shore where they might be free from the depredations of their constantly quarrelling neighbours. One night they began to build a causeway across the harbour, but though they toiled frantically and without pausing to rest, by the time the sun had begun to rise they had not completed their task—and once the sun's rays had touched their work, it could not be continued. Today their "work" lies unfinished, a curious tongue of fragmented lava which extends well out into the Waitemata not so very far from the southern terminal of the harbour bridge. *(Best seen from the reserve at the end of Point Chevalier Rd, off Great North Road.)*

A WALK AROUND THE CITY

Allow upwards of 2 hrs. Start at Albert Park, by the University Tower (Princes St). The University gardens are worthy of a stroll, with many identified species.

Albert Park ★★: Once the site of Albert Barracks (part of whose rifle-slit stone walls (1846-52) still stands behind the university administration building), the park is overlooked by the crenellated tower of the university. Bedecked with the memorabilia of over a century, only two blocks from Queen Street and shaded by towering trees, the park provides a favoured lunch spot for office workers and students.
Walk down through the park, passing a statue of Sir George Grey and a memorial to troopers who fell in the Anglo-Boer War in the Cape he once governed. Turn left along Kitchener St to pass the:

Auckland City Art Gallery ★★★: A visit should be made to inspect its splendid collection (*described under "Museums and Art Galleries", below*).
Continue along Kitchener St and turn down Wellesley St East, passing the Auckland Public Library (see "Museums and Art Galleries", below) to reach Queen St, the city's premier street. Turn up Queen St, towards the clock-domed and wedge-shaped:

Auckland Town Hall (*cnr Grey's Ave and Queen St*)**:** the building's facade is of Oamaru stone and its base of Melbourne bluestone. In the vestibule is a massive **kauri slab,** the timber used to panel the semi-circular Council Chamber. To the right is the low, sleek **Aotea Centre ★ ★ ★,** built at the behest of locally-trained international opera star Dame Kiri Te Kanawa as the country's foremost concert hall. The contemporary **art** within the Centre is itself well worth seeing. In the far left corner of Aotea Place is a statue of **Lord Auckland.**
Now walk back down Queen St, passing several major shopping centres and the Stock Exchange (on left: visitors gallery), whose investors experienced the worst losses of the world-wide crash of October 1987. Continue down to reach, on the right:

Vulcan Lane: A small shopping mall, so named because it was here that Auckland's early blacksmiths plied their trade. *(At this point the walk may be ended by walking up Vulcan Lane turning right into High St and left up Courthouse Lane to return to Albert Park.) Otherwise continue down Queen St. On reaching the mall, turn left into Customs St West to see, on the left at no. 22:*

Old Customhouse (1889): A princely Victorian governmental building given new life by conversion into shops and a restaurant. *Return to the mall and continue, past Downtown, to the foot of Queen St and the waterfront. Turn right along Quay St to reach the wharf gates opposite:*

Britomart Place: It was here that Governor Hobson declared Auckland to be the country's capital. There was then a point on which the ceremony took place, but this has been excavated for harbour reclamation.

Turn up Britomart Place, turn left along Beach Rd and immediately bear right into Anzac Avenue. Turn right again, up Short St, left along Eden Crescent, right up Parliament St and left along Waterloo Quadrant to the:

High Court (1868): Modelled by its architect on Warwick Castle and encrusted with turrets, gargoyles and stone effigies, the building was erected to replace the original "wretched barn" that had previously served as a courthouse. Identified heads range from Queen Victoria, Prince Albert and the then-Duke and Duchess of Kent, to Socrates and Hone Heke!

The High Court deals with the most serious criminal and civil cases and appeals from the District Courts. The public galleries of the courtrooms are usually open to the public. The court has outgrown the building and a new annexe has been built close by.
Now walk back up Waterloo Quadrant to reach Princes St and return to Albert Park.

One Tree Hill, Auckland.

VIEWPOINTS

Extinct volcanic cones are very much a part of the Auckland landscape and the more accessible provide excellent viewpoints. No fewer than 63 separate points of eruption have been recorded, the youngest, a mere 750 years, being the island of Rangitoto. Some of the smaller cones have been quarried out of existence for their scoria, but fortunately the major peaks have been declared reserves. The three viewpoints described are all conspicuously volcanic cones.

One Tree Hill ★★★ (*183 m*): Of the many pa-sculptured volcanic cones, this extensively fortified site is perhaps the most impressive. Built as the pa Maungakiekie ("mountain where kiekie grows abundantly") during the seventeenth and early eighteenth centuries, its massive earthworks could house 4,000 defenders and are today among the largest still surviving.

Clearly to be seen are the terraces of the satellite pa which once surrounded the main site, each then fortified with ditches, earth ramparts and wooden palisades. Large cultivations surrounded the whole complex to provide food for its inhabitants and to stock the rua (kumara pits).

Final architect of the pa was the relentless Kiwi Tamaki, who dominated the district in the 1700s until defeated by the Kaipara tribe of Ngati Whatua—whose losses in these wars with Tamaki were so great that they are said to have avoided conflict with other tribes for a generation, to enable their children to grow into warriors. By the early 1800s successive invasions had shown the area to be untenable and so it came to be virtually deserted. When Auckland was founded in 1840, One Tree Hill's desolate earthworks were littered with pipi shells and the bones of its last defenders.

The summit itself was known as Te Totara-i-ahua, a reference to a single towering totara tree which once grew there and was revered as commemorating the birth of an important ancestor. In 1852 a group of settler vandals cut down the sacred tree, and in an endeavour to make amends Sir John Logan Campbell planted the present landmark tree in 1880. Unfortunately he chose an exotic pine rather than totara, which in 1994 finally provoked some local Maori to attempt to chainsaw it down to dramatise lingering grievances, although it was close to the end of its natural life. There will be consultations when the time for replacement arrives.

A road now leads to the summit where there are superb views over the twin harbours, the city and the trees of Cornwall Park. Occasionally Great and Little Barrier Islands and even the outline of the Coromandel Peninsula may be seen in the distance. Sheep graze on the hill's grassed slopes and present the extraordinary spectacle of a farm in the heart of the country's largest metropolis. On the very tip is Sir John Logan Campbell's grave and a towering 21-metre obelisk to honour his admiration for the Maori people.

On the fringe of One Tree Hill is the **Auckland Observatory** (*see "Other Things to See and Do" (below)*). After an evening demonstration may be an appropriate time to view Auckland by night from One Tree Hill's summit.

For a description of neighbouring Cornwall Park, see "Some Parks and Gardens" (below). Access from Manukau Rd, Greenlane West Rd and Campbell Rd.

Mount Eden ★★★ (*196 m*): Known to the Maori as Maungawhau, Mount Eden marked the southernmost limit of the land purchased from the Maori in 1840 for the site of Auckland. The peak was used by the first Surveyor-General, Felton Mathew, as a starting point for the triangulation of the area and is still the principal trigonometrical station for much of Auckland province.

It is believed that occupation of the still-apparent pa site goes back to the twelfth century and that at its zenith about 3,000 Maori occupied the cone. However, legend tells of the treacherous slaying in the 1500s by the local Maungawhau of a Hauraki chief who was on a friendly visit here. Predictably the Hauraki tribes retaliated by besieging the pa. An unusually long and hot summer saw the defenders' water supply dry up, and the siege culminated in the burning of the pa and the massacre of its inhabitants. As so often happened after bloodshed, the previously impregnable pa was abandoned, never to be re-occupied.

The view from the summit encompasses the whole Auckland isthmus. On the tip of the precipitous crater walls a direction-finder identifies points of interest.

Enter from Mt Eden Rd and drive through the domain to the summit. **Eden Garden** is an area landscaped by thousands of trees and shrubs, especially camellias and rhododendrons. *Omana Ave, off Mountain Rd. Open daily, 9 a.m.–4.30 p.m.*

Mount Albert ★: A road leads to the summit, where the mouldings of pa fortifications are plainly seen. In one of the grassed craters one may picnic in a rustic atmosphere in dazzling contrast with the surrounding sprawl of suburbia. *Summit Drive, off Mt Albert Rd, leads into Mt Albert Domain (open daylight hours only) and on to the summit.*

Mount Victoria: A completely different aspect of the city is gained when viewed from the North Shore. *Devonport.*

City centre viewpoints: Scale two city buildings for stunning view. The Bank of New Zealand Tower Shopping Centre has an observation deck (*125 Queen St; open Mon.–Sat.*) and **Restaurant 360°** revolves gently atop the Telecom Building (*Karangahape Plaza, 501 Karangahape Rd; tel. (09) 358-4360*).

SOME PARKS AND GARDENS

Auckland Domain ★★★: This expanse of parkland and sportsfields was an early reserve where each Sunday the garrison band would serenade Victorian families as they promenaded among the peacocks of yesteryear. The twin wings of the spacious Winter Gardens, linked by a court and statuary, form Tropical and Cool Houses and are a legacy of the financial success of the Auckland Exhibition of 1913.

Nearby is the spring where in 1884 the Auckland Acclimatisation Society propagated the country's first rainbow trout with ova brought from California's Russian River by way of Tasmania. These were the progenitors of all New Zealand's rainbow trout and the strain is now the world's purest, so that ova today are exported back to California.

On Domain Hill (or Pukekawa, "sour hill") stands the city's war memorial, the Auckland War Memorial Museum ★★★ *(see below)*, from which there is an unexpected tree-fringed view of city and harbour. *Entrances off Park Rd, Parnell Rd (via Maunsell St) and Stanley St. Conducted walks leave the museum on Sundays at about 1.30 p.m.*

By the Stanley Street entrance to the Domain is a cluster of curious, perfectly spherical boulders removed from Silverdale in 1971. Formed naturally by the action of lime cementing sand around a small pebble, the Silverdale boulders are less well known than the renowned Moeraki Boulders on Moeraki Beach some 80 kilometres north of Dunedin.

Cornwall Park ★★★: Over 120 hectares of city farmland studded with plantations of kauri, rimu, nikau palms and pohutukawa. The park, a gift from Sir John Logan Campbell, is complete with woolshed, and offers an unusual pastoral scene as sheep and cattle graze in the heart of the city.

The park includes Auckland's oldest building, **Acacia Cottage** (1841), which first stood near Shortland Street and was built by Sir John and his partner, William Brown *(open daily from 7 a.m.–4 p.m.; tel. (09) 630-8485.)*. **Huia Lodge** (1903), built for a park-keeper, serves as an information centre where visitors can taste early twentieth-century Auckland life.

Adjoining the park is Greenlane Hospital, with an international reputation in advanced surgical techniques. *Greenlane West Rd.*

Zoological Gardens ★★: The gardens are as attractive and varied as the animals they house, and include a nocturnal kiwi house, a native forest aviary (housing some of the country's rarest birds), tearooms and many shaded picnic spots. The policy is to keep only animals which have been born in captivity. *Motions Rd, off Great North Rd. Open daily. Feeding times in the afternoons. Keeper talks on Sundays and public holidays; tel. (09) 378-1620.* A vintage tramway links with the Museum of Transport and Technology *(below)*.

Ellerslie Racecourse: Twelve hectares of formal gardens attract visitors even outside racedays. Major events include the Auckland Cup and Railway Handicap *(New Year's Day)*, the Air New Zealand Stakes *(February)*, Easter Handicap and the Ellerslie Sires Stakes *(April)* and the New Zealand Derby *(26 December)*. *Greenlane East. By Greenlane exit.*

MUSEUMS AND ART GALLERIES

Auckland Museum ★★★: Set in the parklands of Auckland Domain, the museum contains one of the country's most comprehensive collections. Pre-eminent are displays of artefacts from the South Pacific region and its hall of New Zealand birds. The excellent museum shop alone is worth a visit.

The collections highlight distinctive tribal styles within Maori decorative design alongside aspects of traditional cultures of the Pacific region. Daily cultural performances add verve to the displays *(11.15 a.m. and 1.30 p.m.; tel. (09) 838-7876)*. Of particular interest in the Maori Court is Hotunui (1878), a carved meeting house which first stood near Thames and depicts the ancestry of the Ngati Maru tribe. Rangitakaroro, a magnificent carved gateway, originally stood at Te Koutou on Lake Okataina, near Rotorua. The smaller pataka (food storehouse), Te Oha, features in Arawa tribal history as it stored the body of a Ngati Haua whose death triggered a bloody clash between the two tribes. The 25-metre war canoe, *Te Toki-a-Tapiri* ("Tapiri's battle-axe"), built *c.* 1836 and regarded as the finest example surviving, once sailed the Manukau Harbour. On the walls hang studies of a number of Maori chiefs by the artist C.F. Goldie (1870–1947), whose portraits today command high prices. *Open daily, 10 a.m.–5 p.m. Visitors may lunch in the restaurant or picnic in the Domain. Free guided tours on most days (tel. (09) 309-0443). Entrances off Park Rd, Parnell Rd (via Maunsell St) and Stanley St.*

Auckland City Art Gallery ★★★: The country's oldest gallery contains the country's best collections of contemporary New Zealand art and its finest group of Gothic works, which date from the 1300s. Displayed are German, Dutch and Italian prints of the sixteenth to nineteenth centuries, French Impressionist and Post-Impressionist prints, contemporary American and European prints and a collection of nineteenth- and twentieth-century Japanese prints. Local artists represented include McCahon, Woollaston, Binney, Mrkusich, Smither and Illingworth. The New Zealand collection dates back to a painting executed by Hodges as he accompanied Captain Cook, and includes a number of paintings by Frances Hodgkins, one of the country's best-loved artists. *Open 10 a.m.–4.30 p.m. daily; free guided tours at 2 p.m. daily. Cnr Kitchener St and Wellesley St East, by Albert Park (above).*

MOTAT (Museum of Transport and Technology of New Zealand) ★ ★ ★: New Zealanders, with characteristic ingenuity, have maintained superseded equipment in working order long beyond most manufacturers' wildest expectations. So it is that this museum has been able to glean a fascinating collection of exhibits. The displays include the development of printing, photography and of calculating machines from abacus to computer, a working tramway, a railway, vintage cars and carriages, and a burgeoning village where colonial buildings are preserved and furnished in the style of their period. The **Science Centre** explores the basic sciences in a hands-on fashion.

War machinery, guns and aircraft are also on show, but of all the exhibits perhaps the most interesting concern the exploits of the pioneer aviator, Richard Pearse (1877-1953). A farmer near Temuka and considered eccentric by the more charitable of his neighbours, Pearse was a mechanical genius who designed and built an aircraft which he twice flew successfully in March 1903 (at the latest), a bare three months after the Wright brothers had made what is regarded as the world's first powered flight. Some claim that Pearse flew in 1902, ahead of the Wright brothers, and it seems likely that the controversy will continue. Displayed are the remains of his plane—which came to rest in a hedge—and also his second aircraft, which never flew and lay for 40 years forgotten in a shed. Pearse also built a motorcycle (1908), on show in the Carriage Hall.

At MOTAT 2 are rare historic aircraft, including a **Lancaster bomber** and the last surviving **Solent Mark IV flying boat.**

The museum began in 1963, sparked by a move to save the huge twin-cylinder, double-acting, compound-condensing Beam Engine (1877) which for generations had pumped Auckland's water supply from Western Springs. Some of those who enter the Pump House (1876) are unaware that they are actually walking about inside a massive engine. *Great North Rd, opp. the junction with Western Springs Rd. Open daily, 9 a.m.–5 p.m. (from 10 a.m. at weekends).* A **vintage tramway** links the museum with the zoo. *Most activity takes place at weekends.*

Racing Museum: A history of the New Zealand thoroughbred industry. *Ellerslie Racecourse. Open on race days, 11 a.m.–4 p.m. and groups by arrangement; tel. (09) 524-4059*

The Navy Museum: Featured is a welter of naval ephemera dating back to the nation's beginnings. HMNZS Philomel, *Spring St, Devonport. Open daily, 10 a.m.–4.30 p.m.; tel. (09) 445-5186.*

Private art galleries: Auckland has a profusion of art galleries worth visiting, whether to browse or to buy. Among them are the Aberhart North Gallery (*54 Wellesley St*), Aotea Centre (*Queen St*), Artis Gallery (*280 Parnell Rd*), Art and Soul (*411 Mt Eden Rd*), Artspace (*6–8 Quay St; works not for sale*), Auckland Society of Arts (*13 Blake St, Ponsonby*), Chiaroscuro Gallery (*cnr Queen St and Durham St E*), Clay Feat (*Level 2, Countrywide Bank Centre, 280 Queen St*), Claybrook Gallery (*1 Claybrook Rd, Parnell*), Fisher Gallery (*Reeves Rd, Pakuranga*), Gow Langsford Gallery (*123–125 The Strand, Parnell*), Judith Anderson Gallery (*54 Wellesley St*), The Lane Gallery (*12 O'Connell St*), Mairangi Art Centre (*Hastings Rd, Mairangi Bay*), Master Works Gallery (*8 York St, Parnell*), Oedipus Rex Gallery (*32 Lorne St*), Portfolio Gallery (*6 Lorne St*), Nathan Homestead (*70 Hill Rd, Manurewa*), Outreach (*1 Ponsonby Rd*), Pots of Ponsonby (*298 Ponsonby Rd*), Pumphouse (*Killarney St, Takapuna*), RKS Galleries (*54 Wellesley St W*), Te Taumata Art Gallery (*Finance Plaza, Victoria St*), and the Warwick Henderson Gallery (*32 Bath St, Parnell*).

HISTORIC HOUSES ★ ★ ★

The city has several historic houses which are open to the public. Each has its own character and each reflects the identity of its earliest residents.

Highwic: An exceptional house in the New Zealand context, it was constructed as a colonial gentleman's residence from 1862 by the enlargement of an even earlier dwelling into a mansion. The typically English gentleman's use of a servants' staircase made it possible to confine domestic staff and minimise their contact with the family areas. The elegance of the family's surroundings contrasts with the utilitarian colonial kitchen.

49

The house was built for Alfred Buckland (for whom Bucklands Beach is named: he had his holiday home and private racecourse there). Buckland became one of the province's largest landowners and his need for a spacious home is reflected in the size of his family—twice married, he fathered 21 children over a period of 36 years. His family retained the home until 1978.

The house (whose vertical boarding, battens and steeply pitched roof are akin to the "Selwyn" Churches) is occasionally let out for weddings and receptions in its ballroom and spacious grounds. *40 Gillies Ave (by Gillies Ave exit from the motorway south). Open daily, 10.30 a.m.–noon; 1–4.30 p.m.; tel. (09) 524-5729.*

Alberton (1862): One of the country's most handsome houses, with imposing towers and gracious verandahs, Alberton stands as a testimonial to Allan Kerr Taylor's (1832-90) successful gold-mining ventures and to his role as a leader of Auckland society. The house was enlarged several times but maintains an external coherence. A curious feature in so large a house is the way in which folding doors could vary the size of the breakfast room by reducing that of the ballroom—the setting of many a crowded ball, archery party and "at home". *100 Mt Albert Rd, Mt Albert. Open daily, 10.30 a.m.–noon; 1-4.30 p.m. (except Christmas Day and Good Friday).*

Kinder House (1856-57): The house serves as a gallery dedicated to the works of the Rev. John Kinder (1819-1903), a talented artist and early photographer who arrived in New Zealand in 1855 to take up the post of Master of the Church of England Grammar School, where his dour approach to life led someone to pen:

> "Twixt Kinder and kinder
> There's no different letter,
> But if Kinder were kinder
> It might have been better!"

The gallery includes reproductions of Kinder's well-known views of early Auckland as well as photographs from his album and a growing number of original works. A feature is the tearooms and the Victorian garden. *2 Ayr St, Parnell (off Parnell Rd). Open Tues.–Sat. from 10.30 a.m.–4 p.m. (staff permitting); before visiting tel. (09) 379-4008 or 529-2759.*

Ewelme Cottage (1863-64): This roomy kauri cottage was built by the Rev. Vicesimus Lush (1817-82, first vicar of Howick) and lived in by his descendants for over a century. It contains much of its original furniture and effects. Lush designed the house himself, doubtless drawing upon his brief time spent studying architecture at Cambridge University as well as upon the Howick vicarage, to which there are similarities. Its name comes from an English village near Oxford where Mrs Lush lived before her marriage. In the garden is a magnificent English oak, planted as a sapling in 1866. Also of note is the curious palm-like tree, *Nolina recurvata,* a native of Mexico which is sited directly in front of the verandah and flowers every 10-15 years. It began its sojourn at Ewelme as one of Mrs Lush's pot plants. *14 Ayr St, Parnell. Open daily, 10.30 a.m.–noon; 1–4.30 p.m.; tel. (09) 379-0202.*

OTHER NOTABLE BUILDINGS

St Stephens Chapel ★★★ (1856-57): In an idyllic setting on a knoll overlooking Judges Bay and the trees of Parnell Park stands the tiny "Selwyn" chapel of St Stephens. An earlier chapel (1843) was built of stone, but as beach sand had been used carelessly in preparing its mortar, it collapsed in a storm. Its wooden successor has a special place in Anglican ecclesiastical history, as it was here in 1857 that the Constitution of the Church of the Province of New Zealand was signed on the table which now serves as the chapel's altar. Many of Auckland's pioneers and soldiers are buried in the churchyard, among them Bishop Cowie (first Bishop of Auckland) and the Rev. Rota Waitoa (the first Maori to be ordained). *End of Judge St, off St Stephens Ave, Parnell.*

Selwyn Court ★★★ (1863): A spired and church-like building, formerly Bishop Selwyn's library and now used for lectures and synod meetings, Selwyn Court is the focal point of an essentially ecclesiastical area. Beside Selwyn Court is **Bishop's Court,** residence of the Bishop of Auckland, and behind is the residence of the Dean.

Close by in Parnell Road is the **Cathedral Church of St Mary** (1888), moved from across the street to its present site in 1982 after considerable controversy and now incorporated in the new **Holy Trinity Cathedral,** whose Marsden Chapel includes windows depicting Christmas Day 1814.

With a number of "Selwyn" churches in the area, Auckland's history is heavy with his influence. George Augustus Selwyn (1809-78) came to New Zealand in 1842 as a missionary bishop with a distinguished academic record and having represented Cambridge in the first Oxford *v.* Cambridge boat race. An indefatigable traveller,

Selwyn covered thousands of kilometres both by boat and on foot to weld a scattering of mission stations into a constituted Church Province. Though he tried to serve both sides in the troubles that followed, he unhappily chose to be chaplain to the Imperial troops during the Waikato Campaigns and so unwittingly contributed to Volkner's martyrdom at △ Opotiki. The Church, it seemed to some Maori, was but another European instrument of oppression. In 1868 Selwyn was recalled to Britain and became Bishop of Lichfield, where he served until his death 10 years later.

The "Selwyn" church, of which several still stand in Auckland, was a deliberate attempt to escape from the ticky-tacky wooden buildings of the time. Basically Gothic in design, the churches featured steep-pitched shingled roofs, diamond-shaped leaded windows and exterior bracing timbers. Among the finest examples are nearby St Stephens Chapel *(above)* and All Saints' at Howick. Selwyn's best-known architect, the Rev. Frederick Thatcher, designed many of the churches and also Selwyn Court. *St Stephens Ave and Parnell Rd intersection, Parnell.*

St John's College: The Provincial Theological College of the Anglican Church in New Zealand was originally founded at △ Waimate North. Its magnificent "Selwyn" chapel (1847), whose interior is rich in atmosphere, contains memorials and stained glass which record New Zealand's century-and-a-half of Christianity.

The distinctive College Hall (1849) dates from the same period. In front of the chapel lies the grave of Margaret Frances Selwyn (1850-51), a short-lived daughter of the Bishop. *202 St John's Rd. Permission should be asked before the buildings are entered.*

Onehunga Blockhouse (1860): Built to protect the infant colony's capital from anticipated attack by Maori tribes to the south, the blockhouse, in the centre of the Fencibles' recreation reserve, was one in a chain of outposts across the city's southern perimeter. Cruciform in shape, the building had loopholes at intervals now blocked by vertical bricks in its exterior walls. Never the subject of attack, the building probably would not have survived had it been built of wood, as were so many others.

For a time the blockhouse served as Council Chambers for the Onehunga Borough Council, a council which in 1893 and only a few months after women acquired the vote itself acquired the British Empire's first woman mayor, Elizabeth Yates. Despite the dire predictions of the day and the machinations of an hysterical all-male council, the borough survived the experience. The blockhouse is today used by local organisations. By the park is another outdoor swimming pool. *Jellicoe Park, Onehunga.*

OTHER THINGS TO SEE AND DO

Kelly Tarlton's Underwater World ★ ★ ★: A moving conveyor ushers visitors under the sea, along a clear acrylic tunnel, to see fish in a variety of underwater habitats — kelp and sand bed, a rocky reef, a submarine cave and finally a shark tank. An audio-visual portrays Kelly Tarlton's exploration of shipwrecks around the New Zealand coast. The aquarium, among the world's largest, has been created ingeniously in the city's former stormwater holding tanks, under Tamaki Drive.

Here, too, is the **Antarctic Experience** ★ ★ ★, with a realistic walk through a recreation of Scott's Antarctic hut (1911), a (heated) snowcat trip through an Antarctic "white-out", passing a live penguin colony and travelling under ice to glimpse the marine life of a most demanding environment, all in a temperature of minus 7 degrees! The snow and ice are real . . . but no special clothing is needed. *Orakei Wharf, Tamaki Drive, Orakei. Open daily (not Christmas Day) 9 a.m.–9 p.m. (occasional private functions from 6–9 p.m.); tel. (09) 528-0603.*

Hobson Wharf Maritime Museum ★ ★ ★: A celebration of Auckland's long links with the sea highlights Polynesian voyaging, whaling, Pakeha immigration, and navigation. Visitors see historic and famous boats and the busy workshops of boat-builders, sail-makers and modellers and enjoy trips on the harbour (*1 p.m. daily*) as well as the daily training and match-racing activities of local yachtsmen. *Eastern Viaduct, Quay St; open daily from 10 a.m.–6 p.m. (9 p.m. Fri–Sun); from 10 a.m.–5 p.m. in winter; tel. (09) 358-3010.*

Parnell Village ★ ★: A shopping complex with a restored Victorian atmosphere. Shops in the vicinity are good for handicrafts and are particularly busy on Saturdays, when many come to browse, to buy and to lunch in the sun. There are several restaurants in or near the complex. *Parnell Rd.*

Auckland Observatory: A 500-mm Zeiss telescope reveals intriguing astronomical phenomena, much of which is invisible from the northern hemisphere. *Open Tues and Thurs evenings, 7.30–10 p.m. (weather permitting); special groups on other nights by arrangement. Off Manukau Rd, by the entrance to One Tree Hill Domain.*

Rainbow's End ★ ★: The country's largest adventure park presents varied challenges, from spine-tingling corkscrew rollercoaster rides and motion simulators through to Nostalgic Theatre and minigolf for the more faint-hearted. *Cnr. Great*

51

South and Wiri Station Rds, Manukau City. Open daily from 10 a.m.–5 p.m.; tel. (09) 262-2030. A Superpass gives entry to all rides.

International Rugby Hall of Fame: New Zealand's favourite sport is honoured here in memorabilia and displays, with opportunities to show your own rugby skills. *Restaurant and bar; shop. Cnr Queen and Victoria Sts. Open daily from 9.30 a.m.–5 p.m.; tel (09) 309-8970.*

Parnell Baths: A large salt-water pool. *Open October-April. Access from Judges Bay (foot of St Stephens Ave, Parnell) and from waterfront Tamaki Drive.*

Lake Pupuke: Here on the North Shore one may fish actually within the Takapuna City boundary. In mythology, the lake was the resting place of Rangitoto before the island submerged to surface again offshore. Small boats and yachts abound where Blondin, the tightrope walker who once crossed Niagara Falls, unsuccessfully tried to walk on the water using tin "feet". Disgusted, he left his "feet" behind, and a local resident is said to have drowned in an attempt to do better. *Fishing licences are available from Wiseman's Sports Store, Lake Rd, Takapuna. Fishing gear is for hire at Wiseman's Store, Queen St; boat hire from Deepacre Motel, Takapuna.*

North Head: For many years this volcanic headland has served as a military post, Fort Cautley. The fort was originally constructed in 1885-86 during one of the several "Russian scares" that swept the country after the opening of the Russian Pacific port of Vladivostock. Three batteries were established, North, South and Summit, and from 1901 to 1907 a minefield was maintained from North Head across to Bastion Point. Although manned through two world wars and used for training purposes, the nearest the batteries came to engaging an enemy was during World War I when the artillery yard at the base of the hill was used as an internment camp for German nationals. Most of the guns were sold as scrap when the batteries were substantially dismantled after 1959, but some have survived, including one of the three "disappearing guns" (so named because after they had fired they recoiled underground for reloading). This adorns the South Battery and is maintained as a memorial. (*Another example is at Dunedin's Taiaroa Head, see South Island volume.*)

Now an historic reserve, the hill is riddled with underground tunnels and chambers, and scarred with abandoned gun emplacements. A pleasant walk with excellent views of the Hauraki Gulf follows a track at near sea level. *End of Takarunga Rd, Devonport. Information from the Department of Conservation.*

Pavilion of New Zealand ★ ★: The country's acclaimed exhibition, the success of Brisbane's World Expo '88, is a celebration of the country's mythology, history and environment. *Montgomerie Rd, near Auckland International Airport. Open daily in January and thereafter at weekends and public holidays from 9.30 a.m.–5 p.m. (tours on the hour from 10 a.m.–4 p.m.); tel. (09) 256-0111.*

Some markets: A bustling marketplace with a carnival air is the **Victoria Park Market** (*Victoria St. West; open daily*). In complete contrast is the **Otara Flea Market** set in the heart of the Polynesian community (*Otara shopping centre carpark; Saturday 6 a.m.–noon*). **China Oriental Markets** offer Asian delicacies and arts and crafts (*cnr Quay St and Britomart Pl. Open daily*). The **Mission Bay handcraft market** operates each Sunday (*Mission House, Tamaki Drive; 10 a.m.–4 p.m.*) and the monthly **Titirangi village market** is a tuneful affair, with an emphasis on live music and natural products (*last Sunday of the month; Titirangi War Memorial Hall, off Titirangi Rd, West Auckland*).

SOME WALKS

In addition to the "Walk Around the City" suggested above, there are conducted walks arranged through the Auckland Visitor Centre.

Pre-eminent is the **Coast-to-Coast Walkway**, a 13-kilometre walk of upwards of four hours. This begins on the Waitemata Harbour at the Ferry Terminal near the foot of Queen Street, and winds through the Domain and over Mt Eden and One Tree Hill before emerging on the Manukau Harbour at Beachcroft Avenue. *The walkway route is marked with distinctive symbols. An excellent pamphlet is available from the Visitor Centre. There are several places for refreshments en route.*

Favoured haunts farther afield are the cool bush walks of the **Waitakere Ranges**, to the west of the city (*information from Arataki Visitor Centre, 5 km from Titirangi, tel. (09) 817-7134*). In addition, the other regional parks — **Tawharanui, Mahurangi, Wenderholm, Shakespear** and **Long Bay** among them — offer easy family walking. In summer, too, tramps are conducted in both the Waitakere Ranges and the **Hunua Ranges** to the south-east. (*Information on walks, tramps and camping reservations from Regional Parks City Visitor Centre, Ferry Building, Quay St; tel. (09) 366-2166*).

SOME BEACHES

City beaches: Part of Auckland's irresistible appeal is the great number and wide variety of its beaches, so much so that it is possible to mention only a few.

Houses crowd the attractive, golden North Shore beaches which string from Cheltenham north to Long Bay, and include such gems as Takapuna and Milford. Swimming at inner harbour beaches is, of course, affected by tidal conditions, but charming Judges Bay and Mission Bay are in particularly appealing settings.

The harbour offers the safest bathing. By contrast great care is needed on the west coast surf beaches where sudden rips can develop and where holes can trap the unwary. It is prudent to swim only in patrolled areas.

Whangaparaoa Peninsula★★: Whatever conditions prevail, a sheltered cove can generally be found on a peninsula liberally scalloped by inlets. Sprinkled with retirement and holiday settlements, and crowded in summer, only Shakespear Regional Park on the tip of the peninsula, host to many pukeko, remains unsettled. The Park's three sandy beaches—Army, Shakespear and Okotomai—provide safe swimming and boating, and its slopes can be explored along signposted trails which start from Army Bay. These lead into open paddocks and climb to the summit, which provides commanding views of Auckland, the Hauraki Gulf and especially Tiritiri Island. *37 km N on Highway 1. Detour along Whangaparaoa Drive.* By the turnoff are examples of concretions—naturally formed and perfectly spherical boulders. Nearby, at **Silverdale,** is a pioneer village.

Piha★★★: The most popular of the west coast surf beaches, with an assortment of seaside homes, Piha is dominated by the reclining mass of Lion Rock, viewed to effect from the road just before it plunges down to the beach. The rock is irresistible to the energetic, and a steep path has been formed to its crest.

Pounding surf, a sheltered lagoon and a ariety of walks make Piha ideal for a family outing. At the southern end of the beach the short Tasman Track leads to the Gap and the Blowhole, spectacular when a heavy sea is running. At the beach's northern extremity, the Laird Thompson Track (*1.2 km*) scales the point to reach Whites Beach.

Tracks lead into the bush of the Waitakere Ranges. From the top of Gander Road a steep climb reaches Maungaroa trig and a superb view. A favoured bush walk is to Kitekite Falls, starting from the end of Glen Esk Road. *(Allow approx. 45 mins.)* *40 km W.*

Karekare Beach: A broad belt of sand caught between two rocky escarpments. Close by the shore one may picnic in a leafy glade at the foot of a waterfall (*a track leads down, 100m beyond the parking area*). Jutting from the sand is old railway iron, a relic of the Parahara railway, built in the 1870s to carry timber to a wharf near Whatipu on the tip of Manukau Harbour but abandoned in 1886. An old tunnel is reached after walking south along the beach, beside which lies a derelict steam-engine boiler jettisoned when it proved too large to fit through. *(Allow ½ day. It is important to leave on an outgoing tide as the southern point is impassable at high tide.)* *40 km W.*

Bethells Beach: Typical of the west coast beaches, Bethells is exposed and often thunderous with heavy surf. Good rock fishing. *The access road crosses private property and a charge may be made. 40 km W.*

Whatipu: Another excellent surf beach lying at the end of a 44-kilometre drive from Auckland, the final section of which winds slowly through dense bush spiked by tree-framed vistas of Manukau Harbour.

An easy day-long walk is along Gibbons Track to Muir's Hut, to return along the beach, passing a series of sea caves shortly before arriving back at Whatipu. A shorter walk, to Paratutai, leads to traces of the bush railway which once ran from Karekare to the wharf there. *(See Karekare, above.)* Excellent surf- and rock-casting.

En route to Whatipu the treacherous Manukau bar, which claimed many ships in Onehunga's days as a busy port, may be seen at the end of a 10-minute walk. Also signposted on the way is a 20-minute walk up to the summit of Mt Donald McLean, from which breathtaking views extend over the Manukau Harbour, the city and the ranges. *44 km via Titirangi, Parau and Huia.*

Muriwai Beach★★: An idyllic seaside settlement with the pounding surf characteristic of the west coast. To the north lie sand dunes presently being stabilised for forestry in the same way as those that back △ Ninety Mile Beach. The same sand dunes create the environment necessary for the toheroa (*p. 162*), a keenly sought shellfish whose numbers have dropped perilously. For some years there has been a total ban on taking them.

53

From the south of the beach a track leads over the bluff to Maori Bay, at low tide also accessible along the beach. From the track there are views of distant Oaia Island. On the closer Motutara Island colonies of gannets and terns may be seen. The gannet colony has expanded to also nest on the mainland, forming the second of the world's two known mainland nesting sites. *(The other is at △ Cape Kidnappers; for a description of gannets, see p.* **123**.) At times the stark black and white plumage of the gannets wheeling in the thermals that lift from the hot, black sand is rivalled by multi-coloured hang gliders, also exploiting the wind currents rising from the beach below the Maori Bay cliffs. *Bush & Beach Ltd run tours from Auckland, Sept. to May; tel. (09) 478-2882.*

△ **Waiwera★★**: Thermal pools contrast with ocean bathing. *48 km N.*

△ **Orewa★★**: The hub of the "Hibiscus Coast" is in summer a rumbustious seaside resort complete with trappings. *40 km N.*

OTHER ENVIRONS

△ **Hauraki Gulf★★★, Islands of the:** A paradise for sailor and day-tripper alike. Pre-eminent are the islands of Rangitoto, Kawau, Waiheke and Pakatoa.

△ **Helensville★** *(50 km NW)*: Thermal pools nearby draw many visitors.

△ **Howick★★** *(22 km SE)*: Founded as a Fencible settlement, its old buildings and restful air give the town a character of its own.

Sheep World ★★: Here every aspect of sheep farming can be experienced. Shows include sheep mustering and shearing exhibitions, and visitors may try their hand at feeding lambs or spinning yarn. *73 km N on Highway 1 (4 km N of △ Warkworth). Shows at 11 a.m., 1 and 3 p.m. daily; tel. (09) 425-7444.*

△ **Puhoi★** *(53 km N)*: A Bohemian settlement whose atmosphere reflects the flavour of its origins.

SUGGESTED DRIVES

TAMAKI DRIVE *(10 km)*: *This suggested trip leads along the southern shores of Waitemata Harbour, past appealing beaches. Start from the Post Office (at the foot of Queen St), and follow Quay St and Tamaki Drive. As one passes on to the causeway to the right is:*

Judges Bay: Pared from the harbour by the roadway, the bay nestles at the foot of Parnell Park. From Tamaki Drive there is pedestrian access to the Parnell Swimming Baths, with Judges Bay a short walk beyond. Above the bay stands tiny St Stephens Chapel. *(See "Other Notable Buildings", above.)*
The road crosses Hobson Bay to reach:

Okahu Bay: One of the principal anchorages for pleasure boats. Note the protective timber wave screen some distance offshore.

Orakei Multi-cultural Marae: A remarkable example of a multi-cultural marae, where social and educational programmes are mounted and where the city's Polynesian community can meet. By having the marae open to all visitors, it serves as a cultural catalyst as well as fulfilling a social need. Mixed teams of Maori and Pakeha have worked on the construction and art work of the massive, 900 square-metre meeting house. The reception area (which visitors should contact on arrival) and meeting house face across the Waitemata Harbour and the Hauraki Gulf from a spectacular site. *Reached via Kitemoana St (off Tamaki Drive). Open Monday–Friday, 9 a.m.–3.30 p.m.; tel. (09) 521-0617 (no photography).*
Immediately beyond Orakei Wharf, detour up Hapimana St to the:

Savage Memorial Park: On Bastion Point, the park occupies a strategic position still studded with concrete fortifications from World War II. In recent years the acquisition by the Government of land nearby has formed a focal point for general Maori dissatisfaction over the alienation of Maori land.
  On the tip of the point is the Labour Party's austere but expansive memorial to their first and wartime Prime Minister, Michael Joseph Savage (1872-1940). A slender column rises above the mausoleum, and looks across the harbour to the triple peaks of Rangitoto.
  Savage, born of Irish stock near Benalla township in Victoria, Australia, came to New Zealand in 1907. A foundation member of the Labour Party, he was elected to Parliament in 1919 and rose to become Leader. His humane, amiable and sincere personality helped win Labour a resounding election victory in 1935. His death in 1940, two years after the comprehensive Social Security Bill (seen by Savage as an act of "applied Christianity") had become law, provoked scenes of public grief without precedent in New Zealand.
Return down Hapimana St to Tamaki Drive and bear right to:

Mission Bay: An attractive bathing beach with a tree-shaded foreshore. *(A signposted walk leads up to the Savage Memorial.)* By night the fountain here forms a foreground to the lights of the North Shore. Adjoining Kohimarama Beach and St Heliers Bay are safe bathing beaches. The old **Melanesian Mission** (1860) is now a restaurant. *At the far end of St Heliers Bay, wind up narrow Cliff Rd to end the drive at:*

Achilles Point: A small memorial here recalls HMS *Achilles,* a cruiser of the Royal New Zealand Navy which with two other ships in 1939 destroyed the German pocket battleship the *Admiral Graf Spee* in the Battle of the River Plate. *Achilles* returned to Auckland to be greeted by an ecstatic crowd of 100,000.

THE AUCKLAND WINE TRAIL: A number of New Zealand's leading wineries are to be found within a pleasant drive from the city in the vicinity of **Henderson** ★ (*18 km W*), an attractive town encircled by orchards and vineyards. Many of these wineries are run by descendants of Dalmatians who originally came to New Zealand to work the kauri gumfields of North Auckland, but who turned to winemaking when the gum petered out. However, the highly-successful Corban's Wines was founded here in 1902 by a Lebanese. *Most of the wineries welcome visitors to inspect their undertakings, to sample and to buy. Visits to a number of these wineries can be readily combined into a round trip, taking in attractive orcharding districts and the scenic Waitakere Ranges en route.*

In the vicinity of **Kumeu** (*25 km NW*), Matua Valley Wines (*Waikoukou Valley Rd, Waimauku*) is in a pretty setting with an adjacent licensed restaurant, and has long been a popular outing on its own account. Nobilos (*Station Rd, Huapai*) also has a reputation of long standing, Kumeu River (*Highway 16, Kumeu*) has a burgeoning reputation and the Selak Winery (*cnr Old North Rd, Kumeu*) is worth a visit.

At Henderson, Pleasant Valley Wines (*322 Henderson Valley Rd*) and Babich's (*Babich Rd*) are among those attracting interest.

WAITAKERE SCENIC DRIVE: *Starting from Titirangi, this 68-kilometre drive follows Waitakere Scenic Drive through the Waitakere Ranges, affording alternating views of distant city and dense bush. Over 16,000 hectares of rugged native forest comprise the Waitakere Ranges Centennial Memorial Park, with a variety of walks and tramps through varied bush. Remnants of timber dams and bush railways date from the days of logging at the turn of the century. At Swanson, the Two Foot Gauge Tramway Society periodically operates a rebuilt locomotive up to the Waitakere Dam (tel. (09) 832-3300, evenings). The Arataki Visitor Centre (5 km from Titirangi) has information on all aspects of the park; tel. (09) 817-7134. A number of walks are signposted on the Scenic Drive.*

A short detour reaches **The Cascades and Kauri Park**, a bush-encircled amphitheatre providing an incomparable setting for a golf course and with a short walk to a spectacular rift cut by the stream in a sheer rock wall. Other tracks lead to stands of kauri in the park.

ORGANISED EXCURSIONS

Harbour and Gulf cruises: No visitor to Auckland should fail to sample the City of Sails from the sea. Short harbour cruises of about 2 hrs cruise past various sights of interest and visit Rangitoto briefly (*e.g. Fullers Cruise Centre, tel. (09) 367-9111; trips leave Pier 3 at about 2-hourly intervals from 9.30 a.m. to 4 p.m.*). Fullers also shuttle between Pier 3 and Rangitoto, a 45 min. journey (*one way; allow 2 hours for the return climb to the summit — or take the tractor train*). Fuller's Quickcat cruises between downtown Auckland and Waiheke Island from Pier 2, an island with more than enough for a fulfilling day's outing (*departing at about 2-hourly intervals from 8 a.m. to 7 p.m. and returning from 8.45 a.m. to 7.45 p.m.*). A full day trip visits Great Barrier Island. *Consult the full selection available from the Visitor Centre before making a final choice.*

Sailing: Experience the harbour and have free sailing tuition. *Rangitoto Sailing Centre, Hobson Wharf Maritime Museum; tel. (09) 358-2324.* At △ Waiuku the *Jane Gifford*, the country's oldest scow, sails the Manukau Harbour (*Jane Gifford Excursions, tel. (09) 235-8924 for details of timetable; bookings essential*). Sailing day tours and charters are also available. *Fun in the Sun Travel, tel/fax (09) 520-5591; Transformer Tours, tel. (09) 534-6046; Max Charters, tel. (09) 834-4463; Chieftan Charters, tel. (09) 416-4743.*

Other adventure activities: Those on offer include abseiling/rock climbing (*tel. (09) 815-1851, 837-5177 or 025-967-014*), rap jumping down the side of a high-rise hotel (*tel. (09) 483-8553*), mountain biking through forest and wilderness areas (*tel. (09) 537-0863 or 357-0502*), exotic Harley Davidson motorbike tours (*tel. (09) 812-8685*), horse riding along endless beaches (*tel. (09) 411-8480, 420-2835, 420-7269 or 422-6275*), hot air ballooning (*tel. (09) 415-8289*), diving the Poor Knights (*tel. (09) 298-1941*), sea or river kayaking in unbelievable settings (*tel. (09) 529-2230 or*

412-9126), windsurfing on the waters that produced brother and sister Olympic gold medallists Bruce and Barbara Kendall (*tel. (09) 528-5277)*, paragliding tandem or solo (*tel. (09) 483-2619)*, and tandem or solo parachuting (*tel. (09) 838-6963)*.

Maori heritage: A rare opportunity to see the capital of Polynesia through Maori eyes. A cultural show and Maori food are included. *Maori Heritage Tours, tel. (09) 486-4138; fax (09) 489-5411 (booking essential)*.

Gannet colony tour: One of only three accessible mainland gannet colonies anywhere is visited daily. *Bush & Beach Ltd, tel. (09) 478-2882. The breeding season is from August to April.*

Wild Coast tour: A 4WD coach lunges over the sand dunes of the wild West Coast beaches, with visits to a macadamia nut orchard and a kiwifruit winery. *Scenic Tours, tel. (09) 634-0189.*

Coach tours: A variety of coach tours of both the city and the surrounding countryside include farm and vineyard visits. The "Explorer Bus" makes a daily and continuous shuttle around major points of interest in the city (*departure and tickets from the Ferry Building, Quay St; tel. (09) 360-0033*).

Scenic flights: Regular and charter flights leave for numerous destinations, affording thrilling views of the city and the islands of the gulf.

BAY OF ISLANDS ★★★ *Northland   Maps 2, 3*

Information Bay of Islands, Marsden Rd, Paihia; tel. (09) 402-7426; Bay of Islands Maritime and Historic Park Visitor Centre (DOC), The Strand, Russell (tel. (09) 403-7685); Fullers Northland, Paihia (tel. (09) 402-7421) and Russell (tel. (09) 403-7866) and King's Tours and Cruises, Paihia (09) 402-8288.

THE "BAY OF ISLANDS" was how Cook described the area two centuries ago, and the simplicity of his name masks the diversity of its charm. The subtleties of its attraction lie as much in the graceful fusion of sea with land as in the manoeuvres of Man—of Maori, whaler, missionary, and later, settler. The Bay, studded with over 150 islands, is a "drowned river system", an area where the sea has invaded and drowned a number of river valleys. Its sheltered waters offer some of the finest boating and fishing to be found anywhere, and the menus of local restaurants reflect the abundance of marine life in the Bay.

Sailing boats, ancient and modern, compete in a Tall Ships Race (*early Jan.*).

SOME HISTORY

First explorers: According to tradition, the Polynesian explorer Kupe visited the Bay of Islands in the tenth century and Toi followed about 200 years later. Cook, in 1769, was the first European to visit the area. As he entered the bay he named Cape Brett in honour of Sir Piercy Brett, one of the Lords of the Admiralty, and with rare humour noted "near [the Cape] is a small Island or Rock with a hole pierced through it like the Arch of a Bridge, and this was one reason why I gave the Cape the above name, because Piercy seem'd very proper for that Island".

The French explorer Marc-Joseph Marion du Fresne (1724-72) followed and in 1772 established a temporary base on Moturua Island. Still buried on the island is a bottle containing the claim of "Austral-France" for King Louis XV of France. Marion du Fresne loaded his two ships with fresh vegetables, water and spars and preparations for leaving were all but complete when Marion du Fresne and about 25 of his crew vanished while visiting what is now called Assassination Cove. A party of 12 set out to look for them but only one man returned to tell of their fate. The reason for the tragedy is not known but probably Marion du Fresne's party had unwittingly violated tapu ground. Other theories are that their deaths were revenge for fellow-countryman de Surville's kidnapping of a △ Doubtless Bay chief three years earlier, or for indignities a chief had been subjected to when caught stealing an axe. The surviving members of the expedition left the Bay of Islands, and New Zealand, after burning a number of villages and killing a great many of their inhabitants. This was a most tragic end to a five-weeks' stay of otherwise most friendly relations, which had culminated in a ceremony interpreted by Marion du Fresne as his own elevation to chiefly rank.

Samuel Marsden and the missionaries: The Rev. Samuel Marsden (1765-1838) promoted the first missionary work in New Zealand. While chaplain in the British colony of New South Wales he had met and befriended two visiting Bay of Islands' chiefs and, at his suggestion, the Church Missionary Society (affiliated to the Church of England) directed Marsden to establish the first mission station in New Zealand. Marsden and a missionary group came to the Bay of Islands in 1814, accompanied by one of the two chiefs, to establish a mission at Rangihoua, and on Christmas Day Marsden conducted the first Christian church service to be held in the country.

Mission stations were then established at different points around the Bay of Islands, at △Kerikeri (1819), △Paihia (1823) and △Waimate North (1830), before they were extended over most of the north of the North Island.

In all, Marsden visited New Zealand seven times. A dynamic personality, he showed great bravery and unflagging zeal in his work, and ranks as one of the outstanding persons of his time. Now venerated as a churchman he was nonetheless a stern disciplinarian and, as Magistrate in New South Wales, showed qualities of brutality and persecution in keeping with the times if not with his creed.

European settlement: The Bay of Islands saw the beginnings of both Christianity and European settlement. From about 1820 an unruly settlement grew up at Kororareka *(see △Russell)*, and when eventually the British Government was induced to annex New Zealand it was at Waitangi that the treaty with the Maori chiefs was first signed. War came in 1845 with the sacking of Kororareka and the defeat of British troops at Ohaeawai (*p. 112*). By the time the war ended, at Ruapekapeka (*p. 117*), the capital had been moved to Auckland (1840) and the Bay of Islands' era of importance was over.

BIG-GAME FISHING

As New Zealand's most popular game-fishing grounds, the Bay of Islands draws fishing enthusiasts from all over the world. The largest striped marlin in the world emanate from these waters, along with blue marlin, black marlin, broadbill, tuna, yellowtail, thresher, mako and hammerhead sharks. The Bay of Islands holds a number of world records. Seasons are: marlin and tuna—January-May; yellowtail—June-September; shark — all year round. *Launches may be chartered by phoning the Bay of Islands Swordfish Club (tel. (09) 403-7857).* The sport here first achieved international acclaim through the writings of the American novelist Zane Grey (1875-1939), and his name is still mentioned locally.

EXCURSIONS AND ACTIVITIES

The **Cream Trip**, a 4½ hour, 64-kilometre cruise among the Bay's enchanting islands, has for years enjoyed the reputation for being the finest launch trip in the country (*p. 174*). Other launch trips are run to **Cape Brett** and fascinating **Piercy Island** (the "Hole in the Rock") at the entrance to the Bay of Islands, and to **Otehei Bay** on Urupukapuka Island, made famous by the author Zane Grey. An enthralling experience is to **Swim with the Dolphins**, an excursion that can be combined (as can several cruises) with a ride on the **Nautilus**, an underwater viewing vessel. Sailing on the tall ship the *R.Tucker Thompson*, is a majestic way in which to explore the islands. Coastal **sea kayaking, diving** (including the wreck of the bombed *Rainbow Warrior), marae visits* and **abseiling** can all be arranged. **Coach trips to Cape Reinga** via Ninety Mile Beach run daily. *Details from Information Centre, Fullers and King's, see above.*

BAY OF ISLANDS MARITIME AND HISTORIC PARK ★ ★ ★

Details of walks and camping are available from the Department of Conservation's Bay of Islands Maritime and Historic Park Visitor Centre at △ Russell (tel. (09) 403-7685) and from the Field Centre at △ Kerikeri (Landing Rd, tel. (09) 407-8474. At Russell, displays and an audio-visual presentation illustrate aspects of the park.

The park, with its many islands and coastal reserves and stretching from Whangaroa in the north to Whangaruru in the south, encompasses some of the most delightful boating waters in the country. To many, nothing could be more blissful than to sail in amongst the enchanting islands, dropping anchor at whim to picnic or to explore. Several have well-marked tracks — Motuarohia (Roberton Island) (*20 mins to a pa site site*), Moturoa (2 ½ hrs), Motukiekie (*30 mins*) and Urupukapuka Island (*5 hrs, archaeological walk*). Informal camping is encouraged on Urupukapuka, but campers must be self-sufficient. There is a modest, "first come, first served" campsite at Whangaruru North Head.

Water taxi services from Paihia, Waitangi and Russell provide a link with islands and remote fishing and picnicking places.

YACHT CHARTERS

There is a special magic to the Bay of Islands for those who sail under canvas. Yachts are available for charter, with or without crews. Novices live aboard and are given instruction for about five days, by which time they are usually competent to sail unaided. *Rainbow Yacht & Launch Charters, Opua Wharf; tel. (09) 402-7821.*

TOWNS AND PLACES OF INTEREST

Assassination Cove: The scene of Marion du Fresne's death. *Te Hue Bay on Orokawa Peninsula. Boat access only.*

Kahuwera pa site: A pa site near Paeroa Bay, this historic reserve, of importance in the days of the whaling trade, is accessible only by boat. *Between Manawaora Bay and Paroa Bay.*

△**Kawakawa:** The principal town in the region and the centre for the Bay of Islands County. Nearby are Waiomio Caves, and Ruapekapeka, scene of the last battle in the War of the North.

△**Kerikeri★★★:** An enchanting town set in citrus orchards, with the country's oldest building on its picturesque inlet.

Moturua Island★: Visited on launch trips, the island was the site of Marion du Fresne's 1772 shore base. A bottle, bearing the Arms of France and containing a document claiming the country for France, awaits discovery. According to one of Marion du Fresne's officers this elusive treasure is buried "four feet under the earth, at 57 paces from the edge of the sea, reckoning from the high water mark, and at 10 paces from the little stream". Both Cook and Marion du Fresne drew water from a stream here. *Details of walking tracks from DOC offices at Russell and Kerikeri. A wildlife nature cruise makes a stop here to see the North Island bush robin and the kiwi (King's, Paihia; tel.(09) 402-8288).*

Opua: A short distance from Paihia, the Opua car ferry provides a quick and inexpensive link with Russell, saving 109 kilometres by road. On the point due east of Opua stood the pa of the Ngapuhi chief Whetoi Pomare II, the third chief to sign the Treaty of Waitangi. Suspected of collaboration with Hone Heke, Pomare was arrested by the Government in 1845 and, despite the flag of truce flown there, the pa was razed to the ground. Tamati Waka Nene, a friendly chief, intervened on Pomare's behalf and he was released. *The pa site is at the end of Ranui Rd, off Waikino Rd, a detour on the road from Opua to Russell. Only traces remain.*

The **Opua–Paihia Walkway** follows the coastline from the wharf and through mangroves (3½ hrs one way; *Paihia Taxis can collect you from the other end*). The **Harrison Scenic Reserve Walk** follows the early stages (*30 mins one way.*)

Urupukapuka Island: Otehei Bay on the island is sheltered and close to first class deep-sea fishing. Zane Grey camped here in the 1920s and used the bay as a base for his famous fishing trips. Many come to the island today to enjoy the archaeological walk or to view marine life on the semi-submersible viewing vessel "Nautilus". *Several Fullers cruises make a stop here and there are cabins for rent.*

△ **Paihia ★ ★ ★:** A beach resort where many activities on and around the water are based, it looks across the water to Russell.

Pakaraka★: At the crossroads near Ohaeawai, this is where Archdeacon Henry Williams (*p. 173*) retired to his Retreat. With members of his family he lies buried in the oak-lined churchyard of Holy Trinity Church (1851), a church endowed by Williams and built by his sons. The original section of the Retreat, Williams's home opposite the church, cannot be seen from the road but may be visited by arrangement. Behind and to the right of the church is the terraced hillock of Pouerua pa, a Ngai Tahuhu stronghold of three centuries ago and heavily populated by Ngapuhi in early European times.

Rangihoua Bay: Here on the Bay of Islands' northern shore is where Marsden established the country's first mission station (1815). Nearby, at Oihi, a Cross marks the place where Marsden conducted the first Christian service in New Zealand, on Christmas Day 1814. Appropriately, the text for his sermon was "Behold I bring you glad tidings of great joy".

The Oihi Reserve borders Rangihoua pa, once the stronghold of Ruatara (*c.* 1787-1815), the Ngapuhi chief under whose protection Marsden brought the first missionaries. In 1809, the enterprising Ruatara travelled to England, crewing a ship, but later found himself deposited on the convict ship, *Ann,* bound for New South Wales. On board he was befriended by Marsden, fortuitously returning to Sydney. The *Boyd* massacre at △ Whangaroa Harbour for a time deterred missionary endeavour, and it was only when Ruatara and his uncle, Hongi Hika, guaranteed their safety that Marsden deemed it prudent to proceed. Ruatara accompanied Marsden across the Tasman, and acted as interpreter at the first Christian service. *Turn off immediately north of Waipapa and follow Kapiro, Purerua and Rangihoua roads. A noticeboard sets out the landowner's conditions of entry for the walk to the Marsden Cross. The Cross is more easily viewed in the course of a launch trip.*

Roberton Island (Motu Arohia): The island was the scene of tragedy in 1841 when a Maori labourer, Maketu, killed his employer and her children. Maketu was taken to Auckland for trial and given the dubious distinction of being the first Maori to be condemned to death by a properly constituted court of law.

The island had previously witnessed the even-handedness of Captain Cook. In 1769, after he had anchored just to the south, he went ashore with a small group that was "surrounded by 2 or 3 hundred people" who "set up the war dance and immidiatly [sic] some of them attempted to seize the two Boats". Some were peppered with small shot, and "only one or two of them was hurt with small Shott, for I avoided killing any one of them as much as possible and for that reason withheld our people from fireing". Tranquillity restored, Cook returned to the *Endeavour,* where "I order'd Matthew Cox, Henry Stevens and Manl Paroyra to be punished with a dozen lashes each for leaving thier duty when a shore last night and digging up Potatoies out of one of the Plantations, the first of the three I remited back to confinement because he insisted that their was no harm in what he had done." For good measure Cox received a further half-dozen lashes the next day. On Cox's return to England he sued Cook over the incident. The Admiralty Solicitor was directed to defend the proceedings but they do not seem to have gone far.

A track leads from the beach to a notable ра site (20 mins up). The land at either end of the island is privately owned. The central portion forms part of the Bay of Islands Maritime and Historic Park.

△**Russell★★★**: A picturesque township and big-game fishing base which was the first centre of European settlement in New Zealand.

△**Waimate North★★★**: Here stands the last of three gracious mission station homes, legacy of a once thriving village.

△ **Waitangi ★ ★ ★**: An historic reserve surrounds the old Treaty House.

Rangitikei Maps 12, 13 Pop. 1,839 **BULLS**

31 km NW of Palmerston North; 44 km SE of Wanganui. Rangitikei Information Centre, 104 Bridge St; tel.(06) 322-0055.

BULLS, a small farming town on a major road junction, is set on fertile river flats close to the Rangitikei River. A nationwide pun is that here is the only place in the world where you can get "milk from bulls".

The town, the oldest in the Rangitikei, is named after James Bull, who founded it in 1859. A wood carver of some note, Bull was responsible for some of the panelling in the British House of Commons and for a time ran a hotel and store here.

ENVIRONS

Flock House Station: Originally run by the Government to provide free farm instruction for one year to youths of between 16 and 18 years, the station was established in 1924 from a fund raised by New Zealand sheep owners to acknowledge their World War I debt to British seamen. At first only the sons of British seamen who died in the war were admitted. *15 km on the road to Scotts Ferry, a small seaside settlement at the rivermouth 21 km from Bulls. The actual "ferry" sits, restored, by the side of the road.*

Wheriko Church (1862): The simple little wooden church at Parewanui has its origins in the Church Missionary Society work of the Reverend Richard Taylor (1805-1873), who worked in the Wanganui and Rangitikei districts on his appointment to the Putiki Mission Station in 1843. The name "Wheriko" is a reference to the radiance of Moses' countenance as he descended Mount Sinai. The charismatic leader, Tahupotiki Wiremu Ratana, leader of the Ratana movement spent his childhood at Parewanui (*see p.188*). *9.5 km SW on the way to Scotts Ferry.*

Ohakea RNZAF Wing Museum ★ ★: From aero engines to uniforms and photographs, the paraphernalia associated with aviation portrays the history of the RNZAF in a hands-on fashion. *3 km S on Highway 1. Open daily; tel.(06) 351-5020*

Waikato Maps 6, 8 Pop. 10,533 **★ CAMBRIDGE**

24 km SE of Hamilton. Information Centre, Queen St; tel. (07) 827-6033.

A CHARMING TOWN on the Waikato River, Cambridge is given a more-than-English atmosphere by stately exotic trees, old churches and a village green, idyllic setting of many a cricket match and the scene of countless picnics by through-travellers. The bells of graceful St Andrews Church add to the character of the town, with its tradition of bell-ringing.

59

Cambridge was chosen, too, by an English millionaire who toured the world in search of the ideal site for his St Peter's School (1936). Closely modelled on the English public school, it is set in rolling farmland close to the river.

Dairying, sheep and cattle raising and pigs are the main local farming activities. A number of stud stables produce yearlings for an international market. The local all-weather trotting course is well patronised.

SOME HISTORY

A military settlement: The town, which shares the war-torn history of △ Hamilton, is on the site of Horotiu pa. In 1864 the pa was chosen for a military settlement as it stood as far upstream as the British gunboats could steam. A redoubt that could accommodate over 1,000 men was built by the 3rd Waikato Regiment, and when hostilities ended some of the soldiers were allotted a town acre (0.4 ha.) in Cambridge, together with a block of farmland. The village green (officially Victoria Square) was dubbed "the government acre". *The redoubt stood on the lip of the river terrace in Fort St. (opp. ambulance station).*

The town's name is said to have been given either because the Waikato River here resembled the River Cam in Cambridge, England, or to honour the Duke of Cambridge, then Commander-in-Chief of the British Army.

POINTS OF INTEREST

Cambridge Country Store: An extensive range of craftwork drawn from all over the country is offered for sale in a restored century-old Gothic church. Local farm stays can also be arranged here. *93 Victoria St. Open 9 a.m.–6 p.m.; tel. (07) 827-8715.*

Cambridge Museum: The district's museum holds records of the early history of the area. *Courthouse, Victoria St. Open Tues–Sat 10a.m.–4 p.m.; Sun 2–4 p.m.*

Stud tours: A store with a bewildering array of equine ephemera can arrange tours of thoroughbred stud farms. *The Gift Horse, Empire Arcade.* Stays on stud farms can be arranged through the Visitor Centre.

ENVIRONS

Karapiro hydro-electric power station: The farthest downstream of the Waikato chain and the second to be built, the station was completed in 1948. The arch-design, 335-metre dam raises the water about 30 metres above normal river level, and its lake extends some 24 kilometres to Arapuni. *8 km SE.* Karapiro Domain includes a complex built for the 1978 World Rowing Championships, a golf course and a camping ground. *On the lake's left bank, 800 m from the dam.*

Karapiro Lookout★: A picturesque picnic area by the main highway looks out over the eight square kilometres of Lake Karapiro, scene of the rowing events for the 1950 British Empire Games and the 1978 World Rowing Championships. The view across the lake extends to the distant wooded slopes of Maungatautiri. *13 km SE.*

Maungakawa Scenic Reserve: The road through the reserve on nearby Sanatorium Hill affords a magnificent panorama of the rich Waikato plains. There are several walking tracks through regenerating bush mixed with exotic species—these survive from times when a homestead here was a garden showpiece. The homestead (traces of which remain in the Gudex Memorial Park) served as the country's first sanatorium for the open-air treatment of tuberculosis. A 30-minute walk back to the main road from the park is popular with car passengers. *10 km NE of Cambridge. Maungakawa Rd. Signposted.*

CARTERTON   *Wairarapa   Map 12   Pop. 6,913*

14 km SW of Masterton.

THE FARMING CENTRE of Carterton, surrounded by the wide plains of the lower Wairarapa valley, sprawls along the main highway which gave it birth. The plains are predominantly dairying and fat-lamb country, the surrounding hillsides nurture extensive sheep runs, and to the south-west market gardens cater mainly for the needs of Wellington. There is excellent river fishing hereabouts.

The settlement was founded in 1857 by the Wellington Provincial Council but the trials and tribulations inflicted on the first settlers were such that the council did not repeat the experiment, a decision one historian has described as "an act of compassion"!

SOME HISTORY

Three Mile Bush: The site of Carterton was passed over by the Small Farm Association, which favoured △ Masterton and △ Greytown, and it was left to the Wellington Provincial Council to settle the "Three Mile Bush", as the area was then aptly known. In 1857 settlers were recruited from Britain and from the Australian goldfields on the promise of land and two years' work while the "road" between Masterton and Greytown was upgraded. But the sections they were sold, on terms, proved inadequate to support a family, and so when work on the road stopped prematurely public meetings in both Carterton and Greytown warned the Provincial Council to "avert the horrors of anarchy and possible bloodshed [by voting] at once the necessary supplies for resuming the public works". Their appeal was rejected by, among others, the unsympathetic Edward Jerningham Wakefield, who was scathing in his description of the settlers as a "nursery of labourers" supported at public expense—but who gratuitously offered to provide a "well regulated soup kitchen" if claims of starvation could be substantiated.

From roading and farming, the settlers in desperation turned to milling the surrounding areas of totara and white pine. The land claimed from the bush proved good for dairying and, coupled with the advent of refrigeration, brought the unspectacular but sound growth of Carterton.

For a time the town was called "Three Mile Bush", an appellation its residents found far from flattering. Almost at the outset a petition suggested no less than six alternatives, but two years passed before a further petition "that the Three Mile Bush be ... named 'Carterton' in honour of our representative C.R. Carter Esq. ..." brought success. Charles Rooking Carter (1822-96), born in Westmoreland, founded a contracting firm and as a liberal reformer played an energetic part in the affairs of the Small Farm Association. He represented the Wairarapa in both the Wellington Provincial Council and the House of Representatives, and it was his suggestion which gave rise to the land trusts of Masterton and Greytown. Carter's firm constructed the first road bridge over the Waiohine River (1859) to link Carterton with the road to Wellington.

POINTS OF INTEREST

Paua Shell Factory: There are tours of the factory, a video display of the life of the paua, a paua aquarium, as well as scope for buying jewellery and souvenirs. *54 Kent St. Open daily; tel. (06) 379-6777.*

A number of **adventure activities** — from jet boating and white water rafting to hot-air ballooning and helicopter rides — may also be arranged.

ENVIRONS

Carters Bush Scenic Reserve: In a remnant of the native bush that once covered the river valleys hereabouts, a walkway leads through kahikatea (white pine), the country's tallest native tree and one often dominant in swampy areas. *12 km. E. Gladstone Rd.*

Waiohine River Gorge: The road rises gently into the foothills of the Tararuas to reach a gorge with safe swimming and an occasional picnic spot. Beyond, the road continues into the Tararua Forest Park (*see* △ *Masterton*) and the start of tracks south to Omega (*1,118 m*) and north to Mt Holdsworth (*1,464 m*). *21 km. Turnoff signposted 5 km SW on Highway 2.*

Tararua Forest Park ★ ★: There is accommodation, walks, river swimming and secluded camping in the vicinity of **Holdsworth Lodge** (*see p.135*). *22 km. Turnoff signposted 3 km NE on Highway 2.*

Mangatarere Valley: Another area with plenty of pleasant picnic spots and peaceful swimming holes. *Mangatarere Valley Rd. 26 km.*

Honeycombe Rock Walkway ★ ★: Further afield the easy 8-kilometre walk along Wairarapa's south eastern coastline has a remote grandeur (*see p.135*)

CASTLEPOINT ★ ★

Wairarapa   Maps 11, 12   Pop. 554

68 km E of Masterton.

CASTLEPOINT, a seaside settlement dominated by the white pillar of a lighthouse, was named not for the point on which the lighthouse stands, but for the bastion-like rock on the far side of the lagoon. The settlement is much frequented by family groups, as even while heavy surf pounds the ocean beach, in the "Basin" beyond is the safest of bathing. There is good sea fishing from the reef, surf-casting from the beach and flounder fishing in the "Basin".

Castlepoint comes alive once a year when an informal race meeting (dating from last century) is staged on its broad sweep of sandy beach. Crowds come to picnic and to bet somewhat frivolously, as horses are allotted their numbers not before but after the betting windows have closed. *The meeting is generally held on the third or fourth Saturday in March, depending on tide times.*

MAORI LEGEND

A fishing story: Castlepoint (or Rangiwhakaoma, as it was known) was where Kupe began his heroic chase after a monstrous wheke (octopus) which had stripped his fishing line of bait. Furious, Kupe vowed to slay the wheke even though in his homeland of "Hawaiki" they were regarded as pets. The wheke hid in a cave but was tracked down by the vengeful Kupe, who chased it down the coast and across Cook Strait to the South Island before he finally captured and killed it at Whekenui ("big octopus") in Tory Channel. It was Kupe who in legend discovered New Zealand in *c.* 950 A.D. and named it Aotearoa ("land of the long, white cloud"). Other versions suggest that Kupe chased the wheke all the way from "Hawaiki".

SOME HISTORY

"Wharepouri's Mark": Here there was a settlement of Ngati Kahungunu who fought against Te Ati Awa at Wellington until the Te Ati Awa chief, Te Wharepouri, travelled to Castlepoint to make peace. Despite the peace, Te Wharepouri remained anxious for the protection which settlers at Wellington would give his tribe, and he readily sold large areas to the New Zealand Company for the site of Wellington when Col. William Wakefield arrived there in 1839.

Shortly before his death in 1842, Te Wharepouri erected a sandstone pillar on nearby Whakataki Beach to commemorate the peace he had brought about. *Known as Wharepouri's Mark, a stone cairn has replaced the original pillar and is by the roadside, by the beach, 2.5 km on Mataikona Rd.*

Deliverance Cove: Although Captain Cook had named Castlepoint in 1770, it was not until 1843 that the first Europeans came ashore, among them Archdeacon William Williams and the Rev. William Colenso. Their missionary schooner, *Columbine,* had been caught for 15 days in a storm, and their relief at finding a break in the "perpendicular line of cliff" where there was both food and water prompted a grateful Colenso to name the place "Deliverance Cove", a name which persisted until the 1890s. Five years after the missionaries had called, Thomas Guthrie, an early sheep runholder, drove his stock round the coast from Wellington to an area here—then, as now, largely free of bush.

For some time Castlepoint was a regular port, a role it lost in 1880 when the Wellington-Masterton railway opened.

Nearby Tinui was where the first Anzac Day ceremony was held in 1916, just one year after the Gallipoli landing, when a Cross was erected on the large rock outcrop that dominates the area. The country's first commercial aerial-topdressing flight was made from the Tinui sportsground (*see p.* **134**).Today, the village is a centre for arts and crafts.

CASTLEPOINT LIGHTHOUSE

The lighthouse dates from 1913 and is of special assistance to vessels coming from Panama which often make the light their landfall. The coast can be treacherous for fishermen as well as ships. Several fishermen have been drowned close by, and in 1922 one of the keepers was killed when he fell from the tower.

The tower stands 52 metres above sea level and is 23 metres in height, one of the tallest in the country. Sending three quick flashes each 45 seconds, the light is visible for 30 kilometres. *Access is across a long board-walk and there is a 15-minute walk to the tower. Under the rock on which the lighthouse stands is the sea cave in which the wheke is said to have taken refuge. The cave may be reached and explored safely only at low tide.*

★★ COROMANDEL

Coromandel Peninsula Map 5 Pop. 1,396

56 km N of Thames (via Tapu). Information Centre, Kapanga Rd; tel. (07) 866-8598 and Department of Conservation Field Centre, Kapanga Rd; tel. (07) 866-6869.

SNUG AT THE FOOT of the Coromandel Range, the town's buildings straggle over a surprisingly large area for so small a population. Chief delight to the visitor is the quaintness bestowed by Victorian buildings, thinned in less prosperous later years but with excellent examples of colonial architecture. These reflect the flush of prosperity in which the town was born.

The town serves local farmlands, most of which focus on dairy cattle. The district is a favoured refuge for those practising alternative lifestyles and with Aucklanders for weekend and holiday baches. Several local gardens are open to the public.

Coromandel was named after HMS *Coromandel*, which in 1820 called to load kauri spars and timber.

SOME HISTORY

Coromandel goldfields: Sawmiller Charles Ring went from Coromandel Harbour to the Californian goldfields with a load of kauri timber in 1850 and returned to find rumours of gold rife, for it was widely believed that a log had floated down Driving Creek and emerged with a lump of gold-bearing quartz embedded in one end.

First the Californian and then the Australian gold discoveries had lured settlers away from New Zealand so, with labour scarce, £500 was offered by an Auckland committee for the finder of a "payable" goldfield. Within two days of his return to Coromandel, Ring was back in Auckland with gold-bearing quartz to claim the reward. Immediately, about 40 square kilometres around Coromandel harbour were leased for three years from local Maori, and New Zealand's first gold rush was under way. However, the expensive machinery needed to extract the gold quickly discouraged the 300 miners who had gone there, the goldfield was not considered "payable" and Charles Ring was refused the reward. Within a few months the diggers had gone.

Coromandel's fortunes revived after the South Island discoveries, with fabulous finds at Thames in the 1860s, but by 1872 they had slumped once more.

Today Coromandel's old Gold Warden's Court houses offices and on a small bridge on the northern exit from the town a plaque records the place near which Charles Ring in 1852 made the country's first recorded gold discovery.

POINTS OF INTEREST

Coromandel School of Mines Museum: Housed in the original School of Mines building (1897), the extensive collection comprises rock samples, local gemstones and old photographs of the Peninsula's mine workings. *Signposted. Open during holiday periods.*

A restored **stamper battery** on its original site once separated gold from quartz. Both the berdan and the ballmill processes are displayed. *Buffalo Rd; N of town.*

Driving Creek railway and potteries: Here a narrow gauge railway delights as it winds through regenerating native bush, offering spectacular views as it dips and turns. There are bush walks and a working pottery. *Driving Creek Rd; tel. (07) 866-8703. Train runs daily, 2 and 4 p.m. Also 10.30 a.m. end October to April. More frequently in holiday periods, when it is advisable to book.*

Long Bay: A good picnic and camping area by a safe, if tidal, beach. A 24-hectare reserve here, half of which is in native bush, has signposted tracks leading to a clump of kauri. The road to Long Bay skirts the harbour and passes a fish-processing plant and oyster-farming beds. *Signposted. 3 km.*

NORTH FROM COROMANDEL
(arranged in alphabetical order)

Colville: A tiny settlement with the last store for the northbound traveller. Colville was once the centre of a kauri-milling district, *26 km.*

Coromandel Peninsula Farm Parks: Farm parks at Waikawau Bay and Fletcher Bay (Cape Colville) offer sandy swimming beaches, coastal walks and good fishing. There is camping at Waikawau Bay, Stony Bay, Fletcher Bay, Port Jackson and Fantail Bay and some rental accommodation at Waikawau Bay and Fletcher Bay. *Apply to Department of Conservation offices.* The **Coromandel Walkway** leads from Fletchers Bay to Stoney Bay (*3 hrs one way*).

Kennedys Bay: A popular camping, crayfishing and yachting haven over Tokotea Hill from Coromandel. The bay is named after its first settler, John Kennedy, who in 1843 and after years of successful timber deals, sailed for Auckland with £4,000, only to be robbed and murdered by his crew. A goldfield was proclaimed here in 1868. *21 km NE from Coromandel.*

Mt Moehau (892 m): The highest peak in the Moehau Range and the centre of a sacred Maori Reserve affords a strenuous all-day climb rewarded by the peninsula's most spectacular views. According to tradition, Tamatekapua, captain of the *Arawa* canoe, is buried near the summit, and the name of Moehau ("windy sleeping place") was given to the peak by his son.

A tiny native frog, *Leiopelma archeyi*, although rarely found off the Coromandel Peninsula, is sometimes seen here. Protected by law, it possesses the most primitive skeletal and anatomical features of any known frog and is even more unusual in that its young are hatched from eggs and bypass the free-living tadpole stage. *Allow 7 hrs for the return tramp. Start from Te Hope Stream 35 km N of Coromandel. First follow the left bank of the stream and then a clear spur to the S. A Forest Park sign at the start of the track gives the conditions for crossing private property and indicates the route to be followed. A companion with local knowledge is an asset.*

Port Charles: A remote but charming holiday spot with baches tucked away in the bush. A marine radio station operates here, a notice addressed to "overseas shipping" on its door. Beyond is Sandy Bay, a sheltered, safe and splendid sweep of sand. The Coromandel Walkway starts at Stony Bay, just beyond Port Charles, and extends some 7 km to Fletchers Bay. *Allow 3 hrs each way. Stout footwear is recommended. 45 km N from Coromandel.*

Port Jackson: After the rugged coastline to the south where the road passes a granite quarry, its wharf by the roadside, the long open beach of Port Jackson, backed by lupin but with little shelter, comes as a surprise. Six kilometres on, at the present road's end, Fletchers Bay is a delightful pohutukawa-shaded cove with good fishing and a walk for the more energetic over the eastern headland to climb the 150-metre Needles, a spectacular viewpoint. *56 km N from Coromandel.*

Tokatea: Mine tunnels and dangerous, deep, open shafts pockmark the crest of Tokatea Hill where the nostalgia of a vanished gold town combines with a magnificent panorama west over Coromandel Harbour and the Hauraki Gulf and east to Kennedys Bay.

Tokatea means "white rock". *8 km from Coromandel on the road to Kennedys Bay.*

COROMANDEL PENINSULA ★★★   Map 5

Department of Conservation Offices: Kauaeranga Field Centre, Kauaeranga Valley, tel. (07) 868-6381; Coromandel Field Centre, Kapanga Rd, Coromandel, tel. (07) 866-6869.

THE PENINSULA juts claw-like from the South Auckland coastline to separate the Hauraki Gulf from the Bay of Plenty. Like vertebrae, the volcanic Coromandel and Moehau Ranges run out to Port Jackson and invest the peninsula with raw grandeur, well forested and wild. Deep in the bush lie abandoned mining machinery, old kauri waterdams and timber-milling equipment.

The peninsula is full of contrasts. In places the sea laps on lazy golden beaches, at times it crashes on jagged rocks at the feet of precipitous cliffs which seem to be supported only by the roots of gnarled pohutukawa trees. The farmland is in places fertile, and in others manuka and gorse have reclaimed vast areas and the arduous process of clearing continues.

For sports lovers the area offers wide variety. Wild pig abound in the bush, duck and pheasant are plentiful in season, and skindivers find both fascination and fish off the many bays and islands. On the eastern shore surf-casters and big-game fishermen are well rewarded, and the sheltered western coast is often flecked with yachts. The peninsula has also become a mecca for artists and craftspeople and in recent years growing numbers of Aucklanders have established holiday homes around the coast.

A glossary of Maori words appears on *pp.* **313-15.**

SOME NOTES

Gemstones: The widest variety of gemstones in the country is to be found on the peninsula. Both agate and jasper are found in rivers and creeks near Thames, and on the road north many of the beaches yield varieties of cornelian, beach agates, chalcedomy, jasper and petrified wood. Te Mata Beach is particularly rich in magnificent specimens of cornelian-agate. Among the deserted minetips at Tokatea, amethysts and quartz crystals may be collected. *The derelict tunnels are potentially dangerous.*

On the peninsula's east coast, at Kuaotunu, Black Jack Hill offers clear quartz crystals, sinter, variously coloured chert and pseudomorphs. In streams near Coroglen, jasper, agate and banded chert may be found, and at Hikuai the river contains a variety of stones including banded chert, onyx, jasper and plasma. The very rare precious opal has been found near Tairua. *Inquire at the Department of Conservation if you wish to fossick for gemstones in the Forest Park itself.*

Kauri, gum and gold: Like Northland's, the peninsula's natural fascinations are gilded by two short periods of uncontrolled exploitation. Kauri timber, gum and gold drew men to New Zealand from all over the world, and the Coromandel Peninsula offered all three. In the early 1800s its kauri forests were ravaged by overseas timber traders whose pit-saws few trees survived. They were followed by gum diggers and miners who by the end of the century had plundered most of the accessible gum and gold. The peninsula's population fluctuated as wildly as its fortunes and today is relatively sparse.

COROMANDEL RANGE ROADS

The coasts are linked by four main roads, each crossing the rugged Coromandel Range:

Coromandel–Whitianga Road (via Kuaotunu) (Highway 25), *48 km:* The longer of the two roads which link Coromandel and Whitianga, Highway 25, winds slowly to a height of 347 metres and affords magnificent views of Coromandel Harbour, Whangapoua Harbour and Mercury Bay. The road skirts Whangapoua Harbour and passes through the old gold settlement of **Kuaotunu**, turnoff point to Otama Beach and Opito Bay *(see below).*

Coromandel-Whitianga Road (direct route) (Highway 309), *33 km:* Narrow and winding, the road passes through fine stands of bush and affords wide views of the Coromandel coast. Signposted are the Waiau Falls *(11 km from Coromandel),* with a swimming hole below the falls. At the Kauri Clump Scenic Reserve *(signposted, 12 km from Coromandel),* a short walk leads to a number of kauri trees which tower above surrounding native bush. Near the reserve is the best point from which to climb Castle Rock *(525 m),* a hill easily recognised from its name and which offers a magnificent view. *(Allow 1½ hrs return.)*

Tapu-Coroglen Road: The road winds along the Tapu and Waiwawa River valleys. The horizon is dominated by the Camel's Back *(819 m)* with its camel-humped twin peaks. According to tradition the mountain was the scene of a Maori battle which ended with a number of Ngati Terangi being hurled to their deaths.

At **Rapaura** *(7 km from Tapu)* in summer one may pause at the Rapaura Water Gardens, where spring water cascades through native bush to feed water-lily ponds *(open Oct. 1-April 30, 10 a.m.-4 p.m.).*

A **"square" kauri** *(signposted 26 km from Tapu),* said to be at least 1,200 years old, is reached after a short walk up a stepped track. The tree can be seen from the road but the five-minute walk is necessary to appreciate properly its nearly square trunk.

Kopu–Hikuai Road, *32.5 km:* The newest of the peninsula's roads, completed in 1967, the route cuts deeply through rugged country. At its highest point the road follows an old horse trail which at the turn of the century led from Thames to the Tairua Valley mines.

COROMANDEL FOREST PARK

Coromandel Forest Park (63,400 ha.) extends over much of the peninsula's bush-covered uplands and includes about 8,000 hectares of regenerating kauri. A well-designed and expanding system of tracks leads to a variety of points of interest, including dams built to store water which could be released suddenly and so drive kauri logs down to creeks, rivers or tidal waters. Much of the park is the subject of prospecting licences as the search continues for gold, silver, sulphur, zinc, lead and copper. There is some rental accommodation at Waikawau Bay and Fletchers Bay (Cape Colville). *Information from Department of Conservation offices.*

TOWNS AND PLACES OF INTEREST

Aldermen Islands: Named by Cook in a moment of whimsy at the same time as neighbouring Mayor Island, the islands form part of the Hauraki Gulf Maritime Park. Now a sanctuary, the islands are abundant in tuatara, and one—Flat Island—is home to the country's largest colony of the white-faced storm petrel, "Mother Carey's Chicken". *A permit is required before landing.*

Colville: A tiny settlement with the last store for the northbound traveller.

△ **Coromandel★★:** A picturesque town of Victorian and gold-rush memories. From here roads lead north to Port Jackson, Port Charles and Kennedys Bay.

Hahei★: An idyllic seaside spot favoured by skindivers, the sands of its island-sheltered beach are tinted pink with crushed shell. There are two pa sites at the southern end of the beach—one on the headland, the other high above it. Beyond are two blowholes, most spectacular at high tide when a swell is running. At the northern end of the beach a two-hour return walk over the bluff leads to Cathedral Cave, a huge sea-formed cavern which faces "The Lion's Head".
  In tradition, a group from the *Arawa* canoe settled here under the leadership of a chieftain, Hei, and became the progenitors of a strong and powerful tribe. Hahei is a contraction of Te O-a Hei ("the exclamation of Hei") and refers to an incident when Hei, pointing to a high, curving island off the coast, exclaimed that "it is the outward curve of my nose". Off-shore, the **Te Whanganui-A-Hei marine reserve** protects all forms of marine life.

Hotwater Beach★★: A long beach named after the hot springs which seep up through the sand. At high tide the area of the springs is flooded, but between low and mid tides visitors may scoop out their own hot pools in the sand—the deeper the pools the hotter they become. *The springs are at the mouth of the Tauwaiwe Stream. Signposted. Cross the stream and dig between the cliff and the sea-girt rock.*

Kuaotunu: Once a thriving gold town complete with racecourse, rifle range and brass band, Kuaotunu has today but a single store. At Powell's Point, immediately south of the settlement, bare patches of clay on Bald Spur mark the site of the Try Fluke Reef which began the rush of Kuaotunu in 1889. Kuaotunu's beaches and excellent fishing spots are attracting increasing numbers of campers. The 18-kilometre journey along Black Jack Road to Opito Bay (popular with surf-casters) affords magnificent seascapes. On the point is Opito pa, a site dating from the 18th century where an interesting burial site with 14 stone adzes has been discovered *(permission to visit is not required)*. The best of the local beaches are Kuaotunu Beach and Rings Beach. Kuaotunu means "roasted young", a reference to muttonbirds.

Mercury Islands: Offshore to the east of the peninsula lie the Mercury Islands, a group of seven. All but the largest—Great Mercury—are included as nature reserves in the Hauraki Gulf Maritime Park. The islands interest ecologists, who study the effects of the kiore (Polynesian rat). Where there are large numbers, those of the tuatara, lizards and certain bird species are small, but the converse also applies. The islands are rocky and steep, with few landing places, for the beaches are frequently ringed with boulders and cliffs. Landing is difficult, and dangerous in some conditions. *A permit is required before landing.* The island group is favoured by skindivers.

Pauanui ★★ : A rapidly growing seaside town is set on a broad, sandy beach facing across to Tairua, with which it is linked by ferry. Its permanent population, boosted by a recent canal housing development, explodes to about 10,000 in the height of summer. A walking track leads from the southern end of the beach to the trig on Mt Pauanui *(387 m)* and a splendid panorama *(allow 1 hr)*. Half and full-day guided tours explore the hinterland. These include walking trips to seek out abandoned gold workings, old kauri dams and gold mines inhabited by glow-worms. In a bush setting luxury **Puka Park Lodge**, with its accommodation units scattered discreetly among the trees, attracts the more discerning (and affluent) traveller *(tel. (07) 864-8088.)* Canoe safaris probe the Tairua River and special guides explore relics of the kauri milling and goldmining eras *(Pauanui Information Centre, tel. (07) 864-7101). 15.5 km S of Tairua, detour 11 km.*

Port Charles: A remote but charming holiday spot. *(See under △ Coromandel.)*

Port Jackson: An open beach on the tip of the peninsula. *(See under △ Coromandel.)*

Tairua★: A rapidly growing holiday town in a spectacular setting. The pa-sculptured twin peaks of Paku *(178 m)*, once an island, afford unequalled views of the harbour out to Slipper and Shoe Islands. Tairua means "two tides".
  To the north is the Twin Kauri Reserve *(4 km)*, with the twins by the road, while at the end of Sailors Grave Road *(5 km N)*, one may visit the grave of a sailor from HMS *Tortoise* who drowned in the surf in 1842. *(After crossing the creek, walk along the beach. The grave is on the knoll.)* Information Centre, tel. (07) 864-7055.

Southwest, up the **Puketui Valley**, the fossicker can spend days exploring the **Broken Hills**. As well as being a rockhound's paradise, there are walks amongst old gold workings, including a 400-metre tunnel, and camping. *Turn off Highway 25 at Hikuai, 10 km SW.*

△**Thames★**: Overlooking the Firth of Thames is the peninsula's largest town.

△**Waihi★★**: Site of the country's richest gold mine, the town has a magnificent surf beach close by.

Waikawau: Here, near the river mouth, tramcars cluster as holiday baches and face across to the Auckland streets they once plied. *27 km N of Thames.*

△**Whangamata★★★**: A popular summer resort with a splendid surfing beach.

△**Whitianga★★★**: The township site, in Mercury Bay, was visited first by Cook, then by kauri seekers, and is now swollen by big-game fishing enthusiasts and summertime holidaymakers. Nearby are Hahei and Hotwater Beach *(see above).*

DANNEVIRKE

Hawke's Bay   Map 12   Pop. 5,663

105 km SW of Hastings; 55 km NE of Palmerston North. Information Centre, 156 High St; tel. (06) 374-8983.

DANNEVIRKE, bustling centre of the southern Hawke's Bay farmlands, has little to remind visitors of its origins as a Scandinavian settlement in the giant totara forest known as the "Seventy Mile Bush". Although the forest, which once extended virtually from Masterton to Takapau, has vanished and the Scandinavians have been absorbed, the town's beginnings are still reflected in the names of many of its residents.

Dannevirke means "The Danes' Work", and was the name given to a great wall built across the Danish isthmus in the ninth century for defence against the Saxons but which was lost by Denmark in the Prussian invasion of 1864. Here the name can be taken as a reference to the construction of the road and to the rich pasturelands won from the forest.

Dannevirke's **Domain**, shaded by gracious old trees, is a pleasant place in which to picnic.

SOME HISTORY

A Scandinavian settlement: Portions of the Seventy Mile Bush were purchased by the Hawke's Bay and Wellington Provincial Councils, and the Government financed the immigration of Scandinavians both to settle the bush and to complete a road through it, now Highway 2.

In 1872 the first settlers arrived at Napier—Norwegians, Danes and Swedes among them—and were divided into two groups, one going to Dannevirke, the other to nearby △ Norsewood. For two days they trekked through the bush before reaching the rough clearing destined to become Dannevirke. At the sight of high fern and charred tree trunks a feeling of despair swept over the party, some even breaking down to weep at the monumental task which confronted them.

Development was retarded by the high cost of transporting food from Napier, and wages paid for roadmaking barely covered the day-to-day cost of living. So when the Government insisted that the settlers repay their fares before they bought land (at £1 an acre), many families left the district, some moving on to North America.

Sawmilling, coupled with the arrival of the railway in 1884, brought rapid growth, and the hitherto exclusively Scandinavian community was swollen by British migrants.

POINTS OF INTEREST

Coonoor Caves: Groups can be conducted through caves adorned with stalactites and ancient moa bones. *32 km E. Arrange through the Information Centre.*

Akitio: On the Wairarapa coast, sandy Akitio Beach with its reef is attractive for swimming and fishing. There is an historic **landing shed**, which was used to store wool bales in days when wool was shipped round the coast (*c.* 1880–1942). *76 km E. via Weber.* En route, a detour may be made to **Waihi Falls** (some 18 metres across), set in a reserve of predominantly totara and matai. (*At Waipatiki, turn right along Oporae Rd.*)

TOURING NOTE

Those who seek a back-country alternative to Highway 2 can link with Highway 52 and proceed either south (by way of Pongaroa and Alfredton) to △ Masterton, or north (through Porangahau *p.* **257** and Wallingford) to △ Waipukurau.

DARGAVILLE   Northland   Map 3   Pop. 4,773

58 km SW of Whangarei. Information Centre, Normanby St.; tel. (09) 439-8360.

DARGAVILLE, named for the Irish-born Australian, Joseph McMullen Dargaville, who founded the town in 1872, is in the heart of a thriving dairying district and is used by visitors to Northland as a base from which to explore △ Waipoua Kauri Forest and Trounson Kauri Park *(52 km and 35 km N respectively)*. There are wineries near Dargaville, at Turiwiri *(3 km)*.

Originally the town was a kauri timber and gum trading centre where ships of up to 3,000 tons would call after sailing in to Kaipara Harbour and a further 64 kilometres up the Wairoa River to moor at the town's wharf. Many of its first settlers were Dalmatians, whose descendants still inhabit the area.

A feature of the wild, pounded ocean coastline is the restless sand beds. Periodically these move to reveal the hulks of long-forgotten wrecks and fuel the imagination of those who enjoy speculating as to whether the Spanish might have been among the earliest of the country's European visitors!

POINTS OF INTEREST

Northern Wairoa Museum★★: In a hilltop setting which affords sweeping views of the town and the river, the museum portrays the history of the district in displays of Maori artefacts, maritime items and objects from the pioneering era. A seafaring collection built up over 50 years by a local sea captain, Capt. Dandy Vause, has been augmented by masts from the ill-fated Greenpeace vessel, *Rainbow Warrior*, and there is also a "lighthouse restaurant". Of special interest is a pre-European Maori canoe, buried at North Head in 1809 by local Ngati Whatua after invading Ngapuhi had inflicted casualties upon them. Its prow was discovered by a lighthouse keeper in 1900 but the hull was not rediscovered until 1972. As a canoe wholly hewn with stone adzed tools, it is extremely rare. Kauri is depicted in all its facets, the display including a massive 84-kg specimen of gum. *Harding Park. Follow signposts. Open daily. Tel (09) 439-7555.*

ENVIRONS

Baylys Beach: A popular summer holiday and camping spot, and home to all too few toheroa (*p.* **162**). The taking of toheroa is often banned, but the tasty tuatua is plentiful and the shellfish may be gathered south of Baylys Beach *13 km W of Dargaville.* At **Moremunui**, a plaque marks the site of a major battle between the Ngapuhi and Kaipara tribes in which muskets are said to have been used for the first time. *Access by beach 10 km N of Baylys Beach.*

Pouto Lighthouse ★★: More than a century old, the kauri-timbered lighthouse on North Kaipara Head was one of the last to be built of wood. Built in 1884, the three storey building was decommissioned in 1947 when the Kaipara was closed as a port of entry. *A 2-hr walk starting at the end of Poutu Point Rd, 67 km SE of Dargaville on △ Kaipara Harbour. Four-wheel-drive trips run from Dargaville.*

The sand bar at North Spit proved in the past to be a graveyard for many ships, and beyond the lighthouse in an area of the sand dunes known as the "Ships Graveyard", beachcombers still find bottles and pieces from the wrecks of past generations.

Kai-iwi Lakes (Taharoa Domain): Three freshwater lakes, known as dune lakes, offer swimming, sailing, water-skiing and trout fishing. Camping at the main lake is popular in summer (*book through the Information Centre*) and the sandy shores make good picnic places. *35 km N.*

"Only fools want to travel all the time; sensible men want to arrive." *Klemens von Metternich*

Northland   Map 1   ★★★ **DOUBTLESS BAY**

35 km NE of Kaitaia to Coopers Beach.

DOUBTLESS BAY contains a series of spendid beaches which make the area a choice holiday spot. There is good big-game fishing at the entrance to the bay. Matai Bay and Cape Karikari attract skindivers.

From Mangonui, tours run up △ Ninety Mile Beach to Cape Reinga. The Nocturnal Park and Glow Worm Grotto (p. 114) and the Wagener Museum at Houhora Heads (p. 190) can also easily be visited from Doubtless Bay.

SOME HISTORY

Kupe's first landing: Kupe, credited with the first discovery of New Zealand *(see p. 9)*, is said to have made his initial landfall at Taipa, in Doubtless Bay. Kupe is almost the only Polynesian explorer reputed to have returned to his homeland and, according to tradition, his descendants migrated here several hundred years later to land in the same place.

European exploration: The bay was named in 1769 by Captain Cook who, after wondering whether the northern extremity was a peninsula or an island, concluded: "Doubtless, a bay."

Only eight days after Cook had sailed past, the French explorer Jean Francois Marie de Surville (1717-70) became the first European to enter Doubtless Bay. During an ill-fated voyage in search of a fabulously rich island believed to lie in the direction of Peru, de Surville was forced to sail south to the land discovered by Tasman in order to get food and rest for his scurvy-stricken crew. At Doubtless Bay an incident involving a boat which had broken loose in a storm ended tragically. De Surville set out to retrieve the dinghy but the Maori, possibly believing it to be theirs by virtue of muru (the plundering of a person who had suffered a misfortune), hid it from him. Relations had hitherto been amicable but in a rage de Surville now burned Maori huts and other property and captured a chief called Ranginui. He then sailed for South America, taking with him Ranginui, who soon died of scurvy. De Surville himself was drowned not long afterwards when a small boat in which he was attempting to land capsized in heavy surf.

One theory for the murder of Marion du Fresne at the Bay of Islands three years later is that the Maori there remembered the brutality of his fellow-countryman de Surville. Yet this, the third recorded European expedition to visit New Zealand, is remarkable in that no Maori or European was injured in the meeting of the two peoples.

While in Doubtless Bay, de Surville was forced to abandon three of his anchors when his ship, *St Jean Baptiste,* was battered in the gale which caused the loss of the dinghy. Two of the anchors were located in 1974 and the third in 1982. One is now displayed in the Kaitaia Museum; a second is in the Museum of New Zealand at △ Wellington. They represent the oldest authenticated relics of European New Zealand. *A plaque at Whatuwhiwhi records de Surville's visit.*

POINTS OF INTEREST

Karikari Peninsula: The western arm of Doubtless Bay arches through the lengthy sweep of Tokerau Beach to conclude in the knuckle of the Rangiawhia Range. Whatuwhiwhi, on the northern curve of the Bay and visited by de Surville in 1769, has a good beach. By the shore here is a rock which, in legend, is Kupe's daughter, transformed into stone by her father in a fit of anger. Towards the north, **Matai Bay**, with a DOC camping ground, is a picturesque spot in which to picnic and to swim. From near here the white silica sands of **Karikari Beach** on the western coast can be reached along a track.

Lake Ohia: By the turnoff to Karikari Peninsula from Highway 10, the lake has been substantially drained to expose hundreds of ancient kauri stumps carbon dated to 40,000 years. The trees died as the sea rose to swamp the area, but the stumps were preserved by the peaty, acidic water of the lake. *(Best seen from a short track on the left, 1 km from Highway 10.)* Also of interest are a series of pits dug by kauri gum diggers. *(By the roadside, to the right, 2 km from Highway 10).*

Taipa★: By the mouth of the Taipa River are a fine beach and boating facilities but few of the trees characteristic of other beaches in the area. A memorial by the river bridge marks Kupe's traditional first landing in New Zealand.

Cable Bay ★ : Tucked into a bluff and with good bathing and picnicking, Cable Bay is an appealing corner of the Bay. An early overseas telegraph cable from Norfolk Island made its landfall here, and between 1902 and 1912 a cable station operated in the bay. *There is a small display in the store.*

Coopers Beach ★★★: A brilliant sweep of sheltered sand arching between two pa
sites and trimmed with old pohutukawa is an idyllic holiday setting, but those who
prefer tranquillity should visit out of season.

Of the two pa, Rangikapiti *(on the point between the beach and Mangonui)* is the
larger and more interesting. It is said to have been built when the local Ngati Kahu
tribe first arrived at Mangonui on the *Ruakaramea* canoe from their legendary
Polynesian homeland, Hawaiki. *Detour 800 m at the eastern end of the beach.* From
the pa there are splendid views of the beach, Mangonui and Mill Bay.

Mangonui ★★: Houses spill down well-wooded slopes to the Mangonui shore and
present a most attractive scene. The town grew up as a port for ships engaged
in the kauri trade, timber was milled here and overseas ships revictualled. Trees
were felled around the bay and floated to Mangonui to be milled. Mill Bay provides
safe anchorage for small boats and good sea-fishing. Close by, the cluster of restored
buildings around the old post office exudes an old-world air.

The **Aquarium** on the wharf displays local sealife, including giant packhorse
crayfish and colourful live sponges and corals. *Open daily.*

Hihi: Facing across the water to Mangonui is the restful holiday settlement of Hihi.
Good swimming, rock fishing and the possibility of harvesting a few Pacific oysters
make this an attractive spot. *6 km off Highway 10.*

On Butler Point, the venerable **Butler House** stands in a peaceful setting, and
nearby is a small **whaling museum** *(private property; visits by appointment only,
tel. (09) 406-0006; there is a small admission charge).*

EAST CAPE ROAD ★★★   *East Cape Maps 9,10*

Gisborne to Opotiki via Hicks Bay 342 km; via Waioeka Scenic Highway 147 km.

THE COAST ROAD between △ Gisborne and △ Opotiki, which passes the most
easterly point in New Zealand, is popularly known as the East Cape Road. The
coastal route, though both longer and slower, is of infinitely greater scenic value
than the direct road, but the two combine to make a satisfying round trip of some
490 kilometres. The East Cape Road is seen at its best shortly before Christmas,
when flowering pohutukawa add crimson brilliance to the vivid seascapes. The coast's
numerous fine beaches are often quite deserted, and its exceptional climate attracts
increasing numbers of visitors.

Though the East Cape was where Europeans first landed in New Zealand, for a
long time it remained isolated from the rest of the North Island. Communications by
land were made difficult by the jagged Raukumara Range and the forbidding bush of
the Urewera. For this reason European settlement took place slowly, and a heritage
of its isolation is the region's comparatively large Maori population.

SOME NOTES

The East Cape Maori: Maori form a third of Gisborne's total population and over
half of the region's rural population. The Ngati Porou, centred on Ruatoria and
Tikitiki, is the major tribe in the region.

About one quarter of the land on the East Cape is occupied by Maori owners, and
further land is leased to European farmers. To overcome the many problems created
by a multiplicity of owners, it is usual for a Maori-owned farm to be run by a
manager, supervised by an elected committee of owners. The unsatisfactory state of
much of the land is largely the result of its abuse by early European leaseholders
whose leases contained no compensation clauses for improvements and who let the
land run down as their leases came to an end.

The region was the home of Maori carving in perhaps its finest form, but relatively
few examples remain. Some magnificent specimens have left the district—such as
the war canoe *Te Toki-a-Tapiri* (c. 1840), now in the Auckland Museum, and the
meeting house Te Hau-ki-Turanga (c. 1844) and the storehouse Nuku te Whatewha,
both in the Museum of New Zealand in Wellington. Good examples among those
that remain are at Hicks Bay, Te Kaha, Tikitiki, Gisborne and Mataatua. Many older
carvings were allowed to rot away, and missionaries urged the abandonment of
features in the carving they considered obscene.

PLACES OF INTEREST
In geographical order, from south to north:

△**Gisborne** ★★★ *(147 km from Opotiki direct; 342 km via East Cape)*: A prosperous city which belies Cook's name of "Poverty" Bay.

Wainui Beach *(5 km)*: A fabulous stretch of surf which unfortunately can be prone to dangerous potholes. Whales who often visit the coast can also find the area unfriendly. At the northern end of the beach a pod of 59 sperm whales were buried in the sandhills in 1970, after they became disorientated and were stranded on the beach.

Whangara *(turnoff 27 km from Gisborne; 314 km from Opotiki), detour 3 km*: A small Maori seaside settlement which also has links with whales.. According to legend, Paikea travelled to New Zealand on the back of a whale. He walked south from the Coromandel Peninsula, with his faithful whale following him along the coast. When they reached Whangara the whale turned into stone, now Paikea Island, and Paikea built his home on its back. The **Whitireia meeting house** at the road's end has as its tekoteko a black whale being ridden by Paikea. *Permission should be sought before entering the marae.* Whangara means "sunny bay".

Waihau (Loisels) Beach ★★★ *(turnoff 40 km from Gisborne; 302 km from Opotiki), a slow, 6 km detour*: A magnificent, isolated beach ideal for the independent camper. Waihau means "windy water".

△**Tolaga Bay** ★★★ *(55 km from Gisborne; 286 from Opotiki)*: An attractive bay with swimming, fishing and a walk to fascinating Cook's Cove.

Anaura Bay ★★★ *(turnoff 69 km from Gisborne; 273 km from Opotiki)*: This superb stretch of golden sand was where Captain Cook landed for the second time in New Zealand and where he received a friendly reception from local Maori in sharp contrast to the bloodshed at Gisborne. The *Endeavour* stayed for two days, but surf hindered the crew in their efforts to fill the watercasks and so when Cook was told of a better watering place at Tolaga Bay he sailed south. Anaura means "red cave". Good independent camping. The iron cladding of Hinetamatea masks a Ngati Porou meeting house with an astonishing painted interior dating from the 1880s. *(Seek permission to visit.)* The **Anaura Bay Walkway**, at the northern end of the bay, affords both panoramic views and the dense shade of native bush. *(The 3.5 km track, an easy walk, takes about 2 hrs. Signposted detour 7 km.)* Beyond Anaura Bay the road continues through farm gates to a series of views down to secluded beaches.

Tokomaru Bay *(92 km from Gisborne; 250 km from Opotiki)*: Named after the *Tokomaru* canoe of the Polynesian migration of six centuries ago, Tokomaru Bay was once the centre of much commercial activity, as is shown by the disused freezing works and shipping offices by the wharf at the northern end of the bay. On the way to the wharf, on the Pakirikiri marae, stands a well-carved modern meeting-house (1934).

In August 1866, a band of Hauhau held Pukepapa, a pa midway along the bay, and Ngati Porou, fighting for the Government, had fortified an old pa on Te Mawhia headland *(the point at the southern tip of the bay)*. The headland was almost an island, joined to the mainland by a narrow neck and approachable only at low tide. Three old whalers joined the Ngati Porou and were left at the pa with two warriors and the women while the main force went along the coast to recruit more men. A large Hauhau party, discovering the garrison's absence, attacked Te Mawhia at low tide, clambering up a precipitous rock face on the seaward side. The two warriors and three whalers, armed with muzzle-loading shotguns, and the women, who hurled rocks down on the heads of the climbing Hauhau, successfully beat off the attackers, but one of the whalers later died from his wounds. The main body of Ngati Porou returned to find the pa safe, to rout the Hauhau and force them to retreat south.

Te Puia *(103 km from Gisborne; 239 km from Opotiki)*: Natural hot pools make a restful break. A short walk to the source of the springs leads to "Mount Molly" and a pleasant view of the area. For many years natural gas has been used locally for domestic heating and is occasionally seen burning in vents along Ihungia road. *(Detour inland just N of the town.)* A hospital dominates the town and adds to its importance. A short detour to Waipiro *(below)* is of interest. Te Puia means "hot springs".

Waipiro Bay: Once a bustling port, along with the vanished Port Awanui and Tuparoa, it now presents a nostalgic scene. Waipiro Bay in the early 1900s was the largest settlement on the East Coast and the focus of county administration. The bay was a recognised calling place for shipping, where sheep, cattle, and horses were all brought ashore in surfboats and wool was taken out. Timber was simply thrown overboard and left to be washed ashore by the next tide.

The present main road bypassed the town in the 1920s and spelt the end of its importance. Life today revolves around the **Iritekura marae**, with a venerated house embodying the ancestors of the local Whanau-a-Iritekura, a hapu of Ngati Porou. Sir Robert Kerridge, founder of a nationwide chain of theatres, had his first cinema here, now the marae dining hall. Waipiro means "stinking water". *Detour 14.5 km along a loop road, increasing the through distance by 3 km. Turn off either at Te Puia or at 17 km S of Ruatoria (116 km from Gisborne; 226 km from Opotiki).*

△**Ruatoria** *(turnoff 130 km from Gisborne; 212 km from Opotiki)*: Centre of the Ngati Porou and once the home of Sir Apirana Ngata.

Tikitiki ★★ *(150 km from Gisborne; 192 km from Opotiki)*: St Mary's Church here, built in 1924 as a memorial to Ngati Porou servicemen killed in World War I, is one of the most ornate Maori churches in the country. The poupou (carved panels) and kowhaiwhai (rafter patterns) tell the history of the Ngati Porou tribe. Two of its soldiers, Captains Pekama Kaa and Henare Kohere (both brothers of local clergy) are depicted in the east window.

According to local tradition, when the mythical Maui *(pp.* **7-8***)* dragged up the North Island the first place he landed was at the mouth of the Waiapu River, immediately south of Tikitiki. Tikitiki ("knot of hair") is a contraction of Maui's full name. He was born prematurely and, as his mother Taranga did not expect him to live, she cut off some of her hair, wrapped up the baby and threw the bundle into the sea. Not surprisingly, Taranga did not recognise her son when he reappeared unexpectedly several years later. Maui's full name was Maui-tikitiki-a-Taranga ("Maui, the knot of hair of Taranga").

Te Araroa *(177 km from Gisborne; 165 km from Opotiki)*: The town has New Zealand's (and for what it's worth, the world's) most easterly hotel. On the foreshore near the hotel stands an enormous pohutukawa named Te Waha-o-Rerekohu ("the mouth of Rerekohu"), a chief who once had a pataka (storehouse) by the tree. It is over 600 years old and, when measured in 1950, was the country's largest, with 22 trunks, a girth of 19.9 metres and a spread of 37.2 metres. Te Araroa ("the long path") may have been the name given by local Maori to a local mission station at which the Rev. George Kissling (1803-65) had formed a long box-edged path from the gate to the front door. The beach is not safe for swimming.

In 1820, in one of a series of devastating raids in the area, a Ngapuhi raiding party from Northland, armed with guns, overwhelmed Ngati Porou living here. They had no guns of their own and no experience of European weapons. About 3,000 Ngati Porou are said to have been killed or taken prisoner.

The East Cape Lighthouse ★★ *(21 km E of Te Araroa)*: The lighthouse marks the most easterly point of the New Zealand mainland. The Cape was named by Captain Cook in 1769, for he shrewdly suspected this, though it was before he had circumnavigated and mapped the country. Just off the Cape is East Island which, with no beach, proved difficult to land on. Keepers of the original lighthouse (1906) found life unpleasant here as the cliffs kept slipping, endangering the buildings. After four men were drowned while attempting to land supplies, the light was moved to its present site. The light, reputedly the most easterly in the world, stands 139.9 metres above sea level in a 14–metre tower. It flashes once every 10 seconds and is visible for 48 kilometres.

There have been many small craft wrecked in the area, and in 1924 the 4,664–ton SS *Port Elliott* was lost off the Cape. *42 km return. Detour from Te Araroa. Allow 1 hour plus 40 mins for the walk to the light. Starting behind the keeper's house, the track to the light leads up about 600 steps. (The precise number of steps is a matter on which few* Guide *users have been able to agree!)*

Hicks Bay ★★ *(turnoff 189 km from Gisborne; 153 km from Opotiki)*: An area increasingly popular with campers, Hicks Bay was named by Captain Cook in 1769 after one of his officers. In 1830 two European ship deserters were living here with local Maori when their settlement was attacked by a war party from the Bay of Plenty, come to avenge the murder by Ngati Porou of one of their tribe on board the *New Zealander* at Whakatane. One of the Europeans, who had acquired a wife that day and knew nothing of the murder, was killed and eaten on his wedding night and it is said that the invaders complained that he was so thin and tough that their meal was tasteless. The other was kept prisoner until rescued by the fortuitous arrival of a whaling boat.

The grey shell of the derelict freezing works *(near the wharf)* recalls days of intensive coastal shipping on the Cape before the road was developed. Of three freezing works, at Tokomaru Bay, Hicks Bay and Gisborne, only that at Gisborne has survived.

The Tuwhakairiora meeting house here is one of the finest on the East Cape. The internal carvings were completed in 1872 and the house was erected on its present site as a memorial to local Ngati Porou soldiers who died overseas. The painted mangopare rafter design is found only on the Cape and signifies the supreme death for the warrior, in battle. The tukutuku (woven panels) are of the single poutama design, the diagonal ascent of the panel symbolising man's growth from childhood to manhood, the horizontal lines indicating periods of learning. The meeting house is named after a local chief who avenged the murder of his grandfather in the grand manner, by annihilating the tribe concerned. *(Turn left at the Post Office.)*

At Hicks Bay Motels, which overlook delightful Horseshoe Bay, is a glow-worm grotto *(visitors welcome in the evenings)* and opposite its entrance a bush walk leads to some old puriri about 2.7 and 3.4 metres in diameter. *(20 mins.)*

Lottin Point *(turnoff 206 km from Gisborne; 136 km from Opotiki; 4 km from the signposted turnoff)*: A drive through pleasant farmland leads to an attractive coastal scene where grasslands run down to the water's edge.

Whangaparaoa *(224 km from Gisborne; 118 km from Opotiki)*: It was at Whangaparaoa (the bay of whales) that the canoes *Arawa* and *Tainui* traditionally landed on their arrival from "Hawaiki". Their captains argued as to which had arrived first and could so claim ownership of the stranded whale after which the bay was named. The *Arawa* finally conceded both the land and the whale to the *Tainui,* and sailed on, her crew members travelling widely in the Bay of Plenty and inland as far as Tongariro, naming and claiming the land as they went. Later the *Tainui* left for Kawhia, where the canoe is said to be buried. Other canoes also apparently made their landfall here, and the frequency with which Whangaparaoa appears in Maori legend suggests that it was once a settlement of some size.

The wife of Hoturoa (captain of the *Tainui* canoe) is credited in Maori tradition with introducing the kumara, a sweet potato, to New Zealand. Today some scholars consider that the kumara was brought by the earliest Polynesian settlers; others believe it was introduced by later arrivals and that its cultivation was a crucial factor in the transition from the Archaic to the Classic phase of Maori culture.

Cape Runaway: The eastern extremity of the Bay of Plenty was named by Captain Cook on 31 October 1769 on his way from Poverty Bay (where he first landed) to the Coromandel Peninsula, where he claimed the land for the British Crown. As he passed, five canoes manned by warriors came out from the Cape but Cook "at this time being very busy" could not stay on deck to watch them. Instead he ordered grapeshot to be fired wide of them and over their heads. This frightened the Maori who paddled furiously for the shore, and Cook watched them "Runaway".

Waihau Bay *(turnoff 236 km from Gisborne; 106 km from Opotiki)*: Waihau Bay Lodge, a guest house with licensed restaurant established in 1914, stands out in this tiny settlement which looks across the bay to Cape Runaway *(above)*.

Raukokore *(245 km from Gisborne; 97 km from Opotiki)*: Here two churches, the one Catholic and the other Anglican, nestle in a sea-girt setting of Norfolk pines.

Te Kaha ★★ *(273 km from Gisborne; 69 km from Opotiki)*: The town is set in a delightful cove, one of the most picturesque of the whole drive. A pa once encircled the inlet and its remains may be seen *(on private property behind the Te Kaha Motel)*. The cove was the scene of many intertribal battles. In one such battle the pa, held by Whenau-a-Ehutu (a sub-tribe of the Ngati Apanui) in *c.* 1834, withstood the siege of Ngati Porou who attacked because in an earlier clash here the nephew of a prominent Ngati Porou chief had been killed. After both sides had suffered heavy casualties the Ngati Porou withdrew. The coastal setting had enabled the defenders to bring in supplies and reinforcements by night. They had been undeterred by a long fence which the Ngati Porou had built in front of the pa on which they had draped a large number of Whenau-a-Ehutu dead.

In the 1830s many whalers from the Bay of Islands moved to the East Cape which for a time saw intense activity. As recently as the 1930s open-boat whaling was carried on from here and whales were being landed on the beach. There are few relics of the whaling era, but the Te Kaha Motel has a small collection of early photographs. The *Greyhound* whaling boat by the Gisborne Museum was originally used here.

The richly carved Tukaki meeting-house (1950) *(opp. the Post Office)*, named for a fabled practitioner of the Te Kaha style of carving, has an elaborate and intricately carved lintel. Early and exquisite examples of Te Kaha carving are displayed in the Auckland Museum. *(Permission should be sought before entering the marae.)*

Omaio Beach *(286 km from Gisborne; 56 km from Opotiki)*: The beach has a variety of camping and picnic places.

"One of the pleasantest things in the world is going on a journey; but I like to go by myself." — William Hazlitt *(On Going on a Journey).*

Torere *(319 km from Gisborne; 23 km from Opotiki)*: Holy Trinity Church, beside the meeting house, has a simplicity which contrasts with many other Maori churches. A pebble beach, unsuited to swimming, affords good fishing.

△**Opotiki** ★ *(342 km from Gisborne)*: A farming centre whose unique martyr's church has a chilling history.

EGMONT NATIONAL PARK ★★★

Taranaki   Map 7   33,543 hectares

Information from Department of Conservation Field Centre, 220 Devon St West, New Plymouth (tel. (06) 758-0433); North Egmont Visitor Centre, Egmont Rd, Inglewood (tel. (06) 756-8710); Stratford Field Centre, Pembroke Rd (Stratford approach to the park) (tel. (06) 765-5144), Dawson Falls Display Centre, Upper Manaia Rd, Kaponga (tel. 025-430-248). Visitor Information Centre, 81 Liardet St, New Plymouth (tel. (06) 758-6086). Hunting permits for feral goats and possums from the Department of Conservation, New Plymouth.

EGMONT NATIONAL PARK preserves the last of the dense bush which once cloaked most of the Taranaki region. From the bush rises the loneliest and loveliest of the country's mountains, Taranaki, to dominate the surrounding dairylands. The mountain's dominance is more than visual — its eruptions provided the district with its rich and fertile coating of volcanic ash, and the mountain today plays a vital climatic role.

In winter the slopes draw increasing numbers of skiers, and in the North Island they are ranked second only to Mt Ruapehu. There is a magnificent 3-to-5 day "Round the Mountain" trek, staying in huts en route *(details from DOC).*

For points of interest around the park see △ Egmont/Taranaki, Road Around.

SOME MYTHOLOGY

Lovers' quarrel: According to one version of the Maori myth, Taranaki (for generations known to the European as Mt Egmont) lived with the other mountains in the centre of the North Island. While Tongariro was away, Taranaki wooed and won Tongariro's wife, the graceful Pihanga. Tongariro returned to surprise the guilty pair and in the titanic struggle which followed, Taranaki was banished. The depression under Fanthams Peak was caused by a kick from Tongariro, and the *coup de grace* caused the cleft in Taranaki's summit.

Taranaki retreated ignominiously to the west coast of the North Island, carving the course of the Whanganui River as he went, and then moved north to his present position. While resting near Stratford, his vast weight caused the depression which became Te Ngaere Swamp. When he paused to rest again near the coast, the Pouakai Range threw out a spur, and when Taranaki awoke he was a prisoner. The rock which is said to have guided Taranaki on his journey may be seen near Puniho.

Today Taranaki gazes silently at his lover and his rival. Pihanga still loves Taranaki and sighs occasionally when she thinks of him while Taranaki, when covered in mist, is said to be weeping for his lost love. Meanwhile Tongariro, the enraged and jealous husband, still smoulders with fury. The Tuwharetoa of Taupo have a different version: *see △ Tongariro National Park.*

SOME HISTORY

A tapu mountain: The peak was shrouded in cloud when Tasman sailed by in 1642, so Captain Cook in 1770 was the first European to sight the summit. He named it after the Earl of Egmont, then First Lord of the Admiralty. Two years later the French explorer Marion du Fresne named the mountain "Le Pic de Mascarin" after his ship, the *Mascarin.* Today the mountain is reverting to its Maori name of Taranaki.

The first ascent is attributed to Tahurangi, who is said to have climbed it centuries ago to light a fire on the summit as proof that he had taken possession of the mountain for the Taranaki tribes. Wisps of smoke-like cloud clinging to the summit are said to be Te Ahi a Tahurangi, "the fire of Tahurangi". The first recorded ascent was made in 1839 by Dr Ernst Dieffenbach, a naturalist attached to the New Zealand Company, and a whaler, James Heberley. Their Maori guides would climb no further than the perpetual snowline, where they stopped and prayed for the safe return of the Pakeha. The higher slopes were tapu to the Maori, though they scaled them to bury chiefs and tohunga in secret caves and to collect red ochre. Early climbers often saw elderly Maori sitting alone above the bushline, communing with the spirits of their ancestors.

In 1978, in a symbolic gesture, the mountain was restored temporarily to the ownership of the Taranaki tribes by Act of Parliament to enable them of their own free will to give it to the people of New Zealand rather than by way of disputed confiscation.

SOME GEOLOGY

Dormant volcano: Taranaki's veneer of tranquillity masks a dormant volcano which last erupted as comparatively recently as *c.* 1636.

Volcanic activity has formed a chain from Moturoa (New Plymouth) south to Taranaki. The oldest volcano in the chain is today evidenced only by the Sugar Loaf Islands, and the mountains of Kaitake *(683 m)* and Pouakai *(1,399 m)* were possibly once as high as Taranaki is now — 2,518 metres. It is thought that when Taranaki had grown to about 1,525 metres it became dormant for a long period which ended when a sustained series of eruptions built up the majestic sweep of its peak.

Perfect symmetry is marred only by Fantham's Peak, a subsidiary cone named after Frances Fantham who, in 1885, became the first woman to reach it.

Small amounts of copper, silver and gold have been found in the Kaitake region, but not in commercial quantities.

FLORA

The isolation of Taranaki from other mountains has given it a distinctive flora. Mountain beech and over 100 other species common elsewhere are absent, but present are a number of plants unique to Taranaki.

Climatic variations, too, give the mountain an unusually varied flora, for on the north face the annual rainfall rises from 1,524 mm at sea level to a torrential 7,620 mm at 900 metres, and on the south-east slopes the range is from 1,143 mm to nearly 6,350 mm.

Broadly, the lowland forest is scattered with rimu and rata, and the upland forests contain kamahi, totara and kaikawaka. Above the forest are sub-alpine scrub and tussock lands.

THE MOUNTAIN HOUSES

The "mountain houses" on Taranaki are easily reached by car and provide bases for climbers, trampers and, in winter, skiers.

Stratford Mountain House *(845 m), 14.5 km W of Stratford,* is close to the Manganui skifields. Details of a variety of bush tracks are available at the house. Popular walks are the short Kamahi walk and those to Curtis Falls *(at 975 m; 2½ hrs return)* and to Dawson Falls *(3½ hrs return).* Beyond, the road winds on a further 3 kilometres to a lookout tower and public shelter.

Dawson Falls Tourist Lodge *(924 m), 29 km N of Manaia,* takes its name from the twin 18-metre columns of Dawson Falls, a short distance from the roadside *(signposted).* Good walks are to Lake Dive *(at 914 m; 5 hrs return)* and to Stratford Mountain House *(3½ hrs return).* Details of shorter walks are available from the Lodge.

North Egmont *(936 m), 26 km from New Plymouth,* features a modern visitors' centre with comprehensive displays. Light refreshments are also available. An excellent walk is to Holly Hut and then on to the 30-metre drop of Bells Falls, where the Stony River drains the Akukawakawa Swamp over a spur of the Pouakai Ranges *(6½ hrs return).* Shorter walks are signposted.

CLIMB TO THE SUMMIT

Under favourable conditions the climb is not difficult, and each summer hundreds of people of all ages reach the summit—indeed a feature of New Plymouth's New Year celebrations is a midnight climb to light a bonfire on the highest point. However, weather conditions can change rapidly and so for the inexperienced a guide is advisable. *Contact may be made through the New Plymouth Public Relations Office.* The return climb may be made comfortably in a day. In late January, open summer climbs for the public are organised by the local alpine clubs.

On a clear day, there are fabulous views inland across to the snow-capped peaks of Tongariro National Park and out over dimpled dairylands to the expanse of the Tasman Sea. *Time to summit—from Dawson Falls via Fanthams Peak, 4½ hrs; from North Egmont, 4 hrs; from Stratford Mountain House, 4½ hrs.*

EGMONT/TARANAKI (Road Around) ★ ★ ★

THE ROAD AROUND Taranaki (Egmont), a 179-kilometre (plus detours) "round the mountain" trip, is a comfortable day's drive which offers contrasting views of mountain, bush and sea and leads through lush farmland rich also in historical interest. Short detours may be made to see the Koru and Puniho pa, Cape Egmont, Parihaka and Manaia's blockhouses.

PLACES OF INTEREST

Listed in the order in which they are reached, starting from New Plymouth and travelling in an anti-clockwise direction:

Omata *(6.5 km)*: Near New Plymouth's western city boundary stands picturesque Omata Church, and nearby in a reserve is the site of Omata Stockade, most southerly of the New Plymouth defences during the Taranaki Campaigns.

Angered by troops invading the △ Waitara in 1860, 500 neighbouring Maori massed at Waireka *(2.5 km seaward from Omata)* for an attack on New Plymouth. First, two farmers were shot and tomahawked in ambushes on the main road *(memorial just W of church)* and the next day two boys were killed. New Plymouth immediately sent an expedition of Regulars and Volunteers and men from HMS *Niger* to rescue outlying farmers. The expedition made so many blunders that a court of enquiry was held later, but the threat of attack was removed, to the great relief of the infant settlement at New Plymouth. The hero of the expedition was William Odgers, coxswain from the *Niger*, who was first over the palisades of nearby Kaipopo pa where he hauled the Maori ensign down from its flagstaff. He won the Empire's highest award for gallantry, the Victoria Cross—the first awarded in New Zealand.

Oakura *(14 km)*: Oakura Beach, a popular holiday spot, saw the outbreak of the Second Taranaki Campaign. A group of Maori, hoping to assassinate Governor Sir George Grey, ambushed a detachment of soldiers in 1863 and killed all but one.

On the main road, 1.5 km south of Oakura, the Hauhau *(p. 167)* phase of the Land Wars began the following year, with an attack on troops who were returning from destroying crops in Maori cultivations. The heads of the victims were dried and sent from tribe to tribe all over the North Island to help recruit volunteers to the Hauhau cause.

Immediately south of Oakura *(opp. the road to the beach)* is the signposted turnoff to **Koru pa★★**. Koru pa was a fighting centre for the Taranaki tribe which occupied land around Oakura, and was a very early Maori settlement, dating from *c.* 1000 A.D. The densely wooded pa stands high above the Oakura River and was virtually impregnable as a series of invading war parties discovered to their cost in the early 1800s. The pa was eventually evacuated in 1626 when the local tribes migrated south to escape the invading and better-armed Waikato. The stone-work in the fortifications is most unusual. *Allow 1 hr. Detour 4 km. Signposted inland up the road opp. the turnoff to Oakura Beach; continue through mill to carpark. A 500-m walk leads to the riverside pa.*

Tataraimaka pa/Fort St George historic reserve *(detour turning seaward at 26.5 km along Lower Timaru Rd)*: One of the area's major pa sites, this was the scene of battles in the eighteenth and nineteenth centuries and gave way to a pakeha fort in 1863 during the Land Wars. *(Return to the main highway.)*

Puniho *(31 km)*: Nearby is Puniho pa and the rock **Toka-a-Rauhoto ★**, which in mythology guided Taranaki on his journey from the centre of the North Island *(recounted under △ Egmont National Park)*. The rock halted only when it saw that Taranaki was pinned down by the Pouakai Ranges, and it is said that the mountain will move on when Toka-a-Rauhoto leads the way.

For centuries, as befits such a tapu object, on ceremonial occasions Maori dressed the stone in a chief's cloak, and in the 1800s it was annually annointed with oil.

The rock is still tapu. A local tale tells of 70 invading Ngati Tama who defied its tapu and removed the stone. But the very same day all 70 died, and that night the rock returned to its rightful resting place. The rock lost much of its tapu on the coming of the Pakeha, and it no longer proves fatal to those who touch it. *Detour inland up a short road 800 m S of Puniho. The rock is now set in concrete some distance in front of the meeting-house. Permission should be sought locally before entering the marae.*

Pungarehu (40 km): Turn off here to visit Cape Egmont and (a short distance south) Parihaka (see both below).

Cape Egmont *(detour 5 km)*: The lighthouse which stands here is the most westerly point of Taranaki. The lighthouse was moved here from Mana Island in 1881, and because of Te Whiti's strenuous opposition to settlement in the area was put under the protection of the Armed Constabulary. The *Harriet* with the Guard family aboard, was wrecked off Cape Egmont in 1833. What is believed to be her anchor is mounted by the Rahotu Tavern. *(See △ Manaia.)*

Hereabouts are many curious conical mounds (lahar deposits), formed when water charged with rock debris swept down from the mountain during periods of volcanic activity. Many of the larger hillocks were fortified in pre-European times.

Parihaka *(detour 3 km—inland up Parihaka road)*: Parihaka is of great historical significance as it was the scene of one of the Colonial Government's most outrageous acts.

From 1866 to 1907 Parihaka was the base for the Maori prophets Te Whiti and Tohu who, in their rejection of all things European, fought an obstructive "civil disobedience" campaign at the end of the Land Wars and preached non-violent opposition to the colonists.

The tribes to which these chiefs belonged owned land from Taranaki to the coast, and colonists' attempts to settle this area were keenly opposed. Settlers' paddocks were ploughed up, surveyors' pegs torn out, and workers on the coast road (which Te Whiti vowed would never be completed as it would cut Parihaka off from the sea) were constantly impeded by fences. As Maori fencers and ploughmen were arrested, never resisting and almost jubilant at being captured, more men were sent out from Parihaka to follow them into gaols soon crowded to capacity.

The climax came on 5 November 1881, when troops marched on Parihaka. Contrary to Government propaganda, the soldiers found no fortifications and the only "resistance" came from a group of children who skipped in their path. Sitting on the marae they found some 2,500 Maori, unarmed and under orders from Te Whiti not to resist "even if the bayonet is at your breast". After a lengthy period during which food and hospitality were offered to the bewildered troops, the two prophets were arrested and, like most of the fencers and ploughmen before them, held in custody without trial under special legislation which denied them their civil rights and forbade any court to grant them bail. After 16 months, during which the Maori had petitioned the Queen, an amnesty was declared and the prophets released.

One of Te Whiti's predictions was that the Pakeha would voluntarily leave the country on a "Day of Reckoning". A special fund was set up for that day, but although both prophets led simple lives without signs of extravagance, the huge fund was never satisfactorily accounted for. Te Whiti's "business manager", Charlie Waitara, was said to be worth £250,000 at his death in 1910. Early in the 1890s the two prophets fell out over the use of the fund, and the movement split.

Te Whiti's death in 1907 shocked many of his followers who had believed him immortal, but many of the traditions originated by the prophets are still carried on.

The land question was not resolved until 1926, when the Government granted £5,000 annually in perpetuity to the Taranaki tribes.

At the pa is Te Whiti's tomb, situated on his great marae, scene of so many eloquent speeches and of the Parihaka Affair. Charlie Waitara is also buried inside the railing. On Tohu's marae, a short distance away and established after the split, stands a meeting house built as a memorial to Tohu. After falling into disrepair, in recent times the pa has been rejuvenated and its role as an important Maori centre restored. *The site is deeply revered and visitors are asked both to respect it and to seek permission locally before visiting.*

Oaonui *(53 km)*: Home to the processing plant for the Maui offshore gasfield. At the main gate *(Tai Rd)* is an information centre *(open daily)* with a video and scale models of the Maui A offshore platform and the processing plants. Two platforms, Maui A and Maui B, lie offshore and are serviced from here by helicopter. *For notes on the region's energy-based industries, see pp.* **152-53.**

△**Opunake** *(61 km)*: A dairying centre best known for its beach and good sea fishing.

△**Manaia** *(90 km)*: A farming centre near the Kapuni gasfields, with two blockhouses (1880-81) built for protection against the imagined threat of Te Whiti.

Kapuni *(at Manaia detour 10 km N)*: The tiny village here became a household word when in 1962 natural gas was discovered nearby in commercial quantities. Gas is piped from the wellhead installations to various parts of the North Island, and oil condensate is piped to New Plymouth's port where it is shipped out to the oil refinery at Marsden Point, near △ Whangarei. By night the landscape for miles around pulses in the red glow of the flares. Close by is the urea (fertiliser) plant of Petrochem *(see p. 152)*.

△ **Hawera** *(105 km)*: A feature of the principal town of South Taranaki is the well-preserved **Turuturu-mokai pa** site. Nearby is the intriguing **Tawhiti Museum**.

Normanby *(113 km)*: Situated about 1.5 kilometres from the site of Ketemarae, this former Maori village was once used as a meeting place by west coast tribes and was one of those attacked in the course of General Chute's epic march *(see △ Hawera)*. A memorial in the domain to the soldiers of the Land Wars also marks the site of the Normanby Redoubt *(opp. the railway station)*. Several Parihaka ploughmen were arrested near here.

△**Eltham** *(126 km)*: A dairying centre renowned for its cheeses.

△**Stratford** *(137 km)*: A departure point for Dawson Falls.

△**Inglewood** *(155 km)*: Nearby are the spectacularly sited fortifications of Pukerangiora. On either side of Inglewood can be seen conical hills formed by fine debris deposited around large blocks of lava during an immense mud flow. *If time allows, the return from Inglewood to New Plymouth may be made by way of △ Waitara.*

EKETAHUNA   *Wairarapa   Map 12   Pop. 585*

40 km N of Masterton.

IN CONTRAST TO other Wairarapa towns, the small centre of Eketahuna occupies a pretty site. Approaching from the south one glimpses the spire of a church reaching up from a cluster of buildings set above the gorges of the Makakahi River. There is good trout fishing hereabouts in the "5-M" rivers—the Makakahi, Mangatainoka, Makuri, Mangahao and the Manawatu.

Eketahuna means "to run aground on a sandbank", probably as this was as far south as the Makakahi River could be navigated by canoe. The **Makakahi River Gorge**, deep below the township is a well-shaded picnic and swimming spot *(1 km)*.

SOME HISTORY

Scandinavian bush settlement: The town's first if short-lived name was "Mellemskov" ("the heart of the forest"), bestowed by Scandinavian settlers who in 1872 carved the town site out of the dense "Seventy Mile Bush" (which stretched from Mt Bruce to Takapau) even as they drove a road north towards Hawke's Bay.

The surrounding bush was quickly cleared, a process accelerated by a number of disastrous bushfires. For although the evergreen native rain forests were not fire-prone, as areas were cleared and dead timber left to dry out, hazards were created and as often as not a bush settlement would be ravaged by fire.

As a Scandinavian bush settlement, Eketahuna shares its origins with △ Dannevirke and △ Norsewood, among others.

POINTS OF INTEREST

Eketahuna Museum: The collection of a local society. *Bengston St. Open Sun. 2–4 p.m.*

Mt Bruce National Wildlife Centre ★ ★ ★: The country's leading wildlife centre, where rare and endangered native birds are bred in an effort to save them from extinction. *16 km S on Highway 2. Description under △ Masterton.*

Mauriceville: This railway township where lime is quarried is a shadow of the settlement from which a party of Scandinavians ventured in 1872 to found Eketahuna. Two nearby churches are of interest, one at Mauriceville North for its typically Scandinavian tapering spire, and the other at Mauriceville West for the grave of Lars Andersen Schow. Schow (1835-1920), an eccentric Scandinavian settler, was locally if generously known as "the Poet". His doggerel was rendered even worse by a local printer who lacked the Scandinavian characters necessary to spell his verses properly. In his lifetime Schow explained his choice of a somewhat costly, built-up burial plot— it enjoyed a view of the road, and he was anxious to be able to keep an eye on local comings and goings. Schow's surviving poetry extends over both sides of his headstone. His "Poet's Cottage" still stands *(ask directions locally). At 8 km S of Eketahuna on Highway 2 turn left. At 16 km turn right, signposted "Mauriceville West", to pass Mauriceville North Church on a hillside to the left at 18.5 km. Turn left again to pass Mauriceville West Church on the left, and continue on to Mauriceville. From Mauriceville either return to Highway 2 or follow the signposted 21 km route to Masterton, although this is to bypass the Mt Bruce National Wildlife Centre.*

Taranaki   Map 7   Pop. 2,411   **ELTHAM**

53 km SE of New Plymouth.

ELTHAM was established in 1884 on what had been an ancient Maori trail which was also used by early settlers as the route north to New Plymouth, the way being much safer than the coastal track. At first the township was dependent on timber milled from surrounding bush, but today, the bush cleared, Eltham is primarily a dairying centre and is renowned for the variety and quality of its cheeses.

The town is probably named after Eltham, in Woolwich, England.

SOME HISTORY

Taranaki's dairy exports begin: Taranaki's tradition of exporting dairy produce began with Chew Chong, a Chinese who came to New Zealand during the 1866 Otago gold rush and stayed to buy up scrap metal to ship to China. While travelling in Taranaki he discovered an edible fungus, similar to a Chinese delicacy, growing on newly felled trees. Farmers found that collecting and selling the fungus to Chew provided their only source of cash—needed to meet deferred payments for their land—as all their produce was exchanged with local traders for provisions. The fungus is still known as "Taranaki Wool".

In 1885 Chew sent two kegs of Eltham butter to England from his dairy factory here, an experimental move which lost him money but which marks the beginning of the province's huge dairy export trade. Four years later Chew won first prize at the Dunedin Exhibition for the best entry of export butter. Before long a co-operative dairy opened in Eltham, effectively ending Chew's reign as a dairy pioneer, and forcing his retirement.

Ngaere Swamp: At nearby Ngaere *(north),* in the closing stages of the Taranaki Campaigns, Titokowaru's *(p.* **129***)* Hauhau band was chased by night across a dangerous swamp which had earlier, during the intertribal wars, claimed the lives of about 500 invading Waikato. The Regulars crossed on a footway made from bundles of timber, but the Hauhau escaped.

According to mythology, the swamp filled a depression made by Taranaki (Mt Egmont) as he rested on his journey from the centre of the North Island *(for the myth see △ Egmont National Park).*

CHEESE

A feature of Eltham's dairy industry is its wide range of speciality cheeses. A factory cheese bar offers blue vein, gruyère, gouda, danbo and French-styled soft cheeses to sample and to buy. *NZ Rennet Co., Bridge St. Open weekdays, 8.30 a.m.–5 p.m.*

ENVIRONS

Dawson Falls★: Eltham is a point of departure for the southern slopes of Taranaki. *32 km. See △ Egmont National Park.*

Lake Rotokare: An 18-hectare lake, fed by natural springs, adjoins a remnant of the dense bush which once covered much of the province.

A walkway starts at the Rotokare Domain picnic area and passes through native bush as it skirts the lake. *Allow 2 hrs and wear stout walking shoes when conditions are wet.* The reserve contains a variety of vegetation types, from coastal karaka to montane kamahi, and from swamp-dwelling pukatea, kahikatea and maire to tawa and rewarewa, usually features of drier habitats. Bellbirds, tui and pigeons may be seen and, by night, the kiwi may be heard. *11 km E. Signposted from Eltham.*

Te Ngutu-o-te-manu battle site: The scene of Titokowaru's triumph over the Colonial forces is now a heavily bushed domain. *Ahipaipa Rd. 16.5 km SW. See △ Manaia.*

Kapuni Natural Gas Plant: *25 km SW. See △ Hawera.*

FEATHERSTON

Wairarapa   Maps 12, 13   Pop. 2,580

31.5 km E of Upper Hutt; 36 km SW of Masterton. South Wairarapa Information Centre, The Old Courthouse, Fitzherbert St (Highway 2); tel (06) 308-8051.

FEATHERSTON nestles under the shadow of the Rimutaka ranges. From a coaching stop it became a railway settlement, and then in turn served as military camp, prisoner-of-war compound, and a public works centre while the Rimutaka rail tunnel was constructed.

The gorse-gilded Rimutakas, which sever the Wairarapa from the Wellington region, are notorious for the strong gales which periodically sweep their slopes.

SOME HISTORY

A duelling doctor: For a time known as "Burlings" (after the first local publican, Henry Burling), the settlement was later named for Dr Isaac Featherston (1813-76), first Superintendent of Wellington Province, who chose the town site. The streets are named after members of the Provincial Council of the time—Fox, Wakefield, Johnston, Fitzherbert, Clifford, Bell and Revans. Born in Durham, England, Featherston qualified as a doctor of medicine at Edinburgh before migrating to Wellington, where he practised until politics fully occupied his time. As Superintendent he was a passionate supporter of provincialism, and it was his appointment to London as New Zealand's first Agent-General that paved the way for the eventual abolition of provincial government. Previously, as editor of the *Wellington Spectator*, Featherston had attacked the New Zealand Company's land policy so vigorously that a famous if inconclusive duel was fought between Featherston and the New Zealand Company's principal agent in New Zealand, Col. William Wakefield. Featherston fired first but missed, whereupon Wakefield simply fired into the air—and remarked that he would never shoot a man who had seven daughters.

Featherston's varied roles: The first Maori inhabitants of the lower Wairarapa are said to have been Rangitane, descendants of the *Aotea* canoe who came to the valley by way of Wanganui and Wellington, following the Hutt Valley and finally crossing the Rimutakas. It was from the summit of the Rimutakas, as they looked down on the shimmering lake, that the Rangitane named the valley Wairarapa ("glistening waters"). Later, in exchange for six canoes, the area was ceded to the Ngati Kahungunu, the Hawke's Bay tribe who also occupied the upper valley.

Centuries later Europeans followed, and in 1840 the German surveyor Ernst Dieffenbach became the first European to look down into the valley.

Although Featherston was surveyed in 1857, land was overpriced at up to £32 per town acre at a time when, at △ Greytown and △ Masterton, Small Farm Association settlers could buy for as little as £1. Until railway construction began on the Featherston side of the Rimutakas, the settlement was little more than a resting-place for coaches and wagons.

After the railway to Wellington opened, Featherston was an important railhead for two years until the line was completed to Masterton. The railway workers moved on, and the Featherston Military Camp was established nearby. Cavalry, artillery and infantry were trained here, and over 30,000 men passed through on their way to World War I. The camp was re-opened on a reduced scale during World War II and eventually housed Japanese prisoners-of-war *(see below)*. With the war's end came further work on the railway, when a nine-kilometre tunnel was driven through the Rimutakas (opened 1955). Perhaps the ranges will be pierced yet again, to provide a road connection with Wellington more rapid than the present slow climb to 554 metres over the ranges.

Prisoners-of-war riot: At the request of American authorities, in 1942 Featherston Military Camp was converted into a prisoner-of-war compound to house Japanese prisoners taken during the Pacific campaigns. The 800 prisoners housed here gave their captors no less trouble than did New Zealanders in a similar predicament overseas. The climax came in February 1943 when a captured naval officer refused to parade a working party and was taken off to the cells. None of the remaining 300 men left in the compound would move, and tension mounted as guards forcibly extracted one of their number, who was in the wrong sector. Despite appeals for his assistance, the senior Japanese officer, Lieut. Commander Adachi, would not use his influence to quell the developing confrontation, and in despair the adjutant shot Adachi in the shoulder. If the adjutant thought his act would subdue the prisoners, he was immediately proved wrong, for the prisoners rushed the 30 or so guards, who opened fire with machine-guns and rifles, killing 48 prisoners and wounding 74. Seven guards were injured (most from bullet ricochets) and one of them later died.

The Prime Minister, Peter Fraser, immediately stated that the "firm action . . . was necessary to quell the riot and restore order", a verdict borne out by a subsequent Court of Inquiry presided over by Col. C.G. Powles (whose son, Sir Guy, became the first Ombudsman outside Scandinavia). It was said that a failure by the prisoners to understand that the Geneva Convention made them liable to compulsory work contributed to the tragedy. Only after the riot were Japanese translations of the Convention made available at the camp. As the Protecting Power, Switzerland prepared its own report of the affair, but this is under a 50-year embargo.

Death was no stranger to the Featherston Camp, for towards the end of World War I during a world-wide epidemic, pneumonic influenza swept through the military establishment here, infecting over 3,000 men, 173 of them fatally. Throughout the country nearly 8,000 died. *A memorial and the graves of many of the influenza victims are in a corner of the Featherston cemetery, 800 m along the road signposted "Western Lake" on the town's western exit.*

The site of the camp is today marked by a **Japanese War Memorial** *beside the main highway 3 km N of Featherston.*

LAKE WAIRARAPA

Lake Wairarapa is the scene of the largest conservation and flood control project yet undertaken in New Zealand. The 20-year plan involved the diversion of the Ruamahanga River from Lake Wairarapa directly into Lake Onoke. With floodgates across the Lake Wairarapa outlet, a flood-free flow of 45,000 cusecs can be directed straight into the sea, and flows above this volume are diverted across a controlled floodway into Lake Wairarapa for storage until levels permit the opening of the outlet floodgates.

The lake is very shallow but by controlling the Ruamahanga (which in flood carries a greater volume of water than does the Waikato) it is possible to maintain the lake at its summer level—even in the 10-yearly peak floods which previously have raised the lake by up to 4.3 metres. This will free about 16,000 hectares of highly productive farmland from flood threat, some 10,000 hectares will be increased from 60 to 100 per cent productivity, and over 5,200 hectares of good-quality marginal land will be developed by the Department of Lands and Survey from near zero to 80 per cent of its high potential, and then sold.

Over 1.5 million trees will be planted in tributaries feeding the Ruamahanga to check metal from being washed down from the ranges.

The lake bed was owned by the Ngati Kahungunu until 1896 when it was sold to the Government. The lake is a valuable fishing ground, particularly for eels, and each February and March, when the eels are migrating, Maori come from as far as Hawke's Bay and Wellington to exercise traditional fishing rights. Southerly storms periodically sweep up sand and shingle to close the outlet of Lake Onoke, and the lake then needs to be "opened" to prevent extensive flooding.

The Ruamahanga diversion channel *(signposted E of Featherston)* draws powerboat enthusiasts, and in season there is good duck and swan shooting.

THINGS TO SEE AND DO

Fell engine ★: Last century, opponents of the scheme to take the railway from Wellington into the Wairarapa pointed to the forbidding Rimutakas and described them as insurmountable. Indeed they would have been but for the nuggety Fell engine, designed to grip a centre rail and so tackle slopes beyond the capability of the conventional locomotive. Patented in 1863 by the Englishman John Fell, it was first used commercially five years later on the railway over the Mont Cenis Pass between France and Italy. The Fell engine had an auxiliary steam engine which drove four horizontal wheels arranged to grip each side of a large double-headed rail mounted in the centre of the track between the two running rails.

Six 0-4-2 tank Class "H" Fell locomotives were built in Britain for the Rimutaka Incline, and from 1878 for nearly 80 years they toiled on its steep 1-in-15 grade. Speeds were restricted to about 5 km/h, and to control the speed of descending trains powerful handbrakes were used on the centre rail, augmented by special Fell brake-vans. In all this time only one fatal accident occurred on the Incline, when in 1880 several carriages and wagons were literally blown from the line at a windswept point known as "Siberia". Three passengers were killed and six injured, and to combat the gales at this bleak spot, massive wooden windbreaks were erected.

With the opening of the Rimutaka rail tunnel in 1955 (at 8.79 km the longest in the Commonwealth and fourteenth among the great rail tunnels of the world), five of the Fell engines were scrapped and the sole survivor presented to Featherston as a memento of this adventurous era. A Fell engine, over a century old, is the centrepiece of the **Fell Engine Museum**. *Main highway; open Sat and school holidays, 10 a.m.–4 p.m.; Sun October to April, 10 a.m.–4 p.m.; May to September, 1 p.m.–4 p.m.; tel. (06) 308-9777.*

Heritage Featherston Museum: The collection illustrates the town's links with the Featherston Military Camp and the Japanese Prisoner of War Camp. *Fox St. Open Sat noon–4 p.m.; Sun and public holidays, 10a.m.–4 p.m. and by arrangement; tel. (06) 308-9193.*

Rimutaka Incline Walkway: The route follows the abandoned 16-kilometre Rimutaka Incline, once the steepest railway in New Zealand, which, using the Fell engine *(see above)* at one time provided a hair-raising rail link between Upper Hutt and Featherston. The walkway *(4 hrs one way)*, through tunnels and across bridges, lies between Kaitoke, on the Hutt Valley side *(entrance off S.H. 2)* and Cross Creek *(at 8 km S of Featherston turn off Western Lake Rd for 1 km to reach the carpark, itself a 2 km walk from Cross Creek).*

△**Palliser ★ (Cape), Road to:** A drive down the eastern side of Lake Wairarapa leads to the savage coastline of Palliser Bay and the North Island's most southerly point. Time should be allowed for the detour to glow-worm caves *(see △ Martinborough)* and the walk into the Putangirua Pinnacles. *76.5 km.*

Road to Western Lakes: After a pleasant run along Lake Wairarapa's western shores, the road rises for views of both Lake Wairarapa ("glistening waters") and tiny Lake Onoke ("place of the earthworm") before swinging west to Wharekaukau Station and a series of superb seascapes. The walk out along the spit at Lake Onoke is a must for birdwatchers. *Western Lakes Rd. The return may be made on the eastern side of the lake, via Kahutara (see above).*

Tauherenikau: The informality of race meetings here, particularly in summer months, draws many Wellingtonians to picnic and to congregate at the hotel affectionately known as "The Tin Hut". Tauherenikau means "overhanging nikau palms". *4 km E on Highway 2.*

FEILDING   *Manawatu   Map 13   Pop. 13,370*

19 km N of Palmerston North.

FEILDING, a bustling country town, has an unusual layout which centres on twin squares from which the main streets radiate. Its stock saleyards are among the largest in the country. The Manfeild Park circuit hosts major car, motorbike and truck races.

SOME HISTORY

"The Manchester Block": Feilding came into existence as one of the "special settlements" so much a feature of the 1870s. For a country whose economy was in the doldrums, Sir Julius Vogel (1835-99) prescribed massive overseas borrowings to finance public works and assist immigration, which for a decade saw the economy boom as never before. In the case of Feilding, an English group, the Emigrants' and Colonists' Aid Corporation, headed by the Duke of Manchester, purchased the 42,000-hectare "Manchester Block" for £75,000. The corporation agreed to send 2,000 immigrants over a five-year period, with the Government providing free passages and some guaranteed employment close to the town site.

The block itself was selected by Lt-Col. William Henry Adelbert Feilding, who came to New Zealand for that purpose and whose name was later given to the settlement. Nearby Halcombe was named for the corporation's local agent, A.W.F. Halcombe.

Although the enterprise was embarked upon as a work of charity, it was blessed with the rare good fortune of returning a handsome profit to its shareholders—due in no small measure to the corporation preserving a harmonious relationship with the New Zealand Government of the day and modelling its administration on commercial lines to minimise anticipated losses. As in a number of such settlements, the layout of the town was planned in England, and in this instance was patterned on the city of Manchester.

The first settlers arrived in 1874 to tackle the dual tasks of winning farmland from dense bush and of establishing links with Foxton, then the area's main centre. Their lot was lightened two years later when the rail link with Palmerston North was completed, and further when the line to Wanganui was opened.

POINTS OF INTEREST

Feilding sale yards ★: In an area of over three hectares, stock sales take place each Friday. Specialised sales attract overseas interest. *Manchester through to Warwick Sts.*

"Lookout": The site offers a view down on the town and over the plains to beyond Palmerston North. *Highfield Rd, off West St.*

Kowhai Park: A garden area with aviaries, lake and sportsground. *South St.*

Steam Traction Museum: Vintage equipment is displayed. *5 km. Lethbridge St, off Makino Rd (by cemetery). Open November to April every third Sunday in the month.*

ENVIRONS

Picnic places: Menzies Ford is a willow-shaded, riverside picnic place with trout fishing. *6 km on Colyton Rd, turnoff beyond the town on the road to Kimbolton.* Londons Ford, a picnic and swimming spot on the Oroua River, also attracts trout fishermen. *32 km, 5 km beyond Kimbolton.*

Mt Stewart Memorial: From here one obtains a wide view of manicured farmland. *8 km on the road to Bulls.*

Kitchener Park: A stand of original bush with stream and shady walks. *4 km on Awahuri Rd.*

Mount Lees Reserve ★★: A fine example of a private garden, with interesting combinations of exotic and native trees, shrubs and flowers. One can stroll through the garden, enjoy bush walks and picnic. *11 km. Ngaio Rd, off Mt Stewart-Halcombe Rd. Open Wednesday-Sunday.*

Cross Hills Gardens★: Thousands of rhododendrons and azaleas make a glorious display in season. *On Highway 45 at 5.5 km from Kimbolton. Gardens open daily from September to April, 10.30 a.m.–5 p.m. Nursery open May–Nov; tel. (06) 328-5797.*

Apiti Museum: A small museum reflects the pioneering era. The bush settlement of Apiti itself was carved out of the forest in 1886. *44 km NE; tel. (06) 328-4806.*

Manawatu Maps 12, 13 Pop. 4,195 **★ FOXTON**

116 km NE of Wellington; 38.5 km SW of Palmerston North. Information Centre, Tram Station Complex, Main St; tel. (06) 363-8940.

FOXTON is a town now energetically reliving its past. Activities centre on the "Tram Station", and local shops are encouraged to adopt turn-of-the-century styles. In truth, Foxton has not yet found its destiny. A promising communications role was lost to △Palmerston North, and the flax trade which once distinguished the town has ceased. The settlement, named for Sir William Fox *(p.133)*, a nearby settler and one-time Prime Minister, has fragmented into two — Foxton Beach and Foxton proper, on Highway 1. The first settler was the Rev. James Duncan, the country's first Presbyterian minister.

SOME HISTORY

A river port: The town, the oldest in the Manawatu-Horowhenua district, grew up as a small coastal port at the mouth of the Manawatu River. Originally the settlement was planned for farther upstream, near present-day △ Shannon, but the severe 1855 earthquake prompted settlers to opt in favour of Foxton's firmer ground. As the main outlet for large quantities of dressed flax and timber, Foxton quickly became the hub of the Manawatu. But the combination of the railway (1886) bypassing the town and the river proving too shallow for larger vessels saw the town diminish in importance and its commercial role gradually assumed by Palmerston North. *(How the railway bypassed the town is told under △ Palmerston North.)*

Flax: There are about 100 species of flax throughout the world, but "New Zealand flax", called harakeke by the Maori, is native to New Zealand and Norfolk Island. A perennial with slender leaves up to 2.7 metres long, flax grows in lowland swamps and alluvial soils, and has a distinctive red or yellow flower. Botanists on Cook's second voyage gave the plant its botanical name, *Phormium tenax* ("strong basket"), an allusion to the kits made by the Maori. As a member of the Agave family, it is related to the cabbage tree.

Flax traders were among the first Europeans to come to New Zealand. As well as for baskets, the Maori had used flax for clothing, mats, fishing lines, ropes, eel-pots, nets and house-building, and the traders found them ready to trade up to a ton of flax (then worth about £45 in Britain) for a single musket. The roaring trade touched off an unparalleled period of slaughter as the Maori used their new weapons to decimate their own numbers in attempts to settle age-old intertribal quarrels.

Early settlers, too, were quick to exploit this natural resource, and by 1873 over 300 flax mills were operating throughout the country. In the heyday of the industry there were over 50 flax mills in the Foxton area alone.

Although manila and sisal were superior for cordage, overseas wars caused periodic shortages of both, to the benefit of the local flax industry. The Depression of the 1930s brought a virtual end to the flax export trade, but until 1973, when the industry ceased, flax was being processed here into floor coverings, hemp, underfelt and upholstery padding, and wool-packs.

POINTS OF INTEREST IN THE AREA

Tram Station: The centre point of Foxton's reclaiming of its past, the Tram Station houses photographic displays, crafts and tea-rooms. From here, horse-drawn trams leave to make a circuit of historic local sights, including the locations of early flax-mills. Most of the country's redundant trolley-bus systems, too, are represented in a **trolley-bus museum** which operates along a small stretch of track from here. *Main St. Open daily. Tram operates on Fri and Sat, subject to demand; trolley buses from Tues–Sun.*

Other museums: At the **Foxton Flax Stripper Museum** demonstrations are given of the flax stripping on which the town depended (*Main St; open Sat. 11 a.m.–1 p.m.; other times by arrangement through the Information Centre*). The collection of the **Foxton Museum** is housed in the old courthouse (*Cnr Avenue Rd and Main St. Open Sundays, 2–4 p.m.*).The **Museum of Audio-Visual Arts and Sciences** has millions of metres of early film (*book through the Information Centre or tel. (06) 329-9663*).

Foxton Beach: Sprawling at the mouth of the Manawatu River, the beach settlement is largely made up of holidaymakers and retired people. Its beach draws many visitors from the surrounding area. *6.5 km. Signposted.*

Moutoa floodgates: The Manawatu River was one of the district's life lines as it provided a canoe and supply route to the central Manawatu, but the close farming it encouraged has made extensive flood control necessary. These measures include a series of massive floodgates and floodway at Moutoa. The floodway, hemmed in by stopbanks between which flood waters can be channelled, is designed so that the flood waters do not scour it, thus enabling it to be farmed when not actually in use. The road to Shannon passes over the floodgates, from which the broad floodway can be seen. *9 km E on the road to Shannon.*

Himatangi Beach: A good beach and a favoured toheroa spot. *16.5 km N of Foxton. Signposted off the main road N, at Himatangi.*

A table of distances between major centres appears inside the back cover.

GISBORNE ★★★

Poverty Bay   Map 10   Pop. 44,400 (district)

245 km NE of Napier. Visitor Information Centre and Department of Conservation Information, 209 Grey St; tel. (06) 868-6139.

THE FERTILITY of Gisborne's market gardens, the appeal of her sun-drenched ocean beaches and the obvious prosperity of the city itself clearly evidence how mistaken Captain James Cook was when he named the area "Poverty Bay". But the name is so obviously a misnomer that its irony has been preserved.

For a long time Gisborne was by its geography isolated from the rest of the North Island, but though transport today presents no problem the feeling remains, however unjustified, that Gisborne is in some way remote. Yet it was here that Europeans landed for the first time on New Zealand soil, is here that the first city in the world sees the new day's sun, and here that the highest North Island temperature was officially recorded until the record was lost to △ Ruatoria in 1973.

Gisborne's port, home to a rapidly expanding fishing fleet, handles a variety of exports. Secondary industries in the city range from canning and food processing to the manufacture of hosiery.

SOME HISTORY

The naming of Gisborne: A local legend tells how Kiwa, tohunga of the *Horouta* canoe, declared ownership of the district by setting up a mauri (a material symbol of a hidden protective force) and bestowed the name of Turanganui-a-Kiwa—"the long standing place of Kiwa", later shortened to Kiwa.

To avoid confusion with Tauranga (Bay of Plenty), in 1870 the area was renamed "Gisborne" after the then Colonial Secretary, Sir William Gisborne. Local settlers and Maori refused to accept the change of name until in 1874 both Tauranga and Turanga requested new government buildings. A large sum was voted for a courthouse, gaol and police quarters at Turanga—and great was the settlers' chagrin when the buildings were erected at Tauranga.

Historic first landing: Captain Cook, on his way from Tahiti under orders to see if a continent lay to the east of "the land discovered by Tasman and now called New Zealand", arrived off the New Zealand coast on 7 October 1769. Two days later he led a party ashore, and the first Europeans to set foot on New Zealand soil landed at Kaiti Beach *(marked by a memorial)*. Cook was anxious to establish friendly relations with the "natives", but a series of misunderstandings led to bloodshed. The first landing party killed a Maori they thought was about to attack one of their landing boats; the next day another was shot when snatching a sword, and four Maori in a canoe were killed when they resisted being taken on board. Indeed on 10 October the naturalist Banks wrote: "Thus ended the most disagreeable day my life has yet seen. Black be the mark for it and Heaven send that such may never return to embitter future reflections." On 11 October the *Endeavour* sailed "out of the bay which I [Cook] have named *Poverty Bay* because it afforded us no one thing we wanted".

While to Cook the Maori were unpredictable "Indians", the Maori saw the *Endeavour* as a huge bird with enormous white wings, carrying a household of gods. The gods, "parti-coloured but apparently in the human shape", were so ferocious they could kill from a distance with thunderbolts and make mortals ill merely by looking at them. There is doubt about the original intentions of the Maori—Cook was naturally ignorant of Maori custom and may have misconstrued their challenging haka—but according to local tradition the intrepid Maori were determined to attack the "gods" and, as they did with Tasman, chase them away.

"The uncrowned king": Bay whaling bases sprang up all around the East Cape in the 1830s and with them came traders, among them Captain G.E. Read (1815-78), the "Uncrowned King of Poverty Bay", credited with the founding of the city. Read arrived in 1853 and quickly became the area's most prosperous trader. Until banks opened in 1873, his promissory notes were the local currency and although cattle raising and sheep farming were added to his other interests, Read's selling of land at almost cost price to attract settlers showed him to be less mercenary than most. He died in 1878, eight years after the town of Gisborne had been laid out. Settlement in the district was hampered by the Hauhau conflicts and the presence of Te Kooti *(see below)*.

Hauhau "rebellion": When the Hauhau prophet Kereopa (who a fortnight earlier had been at △ Opotiki when the missionary Volkner was killed, and who was blamed by the settlers for his death) arrived in the Poverty Bay in March 1865 to recruit converts to the Hauhau cause, he effectively ended a period of peace and prosperity. Although many of the Ngati Porou, the principal East Coast tribe, sided with the Government, a large number of local Maori joined the Hauhau and the district saw a series of conflicts which culminated in two key battles. The first took place near Ruatoria, ending when 500 Ngati Porou Hauhau were captured. They were released only after they had taken an oath of allegiance to Queen Victoria. The second was at Waerenga-a-hika *(NW of Gisborne)* and raged for a week. Government forces besieged Waerenga-a-hika pa and after two rounds of home-made shrapnel crammed into salmon tins had landed in the pa, the 400 defenders were induced to surrender. They "could hardly be recognised as men as they came out after their long defence; they were covered in mud, and their hair was long and shaggy".

These battles ended the Hauhau threat in the district, but it was at Waerenga-a-hika that Te Kooti was suspected by the settlers of duplicity and a further challenge to the settlers emerged.

Te Kooti *(c. 1830-93):* Though not a chief, locally born Te Kooti was of high birth as he could trace his ancestry back to the captains of several canoes. He fought for the Government in the campaigns against the Hauhau until 1866, when he was arrested on suspicion of aiding the enemy and, without the trial he so often demanded, was shipped to the Chatham Islands with 300 Hauhau prisoners. Some contemporaries believed that Te Kooti would have been acquitted had he been brought to trial and that local settlers (who disliked his trading competition) and "friendly" Maori (angered by his successful amorous adventures) had combined to deport him.

At the Chathams, Te Kooti founded a new religion, Ringatu ("the uplifted hand"), which superseded Hauhauism and still survives to the present day. The two most recent Census figures put the number of followers at a little over 6,000. Based on the Old Testament, it compared the plight of the Maori under European domination with that of the Israelites enslaved in Egypt—Te Kooti was to be their Moses and restore the Maori to their promised land. Ringatu services were made all the more sensational by Te Kooti's introducing stage effects. He would smear his hand with phosphorus to display it as a hand of pale flame, gleaming in the gloom of the dimly lit meeting house—it was the "hand of the Holy Spirit", a "token from God"—not, as in Hauhauism, a means of averting bullets.

After a brilliantly contrived escape, Te Kooti and his 300 followers sailed from the Chathams and landed their stolen ship just south of Poverty Bay. Two parties sent from Gisborne to arrest them were beaten off, and each time Te Kooti wrote to the Government asking to be left alone. But after a third attack Te Kooti wrote again, saying that if the Government wanted war, it would begin in November.

True to his word, at dawn on 10 November 1868, Te Kooti attacked the unprepared settlement at Matawhero *(7 km W of Gisborne)*, killing 33 Europeans and 37 "friendly" Maori in what became known as the Poverty Bay Massacre.

Only a month passed before the bloodshed of Matawhero was more than matched by Government forces at Ngatapa *(W of Gisborne)*. Te Kooti had occupied an ancient pa site high in the mountains above Ngatapa. It was a formidable position, but, like many Maori pa, had no fresh water supply within its lines. So when "friendly" Ngati Porou cut Te Kooti's only access to a spring, he was forced to withdraw. Over half of Te Kooti's followers were taken prisoner and 120 were summarily executed— "We just stood them on the edge of a cliff and gave them a volley," said an Armed Constabulary scout.

The next four years saw a series of engagements between Te Kooti and Government forces, interspersed with lightning raids of Whakatane, Mohaka and Rotorua launched from Te Kooti's Urewera retreat. Apart from his defeat at Te Porere *(S of Lake Taupo)*, where he departed from his usual tactics, Te Kooti proved to be a brilliant guerrilla leader and more than a match for the Colonial troops.

The Land Wars in effect ended in 1872, when after years of harassment Te Kooti slipped through to Te Kuiti to live under the protection of Tawhiao (the second Maori King) until pardoned in 1883, two years after formal peace had been made.

Te Kooti, about 1.75 metres tall and with regular, aquiline features, had a mild manner which surprised Europeans who met him. His face was not tattooed but embellished with pointed beard and moustache. In 1891 the Government granted him land at Ohiwa, near Whakatane, where he died two years later. He was buried in a grave known only to three of his followers.

THINGS TO SEE AND DO

Titirangi Scenic Reserve (Kaiti Hill) ★ ★ ★: A natural pa site commanding a strategic position, the main area of **Titirangi pa** is still venerated as its first occupiers arrived on the *Horouta* canoe over five centuries ago. However only the lower slopes were inhabited when Cook landed.

The hill offers a magnificent view of the city, its harbour, rivers and surrounds. Seaward the view extends across Poverty Bay to **Young Nicks Head**, the white-cliffed headland that marks the southern extremity of the Bay. The point is named after Nicholas Young, the surgeon's boy who sighted New Zealand on 7 October 1769.

Captain Cook, knowing the *Endeavour* was near land, had offered a gallon of rum to the man who should first sight land by day, and two if he saw it by night. Cook had also promised that part of the coast would be named after him. One can imagine the crew's dismay when it was a 12-year-old boy who won the prize, but we may assume that he required assistance in disposing of the rum. Contrary to popular belief, Nicholas Young would have seen high land in the interior well before the headland named after him. The Titirangi Domain also includes the **Observatory** *(Titirangi Drive)* and, close by, a Second World War **gun emplacement**. *Lookout signposted on the right, across Gladstone Bridge. 3 km return.*

At the foot of the hill on the way to the lookout the road passes the **Poho-o-rawiri meeting house** ★ (1925), one of the largest meeting houses in the country. It is more accurately described as a "decorative hall": because of its size the traditional construction (which depended on a single ridgepole supported by pillars) was passed over in favour of a modern design. It has been called an "Arawa" house because all its carvings were executed in Rotorua. *A visit may be arranged through the Information Centre.* Above the meeting house is a small **Maori church**.

Cook Landing Site Monument: An obelisk marks the place where Captain Cook first landed on 9 October 1769; subsequent calculations have shown it was not on 10 October, the date shown on the inscription, for Cook had been keeping ship's time. *At the foot of Kaiti Hill, on Kaiti Beach Rd, by the mouth of the Turanganui River. Detour from Gladstone Bridge. Kaiti Beach is unsuitable for swimming.* A track leads up Kaiti Hill opposite the monument. Recorded is the site of **Waikahua cottage** (*above the road*) built in 1865 for the Williams family when Hauhau unrest curtailed their missionary work further inland.

As well as those atop Kaiti Hill, memorials to Cook include a giant Canadian **totem pole** (*Alfred Cox Park, Grey St*), presented by the Canadian Government to mark the bicentenary and to record the countries' common debt to the navigator; and a **statue of Young Nick**. *In the Olympic Pool complex; end of Awapuni Rd.*

Botanic Gardens: A pleasant, shaded riverside spot. *On the banks of the Taruheru River, off Roebuck and Aberdeen Rds.*

Gisborne Museum and Arts Centre★: To illustrate the history of the East Coast, included are a small Maori collection, a whaling boat used at Te Kaha and a diorama depicting Cook's landing on Kaiti Beach. An early dwelling, Wyllie Cottage (1872), is furnished in the style of the late nineteenth century. The art gallery mounts both touring and local exhibitions, and has a collection of contemporary New Zealand works. *Stout St. Open Monday–Friday, 10 a.m.–4.30 p.m.; weekends and public holidays, 2–4.30 p.m. Closed Christmas Day and Good Friday.*

Now included in the complex is a **maritime museum**, housed in the superstructure of the *Star of Canada* (7,280 tons), a vessel built in Belfast in 1909 which was caught in a squall and wrecked on Kaiti Beach. The superstructure was salvaged and served as a house for many years before finding its home here on the riverbank.

Museum of Transport and Technology: A museum project with a predominantly agricultural flavour is taking shape at the A & P Showgrounds. "Live days" are held occasionally. *4 km on road to Makaraka. Open mid-December–end February, 2-4.30 p.m.; other times by arrangement with the Museum and Arts Centre.*

Margaret Sievwright memorial (1844–1905)**:** A trained nurse and passionate social worker, Scottish-born Margaret Sievwright campaigned against all forms of social injustice. She was a founder member of the Women's Temperance Union and in the course of campaigning for universal suffrage she formed a women's political association in Gisborne in 1893, where she lived with her husband. To consolidate her work she later established the National Council of Women. *By the Peel St Bridge.*

Waikanae Beach: Close to the city, the beach is crowded in summer. *At the clock tower turn south down Grey St.*

ENVIRONS

Note: The first four points of interest can be combined into a round trip of some 68 km.

Matawhero Presbyterian Church ★: The oldest church in Poverty Bay and the only building in the area spared by Te Kooti in the 1868 Poverty Bay Massacre. Victims of the massacre are buried in a common grave in Makaraka Cemetery *(opp. the showgrounds, W of Gisborne on the main south road).*

The kauri building was reputedly erected by Captain Read in 1862 as a store-house. Later used as an Anglican church, it was by the late 1860s the centre of a military settlement. In 1872 it was acquired by the Presbyterian Church. *At 7 km W of Gisborne on the main road south, detour 800 m from the signposted turnoff.*

Manutuke ★★★: Here the magnificent carvings of Manutuke's two meeting houses manifest the inspired art of the nineteenth-century Maori carver. The celebrated Turanga School of carving reached its zenith under the leadership of Raharuhi Rukupo (1800-73), a local chief whose style of carving is still perpetuated by carvers today. The meeting house **Te Mana ki Turanga** (1883), one of the oldest in the district and one on which Rukupo himself worked, stands on the Whakato Marae. The maihi depict both Tane Mahuta forcing the separation of Rangi (Sky Father) from Papa (the Earth Mother) and also Maui-tikitiki-a-Taranga hauling his mammoth fish to the surface (both myths are recounted in the Introduction). The amo slant inwards in the manner of some early houses.

The finest meeting house in the country is **Te Hau-ki-Turanga** (1842), also a product of Rukupo's era. It stood near here but was removed to Wellington in 1867, where it stands in the Museum of New Zealand.

The recently restored house **Te Poho Rukupo** (1887) stands on the Manutuke marae. Intriguing for its beautifully painted kowhaiwhai patterns on ceiling, heke and poupou, it was built as a memorial to Rukupo and moved here in 1913 from his Pakipaki burial place. Also of interest on this marae are the Maori Battalion Dining Hall, and the

Epeha meeting house with carvings of the Te Arawa. *At Manutuke, 14 km S of Gisborne on the road to Wairoa. (It is courteous to seek approval locally before visiting a meeting house or marae.)*

Rongopai meeting house (1888): Rongopai was built hurriedly when Te Kooti announced his intention of visiting the district—a prospect which dismayed local Pakeha. The interior paintings are of considerable interest. A riot of colour, they mark in their exuberance an abrupt departure from tradition and constitute examples of the Maori folk art that developed under European influence when traditional religious and social structures were disappearing. Largely the work of young artists, the paintings in their time shocked older Maori who saw irreverence in the artists' lighthearted and whimsical approach to their task. *N of Patutahi on Lavenham Rd, the house is set back by a bend in the road. Permission should be sought before entering the marae; tel. (06) 862-7680.*

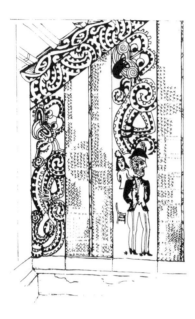

Rongopai meeting house, Waituhi, near Gisborne.

Gray's Hill ★★: From the lookout is a view down over the rich Poverty Bay plains, quilted with market gardens. *10 km via Back Ormond Rd, or on the road to Waiherere Domain turn right at Waimata Valley road. Signposted.*

Northern beaches: To the north-east of Gisborne lies a chain of beaches which offer unsurpassed swimming, surfing and fishing. Wainui Beach *(5 km)* has excellent surf, but care is needed as the beach can develop potholes. Beyond the bathing beach of Makarori *(13 km)* is Tatapouri, which has good crayfishing and is a base for big-game fishing. Farther north lie Whangara *(28 km)*, Waihau ★★★ (Loisels) *(55 km, turnoff signposted at 49 km)*—both described under △ East Cape Road—and △ Tolaga Bay ★★★ *(55 km)*.

Eastwoodhill Arboretum ★★: A vast sanctuary of trees and specimen plants, the arboretum was originally developed when in the late 1920s, after war service in Europe, the late Douglas Cook resolved to transform part of his farm into an English park. In spring the soft green foliage of hundreds of deciduous trees mingles with many magnolia, flowering cherries, wisteria and azaleas and in autumn the deeper, richer colouring of turning leaves is equally spectacular. *35 km NW via Ngatapa. Open daily, 10 a.m.-4 p.m. (A visit may be combined with a trip to Rere Falls (see below).)*

Rere Falls ★★: A drive through pleasant farmland leads to the falls, a favoured picnic and swimming place. The road passes through Ngatapa, near where Te Kooti suffered a major setback when many of his men were executed. *50 km. Leave Gisborne on the main road south, turn right over the Waipaoa River Bridge and continue through Ngatapa to the falls.*

△**Mahia Peninsula:** This somewhat barren promontory which separates Hawke from Poverty Bay has a number of isolated beaches and a sprinkling of holiday homes. *40 km S.*

△**Morere** ★: The hot springs here are set in a delightful bushed reserve with a host of secluded picnic spots. There is good river swimming. *64 km S.*

WALKS IN THE VICINITY

There are several interesting walks in the region. North of Gisborne on the coast at **Anaura Bay**(*85 km N*), a 2-hour walk affords panoramic views (*see p.* **71**). Also north is the fascinating **Cooks Cove** track (*52 km N*) to the "Hole in the Wall", a curious geological formation recorded when Cook visited in 1769 on his first voyage to New Zealand.

Inland at **Otoko**(*Highway 2, 46 km NW*) a 3-hour walkway follows part of the old Gisborne to Moutohora railway (*see Waioeka Scenic Highway, below*). South, in an exotic forest, the **Wharerata** track follows the course of the Waiau Stream (*5½ hrs*) (*Highway 2, 45 km S*).

Note: The Anaura Bay, Cooks Cove and Otoko walkways are closed during the lambing season, 1 August–30 September.

TOURING NOTES

△**East Cape Road ★★★:** The name popularly given to the coast road between Gisborne and Opotiki which passes the most easterly point on the New Zealand mainland. This coastal route, although both longer and slower, is of infinitely greater scenic value than the direct road, but the two can be combined to make a satisfying round trip.

Waioeka Scenic Highway to Opotiki (Highway 2): A magnificent drive which winds through native forest. The route may be varied by turning off at Matawai to follow the attractive if tortuous old coach route. This passes through virgin bush over the Motu Hills and down to the coast, but is not recommended in wet weather. *At Motu a 5-km detour may be made to see Motu Falls.* A further variation is afforded by the **Otoko Walkway.** Passengers may be dropped off at the Mahaki Tunnel *(45 km from Gisborne)* to walk 5 km along the disused Gisborne-Moutohora railway line *(an easy, 2½-3 hr walk)* and be collected opposite the Otoko Hall. Wooden culverts, concrete sumps, fish plates and spikes are seen en route, and near the end of the walk a short detour leads to a pretty waterfall set in native bush, ablaze with flowering kowhai trees in spring.

Routes to Wairoa: The coastal road to Wairoa (Highway 2) passes both △ Morere Hot Springs and △ Mahia Peninsula and affords a spectacular view of Poverty Bay from the crest of the Whareratas. The more demanding inland route is generally considered inferior; however, the 18-metre drop of Te Reinga Falls and Doneraille Park (a secluded area of native bush with good river swimming and fly fishing) both make pleasant stops, and there is also an outstanding view of Poverty Bay from the 354-metre summit of Gentle Annie.

Wairarapa Maps 12, 13 Pop. 1,797 **GREYTOWN**

34 km SW of Masterton.

IT IS DIFFICULT to imagine today that quiet, modest Greytown was once the main centre of the Wairarapa. However, its older buildings do give a hint of history and its stately trees befit the settlement which in 1890 brought Arbour Day to New Zealand. One tree is of particular interest, a massive gum in the grounds of St Luke's Church. As a sapling it is said to have come over the Rimutakas in Samuel Oates's wheelbarrow as he initiated the first regular mail service to the Wairarapa in 1856. The story is told that Oates stayed the night with the local vicar, who surreptitiously removed the sapling and later planted it in the churchyard.

This orcharding and market-gardening town is set on rich silt loam, some of the most fertile soil in the Wairarapa. But while intensive farming yields Greytown's clusters of roadside fruit and vegetable stalls, the river which so enriched the settlement also bedevilled it from the first.

SOME HISTORY

A Small Farm settlement: Greytown, like △ Masterton, was a Small Farm settlement, established in 1854, and was named for Sir George Grey, then Governor, whose help saw the Small Farm Association succeed in its aim of placing small runholdings within the reach of colonists who would otherwise have been labourers.

The town site was originally set in dense bush cut only by a surveyor's line along what is now the main street. It was separated from Masterton not only by the

Waiohine River (which flooded periodically) but also by the "Three Mile Bush" (later the site of Carterton). It was the Waiohine's unpredictable changes of course which in the 1870s led the surveyor John Rochfort to revise his planned course for the railway from Wellington so that it bypassed the Wairarapa's leading centre. Uproar produced delegation after delegation, but no amount of agitation could bend the railway's iron will and Greytown was never to recover its former position of prominence.

THINGS TO SEE AND DO

Papawai Marae ★★: In the 1890s, the marae was a focal point for the Kotahitanga or Maori Parliament movement, a rival to the Maori King movement. In a spirit of Maori nationalism, the Kotahitanga advocated complete self-government for the Maori, as it felt Maori Members of Parliament were unable to convince the European majority of their people's needs. In 1900 the Maori Councils Act created a degree of local Maori administration and so took force from the Kotahitanga movement, which was soon largely absorbed by the Young Maori Party.

At this time Papawai claimed the title of "Maori capital" of New Zealand. Up to 3,000 were living here when, in 1898, Prime Minister Richard Seddon came to discuss with tribal delegations from all over the North Island (King Mahuta from Ngaruawahia among them) Government proposals to open up vast areas of Kingite land.

Tamahau Mahupuku (1840-1902), a Ngati Kahungunu chief, took a prominent part in the affairs of the Kotahitanga and officially represented the Maori people at the inauguration of the Australian Commonwealth. His memorial, unveiled in 1911 by Sir James Carroll, then Acting Prime Minister and himself a Maori, stands on the marae. It was badly damaged in the earthquake which jolted the region in 1942, but has been reconstructed from the remains.

The **whakapakoko** (carvings) which surround the marae and range from small to larger than life-size counter tradition by facing inwards and are said by some to symbolise harmony between Wairarapa Maori and settler. Facing outwards they would offer protection to the marae. Other explanations are that they face inwards in order to find their own solutions within the pa, or that they do so as a sign of peace. The older building, Hikurangi, is a whare wananga, where the tohunga (priest) would initiate selected pupils to religious, occult and celestial knowledge. *3 km. Turnoff signposted on the main south exit from the town; tel. (06) 304-9623.*

Cobblestones Museum ★: The museum is on the site of one of the settlement's first stables (1858), still with its cobblestoned yard, used as a depot by the proprietor of the Cobb & Co. Royal Mail coaches. The "Pride of the Valley", the original Cobb & Co. coach which ran from Martinborough to Featherston, is housed here along with other horse-drawn vehicles. *169 Main St.*

ENVIRONS

Waiohine River Gorge: The road rises gently into the foothills of the Tararuas, to reach a gorge with safe swimming and an occasional picnic spot. Beyond, the road continues into the Tararua Forest Park *(see under △ Masterton)* and the start of tracks south to Omega *(1,118 m)* and north to Mt Holdsworth *(1,474 m)*. *20 km. Signposted from the main road at 4 km NE.*

HAMILTON ★★

Waikato   Maps 5, 6   Pop. 148,625 (urban area)

129 km S of Auckland. Visitor Information Centre, Municipal Bldg, Garden Place; tel. (07) 839-3360.

HAMILTON, the country's largest inland city, sprawls pleasantly across the △ Waikato River in the heart of the lush Waikato plains, among the world's richest farmland. The city grew up as a military settlement on the banks of the river, once the district's principal means of access, and a feature of the city today is its restful riverside parks. Hamilton's natural role as a farming and administrative centre is supplemented by a wide variety of industries, farming experimentation and research and a major university. The region's long tradition of dairy farming has diversified to include goat and deer farming, orcharding, and berry and market gardening.

Crowds flock to the New Zealand National Agricultural Field-days at Mystery Creek *(June)*, and to an annual Hot-air Balloon Fiesta *(about April)*.

SOME HISTORY

Inter-tribal wars: The Waikato was not spared the devastation that followed the introduction to New Zealand of European weapons and ideas of conquest. Te Rauparaha (*pp.* **115-16**), the Ngati Toa chief later responsible for considerable conquests throughout much of the country, lived originally at Kawhia, and it took several years for the remaining Waikato tribes to rid themselves of their neighbour.

Maori agriculture: Archaeological evidence in the Waikato reveals sophisticated horticultural practices in pre-European times. Sand and gravel were used to improve soil friability and drainage; periodic firing of regenerating scrub replenished the soil with nutrients, and the fire-blackened soil, too, captured and retained more of the sun's warmth. Some 2,000 hectares of pre-historic gardens are to be found, mainly along the banks of the Waikato River, between Huntly and Arapuni. Kumara cultivation was an important aspect of an economy which also made use of the rich protein resources of rivers and lakes, the latter being renowned for their "swamp pa". The Waikato, Waipa and the latter's tributary streams provided navigable waterways for the canoeing of people and produce to and from the strongly defended settlements situated in the foothills and uplands of the eastern basin, which formed by far the most intensively settled hinterland area in Polynesia.

In such a setting, the Waikato Maori were poised to adapt quickly to meeting the needs of the settlers, and as early as 1848 the town of Auckland was dependent on Maori agriculture. European crops and farming methods introduced by missionaries were also quickly adopted by the Waikato Maori. The Governor, Sir George Grey, reported that he had "never seen a more thriving or contented population [than the Waikato Maori] in any part of the world . . . there would be no difficulty in acquiring any quantity of waste land [for European settlers]".

Invasion of the Waikato: Against this prospering background, war seemed improbable. But the religious upheaval created by the introduction of Christianity had left the Maori susceptible to further forms of idealism such as those of the Maori King Movement (*pp.* **159–60**). This instability was coupled with a slump in 1856 which saw the price of wheat tumble from twelve to three shillings a bushel and so disillusion the Waikato Maori. For their part, the new settlers were envious of the rich Waikato riverflats. In the Taranaki the Government enforced the infamous △ Waitara Land Deal in 1860, and during the uneasy peace that followed the first Taranaki Campaign, Sir George Grey was instructed to make peace if he could, but to end the idea of Maori independence if he could not.

Though he professed peace, Grey extended the military Great South Road from Auckland through the Bombay Hills, and its inexorable advance into the Waikato brought with it the resumption of fighting which developed into the Waikato Campaign.

False, probably malicious, reports circulated of attacks on the Auckland settlement, soldiers were recruited from the Otago goldfields and from Australia to "protect" the settlement, and a series of redoubts was built south of Auckland. In July 1863, all Maori in South Auckland were ordered to swear allegiance to Queen Victoria and lay down their arms, or to retire to the Waikato. Those who refused to do either were ejected. Inevitably fighting broke out. Bombay, △ Pukekohe and Pokeno saw skirmishes, and a river fleet was assembled to take the war up the Waikato River and into the heart of Kingite territory. The gunboats enabled General Cameron to outflank Maori positions at Meremere and Rangiriri, to capture △ Ngaruawahia (the Maori King's "capital") virtually unopposed, and to supply his troops on the Waipa Plain as they took △ Te Awamutu and Kihikihi. An heroic stand at Orakau marked the end of the campaign—Rewi Maniapoto and 300 followers, besieged by 2,000 troops, survived for three days vowing, "Kaore e mau te rongo—ake, ake!" ("Peace shall never be made, never never!").

The army spent the winter of '64 at Te Awamutu, but no attempt was made to drive the Kingites farther south than the Puniu River (*S of Te Awamutu*), the confiscation or aukati line set by the Government. The soldiers were then settled in villages, each with a redoubt, which were to develop into towns as time passed. The 1st Regiment of Waikato Militia were given their plots of land at Tauranga, the 2nd at Pirongia, the 3rd at Cambridge and the 4th—by far the greatest number—at Hamilton. Each Waikato military settler received a grant of one town acre (0.4 hectare) and a section of from 50 acres (20 ha.) upwards according to rank.

The embittered Waikato Maori had lost much of their land and many escaped to the King Country, where they remained an apparent threat until in 1881 King Tawhiao made formal peace.

Historians now consider that the invasion of the Waikato was simply a war of conquest, the soldiers being paid with blocks of confiscated land. Certainly a vocal element among the Auckland settlers were envious of the lush, Maori-owned river flats and were infuriated by the Maori King supporters' refusal to sell them any. The Government, too, comprised large, or would-be large, landowners.

Problems of settlers: The story did not end with the Maori being forced from their land. Although rich, the Waikato in its central region was swampy, and a Government impoverished by war had no resources for large-scale road building and drainage schemes. Matters were not helped by the fact that the military settlers' pay was stopped as soon as they were allotted their land, and Auckland moneylenders were loath to advance on the security of Waikato properties. Basically the problem was a shortage of capital, and this was eventually overcome when a number of wealthy settlers bought land in the district. By 1875 immigrants were arriving at Hamilton and finding work readily.

But in the next five years, as the result of a world-wide depression, farm prices fell by 23 per cent and it was not until the 1900s that the Waikato became the pleasant prospect it is today—rich, undulating farmland with scarcely a vestige of unworked land and no trace of the price paid in blood, sweat and tears.

The founding of Hamilton: Hamilton was founded in 1864 when military settlers took up land on the site of the deserted Maori village of Kirikiriroa as one of four military settlements in the area (the others being at Cambridge, Te Awamutu and Pirongia). The city was named after Captain John Fane Charles Hamilton, heroic commander of HMS *Esk*, who was killed at △ Tauranga during the Battle of Gate Pa in the same year. Captain Hamilton lies buried in Tauranga's Mission Cemetery but his sword and medals are displayed in the Waikato Art Museum.

The town was planned as a defensive position around three redoubts on both sides of the river. These were positioned to resist any attempt by the Waikato Maori to regain the land that had been confiscated from them. The remains of one of these, the Narrows Redoubt (1864) *(cnr Howell Ave and Cobham Drive)*, are still apparent, looking down on the river from on high and now marked by a trig station. The redoubt was occupied for only two years, and saw no fighting. A survivor from military times is Beale Cottage (1872), built for the surgeon with the 4th Waikato Militia Regiment *(11 Beale St, cnr Beale and Grey Sts)*.

Divided by the river, the two military settlements were linked only by a ferry below Grantham Street. In 1877, the first Union Bridge was built at the south end of Victoria Street, so that Hamilton could be combined into a single borough. Six bridges now span the river.

The arrival of the Main Trunk railway in 1878 confirmed Hamilton's role as the Waikato's primary town. In the same year its first substantial commercial building was erected for the Bank of New Zealand *(still standing on the cnr Hood and Victoria Sts)*. It is now planned for use as a cultural centre.

Traces of pre-European Maori occupation remain in the earthworks of Miropiko pa *(seen about 30 m inside the boundary of 339 River Rd)*, a survivor of more than 20 pa which once stood within the city's boundary.

THINGS TO SEE AND DO

Waikato Museum of Art and History (Te Whare Taonga o Waikato)★★★: The museum has distinguished collections of Waikato social history, fine art and Tainui tribal history from which vigorous changing exhibitions are drawn. In addition, international touring exhibitions cater for a wide range of interests. On permanent display is the finely carved war canoe Te Winika (1838-45) on loan from the Maori Queen, Dame Te Atairangikaahu, together with contemporary Tainui carving and weaving commissioned for the building. One may lunch in a licensed restaurant, and browse among choice works by leading craftspeople in the museum shop. *Cnr Victoria and Grantham Sts. Open daily, 10 a.m.-4.30 p.m. (except Good Friday and Christmas Day). Tel. (07) 838-6533.*

Hamilton Lake (Rotoroa): A wildlife sanctuary not far from the city centre offers a variety of pastimes ranging from yachting and boating to roller-skating and minature golf. A pleasant walk leads around the lake. *Ruakiwi Rd.*

Hamilton Gardens ★★: A host of picnic spots and riverside walks add to the appeal of gardens of infinite variety. Special features are over 4,000 rose bushes and Molly MacAlister's bronze, "Little Bull". *Cobham Drive, Hamilton East.*

Rangiriri riverboat: The remains of the PS *Rangiriri*, a sternwheeler which plied the Waikato from 1864 to about 1889, lies in **Memorial Park**, by the river's eastern bank. It was twice subjected to arson attacks in the summer of 1994-95, in protest at government proposals to force an end to Treaty of Waitangi land claims.

Built in Sydney and assembled at Port Waikato, the boat had been ordered by the military. Although she arrived too late for the fighting, she was in time to carry the first contingent of soldier-settlers to form the settlement of Hamilton. Popularly believed to have been a gunboat, the *Rangiriri* was in fact a steam tug, designed to tow barges. After sinking several times, she was finally abandoned in 1890 and left, stuck fast by the river bank here. In 1982 her hulk was raised for preservation as perhaps the most tangible link with the Waikato campaigns and the founding of the city. The trees in Memorial Park, their numbers thinned by the years, each commemorate a Hamilton soldier who fell in World War I. *Memorial Drive.*

Across the river lies **Ferrybank Park**, the early landing place for both Maori and European settler, where the cross-river punt landed and where the first businesses were sited. *Foot of Grantham St.*

Hockin House (1893): The headquarters of the Waikato Historical Society are furnished in late Victorian style. *Selwyn St. Open Sundays, Nov–May, 2–4 p.m.*

Exscite: A hands-on science and technology centre also stages special events. *Collingwood Court, Collingwood St; open daily, 10 a.m.–4.30 p.m.; tel. (07) 838-3470.*

Central city river walks: Riverside paths may be linked by crossing any of several road-bridges, to make pleasant circular walks. *Leaflets from the Visitor Information Centre.*

Waipa Delta river cruises ★ ★ ★: On the paddleboat MV *Waipa Delta* one may cruise on a floating restaurant, for morning or afternoon tea, for lunch or for an evening meal with music by moonlight (*daily from Oct–March; otherwise Wed–Sun; tel. (07) 854-9415*).

The Ice Bowl ★ ★ ★: Ice-skating sessions for all. *4 Kells Pl; tel. (07) 846-7371.*

Marae visits: These may be arranged through the Visitor Information Centre.

ENVIRONS

National Agricultural Heritage (Mystery Creek) ★ ★ ★: From bush-felling of pioneer agricultural times through to diversification into such horticultural pursuits as kiwifruit and blueberries, farming past and present is displayed at the Mystery Creek complex. Live animals are a feature, including cows used to demonstrate modern milking methods but which can also be milked by hand by visitors.

Exhibits of venerable machinery and traditionally furnished pioneer cottages in the **Clydesdale Museum** emphasise how life on the land has changed over the years. Clydesdale horses take visitors for wagon rides. The **National Dairy Museum** depicts the evolution of today's highly sophisticated milking machinery both on the farm and in the factory.

Other attractions include a working fire-station, a children's farmyard, a working smithy and a colonial village. A craft shop specialises in woollen, angora and mohair garments.

For three days each June, the complex hosts the New Zealand National Field-days, a showcase of agriculture and horticulture, when visitors from both town and country throng the region.

16 km S (2 km from Hamilton airport). Follow signs from Highway 1 or Highway 3. Open daily 9 a.m.–4.30 p.m. (extended hours in holiday periods); tel. (07) 843-7990.

Temple View ★: Dominating the complex that forms the New Zealand headquarters of the Church of Jesus Christ of Latterday Saints and including its Church College of New Zealand is the distinctive Mormon Temple (1958), focal point for South Pacific Mormons. *The interior of the Temple is open only to members of the faith. Information centre open daily, 9 a.m.–9 p.m. A Genealogy Centre makes no charge for helping with family trees (open Tues–Sat). 7 km SW on Tuhikaramea Rd.*

Hamilton Zoo: The park contains extensive picnic areas and displays a wide variety of wildlife, from zebra and llama to primates and native birds. *8 km. Brymer Rd, Rotokauri (access from Western Bypass). Open daily, 9 a.m.–5 p.m.; tel. (07) 838-6720.*

Gails of Tamahere ★ ★: Delightful gardens specialise in dried flowers, with old wooden churches festooned with blooms. One was an early church (1867) on the Coromandel Peninsula. The gardens are seen at their best in Oct–May. Morning and afternoon teas are served. *A pleasant stop en route to △ Cambridge. 12 km S on Highway 1.*

Tauwhare Military Museum: A private collection of militaria. *Victoria Rd., Tauwhare. Open Sat–Mon; tel. (07) 829-0867.*

"Candyland": The "largest candy store in the country" also lays claim to making the world's largest lollipop. Candymaking demonstrations are given (*1 p.m. daily*) and there is a small museum. *Henry Rd, Komakorau. 22 km N off the Gordonton–Taupiri Rd. Open seven days; tel. (07) 824-6818.*

Waterworld: An indoor–outdoor complex of pools, hydro-slides and diving towers draw families from far and wide. *Garnett Ave, Te Rapa. Open daily and evenings; tel. (07) 849-4389.*

Waingaro Hot Springs: Three hot mineral pools (and a long hot-water slide which twirls and winds for 137 metres) are open daily and in the evenings. There is also accommodation, good camping and barbecue facilities scattered through the park. *Waingaro, 42 km NW; tel. (07) 825-4761..* Also within easy reach of Hamilton are thermal springs at △ Matamata (*62 km E*) and △ Te Aroha (*53 km NE*).

△Raglan ★★: Hamilton's nearest beach. *48 km W.*

△Waitomo Caves ★★★: A fantasy land of glow-worms and delicate limestone statuary. *77 km S.*

HASTINGS ★★

Hawke's Bay   Map 11   Pop. 57,748 (urban area)

306 km NE of Wellington (via Shannon); 21 km S of Napier. Visitor Information Centre, Russell St; tel. (06) 878-0510.

HASTINGS, a city of parks and gardens on the closely cropped Heretaunga Plains, is both Napier's traditional rival and her twin city. Napier's port handles the vast output of Hastings' food-processing factories and freezing works, but both claim to be *"the"* principal centre" as each is, albeit in different ways. In spring the blossom of Hastings' many orchards embellishes the landscape, but in all seasons visitors are drawn to the several flourishing wineries which produce some of the country's finest wine.

The city is named after Warren Hastings, first Governor-General of the East India Company (whose acquittal after a seven-year trial for corruption, instigated by the dramatist Richard Brinsley Sheridan, was one of the sensations of late eighteenth-century Britain). The name reflects the interest of the colonists in Indian affairs. Hastings is fortunate to have escaped its original title of "Hicksville", after Francis Hicks who first laid out the town.

Festivals: Hastings' Easter Highland Games ("The Braemar of Australasia"), Spring Festival (*October*) and the Hawke's Bay Agricultural and Pastoral Show each Labour Weekend (*October*) draw visitors from all over the country.

MAORI LEGEND

A giant bite: Looking straight down Heretaunga Street, some see in the silhouette of the ranges behind Havelock North the outline of a giant lying on his back. Legend recounts that the giant Te Mata was a troublemaker and, to get rid of him, local chiefs used a beautiful maiden. The giant in falling for the girl fell for the ploy, but before she would marry him she set him a series of Herculean tasks which Te Mata somehow accomplished until he reached his final hurdle—to eat through the mountain range behind Havelock North. His goal in sight and impatient to finish, Te Mata took one enormously greedy bite, choked, and fell dead. One particular gap is said to be the place from which he took his mouthful.

SOME HISTORY

"The Twelve Apostles": In 1864 a syndicate of 12 settlers known as "The Twelve Apostles" purchased the Heretaunga block, and nine years later Francis Hicks, one of the 12, laid out the town. In the same year the purchase was investigated by a Royal Commission and confirmed after acrimonious argument. The area developed steadily, but at an early stage there was such an acute shortage of labour that a ploughman could earn payment in the form of one acre (0.4 ha.) of land near Heretaunga Street (Hastings' main street) for every three that he ploughed.

Earthquake: In the 1931 earthquake Hastings suffered as disastrously as Napier. Its main street was reduced to rubble, 93 people were killed and damage estimated at the time at £1 million resulted. Despite popular usage elsewhere, the event is most assuredly not known here as the "*Napier* earthquake". *There is a memorial at the foot of the Hastings clocktower.*

FOOD AND WINE

Food processing: The city has numerous food-processing factories including those of H.J. Heinz. Sir James Wattie (1902–74) began his remarkable career earning five shillings a week delivering milk — and milking cows as well, twice daily, seven days a week — while studying accountancy. The backyard cannery he founded in 1934 grew into the largest manufacturing, processing and distributing food operation in the country. It dominated the national scene and was exporting to more than 40 countries around the world before it was incorporated into the Goodman Fielder Wattie group.

Other firms with large plants include the Hawkes Bay Brewery and the Apple and Pear Marketing Board, which has built the country's largest coolstore here. The Tomoana and Pacific freezing works process several million head of sheep and cattle annually.

Winemaking in New Zealand: The first vines were planted, at the Rev. Samuel Marsden's behest, at Kerikeri in 1819, but it was the British Resident at the Bay of Islands, James Busby, who really pioneered the country's winemaking industry. His passion for wine, nurtured by a youth spent in the wine districts of France, earned him in Australia the title of the wine industry's "Australian Prophet", and he was quick to plant grapes on his arrival in the Bay of Islands, in 1833.

Dalmatians, Germans, French, Spaniards, Lebanese, even Chinese and Russians all played their part in establishing today's flourishing wineries, but it was the French brothers of the Society of Mary who introduced winemaking to Hawke's Bay, for altar purposes (the missionary Colenso had earlier brewed fruit wines here). "The Mission" at Greenmeadows is today the country's oldest winery, although in 1897 it was forced to move to its present site by a series of floods on the plains.

Phylloxera, the aphid scourge which destroyed French vineyards in the 1870s, reached this country 20 years later and the industry was set back not just by the need to destroy infected vines but by a Government refusal to pay compensation. No sooner had grafted stock immune to Phylloxera been established than came the double blows of temperance propaganda and then the great Depression of the 1930s. But the resolution of the winemakers overcame all, and today the country's wine industry is flourishing as never before, with New Zealanders taking an ever-increasing interest in wine in general, and domestic vintages in particular.

The wines of Hawkes Bay * * *: The region ranks as one of the country's premier wine-producing districts. Several vineyards may be visited in the course of a tour, with the option of lunch. *Bay Tours; tel. (06) 843-6953.*

There is also a fascinating tour of the **Mission Vineyards and Winery**, the oldest vineyard in the country (*Church Rd, Taradale; Mon–Sat 10.30 a.m. and 2 p.m.; tel. (06) 844-2259*). Another is of the **McDonald Winery**, with a winemakers' museum and the possibility of lunch (*200 Church Rd, Taradale; tel. (06) 844-2053*).

Close to Hastings are the renowned **Te Mata Estate**, with its much photographed homestead designed by Wellington architect Ian Athfield (*Te Mata Rd, Havelock North; tel. (06) 877-4399*); **St George Estate**, with a restaurant and art exhibitions (*St George Rd S, Havelock North; tel. (06) 877-5356*); **Vidals** (*913, St Aubyn St E; tel. (06) 876-8105*) and **Stonecroft Wines** (*Mere Rd; tel. (06) 879-9610*). Further afield are secluded **Sacred Hill** (*Dartmoor Rd, Puketapu; tel. (06) 844-5666*) and **Crab Farm Winery** (*125 Main Road North, Bay View; tel. (06) 836-6678*).

THINGS TO SEE AND DO IN HASTINGS

Spanish Mission buildings * * *: As in △ Napier, in the aftermath of the Hawkes Bay earthquake of 1931 a host of Art Deco and Spanish Mission buildings were erected in Hastings to add to others which had survived the disaster. Particular gems include the **Municipal Theatre** (1914), with an Art Nouveau interior behind a Spanish Mission facade (*Heretaunga St*) and the buildings from the **DIC** to the **CML building** (*Russell St*). *Further details from the Visitor Information Centre.*

Hawkes Bay Exhibition Centre * *: Administered in conjunction with Napier's Art Gallery and Museum, the centre includes Te Whare O Nga Tipuna (a Maori artefacts room) and the Ebbett Collection, assembled by a former mayor of Hastings from the early 1900s to 1940. There are changing displays of arts, crafts and touring exhibitions. *Eastbourne St, Civic Square (at Karamu Rd); open daily.*

The Maori Art and Craft Centre (Nga Tuke Mata O Kahungunu): *340 East Heretaunga Street; open Mon–Sat, 10 a.m.–4 p.m.; tel. (06) 878-7696.*

Cornwall Park: A blissful setting for cricket matches, the park has formal gardens together with an aviary, a fernery and a hot house crammed with colourful exotics. *Signposted. Bounded by Tomoana and Cornwall Rds and Roberts St.*

Frimley Park: Features include an Olympic swimming pool, rose gardens and a wide variety of towering exotic trees which make it ideal for picnics. *Frimley Rd, off Pakowai Rd.*

Fantasyland ★★: An unusual children's playground with fairy-tale castle, pirate ship, moon rocket and many other fantastic structures. Hire boats navigate the castle's moat and an elevated train circles the playground. Fantasyland is set in **Windsor Park**, 25 hectares of sports grounds shaded by stately English trees. *Camping. Windsor Ave, Grove Rd and Sylvan Rd.*

Ice cream parlours: Delectable ice creams are a local speciality in particular Rush Munro's *(704 Heretaunga St West).*

ORGANISED EXCURSIONS

Cape Kidnappers ★ ★ ★: From **Te Awanga**, a tractor-drawn trailer takes groups along the beach followed by a short climb and walk to the actual sanctuary (*Gannet Beach Adventurers; tel. (06) 875-0898).* Alternatively, 4-wheel drive vehicles leave Summerlee Station and cross farmland to reach the sanctuary. *(Gannet Safaris tel. (06) 875-0511).* The viewing season runs from October to late April. The trip can also be made independently.

Industrial tours: The Visitor Information Centre can arrange visits to a variety of local industries. The **Hastings Brewery** conducts tours on Monday, Wednesday, and Friday at 10.30 a.m. *(407 Warren St; tel. (06) 878-5199.).*

Adventure activities: Early Morning Balloons drift across the plains *(tel. (06) 858-8480)* and hang-gliders *(tel. (06) 877-7864)* and paragliders *(tel. (06) 844-5888)* take off from Te Mata Peak. There is also tandem sky diving *(tel. (06) 877-4588).*

HAVELOCK NORTH ★★
5 km SE from Hastings

Havelock North spreads along the foothills of the Havelock Ranges and is at once recognisable as "the Village". A choice residential area, its houses often hidden among trees, the township is a comfortable distance away from Hastings' commercial districts both to preserve its rustic qualities and for residents to enjoy the best of both worlds.

Nationally, Havelock North is known for its private schools—Woodford House, Iona (both girls' secondary) and Hereworth (boys' preparatory).

The township (pop. 8,900) is named for Sir Henry Havelock, winner of the Victoria Cross during the Indian Mutiny, who for a time commanded Imperial troops during the Land Wars.

Te Mata Peak ★★★: A road snakes to the peak's crest which offers perhaps the finest of all views in Hawke's Bay. Below nestles the hamlet of Havelock, and in the middle distance the grid pattern of Hastings' streets dissects a city girt with orchards and market gardens. A sweep of coastline curls past Napier to end in △ Mahia Peninsula, and the rugged Kaimanawa Ranges form a backdrop to plains spiked with poplars. Behind, the peak drops abruptly to the tranquil Tukituki River Valley, a scene which belies the river's name—literally, "to demolish or batter". Ruapehu may be seen on a clear day. *The 6-km road to the summit is signposted off Te Mata Peak Rd.*

The **Te Mata Peak Walkway** *starts at the picnic area 200 m above the Peak House Restaurant on Te Mata Rd and finishes at Waimarama Rd. Allow 30 mins.*

Havelock's honey ★: An astonishing array of honey and honey-based products at **Ashcrofts Honey House** is augmented by a glass-walled hive. Processing can be seen in the summer months. *Arataki Rd, off Karanema Rd; tel. (06) 877-7300.*

In Arataki Road, off Te Mata Road, is **Arataki Honey**, one of the largest producers of honey in the Southern Hemisphere with about 17,000 hives, each with up to 50,000 honeybees per hive and an annual production exceeding 400 tonnes. Hives are hired out for pollination in orchards, and bees are exported to Canada (where bees die in the bitter winter). *Tel. (06) 877-7300.*

A glossary of Maori words appears on *pp.* **313-15.**

Weleda herb gardens: One may walk through the gardens where a wide range of herbs are grown on the slopes of Te Mata Peak, to provide ingredients for the manufacture of natural cosmetics and medicines. Plants as well as herbal products are for sale. *Te Mata Peak Rd.*

Te Mata Road: A feature is John Scott's striking contemporary church, Our Lady of Lourdes. In Arataki Road, off Te Mata Road, is Arataki Honey Ltd, one of the largest producers of honey in the Southern Hemisphere. Also in Te Mata Road is the world-renowned Te Mata Estate Wines, with the oldest commercial cellars in the country, and the Lombardi Vineyards whose wines, as the name suggests, include a number of Italianate varieties. *(See "Hawke's Bay wine trail", above.) Te Mata Rd leads off the roundabout.*

Keirunga Gardens: Here one has the opportunity to stroll or to picnic in one of Havelock North's enchanting gardens. The house itself provides a focal point for the township's cultural activities. *Signposted at the roundabout. Follow Joll Rd to Pufflett Rd.*

OTHER ENVIRONS

△ **Cape Kidnappers ★ ★ ★:** One of only three mainland gannet colonies worldwide (the others are at Muriwai, in △ Auckland, and on Farewell Spit). *21 km to Clifton.*

Pakipaki: In this Maori settlement are a number of whare, but of particular note is the carved meeting house, Houngara (1916). Unusual are both the height of the amo (which almost equals that of the apex of the maihi) and the tekoteko figure (a kneeling warrior whose right hand rests a patu on his head). The heke tipi and poitoito of the porch are carved with manaia and human figures. *6.5 km S on Highway 2. Houngara is opp. a stone church.*

Te Aute College ★: An Anglican-founded school predominantly for Maori, opened in 1854 by Archdeacon Samuel Williams with the help and encouragement of Sir George Grey. The school, which stands in a peaceful setting among trees, achieved its objects far sooner than most had hoped, for among its first pupils were Sir Maui Pomare, Sir Apirana Ngata and Sir Peter Buck. Among other illustrious ex-pupils was Sgt. Ngarimu, VC *(for all see index).* In the foyer of the great hall are medals, citations, awards and insignia won by Buck and Pomare. The hall itself is carved and decorated like the interior of a meeting house, but the small chapel is devoid of embellishment save for a stained-glass window, a memorial to Archdeacon Williams and his wife, which depicts the Shepherds as Maori. A plaque above the chapel's west door declares Williams to be "the life long friend of the Maori race and one of the Fathers of the Church in New Zealand".

The school has had its share of setbacks. Dependent on Government support, it was forced to close when Sir George Grey (who had endowed Te Aute with 1,600 hectares) left the country in 1859. The school reopened in 1872 but complaints were made that Williams was farming the estate to his own advantage. These grew in volume and culminated in the appointment of a Royal Commission which, after careful consideration, concluded that "the endowments are earning as much as possible, are leased to an excellent tenant [Williams], who takes a deep interest in the school, whose farming is of the highest quality and who, when his lease expires, will doubtless leave the property in the highest condition. . . ." In 1918 fire destroyed many of the buildings, and a year later another mysterious outbreak destroyed the rest. Most of the present buildings date from this time, but two of these were also destroyed, in the earthquake of 1931.

28 km S on Highway 2. At convenient times a pupil may be assigned to conduct visitors.

Waimarama Beach ★★★: A superb stretch of golden surf beach looking out to the stark grey cliffs of Bare Island. *31 km S. Signposted from Havelock North.*

Ocean Beach: An attractive beach to the north of Waimarama, its comparatively difficult access deters some visitors. *24 km S. Signposted from Havelock North.*

Lemmon Trust Museum (Puketitiri): A large collection of colonial antiques, early agricultural machinery and vintage cars. *Open most days, 9 a.m.-5 p.m. 63 km NW Hastings, via Rissington and Patoka, with unsealed road the last 10 km from Patoka. Check opening hours with the Public Relations Office.*

Also at Puketitiri is Balls Clearing, a picnic area and reserve which contains the last remnant of the Puketitiri Bush in its virgin state. About three-quarters of the vegetation comprises rimu and kahikatea (white pine).

"He that travels far, knows much." *Clarke* (1639)

HAURAKI GULF, Islands of the ★★★

Auckland   Map 4

Information from the Department of Conservation office, cnr Karangahape Rd and Liverpool St, Auckland; tel. (09) 307-9279. Permits are required to visit some islands.

THE HAURAKI GULF is trapped between the mainland and the long arm of the △ Coromandel Peninsula, whose tip at Cape Colville is actually farther north than Waiwera. Within the gulf lie numerous islands and good deep-sea fishing waters. As the gulf is sheltered from all but northerly winds (Hauraki means "north wind"), it is a perfect haven for yachts. A number of the islands are included in the Hauraki Gulf Maritime Park. Of these, perhaps the most popular with visitors are Kawau, Waiheke and the resort of Pakatoa. Most of the islands are served by ferries and launches from the Auckland wharves as well as by amphibian aircraft.

On a number of the islands, the Department of Conservation is re-establishing rare or endangered species of birds and insects.

ISLANDS OF THE HAURAKI GULF ★★★

In geographical order, from N to S. Access to each island varies; details of modes and timetables available from the Visitor Centre, Aotea Quay, Auckland; tel. (09) 366-6888. Cruise operators (who allow time for walks) include Fullers Cruise Centre, Ferry Bldg, Quay St, Auckland; tel. (09) 367-9102.

Great Barrier Island: Named in 1769 by Captain Cook because it seemed to bar the entrance to the gulf, part of the island is included in the Park. Walkers, campers, fishing enthusiasts, scuba divers, kayakers and horse-trekkers are drawn to this remote spot. Its rugged coastline, trimmed with pohutukawa, has claimed several ships, among them the *Wairarapa* (1894), some of whose 135 ill-fated passengers and crew are buried on the island. An abandoned kauri mill and wharf lie at the head of Whangaparapara Bay. There are two airstrips and three ports served by ferries.

The island may have originated regular airmail postage when in 1898, complete with stamps and air-letter forms and about six years before the Wright brothers first flew, pigeons carried mail to the mainland.

Little Barrier Island: Named by Cook at the same time as Great Barrier, the island is now a closely-protected sanctuary remarkable for its birdlife. Often cloud-capped (the island's Maori name of Hauturu means "the wind's resting spot"), the island is the last refuge of the stitchbird, and at night the *ti-ti-ti* call of incoming grey and white Cook's petrels (*Pterodroma cooki*) leaves a lasting impression. The rare black petrel (*Procellaria parkinsona*) breeds on the higher reaches. Other birds include the brown kiwi, native pigeon, North island saddleback, robin and the endangered kakapo. The island contains the country's last remaining large afforested area undisturbed by introduced browsing animals.

The **Hauturu Stone**, on the beach at West Landing, is said to have once been a dog; the mark on its "back" represents a fatal injury inflicted by one of Toi's slaves when the dog refused to go ashore with him. The stone was wahi tapu (a sacred place) and in the uru-uruwhenua ceremony fishermen would place offerings of fish on it to propitiate the sea spirits. *Some excursions land here but there is no ferry service. Permits to land from DOC. There is a resident ranger.*

Goat Island: A scenic reserve of barely nine hectares and about three kilometres from Leigh *(NE of △ Warkworth)*, lies about 100 metres offshore in an unpredictable and treacherous channel. Its awkward coastline and the variety of the surrounding waters make it an excellent site for Auckland University's marine laboratory. Little blue penguins frequently come ashore on the island's tidal beach. *There are no landing restrictions but visitors are asked to protect the flora by keeping to the walking track.* Offshore is a marine reserve, popular with divers.

Kawau ★★★: The island still lingers in the memory of Sir George Grey, an early Governor and later Premier who transformed its dense forests into a sub-tropical paradise "as pretty as Adam's garden before the fall" by importing trees, plants and animals from the world over.

One visitor was moved to note that "the fauna might puzzle the visitor as to his whereabouts on the face of the earth. The deer of Britain may be seen hurrying past to the covert; the kangaroos of Australia, spanning across the path, pull up erect to view the stranger; tree kangaroos from New Guinea are seen hopping up and down puriri trees; the visitor is kept ever on the alert by the whirr of Californian quail, or Chinese pheasants, and the wallaby kangaroo, in numbers, keep zig-zagging across his path; the Cape Barren goose might also exhibit to him the unusual sight of a bird carrying her young under her wings. . . ."

Many of the exotics Grey established still flourish, although the fauna is less remarkable than it once was. The kookaburra, however, may still be heard, and of the six species of surviving wallaby, white-throated Parma from here have been reintroduced to their native Australia where they had become almost extinct.

Grey's home, which became known as **Mansion House** ★★★ (1844; enlarged 1867), still stands. The house began life as the mine manager's house for the copper mine on the island, but shortly after purchasing the island for £3,700 in 1862, Grey set about redesigning and greatly extending it. Plans to retire here were thwarted temporarily by recall to Britain, but in 1870 he returned to take up residence with his niece, Anne Matthews, and complete the radical transformation of the island. For a time Grey entertained the gifted and the intellectual from many parts of the world, but when, in failing health, he finally sold the island in 1888, much of the gardens fell into disrepair. The house has been restored, furnished in the style of Grey's period and is open to the public. Of particular note is Grey's library, which features four kauri pillars and pit-sawn kauri panelling. *Opening hours vary.*

Grey (1812-98) served in various colonial appointments—Governor of South Australia (1840-45) when only 28, twice Governor of New Zealand (1845-53; 1861-68) and Governor of Cape Colony, South Africa (1854-61). In his first term in New Zealand he quickly quelled the War in the North, personally directing operations at the Battle of Ruapekapeka, and established friendly relations with prominent chiefs in the peace that followed. When war broke out again Grey was Governor of Cape Colony and it was natural that he be posted back to New Zealand to try to restore peace. But while he tried, he also armed for war and precipitated the Waikato Campaigns. His hostility towards local politicians and his disregard of orders from London eventually saw his appointment cancelled in 1868. Grey re-emerged in New Zealand politics and became Premier (1877-79), but his liberal policies were at that time considered too radical (although many of his aims have since been achieved) and his lack of self-restraint denied him popular support.

A bizarre incident occurred on Kawau in 1864 after a shipload of Maori prisoners taken at the Battle of Rangiriri had been brought to the island after Grey had complained of their ill-treatment at Auckland. Alarmed by a malicious rumour that their ship, complete with captives, was to be towed out to sea and sunk, the Maori crowded into fishing boats and with planks and shovels rowed to the mainland near Warkworth, where some of their descendants still live. Opponents thought the Maori intended to join the "rebels" in Taranaki, where war was raging, and accused Grey of helping in the escape.

Dating from before Grey's time are old miners' cottages, mine shafts and other relics of a copper-mining industry. In the 1830s manganese was found here, and in Aberdeen, Scotland, a company was formed to mine the deposits. It switched to copper when a rich lode was struck in 1842. A shaft was sunk under the cliffs near the ruined shoreside engine house, and a stone smelting house was built at Bon Accord Harbour. The mine manager's residence, built of brick and timber shipped from Melbourne, later formed the nucleus of Grey's Mansion. Flooding, engineering problems and the lure to labourers of the Australian goldfields saw production dwindle and finally cease when the island was sold to Sir George.

In summer Kawau is a mecca for yachts—indeed, Harry Jack Island, barely visible at low tide, actually changes hands annually as a race prize on Squadron Weekend. But in all seasons the island has compelling allure for the naturalist and the historically minded. Kawau means "cormorant". *The island may be reached by ferry from Sandspit, near △ Warkworth, or from Auckland.*

Motuora: Approximately four kilometres east of the Mahurangi Heads, Motuora is an attractive, 80-hectare farm included in the Maritime Park. Noteworthy is the variety of marine life in the intertidal zone. A Maori legend tells of the boat-shaped island being towed away from the Bay of Islands after it ran aground and could not be freed. Three caves mark the places where the towline is said to have been secured. Camping is permitted near the caretaker's cottage. Motuora means "wedge-shaped island".

Tiritiri Matangi: Grazed by stock for many years and now a bird sanctuary, the 207-hectare island is being allowed to revert to native bush, a process underpinned by an energetic reforestation programme (much of it by volunteers). Endangered native birds such as the takahe are being released in several of the well-wooded and well-watered gullies. Board walks lead through the bush, and there are viewing boxes to see little blue penguins. There is one good sandy beach, Hobbs Beach, with the rest of the coastline rising sharply. The lighthouse (1864), now solar-powered, was once the most powerful in the southern hemisphere. *Public access limited to daylight hours. Information centre.*

Tiritiri Matangi is not readily translatable: tiritiri is a twig placed in the ground to indicate the position of a kumara tuber; matangi, the warm north-east breeze.

Rangitoto: While the island's sweeping silhouette characterises so many views around Auckland, it was one of the few peaks not fortified by the Maori—and understandably so as in legend the island was still erupting when the ubiquitous Polynesian explorer Toi (*p.* **300**) arrived here hundreds of years ago. With little soil and no permanent source of water, flora is regenerating under the harshest of conditions.

Purchased for £15 in 1857 by "Wikitoria and her heirs for ever", the island has been a scenic reserve and popular picnic place for nearly a century. It is now part of the Maritime Park. Plans for a quarantine station and prison never materialised, a salt works near the Beacon failed and the quarrying of scoria and rock is now prohibited. During World War II the island was declared a restricted area and its summit used as a base for harbour defence.

A causeway now links Rangitoto with Motutapu across narrows through which the Rev. Samuel Marsden once mistakenly tried to sail a boat in 1820. Doggedly refusing to acknowledge his error, and to the consternation of those on board, Marsden pressed on to run aground. Fortuitously, a group of Maori passed by and dragged the boat to the safety of deeper water.

The island's recent volcanic activity is reflected in its name, a contraction of Nga Rangi-totongia-a-Tama-te-kapua, "the days of the bleeding of Tama-te-kapua", captain of the *Arawa* canoe. Islington Bay was earlier known as Drunken Bay as it was there that ships outward bound from Auckland would pause while their crews regained sobriety.

The walk to the summit (*one-hour one way*) affords an unparalleled **view** of the gulf and of Auckland city. A short detour leads to the curious **lava caves**. *Visitor Information and shelter at Rangitoto wharf. No camping on the island.*

Motutapu: Across the causeway from Rangitoto lies the 1,509-hectare island of Motutapu ("sacred island"), the focus of a concentrated reforestation programme. Last century, after the island passed into European hands, massive Victorian picnics were held here with crowds of up to 5,000 at a time. According to tradition, a very early Maori settlement here was buried under an eruption from Rangitoto about 900 years ago.

Today the visitor may cross the island by way of the 3½-kilometre **Motutapu Farm Walkway**, starting at Islington Bay. There is a camping ground at Home Bay. *A DOC conservation officer lives on the island.*

Waiheke Island: Largest of the islands in the Gulf proper, Waiheke is home to a growing population. With swift connections to Auckland, residents can combine an idyllic island lifestyle with the opportunities of city-based careers. The island's **vineyards** attract considerable interest.

White sandy beaches such as Oneroa, Palm Beach and Onetangi (all on the northern coastline) offer safe swimming, and at the island's eastern end a series of tracks thread through the Stony Batter Historic Reserve. Horse-trekking, sea kayaking, sailing, bus and cycling tours, wine-tasting and helicopter trips are all available. Waiheke means "ebbing water". *Information Centre, Oneroa, tel. (09) 372-9999.*

Pakatoa: Due east of Waiheke, Pakatoa has been developed into a holiday resort with self-contained chalets. Its comforts and the island's obvious charm find favour with many honeymooners. Pakatoa means "to flow, as the tide".

Motuihe: Barely 180 hectares in area, Motuihe is a Maritime Park recreational reserve which provides a popular day's outing. A gnarled olive grove is said to have been planted by Sir John Logan Campbell, who farmed the island for a time in 1843. During World War II the island was used as a prisoner-of-war camp and it was from here that the intrepid Count Felix von Luckner escaped in 1917. "The Sea Wolf", as he was known, was the most colourful commander in the Kaiser's Navy and every inch the impeccable gentleman. He took heavy toll of allied shipping before he was captured in the Cook Islands and brought here to be interned. During a carefully staged Christmas concert the Count escaped from the island via the commandant's yacht and commandeered the scow *Moa,* ran up a contrived German flag and set off on a 650-kilometre journey to the Kermadecs. After a sensational chase, the Count and his crew were recaptured at the Kermadecs and returned to captivity on an island in Lyttelton Harbour, near Christchurch. For many years the island served as a quarantine station. Motuihe means "island of Ihenga".

Motukorea (Browns Island): This eroded lava and scoria cone (with virtually unmodified volcanic landforms) bears evidence of lengthy occupation. The largest of several settlement sites is on the rim of the main crater. The **coastal breeding area** for the threatened New Zealand dotterel is of particular interest. It was here in 1840 that the two founding fathers of Auckland city — William Brown and John

Logan Campbell — first settled. Early in the century, a ferry company owned the island and ran picnic parties out from the mainland. However, the once-busy wharf has collapsed into the sea, joining the hulks of five ferries beached to rot at the end of their usefulness. Purchased by Sir Ernest Davies (a successful businessman and mayor of Auckland) and given to the city as a memorial to his father, the island now forms part of the Maritime Park. A **plaque** recording the gift is set in stone salvaged from London's Waterloo Bridge at the time of its replacement. Motukorea is variously translated, with one version, Motu Koreha ("island sinking out of sight"), referring to certain easterly conditions when it can appear to be floating. *Access in daylight hours. Landing is recommended only during the two hours on either side of high tide.*

HAWERA

Taranaki   Map 7   Pop. 11,152 (urban area)

74 km SE of New Plymouth via Inglewood; 105 km via Opunake; 92 km NW of Wanganui. Information South Taranaki, 55 High St, at the foot of the water tower; tel. (06) 278-8599.

HAWERA, principal town of South Taranaki, is a farming centre with an assortment of secondary industries. Its level setting, on the eastern fringe of the Waimate Plain, denies the town any obvious character but when neighbouring Taranaki/Egmont is viewed from the water tower across jumbled rooftops, Hawera assumes a fresh perspective.

Hawera (or Te Hawera, "the burnt place") takes its name from an incident in which an invading war party set fire by night to a large whare in which many warriors were sleeping. Those who escaped from the blaze perished to the taiaha and the mere.

SOME HISTORY

General Chute's march: During the Taranaki Campaigns of the 1860s General Chute, irked by the colonists' contempt for Regular troops who had refused to adapt to the bush techniques required to counter guerilla warfare, slashed his way into the area and established a base near the present town. Chute then began his epic march through dense bush to New Plymouth via Normanby and Stratford, along an ancient Maori trail. In six weeks he marched his men 420 kilometres from Wanganui to New Plymouth and back around the coast, capturing seven fortified pa and sacking 20 villages as he went, with very few casualties. The rugged going was made worse by a food shortage which drove the troops to eat several of their horses.

Chute's impetuosity led him to wreak more havoc than the situation required, but he did succeed in showing that Regulars could fight in the bush without the heavy equipment previously thought essential.

"Hawera Republic": After Chute had re-opened the inland route north to New Plymouth, the ferocious Hauhau movement (*p. 167*) gained control of the area and local settlers withdrew to Patea until, in 1870, a blockhouse was built at Hawera and the present township sprang up around it. Frustrated by apparent Government inactivity to counter Te Whiti's campaign against the sale of Maori land based at Parihaka (*p. 77*), the Hawera settlers in 1879 formed their own volunteer regiments. Then, when Te Whiti's men began ploughing up land worked by the colonists and the Government still did not act, the settlers themselves forced the Maori ploughmen back across the Waingongoro River and later that day at a public meeting declared Hawera's "Independence".

The "Hawera Republic", of dubious legal standing and whose only boundary was the Waingongoro River, was dissolved a fortnight later when Government assistance reached the district.

Cricket under fire: Near Hawera was played an extraordinary cricket match at Easter, 1866, between the "Pigskin Polishers" (Troopers) and the "Footsloggers" (Rangers), to celebrate the completion of a new fort. Because Hauhau were known to be in the vicinity, every player was belted with a revolver and 50 rounds of ammunition, each fieldsman stood with a carbine at his feet and the umpires (along with the usual paraphernalia) held guns for each of the batsmen. As the game progressed a group of bemused Hauhau assembled at the edge of the bush to watch the peculiar ritual and performed a haka in a vain attempt to distract the participants. Tension mounted, and when the Rangers' last pair was at the crease with 10 runs still needed for victory, a hail of musket balls suddenly swept the ground and the players dived for cover. But every man had wagered his grog ration on the outcome, and while spectators gave chase to the Hauhau the game was resumed—to the mortification of some of the Hauhau, who reappeared to let loose a second volley. The interruptions, however, proved too much for the tailend batsmen, who could only manage a further three runs before the game ended in a win to the Troopers. (Unfortunately, the account is of doubtful validity, contained as it is in an "autobiography" which, when it appeared in 1911, caused much offence, and many asserted that "Maori Browne"—as the author described himself—had not even arrived in New Zealand before the fighting had ended. Indeed James Cowan records that all anyone knew of Col. Hamilton-Browne was that he had been placed on probation for forging a cheque. The tale is told in *With the Lost Legion in New Zealand,* by Col. Hamilton-Browne.)

POINTS OF INTEREST

Turuturu-mokai Pa ★★★: The pa is of special interest as it was built in pre-European times and so was designed for hand-to-hand fighting. It stands in a 10.5-hectare reserve by Tawhiti Stream and comprises a main pa and five satellite pa, one of which is connected to the main pa by a tunnel under the stream *(the entrance has been closed for safety).* Many dug-in house sites and rua (food storage pits) may be seen on the summit of the main pa.

The pa was built 400 years ago by the Ngati Tupaea, who were attacked by a rival sub-tribe, the Taki-Ruahine, in the mid 1600s. In an inspired act of treachery the Taki-Ruahine had offered the unsuspecting Ngati Tupaea the services of their famous tattooist, who generously applied his art to the Ngati Tupaea, concentrating on their hips and thighs "to give them speed in battle". Tattooing was extremely painful, carried out with uhi (serrated-edged bone) and mallet, and warriors took some time to recuperate. But as soon as the tattooist had finished his work, the Taki-Ruahine attacked, sacking the pa and massacring its crippled defenders.

Turuturu-mokai means "dried heads on stakes" and refers to the custom of impaling the heads of slain chiefs on stakes driven into the ground.

Near the pa and across a stile is a stone memorial to a redoubt built alongside the deserted pa during the Taranaki Campaigns. At dawn on 12 July 1868 the redoubt was stormed by a Hauhau war party of 60 which included Kimble Bent, a pakeha deserter. The canteen-keeper was the first to be killed and the Hauhau war-priest immediately cut out his heart and singed it with a match not only to ensure the success of the attack but also to terrify the Pakeha who would hear of it. Nine more, including the commander, were killed and six wounded before Regulars from the Waihi Redoubt, five kilometres away, reached the scene and the war party withdrew. An unsuccessful attempt to avenge this attack led to the disaster at Te Ngutu-o-te-manu, near △ Manaia.

In 1938, on the seventieth anniversary of the attack on the redoubt, a carved post was erected on the pa crest, to protect visitors to the pa from the ancient evil influences which had previously kept Maori away from the area. *2.5 km N.*

Hawera watertower: From a height of over 50 metres, the tower affords a splendid view of the surrounding countryside. *Cnr High and Albion Sts. For tour times contact the information office in the tower grounds.*

King Edward Park: The park surrounds a lake with pleasant lawns and gardens. In the centre of the azalea gardens is a quaint statue of Peter Pan's "Wendy", and a willow-pattern garden depicts the traditional plate design. There is also a George III cannon used by the Taranaki Volunteers. *Main St.*

Elvis Presley Memorial Room: An admirer once voted "New Zealand's Most Devoted Elvis Fan" maintains a memorial collection of records, tapes and souvenirs. *51 Argyle St; tel. (06) 278-7624.*

Tawhiti Museum: Here, in a former dairy factory, both life-sized models and miniatures are used to create a visual history of the region. The **Tawhiti Bush Railway** takes passengers on a reconstructed logging railway, once a feature of the district. *47 Ohangai Rd, 3 km NE. Open Friday to Monday from 10 a.m.-4 p.m.; winter Sunday only; tel. (06) 278-6837.*

ENVIRONS

Ohawe Beach: Some of the first moa bones discovered were found in 1844 at the mouth of the Waingongoro River. These were shipped to England where an accurate reconstruction was made of this remarkable bird, which was not unlike a giant emu. In the 1300s several species of moa roamed the Taranaki. A moa skeleton is displayed in the Taranaki Museum, New Plymouth. *At 6.5 km W, detour 2 km. Signposted.*

Te Ngutu-o-te-manu battle site: The scene of an unsuccessful attempt to avenge the attack on the redoubt at Turuturu-mokai *(above),* the site is now heavily bushed reserve. *Ahipaipa Rd. 23 km NW, via Okaiawa. (See △ Manaia.)*

Kapuni Natural Gas Plant: Here gas is processed from the Kapuni Gas Field. *(Tours are conducted occasionally.)* A neighbouring petrochemical plant produces urea and ammonia from natural gas for use as fertiliser. *For notes on Taranaki's energy-based industries, see pp.* **152-53.**

Lake Rotorangi: *Described on p. 181.*

★ HELENSVILLE

Auckland   Map 4   Pop. 1,360

51 km NW of Auckland.

WITH A MELLOW AIR which suggests a town of greater substance, Helensville lies near the southernmost shores of △ Kaipara Harbour. The northbound traveller soon overlooks the mangrove-bordered Kaipara River, and to the south Highway 16 leads through mixed farming country, orchards and vineyards to reach Auckland.

SOME HISTORY

A timber town: Like so many other towns, Helensville began as a timber-milling centre. Rafts of kauri logs were towed here from points around Kaipara Harbour, rafts known as "herringbones" as each comprised a heavy long chain "backbone" with short toggle chains securing logs to it.

The earliest settlers' initial link with Auckland was by sea, a lengthy voyage round North Cape to the Waitemata. However, the hazardous bar at the Kaipara Harbour entrance quickly forced the establishment of a bullock track to Riverhead on the northernmost arm of the Waitemata. A rail link with Riverhead was forged in 1875, when Helensville settlers guaranteed to rail out minimum quantities of timber. Six years later the railway was completed to Auckland.

Depression struck at the turn of the century when, the kauri exhausted, the mills were closed and several houses were uprooted and moved to Auckland. A soap factory, too, failed; although its soap was of good quality it is said that its maker's name, Horatio Hjorth, proved so difficult to pronounce that though customers gazed longingly at the local product, they asked for an English brand. The start of the butter export trade saw the township recover and assume a dairying role.

Helensville (at first, "Helensvilla") is named after Helen McLeod, wife of John McLeod, a pioneer settler born in Nova Scotia who came here in 1862 by way of the Californian goldfields and who prospered in the timber trade. John returned to Nova Scotia but his brother Isaac remained to found the present large clan of McLeods.

THINGS TO SEE AND DO

Parakai Thermal Springs ★ ★: A regular drawcard for many Aucklanders. A cluster of motels has private pools but most people are attracted to the modern hot mineral swimming pools in the Parakai Domain *(open daily, 10 a.m.–10 p.m.).* Also in the domain are shaded picnic areas and a camping ground. *3 km S. Turnoff signposted at 2 km S.* There is also a complex of privately owned pools nearby.

Pioneer Museum: Displayed in a pioneer cottage are various Maori artefacts, kauri gum, pioneer exhibits, photographs and maps of early Helensville. Adjoining is the former **Courthouse** (1864). *Commercial Rd. Hours vary.*

"Iron Park": A collection of restored tractors and machinery. *Te Pua; 3 km SW.*

Cruises on Kaipara Harbour: A vast enclosed waterway, the harbour is Auckland's "third" whose contrasts extend from dense bush and sandy beaches to the indescribably wild West Coast. Historical journeys of up to 4 hours retrace journeys of the distant past. Some combine with a **Sand Safari** to visit old shipwrecks near Poutu Point, *p.* **68.** *Kaipara Cruises; tel. (09) 420-8466.*

★★ HOKIANGA HARBOUR

Northland   Map 3

NW of Whangarei. Information Centre, Omapere Beach, tel. (09) 405-8869.

HOKIANGA HARBOUR, a jagged claw in Northland's western coastline, attracts visitors to its twin beach resorts of Omapere and Opononi. Bleached with high, shifting sand dunes, the harbour's north head is in arid contrast with the green of its southern arm. The entrance has a dangerous bar on which a number of ships have foundered. The harbour saw much shipping in its heyday, and today sand is barged from the north heads the length of the harbour to supply local builders. A vehicular ferry links Rawene with Kohukohu.

SOME HISTORY

Kupe's departure: The Polynesian explorer is traditionally said to have left for home from here after exploring the New Zealand coast, and so the harbour's full name, Hokianga-nui-o-Kupe, means "the final departing place of Kupe".

An early settlement: Ships probably called here from about 1800, as they did at the Bay of Islands, and the two areas developed more or less contemporaneously. Hokianga's population was probably no less wild than Russell's and included "Cannibal Jack" (Jacky Marmon), who arrived about 1824 and is the area's earliest known settler. A ship deserter, he is reputed to have taken part in cannibal feasts. From Horeke jetty can be seen Marmon's Point, above which, on Rawhia Hill, Jacky is reputed to be buried.

In 1827 the first London-based New Zealand Company purchased land for a settlement here but for reasons uncertain the intending colonists departed for Australia only days after the deed of sale was signed. An export trade in kauri built up, for the giant trees grew close to the water's edge, and timber and kauri gum industries boomed up to the early 1900s. Today, with the timber millers and gum diggers gone, the region is predominantly a farming district. Stands of kauri in the △ Waipoua and Trounson Kauri Forests and in Omahuta Forest (*p.* **115**) recall its earlier glory.

"Sovereign Chief of New Zealand": Baron de Thierry (1793-1864), an eccentric expatriate Frenchman, met the chiefs Hongi Hika and Waikato at Cambridge in 1820 during their visit to England. His interest quickened, he came to New Zealand in 1837, bringing with him an assortment of colonists to take up 16,000 hectares of land allegedly purchased from Hokianga chiefs for a mere 36 axes. A bizarre figure, he proclaimed himself "Sovereign Chief of New Zealand", adding this title to his claim to be "King of Nukuhiva" (an island in the Marquesas group). His grandiose scheme to colonise the area collapsed when most of his followers deserted and the title to his land was repudiated. Ridiculed by many and feared by some (at this time rumours were rife that France might annex New Zealand), the impoverished de Thierry settled on the upper reaches of the harbour and later moved to Auckland, where he died in 1864.

One of New Zealand's finest historical novels, *Check to Your King* (1936), by Robin Hyde, concerns this extraordinary character. *A plaque, on Highway 1, 400 m S of the Rangiahua turnoff to Horeke, marks his land and indicates the site of his hut. The plaque is above a concrete railway siding, built for a railway that never came.*

TOWNS AND PLACES OF INTEREST

Described in order approaching from the east.

The magic of the harbour and its many tentacles is best savoured from the water. For those moving at a leisurely pace, a lengthy boat trip on the "mail run" leaves Opononi on the restored Sierra *(1912) (tel. (09) 405-8753). Penetrating some 20 km inland, it affords a feel of the "old Hokianga". Dolphin tours, fishing trips and water taxis are based on Opononi: Hokianga Harbour Water Taxis; tel. (09) 405-4851 or (09) 405-4890; Orca Harbour Tours, tel. (09) 405-8765.*

Horeke: This small harbourside settlement, remarkable for its buildings on stilts over the water, was the site of early shipyards which, promoted by Sydney merchants, enjoyed notable if short-lived success. The first ship built, the 40-ton schooner *Enterprise* (1827), foundered north of Hokianga Heads after only her second trip to Sydney.

The 140-ton brigantine *New Zealander* (1828), in its time the fastest ship sailing out of Port Jackson (once making the Tasman crossing in just six days), the 392-ton barque *Sir George Murray* (1830), named after the Secretary of State for Colonies, and several smaller craft followed. When visiting Sydney, the two larger ships were seized temporarily by the New South Wales authorities for sailing without a register, a fate which dogged the first New Zealand-built vessels. In 1830 the promoters went bankrupt as drought in New South Wales had prevented them from fulfilling a Government contract there for the supply of milk and bread. The *Sir George Murray* and the shipyards were then auctioned in Sydney. A plaque marks the approximate place where the *Sir George Murray* was built.

Offshore lies sleek, low **Ruapapaka Island**, the scene of the first execution in European times when, in 1838, a local Maori was shot for having murdered a

European he had agreed to ferry across the harbour. The incident threatened the wider relationship between local traders and the Ngapuhi here, and was dealt with by Busby, the British Resident (*pp.* **23-24**), who organised and presided over the trial (which took place in the Wesleyan chapel at Mangungu). Thereafter, the hapless Kite stood on the edge of his grave to be shot. Busby appears to have been quite pleased with his wholly unauthorised action. The only explicit function he had in New Zealand, in accordance with his instructions, was "to conciliate the goodwill of the native chiefs, and establish on a permanent basis that good understanding and confidence which it is important to perpetuate".

Mangungu Mission House ★★★ (*c.* 1838): Standing on a ledge above the harbour, the simple timber Wesleyan mission house enjoys a sun-drenched panorama of the inlet and proffers a verandah on which those who make the detour may choose to picnic.

Missionary endeavour began here in 1828, the year after the first Wesleyan mission, at Kaeo near Whangaroa Harbour, had been abandoned. The site was chosen for its proximity to European business settlements on the harbour and because adequate protection could be afforded by the Ngapuhi chief, Eruera Patuone (*c.* 1770-1872). Patuone had established a formidable reputation as a warrior during the tribal wars earlier in the century. He was one of the chiefs who in 1831 petitioned William IV for British protection and was subsequently one of the first to sign the Treaty of Waitangi. It was his claim that, as a child of eight, he had gone aboard Cook's *Endeavour* at the Bay of Islands.

The leader of the missionary band was John Hobbs (1800-83), son of a Kentish coachbuilder, who had served at the Kaeo mission and become fluent in the Maori language. He quickly established himself with local Maori, modelling his style as a preacher on the traditional Maori orators, adopting their gestures and illustrating his message with scenes from their daily life. Some of the hymns he composed are still sung. Under Hobbs' leadership the mission flourished, and it was he who planned this the first permanent mission house which replaced the earlier dwellings. Shortly afterwards, Hobbs interpreted for William Hobson, the British Governor-designate, at the great gathering which took place at Mangungu when local chiefs congregated here to add their own names to the Treaty of Waitangi. (Hobson had planned a series of such meetings throughout the country, but illness forced him to abandon the scenario.)

The Wesleyan success at Mangungu led to the establishment of other mission stations, principally down the west coast of the North Island. By 1846 there were 14 mission stations, with 17 missionaries and 5,000 children in school. In 1840, the Wesleyans established the first Christian mission in the South Island, at Waikouaiti.

In time, the local population dwindled and Mangungu's importance waned so much so that when Hobbs moved to Auckland in 1855 the mission house was dismantled and moved to Onehunga for use as a Methodist parsonage. After being moved again within Onehunga, it was finally returned to Mangungu in 1972, to stand near its original site.

The house is furnished to period, and includes a copy of a drawing by 10-year-old Emma Hobbs who sketched the scene as it was in 1838 before the largest of the temporary buildings burnt down. The rock to which canoes could be moored is depicted in the foreground, and may still be seen on the harbour shore just opposite the entrance to the driveway. The mission church has gone (the church here is a relative newcomer) but the small mission cemetery has survived. The headstones include that of David Clark (1766-1831), first superintendent of the Horeke shipyard. The inscription is still apt: "Is it nothing to you, all ye that pass by?" (Lamentations 1:12). Further relics from missionary times are venerable exotic trees, planted as aids to navigation. *The mission house lies a little off the beaten track. From the east, the best route in to Horeke and Mangungu (only part of which is unsealed) is by way of Rangiahua. The house, administered by the Historic Places Trust, is open at weekends and summer school holidays from 12 noon to 4 p.m. Other times by arrangement. Tel. (09) 401-9640. 17 km N of Taheke; 12 km SW of Rangiahua.*

Kohukohu: An early timber settlement, once the largest on the harbour and today a small service centre, looks across the water to Rawene, to which it is linked by a car ferry. Much of the land by the water's edge was reclaimed with sawdust from the mill, in its time reputed to be the largest in the Southern Hemisphere. The library houses a collection of historical photographs.

What has been claimed as the country's oldest bridge (possibly pre-1840), a tiny arch of Sydney sandstone, crosses a creek in the school grounds, but its construction date is uncertain.

The Centennial Plinth (1938) on Totara Point marks the site of the home of Thomas Poynton, who received Bishop Pompallier (*p.* **205**) when he landed here, and in whose home the first known Mass was offered in New Zealand, on 13 January 1838. *A 1-km walk at 8 km NE of Kohukohu.*

Mangamuka Bridge: It was here that in 1828 the great Ngapuhi fighting chief Hongi Hika (*p.* **122**) received the wound from which he eventually died. One of the largest of the country's kauri trees lies in nearby Omahuta Forest (*p.* **115**).

Omanaia: A tiny Maori settlement which has a Methodist church (1884) perched in solitude above the road. In its graveyard are examples of the curious carved headboards peculiar to Northland, and also the grave of Peretane Papahurihia, a great tohunga of last century. As Hone Heke's chief priest and an opponent of Christianity, he led the Nakahi, the first of the Maori nationalist cults, but was later converted to Christianity. His grave is said to have moved whenever his followers erred in the words of their prayers. Known as the "Blackouts", they recited their prayers in the dark. A more likely explanation for any movement is the district's generally unstable ground. Omanaia means "place of the manaia" (a bird-like human figure), or "place of Manaia" (captain of the *Tokomaru* canoe). *Allow 20 mins. The churchyard gate is by the school entrance. The burial ground is tapu and the permission of a local marae elder should be sought before it is entered.*

Omapere: Approached from the south, Omapere presents a dramatic scene as the harbour suddenly unfolds ahead. Excellent sea fishing can be enjoyed hereabouts. A 30-minute walk along the beach to the heads leads to a blow-hole, most spectacular at high tide. On the south head, above the beach, is an old signal station. Omapere means "place of the plume grass". *Hokianga Visitor Information Centre, tel. (09) 405-8869. The Centre houses a small museum which features photographs of Opo the Dolphin.*

Onoke: Still standing here is author-trader Frederick Maning's old home (*c.* 1860), close by a hut once used as a courthouse for Maori Land Court hearings. Maning (1811-83), born in Dublin, came to live permanently at Hokianga in 1833 and traded here for over 40 years. The best known of his books is *Old New Zealand* (1863), written under the pen-name "A Pakeha-Maori". He played an important part in establishing the Northern Native Land Court, of which he was judge, but towards the end of his life his love for the Maori turned to the bitterness which characterises his later writings. Onoke means "place of the earthworm". *On Brindle's Rd, near the mouth of the Whirinaki River. Detour 8 km from Whirinaki along a narrow road.*

Opononi: A small seaside holiday town a short distance from Hokianga Heads, it has safe bathing and boating, and good sea fishing. *Several trips on the harbour (including dolphin watching) leave from here (see above).*

The town is remembered for the antics of "Opo", an affectionate dolphin which played with children and gave them rides in the summer of 1955-56. Opo made Opononi world-famous as this was only the second time in recorded history that a wild dolphin had behaved in this way, the first occasion being at Hippo in North Africa about 100 A.D. Like "Pelorus Jack" (which "guided" ships in Pelorus Sound), Opo was given protection by law, but the country was saddened when Opo was killed the day before the law was to come into force. On the shore opposite the hotel and above the dolphin's grave is a status of a child with Opo, the gift of the Christchurch sculptor, the late Russell Clark. A full account of the incident is given in *A Book of Dolphins* by Anthony Alpers, and it also forms the basis of Maurice Shadbolt's novel *Last Summer's Dolphin.*

The impressive old Webster Home (*c.* 1870) was the centre of the district's social life in the 1880s and the setting for many balls. In the grounds are two cannons said to be from the *Culgoa*, wrecked on the harbour's bar in 1856. *(Above the road on the town's western exit.)* To the east, high on a pa top, stands a slender column, a memorial to the legendary Kupe. *(At Pakanae 2 km E).* Opononi means "the place of Ponoui".

Rawene ★ (pop. 359): An old timber town in a pleasant setting on the tip of Herd's Point, it is given added quaintness by seaside buildings which jut out over the water.

Of interest in the town is an old Maori fishing canoe (c. 1877; *displayed by the main road*). A car ferry across to Kohukohu on the northern shore provides an alternative route to Kaitaia. *Ferry leaves Rawene about once an hour from about 7.30 a.m. to 5.45 p.m. and returns from the Narrows hourly from about 7.45 a.m. to 6 p.m.* Boats and yachts are available for charter at Rawene from Hokianga Heritage Charter *(tel. (09) 405-7728).*

The comic Dog Tax Rebellion here in 1898 arose when nearby Waima Maori refused to pay a dog-registration fee imposed by the county council. The local magistrate, who had fined a number of dog-owners, was, in the traditional manner, challenged to fight at Rawene. The town was evacuated but tragedy was averted when a local Wesleyan missionary intercepted the war party and persuaded it to withdraw. In this way the last Maori uprising against the Government ended with just one shot fired, and then only as a signal.

Clendon House ★★: Rawene's most famous house was built in the late 1860s by James Reddy Clendon (1800-72), a Kentish sea captain who first visited New Zealand in 1828 after shipping a load of convicts from England to New South Wales. He spent about 20 months on the New Zealand coast procuring a suitable cargo, including kauri spars, for the return journey. In 1832 he returned with his wife and family and established a chandlering business at the Bay of Islands which brought him into contact with American whalers. He was eventually appointed the United States' first honorary consul—a post which did not deter him from helping Hobson with negotiating the Treaty of Waitangi. During the lawless 1830s, Clendon exercised greater authority than did Busby, the British Resident: Clendon was in close touch with the European traders and settlers at Kororareka (Russell) while Busby was at Waitangi, preoccupied with his plaintive letters to London.

After holding various other appointments at Russell (Justice of the Peace, Police Magistrate and Member of the first Legislative Council, 1841-44), he moved to Hokianga as Resident Magistrate. Eventually his plea for land was granted and he built the last of his four or five substantial houses. Surprisingly, as many as three have survived: The Bungalow at Russell and his house at Manawaora (Clendon Cove), as well as the house at Rawene. His first house, at Okiato, served as the infant colony's first Government House but was destroyed by fire in 1842.

Two pictures damaged in the fire at Okiato hang in the drawing room here at Rawene. Also displayed are various certificates of Clendon's official appointments (signed by various early luminaries, among them FitzRoy, Gore Browne, Grey and Wynyard), a register of land transactions in the area from 1860 in both English and Maori, Clendon family furniture and the "Laws of England in the Maori Language" (1858), in which the criminal law extends to a mere 37 pages. *The Esplanade, Rawene. Open daily, 10 a.m.-4 p.m. Closed Christmas Day. Tel. (09) 405-7874.*

Auckland   *Map 4*   *Pop. 13,866*   ★★ **HOWICK**

23 km SE of Auckland.

THE PLEASANT SEASIDE town of Howick, once a remote pioneer community, is today a substantial residential area for greater Auckland but has managed to retain some of its original village character. The surrounding undulating farmland is steadily being eaten way as the city creeps inexorably south. The area is proving popular with South East Asian immigrants, many of whose homes are distinguished by their grand porticoes.

SOME HISTORY

A Fencible settlement: Local Ngaitai had suffered their share of Hongi Hika's devastation, and when Sir George Grey in 1847 established a Fencible settlement here the area was a near-deserted wasteland of scrub and fern. Grey planned a series of defensive military settlements across the isthmus, designed to protect the infant capital at Auckland from restive Maori tribes to the south. In Britain, "Fencibles"—soldiers liable for home service only—were enlisted from those who had completed their time in the British Army. In return for signing on for seven years they received a free passage to New Zealand and the use of a cottage and land which became their own property when their term expired.

Similar Fencible settlements were established at Onehunga (1847), Panmure and Otahuhu (both 1848) to complete Grey's strategy. At the end of 1847 over 200 Fencibles, their wives and families, arrived on Howick Beach where they were "stowed away like herrings in a barrel" until cottages were built. The gracious "Selwyn" Church of All Saints was the first building to be completed, and to cater for other spiritual needs, the Wet Canteen was next—"The antidote was but a few weeks in advance of the bane," Bishop Selwyn commented. Both buildings are still standing.

Although the settlement was never actually attacked, there were a number of alarms, such as in 1863 when two young brothers were murdered. For a time when war seemed inevitable, men came to church fully armed, many settlers spent their nights in the redoubt on Stockade Hill and the Rev. Vicesimus Lush, the local vicar, had cautiously packed up his belongings and buried his plate "for the sake of concealment".

Tied to Howick by their contracts, the Fencibles were spared the temptation to join in the early gold rushes, and the area soon became self-supporting.

The town is named after Howick Hall, Northumberland, seat of Earl Grey who, as Secretary of State for War and the Colonies, approved Sir George Grey's scheme for the Fencibles.

THINGS TO SEE AND DO

All Saints' Anglican Church ★★★ (1847): One of the characteristic "Selwyn" churches designed by the Rev. Frederick Thatcher. Bishop Selwyn is believed to have personally carried some of the kauri beams up from the beach to the site and helped nail shingles to the roof. The vertical weatherboarding, in the Selwyn tradition, is battened over the joints, but missing are the usual hoop-iron windows. External crossbeams, picked out in brown, are a visual feature as well as giving added strength. The building was in the shape of a perfect cross before the nave was enlarged in 1862.

The lychgate is a memorial to the Fencibles, and the graveyard reflects the epidemics that occasionally swept the village; buried here are many of the Fencibles along with the murdered brothers, Nicholas and Richard Trust, and three of the Rev. Vicesimus Lush's children who died in a single month. *Cnr Picton St and Selwyn Rd.*

All Saints' Anglican Church, Howick.

Shamrock Cottage (1847): Once a hotel and the original Wet Canteen for the Fencibles, the cottage stands close to the beach. It has been restored and furnished in character and is open to the public as a restaurant. *Selwyn Rd.*

A suggested walk: An excellent pamphlet (*available locally*) suggests a leisurely walk passing the surviving Fencible cottages.

ENVIRONS

Howick Colonial Village ★★★: Several Fencible cottages have been relocated here to create a Fencible settlement of the 1840-80 period. Examples of each of the various types of military housing may be seen: double-unit cottages for privates; single cottages for sergeants and homesteads for officers. Completing the village are the 1848 Howick Courthouse, the 1852 Howick Methodist Church, a variety of early commercial buildings and a reconstruction of an early settler's sod cottage. Centrepiece is Bell House (*administered by the Historic Places Trust*), built in 1852 for Captain C.H.W. Smith and now used as a restaurant. *Bells Rd, Lloyd Elsmore Park, Pakuranga. Open daily, 10 a.m.–4 p.m. (5 p.m. in summer); tel. (09) 576-9506.*

Musick Point: This headland pa site affords a wonderful panorama. It is named for Captain Edwin Musick and the courageous crew of the *Samoan Clipper,* a plane lost at sea in 1939 during a survey flight from America to New Zealand. Inside, **plaques** depict Captain Musick and a plan shows details of Waiarohia pa. The **"Tainui" tree** by the radio building is said to have originated as flooring on the *Tainui* canoe. *5 km N.*

Beaches: The expanse of sheltered **Bucklands Beach**, on the Tamaki River estuary, is frequented by boat owners. Across the narrow peninsula lies **Eastern Beach**, exposed to the open sea and looking across to Waiheke Island. **Cockle Bay** is favoured both for shellfish (at low tide) and swimming (at high tide).

St John's, East Tamaki (1860): This stone hilltop chapel has been the scene of witchcraft rituals, and in 1965 was burnt out after a Black Mass ceremony. Completely restored, the church is generally closed but its curiosity value attracts a number of visitors. The scoria stone walls in the vicinity are a legacy of "Hampton Park", a grandiose English estate scheme conceived by the Rev. Gideon Smales, who in the 1850s had no less than eight kilometres of stone walls built to subdivide his holding. The church, too, was fashioned by Smales' tireless stonemason. *10 km SW on the road to Papatoetoe.*

Awaroa Walkway: The coastal walkway follows beaches at low tide and reserves when the tide is full. As well as astonishing seascapes, the walk encapsulates the country's history, with legacies of the first Polynesian arrivals, the tribal wars, military settlers and World War II all in evidence. *The full walkway, extending from Shelly Park to Musick Point, takes about 5 hours one way. Pamphlet available locally.*

Rangitikei Maps 12,13 Pop. 565 **HUNTERVILLE**

52 km SW of Taihape; 67 km N of Palmerston North (via Bulls).

HUNTERVILLE, a small farming centre on the main state highway, began in 1884 when a store opened here to supply workers clearing the heavy bush, which then covered most of the district.

POINTS OF INTEREST

Hunterville District Settlers' Museum and Art Gallery: Included are collections of tools, farm equipment and sports gear. *Bruce St. Open Friday and Sunday, 2-4 p.m.; other times on request.*

Bush reserves: Reminders of how hard it was to win the now-spruce farmland are several. **Bruce Park** is particularly noted for its magnificent rimu *(3.5 km S);* **Vinegar Hill Reserve**, a splendid picnic, swimming and fishing spot *(8 km N. Continue 11 km beyond the reserve entrance, along Rewa Rd to Stormy Pt, for a magnificent view of the papa cliffs of the Rangitikei Valley)* and **Pryce's Bush**, an area of virgin bush on the banks of the Rangitikei River, with good swimming *(by the Rata Dairy Factory, 9 km S, follow Putorino Rd to its end).*

River rafting: White-water rafting on the Rangitikei river can be arranged; *tel. (06) 382-5747.*

TOURING NOTE

A slower but more interesting route south is to follow the Mt Curl Road, pass through Marton and rejoin the main route. *Turnoff 5 km S.*

Waikato Maps 5, 6 Pop. 6,534 **HUNTLY**

33 km N of Hamilton.

HUNTLY, centre of the country's largest coalfields, is bisected by the Waikato River. It came to be called Huntly Lodge as the first postmaster, James Henry, used an impress stamp he had acquired when employed by the Marquis of Huntly, in Aberdeenshire. Brickworks have been a feature of the town since 1884, with the well-known "Huntly brick" being seen throughout the country. However, since 1960 the brickworks have mainly centred on the manufacture of refractory bricks. Dominating the skyline are the twin chimneys of the Huntly coal-fired power station.

Rahuipokeka, the Maori name for Huntly, had its origins in a quarrel over the fishing rights to the eels in two lakes, Hakanoa to the east and Waahi to the west. The local chief settled the matter by placing a rahui (a mark indicating imposition of a tapu to conserve temporarily supplies of fruit or game) on the west bank of the river and told his people: "While the rahui is there, no-one is to fish the lakes for eels. When I remove it the tapu is lifted. Then the people on the east bank will fish the east lake, and those on the west will fish the west lake." So it proved to be. Hence also the names of the lakes, Hakanoa ("dance of the lifting of the tapu") and Waahi (or Wahi, "dividing into portions").

COAL

Coal was first mined in the locality in the 1840s by a Church Missionary Society missionary, the Rev. B.Y. Ashwell, who had established a mission station on the river bank nearby. Extensive deposits were identified in 1859 by the Austrian geologist, Dr Ferdinand von Hochstetter, during his nine months' assignment with the colonial government. Local coal was used to fuel gunboats on the river during the Waikato Campaigns, with soldiers carrying it on their backs down from the West Mine to the river until a chute was built. After the war the coal was used by river steamers. Mines were then opened on the east bank, and at the turn of the century the various undertakings were amalgamated to form the Taupiri Coal Company.

Tragedy first struck in 1890, when five men died after a collapse in the original mine, and in 1914 the use of naked lights triggered an explosion in the Ralph Mine, in the centre of the town, killing 43 men and proving that the lesson from the tragic Kaitangata Disaster of 1879, near Balclutha, had not been learned. *(The Ralph Mineshafts are beneath the town but no surface features remain.)* On a third occasion, 25 years later, 11 men were overcome and asphyxiated by poisonous gas following a fire in the Glen Afton Mine.

Since 1940, extensive opencast mining has been carried out to both the east and the west of the town, Lake Kimihia being drained in the 1950s. Subsequently, two underground mines were opened, the East Mine (with its headquarters at the old Kimihia Mine) and West Mine No. 1 (to supply the Huntly Power Station).

OTHER THINGS TO SEE AND DO

Huntly Power Station: The country's largest power station stands on the west bank of the Waikato River, whose waters it uses (at the rate of 34,200 tonnes per hour for each of its four units) to cool condensers before returning the water to the river downstream. Completed in 1981, Huntly is a baseload station (i.e. designed to run for considerable periods on full load) with a generating capacity of 1,000 mW. In a full year it can generate up to 50 per cent more electricity than the combined output of all eight hydro stations on the Waikato River. Each unit is designed to run on both natural gas and coal.

Steam is produced under pressure at a temperature of 538°C. This passes through the high-pressure section of a turbine before returning to the boilers for reheating. It is then passed through intermediate- and low-pressure sections before being discharged into condensers, converted back to water and returned to the boilers to commence a further cycle. Exhaust gases are dispersed through two 150-metre, double-flue chimneys. *Signposted. On the river's left bank, across the river from Highway 1. Free tours by appointment; tel. (07) 828-9590.*

Huntly Mining and Cultural Museum ★: An intriguing collection focuses on coal and coal mining with a display of mining gear, coal testing equipment and a replica of a mine face. *Harlock Place. Open daily, 10 a.m.-4 p.m.*

Te Tumu ancestral tree: An elaborately carved block of totara unveiled in 1981 serves as a visual whakapapa (genealogical table) for the young of the Tainui tribes. *Waahi marae, near the power station. Permission from tribal elders must be obtained before the marae is entered.*

ENVIRONS

Rangiriri battle site: A **heritage centre** with audio-visual presentations portrays the significance of the events here.

On 20 November 1863, three weeks to the day after British troops had taken the Meremere positions (near △ Mercer), an attack was launched overland and from the river on Maori entrenchments here. After an artillery bombardment the troops charged the Kingite trenches to capture the outlying earthworks, known as Te Wheoro's redoubt, and defenders of two outlying pa swam and paddled furiously across Lake Waikare to safety. But on attacking the strong, cleverly constructed central redoubt, the British were repulsed with heavy casualties. General Cameron ordered further assaults but these too ended in disaster. Thirty-seven Europeans were killed and 93 wounded in a day of furious fighting, and when night fell many Maori defenders slipped away. Shortly after daybreak those remaining allowed the troops to approach under the mistaken impression that a parley had been requested and were captured without further bloodshed. The **central redoubt**, scene of the most bitter fighting, is preserved on the west side of Highway 1. Double ditches ran down the hill to the river's edge. To the east lies **Lake Waikare**, now a bird sanctuary. **Te Wheoro's redoubt**, also preserved, is about 400 metres to the south-east of the main earthworks.

Visitors can help paddle and learn chants on **waka rides** aboard the *Te Ia Roa*, built for the 1990 commemorations, along what was once a well-used water highway. *17 km N of Huntly.*

Bush tramway rides: Volunteers run small steam engines from Rotowaro up to the coalmining town of Pukemiro. *8 km. First Sunday of the month from April to December.*

Taranaki   Map 7   Pop. 2,839   **INGLEWOOD**

22 km SE of New Plymouth.

INGLEWOOD, officially christened in January 1875, began like other settlements in the vicinity as a milling town set in dense bush. Today the township services surrounding farmland and processes casein and butter for export. The Moanui dairy company, based here, is one of the largest in the province.

At times variously called "Milton" and "Moa", "Inglewood" was finally decided upon, for the town was in a corner, an "ingle", of the bush. The name is still apt, as here the main route north forks to New Plymouth and to Waitara. Behind the war memorial, tucked into the "ingle", is a massive rhododendron.

SOME HISTORY

Migrants from Poland: During the 1870s a significant number of Polish migrants settled in the district as farm labourers. Buying forest land on deferred-payment terms, they engaged in road building and bush felling to gain cash while they devoted their meagre spare time to clearing their holdings. Family traditions vary as to why they came. Some say most came from one vast estate, where conditions were so bad that they opted to emigrate; others suggest that it was a reaction to Poland's Prussian rulers wishing to "Germanise" the Poles.

POINTS OF INTEREST

Fun Ho! Toy Museum ★: A museum of sturdy toys, now collector items, arouses nostalgia in those who can remember the household brand name "Fun Ho!" The small, colourful toys, at first manufactured in 1939 from lead, finally ceased production in 1982 when the lifting of import restrictions allowed plastic to dominate the market. Short re-runs are occasionally offered for sale. *Mamuka St. Open Saturday afternoons or by appointment; tel. (06) 756-8394.*

Pukerangiora Pa ★★: A heavily bushed pa site in a most dramatic setting. *8 km NE. See △ Waitara.*

Kerikeriringa Pa: Situated on a neck of land across the Waitara River from the Tarata Domain, the pa was the scene of an attack by invading Waikato warriors after their repulse at nearby Pukerangiora in 1819-20. A hero of the day, Tutahanga, a renowned warrior, slew four of the attackers before he himself was shot, but despite his bravery the pa eventually fell. *Tarata. 19 km E.*

Northland   Maps 2, 3 Pop. 3,663   **KAIKOHE**

88.5 km NW from Whangarei (via Kawakawa). Information Centre, Cnr Broadway and Kowhai Ave; tel. (09) 401-1693. Department of Conservation Field Centre, 91 Mangakahia Rd; tel. (09) 401-0109.

KAIKOHE is strategically set in level farmland in the very centre of Northland. The name recalls an incident in which a raiding tribe forced local Maori to hide in the kohekohe trees on Kaikohe Hill and to subsist on their berries. At first Kai Kohekohe ("kohekohe food"), the name was later shortened to Kaikohe. Close by are unusual mercury springs, whose warm bubbling waters have long been credited with healing properties by local Maori.

The district was the scene of considerable fighting, both inter-tribal and during the War in the North, when Hone Heke engaged Imperial troops. The British troops suffered two resounding defeats nearby (*see below*). Once hostilities ceased, Heke settled and spent his last years here. The town was for decades little more than a Maori settlement until its development forged ahead after World War I, when nearby land was opened up for returned servicemen.

POINTS OF INTEREST

Hone Heke Monument (1911): The memorial stands on Kaikohe Hill, a good picnic place with a pleasant view of the area. The monument is not to the fighting chief but to his great-nephew (1869-1909), a Member of the House of Representatives for Northern Maori from the age of 24, who also prepared the way for the Young Maori Party. His promising career was cut short by tuberculosis at the age of 40. *Detour 1 km. Signposted at western exit from the town.*

Pioneer Village ★: The growing village includes Maioha Cottage (*c.* 1875); the tiny Kaikohe gaol (1890) complete with graffiti; a Waimate North courthouse (1862); a working bush railway and a blacksmith's shop. *Recreation Rd. Open weekends; weekdays by arrangement.*

Reed Memorial Park: A well-bushed picnic spot. *200 m N, off Broadway. Signposted.*

Aperahama Church (1885): An appealing, steep-roofed building of weatherboard pit-sawn at Horeke, on the Hokianga Harbour. Aperahama Te Awa, a prominent Maori churchman, lies buried in the churchyard. *Taheke Rd.*

ENVIRONS

Ngawha Hot Springs ★★: The soda mercury springs here range in colour from slate to milk, vary in temperature, and are said to have curative properties for a number of skin and rheumatic disorders. The two sets of pools are small and are for soaking rather than for swimming. Exploratory drilling for steam for a possible geothermal power station has been carried out in the locality.

From 1928-34, a British company mined mercury here, but although nearly 20 tonnes of metal were won the operation may have been started only to strengthen the company's bargaining position with Spain, its traditional supplier. For as soon as its Spanish contract was renewed, operations were abandoned. *Detour 2.5 km. Signposted off Highway 12 to Ohaeawai at 6.5 km.*

Lake Omapere: The lake has a depth of only 2.4 metres and is fed by hot soda springs near its south-western shore. Signposted on the lake's edge is the scene of the first engagement between British troops and Hone Heke, in May 1845, two months after the sacking of Kororareka (*pp.* 204-05). It was the first time British troops had operated inland and saw the first of several devastating bayonet charges which inflicted heavy casualties on the Maori but left them, bloodied but unbowed, still holding their lakeside pa. The British lost 14 dead and 40 wounded, the Maori 30 dead and 50 wounded. *The battle site is signposted on Highway 1 at 5 km NW from Ohaeawai; 9 km NE from Kaikohe.*

Ohaeawai battle site: The attack on Hone Heke at Lake Omapere had been criticised as hurried and ill-considered, but worse was to follow when Heke converted Ohaeawai pa into a brilliantly designed fort. In mid-winter 1845, the British attacked, charging up from the valley to the west of the pa site, "the regulation 23 inches between each rank", only to be met with a blaze of rifle fire which felled a third of their number. The pa was later evacuated (it was customary for the Maori to vacate a pa once blood had been spilt in it) and was destroyed by soldiers who were shocked to find the mutilated body of one of their number. He had been the victim of ceremonial cannibalism on the only occasion it occurred during the War in the North. After such a resounding victory, Heke's mana knew few bounds, but six months later the war ended with his convincing defeat at Ruapekapeka (*p.* 117).

In the battle of Ohaeawai the British lost 41 dead and 73 wounded to the Maori's 10 dead.

St Michael's Church (1871), a simple Maori church, stands on a rise to the north of Highway 12, within the scoria walls that are the remnants of the outer fortifications of the pa. *3 km W of Ohaeawai; 9 km NE of Kaikohe.* Around Ohaeawai township itself, pa-sculpted hillsides are much in evidence.

KAIPARA HARBOUR ★   *Northland   Map 4*

NW of Auckland.

THE TENTACLES of isolated Kaipara Harbour probe wide and deep into the dairylands north-west of Auckland. The harbour's serenity gives no hint of the hustle of earlier times, when shipping braved its dangerous bar to ply round the harbour shores with loads of kauri, gum and produce bound for Auckland.

The main highway north from Auckland affords glimpses of the coastline only near Bryderwyn, and the harbour's impressive expanse is better seen from the secondary road between Helensville and Wellsford.

POINTS OF INTEREST

Cruises on Kaipara Harbour run from △ Helensville, including historical journeys of up to 4 hours that retrace journeys of a distant past. Some combine with a **Sand Safari** *to visit old wrecks near Pouto Point, on the northern side of the harbour entrance. Kaipara Cruises; tel. (09) 420-8466.*

△**Helensville★:** A dairying centre, known for nearby Parakai Hot Springs, a spot favoured by Aucklanders. *51 km NW of Auckland.*

Port Albert: Now an isolated cluster of houses on a headland above the harbour, this was once the port for the since-vanished nonconformist settlement of Albertland. Among the last of the "special settlements", it was organised by a young English journalist, William Brame (1833-63), who died not long after his arrival with the colonists, but not before they had completely lost faith in him. A lack of roads, the uncertainties of the tidal harbour and a plague of crop diseases saw the settlement of about 3,000 fail, even though a kauri gum industry had boomed and oyster farming, orcharding and tobacco growing had all been tried. Today the district is predominantly a dairying one.

The Albertland Museum has a collection of photographs and items of local interest and includes an original plan of the town of Port Albert. *Port Albert Domain, 5 km E of Port Albert. Turnoff signposted on road to Wellsford. Open by arrangement. Inquire locally.*

The minute Minniesdale Chapel★ (1867), in a delightful, solitary setting overlooking Kaipara Harbour, has many ties with the Albertlanders. The Chapel's pre-cut framing, coloured glass and bell were shipped from England by the Rev. Edwin Brookes when he followed his three pioneering sons to Albertland. The stylish colonial homestead of the Brookes family nestles in the trees below and is best seen from the road just past the chapel. Minniesdale takes its name from the Rev. Brookes's wife, Jemima, known as "Minnie". *6.5 km S from Port Albert. Follow the road towards Wharehine, turn right into Pah Hill Rd and then along Shegadeen's Rd.*

Brynderwyn: A memorial at the junction of State Highways 1 and 12 is to J.G. Coates, New Zealand's first native-born Prime Minister, buried at △ Matakohe.

Whakapirau: A secluded spot on the harbour shore opposite Pahi. Its deep-water anchorage once saw ships loading kauri for Australian and southern New Zealand ports. *10 km from the main road. Turnoff signposted 6.5 km E of Paparoa.*

Paparoa: A local servicing centre (established in 1862 as part of the Albertland movement) from where Pahi (*below*) is reached. Kauri Bushman's Park includes a dense stand of kauri rickers and offers attractive bush walks and picnic spots. *(Turnoff signposted 1.5 km W. Detour 1.5 km.)*

Maungaturoto: A county town which strings out its small population along a surprisingly long length of highway.

Pahi: The town faces Whakapirau across a narrow inlet and affords excellent swimming, boating and camping. Its old boarding-house seems somewhat incongruous on the wide, grassed domain hard by the beach. There can be few larger than the monstrous Moreton Bay fig tree, also on the domain. *7 km S from Paparoa.*

△**Matakohe★★:** A tiny settlement with a memorial church to J.G. Coates and a splendid kauri museum.

Ruawai: A farming centre, once a port of call for steamers on the harbour, where much swampland has been reclaimed. *30 km S of Dargaville.*

△**Dargaville:** A starting point from which to visit the mighty △ Waipoua and Trounson kauri forests.★★★

Tinopai: A small fishing settlement on the tip of a forested peninsula. With wide views of the harbour and good swimming at high tide, it presents a delightful camping spot. The road from Matakohe to Tinopai passes Hukatere Church (*see △ Matakohe*). *22 km S from Matakohe.*

Pouto: A tiny farming centre at the tip of North Head. Nearby, in hollows between sandhills, a variety of waterfowl nest in freshwater lagoons, ducks, dabchicks, shags and seabirds among them. The sandbar at North Spit proved in the past to be a graveyard for ships, some of whose skeletons are still to be seen.

The century-old kauri-timbered lighthouse on North Kaipara Head was one of the last to be built of wood. In use from 1884-1952, it is now preserved by the Historic Places Trust. *A 2-hr walk starting at the end of Poutu Point Rd, 67 km SE of Dargaville.*

KAITAIA   *Northland   Map 1   Pop. 5,209*

157 km NW of Whangarei (via Mangamuka). Northland Information Centre, Jaycee Park, South Rd; tel. (09) 408-0879. Department of Conservation Field Centre, Pukepoto Rd; tel. (09) 408-2100.

KAITAIA, principal town of the Far North and a shopping centre serving surrounding farmlands, has visibly prospered from the surge of interest in Northland as a holiday area and more particularly from the many visitors attracted by entertaining bus trips run from here to Cape Reinga via △ Ninety Mile Beach. A landmark is the slender needle column of the town's clock tower. Close by, the Yugoslavian Social Club building is a tangible legacy, along with very many of the local surnames, of the kauri gum digging days and the many Dalmatians the fields attracted.

In about January, the annual Ninety Mile Beach Surfcasting Contest is held, a fishing competition with large cash prizes in which novices have been conspicuously successful.

Kaitaia means "an abundance of food".

SOME HISTORY

"The Winterless North": The town was a Maori village when, in 1834, a Church Missionary Society mission station was established by W.G. Puckey and Joseph Matthews on the site of the present St Saviour's Church *(Panakareao St)*. Their graves, along with that of Nopera Panakareao, a local chief who protected the mission and supported the Treaty of Waitangi, are in the churchyard of the present church (1887).

Kaitaia expanded as kauri gum diggers invaded Northland towards the end of last century. Yet as late as 1914 its main street was little more than a country road. After World War I the district, and with it the town, developed rapidly, largely through the efforts of Col. Allen Bell, who coined the phrase "The Winterless North" in his energetic promotion of the region.

THINGS TO SEE AND DO

Far North Regional Museum★★: The museum's small but vital collection includes a splendid display of polished kauri gum, the huge anchor lost by de Surville at Doubtless Bay in 1769 and recovered over 200 years later, a replica of the famous Kaitaia lintel (the original carving is in the Auckland Museum), and a cast of rock carvings fortuitously found near Houhora. Other displays concern the wreck of HMS *Osprey* off the entrance to Herekino Harbour in 1846 and the establishment of the international telephone cable at Cable Bay. *6 South Rd. Open daily.*

Reservoir Hill: From the lookout the view takes in both the east and west coasts. *Okahu Rd, off Redan St.*

ENVIRONS

△ **Cape Reinga★★★:** A pleasant drive to the northernmost tip of New Zealand.

△ **Ninety Mile Beach★★★:** A magnificent sweep of unbroken sand.

Sullivan's Nocturnal Park: In a natural setting of native bush, both glow-worms and kiwi may be seen. Best viewed by night or in the late afternoon. Barbecue facilities. *18 km E, in Peria Rd, near Fairburn: tel. (09) 408-4100.*

Mangamuka Scenic Reserve: An area of bush which includes a small potable soda spring *(29 km S on Highway 1)* and a double-headed korau, a large tree fern *(26 km S).* Both signposted.

Wagener Museum ★ ★: Included are extensive displays of Maori artefacts, natural history, firearms, kauri gum, whaling and Victoriana. Less usual is a collection of early automatic vending machines. There are various working exhibits and the old homestead may be visited. *40 km NW of Kaitaia, at Houhora Heads. Open daily (except Christmas Day and Good Friday), 9 a.m.– 5 p.m.*

The country's most northern golf course is situated here and there is also good camping. *(Tel. (09) 409-8564.)*

Kaitaia Walkway: Originally formed as a proposed roadway early in the century, the track *(9 km)* extends between Larmers Road and Diggers Valley Road. *Start near the Kiwanis Bush Camp, signposted off Highway 1 at 3 km S. Allow 6–7 hrs one way. Boots recommended in wet conditions.* There are splendid views en route. For more experienced trampers the **Mangamuka Gorge Route** *(19 km)* between Takahue Valley and Mangamuka Gorge is a good challenge. *Its principal access is from Highway 1 at the summit of the Gorge, some 26 km SW of Kaitaia.*

ORGANISED EXCURSIONS

△ **Cape Reinga and** △ **Ninety Mile Beach:** Entertaining all-day trips are run to the lighthouse on the tip of Cape Reinga, a revered spot where the spirits of the dead depart down the roots of an ancient pohutukawa tree to make their journey to Hawaiki (*see full legend p.* **189**). A feature of the trip is the journey along Ninety Mile Beach and the bed of the Te Paki Stream. *The round trip cannot be followed privately. The Te Paki stream route, with its potentially lethal quicksands, is closed to the general public. Sand Safaris, 221 Commerce St; tel/fax (09) 408-1778. Departs 9 a.m. daily.*

"Seaspray Trail": From the southern end of Ninety Mile Beach a fascinating trip first climbs into the hills for magnificent views and a stop at the Ahipara Hill Gumfield. It then drops down to the coast to make the return journey along the beach, inside the Tauroa Point reef. There is an opportunity to sand toboggan while awaiting a grilled sausage! *Tu-Tu Tours Ltd; tel. (09) 408-0200.*

TOURING NOTE

Omahuta Kauri Sanctuary Walk ★ ★ ★: A splendid stand of kauri is reached after a half-hour walk through the bush. The bright colours of the rosella parakeet, a native of Australia, may also be in evidence. The largest kauri, Hokianga, stands some 54 metres high and is ranked as the country's eighth largest. An even taller tree, Kopi (at 56 metres the country's third largest) collapsed in 1973. *The carpark is reached from a signposted turnoff 1 km S of Mangamuka Bridge, on Highway 1, at 38 km SE of Kaitaia. The access road, narrow in places, is 13 km long; the last 5 km are within Omahuta Forest.*

Horowhenua   *Map 13*   **★★ KAPITI ISLAND**

6.5 km offshore from Waikanae. Permits to visit from DOC, Wellington (tel. (04) 472-5821). No overnight stays are permitted other than on the privately owned farm. Access is generally by a licensed commercial operator (e.g. Kapiti Marine Charter, tel. (06) 297-2585; Wed to Sun inclusive). Boats can take divers to the marine reserves.

THE SOFT FORESTED FACE which Kapiti turns to the mainland is in stark contrast to the abrupt cliffs of her western shores, where shingled slopes rise a sheer 30 metres from the sea.

Before regaining her pristine peacefulness, the 1,760-hectare island resounded first to the clash of war (as it was here that the warrior-chief Te Rauparaha made his headquarters), and then to the frantic comings and goings of seven whaling stations. During a subsequent farming era, about half of the island was cleared, and the natural reafforestation is of particular interest as it provides a rare example of native forest re-establishing itself in the absence of hoofed animals.

Off-shore lie two **marine reserves** on the confluence of two sea currents, one warm and one cold, whose exceptionally clear waters support a divergence of marine life. Reefs are coloured with yellow and orange sponges, and beds heavy with seaweed feed kina, paua and butterfish.

SOME HISTORY

The "Maori Napoleon": To Cook, Kapiti was simply "Entry Island", an island at the western entrance to Cook Strait, but to Te Rauparaha 50 years later it was the gateway to a dream.

Forced with his tribe to flee his ancestral homelands at △ Kawhia, Te Rauparaha (c. 1768-1849) led his Ngati Toa and related Ngati Raukawa south down the west coast, slaying enemies and winning allies in the year it took them to reach the Horowhenua. There the local Muaupoko were decimated, and once Kapiti had been taken Te Rauparaha was free to implement his plan—to curry favour with Pakeha traders, acquire muskets and embark on a widespread campaign of conquest. His warriors ranged as far south as Kaiapoi (near Christchurch) in the course of campaigns paralleled only by those of the Ngapuhi under Hongi Hika, and Te Rauparaha was inevitably compared with Napoleon—with whom he shared "consummate skill in the art of war ... a lack of inconvenient scruples, and an overwhelming thirst for conquest".

The Ngati Toa chief was careful to preserve good relations with the Pakeha, but could not prevent his Te Ati Awa allies from feuding with Ngati Raukawa, a state of affairs which eventually worked to the benefit of the New Zealand Company settlers at Wellington. For when Te Rauparaha's nephew, Te Rangihaeata (with his uncle's secret support), challenged the company's land purchases, the settlers found Te Ati Awa only too eager to help them in the fighting that followed.

'Suspecting Te Rauparaha's duplicity, Governor Grey arrested him at Plimmerton and held him captive for two years, by which time the old chief's thirst for conquest had subsided.

Although never converted to Christianity (he would sooner discuss the prospects for forthcoming race-meetings), Te Rauparaha actively assisted both Williams and Hadfield in the building of Otaki's elegant Rangiatea Church, in whose grounds he lies buried. *(See △ Otaki).*

Not born to the highest rank and less than 1.5 metres tall, Te Rauparaha won leadership of his tribe through his audacity and the cunning which earned him among his enemies a reputation for treachery. Though his sister, Waitohi, may have masterminded many of his strategies, in the heat of battle the inspired Te Rauparaha invariably turned his enemies' tricks against themselves.

Kapiti is an abbreviation of Te Waewae-Kapiti-o-Tara-raua-ko-Rangitane (signifying the junction line of the boundaries between Ngai Tara and Rangitane tribal lands), a demarcation which the presence of Te Rauparaha rendered academic.

A BIRD SANCTUARY

Kapiti is today a bird sanctuary where are found several species of native birds whose numbers on the mainland are dwindling. As well as the more common forest birds — kaka, parakeet, tui, wood pigeon, weka, saddleback, fantail, robin and whitehead — endangered species such as takahe, kokako, and stitchbird (the rarest of the country's honey-eaters) have been introduced from other parts of the country to Kapiti's more secure environment.

Many varieties of water birds are seen around the coast and on Okupe Lagoon.

POINTS OF INTEREST ON THE ISLAND

Rangatira: An area of about eight hectares of level land where the ranger's house is located is the landing place for visitors. Here can be seen the earthworks of a Ngati Toa pa, traces of a whaling station and the red whare of Malcolm McLean, who farmed the island until 1905. The borer-like pitting of the whare's weatherboards was caused by hundreds of rat skins being tacked on its walls to dry.

Tuteremoana *(521 m)*: An absorbing walk leads to the island's highest point, from which is seen a magnificent panorama of the west coast of the North Island and of the northern reaches of the South. The point was used as a lookout by early whalers, and Tuteremoana means "to keep watch over the sea".

Okupe Lagoon: Situated near the island's northernmost tip, the lagoon is noted for its waterfowl. In 1822 a great battle was fought around the shores of the lagoon when a number of outlying tribes combined to attack the island as they feared the further growth of Te Rauparaha's power. A slave on the island caught sight of a huge flotilla of canoes as they poised offshore for a dawn attack. Quickly he warned his mistress, Te Rau-o-te-Rangi, whose husband, with many of his tribe, was on the mainland. Wasting no time she slipped into the sea, her daughter on her back, and after a perilous swim reached the mainland. Reinforcements rushed across to Kapiti but were in time only to join in the victory celebrations, as the Ngati Toa on the island had already put the attacking force to flight.

KATIKATI

Bay of Plenty   Map 8   Pop. 2,232

39 km NW of Tauranga. Information Centre, Main St; tel. (07) 549-1658.

KATIKATI, with its gaily painted buildings has found a vibrant identity as the "mural town". A painting of "The Pioneer Kitchen" commemorates the centenary of women's suffrage.

Katikati was settled in 1875 by colonists organised by George Vesey Stewart (1832-1920), an Irishman who planned a special settlement of Ulster gentry with himself as its patriarch. However, the settlers found conditions far more severe than Stewart had led them to believe, and it was not until his last years that he won their admiration and respect. It is estimated that Stewart brought over 4,000 settlers to New Zealand.

Today Katikati is a dairying and fruit-growing centre, with a number of dairy farms switched to kiwifruit, which grow prolifically hereabouts. The Morton Estate winery *(Main Rd)* is renowned internationally.

Katikati means "nibbling", and refers to an incident when the captain of the revered *Arawa* canoe is said to have merely nibbled at his food here while his men ate quickly.

THINGS TO SEE AND DO

Sapphire Hot Mineral Springs ★ ★: Fresh thermal pools for swimming or soaking are set in a bush reserve. *6 km. Turn off 3 km S. Open daily, including evenings. Accommodation and camping; tel. (07) 549-0768.*

Katikati Bird Gardens: *Walkers Rd East. Turn off 6.5 km S of Katikati.*

Beach horse riding: Ride along an open, wild ocean beach and, at low tide, cross to camp on Matakana Island. *Arrange through the Visitor Centre.*

Northland Maps 2, 3, 4 Pop. 1,624 **KAWAKAWA**

55 km NW of Whangarei.

THE FARMING CENTRE and service town of Kawakawa is remarkable for its railway line, which shares the main street with more usual traffic. Its solitary service is provided by the J-Class locomotive which chugs its way along the line between Opua and Kawakawa, pausing in the main street here to allow time for a drink at the Star Hotel before returning to Opua. The township began with a small flax-milling industry in about 1814 and settlement was boosted by the opening of coal mines in the 1860s, since closed. Coal was once shipped out through Opua.

Periodically the Star Hotel hosts a chainsawing competition, with races and prizes for chainsaw sculptures.

Bay of Islands Vintage Railway: *Trips to and from Opua take about 45 mins. Two or three times daily in peak periods; reduced service at other times; tel. (09) 404-0684.*

ENVIRONS

Ruapekapeka Pa ★★★: Ruapekapeka was the scene of the final battle in "Heke's War". While the War in the North was raging, Sir George Grey arrived in New Zealand to replace FitzRoy as Governor and promptly ordered all available troops, numbering over 1,600, to attack Ruapekapeka pa.

Here the Ngapuhi under Heke's ally, Kawiti, had built a massive pa. About 90 metres long and 64 metres wide, it had tunnels roofed with heavy logs and earth to connect its trenches and was completely encircled with palisades up to 6 metres high. Several wells ensured that a lengthy siege could be resisted. From here, too, the Ngapuhi could see ships in the bay at Russell.

Smarting under the ignominy of defeats at Lake Omapere and Ohaeawai, the British were anxious to regain a little of their lost prestige. Governor Grey, who personally supervised the operation, on 10 January 1846 directed a lengthy bombardment which battered gaping holes in the palisades. As soon as the first gaps appeared Grey's commanders urged him to attack, but shrewdly Grey continued the bombardment and so avoided a repetition of the earlier British defeats. Hone Heke, who had arrived at the pa only the night before the bombardment began, advised Kawiti to withdraw and to fight the British in the forest where their heavy guns would be useless; but Kawiti was determined to hold his pa to the last. The next day, a Sunday, the British troops stormed the pa, to the astonishment of Kawiti's unsuspecting Ngapuhi, who had naively imagined that the day would be dedicated to rest and prayer. The pa was quickly abandoned and fighting in the forest lasted several hours before the Ngapuhi withdrew.

The British success ended the War in the North, and Governor Grey's Proclamation which allowed the Ngapuhi to return peacefully to their homes was received with gratitude. In the battle the British lost 12 killed and 30 wounded, the Ngapuhi 20 killed and 30 wounded.

Ruapekapeka means "the bat's nest". *Turnoff 16 km S of Kawakawa on Highway 1 and continue 5 km. Signposted. An easier route than the direct road from Kawakawa. The cannon within the pa was used in its defence, and the earthworks and one of the wells give some idea of how extensive the fortifications once were. A total of 20 mins walking is included.* The pa affords far-reaching views of Northland.

Kawiti Caves ★: Owned by the Kawiti family, whose forebear fought with Hone Heke at nearby Ruapekapeka, the caves are a series of caverns set in a massive limestone outcrop and feature a spectacular **glow-worm gallery** and limestone formations. There are also a number of small tapu **burial caves** nearby. *Waiomio. The turnoff is signposted 3.5 km S of Kawakawa on Highway 1. Detour 800 m. Open daily. Daytime lantern tours run regularly and last 30 mins; tel. (09) 804-0024.*

Taumarere Church (1875): The third to be built at △ Paihia, it was moved here in 1925 when it was replaced at Paihia by the present stone memorial church. *1.5 km from Kawakawa on the road to Opua.*

Otiria meeting house: On the marae at Otiria stands the modern (1964) carved meeting house, Tumatauenga. *1.5 km W of Kawakawa.*

KAWERAU

Bay of Plenty   Map 9   Pop. 8,135

32 km SW of Whakatane. Information Centre, Plunket St; tel. (07) 323-7550.

KAWERAU is a planned model town at the foot of Mt Edgecumbe and near the vast Kaingaroa State Forest. The town was built in 1953 to serve the huge pulp and paper mills around which its life revolves. Many of its streets are named after former Prime Ministers and Governors-General.

There is excellent trout fishing in the Tarawera River, and horse riding close by.

TASMAN PULP AND PAPER MILL

The Tasman Pulp and Paper Company's plant at Kawerau is New Zealand's largest exporter of manufactured goods. Its newsprint machines, among the fastest in the world, have an annual production capacity of about 400,000 tonnes. Other products include 185,000 tonnes of chemical pulp for sale, 200,000 cubic metres of sawn timber, 1,000 tonnes of sulphate turpentine and 3,300 tonnes of tall oil. Such products are sold in New Zealand, in Asia and the Pacific, but Australia is the major market.

The principal source of logs is the Kaingaroa Forest from whence 1,900,000 cubic metres of logs a year are railed from Murapara. Tasman is also a forest owner in its own right, currently holding 77,000 hectares of forest land, with a sizeable nursery at Te Teko. The operations are expanding to incorporate a high-tech recycling fibre mill which will recover some 75,000 tonnes of waste paper and processes it into 60,000 tonnes of de-inked fibre. Eventually recycled fibre will provide about 20 percent of the content of the paper produced annually.

Tours daily (1 hr) from the main gate at 2 p.m. (except weekends and public holidays). Minimum age 12 years. Shoes must be worn. Tel. (07) 323-3999.

Beside the Tasman plant is the Caxton Paper Mill, separately owned and operated, which manufactures tissues and other light-weight papers.

ENVIRONS

Putauaki ★ ★ (Mount Edgecumbe) (*830 m*): There is an annual "King of the Mountain" race, and although the record for a race to the summit and back stands at about 70 minutes, most should allow a full day for the climb. To add to the extensive views from the top, an unexpected reward is a swim in the crater lake. The mountain is regarded by the Ngatiawa as a symbol of their tribe and is used as their burial ground. For many years the tribe objected to its being planted by the forestry company. *Start from Centre Rd, off Waterhouse St, off River Rd. A 4-wheel drive safari operates for the less energetic (tel. (07) 323-8755).*

Tarawera Falls ★ ★ ★: Located about a kilometre from the outlet of Lake Tarawera, where the Tarawera River disappears underground, the falls emerge through natural tunnels in the face of a sheer rock wall and plunge some 60 metres onto jumbled rocks below. *Tarawera Rd, off Waterhouse St, off River Rd.*

The road passes near Te Whanautanga-o-Tuhourangi (*5.5 km*), a rock said to mark the birthplace of Tuhourangi, a revered Arawa ancestor. Those who pass the rock should observe the Maori custom of uruwhenua by placing a branch or twig at its base to ensure a safe journey. *Marked by chained white posts.*

Horse treks: Riding through unspoiled countryside is possible at all times of year Others may enjoy delightful walks. *Tui Glen Farm Horse Treks, 2 km; tel. (07) 323-6457.*

Awakeri Hot Springs: Here are soda thermal pools alongside a picnic area and camping ground. *19 km NE of Whakatane on the road to Whakatane. Open daily to 9.30 p.m.*

KAWHIA HARBOUR ★★

King Country   Map 6

60 km W of Otorohanga.

FOR THOSE who seek a remote and timeless corner, Kawhia Harbour has a compelling fascination. Here land and sea blend, and even the jumbled cottages of Kawhia township (pop. 345) seem not incongruous in a harbour whose spell owes as much to isolation as to its languid landscape. There is a small **museum** (*Kaora St*).

SOME HISTORY

The primitive brink: Kawhia's history begins with the arrival of the revered *Tainui* canoe in the Polynesian migration which is said to have brought the Ngati Maniapoto and Waikato tribes to New Zealand, Kawhia being the traditional final resting place of this canoe.

Kawhia is a contraction of the name Ka-awhia given the place by Turi, captain of the *Aotea*, a canoe of the same migration. "Whiawhi" was a ceremony performed by Polynesian explorers as they entered a new land to protect themselves from evil influences, and each phase of the chant used by Turi began with the word "ka".

Well stocked with fish, the sheltered harbour for centuries was the scene of incessant tribal battles until finally, in 1821, a force of some 5,000 raised from the remaining Waikato tribes invaded Kawhia simultaneously by land and by sea, contriving to defeat the belligerent Te Rauparaha and force him to migrate with his Ngati Toa and Ngati Raukawa followers south to △ Kapiti Island.

Gradually traders settled round the harbour and in 1834 the Wesleyan missionary the Rev. William Woon established a mission station at Papa, Karewarewa, on the north side of the harbour. This, however, was abandoned in early 1836. Another station, founded in 1835 by his colleague the Rev. John Whitely at Ahuahu, on the south side of the harbour, was initially even more short-lived but was re-established in 1839.

The township grew into an important timber- and flax-trading centre. Sydney for a time was supplied with much of its grain, and wheat, apples and onions were shipped to the Californian goldfields in the 1850s. Inevitably some settlers purported to buy up large land holdings, and one story tells how the township site changed hands on the fall of a card in a game of pontoon. But when the Land Wars broke out, white traders and settlers were expelled from Kawhia and for 20 years were barred from the whole of the King Country. Once peace was restored in 1881, the Government surveyed the town and auctioned sections without hindrance, but when the Government tried to re-open the port it was for a time frustrated by Kingites, who smashed navigation beacons. A force of 120 was sent from Wellington to avert further trouble.

Since then development has been slow. Kawhia, with the finest natural harbour on the North Island's west coast, might well have blossomed into a major export port, but the dual lack of railway and adequate roading, coupled with Government uninterest and finally the intervention of World War I, saw the chance pass by. So it is that in some ways even today Kawhia may still be described as resting "on the very brink of primitive New Zealand".

THINGS TO SEE AND DO

Te Puia (Hot Water) Beach ★★: Here, as on the Coromandel Peninsula, hot springs well up through the sand. Between low and mid tide visitors may scoop out their own hot pools, the best time being when the tide has turned. *Ocean Beach. Signposted. 4 km.*

"Tainui" canoe's resting place: According to tradition, the *Tainui* canoe (said to have brought the first kumara plants to New Zealand) is buried on the lower slopes behind the Anaukiterangi meeting house. The canoe was buried and two upright stone slabs were erected 23 metres apart, above both bow and stern. The meeting house features the canoe's captain, Hoturoa, on its tekoteko, and on the pou-koukou-aro below him are carved the figures of his descendants. Inside are poupou depicting various *Tainui* tribal ancestors. Of particular interest is Nga-toko-waru *(fifth poupou on right)*, who faces the man he murdered, Te Putu *(fifth on left)*. As a prisoner of the Waikato at a pa on Mt Taupiri, Nga-toko-waru asked as his last wish that he be allowed to gaze upon the face of Te Putu the Great before being put to death. Suddenly he fatally stabbed Te Putu and smeared himself with the great chief's sacred blood, thus rendering himself tapu. Some say Nga-toko-waru was then killed but was spared the final ignominy of being eaten because of the tapu; others aver that because of the tapu none dared touch him, and he escaped. The tribal breach was later healed by a convenient marriage, from which the line of Maori Kings is descended. *Karewa Beach.*

Fabled pohutukawa trees ★★★: Tangi te Korowhiti is the name given to a venerable pohutukawa (which now resembles a clump of trees) which in tradition was used some six centuries ago to moor the *Tainui* canoe. As such it has been venerated by generations of descendants of its crew as the place where their history in Aotearoa began, and as such ranks with the taonga (treasures) of the Tainui tribe. As erosion now threatens the tree, seedlings are being raised from it. Nearby Te Hikitanga was also revered as a tree beneath which tohunga conducted sacred rites, where they built shrines and where, with due ceremony and incantation, they would consult the atua. *On the shore, in Karewa St. Tangi te Korowhiti is at the road's end.*

Kawhia Memorial Church: The church contains miniature panels of the *Tainui* and *Aotea* canoes, from whose passengers most of the Maori on the west coast from Cook Strait to Kaiparā claim ancestry. *Waiwera St, off Tainui St.*

Harbour launch trips: Excursions are run from the wharf out to the heads and round the harbour's shores. *Details at the wharf.*

ENVIRONS

Arawi pa site: It was here that Te Rauparaha made his final stand against the overwhelming forces of the Waikato tribes. A close siege lasted for several months, but as many of the besiegers were related to the Ngati Toa chief, there was an element of sympathy which undermined its effectiveness. The well-photographed peninsula is accessible only on foot and only at low tide. *On the harbour's southern shores. Ask directions locally.*

Taharoa: South of the harbour entrance, at Taharoa, the coast is particularly rich with ironsand. Several hundred million tonnes of concentrate have been sold under a long-term contract to Japanese interests and may return the area's Maori owners as much as $10,000 million. To extract the iron and ship it to Japan, mining rigs, an extraction plant and offshore port facilities were established—and facilities subsequently doubled—so that in recent times what had been one of the most isolated of Maori communities has undergone perhaps the most intense period of social and economic change experienced anywhere since the arrival of the Pakeha in New Zealand. *47 km.*

Oparau: There is a small pioneer museum in Te Kauri Park. *13 km from Kawhia on Highway 31 to Otorohanga.*

KERIKERI ★★★

Northland   Maps 2, 3   Pop. 2,632

88 km NW of Whangarei. Department of Conservation Field Centre, Landing Rd; tel. (09) 407-8474.

KERIKERI is the idyllic settlement of which the city dweller dreams. Tall hedgerows hide the orchards which flourish in the district's rich soil, and people from many countries give the village a quaintly cosmopolitan flavour and contribute to its reputation as a centre of pottery and handicrafts. Kerikeri Basin, close by, with its old mission house, Stone Store and terraced pa, presents a restful scene.

SOME HISTORY

Mission settlement: Like Paihia, the settlement began as a mission station. The Rev. Samuel Marsden of the Church Missionary Society, on his second visit to New Zealand, established the country's second mission station at Kerikeri Basin in 1819 (the first being at Rangihoua in 1814).
    The Rev. John Butler (1781-1841), New Zealand's first ordained missionary, was its superintendent and after more than 18 months of discomfort he moved his family into the distinctive mission house which still stands today. With the Ngapuhi fighting chief Hongi Hika periodically alarming the missionaries with cannibal practices at the pa across the Basin, and with Butler endeavouring to stop Hongi and other chiefs from acquiring muskets, the missionaries' position was precarious.
    However, the mission achieved much of its work with local Maori, and Butler, energetically breaking in the land, became the first to plough New Zealand soil. On 3 May 1820 he wrote: "The agricultural plough was for the first time put in to the land of New Zealand at Kideekidee, and I felt much pleasure in holding it after a team of six bullocks brought down by the *Dromedary* [a visiting naval ship]. I trust that this day will be remembered with gratitude, and its anniversary kept by ages yet unborn. Each heart rejoiced in this auspicious day, and said, 'May God speed the plough'." Appropriately, Kerikeri means "to keep on digging". (In an annual nationwide competition ploughmen compete for a silver replica of the plough used by Butler.) *The plough itself is displayed in the Stone Store.*
    A clash of personalities between Butler and Marsden culminated in Butler's suspension on a dubious charge of drunkenness and his recall to England. In 1839 he came out to the settlement at Wellington and died there two years later.

Citrus orchards: These date from the 1920s when the land was subdivided as part of an intensive development scheme. In Kerikeri's pleasant climate subtropical fruits thrive, and today huge quantities of grapefruit, mandarins, passionfruit, navel oranges, tamarillos, feijoas, kiwifruit and lemons are grown for both national distribution and export. The Orange Centre conducts visitors around its holding on an "Orange-Mobile" (*see below*).

POINTS OF INTEREST AT KERIKERI BASIN

There is a car park by the Kerikeri River bridge, opp. Rewa's Village, and tearooms in an historic setting by the Old Stone Store.

Kerikeri Mission House ★★★: Completed in 1822 and overlooking Kerikeri Basin, it is the oldest building in the country. It was built for the Rev. John Butler, who was able to live in it for only a year. A succession of missionaries followed until finally James Kemp (1798-1872), a member of the original group of Kerikeri missionaries, moved into the house in 1832. It is remarkable that for 142 years the building was lived in continuously by members of the Kemp family, and but for their care it would not have survived. For this reason it is popularly known as the Kemp House. Comparatively few changes have been made through the years. The lean-to (or skilling) at the rear was added in 1834, and the verandah has been renewed twice.

In 1981 the house was inundated by severe flooding when the Kerikeri River burst its banks. In the course of making good the damage, the opportunity was taken to restore the appearance of the house to that of 1840—somewhat more stark than the stylish late-Victorian atmosphere it had previously exuded, but perhaps less misleading in that it dispels any impression of the missionary's lot being rather more comfortable than in fact it was. Downstairs the house is furnished as at 1840 and upstairs to a later period. *Open daily in summer (except Christmas Day and Good Friday). Closed Thursday, Friday, from June–August. Tel. (09) 407-9236.*

Close by, inviting tearooms now occupy a house which traces its origins back to the times of the mission station.

Stone Store ★ ★ ★: The store, presently closed for major conservation works, was built from 1832–35 to replace an old wooden store dating from 1819 which had become a fire hazard. Most of the stone was obtained locally, but arches, quoins and keystones are of Sydney sandstone. By the time the building was completed it was the centre of controversy. It had proved a costly project and as the Maori population dwindled the Kerikeri mission had greatly declined in importance. The Rev. Henry Williams (*see p.* **173**) had vigorously opposed the project and was infuriated by the extravagance of the turret and clock which originally crowned the building.

The store was seldom used as such. From 1842–44 its upper floor housed Bishop Selwyn's library, the Bishop thinking little of walking the distance from Waimate North to consult his books, as he much preferred them to be in the safety of a stone building. In 1845 it served as an ammunition magazine for troops fighting Hone Heke, and by 1853 it was empty. *Both the Mission House and the Stone Store are close by the road at Kerikeri Basin.*

St James Anglican Church (1878): Here are memorials to the missionaries Butler and Kemp.

Rewa's village ★★★: A full-scale reconstruction of a Maori village which recaptures the atmosphere of the average kainga in pre-European times. Traditionally each sub-tribe built a pa (fortified village) on a hilltop or some other easily defended position. In contrast, the kainga (unfortified village) was a temporary arrangement built close to the kumara fields or to other sources of food. In times of peace most would live in the kainga, but in times of danger would desert the kainga for the greater safety of the more permanent pa.

An unexpected feature of the kainga is an almost complete lack of carving. There was never much carving in evidence in the kainga, as tribal treasures were better protected in the pa, and it was there that the more permanent buildings such as the meeting house were built. The kainga here is as authentic as is possible and closely follows sketches made by early artists. It is named for Rewa, Hongi's second-in-command. Buildings such as these also served as the first homes for the earliest missionaries. *Open daily.*

The site of Rewa's actual village is on the opposite side of the Basin.

Kororipo Pa: An historic reserve on the terraced point across the Basin, is associated with the famous fighting chief Hongi Hika (*c.* 1780-1828). There he kept his canoes and thence he set out on his military expeditions. Hongi was quickly impressed with the effectiveness of firearms against the traditional Maori weapons and lost no opportunity in acquiring them for his followers. With them the Ngapuhi wrought devastation as far afield as Wellington and the East Cape.

Hongi appealed to the Europeans who met him as one quick to learn and insatiably curious about European culture and customs. In 1814 he visited Sydney where he met the Rev. Samuel Marsden, whom he later helped to found mission stations at Rangihoua and Kerikeri.

121

In 1820, with the chief Waikato and missionary Thomas Kendall, Hongi visited England and helped to compile a Maori dictionary for the Church Missionary Society. While there he was received by George IV who gave him a suit of chain mail. On his return by way of Sydney he exchanged for firearms most of the presents which had been showered on him by London society as he prepared for fresh campaigns of conquest. In turn the Waikato, the Bay of Plenty and Rotorua were invaded, and Hongi's superior firepower carried all before him in his bid to give New Zealand a single paramount chief and so emulate the King he had met. Wounded at Maungamuka, he died at Whangaroa a year later, in 1828.

The **Kororipo Pa Historic Walk** to the grassed terraces of the pa has a number of interpretative notice-boards. *The 30-min walk to the pa begins 50 m up the Kerikeri Rd from the Stone Store and is rewarded with pretty views of the Basin.*

Other Kerikeri Basin walks: The easy **Wharepoke Falls Track** (*1 hr return*) starts from the road about 100 metres up from St James Church, and leads through bush to the Wharepoke (Booth) Falls. It continues on a further 30 mins to Fairy pools. On the opposite riverbank, the **Kerikeri River Track** (*a good 1 ½-hr walk*) links the car park by Rewa's Village with Rainbow Falls, a distance of 3.5 km. As it follows the river, the track passes Wharepoke Falls and through stands of native bush, among them clumps of kauri and totara. The **Hongi Hika Track** (*30 mins. one way*), shaded by gum trees, links Hone Heke Road with Kororipo Pa.

River trips: Hour-long trips on the tiny MV *Belfast* explore the secrets of the river and the inlet. *Kerikeri Riverboat Cruises, Stone Store Wharf; tel. (09) 407-8276 (after hours). (Limited service in winter.)*

OTHER POINTS OF INTEREST

Rainbow (Kerikeri) Falls ★ ★: Situated on the Kerikeri River, the falls fascinated early artists with their attractive bush setting. Behind the falls is a cave where, according to tradition, a war party successfully hid to escape from enemies. *4 km beyond Kerikeri Basin, off Waipapa Rd. A 10-min. walk from the parking area at end of Rainbow Falls Rd.*

Kerikeri Methodist Church (*c.* 1870): Originally built to serve as the Whangaroa County courthouse, it stood near Whangaroa Harbour. In 1940 it was moved to its present site and rebuilt to serve as a church. The dock was adapted for use as a pulpit, the communion rail once confined the jury and the judicial bench is now a communion table. *On the Kerikeri Basin exit from the town.* The wooded park behind the Methodist Church is a pleasant picnic place named "Fairy Pool", unusual for its large number of gum trees.

The Orange Centre: A working orchard where visitors tour on an "Orange Mobile" and sample fresh orange juice along with Devonshire teas and light meals. *Highway 10, 4 km W of Kerikeri. Open daily 9 a.m.–5 p.m. Tel. (09) 407-9397.*

ENVIRONS

Opito Bay: A bathing beach with a walking track into the **Ake Ake Historic Reserve** (*30 mins.*). *13 km. Signposted off Walter's Flat Rd, beyond Kerikeri Basin.*

Puketi Forest: Acquired by the Government from its Maori owners in 1859 for a mere £125, the forest includes a stand of young kauri. A group of Canadians are recorded as logging here in 1860; rimu logging continued until 1975, and kauri logging until 1979. For the visitor there are pleasant picnic spots and bush walks through stands of kauri to see the remains of old kauri water-dams. *Turn W off Highway 10 (signposted N of the Kerikeri turnoffs) and continue 14 km.* A Department of Conservation leaflet describes a variety walks, short and long.

△ **Bay of Islands ★ ★ ★:** A description of the area is given under this heading.

"As the Spanish proverb says, 'He who would bring home the wealth of the Indies must carry the wealth of the Indies with him'. So it is in travelling: a man must carry knowledge with him, if he would bring knowledge home." *Samuel Johnson*

★★★ KIDNAPPERS (Cape)

Southern extremity of Hawke Bay Map 11

HARBOURING ONE of the world's three known mainland colonies of gannets, Cape Kidnappers resembles the tail of the tuatara dipping gently into the sea. There is a much smaller colony at Muriwai Beach, near Auckland and on Farewell Spit, the northerly tip of the South Island, the birds have recently started to establish a colony. The colony on Cape Kidnappers is the largest and most accessible.

The Cape was known to the Maori as Te-Matau-a-Maui ("Maui's fishhook"), as it was said to be the snare with which Maui foul-hooked his legendary "fish" and hauled the North Island to the surface. The Cape was the hook's point, the sweep of coastline north its shank. *(For the legend, see p. 8.)*

SOME HISTORY

Kidnappers off the Cape: Captain Cook, after his tragic first landing at △ Gisborne, sailed south, skirting the Hawke Bay shoreline, and stood *Endeavour* off the Cape overnight. In the morning canoes came out to trade "some stinking fish". To one trader Cook offered a piece of red cloth in exchange for a dogskin cloak, but after inspecting the offering the Maori paddled off, with both the captain's cloth and the cloak aboard. A little later the same canoe returned; unbeknown to Cook, some of those on board *Endeavour* had planned to capture it as "punishment", hoping to throw a rope over the head of the canoe and hoist it up to *Endeavour*'s anchor. However, the Maori unwittingly forestalled the scheme by seizing Taiata (a young boy-servant to the interpreter Tupaia), who was in the main-chains. Cook's men fired on the canoe—with "an equal chance of killing the Boy or the Thieves"—and in the confusion Taiata dived overboard to be rescued unhurt. Cook noted that "this affair occation'd my giveing this point of Land the name of *Cape Kidnappers*".

Neither Cook nor the others keeping journals on board appear to have noticed the gannets, but two months later, on Christmas Eve, Banks shot several gannets off the Three Kings "to make a Goose pye for tomorrows dinner". Banks noted that the pie "was eat with great approbation", but on 26 December he ruefully recorded: "This morn all heads achd with yesterdays debauch."

CAPE KIDNAPPERS GANNET SANCTUARY ★★★

The gannet is a predominantly white bird, with a golden crown and black-tipped flight feathers. Those usually seen about New Zealand are the Australasian gannet *(Sula bassana serrator)*, which breeds in both New Zealand and south-eastern Australia and ranges from Western Australia to the Chatham Islands. Large seabirds with long, pointed wings and tails and strong beaks, the gannets fly with powerful wingbeats and occasional glides. Most spectacular is their method of fishing, when whole flocks suddenly dive straight into the sea from a great height at speeds of up to 145 km/h.

The birds breed on land, usually on isolated islands, where they perform elaborate and involved mating rituals. Chicks are born naked and grow a white down which, after four months, gives way to grey down-plumage—by which time the chicks are ready to leave the colony for the eastern Australian seaboard, not to return here to breed until four years old.

Gannets congregate at the sanctuary from late July, eggs are laid in hollow mounds during October and November, and chicks appear about six weeks later. Migration begins in February and March, and by April most of the birds have gone.

Access: From **Clifton Domain** the journey on foot can be made only at low tide. Suggested starting times are no earlier than three hours after high tide and, from the Cape for the return walk, no later than four hours before high tide. However, unfavourable wind and sea conditions can reduce these times. It is a pleasant, easy walk of about two hours along eight kilometres of sandy beach. There is a rest hut for visitors 800 metres beyond Black Reef. Visitors then climb a grassed track to the plateau for a close view of the gannets' nesting ground. *Drive to Clifton Domain, Clifton, at the end of the road optimistically signposted "Cape Kidnappers", 21 km SE from Napier and 21 km E from Hastings. Good beach and facilities at the domain. Tide times available from the Visitor Information Centres at △ Napier and △ Hastings.*

Organised Excursions: From **Te Awanga**, a tractor-drawn trailer takes groups along the beach followed by a short climb and walk to the actual sanctuary (*Gannet Beach Adventurers; tel. (06) 875-0898*). Alternatively, 4-wheel drive vehicles leave Summerlee Station and cross farmland to reach the sanctuary. (*Gannet Safaris tel. (06) 875-0511*). The viewing season runs from October to late April.

LEVIN

Horowhenua   Maps 12, 13   Pop. 18,963 (urban area)

94 km N of Wellington. Information Office, Regent Court Arcade, Oxford St; tel. (06) 368-7148.

SET BETWEEN the bush-clad Tararuas and the sea, Levin is marked by streets tree-lined to temper its warm summer weather. Inland, the changing moods of the mountainous Tararuas lend variety to a generally lush landscape.

The surrounding Horowhenua district is predominantly concerned with market gardening and the supply of whole milk to Wellington, but sheep farming prevails on the Tararua foothills. Tuesday is "sale day" in Levin, when through large saleyards pass much of the livestock which feeds Wellingtonians in the coming week. To the south a multiplicity of wayside stalls tempt the traveller with flowers, fresh fruit and vegetables. Local river mouths are popular with whitebaiters.

SOME HISTORY

A railway settlement: Levin, founded in 1889, in common with a number of nearby settlements owes its origins to the construction of the Wellington-Palmerston North railway. The most successful of all the railway settlements, it is named after W.H. Levin, a director of the railway company. *(For notes on the railway, see △ Palmerston North.)*

Woman in a whare: The kink in the town's main street a block south of the Post Office has a local explanation. It is said that there was once talk of widening the road but an old woman who lived in a whare on the corner was so indignant at the prospect of being moved that she armed herself with a shotgun, and vowed to shoot the first man who touched her home.

POINTS OF INTEREST

Factory Shops: A feature of the town is the number of manufacturers offering goods, generally clothing and fabrics, at factory prices.

Thompson House (1922): A pleasant gabled house, used for exhibitions and cultural events, is the focal point of public gardens which include an interesting Begonia collection. *Kent St.*

Lake Horowhenua: Today rowing regattas are held and yachts sail where canoes once paddled. Four of the lake's artificial island pa, built of bundles of fibrous vegetation topped with sand and encircled with sharpened stakes to hole attacking canoes, have now sunk beneath the surface, but two others remain visible—Waikiekie and Roha-a-te-Kawau. The lake bed and the fish are owned by the local tribe of Muaupoko. The lake shore has become a family picnic spot. *Follow Queen St from the Post Office west to its end, 2.5 km.*

Waiopehu Native Reserve: One may picnic here beside dense native bush. *At the end of Queen St East, across Arapaepae Rd. Turnoff by Post Office. 4 km.*

Ohau track: The track climbs into the Tararua Forest Park to link with a wide-ranging network. *Start signposted on Gladstone Rd.*

ENVIRONS

Waitarere Beach: One of the most popular of the district's beaches. Gently shelving, it is ideal for bathing and holds rewards for both line and net fishermen.

Afforestation on the sand dunes which back the beach not only saves adjacent good farmland from the shifting sand but also makes use of otherwise unproductive areas. *(For notes of the process see △ Ninety Mile Beach.)*

A magnet for visitors is the hulk of the Glasgow-built (1865) *Hydrabad* (1,349 tons), a full-rigged sailing ship which in 1878 was blown ashore here while en route from Lyttelton to South Australia with a cargo of railway rolling stock. In the storm her sails were shredded, and when her anchors dragged she was run ashore in a successful attempt to save the lives of her crew.

Pleasant drives along the beach are south to Hokio Beach *(5 km)* passing the wreck of the *Hydrabad (1.5 km)*, and north to the Manawatu River mouth *(8 km— no exit)*. *14.5 km. Turnoff signposted on the main road 8 km N of Levin.*

Hokio Beach: A settlement older than Levin, Hokio was once a Cobb & Co. coaching stop on the beach route north from Wellington. The beach is safe for bathing. A drive up the beach to Waitarere *(5 km)* follows the coaching route and passes the wreck of the *Hydrabad (3 km)*. *10 km from Levin. Turnoff signposted on southern exit from the town. The road skirts Lake Horowhenua (above).*

Papaitonga Scenic Reserve★: The reserve is centred on Lake Papaitonga (Buller Lake), and is notable both for its birdlife and as an historic spot. It was here that Te Rauparaha *(pp.* **115-16***)* was very nearly taken by surprise at a great feast of eels to which he had been invited by local Muaupoko, who rightly feared that he would attempt to dispossess them of their land, and planned to kill him. Te Rauparaha and only one other member of his party managed to escape, by breaking through the walls of the burning whare in which he was intended to die and then hiding in the stream which flows from the lake. Te Rauparaha subsequently exacted a terrible vengeance, returning to sack the island pa, to slay some 600 Muaupoko, and to drive from their land the few who escaped.

With the disappearance of much of the region's bush and swamplands, the reserve has become a refuge for such birds as the Australian bittern, the spotless crake, the New Zealand dabchick and black swan from as far away as Lake Rotorua. *8 km. At Ohau, 5.5 km S, detour along Muhunoa West Rd and take the second road on the right.*

Perenara Maori Craft Centre: Locally made jewellery, woven baskets and carving are on sale. Demonstrations of action songs and haka, and a guided tour of the marae, can be arranged. *Main Rd, Ohau, 5 km S; tel. (06) 367-9312.*

Tatum Park: Headquarters of Scout training in New Zealand, and where top-level management courses are conducted. A small **museum** is open to the public. *At Manakau, 10 km S.*

LOWER HUTT

Wellington   Map 13   Pop. 94,540 (urban area)

14.5 km NE of Wellington. Visitor Information Centre, 25 Laings Rd; tel. (04) 570-6699; DOC Catchpool Valley Field Centre (Rimutaka Forest Park) Coast Rd, Wainuiomata; tel. (04) 564-8551.

THE CITY OF LOWER HUTT, hemmed in between steep hills, sprawls over the alluvial plains of the lower Hutt River valley as far as the Taita Gorge.

The neighbouring borough of Petone, where Wellington's first European settlers stepped ashore in 1840, might today have been the heart of the capital had not the Hutt River flooded and induced the pioneers to move their infant settlement round the harbour to Thorndon. Once Governor Grey had forcibly resolved the land question with local Maori, timber milling began and slowly the valley was cleared of its dense forest. Its rich soil was used increasingly for market gardening as the needs of Wellington grew. Finally the capital, hindered by the lack of hinterland, overspilled; State housing projects flooded the valley with people, and market gardens gave way to manufacturing industries.

Lower Hutt has long been home to a variety of internationally respected research institutions. Its industrial role, too, is of national importance. Large television studios at Avalon are responsible for many of the domestically produced drama programmes.

The city's name contrasts with nearby Upper Hutt and is taken from the river, which remembers Sir William Hutt, sometime chairman of the New Zealand Company.

SOME HISTORY

The Battle of Boulcott Farm: As elsewhere, misunderstandings over the nature and extent of the land "purchases" made by the New Zealand Company led to violence. After an investigation of the transactions, in 1845 the Land Commissioner, William Spain, awarded the company 28,760 hectares at Wellington and in the Hutt Valley, but excluded Maori villages, Maori-occupied land and 39 native reserves. There was much uncertainty as to the precise location of the excluded areas, and a chief of Ngati Tama, with the backing of Te Rangihaeata *(see index)*, had already cut a line across the Hutt Valley, claiming the upper valley for his tribe and stating that Te Ati Awa had had no right to try to sell the area to the New Zealand Company. As tension mounted, war seemed inevitable; the settlers fortified the township at

Wellington and built blockhouses in the outlying areas, including Fort Richmond at Hutt Bridge. Volunteers drilled with flintlock muskets, and defences were swollen with the arrival of regular troops withdrawn from the Bay of Islands at the conclusion of the War in the North.

Before long the troops had high-handedly razed the Ngati Tama's principal village on the banks of the Hutt River (established on land allegedly sold to William Swainson), and the Ngati Tama retaliated by plundering the farmer settlers in the Hutt of all they possessed, leaving them and their families no choice but to straggle back to Wellington.

Despite legal advice that the Ngati Tama's actions were justified, Governor Grey declared martial law, shots were exchanged, and Andrew Gillespie and his young son (who had taken possession of land from which Ngati Tama had just been evicted) were tomahawked to death. It was only a matter of time before the Ngati Toa chief Te Rangihaeata struck.

The blow fell one foggy morning at a stockade at Boulcott Farm in May 1846 when an outlying picket was overwhelmed. Among the defenders was the heroic bugler, 21-year-old William Allen, who seized his bugle in an attempt to give the alarm, only to have his right arm all but severed by a blow from a mere. Incredibly he struggled to his feet once more, his bugle in his left hand, and was still trying to sound a call when he was struck a second and mortal blow. But shots had already been fired by a lieutenant and the main outpost was alerted without the bugle call. After a torrid engagement, the 200 Maori withdrew, leaving six of the 45 defenders dead and four wounded. *The stockade was on the site of the Hutt Golf Club's course; a memorial stone stands on the corner of High St and Military Rd, and a memorial headstone is in St James's Churchyard, Woburn Rd.*

So began the war at Wellington and the campaigns against Te Rangihaeata at Pauatahanui *(see △ Wellington).*

THINGS TO SEE AND DO

Avalon NFU Television Studios ★: A major film and television production complex. *Percy Cameron St. For details of conducted tours tel. (04) 385-6382.*

Avalon Park: The 30-hectare park has an adventure playground with a large lake and canoe, boat and train rides most weekends and holidays. *Between Taita Drive and Harcourt Werry Drive.*

Dowse Art Museum ★ ★ ★: Displayed here is an excellent collection of New Zealand art, with a strong emphasis on crafts — textiles, glass, jewellery and ceramics. The beautifully carved pataka (storehouse), Pataka Whakairo Nuku Tewhatewha, is also of special interest. Changing exhibitions are well displayed. *Laings Rd. Open weekdays, 10 a.m.–4 p.m.; weekends and public holidays, 11 a.m.–5 p.m.; tel. (04) 570-6500.*

Opposite are the Tutukiwi Orchid and Fern House, and a Conservatory.

Percy's Scenic Reserve ★: A tiny bushclad valley where for decades stood J.H. Percy's water-driven flour mill. A bush track climbs to a pleasant vantage point. *Highway 2, S of Melling Bridge, Petone.*

Christ Church (1854): The quaint and minute church, Wellington's oldest, has been carefully restored after being gutted by fire in 1989. In the original pit-sawn timber construction, no nails were used. *Eastern Hutt Rd.*

Marae visits: It is possible to visit a number of Maori marae, the focal points for cultural and social events in Maori life. These include the Waiwhetu Marae *(Puketapu Grove, Waiwhetu; tel. (04) 569-3326)*, the Kokiri Marae *(5 Barnes St, Seaview; tel. (04) 568-7906)*, the Petone Marae *(Wione St, Petone; tel. (04) 568-8220)*; and the Wainuiomata Marae *(Wise Park, Fitzherbert St, Wainuiomata; tel. (04) 564-8395).*

Rata St loop walk: A walk on the eastern hills, behind the suburb of Naenae, offers good views of the valley. *Rata St. Entrance to the left of Wesleyhaven Eventide Home. Allow 1¼ hrs.*

Korokoro Dam walk (Belmont Regional Park): The easiest of the several tracks that thread through lofty pine trees and dense bush on the Belmont Hills. The walk leads to an observation deck overlooking the dam, Petone's original water supply. *Oakleigh St — Maungaraki Rd; park off Dowse Drive, Maungaraki. 1 hr return.*

Markets: Settlers Market *(Jackson St, Petone: weekends)* draws customers from far afield. Of interest, too, is the Station Village Market *(cnr Hutt Rd and Railway Ave: Thursday to Sunday)* and the Homecraft Market *(Horticultural Hall, Laings Rd: Thursday mornings, May to December).*

ENVIRONS

(See also points of interest listed under △ Wellington and △ Upper Hutt.)

Petone Settlers' Museum (Te Whenua Te Iwi o Pito-one) ★★: An interesting museum with attractively presented displays relating to the history of the area. The Charles Heaphy Gallery mounts changing exhibitions. Held here are computerised records of early European immigrants, useful for tracing forebears. *(The Esplanade; open daily in afternoons, except Monday.)*

The building, the **Provincial Memorial** (1940), records the landing of the first New Zealand Company ships and the names of the settlers they carried. The Petone settlement on the harbour's shore (its name a corruption of Pito-one, "end of the sandy beach") might as "Britannia" have been the country's capital but flooding induced the settlers to moved around the harbour to Thorndon (*see p.* **283**). Nearby an Ionian Cross commemorates the site of the infant settlement's first religious service *(on the Esplanade)* and a short distance away lies the grave of Te Puni (*see p.* **298**), the Ati Awa chief who welcomed and assisted settlers *(Te Puni St).*

A **Leisureland** and **Lilliput Fun Park,** well patronised in summer, also operate on the foreshore.

Eastern Bays: See △ Wellington, "Eastern Bays Drive", for a description of the drive along the Petone foreshore to the Eastern Bays, and "Some Short Walks" for walks to Butterfly Creek and to the historic Pencarrow lighthouse.

Wainuiomata Valley: The signposted road over Wainui Hill climbs to afford a spectacular view of the lower Hutt Valley, the harbour and Wellington city. Below may be seen the Hutt Park raceway and the extensive railway workshops.

From Wainuiomata *(6.5 km),* Wainuiomata Valley Road leads a further 21 kilometres to a bleak and wild stretch of Cook Strait coastline. From the road's end, on private property, a half-hour walk leads to a seal colony and to the **Cape Turakirae Terraces** *(stout footwear essential).* Five separate marine terraces or "raised beaches" correspond with earthquakes of 100, 600, 3,100 and 4,900 years ago. The most recent uplift was in 1855, and the highest and most ancient beach was raised 6,500 years ago. Each uplift has made the sea retreat further, to form a new beach and to leave exposed a strip of rocky sea bed cut by the sea. The terrace sequence enables geologists to assess the amount, type and frequency of past land movements, and forms the basis for predicted future movement. Similar terraces were undoubtedly formed elsewhere around Wellington but have been eroded away. The terraces here have survived as they were cut from the hard greywacke rocks that form the core of the Rimutaka Ranges.

Some nine kilometres south of Wainuiomata is the **Catchpool Valley** of the Rimutaka Forest Park, in which are found camping and picnic areas. Several tracks provide good walks for people of all ages. Among them are the well-known Five Mile Track to the Orongorongo River *(4 hrs return and muddy in all seasons),* the Middle Ridge Track *(1¾ hrs return; branching off the Five Mile),* and Butcher Track, a one-hour stiff climb for magnificent views of Wellington Harbour and, on a clear day, the South Island.

Details of walks in the park are available from the DOC Catchpool Valley Field Centre, Coast Rd, Wainuiomata; tel. (04) 564-8551.

MAHIA PENINSULA

Northern extremity of Hawke Bay   Map 10

43 km E of Wairoa.

THE MAHIA PENINSULA is a somewhat barren promontory which separates Hawke Bay from what is commonly, if inaccurately, called Poverty Bay—Poverty Bay is strictly only the small bay in which Gisborne stands, but is loosely applied to a larger area. The peninsula, favoured by campers, affords good fishing, crayfishing and skindiving. Its highest point is Te Kapu *(397 m).* The largest centre is Mahia Beach township, at the southern end of Opoutama Beach.

The peninsula is a typical *tombolo,* an island which, with the accumulation of sand and debris, has "tied" itself to the mainland.

POINTS OF INTEREST

Whangawehi rock font: According to tradition this hollow rock was used as a baptismal font by the Ven. Archdeacon William Williams when no fewer than 245 Maori converts were baptised in 1842. Across the road is a recess in the rock where records are said to have been kept. *On the eastern side of the peninsula on a rocky headland. Signposted 4 km E of Mahia on the Whangawehi Coronation Reserve.*

Mangawhio lagoon: An important wetland area on the narrow neck of land to the north of the peninsula, this is the last fragment of water to survive the continuing filling-in process as Mahia, once an island, ties itself to the mainland.

Beaches: Opoutama and Mahia Beaches are favourites with summer campers, but surfers prefer the waves of Blacks Beach, further south. Everywhere are good spots for fishing and scuba diving.

The peninsula has always been of importance for its abundance of fish. Both in pre-European times and since, Mokotahi Hill was a useful lookout point. At the peak of the whaling activities in the 1830s and 1840s, whaling bases were established on the beach at Mokotahi and across the bay at Waikokopu, whose role in the fishing industry continues to the present day.

Portland Island: Just off the southern extremity of the peninsula lies the island from where the original lighthouse was moved to △ Wairoa. Some time might be spent looking out to sea here, as did the captain of the schooner *Glencairn* in 1891. He reported seeing a slate-coloured serpent near the light, and claimed that it was longer than his ship, fully five metres across, and had a small head and a fin running down its back!

MAKETU   *Bay of Plenty   Map 8   Pop. 755*

45 km E of Tauranga. Information Centre; tel. (07) 533-2343.

MAKETU, once a thriving Maori settlement, is today a small coastal village at the mouth of the Kaituna River.

A major stronghold, Maketu for centuries provided a coastal outlet for Rotorua's Arawa tribe. It was here, too, that the *Arawa* canoe of the Polynesian migration is said to have finally landed.

Maketu is named after a place in "Hawaiki", the Maori's traditional homeland.

SOME HISTORY

Thrice wed: Philip Tapsell (*c.* 1777-1873), a Danish sailor, established a flax-trading post at Maketu in 1828 which flourished for a time but ended seven years later when Te Waharoa invaded from the Waikato and wrecked the settlement. Tapsell, in many ways a remarkable character, was married no less than three times, and by three of the most famous of the early missionaries—Kendall, Marsden and Pompallier.

A hasty return: By 1863 many of the Arawa had gone to the kauri gumfields of North Auckland where they operated a fleet of small ships along the Northland coast. When they heard that some East Coast tribes planned to march through Arawa land in the Bay of Plenty to reinforce followers of the Maori King who were fighting against the Government in the Waikato, the Arawa could not return too quickly. On arrival at Maketu they either ran their ships aground or abandoned them in the estuary in their haste to defend their land. The ships were left to rot, sink and ruin the harbour. Unpredictably the Government spurned their offer of help and refused the Arawa the arms they needed to repel the intruders. William Mair (1832-1912), a visiting magistrate, saw their plight and induced officers at Tauranga to give the Arawa their sporting ammunition and shopkeepers to provide lead from tea-chests for making bullets. So it was that at Lake Rotoiti the Arawa were able to repulse the East Coast war party. When the intruders then attacked Maketu, the Arawa were supported by a small detachment of troops who had converted an old Maketu pa site into the Pukemaire Redoubt. The guns of Pukemaire, combined with the gunboats *Falcon* and *Sandfly*, soon drove the intruders out of their entrenchments near Waihi Lagoon, and the engagement ended with the Arawa pursuing the enemy along the beach to Matata, where a number of canoes were waiting.

POINTS OF INTEREST

"The Monument" (1940): A centennial memorial cairn by the river mouth marks the traditional final landing place of the *Arawa* canoe. The side facing the sea depicts the revered navigator, Tama-te-Kapua, on stilts gathering breadfruits in his homeland Hawaiki. Tradition has it that for generations two trees stood where the stern and the prow of the waka rested on the shore. *By the surfclub.*

St Thomas' Church (1868): The church stands on the site of the first mission station, established in 1842 by the Rev. Thomas Chapman, who also raised the money for the church. In the graveyard is a Government-built memorial to Winata Pekanui Tohiteururangi, a local chief killed in 1864 while leading Arawa tribesmen to the defeat of the invading East Coast force. Behind the church stood the Pukemaire Redoubt that featured in the fighting.

Te Awhi-o-te-rangi meeting house ("the embrace of heaven"): The meeting house stands on the site of the original Arawa pa *(turnoff by the Arawa memorial and bear right).* **Whakaue meeting house** is a well-carved building, largely a copy of an earlier Tamatekapua at Ohinemutu, △ Rotorua. Unusual features are the porch rafters (standing on edge as in a European building), the two carved figures beneath the porch window, and the large carved figure in front of the porch but not part of the pou-koukou-aro. Whakaue is an ancestor of a large hapu of Arawa, the Ngati Whakaue, and father of the renowned Tutanekai. *(A short distance upriver from the township.)*

Taranaki   Map 7   Pop. 992   **MANAIA**

15.5 km W of Hawera.

THE FOCAL POINT of Manaia, a prospering Taranaki farming centre, is a rotunda flanked by war memorials. One is dedicated to the Armed Constabulary killed in local campaigns and bears among others the name of the soldier-artist Major Von Tempsky *(see below).*

To the north lie the Kapuni natural gasfields, from which gas is piped to various parts of the North Island. They also provide oil condensate which is piped to New Plymouth and shipped on to the oil refinery at Marsden Point, near △ Whangarei.

Manaia is named for the captain of the *Tokomaru* canoe.

SOME HISTORY

Guard family incident: The mouth of the Kapuni Stream *(SE, near Kaupokonui Beach)* saw the final scenes of the tragedy now known simply as the "Guard Family Incident".

When the *Harriet,* a trading ship, was wrecked near Cape Egmont in 1834, 12 of her crew were killed and eaten by local Maori. In a desperate bid to save the lives of his family and the remaining crew members, the captain, John Guard *(c. 1800-?),* persuaded his captors to release him and promised to return with a ransom of gunpowder. This the Taranaki tribes badly needed to counter sporadic invasions by their better-armed Waikato neighbours.

Guard made his way to Sydney where his story aroused so much interest that the Governor sent the naval ships *Alligator* and *Isabella* to the rescue, but at no stage was payment of the ransom of gunpowder ever contemplated. The surviving crew members were found at Mikotahi (New Plymouth), where a chief was taken on board as a hostage. The ships sailed south to Waimate pa on the mouth of the Kapuni Stream, where Guard's wife and children were rescued over a period of several days—during which time the pa was wantonly shelled.

To further avenge their murdered shipmates, and as soon as Guard's family were safe, the rescued crew members attacked the Maori on the beach, while soldiers posted on the cliffs above mistakenly opened fire and massacred the Maori. The sailors' attitude seems to have been shared by Guard who, when asked how he would civilise the Maori, is said to have replied, "Shoot them, to be sure!"

The inglorious incident created a furore and was investigated by the British House of Commons.

Guard had earlier founded the whaling industry in Cook Strait in the 1820s, and in the 1840s probably retired to farm land near Kakapo Bay (Marlborough Sounds), where his descendants still live.

BLOCKHOUSES ★★

On the golf course stand two of the best-designed and best-preserved blockhouses, built by the Armed Constabulary in 1880-81 to counter the imagined threat of Te Whiti at nearby Parihaka *(p. 77).* Between the blockhouses is a replica of the original wooden tower known as "The Watchtower of the Plains". The fortifications were never the subject of attack. *At the town's eastern exit, follow signposts to the Manaia Golf Course. There is a pleasant walk through stately trees. The blockhouses are 100 m from the clubhouse. Detour 1.5 km.*

ENVIRONS

Kaupokonui Beach: A popular picnic and fishing spot. *6.5 km SW.*

Te Ngutu-o-te-manu battle site: Te Ngutu-o-te-manu ("the bird's beak") was a palisaded village whose real strength lay in its tangled forest setting, with no roads and no defined tracks into it. It was also the pa of the Ngati Ruahine chief and Hauhau warrior Titokowaru *(d. 1888),* a master of guerrilla warfare ranking second only to Te Kooti. He specialised in surprise attacks and in enticing untrained troops to fight in unfamiliar territory.

To intimidate the Pakeha troops, Titokowaru arranged for a trooper to be ambushed and his body brought here to be cooked and eaten. He then launched a successful surprise attack on the redoubt at Turuturu-mokai *(see △ Hawera)*. To avenge their defeat at the redoubt, British troops moved against Te Ngutu-o-te-manu, but to end the resulting skirmish the Ngati Ruahine faded into the forest, and little was accomplished. But a fortnight later, on 7 September 1868, the same troops, lost in the dense bush, stumbled on the pa again. Totally unprepared they were shot down by unseen riflemen and their commander, Lt-Col. McDonnell, turned defeat into disaster by retreating without properly informing his other commanders. The troops suffered 51 casualties, and as news of Titokowaru's further triumph spread, fresh converts flocked to join him and the Hauhau cause.

Among the dead was Major Gustavus Ferdinand Von Tempsky (1828-68), a Prussian soldier of fortune whose penchant for action had led him to New Zealand by way of Central America and the Californian goldfields. One of the most controversial figures in the Land Wars, Von Tempsky was also an accomplished water-colourist, and his action scenes are held in the collections of the Alexander Turnbull Library (Wellington) and the Hocken Library (Dunedin).

Titokowaru's prestige and influence soon declined as a result of an association with another chief's wife, and after being harried by Wanganui Maori fighting for the Government he abandoned warfare, later to lead peaceful ploughing parties from Parihaka.

The battle site is now a 20-hectare domain and picnic place, mostly heavily bushed, and containing a memorial near where Von Tempsky died. *Signposted 12 km from Manaia, 3 km E of Kapuni on Ahipaipa Rd.* Within sight of the main gates are the Kapuni Natural Gas Plant and Petrochem's urea plant.

Kapuni Natural Gas Plant: *14 km N. See △ Hawera.*

MANGAKINO

Volcanic Plateau   Map 8   Pop. 1,542

71 km NW of Taupo; 37 km SW of Tokoroa; 86 km E of Te Kuiti.

BY THE DAMMED WATERS of the Waikato River at Maraetai, Mangakino bears the unmistakable architectural imprint of a Ministry of Works township. It was built on a semi-permanent basis in the late 1940s and early 1950s to house initially the workforce for the hydro schemes at Maraetai, Waipapa and Whakamaru *(see △ Waikato River)*.

With the schemes completed and construction staff moved on, Mangakino augmented its permanent population with farm and timber workers and retired people. Exceptionally cheap housing, excellent trout fishing and hunting, and the proximity of several hydro lakes on the Waikato River have led a number of people to buy houses here for use as holiday homes.

Hidden deep in the surrounding bush are mystical metre-high ancient posts of carved totara, standing in clearings where, it is said, nothing will grow properly. The taonga are at the corners of a triangular map drawn by a Waikato elder on his deathbed in 1976, to show where unknown influences had triggered unexplainable events.

Mangakino means "bad stream".

MANUKAU CITY

Auckland South   Map 4   Pop. 237,705 (urban area)

22 km SE of Auckland. Information Centre, George Bolt Memorial Drive (2 km from Auckland International Airport); tel. (09) 275-5321.

MANUKAU CITY, stretching from coast to coast south of the Auckland isthmus, is the country's largest city by area and largest local authority by population. However, such is its generally rural character that the visitor may be excused any lack of awareness of its city status. Manukau was predominantly a farming community until after World War II, when Auckland's population exploded and both people and industry spilled south.

Otara: The "new town" of Otara is an exciting and vibrant multi-cultural community. The Saturday morning flea market has a unique Pacific Islands atmosphere, in the heart of the country's largest Polynesian community *(Newbury St, off East Tamaki Rd)*.

Cultural centres: The distinctive brick-and-timber **William Massey Homestead**, set in park lands, became the politician's home in 1890. It now serves as a community and cultural centre, and displays exhibitions. Massey (*see p.* **292**) was Prime Minister from 1912–25. (*351 Massey Rd, Mangere East; tel. (09) 275-0482.*) The **Nathan Homestead**, another cultural centre, also offers relaxed lunches and attractive gardens. (*70 Hill Rd, Manurewa; tel. (09) 267-0180.*)

Rainbow's End ★ ★: An endlessly entertaining adventure park (*see p.* **51**).

MARTINBOROUGH

Wairarapa   Maps 12, 13   Pop. 1,347

19 km SE of Featherston; 19 km S of Greytown. Information Centre, Kitchener St; tel. (06) 306-9043.

THIS SMALL but mellow farming centre is given identity by its central square which has no fewer than eight streets leading into it. Its extraordinary plan underlines the colonists' passionate loyalty for all things British, for when Sir John Martin subdivided a portion of his land in the 1870s, he actually planned the central portion in the shape of a Union Jack whose "cross-bars" are the streets radiating from a central reserve. The streets themselves he named after various places he had visited on a world tour—Venice, Cologne, Dublin and New York among them. St Anthony's Church now stands where Sir John had optimistically planned a railway station.

Two large country fairs (*first Saturday in February and March*) draw many visitors to handicraft stalls in the town square and later in the year local, highly acclaimed wineries draw devotees to "Toast Martinborough" (*November*).

SOME HISTORY

New Zealand's first sheep stations: Captain Cook made the first attempt to introduce sheep to New Zealand when in 1773 he set ashore at Queen Charlotte Sound a ram and a ewe, the survivors of six he had brought from the Cape of Good Hope. The experiment was a failure, for within a few days both had died.

Sixty years later, a number of early settlers and missionaries all had sheep on their mixed runs, but pastoral farming dates only from 1843, when Charles Bidwill (1820-84) left Sydney for Nelson with 1,600 sheep. Many did not survive the crossing, more died from drinking salt water after being landed, and others he sold. But the remaining 350 he shipped to Wellington, and (helped by Hutt farmer William Swainson) he drove them around the coast into the Wairarapa. On a previous visit to the district, made with the partners Charles Clifford, William Vavasour and Henry Petre, both Bidwill and the partners had made separate arrangements with local Maori to lease grazing land. The prospective farmers drove their stock around the coast together, and for some time all were camped on the west side of Lake Wairarapa while they negotiated at length with the Maori to canoe their flocks across. Before a bargain was struck, Bidwill elected to return to Wellington for cattle, and the three partners were actually the first across.

Progress was slow; Vavasour returned to Britain and after three years Petre and Clifford left for land in Marlborough which seemed to offer better prospects. But Bidwill persevered, and today a number of his descendants still farm in the district.

Droughts in Australia during the 1850s meant that sheep, mainly Merino, could be purchased there fairly cheaply. The infant farming industry was further boosted by the decision of a number of Australian squatters who despaired of that country's fickle rainfall to migrate to New Zealand, bringing with them both capital and expertise. They also brought a spirit of gloom and earned the collective description of "The Prophets", as they constantly predicted the failure of the small farmer.

British breeds were also imported and were crossbred with the Spanish-originated Merino which, if excellent for fine wool, were poor breeders and provided indifferent meat carcasses. Quickly the colonial cross-bred emerged as larger, as better breeders and as heavier fleeced, and their success led to the wholesale conversion of Merino flocks to half-bred.

With the introduction of refrigerated cargo ships in the 1880s and with meat-hungry markets on the other side of the world now within reach, emphasis switched from wool to meat, and today's three-tiered system of production emerged. On the high country, with pasture sufficient only for slower-growing sheep, wool remains paramount. The hill areas of both islands are breeding country, in the main dependent for income on wool and the sale of breeding ewes. The remaining "fat lamb" farms principally breed export lambs from ewes bought from hill-country areas each year.

The sheep population today stands at about 70 million. Of these, the breeding ewes are predominantly cross-bred, and for export lambs are mated to one of the established breeds of ram, in the main either Romney or Southdown.

The country's first sheep stations were established on the outskirts of Martinborough in 1844 *(marked by noticeboard 8 km on the road to Lake Ferry).*

THE WINES OF MARTINBOROUGH

Long, dry summer spells render the Wairarapa a very competitive wine-producing area. Some of the world's finest sauvignon blancs are produced by the twenty-odd and growing number of vineyards in the vicinity of the town and several have won international accolades. Most welcome visitors, and at Te Kairanga Vineyards wine may be tasted and purchased in an 1860s pit-sawn cottage. Moved from the township, it was originally built for a farm-worker by Martinborough's founder, John Martin.*The Martinborough Wine Makers Association, PO Box 148 (tel. (06) 306-9495) can arrange tours of the vineyards.*

POINTS OF INTEREST

Martinborough Museum: A small local collection housed in an 1897 cottage. *In the Square, cnr Oxford St. Open weekends and school holidays or by arrangement; tel.(06) 306-9796.*

Ruakokoputuna glow-worm caves: Unlighted limestone caves in which glow-worms may be seen. *18.5 km. Leave Martinborough on the road to Lake Ferry and at 6.5 km turn left along Dyerville Rd. Obtain permission at Blue Creek homestead 1.5 km before the caves. The caves themselves, only about 10 metres from the access road, are signposted. A torch and waterproof footwear are advisable. Tel.(06) 306-9393.*

Nearby is the **Ruakokoputuna Chasm,** a pretty 4-hour return walk into a limestone chasm. *Patuna Farm; (tel. (06) 306-9994.*

△ **Palliser (Cape), Road to ★:** A drive down the eastern side of Lake Wairarapa leads on along the rugged coastline of Palliser Bay. *66 km.*

MARTON   *Rangitikei   Maps 12, 13   Pop. 4,858*

38 km SE of Wanganui; 48 km NW of Palmerston North. Information Centre, 23 High St; tel.(06) 327-6664.

BYPASSED by the main highways and unruffled by through traffic, Marton is the prospering centre of a rich farming district. The town, originally a watering place for stock drovers, was established by private speculators in the 1860s and has been fortunate in acquiring the parks and reserves which were predictably omitted from the speculators' plans. The railway reached Marton in 1878 and once the Wanganui and Wellington districts were linked, survey parties left Marton to establish the Main Trunk Line north to Auckland.

Added significance is given the town by its several nationally known schools— Huntley, an Anglican preparatory school for boys; Nga Tawa, an Anglican secondary school for girls, and Turakina Maori Girls' College conducted by the Presbyterian Maori Trust.

SOME HISTORY

The importance of being Marton: To begin with the town was known as Tutaenui, but at a public meeting in 1869, the centenary of Captain Cook's first landing in New Zealand, it was changed to Marton to commemorate the explorer's Yorkshire birthplace. The change was made less to honour Cook than to rid the town of a Maori name whose distressing meaning ("a dung heap") had only just been discovered.

THINGS TO SEE AND DO

Church of St Stephen (1871-73): The church stands on the site of a redoubt built in 1868 in anticipation of an attack which never came. It was originally planned as a distant imitation of Salisbury Cathedral, but first lack of funds and later alterations caused considerable departures from the intended design. The main timbers are of totara, a feature being the fine interior panelling which at times captures the spirit of stone. *Maunder St.*

Bishop Hadfield (*p.* **169**) died at Marton and lies buried in Tututotara Cemetery at Porewa.

Captain Cook Pioneer Cottage: A small colonial cottage which has no links with the explorer but reflects the origins of the town's name. *Wellington Rd. Open Sundays, 2.30-4.30 p.m., and at other times by arrangement.*

ENVIRONS

Dudding Lake Reserve: A popular picnic, bathing, boating and trout-fishing spot. *11 km from Marton on the Bulls-Wanganui Highway.*

"Westoe": The property which was acquired by the pioneer statesman and reformer Sir William Fox (1812-93) in 1849. Fox had hoped to establish a thriving town named Crofton on his estate *(3 km S of Marton)*, but as thirsty labourers were to be denied alcohol—Fox was later to found the New Zealand Alliance—Crofton could never boast much more than a post office. The remarkable Italianate homestead, of heart matai and totara, with an unusual high tower, was built by Fox in 1874 and was his home for 11 years.

Fox, four times Prime Minister, was in his element when in Opposition but proved an ineffectual leader in Government. Although of idealistic aims, he lacked the ability to translate them into action. Fox was a competent water-colourist, and today his paintings find a ready market. *2 km from Highway 1 on the Kakariki Rd. The property is in private ownership but the magnificent* **woodland gardens and nursery** *are open to the public Tuesday to Saturday, 10 a.m.–4 p.m. or by arrangement; tel. (06) 327-6350.*

*MASTERTON

Wairarapa   Map 12   Pop. 20,007 (urban area)

100 km NE of Wellington. Visitor Information, 5 Dixon St; tel. (06) 378-7373.

MASTERTON, centre of a rich farming district, might well have been "Christchurch", as the New Zealand Company considered establishing a church settlement on the wide plains of the Wairarapa Valley before its offshoot, the Canterbury Association, finally chose a South Island site. Indeed, there is also a visual parallel, as in parts of the valley views across level plains to the abrupt Tararua Ranges are not unlike those charactertistic of the Canterbury Plains. There are some three million sheep within a radius of 16 kilometres.

SOME HISTORY

A Small Farm Association settlement: While most districts are given individuality by war or the quest for gold, the Wairarapa was spared both the scourge of the former and, despite a 30-year search, the blessings of the latter. The manner in which it was settled gives the Wairarapa its distinction.

The first European explorers visited the Wairarapa in 1840-41, at a time when local Ngati Kahungunu were returning from exile in Mahia where they had earlier retreated with their kin from Hawke's Bay. Within four years, Charles Bidwill and others had driven sheep around the coast from Wellington *(see △ Martinborough)* and within a decade runholders had illegally leased most of the Wairarapa coastline. The time had then arrived for closer settlement.

The "Wakefield scheme" of colonisation adopted by the New Zealand Company had made no provision for small runholders. Indeed there was no place in the plan's amalgam of capitalist and labourer for the labourer ever to acquire a holding as large as 16 hectares. So it was that when a controversial and overly aggressive Derbyshire cooper named Joseph Masters (1802-74) arrived in Lambton Quay by way of Sydney and Tasmania, he soon hardened opposition to the "Wakefield scheme" into the Small Farm Association. The association approached the Governor, Sir George Grey, for help. The liberal Grey was sympathetic to their plans as he had himself earlier halved the Crown's selling price of rural land in the hope that the small farmer might then be able to buy it—a wish unfulfilled as large areas were promptly snapped up by wealthy speculators and pastoralists. It was at Grey's suggestion that a party of Small Farmers travelled to the Wairarapa in 1853 and induced the Maori to sell land to the Government. The association, now able to proceed with its plans, drew up rules providing for towns of 80 hectares, with one town acre (0.4 ha.) for each of the first 200 settlers. With each town acre there were to be corresponding suburban and rural sections of 16 and 40 hectares respectively.

Two town sites were chosen, the sections ballotted for, and amid songs and toasts the new towns were named "Masterton" (to honour the founder of the scheme) and "Greytown" (to record the help given by the Governor).

For Masterton there was not the degree of public works that helped to establish Greytown, and there were lean years while land was broken in by farmers dependent from the outset on produce for survival. Matters were not improved by dissension— as one historian has noted, "Whatever they did they did wholeheartedly and when they quarrelled . . . they made the most of their differences." It was not until the 1870s that Masterton drew ahead of Greytown as the centre of the Wairarapa. By this time the "Seventy Mile Bush" to the north was being opened up, rivers to the south bridged, and more prosperous times had come with the Vogel administration's policy of free-spending on public works. During the 1870s, too, the railway advanced from Wellington to Featherston and on up the valley to Masterton—bypassing an irate Greytown.

The first issue to unite the "Small Farmer" and the outlying large sheep runholder was an energetic no-licence campaign. The Masterton Temperance Society was formed in 1877—the year the Masterton brewery opened—and a hard-fought campaign brought local no-licence in 1908 which only ended in 1946-47 with the introduction of licensing trust control. The now-popular concept of local but public ownership and control of taverns began in Masterton, and the town has prospered visibly on the profits. *An embroidered "history" is in the public library (Queen St).*

AERIAL TOPDRESSING

Aerial topdressing, a relatively inexpensive way of spreading fertilisers and weedicides on hill country previously too costly to cover, produced a revolution in farm management. Fully two-thirds of the country's 20 million hectares of farmland is too steep for farm machinery and until aerial topdressing began in earnest its mineral fertility, and so its carrying capacity, had been declining.

The concept of aerial topdressing in New Zealand dates from about 1926 when it was rejected as impractical, and it was only after World War II that tests led to the first commercial aerial topdressing flight. This was made from the Tinui sportsground (near △ Castlepoint) in 1947, when clover seed was spread from a Tiger Moth. Today hundreds of thousands of tonnes of fertilisers and lime are applied annually in this way. In addition, clover is sown, insecticides, fungicides and weed-killers are sprayed, and poison is spread for rabbits and opossums. Aerial topdressing is one of the most important features of the country's farming industry and there are no fewer than 10,000 privately owned airstrips, many serving several properties.

The district's concern with farming is also reflected in the Taratahi Agricultural Training Centre (*Cornwall Rd, East Taratahi. Tours of the farm are available; tel. (06) 378-2116.*)

THINGS TO SEE AND DO

Queen Elizabeth Park: A peaceful corner which includes a cricket oval ringed by tall trees, an aviary, an aquarium with a variety of small fish *(open daily)*, an adjacent deer park and a small lake where boats may be hired. A memorial records the tradition of friendship between Maori and Pakeha in the Wairarapa. *Park St, off Queen St.*

Henley Lake: A recreational lake created in 1988 as a water sports centre, where windsurfing, jet-skiing, dragon boating, model yacht sailing are possible as well as trout fishing. The **NZ Rare Breeds Conservation Society** nurtures rare pastoral animals that might otherwise not survive such a small Irish house cow the size of a dog, and the kuri, a Maori pig of East Asian origin. *Signposted off Colombo Rd.*

Wairarapa Arts Centre: This small gallery, in a centre that incorporates the Wesley Methodist Church (1878), displays touring exhibitions along with its own small permanent collection, which includes a Hepworth sculpture. Of special interest is the **Stidolph Museum of Early Childhood**, a delightful array of items from antique dolls to clockwork toys. *Bruce St, off Queen St. Open Mon–Fri, 9 a.m.–5 p.m.; weekends, 1–4 p.m.; tel. (06) 377-1210.*

Nukutaimemeha meeting house (1908): The meeting house has been moved to its present site from Carterton to serve as the Anglican Maori Mission centre. Named after the mythical canoe from which Maui "caught" the North Island, the whare runanga has carvings portraying the myth in a design copied from a much older house. The tekoteko depicts Maui holding in both hands a carved rope which descends the poutahu (the post supporting the ridgepole) to enter the mouth of a most realistic fish. The fish's tail disappears behind a carved head only to reappear through the head's mouth as its tongue. *131 Cole St.*

"Golden Shears": Masterton is both birthplace and venue of the international "Golden Shears" shearing event, the premier event of its kind and staged annually. With bewildering ease, shearers strip 20 sheep of their wool at the rate of more than one a minute, but are judged on the quality of their shearing as well as on their speed. *First week in March.*

Vintage Aviation Museum ★: The New Zealand Sport and Vintage Aviation Society is housed at Hood Aerodrome and runs **scenic flights** in vintage aircraft. *Turnoff signposted on exit south from Masterton. Usually open Sundays or by request; tel. (06) 377-3466.* Updrafts created by winds crossing the Tararuas provide excellent conditions for gliding, and many records have been set in the vicinity.

Horse-trekking: Guided treks leave at 10 a.m. and 2 p.m. *Windana Run Pony Trekking, South Rd; tel. (06) 378-8985.*

Canoeing: There are possibilities for exploring both the Ruamahanga River in the southern Wairarapa and the Whareama River, towards △ Riversdale. *Kahutara Canoes; tel. (06) 308-8453 and Seven Oaks Canoeing Adventures; (06) 372-3801.*

Marae visits: Maori concerts and marae visits can be arranged. *Details from the Visitor Information Centre.*

ENVIRONS

Mt Bruce National Wildlife Centre ★★★: The Centre, on the slopes of Mt Bruce, is dedicated to the conservation of native wildlife. Here, birds both common and extremely rare are held in the most natural habitat possible. Opportunities are provided for the public to see and study the birds, and captive breeding programmes are carried out to supplement those species which have become endangered or are rare in the wild. Two of the most notable birds are the takahe *(Notornis mantelli)*, a flightless relative of the pukeko, and the black stilt. Rarely seen in the last century the takahe was for 50 years believed to be extinct until a small colony was discovered in 1948 near Lake Te Anau in the Fiordland National Park. The black stilt is now one of New Zealand's rarest mainland birds, with the only known breeding population being in the South Island's Mackenzie Basin.

The kokako (North Island blue wattled crow), saddleback, kiwi, parakeet, native pigeon and falcon are among other species held. A pond within the reserve complex is home to most species of native waterfowl. *30 km N on Highway 2. Open daily, 9 a.m.–4 p.m. Administered by the Department of Conservation.*

En route from Masterton is the **Mt Bruce Pioneer Museum** (*18 km*).

Tararua Forest Park ★ ★: The well-bushed and rugged Tararua Ranges form part of the North Island's mountain backbone and sever the Wairarapa from the west coast. Indeed there is no road over the ranges between the Akatarawa road and the Pahiatua Track. The park has a number of impressive peaks of which the highest is Mitre (at 1,571 metres almost as high as its better-known namesake at Milford Sound). Many impressive tracks thread through the bush and there is a large number of huts. The park covers over 100,000 hectares and, along with its prime purposes of controlling erosion and preserving water supplies, also caters for the differing needs of the timber industry and of the trampers and hunters of the Wellington region. There is good deer and pig hunting. *Full details, hut tickets and hunting permits available from the Department of Conservation offices at Masterton (tel. (06) 378-2061) and Holdsworth Lodge (tel. (06) 377-0022). There are several access points from the Wairarapa Valley.*

For the comparatively fit with a day or two to spare, a marked track leads from **Holdsworth Lodge** above the bush line of the Tararua Forest Park to the summit of **Mt Holdsworth** (*1,474 m*) for superb views of the Wairarapa and the west coast. The track continues along the ridges to the Atiwhakatu Valley (*two DOC trampers' huts*). Shorter walks include those to Donnelly Flat, Holdsworth lookout (*both 1 hr return*) and the Akiwhakatu Valley (*2 hrs return*). There is river-swimming, secluded camping and picnic spots here and bunk accommodation in the Lodge (*tel. (06) 377-0022). (22 km. End of Norfolk Rd. Turnoff 6.5 km S on Highway 2.*)

Honeycomb Rock Walkway ★: The track *(8 km return)* leads along a remote stretch of Wairarapa coastline, with spectacular rocky outcrops in honeycomb formation. A colony of fur seals and the wreck of the *Tuvalu*, which ran aground in 1967 on its maiden voyage, can also be seen. *50 km S. Follow signposts to Flat Point and Glenburn.*

△ Castlepoint ★★: A beachside holiday settlement in an unforgettable setting, with both open surf beach and sheltered lagoon. A diverting race meeting is held on the beach each summer. *68 km.*

△ Riversdale: The Wairarapa's most-frequented beach resort. *56 km.*

△ **Palliser (Cape), Road to** *: After following the main road south to Greytown, the route swings down the eastern side of Lake Wairarapa to reach the savage coastline of Palliser Bay and the North Island's most southerly point. Time should be allowed for the detour to glow-worm caves *(see △ Martinborough)* and for the walk into the Putangirua Pinnacles. *105 km.*

TOURING NOTE

Mikimikitangaotemataongauteretawhaoatawhirimatea: This monument records in its name the surprised look on the face of Tawhirimatea when, in the mid 1860s, he confronted a much larger Hauhau war party than he had expected. Nonetheless, the chief managed to persuade the Hauhau to abandon their venture, and as a result preserved for the Wairarapa the distinction of being the only region in the North Island wholly to avoid bloodshed during the Land Wars. *The roadside monument is by Highway 2, at 13 km N of Masterton.*

MATAKOHE ** *Northland Maps 3, 4*

46 km SE of Dargaville.

MATAKOHE, a tiny settlement on the northern reaches of the △ Kaipara Harbour, is well known for its splendid kauri museum. It also takes pride in being the home town of Joseph Gordon Coates (1878-1943), New Zealand's first native-born Prime Minister (1925-28).

Matakohe means "the place of the kohekohe tree".

POINTS OF INTEREST

Matakohe Kauri Museum * * *: The museum here tells the story of the kauri in its entirety. The collection of kauri gum alone, the largest in existence, is absolutely stunning. The range of colours in the gum is quite extraordinary — red, pink, yellow, amber, black, white — and the gum is exhibited in its many stages from the crude form in which it is found to highly polished, carved ornaments and jewellery. Complementing the gum collection are displays in lifelike settings of equipment used in the kauri gum and timber industries, a smithy and a bushman's hut. Also relating to the era is a reconstructed turn-of-the- century colonial house with period furniture and furnishings. In the Tudor Collins Wing, fine kauri furniture and photographs depict aspects of the kauri industry in a wing panelled with native timbers. *Signposted. A short distance from Highway 12. Open daily, 9 am.–5 p.m.*

Coates memorial window, Matakohe.

Coates Memorial Church: This non-denominational church was opened in 1950 as a somewhat austere national memorial to Joseph Gordon Coates (1878-1943), PC, MC (and bar), who lies buried in his family's plot nearby.

Coates, born and educated locally, first entered Parliament in 1912. When he returned from World War I, decorated for bravery and a national hero, he took up his first Cabinet post and in the vacuum created by Massey's death in 1925 became the country's first native-born Prime Minister (if one excludes Sir Francis Dillon Bell—1851-1936—who served for the fortnight before Coates's election victory). He proved unable to match in deeds the extravagant labels his party gave him during the 1925 elections and in 1928 his Reform Party was defeated at the polls. Although never again to be Prime Minister, Coates's finest hours lay ahead. In the Coalition Ministry of 1931-35 he spearheaded ingenious approaches to the economic upheavals of the Depression, and then in 1940 joined Fraser's War Cabinet to serve as Minister of Armed Forces and War Co-ordination until his death in 1943.

Of note in the church is the small memorial window which shows the soldier-statesman as a knight in armour. The oak in the church grounds was planted in 1887 during celebrations of Queen Victoria's Golden Jubilee. The original church (1867) now stands in a corner of the churchyard and is used as a church hall. *The church stands opp. the museum.*

ENVIRONS

St Michael's on the Hill, Hukatere (1861): The church stands in a lonely setting high above Kaipara Harbour. Inside is a copy of the handwritten agreement between Bishop Selwyn's Building Committee of Mangawai and the contractors who built the Chapel School House for £45. *10 km S, on the road to Tinopai.*

Tinopai: A small fishing settlement on the shores of Kaipara Harbour. *22 km S. Described under △ Kaipara Harbour.*

Kauri Bushmen's Memorial Park: A dense stand of kauri rickers and a good picnic place. *4 km on Highway 12 to Paparoa. Detour 1.5 km.*

Waikato   Map 8   Pop. 5,561   ★ **MATAMATA**

62 km E of Hamilton. Visitor Information Centre, 45 Broadway; tel. (07) 888-7260.

THE ONLY TOWN on Highway 27 — a restful alternative to the main route for travellers going north to Auckland or south to Taupo — Matamata is also a useful base for fishing good trout rivers and lakes, and visiting a plethora of private gardens. The lush surrounding country which the town services is noted for its sheep and dairy products and as the birthplace and training ground of a large proportion of New Zealand's race horses. There are more than 20 thoroughbred horse studs in the vicinity, some of which can be visited.

Matamata means "headland", a reference to Te Waharoa's pa near Waharoa, which projected into surrounding swamp.

Centennial Drive: Running through the heart of the town, from Tainui Street to Broadway, it provides more than three hectares of gardens and a host of appealing picnic places.

SOME HISTORY

Two great chiefs: Matamata was home to Te Waharoa (1776-1838) and his son, Wiremu Tamihana (1820-66), both chiefs of the Ngati Haua. As a child Te Waharoa was captured by an Arawa sub-tribe, the Ngati Whakaue of Rotorua, who lived to regret letting him return to his own tribe, for in 1836 he avenged the murder of a close relative by attacking Ohinemutu and sacking Maketu. The missionary Archdeacon Brown saw the return of the Ngati Haua war party, which was quickly joined by "one of the infant children of our school dandling on his knees and making faces at the head of some Rotorua chief who had been slain in the fighting".

Fearful of reprisals against Matamata, the Church Missionary Society ordered Archdeacon Brown to abandon the mission he had only recently established, but his efforts were ultimately rewarded. For when he established the Tauranga mission station parties of Maori from the Matamata district soon began to visit him there.

Te Waharoa died peacefully in 1838, and Brown wrote of him that he had proved "a remarkable character, fierce, bloody, cruel, vindictive, cunning, brave and yet, from whatever motive, a friend of the mission".

His son, Wiremu Tamihana, seems to have inherited his father's finest qualities. He opposed the Treaty of Waitangi (1840), adopting his father's position: "The land will remain forever to produce food . . . while the blankets will wear out, the axes will be broken . . . and the iron pots will be cracked by the heat of the fire."

Tamihana was a key figure in the Maori King Movement (*pp.* **159-60**)—he was instrumental in having Te Wherowhero elected as the first King, Potatau I. As "Kingmaker", Tamihana officiated at the proclamations of Potatau and later Tawhiao, and his senior descendant has by tradition officiated at every proclamation since. Essentially Tamihana's was the voice of reason, and he frequently mediated in disputes, but within the movement the militancy of Rewi Maniapoto eventually prevailed. He spent the last years of his life pleading for the return of confiscated land, but it was not until 1946 that the justice he sought was finally done and the Government granted the Waikato tribes $12,000 annually for 50 years and thereafter $10,000 annually in perpetuity.

Josiah Clifton Firth (1826-97): Josiah Firth leased an extensive area of land from Wiremu Tamihana and by 1884 held 22,400 hectares. He carried out large-scale drainage of swamplands, built a road to the military settlement at Cambridge and cleared the Waihou River of snags to make the river navigable and Te Aroha a port. He yet found time to write the first-published New Zealand play, a political satire titled *Weighed in the Balance* (1882), but the failure of other enterprises six years later saw the break-up of his vast holdings.

ENVIRONS

Firth Tower Historical Reserve: The Waikato Campaign and the skirmishes with Te Kooti had ended some years earlier, so presumably the sturdy Firth Tower (*c.* 1881) was built as a precaution against any future disturbance. A three-storeyed blockhouse about 18 metres high, and with narrow windows designed for fighting, it was never the object of attack. Firth's imposing homestead was destroyed by fire in 1902, but its replacement that same year is now furnished in the period and, along with the tower, is open to the public. Moved here are the old Methodist Church (1912), an early country post office and a one-room, single-teacher schoolhouse. Paintings, pottery and farm implements are exhibited along with possessions from the Firth family. Also featured is a display concerning the construction of the Kaimai tunnel.

Within the complex, too, a cairn marks the place near where the redoubtable Wiremu Tamihana died. A remarkable meeting took place near the site of the monument *(originally 150 m from its present site)* in 1870 when, both unarmed, Firth met Te Kooti, and tried unsuccessfully to persuade him to surrender. The chief replied, as was his wont, that if left alone he would live in peace, but if harassed he would continue to fight.

Stanley Landing, on the Waikato River where Firth had his port, is an excellent summer picnic place. *(Directions from the Reserve management.)*
3 km on the road to Okauia Springs. Open daily 10 a.m.–4 p.m.; tel. (07) 888-8369.

Opal Hot Springs: The springs, set in parklike surroundings, include private hot mineral pools as well as open-air public baths. The naturally hot mineral waters have curative properties for rheumatic and nervous complaints. There is also accommodation, camping and a neighbouring golf course. *6.5 km. Signposted. Open daily, including evenings; tel. (07) 888-8198.*

As well **jet boats** on the Waihou River operate from the Springs. *Opal Jet Tours; tel. (07) 887-2837.*

Kaimai tracks: There are numerous pleasant walking tracks in the Kaimai Ranges, perhaps the easiest and most attractive being the 3-hour return walk to the 150-metre drop of the **Wairere Falls** *(access from Goodwin Rd, off Gordon–Okauia Rd).* The **Thompson Track** follows a disused country road through to △ Katikati *(full day). Details of all walks from the Visitor Information Centre.*

Gliding: Sample the sky by treating yourself to an inexpensive trial flight in a two-seater glider from the Matamata airfield. *9 km N on Highway 27 towards Morrinsville. Wed, Sat, Sun; Piako Gliding Club; tel. (07) 888-1766. Details also from the Visitor Information Centre.*

Paragliding: The Kaimai Ranges afford a challenging take-off point from which to float down onto the plains. *Details from the Visitor Information Centre.*

Matamata garden safari: The Visitor Information Centre can provide details of private gardens which can be visited, both in the town and in the surrounding countryside. *Most owners need to be telephoned in advance.*

Tangata Marae visits: Day visits by tacking on to a group (and overnight stays) may occasionally be arranged to experience life on a marae at Okauia. *16 km. For bookings tel. (07) 888-7260.*

A key to the maps appears on the inside front cover.

MAYOR ISLAND ★★★

Off the Bay of Plenty Coast   *Map 5*

35 km N of Tauranga. Fishing trips and excursions to the island may be arranged through the Visitor Information Centres at △ Tauranga and △ Mount Maunganui.

MAYOR ISLAND, once a Maori stronghold, is now world-famous as a big-game fishing base. Walks through bush filled with native birds, a number of old pa sites, good skin-diving locations and a one-hour walk to the trig station provide competing attractions. In the island's twin volcanic craters are two lakes, both actually below sea level, one green in colour, the other almost black.

With rare whimsy Captain Cook named the island "the Mayor" in 1769, at the same time as he named the Aldermen Islands, off the Coromandel coast, "the court of Aldermen".

BIG-GAME FISHING

The pohutukawa-fringed island rises 387 metres from a sea which teems with such big fish as tuna, marlin, kingfish, and mako and thresher sharks, whose size has brought a number of world-record catches.

The season for heavier fish begins about late December and lasts to early May. Demand makes it necessary to arrange charters well in advance; enquire at the Tauranga Visitor Information Centre *(tel. (07) 578-8103)*, or any of the charter companies. An international competition is staged annually.

The Tauranga Big Game Fishing Club also welcomes enquiries. (*Headquarters, Sulphur Point, Tauranga (opp. the Tauranga Marina); PO Box 501, Tauranga.*)

Trips to the island are run from △ Tauranga and △ Mt Maunganui, and may also be arranged from △ Whangamata.

Waikato   *Map 4*   *Pop. 219*   MERCER

60 km SE of Auckland; 70 km NW of Hamilton.

THE SMALL SETTLEMENT at Mercer, perched on the right bank of the Waikato River, is seemingly snared between railway and river. To the south rise the six huge chimneys of the coal-fired Meremere Power Station, which closed in 1991. These, which once belched waste gases into the country air, and dilapidated wharf buildings on the opposite bank, recall the town's various past roles as a major generator of power and as a wayport on the river.

The township began as a military settlement at the then-extreme end of the Great South Road and, as it marks the gateway to the Waikato, was the scene of fighting at the start of the Waikato Campaign. Just north of Mercer is the Mangatawhiri River, considered a boundary line by Maori to the south. It was when British troops crossed the stream in July 1863 that hostilities in the Waikato began.

Mercer is named for Captain Henry Mercer, of the Royal Artillery, who died in the nearby Battle of Rangiriri at △ Huntly. In England, Mercer's brother (smarting because he personally had fallen foul of the Duke of Cambridge during the Crimean War) published polemic pamphlets arguing that his brother's death was the result of foolhardiness on the part of General Cameron and of a continuing vendetta waged by the British Army against the Mercer family—"he was sent on a forlorn hope . . . in which success was impossible and death certain".

An iron gun turret from the *Pioneer*, a steam tug which saw fighting on the river, serves as the base of Mercer's war memorial and was at one time used as the local gaol. *(By the Post Office, near the river.)*

Meremere coal-fired power station: The power station was once fired by coal brought by aerial ropeways from coalfields some 10 km to the east, across a swamp. *5 km S of Mercer.*

"My heart is warm with the friends I make,
And better friends I'll not be knowing;
Yet there isn't a train I wouldn't take,
No matter where it's going."
Edna St Vincent, "Second April"

Meremere trenches: Maori artillery on a fortified ridge at Meremere overlooked the Waikato and bombarded the first British gunboats to sail up the river. A combined force of over 1,000 supporters of the Maori King had assembled and for two months resisted the invaders by manning a number of ships' guns loaded with improvised ammunition such as pieces of iron chain and pound weights raided from traders' stores. After several exchanges of fire the positions were reconnoitred and in October 1863 a fleet of gunboats assembled while 600 militia were landed. The Maori unsuccessfully attacked the British land force and then forestalled a two-pronged attack on their positions by retreating across the flooded swamps towards Thames. When the British force reached the Meremere trenches all they found were two heavy guns, a musket and three canoes. A redoubt was then built on the highest point. *The remains of the earthworks of the redoubt, which was superimposed on part of the pa site, are in good repair and may be seen by turning off main highway immediately south of the power station, turning left along Meremere Lane then bearing right to reach the reservoir. A short walk leads to the positions.*

Wangamarino Wetlands ★ ★: A board walk provides access to an important and fragile wetlands area, home to up to 50,000 waterfowl, fernbirds and Australasian bitterns. The vegetation includes bladderwort, ferns, orchids and mosses, some unique to the Waikato region. The boards protect the vegetation, necessary as footprints here can remain embedded for years. *Start by Pylon 72. Causeway adjacent to Meremere power station. Access also from Island Block Rd.*

MOHAKA

Hawke's Bay   Maps 9, 11   Pop. 104 (locality)
33 km SW of Wairoa.

THE THROUGH TRAVELLER tends to think of Mohaka only in terms of the spectacular Mohaka rail viaduct *(seen from the main highway)* which, like a massive meccano piece, spans 278 metres across the Mohaka River at a height of 95 metres. One must detour some six kilometres to find the scattering of buildings which comprise the township of Mohaka, on a terrace high above the papa-walled Mohaka River.

The tiny township has its place in history as it was one of several townships devastated by Te Kooti (*p.* **85**) in the closing stages of the Land Wars.

MOHAKA MASSACRE

On 10 April 1869 Te Kooti suddenly descended on Mohaka from his Urewera retreat, taking outlying settlers by surprise and laying siege to Te Huke and Hiruharama (Jerusalem) pa where the inhabitants, Maori and Pakeha, had fled for safety. Some of his men looted and burned the houses, and those who ransacked the deserted hotel became so intoxicated and behaved so recklessly that they were easy targets for the defenders in the pa. Te Huke pa fell when Te Kooti's men, who professed to make peace, were allowed inside and promptly massacred its defenders. Reinforcements rushed from Wairoa in time to save Hiruharama pa, and Te Kooti withdrew with a large supply of liquor to camp only 10 kilometres inland. The commander of the relief force, when told that Te Kooti's men were drunk and there for the taking, could only dither, and the chance passed.

Te Kooti's men killed 60 for the loss of 10 of their own, with much of the killing being done by Urewera Tuhoe, fighting for Te Kooti because local Ngati Pahauwera were their traditional enemies.

POINTS OF INTEREST

Te Huke pa stood on the lip of the precipice above the river, opposite Mohaka School and marked by a small cemetery. The site of **Hiruharama pa** is close to the curious if unprepossessing ironclad **Round Meeting Hall**. The hall does not seem to owe its shape to Rua Kenana, who built a colourful round temple at Maungapohatu in the Urewera at the beginning of the century, but rather to a need to accommodate ballroom dancers more readily. A local explanation is that previously girls had tended to hide in corners(!) — a tale lent credence by the meaning of Mohaka, "a place for dancing".

TOURING NOTE

Although the township is on a loop road from Highway 2, the easiest approach is from the Wairoa side, a route which also affords a fine view of Hawke Bay and Napier.

140

Hawke's Bay   Map 10   ★ MORERE

40 km E of Wairoa; 61 km SW of Gisborne. Administered by the Department of Conservation; tel. (06) 837-8856.

MORERE, a small settlement known for its hot springs, is set in a 200-hectare reserve. The bush, a remnant of the forest which once covered much of the East Coast countryside, contains groves of nikau palms and is home to a variety of native birds. There is a large, developed picnic area as well as a number of secluded picnic glens, which render it a pleasant spot for lunch. A number of walks of varying lengths, including the **Nikau Loop Track** (*20 mins*), lead through the bush. The **glow-worms** are magical at night.

HOT SPRINGS

The hot springs have both public pools and private baths. The waters, with properties similar to but stronger than those of Poland's Kreuznach Spa, are given curative qualities by calcium, sodium chloride and iodides which slightly tinge their colour. *Open daily, 10 a.m.–6 p.m.* The design of the Nikau Pools has won architectural acclaim.

Morere appropriately means "the waters of life which come into this world from the other world". The pools were frequented by local Maori long before being discovered by Pakeha in 1884.

MORRINSVILLE

Waikato   Map 6   Pop. 5,567

33 km NE of Hamilton. Visitor Information Centre, Thames St; tel. (07) 889-5575.

MORRINSVILLE, centre of a flourishing dairy-farming district, has a number of huge dairy factories within a 25-kilometre radius. Yet its prosperity and fertile farmlands, today among the most intensively farmed areas anywhere, belie the grim struggle of the district's first settlers. The town is home to a flourishing mushroom-growing industry *(tours by arrangement)*.

SOME HISTORY

The town of Morrin: The town is set on the fringe of the Hauraki Plains but today it is difficult to visualise this vast area as being almost totally waterlogged; at times it was possible to travel all over the plains by boat. Indeed, the distinct bend in the main street, Thames Street, at its busiest intersection, is attributed to the original surveyors' being anxious to keep the road to higher ground away from surrounding swamps. Even once the Waikato Campaigns had ended, settlers were not drawn by the challenge of the plains until the railway had pushed across from Hamilton, to increase land values and make drainage seem an economic proposition.

Samuel and Thomas Morrin were among those who took up land and, as was the fashion, at a point as far up the Piako River as boats could reach, laid out plans for a village on their 12,000-hectare holding. But contrary to fashion the brothers' vision has been realised and today the resulting town perpetuates their family name.

In the economic depression of the 1890s, along with so many other large Waikato holdings, the farm property fell into the hands of mortgagees and was sold for less than the brothers had spent on development. To add local problems to a national crisis, the nearby △ Te Aroha goldfields had collapsed. Sheep capable of resisting damp local conditions had not been found (later to prove to be the Romney), and the Waikato soils were unable to sustain permanent pastures or yield animal crops economically. Only the one-man farm unit could subsist without employing labour.

So much Waikato land passed into the hands of the Bank of New Zealand that the bank itself was endangered, and in 1894 legislation was rushed through Parliament in a single night to save the bank with Government guarantees. (It was not until 1945 that the bank was nationalised.) It was the establishment of the dairy industry at the beginning of the twentieth century that revolutionised farming in the Waikato and, coupled with topdressing, brought its present prosperity.

POINTS OF INTEREST IN THE AREA

Rukumoana Pa ★: On a lonely rise, sole sentinel a marble statue, stands a successor to the Kauhanganui (Maori Parliament House) which once stood at Maungatautari, where met the Kingmakers of the Maori King Movement.

In one room a whole wall is emblazoned by a large and venerable flag of the King Movement which incorporates a Union Jack, the names of two *Tainui* canoe descendants and a chief with tattooed face and taiaha in hand. Its symbolism is obscure. The building for a time housed the throne used in Maori coronations, now at △ Ngaruawahia. The statue is of the third Maori King, Mahuta (*c.* 1855-1912). Inscriptions trace his genealogy back to a number of ancestral canoes.

Close by is Werewere, a carved meeting house connected with the King Movement. *Both Kauhanganui and Werewere may be visited by arrangement at Rukumoana Pa. 5.5 km from Morrinsville, along the Kiwitahi road to Matamata.*

Mt Kuranui: A 137-metre climb leads to a panoramic vantage point. *Follow Kuranui Rd off exit to Hamilton and select starting point.*

Morrinsville Museum: Housed in a small 1870s farmer's cottage is a general collection of items of district interest. There is also a Maori canoe once used for carrying flax on the Piako River. *Cnr Lorne and Anderson Sts. Open Sundays, 1.30–4 p.m. and at other times on request; tel. (07) 889-7888.*

Horse trekking: Horse treks through bush and over tranquil cattle and sheep farmland. *Waikato Horse Treks; tel. (07) 887-4779.*

MOUNT MAUNGANUI ★★★

Bay of Plenty   Map 8   Pop. 11,391

5 km NE of Tauranga. Information Office, Salisbury Ave; tel. (07) 575-5099.

OVERSHADOWING the township of Mount Maunganui, and dominating much of the Bay of Plenty coastline, is the bold cone of the Mount. A curious feature, the Mount was once an island but is now tied to the mainland by a long, slim peninsula which built up as an offshore bar. It is on this stretch of sand that the town stands.

Mount Maunganui, called simply "the Mount", was for many years a small settlement known only for the attractions of its splendid Ocean Beach. But with the explosion of timber exports through the port of △ Tauranga, the Mount has paralleled the rapid growth of △ Kawerau and Kinleith (near △ Tokoroa). Deep-water installations were built at the Mount to accommodate larger vessels and today they handle the lion's share of the trade. A large chemical plant uses pulp-mill by-products to produce chemicals for paint, detergent, paper and industrial coatings.

Such growth has changed the town's character and given it substance it previously lacked, but it has not altered the boisterousness of the country's most popular beach resort, whose population in summer is swollen to city proportions.

A bridge across the harbour now links the town to Tauranga, reducing a 20 km drive to only 5 km. Maunganui means "large mountain".

POINTS OF INTEREST

The Mount ★ ★ ★: The climb to the 232-metre summit is rewarded by extensive views along the coastline and passes the ancient earthworks of its fortifications, clearly visible to the south-east. Less challenging but with more intimate views is the wide base track around the mountain.

The Mount was a logical pa site, its natural advantages compounded by a narrow pass which served as the summit's only means of access and which could be held by a mere handful of defenders. In the 1700s a series of minor incidents led a party of Ngaiterangi to attack the pa. Daring strategy was called for and the Ngaiterangi proved equal to the task. They divided into three parties; the first feigned friendship and was admitted by night in to the pa and held the attention of its inhabitants while the second party disabled canoes moored on the beach below. In the meantime the main body arrived by canoe to launch an attack on the narrow pass at the same moment as the party inside the pa began to set fire to its raupo buildings. Of those defenders who managed to escape, many were to drown as the disabled canoes sank under their weight. The victory was overwhelming and the Ngaiterangi were able to conquer the rest of the district. *Allow 1 ½ hrs return to the summit. (The record for the annual New Year's Day race up and down the Mount is about 19 mins!) The base track around the mountain offers an unusual perspective with views across to Matakana Island. 45 mins.*

Hot Salt Water Pools ★ ★: A rare phenomenon and a boon on chilly days. *Adams*

Avenue, at the foot of the Mount. There are active, passive and private spa pools within the complex. Open daily 8 a.m.–10 p.m.; tel. (07) 577-7201.

Ocean Beach ★ ★ ★: The famous sweep of golden sand that has made Mount Maunganui a top summer resort extends for some kilometres along the Bay of Plenty coast and is also reached through Papamoa. *Marine Parade.*

Moturiki Island ★ ★: The rugged little island off Ocean Beach is worth the short walk. A **blowhole** here is spectacular in heavy seas, when water funnelled through the rocks forms a thundering salt-water geyser. *On the point off Marine Parade.*

ORGANISED EXCURSIONS

Scenic flights: Excursions operate from the Tauranga Aero Club's airport at Mount Maunganui. A thrilling flight is over volcanic △ White Island. Flights in a glider are also possible. *Book through the Information Centre or the airport; tel. (07) 575-8768.*

Launch trips: Fishing trips and excursions to △ Mayor and Motiti Islands, and elsewhere can be arranged. *Book through the Information Centre. Row boats and outboards are also for hire.*

MURUPARA

Volcanic Plateau   Map 9   Pop. 2,964

65 km SE of Rotorua. Information from the Resource Centre, Civic Square; tel. (07) 366-5359. Department of Conservation Te Ikawhenua Field Centre, Highway 38; tel. (07) 366-5641.

MURUPARA means "to wipe off mud". The name's negative connotations, however, have not deterred the increasing numbers who come to savour the magnificence of nearby Whirinaki Forest, recognised as one of the most beautiful stands of mature native forest in the country.

KAINGAROA FOREST

The establishment of the Kaingaroa State Forest of over 138,000 hectares—among the largest planted forests in the world—owes its origins to a combination of circumstances. From an economic viewpoint only cheap land, sub-marginal for agriculture, could be used and this happened to be plentiful as the cobalt deficiency in the North Island's pumice lands was not identified until the late 1930s. To this was added the rapid growth rate and high productivity of radiata pine, and finally the cheap labour of the Depression era. From 1923-36 some 270,000 hectares were planted throughout New Zealand, over half by the State and much of it on the Kaingaroa Plains.

Unfortunately the main native forests of rimu, miro, matai, totara and kahikatea regenerate extremely slowly and take up to 700 years to reach maturity. As against this, radiata pine grows rapidly, maturing in about 30 years (two-and-a-half times as fast as in its native California), is easy to handle, is adaptable to varying conditions, and the wood it produces is remarkably versatile. So it is that for economic reasons the main timber-producing native forests cannot be replaced in kind.

Today radiata pine is New Zealand's most important house-building material. It is sufficiently versatile to be used for framing, flooring, weatherboarding and furniture. Lower grades are used for boxing and coreboard, and smaller logs for wood pulp from which paper and fibreboard are manufactured.

Most afforestation is now carried out by planting trees raised in nurseries rather than by the sowing of seed direct to plantation areas. On average, 1,200-1,500 trees are planted to the hectare. The large number planted arises from the need to ensure that only well-formed trees are available for final felling. Wood production can be concentrated on only 200-400 trees per hectare, but the practice varies as the size of the log is not the sole basis for fixing the time for the harvesting of the main crop.

To harvest the wood, blocks of up to 80 hectares are clear-felled and the timber recovered. In some localities seedlings regenerate naturally from seed dropped by the original crop to form a significant part of second rotation stands. However, replanting using seedlings raised in nurseries from genetically improved seed is carried out in the majority of cases, and this may follow either burning or windrowing of logging debris. Planting without the benefit of preparation may be carried out on warmer sites.

143

Maori rock drawings: In a rock shelter a short distance from Highway 38 are drawings of an unknown age, depicting canoes. *8 km W of Murupara. Details from the Resource Centre.*

WHIRINAKI FOREST PARK ★ ★ ★

Remote and timeless, Whirinaki Forest (60,900 hectares) exudes a magical air. Sandwiched between the indigenous forests of the Urewera and the exotic plantations of Kaingaroa, its sense of the primeval in ancient flora and uninhibited fauna have led conservationists to battle for its preservation. From the small, isolated settlement of **Minginui**, walks, short and long, thread through some of the North Island's finest stands of podocarp forest — ancient rimu, totara, matai, miro and kahikatea among them. A favourite is the 27-kilometre **Whirinaki Track** (*overnight hut accommodation midway*) which follows the river from its source. There are longer, tougher tramps, too, and trampers' huts and camping sites are scattered through the park. For hunters, red deer and pigs abound, and there are rainbow and brown trout in the rivers.

Minginui is also the starting point for **horse trekking** and **trail biking**. **Whitewater rafting excursions** and **canoe trips** operate on the Rangitaiki River. *25 km S of Murupara. Turn off Highway 38 at Te Whaiti. Information from the Department of Conservation at Murupara.*

NAPIER ★ ★ ★

Hawke's Bay   Maps 9, 11   Pop. 52,468 (urban area)

325 km NE of Wellington (via Shannon); 144 km SE of Taupo; 21 km N of Hastings. Information Centre, 100 Marine Parade; tel. (06) 835-7182; Art Deco Shop, 163 Tennyson St, Clive Square East; tel. (06) 835-0022

NAPIER, the largest city in Hawke's Bay, whose port handles the province's huge volumes of produce, spreads around the wedge of Bluff Hill, sometimes still referred to as "Scinde Island". Napier was almost completely surrounded by water before the calamitous 1931 earthquake flattened the city but uplifted vast areas of surrounding seabed. As a result of this disaster the city was almost completely rebuilt during the 1930s, giving it an Art Deco style of architecture unique to a New Zealand city and creating a "moderne" look surprising in one of Hawke's Bay's oldest settlements.

The city's equitable climate (in 1994 it set the North Island's record for annual sunshine hours with 2,588) and its considerable investment in holiday promotion render it one of the country's most popular holidaying centres. A **Summer Festival** runs for seven weeks (*from Jan 1*); **Harvest Hawkes Bay**, a celebration of food and wine is held annually (*February*) and there is an *Art Deco Weekend*, much more than simply an architectural event (*mid-Feb*).

SOME HAWKE'S BAY HISTORY

Early European contacts: After Captain Cook had made his unfortunate first landfall at △ Gisborne, he sailed *Endeavour* south along the Hawke Bay coastline as far as Cape Turnagain. Passing Bluff Hill he observed that "on each side of this bluff head is a low narrow sand or stony beach; between these beaches and the Mainland is a pretty large lake of Salt water, as I suppose . . ." A situation which an earthquake was to alter radically some 160 years later.

Cook saw a large number of Maori on the shore—Ngati Kahungunu, who suffered at the hands of tribes who attacked from over the western ranges. When traders followed in Cook's wake, the Ngati Kahungunu's traditional enemies gained prior possession of the musket and drove the Hawke's Bay tribes north to settle about the △ Mahia Peninsula.

So it was that when whalers, missionaries and eventually settlers began to arrive, there were few Maori over the greater part of Hawke's Bay. But the coming of the Pakeha saw the end of tribal warfare and they began to return to their homelands.

One of the first to see the province's farming future was W.B. Rhodes (a whaler-trader at Wairoa) who claimed to have purchased the whole Hawke's Bay coastline and inland for 50 kilometres—an area he estimated as exceeding 600,000 hectares—for a mere £150. Unhappily for Rhodes, he was unaware that the Treaty of Waitangi had been signed, and his purchase was void.

William Colenso (1811-99): Missionaries had visited the area from time to time, and in 1844 the Rev. William Colenso was sent from the Bay of Islands to establish a mission station near Clive. *(A marker near the foreshore indicates the approximate site of the Waitangi Mission, the first mission station in Hawke's Bay. Just N of Clive on Highway 2 immediately beyond the second of three bridges.)*

Colenso was a man of varied and brilliant talents—as a printer at Paihia (1834-42) he produced a bewildering number of publications under the most primitive of conditions; ordained in 1844, he toiled ceaselessly as a missionary, and as a botanist he contributed papers to learned journals, achieved Fellowship of the Royal Society, and gave his name to one genus *(Colensoa)* and many species. An affair with a Maori girl saw him dismissed by the Church Missionary Society in 1852, after which he became prominent in Hawke's Bay political life, and at the time of his death he was considered a leading authority of Maori culture. In retirement he was re-admitted to a Church he had really never ceased to serve.

In the same year that Colenso arrived in Napier (or Ahuriri as it was then known), Bidwill pioneered the Wairarapa sheep country, and by the end of the decade flocks had been established up to the fringe of Hawke's Bay—indeed one flock of 3,000 had been driven north up the coastline from Castlepoint to Pourerere and inland to graze illegally near Waipukurau. But Hawke's Bay itself was all but devoid of settlers, so much so that in 1850 the *New Zealand Spectator*, writing of a search for a murder suspect, described Hawke's Bay as "the Alsatia of the colony, whither all the disorderly and desperate characters resort to be out of reach of the law".

Sir Donald McLean (1820-77): At this time Donald McLean was appointed a Land Commissioner and travelled to Hawke's Bay to purchase on behalf of the Government large blocks of land for settlement. But even in "Alsatia" there was time for civilities, and on Christmas Day 1850 McLean noted that he had fared on "a fine rooster and rice pudding for dinner, with a glass of madeira sent by Mr Colenso".

McLean was born in the Hebridean island of Tiree and when only 19 migrated to New Zealand by way of New South Wales. His purchases for the Government of the Waipukurau Ahuriri (Napier) and Mohaka blocks totalling 252,000 hectares opened the way for pastoral settlement of Hawke's Bay. In 1861 he resigned from Government service to farm his various holdings and, with J.D. Ormond, virtually ran Hawke's Bay until provincial government was abolished in 1876. As a member of successive central governments he held various Cabinet posts up to the time of his death. The Te Makarini (The McLean) Trust for Te Aute College, whose income provides scholarships for gifted students, was established by McLean's son in his father's memory. Honoured by some as a father of settlement in the region, McLean is inevitably seen by others as instrumental in separating vast areas of land from their rightful owners.

Provincial Government: As settlers took up more and more land in Hawke's Bay they began to question the use being made by the Wellington Provincial Government of revenue received from Hawke's Bay land sales. After £20,000 had been received in 1857, less than £1,000 of which was spent in Hawke's Bay, public meetings called for separation, with the result that late in 1858 Hawke's Bay was proclaimed a self-governing province with Napier as its capital. Hawke's Bay was, in fact, the first breakaway province (to be followed by Marlborough and Southland), and its population was so small that in the first elections the top-polling candidate received a mere 25 votes. However, with the proceeds of land sales the new province could develop quickly and without taxation; but land sales as a source of revenue were certain to come to an end, and so by the time provincial government was abolished in 1876 there was little opposition in the Bay.

The Battle of Omarunui: Hawke's Bay south of Wairoa was virtually untroubled during the Land Wars, partly because of good relations between the settlers and local Maori, and partly because the only Hauhau attack was dealt with so effectively.

It was in October 1866 that the small but warlike Ngati Hineuru of Te Haroto and Tarawera assembled a small force and marched on Napier. The band divided for a two-pronged attack, about 100 moving down the Tutaekuri to Omarunui, and a handful of 25 following what is now the road from Taupo. The groups were to attack outlying settlements and then join to sack Napier.

The settlers reacted promptly to news of the approaching war parties and local forces were put under the command of Col. George Whitmore, a retired officer-turned-farmer who was later to lead expeditions against Te Kooti, and against Titokowaru in Taranaki. The Ngati Hineuru at Omarunui were surrounded by night. At dawn, once the ritual Hauhau dances around a niu pole had concluded and after a request for them to surrender had been rejected, Whitmore's force opened fire to kill, wound or capture virtually every one of them. At the same time a company of military settlers intercepted the smaller party in a narrow defile in the Esk valley. Cut off front and rear the Hauhau had no choice but to fight it out, and in a brief and hopeless encounter about half were killed.

It has been suggested that the Ngati Hineuru's rashness in thinking their small bands could successfully attack a well-armed settlement lay in their confidence in the supernatural assistance promised by the prophets of Hauhauism—in particular that bullets could be averted by magical incantations. The settlers of Hawke's Bay were never again menaced. *Memorials in Omarunui Rd and at Eskdale mark the encounters.*

145

Hawke's Bay earthquake: As the citizens of Napier and other Hawke's Bay centres were going about their weekday business on 3 February 1931, at 10.47 a.m. a violent earthquake shook the whole area, demolishing or damaging virtually every building in Napier and Hastings, and killing 256 persons. Both cities were reduced to rubble, and fire followed to complete the country's greatest catastrophe. The main shake was recorded as far away as Kew (United Kingdom), Cairo, Bombay and Calcutta, and waves of tremors (over 580) continued for a further 10 days to hamper rescuers.

Although the earthquake is often spoken of as a "Napier" event, it wrought a trail of devastation from Wairoa to northern Wairarapa, but nowhere more vividly than in Napier. Here, the Bluff Hill cliffs crumbled and the Ahuriri Lagoon was raised to return 3,343 hectares of land from the sea. Today this expanse includes industrial areas and farmland as well as the site of the airport and the suburbs of Marewa ("raised from the sea"), Onekawa ("sour soil"), Pirimai ("joining up") and Maraenui ("great expanse"). Damage was estimated at £5 million in Napier alone, but in material terms the new land proved very real compensation as Napier's expansion had been threatened by a shortage of building land. In seconds vast areas of swampy land and lagoon were reclaimed and a 20-year-old argument over the harbour site resolved.

Larger buildings toppled in Napier included the Anglican cathedral, public library, nurses' home, an old-age home, and a departmental store which collapsed on customers and staff. A service was in progress in the cathedral when its roof caved in, killing one parishioner and critically injuring the Dean. Roads and railway lines all over the province buckled and twisted, and bridges cracked and sagged to further hinder relief work.

Thousands of refugees poured out of the district and thousands more camped in tents hurriedly pitched in city parks. Paradoxically, as a world-wide depression was then gripping the country, the unemployed actually flocked towards the stricken area in search of work, so that the district had to be sealed off, and only those with permits allowed in.

Among the many gallant rescuers were the crew of HMS *Veronica*, fortuitously berthed in Napier's port. Her bell now stands on Marine Parade and is tolled each New Year in memory of the city's debt to her crew.

MARINE PARADE ★ ★ ★

More than any other centre, Napier has set out to capture the bustle and atmosphere of a British seaside resort—while enjoying, of course, a superior climate. Distinctively lined with towering Norfolk pines, during summer festooned with thousands of fairy lights, the Parade has many attractions.
Starting from the southern end of the Parade, the points of interest include:

Hawke's Bay Aquarium ★ ★ ★: Displayed on three floors, with a huge central oceanarium, is a wide range of marine life. Many of the fish are drawn from Hawke Bay itself, but tropical and freshwater fish from many parts of the world are also to be seen. Occasionally skindivers venture into the main tank to feed sharks by hand *(usually at 3.15 p.m. at weekends, during public holidays and at peak periods)*. On top of the building is a camera obscura, a series of lenses which rotate slowly to throw an ever-changing panorama of the coastline on to a screen. *Open daily (except Christmas Day) from 9 a.m.–5 p.m.; extended evening hours in summer holidays; tel. (06) 834-4196.* To the north is a boating lake.

Marineland ★ ★ ★: A spectacular show is staged regularly, when dolphins, seals and other mammals give remarkable demonstrations of the rapport they enjoy with their keepers. Other marine life which may be seen includes penguins, otters, sea lions, and gannets. *Open daily from 10 a.m.–4.30 p.m.; performances at 10.30 a.m. and 2 p.m., lasting about ¾ hr; additional performances at peak periods; tel. (06) 834-4195.* It is also possible to swim with the dolphins.

The Stables Museum: Across the Parade, opposite Marineland, is the Stables complex where at **Earthquake '31** one may in safety experience a major earthquake and see both historic film footage and static displays of the catastrophe of 1931. A **Waxworks Museum** portrays scenes from the past. *60 Marine Pde. Open daily.*

Colonnade: Proceeding northwards, a skating rink, sunken garden, putt-putt golf course and soundshell (as well as the Public Relations Office) are passed before reaching the Colonnade, which resembles the skeleton of some incomplete Mediterranean villa. In its sun bay is the *Veronica*'s ship's bell, with which each New Year is "rung in". The memorial to the earthquake is a fitting one, for in the aftermath the rubble of demolished buildings was swept into the sea to reclaim the land hereabouts.

Hawke's Bay Art Gallery and Museum★★★: The museum features "Nga Tukemata — The Treasures of Ngati Kahungunu", an innovative exhibition (including an audio-visual display) of the art and mana of the Kahungunu of the eastern North Island. Also of special interest are displays of photographs and cryptic reports of local newspapers — with advice on drinking water, food distribution and sanitary measures interspersed between casualty lists which, along with a second audio-visual presentation, recaptures something of the magnitude and horror of the 1931 earthquake.

Also illustrated is the emergence from the rubble of "the newest city on the globe" with its unique Art Deco air.

Changing art exhibitions include works by local and overseas artists. The craft collection covers contemporary ceramics and glass, and decorative arts range from the seventeenth century to the Art Deco period. Books, manuscripts and photographs record the history of Hawke's Bay. The **Harold Berry Historical Reference Library** (*open Tues–Fri, 12.30–4.30 p.m.*), within the museum complex, is the Regional Archives Repository. *65 Marine Parade. Open daily Mon–Fri, 10 a.m.–4.30 p.m.; weekends and public holidays, 1.00–4.30 p.m.; tel. (06) 835-7781.*

Statue of Pania: There are three statues on the Parade: the "Spirit of Napier" rising to the south; the fishermen hauling in their catch by the Aquarium, and Pania of the Reef.

As Rotorua has its legend of Tutanekei and Hinemoa, so too has Napier its Pania. Pania was a member of the Sea People but left them to dwell on land with her human lover, Karitoki. Her people were constantly calling her to return and finally, when their call grew irresistible, Pania swam out to meet them for one last time. But her people drew her down into the caverns of the sea and would not let her return to the land and her lover. Today, when passing over an offshore reef, the fanciful may see in the depths Pania with her arms outstretched, still striving to return to Karitoki.

Kiwi House★★★: Beyond the floral clock and the swimming pool is a well-designed nocturnal room where the visitor may see, perhaps for the first time, such creatures of the night as the kiwi, the bush gecko and native land snails. *Open daily, 11 a.m.-3 p.m.; live kiwi show, 1 p.m.; feeding, 2 p.m.; tel. (06) 835-7553.*

OTHER THINGS TO SEE AND DO

Bluff Hill viewpoints ★★★: The Bluff Hill Lookout offers fine views of the Hawke's Bay coastline, north to Mahia Peninsula and south to Cape Kidnappers. The viewpoint looks precipitously down on the wharves, but towering gum trees screen the view of the city itself. Steps lead to an elevated viewing platform atop World War II gun emplacements. *Signposted off Lighthouse Rd.*

On a lower ridge is the City Lookout, from which an intimate view of the city and Marine Parade is obtained. By night it is an excellent vantage point from which to photograph the illuminations. *Clyde Rd.*

Botanic Gardens ★★: The gardens spill down the slopes of the Hospital Hill from the crest where the barracks of the 65th Regiment have given way to the hospital. Zig-zagging down, trees give way to formal gardens and a natural amphitheatre where open-air concerts are staged. By the amphitheatre is an aviary which houses unusual budgerigars and other birds. *Bounded by Napier and Simla Tces, and Spencer and Chaucer Rds.*

Neighbouring the gardens is the old cemetery, some of whose headstones read like an early edition of *Who's Who.* Immediately inside the main gate lies Major-General Sir George Stoddart Whitmore (1830-1903), who led the campaigns against Te Kooti and Titokowaru, and accompanied Sir George Grey to Parihaka in 1879 in an attempt to reconcile Te Whiti. Next is the grave of the Rev. William Colenso (1811-99), the country's first printer and Hawke's Bay's first missionary *(see above).* In a group lie members of the Williams family, among them no fewer than three bishops. The brothers Henry and William Williams were among the country's first missionaries. Of more local interest are the graves of Henry Morrison, a casualty of the Battle of Omarunui, and Sir Donald McLean (1820-77), the Land Purchase Commissioner who opened up the province of which he later became Superintendent. *Enter from Napier Tce.*

Art Deco walk: A leaflet describing in detail an hour-long walk through a group of some of the world's finest small Art Deco buildings, issued by a trust dedicated to their protection, is available locally. Intriguing is the occasional use of stylised Maori motifs (e.g. the old BNZ building, *cnr Hastings and Emerson Sts*). *Leaflet from the Art Deco Shop, 163 Tennyson St, Clive Square East; tel. (06) 835-0022 or the Visitor Information Centre. (See also "Organised excursions", below.)*

Waiapu Cathedral: The Cathedral Church of St John the Evangelist epitomises the renaissance of Napier. As the city rumbled, the old cathedral crumbled, critically injuring the Dean and killing one parishioner. Like the city, the new cathedral has risen from the rubble of the old. By the entrance porch is the original foundation stone (1886), and above it a stained-glass window built of fragments of glass retrieved from the ruins.

In the nave is a Cross of fourteenth-century nails, a gift from Coventry Cathedral (bombed in 1940), from one ruined cathedral to another in the expectation (since fulfilled) that both would rise again.

The south ambulatory leads from behind the lectern (one of the few furnishings rescued from the old cathedral and bearing a Bible autographed by Queen Elizabeth II). It passes a number of plaques, including one erected by fellow colonists to honour two Land War victims, and one by parishioners to commemorate the worshipper "who died amidst the ruins" in the earthquake. It leads to a tiny Maori Chapel, dedicated to the Maori leaders the Rt. Rev. Frederick Bennett (first Maori Bishop and Bishop of Aotearoa) and Sir Apirana Ngata, whose widow wove the cover for the bishop's chair. Along the top panel of the chair, whose decor is otherwise traditional, is carved an interpretation of the Last Supper.

In front of the cathedral is the illuminated Tait Fountain. *Tennyson St.*

Kennedy Park Rose Garden: Over 3,000 bushes present a multi-coloured spectacle. *Storkey St, off Kennedy Rd.* Adjacent is a motor camp.

The Iron Pot: A quaintly named inlet now dredged to form a cosy anchorage for a variety of small craft. It owes its name to early whalers who were reminded of a similar feature in Hobart, Tasmania. The whalers themselves are remembered by a tripot from the Tangoio Whaling Station (*c.* 1870).

At the time of the earthquake HMS *Veronica* was moored at West Quay, around the southern lip of the Iron Pot. The ship was all but left high and dry as the seabed rosé beneath her. On the opposite lip, the Hawke's Bay Game and Offshore Fishing Club has its headquarters.

The Iron Pot is in Ahuriri, the suburb with the city's oldest houses and which bears the original name for Napier.
Leave on Highway 2 proceeding north. At the Pandora Rd–Hyderabad Rd intersection continue straight ahead, bearing right to reach Customs Quay.

ENVIRONS

△ **Cape Kidnappers Gannet Sanctuary** ★ ★ ★: A mainland gannetry, rare beyond the shores of New Zealand, on the tip of a peninsula whose name recalls an incident on Captain Cook's voyage. *21 km SE to Clifton.*

Waimarama Beach ★★★: A superb stretch of golden surf beach looking out to the bleak grey cliffs of Bare Island. *45 km S. Signposted from Havelock North.*

Waipatiki Beach ★★: In complete contrast to the open sweep of Waimarama Beach, Waipatiki Stream has carved a wedge in the rugged cliff-line north of Napier to form a sheltered, sandy cove. *44 km N. Turnoff signposted on the main route to Wairoa shortly after crossing the Esk River Bridge.*

Eskdale Park ★★: A much favoured, tree-draped, riverside swimming spot set in the lush Esk Valley, now ribboned with grapevines. A flood in 1937 devastated the fertile valley. Silt submerged fences and very nearly reached the roofs of some houses. In more distant times, a band of military settlers intercepted and overwhelmed the northern Hauhau party of 25 bent on attacking Napier in 1866. The brief and hopeless encounter is recalled by a memorial on the road to Taupo, just west of the turnoff to Eskdale Park. *19 km NW of Napier on the main road to Taupo. The turnoff is signposted 5 km past the Wairoa road junction.*

Lake Tutira ★★: Fringed by weeping willows which offer idyllic picnicking and camping sites, this tranquil spot was declared a bird sanctuary at the instigation of farmer/author/ornithologist William Herbert Guthrie-Smith (1861-1940) who farmed neighbouring Tutira Station. Guthrie-Smith turned 9,600 hectares of bracken into a station carrying 38,000 sheep. After World War I he subdivided most of his holding for settlement by returned servicemen, and the 810 hectares he retained were eventually left in trust for the nation. But it was as an author rather than a farmer that he made his name. After an unsuccessful venture into fiction, he found his niche in natural history and published a number of works, among them the New Zealand classic *Tutira—The Story of a New Zealand Sheep Station* (1921, reprinted 1969) which meticulously documented Tutira from its geological beginnings to its development as farmland. Throughout his writings Guthrie-Smith urged the preservation of native birds and the conservation of native forests, and he was one of the first writers to lament settlement by Anglo-Saxons whose "rat-like pertinacity has accomplished the

MAPS

See key to map numbers on p. 2.

When looking for a place name, first look in the index at the back of the book.

In the text the symbol △ denotes a place with its separate entry in the alphabetical section.

REFERENCE FOR MAPS IN THIS SECTION

City, or large town	
Town	o
Locality	o
Railways	
Race track	o
Mine	
Plantation	

National State Highways
Provincial State Highways
Other roads
Tracks
590 — Elevations in metres
Rivers, streams
Marsh, swamp, mudflats

1

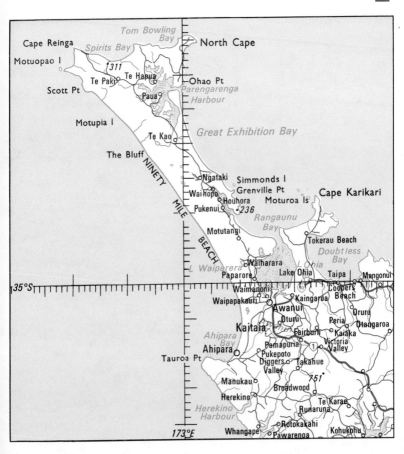

2

Berghan Pt
Stephenson I
CAVALLI IS
Taupo
Bay
Mangonui
Whangaroa Bay
Flat I
Motukawanui I
35°S
Oruaiti
1377
Kahoe
Matangirau
Orura
Matauri Bay
Waitaruke
Whangaroa
Otoroa
Takou
Otangaroa
Pupuke
Kaeo
Bay
Omaunu
Waiare
Te Tii
Mangamuka
Waipapa
Cape Wiwiki
Cape Brett
Mangamuka
Bridge
Kerikeri
Bay of Islands
Umawera
Waibou
Waitangi
Russell
Poketi
Valley
Rangiahua
Okaihau
Waimate
Paihia
Ngaiotonga
North
Puketona
Home Pt
Maraeroa
Taumaterere
Waihaha
Horeke
Ohaeawai
Opua
Whangaruru North
L Omapere
Ngawha
Pakaraka
Karetu
Punaruku
Rawene
Otiria
Kawakawa
Oakura
Whangaruru Harbour
Kaikohe
Moerewa
Pokapu
Waiomio
Rimariki I
Omanaia
Te Iringa
Ruapekapeka
Tapuhi
Helena Bay
Taheke
Ngaphuhi
Opahi
Taikirau
Maromaku
Puhipuhi
Whananaki
Waima
Otaua
Tautoro
Matawaia
Towai
Hokerenui
Opuawhanga
Sandy
Waimamaku
Matapouri
Wekaweka
Kaikou
Riponui
Otonga
Marua
7.74
Awarua
Pipiwai
Tanekaha
Hikurangi
Tutukaka
Waipoua
Nukutawhiti
Purua
Matarau
Kauri
Kiripaka
Ngunguru
Forest
Tutamoe
697
Ruatangata
Glenbervie
Ngunguru
Katui
Pakotai
Kokopu
Kamo
Donnellys
Parakao
Titoki
Poroti Maunu
WHANGAREI
Crossing
Aranga
Houto
Tamaterau
Kaihu
Maungatapere
Otaika
Parua Bay
L Taharoa
Maropiu
Avoca
Whatitiri
Portland
One Tree
Point
McLeod Bay
Mamaranui
Waihue
Kirikopuni
Tangiteroria
Oakleigh
Taurikura
Tangowahine
Maungakaramea
Mangapai Mata
Marsden
Pukehuia
Point

3

Valley
Mangamuka
174°E
Bay of Is
Manukau
751
Kerikeri
Russell
Broadwood
Mangamuka
Bridge
Waitangi
Paihia
Herekino
Te Karae
Waibou
Poketi
Herekino
Runaruna
Umawera
Valley
Opua
Harbour
Rotokakahi
Rangiahua
Okaihau
Waimate
Puketona
Whangape
Kohukohu
Maraeroa
North
Taumaterere
Pawarenga
Motuti
Horeke
Ohaeawai
Whangape
Panguru
Rawene
L Omapere
Ngawha
Otiria
Moerewa
Harbour
Kaikohe
Kawakawa
Oue
Omanaia
Pokapu
Waiomio
Rangi Point
Whirinaki
Te Iringa
Opahi
Taikirau
Maromaku
Omapere
Pakanae
Taheke
Ngaphuhi
Opononi 7.74
Waima
Otaua
Tautoro
Towai
Hokianga Harbour
Waiotemarama
Waimamaku
Matawaia
Wekaweka
626.
Kaikou
Riponui
Awarua
Waimatenui
Pipiwai
Waipoua
Nukutawhiti
Purua
Forest
697
Ruatangata
Katui
Tutamoe
Pakotai
Kokopu
Donnellys
Parakao
Titoki Poroti
Crossing
Houto
Aranga
Maungatapere
Kaihu
L Taharoa
Maropiu
Avoca
Whatitiri
Mamaranui
Waihue
Kirikopuni
Tangiteroria
Tangowahine
Maungakaramea
Pukehuia
Paroro
Omana
Awakino
Point
Dargaville
Waiotira
Baylys Beach
Turiwiri
Rehutai
Aoroa
Arapohue
36°S
Te Kopuru
Mititai
Tokatoka
Te Maire
Whenuanui
Raupo
Naumai Matakohe
Tikinui
Ruawai
Taingaehe
Te Kowhai
Hukatere

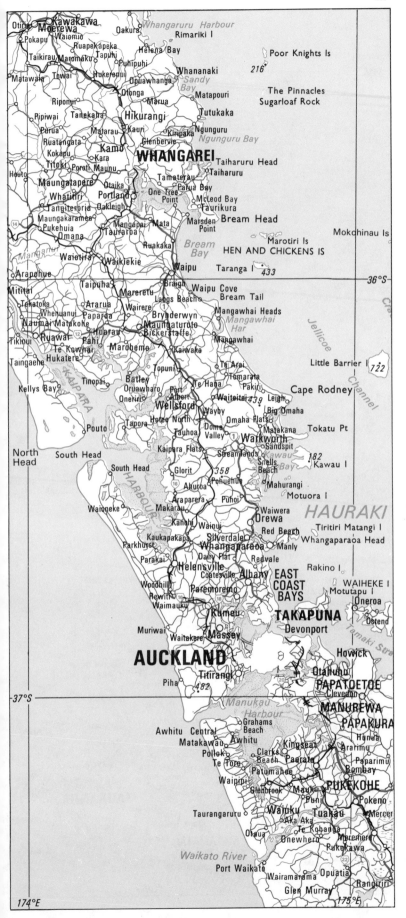

Otinga Kawakawa
Moerewa
Pokapu Waiomio
Oakura
Rimariki I
Whangaruru Harbour
Ruapekapeka Taupiri
Taikirau Maromaku Puhipuhi
Matawaia Towai Hukerenui Opuawhanga
Otonga
Riponui
Marua
Pipiwai Tanekaha
Purua Matarau
Ruatangata Kauri
Kokopu Kara
Titoki Poroti Maunu
Houto

Helena Bay
Whananaki
Sandy Bay
Matapouri
Tutukaka

Poor Knights Is
216

The Pinnacles
Sugarloaf Rock

Hikurangi
Kamo
Glenbervie
Kiripaka
Ngunguru
Ngunguru Bay

WHANGAREI
Taiharuru Head
Taiharuru
Maungatapere
Otaika
Whatitiri Portland
Tangiteroria Oakleigh
Maungakaramea
Pukehuia
Omana
Mangapai Mata
Taurarua
Ruakaka
Waiotira Waikiekie
Arapohue

Tamaterau
One Tree Point
Parua Bay
McLeod Bay
Taurikura
Marsden Point
Bream Head

Mokohinau Is

Bream Bay
Marotiri Is
HEN AND CHICKENS IS

14

Mangawhare
Waipu
Taranga I 433

36°S

Mititai
Tekatoka
Whenuanui Paparoa
Naumai Matakohe
Ruawai
Tikinui
Te Kowhai
Taingaehe Hukatere

Taipuha
Mareretu
Wairere
Brynderwyn
Maungaturoto
Bickerstaffe
Maraeheme
Kaiwaka

Braigh
Waipu Cove
Bream Tail
Laings Beach
Mangawhai Heads
Mangawhai Har
Mangawhai

Jellicoe Channel

Ararua
Pahi
Huarau

KAIPARA

Topuni
Te Hana
Oruawharo
Onerihi
Albert
Port
Hoteo North
Tauhoa
Kaipara Flats
Tapora

Te Arai
Tomarata
Pakiri
Waiteitei 439
Wayby
Omaha Flats
Doma Valley
Matakana
Sandspit

Leigh
Big Omaha

Cape Rodney

Little Barrier I 722

Tinopai
Batley

Te Hana
Warkworth
1

Tokatu Pt

North Head
South Head
Pouto
Kellys Bay

South Head

Glorit 358
Ahuroa
Araparera
Makarau
Kanohi
Waiuku

Streamlands
Snells Beach
Puhoi
Mahurangi
Motuora I

Kawau Bay 182
Kawau I

HAURAKI

Waioneke

Kaukapakapa
Parkhurst
Parakai

Waiwera
Orewa
Red Beach
Waiwera
Silverdale
Whangaparaoa
Dairy Flat
Manly
Redvale

Tiritiri Matangi I
Whangaparaoa Head

Rakino I

Helensville
Coatesville Albany
Woodhill
Rewiti Paremoremo
Waimauku

EAST COAST BAYS

WAIHEKE I
Motutapu I
Oneroa
Ostend

Muriwai
Waitakere
Kumeu
Massey

TAKAPUNA
Devonport

Tamaki Stra

AUCKLAND
Piha
Titirangi 482

Howick

Otahuhu
PAPATOETOE
Clevedon
Manukau Harbour

MANUREWA
PAPAKURA

37°S

Awhitu Central
Matakawau
Pollok
Te Toro
Waipipi

Grahams Beach
Awhitu
Clarks Beach
Patumahoe

Kingseat
Paerata

Hunua
Ararimu
Paparimu
Bombay

Glenbrook
Waiuku
Tauranganui
Otaua
Onewhero

Mauku Puni
Aka Aka
Te Kohanga

PUKEKOHE
Tuakau
Pokeno
Mercer
Meremere
Rukekawa

Waikato River
Port Waikato
Wairamarama
Glen Murray

Opuatia
Rangiriri
22
1

174°E
175°E

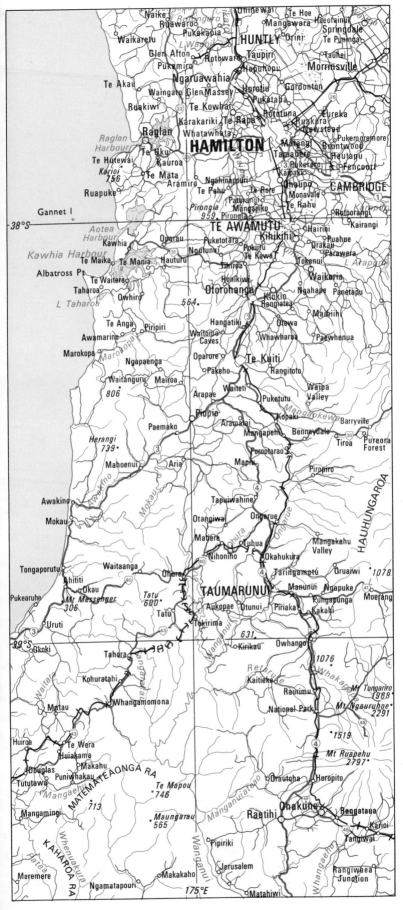

7

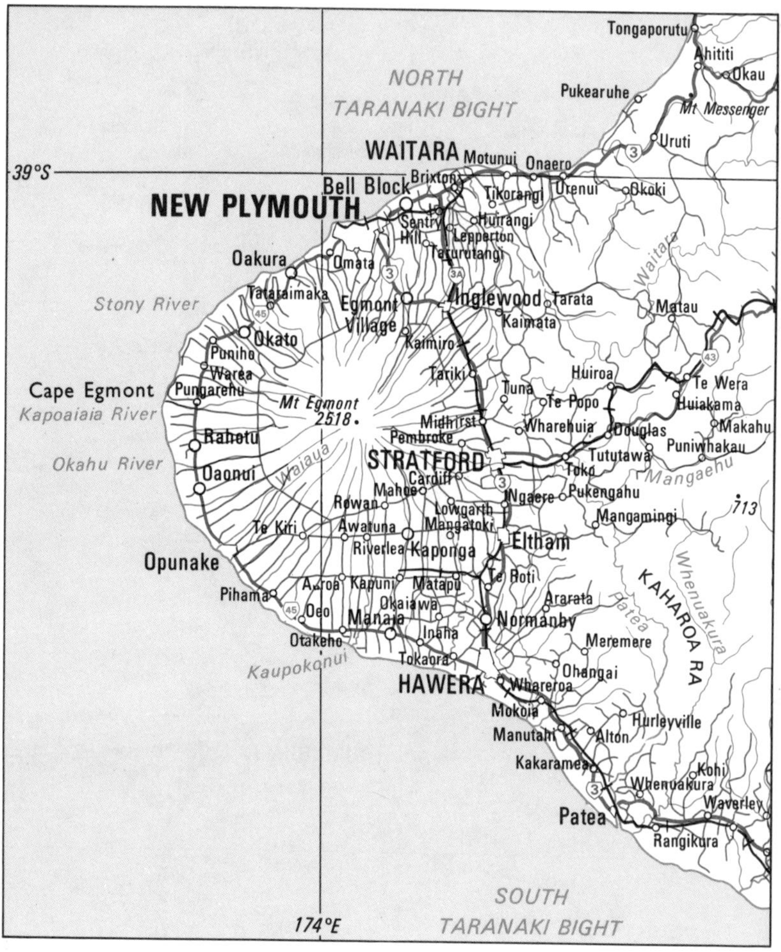

NORTH
TARANAKI BIGHT

Tongaporutu
Ahititi
Okau
Pukearuhe
Mt Messenger
Uruti

WAITARA Motunui Onaero
Brixton
Okoki
Utenui

−39°S

Bell Block
NEW PLYMOUTH
Tikorangi
Huirangi
Sentry
Hill
Lepperton
Tarurutangi

Oakura
Omata
3A
Tataraimaka
3
Egmont
Village
Inglewood Tarata
Kaimata
Matau

Stony River
Okato
Kaimiro
Puniho
Warea
Tariki
Huiroa
43
Te Wera
Huiakama

Cape Egmont
Punarehu
Tuna
Te Popo
Makahu
Kapoaiaia River
Mt Egmont
2518
Midhirst
Wharehuia
Douglas
Puniwhakau

Okahu River
Rahotu
Pembroke
Tututawa
Mangaehu
Oaonui
STRATFORD
Cardiff
Toko
Pukengahu
713

Waiaua
Mahoe
Ngaere
Mangamingi
Te Kiri
Rowan
Lowgarth
Awatuna
Mangatoki

Opunake
Riverlea **Kaponga**
Eltham
KAHAROA RA
Pihama
A roa
Kapuni
Matapu
Te Roti
45
Oeo
Okaiawa
Ararata
Patea

Manaia
Inaha
Normanby
Meremere
Whenuakura
Otakeho
Tokaora
Ohangai

Kaupokonui
Whareroa
Hurleyville
HAWERA
Mokoia
Manutahi
Alton
Kohi
Kakaramea
Whenuakura
Waverley
3
Patea
Rangikura

174°E

SOUTH
TARANAKI BIGHT

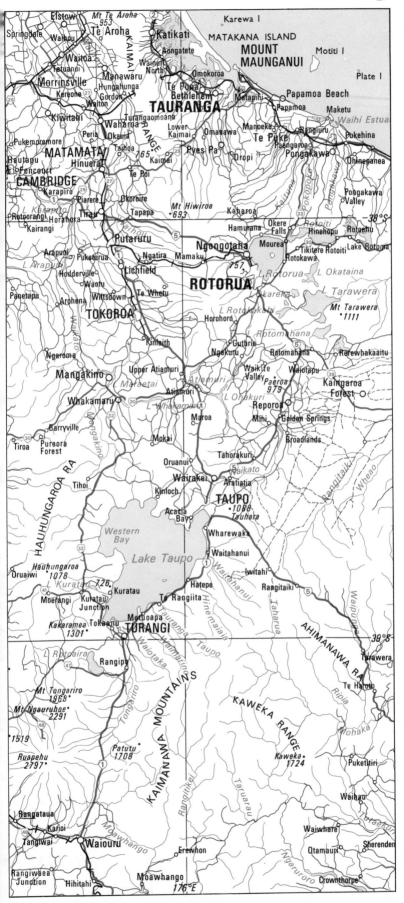

9

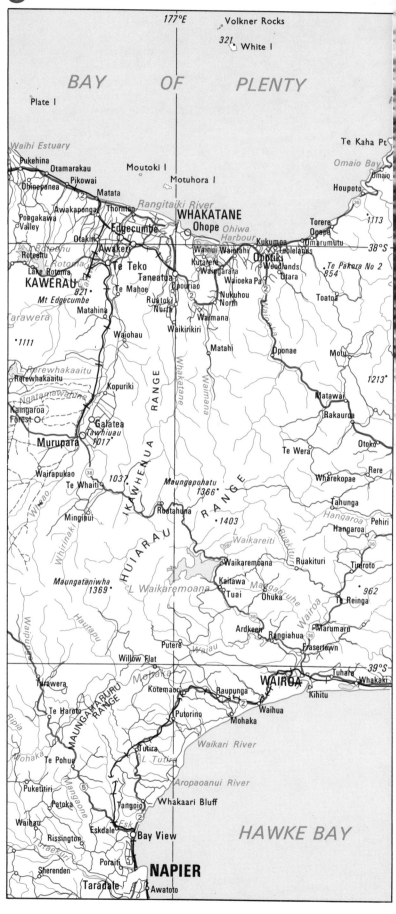

BAY   OF   PLENTY

Volkner Rocks

321 White I

Plate I

Waihi Estuary
Pukehina   Otamarakau   Moutoki I
Ohinepanea   Pikowai   Motuhora I
    Matata
Pongakawa   Awakaponga   Thornton   *Rangitaiki River*   WHAKATANE
Valley   Edgecumbe   Ohope   *Ohiwa*
Otakiri   *Harbour*
Rotoehu   Awakeri   Wainui Wainahi
Rotoma   Kutarere
Lake Rotoma   Te Teko   Waiorarara
KAWERAU   Taneatua   Waioeka Pa
        Te Mahoe   Opouriao   Nukuhou
Mt Edgecumbe   Ruatoki   Waimana   North
821   Matahina   North
Tarawera   Waikirikiri
            Waiohau   Matahi
•1111
Rerewhakaaitu   Kopuriki
Rerewhakaaitu
Ngatamawahine
Kaingaroa   Galatea
Forest   Tawhiuau
Murupara   *1017*
    Wairapukao   *1037*
    Te Whaiti   *Maungapohatu*
        Minginui   Ruatahuna   *1366*

Te Kaha Pt
Omaio Bay
Omaio
Houpoto
1113
Torere
Opape   Umarumutu
Kukumoa   Tablelands   38°S
Opotiki
Woodlands   *Te Pakora No 2*
Otara   *854*
Toatoa
Oponae   Motu
            1213•
    Matawai
Rakauroa
Te Wera   Otoko
        Rere
Wharekopae
Tahunga   Pehiri
Hangaroa
Ruakituri   Tiniroto
•962
Te Reinga
Marumaru
Fraserton

•1403
L Waikareiti
Waikaremoana
Maungataniwha   Kaitawa   *Maggaruhe*
1369•   *L Waikaremoana*   Tuai   Ohuka
    Putere   Ardkeen   Rangiahua
        Willow Flat
        Mohaka   WAIROA
Tarawera   Kotemaori   Raupunga   Kihitu
    Te Haroto   Waihua
            Putorino   Mohaka
                Tutira
    Te Pohue   *L Tutira*   *Waikari River*
Puketitiri   *Aropaoanui River*
    Patoka   Tangoio   Whakaari Bluff
Waihau
    Rissington   Eskdale   Bay View   HAWKE BAY
        Poraiti
    Sherenden   NAPIER
        Taradale   Awatoto

Tuhara
Whakaki
39°S

177°E

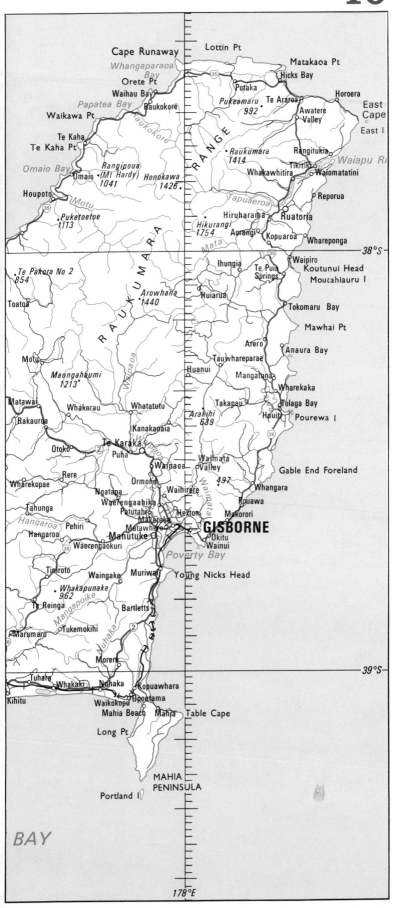

Cape Runaway
Lottin Pt
Whangaparaoa Bay
Matakaoa Pt
Orete Pt
Hicks Bay
Waihau Bay
Potaka
Horoera
Papatea Bay
Raukokore
Pukeamaru
992
Te Araroa
East
Waikawa Pt
Awatere
Cape
Valley
East I
Raukokore
Te Kaha
Te Kaha Pt
Raukumara
Rangitukia
1414
Rangipoua
Waiapu R
Omaio Bay
(Mt Hardy)
Whakawhitira
Waiomatatini
Omaio
1041
Honokawa
Tikitiki
1426
Houpoto
Motu
Reporua
Puketoetoe
Tapuaeroa
1113
Hiruharama
Ruatoria
Wharenga
Mata
Hikurangi
Kopuaroa
1754
Aorangi
———— 38°S
Te Pakora No 2
854
Ihungia
Waipiro
Te Puia
Koutunui Head
Arowhana
Springs
Moutahiauru I
Toatoa
1440
Huiarua
Tokomaru Bay
Motu
Mawhai Pt
Maungahaumi
Atero
Anaura Bay
1213
Tauwhareparae
Matawai
Whakarau
Whatatutu
Huanui
Rakauroa
Mangatuna
Wharekaka
Kanakanaia
Takapau
Tolaga Bay
Arakihi
Hauiti
Pourewa I
Otoko
Te Karaka
639
Puha
Rere
Waipaoa
Waimata
Wharekopae
Ormond
Valley
497
Tahunga
Ngatapa
Waihirere
Whangara
Waerengaahika
Rouawa
Pehiri
Patutahi
Hexton
Makorori
Hangaroa
Makaraka
Hangaroa
Matawhero
GISBORNE
Manutuke
Okitu
Waerengaokuri
Wainui
Poverty Bay
Tiniroto
Waingake
Muriwai
Young Nicks Head
Whakapunake
962
Te Reinga
Bartletts
Mangapoike
Marumaru
Tukemokihi
Nuhaka
Morere
———— 39°S
Tuhara
Nuhaka
Whakaki
Kopuawhara
Kihitu
Opoutama
Waikokopu
Mahia Beach
Mahia
Table Cape
Long Pt
MAHIA
PENINSULA
Portland I
BAY
178°E

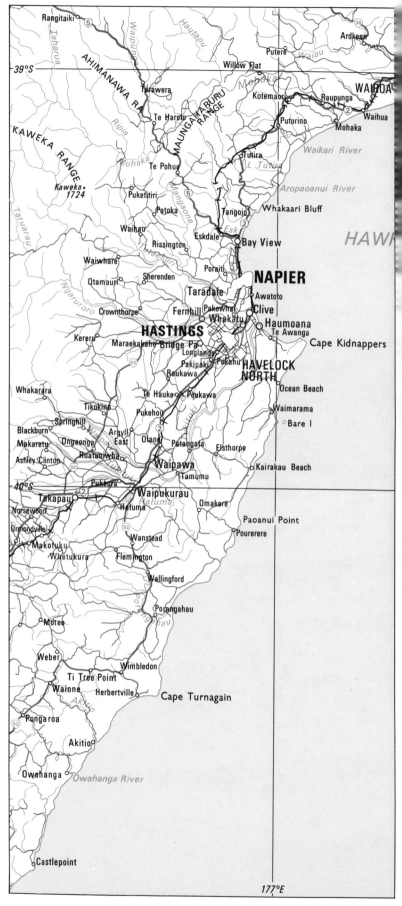

Rangitaiki
Ardkeen
AHIMANAWA RA.
Putere
Willow Flat
39°S
WAIROA
Tarawera
Kotemaori
Raupunga
Waihua
Te Haroto
Putorino
Mohaka
MAUNGAHARURU RANGE
KAWEKA RANGE
Te Pohue
Tutira
Waikari River
Puketitiri
Patoka
Tangoio
Whakaari Bluff
Kaweka
1724
Aropaoanui River
Waihau
Rissington
Eskdale
Bay View
Waiwhare
Poraiti
HAW
Otamauri
Sherenden
NAPIER
Taradale
Awatoto
Crownthorpe
Fernhill Pakowhai
Clive
Whakatu
Haumoana
HASTINGS
Te Awanga
Kereru
Maraekakaho Bridge Pa
Cape Kidnappers
Longlands
Pakipaki Pukahu
HAVELOCK
Raukawa
NORTH
Whakarara
Te Hauke
Poukawa
Ocean Beach
Tikokino
Pukehou
Waimarama
Springhill
Bare I
Blackburn
Argyll
Otane
Makaretu
East
Patangata
Elsthorpe
Ongaonga
Ashley Clinton
Ruataniwha
Tamumu
Waipawa
Kairakau Beach
Pukeora
40°S
Waipukurau
Takapau
Hatuma
Omakere
Norsewood
Paoanui Point
Ormondville
Pourerere
Makotuku
Wanstead
Whetukura
Flemington
Wallingford
Porangahau
Motea
Weber
Wimbledon
Ti Tree Point
Waione
Herbertville
Cape Turnagain
Pongaroa
Akitio
Owahanga
Owahanga River
Castlepoint
177°E

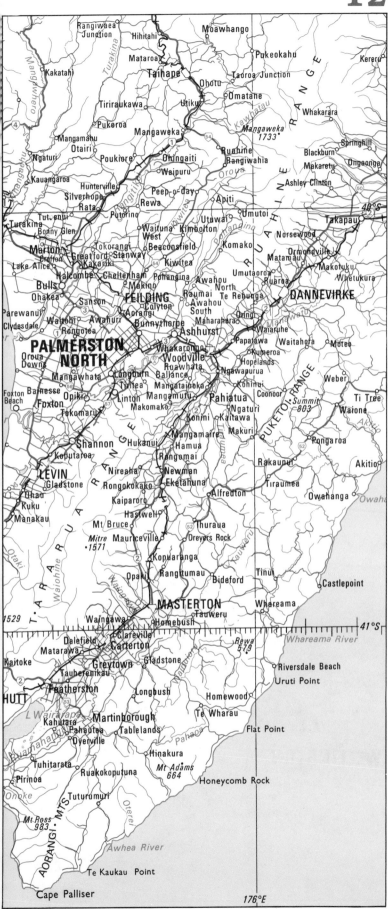

Rangiwaea Junction
Hihitahi
Moawhango
Kakatahi
Mataroa
Taihape
Pukeokahu
Kereru
Tiriraukawa
Ohotu
Taoroa Junction
Omatane
Whakarara
Pukeroa
Mangaweka
Utiku
Mangaweka 1733
Springhill
Mangamahu
Ohingaiti
Ruahine
Blackburn
Ongaonga
Otairi
Poukiore
Rangiwahia
Makaretu
Ngaturi
Waipuru
Ashley Clinton
Kauangaroa
Hunterville
Waituna
Peep-o-day
Apiti
40°S
Silverhope
Rata
Rewa
Umutoi
Takapau
Tut.enui
Putorino
Utuwai
Norsewood
Turakina
Waituna West
Kimbolton
Bonny Glen
Komako
Ormondville
Marton
Tokorangi
Beaconsfield
Matamau
Greatford Stanway
Makotuku
Lake Alice
Kakariki
Kiwitea
Pohangina
Umutaoroa
Whetukura
Bulls
Halcombe
Cheltenham
Awahou North
Ruaroa
Ohakea
Makino
FEILDING
Raumai
Te Rehunga
DANNEVIRKE
Sanson
Awahou South
Parewanui
Waitohi
Aorangi
Colyton
Maharahara
Oringi
Clydesdale
Rongotea
Awahuri
Bunnythorpe
Ashhurst
Waiaruhe
Papatawa
Waitahora
Motea
PALMERSTON NORTH
Whakarongo
Woodville
Ruawhata
Kumeroa
Oroua Downs
Longburn
Ballance
Ngawapurua
Hopelands
Weber
Mangawhata
Tiritea
Mangataioka
Pahiatua
Kohinui
Coonoor
Summit 803
Barnesse
Opiki
Linton
Mangamutu
Ngaturi
Ti Tree
Foxton Beach
Foxton
Makomako
Konini
Kaitawa
Makuri
Waione
Tokomaru
Mangamaire
Pongaroa
Shannon
Hukanui
Hamua
Rakaunui
Akitio
Koputaroa
Rongomai
LEVIN
Nireaha
Newman
Tiraumea
Gladstone
Rongokokako
Eketahuna
Alfredton
Owahanga
Ohau
Kaiparoro
Kuku
Hastwell
Manakau
Mt Bruce
Thuraua
Mitre 1571
Mauriceville
Dreyers Rock
Kopuaranga
Opaki
Rangitumau
Bideford
Tinui
Castlepoint
MASTERTON
Whareama
1529
Waingawa
Tauweru
Homebush
41°S
Dalefield
Clareville
Whareama River
Matarawa
Carterton
Rewa 579
Kaitoke
Gladstone
Riversdale Beach
Tauherenikau
Greytown
Uruti Point
Featherston
Longbush
Homewood
HUTT
Te Wharau
Flat Point
Kahutara
Martinborough
Pahautea
Tablelands
Oyerville
Hinakura
Tuhitarata
Mt Adams 664
Honeycomb Rock
Pirinoa
Ruakokoputuna
Tuturumuri
Onoke
Mt Ross 983
Awhea River
Te Kaukau Point
Cape Palliser
176°E

13

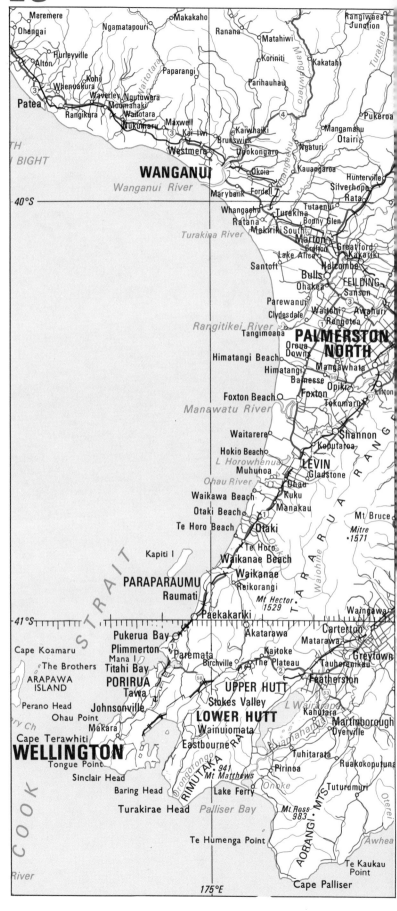

Meremere
Makakaho
Rangiwaea Junction
Ohangai
Ngamatapouri
Ranana
Matahiwi
Hurleyville
Koriniti
Kohi
Paparangi
Kakatahi
Alton
Whenuakura
Waverley Ngutuwera
Parihauhau
Pukeroa
Patea
Moumahaki
Rangikura
Waitotara
Mangamahu
Otairi
Nukumaru
Maxwell
Kaiwhaiki
Kai Iwi
Brunswick
Ngaturi
Westmere
Upokongaro
Kauangaroa
Hunterville
Okoia
Silverhope

WANGANUI
Fordell
Rata

Wanganui River
Marybank
Tutaenui

40°S
Whangaehu
Turakina
Ratana
Bonny Glen
Makirikiri South
Marton
Greatford
Turakina River
Crofton
Kakariki
Lake Alice
Nukombe
Santoft
Bulls
Ohakea
Sanson
FEILDING

Parewanui
Watiohi
Awahuri
Clydesdale
Rangotea

Rangitikei River
Tangimoana
PALMERSTON
NORTH
Oroua
Downs
Himatangi Beach
Mangawhata
Himatangi
Bainesse
Opiki
Foxton Beach
Foxton
Linton
Tokomaru

Manawatu River
Waitarere
Shannon
Hokio Beach
Koputaroa
L Horowhenua
LEVIN
Muhunoa
Gladstone
Ohau River
Ohau
Waikawa Beach
Kuku
Otaki Beach
Manakau
Te Horo Beach
Otaki
Mt Bruce
Te Horo
Mitre
•1571
Kapiti I
Waikanae Beach
Waikanae
PARAPARAUMU
Reikorangi
Raumati
Mt Hector
1529
Waingawa
Paekakariki

41°S
Pukerua Bay
Akatarawa
Carterton
Cape Koamaru
Plimmerton
Matarawa
Mana I
Kaitoke
Greytown
The Brothers
Titahi Bay
Paremata
Birchville
The Plateau
Tauherenikau
ARAPAWA
ISLAND
PORIRUA
Featherston
Perano Head
Tawa
UPPER HUTT
Ohau Point
Johnsonville
Stokes Valley
Kahutara
Makara
LOWER HUTT
Martinborough
Cape Terawhiti
Wainuiomata
Dyerville
WELLINGTON
Eastbourne
Tongue Point
Tuhitarata
Ruakokoputuna
Sinclair Head
Pirinoa
Baring Head
Lake Ferry
Mt Ross
Tuturumuri
Turakirae Head
Palliser Bay
983

Te Humenga Point
Te Kaukau Point

Cape Palliser

175°E

COOK STRAIT

RUAHINE RANGE

TARARUA RANGE

RIMUTAKA RA

AORANGI MTS

ruin of a Fauna and Flora unique in the world''.

The bird sanctuary is a fitting memorial, but Guthrie-Smith played a wider role in alerting the public to the needs of conservation.

There is good swimming in the lake, and excellent trout fishing where a stream flows into its northern reaches. *40 km N on the main Napier-Wairoa road.*

The **Tutira Walkway,** steep in places, passes through Tutira Station and the adjoining Lake Tutira Domain. There are splendid views of coastal Hawke's Bay from Table Mountain Trig. *Allow 5 hrs for the full round trip of 9 km.*

Dartmoor: A picnic spot dense with silver poplars at the confluence of the Mangaone and Tutaekuri Rivers. There is good swimming and trout fishing in both rivers. *24 km W of Napier via Taradale and Puketapu, bearing left at Puketapu to follow Dartmoor Rd to the river bridge.*

To return by way of the Omarunui battle-site memorial, turn off to Fernhill, passing the small Puketapu Church with the graves of members of the Lowry family and a memorial window which reflects their interest in both sheep raising and horse racing. *Bear left over the river bridge to follow the Omarunui road down the right bank of the Tutaekuri, passing the memorial (at 4.5 km from bridge). Continue to the end of Omarunui Rd, then follow signposts back to Napier or Hastings.*

Lemmon Trust Museum (Puketitiri): A large collection of colonial antiques, early agricultural machinery and vintage cars. *51 km NW, via Rissington and Patoka; tel. (06) 839-8894.* At **Balls Clearing,** a picnic area, a reserve contains the last remnant of the Puketitiri Bush, much of it rimu and kahikatea.

Otatara Pa Historic Reserve ★: The pa, beside the Tutaekuri River, is remarkable for its antiquity — it was probably occupied as early as 1150 A.D. — for its lack of earthwork defences and for its immense size, once extending to some 40 hectares. Some 400 years ago, the pa was attacked by a raiding of Kahungungu, under the chief Taraia from Wairoa, but the intruders were thwarted when, overnight, the defenders dug a large ditch between the upper and lower sections of the pa. But, Taraia subsequently returned with more of his people, causing the inhabitants to abandon their land and allowing the Kahungungu to establish their power firmly in the area. As a result they eventually extended their territory as far south as the Wairarapa. Numerous terraced dwelling sites, storage pits for kumara and small-scale defence works (once supplemented by palisades) remain, and there is a magnificent view. *Springfield Rd, 1 km S of Taradale. 10.5 km SW. A loop track (1 hr) starts from the carpark.*

Game Farm and Trout Hatchery: Over 1,000 pheasants are reared and 200,000 trout hatched yearly. *22 Burgess Rd, Greenmeadows. Open daily; tel. (06) 844-2291.*

ORGANISED EXCURSIONS

Art Deco Walk ★ ★: Guided walks thread through Napier's astonishing concentration of Spanish Mission-style buildings, modes of architecture in vogue when Napier was rebuilt after the 1931 earthquake. *Sun and Wed afternoon, 2 p.m. (daily in summer holidays). The walk leaves from the Art Deco Shop, 163 Tennyson St, Clive Square East; tel. (06) 835-0022.*

△ **Cape Kidnappers Gannet Sanctuary ★ ★ ★:** Vehicles take groups either along the beach or across farmland to visit the world's largest mainland gannet colony. *Gannet Beach Adventures (tel. (06) 875-0898); Gannet Safaris (tel. (06) 875-0511).*

Wine tours: Hawke's Bay ranks as one of the country's premier wine-producing districts and several vineyards may be visited in the course of a tour, with the option of lunch. *Bay Tours; tel. (06) 843-6953.* There is also a fascinating tour of the **Mission Vineyards and Winery,** the oldest vineyard in the country (*Church Rd, Taradale; Mon–Sat. 10.30 a.m. and 2 p.m.; tel. (06) 844-2259).* Another is of the **McDonald Winery,** with a winemakers' museum and the possibility of lunch (*200 Church Rd, Taradale; tel. (06) 844-2053). See also △ Hastings.*

Adventure activities: Rafting on the Mohaka River (from white water to scenic drifting), **horse-trekking,** hunting and trout fishing. *Riverland Outback Adventures, tel. (06) 834-9756.* At all times of year **hot air balloons** hover over Hawkes Bay for an hour or so and then offer a traditional balloon picnic. *Early Morning Balloons Ltd., tel. (06) 858-8480.*

Sheepskin factory tours: An introduction to sheepskin tanning and manufacturing. Factory shop. *Free tours 11 a.m. and 2 p.m. daily. Classic Sheepskins Tannery, Thames St, Pandora; tel. (06) 835-9662.* A **"Follow the Wool Bale"** tour traces aspects of the wool industry (*morning tour covers the wool brokers and the wool scour; the afternoon tour, the manufacture and retail of sheepskin products). Bay Tours; tel. (06) 843-2046.*

NAPIER-TAUPO ROAD *   Maps 8, 9

The road links Napier, on the Hawke's Bay coast, with Taupo in the heart of the North Island. 144 km.

THE NAPIER-TAUPO ROAD in a relatively short order runs through as varied a landscape as one could imagine, ranging from gentle plain to rugged mountain ranges, from the lush vineyards of the Esk Valley to the desert-like pumice lands near Rangitaiki, and from well-cultivated fields to marginal farmland.

THE STORY OF A ROAD

The story behind the road is perhaps more fascinating than its scenery. It was used by Taupo-based Tuwharetoa in pre-European times as a track to collect seafood from the plentiful Ahuriri Lagoon (since vanished in the Hawke's Bay earthquake), and one of the first aims of the Hawke's Bay Provincial Council was to open the route as a road—the council appearing to prefer Auckland rather than Wellington as a market. Missionary-explorer William Colenso had walked along the track in 1847 as far as Tarawera, but the council was not deterred by his description of "hills of all shapes and sizes ... very steep, making descent and ascent difficult—in places hazardous".

Before much progress was made, in 1869 the project was taken over by the central Government, intent on opening a supply route to its garrison at Taupo. Through the dense bush the road was forced, despite Te Kooti's followers, whose constant menace forced the Government to pay its roadmen very high wages. Once completed, a chain of military posts and blockhouses was established at strategic points to keep the long line of communication open.

With the war virtually over, a stage-coach was able to link Napier with Taupo in 1874, but the bone-shaking trip took a tiresome two days and involved six changes of horses and the fording of the Esk River no fewer than 43 times. One of the Cobb & Co.-type coaches used on the service is displayed in the museum at Napier. In 1913 a large open Cadillac tourer was introduced and for the first time the journey could be completed in a single day, although the route was still formidable—even in 1919 an average of only six vehicles used the road each day.

From two days, the time taken for the journey has now shrunk to less than two hours but even today the rugged terrain and the surviving stands of bush enable one to appreciate the courage and enterprise of the early road-builders.

POINTS OF INTEREST
In geographical order, from Napier to Taupo:

Eskdale *(Napier 18 km; Taupo 126 km)*: In a narrow defile here, a band of military settlers in 1866 intercepted and overwhelmed a northern Hauhau party of 25 bent on attacking Napier township. In a brief and hopeless encounter its leader and 10 others died. *(For details of the overall strategy, see △ Napier.) A memorial stands just W of the signposted turnoff to Eskdale Park, a popular riverside picnic area.*

Te Pohue *(Napier 44 km; Taupo 100 km)*: An insignificant settlement by a minute lake, this was the first day's lunch stop for the Napier–Taupo coach. As the coach left Napier, a carrier pigeon would be released to advise the hotel here how many to expect for lunch. Te Pohue means "the climbing plant", such as clematis. Just before Te Pohue is the turn-off to **Trenlinnoe Gardens**, landscaped gardens in an "English" style *(5.5km. Open daily Thurs–Sun, mid-Aug to end of May; tel. (06) 834-9703).*

Tarawera *(Napier 80 km; Taupo 64 km)*: This was the Maori village from which the Hauhau left on their abortive attack on Napier in 1866, after which military forces built, near the site of today's tavern, a stockade of special design to counter rifle fire from the higher hills close by. In stage-coach times passengers stayed overnight here in a hotel whose liquor licence the tavern perpetuates.

In a bush setting on a ledge above the Waipunga River are the Tarawera Hot Springs. These are in a state of disrepair since Cyclone Bola but the ten-minute bush walk from the tavern to the old bath site is delightful.

Tarawera means "hot peak", but should not be confused with the famous volcano of the same name near Rotorua.

Waipunga and Waiarua Falls Lookout *(Napier 89 km; Taupo 55 km)*: Twin waterfalls below which a series of rapids run through a bushlined gorge.

Rangitaiki *(Napier 108 km; Taupo 36 km)*: A motel now stands on the site of the old Rangitaiki Hotel (destroyed by fire in 1987), the second lunching stop in coaching times. Hunting, fishing and rafting may be arranged. *Tel. (07) 384-2803.*

150

Opepe Graves *(Napier 127 km; Taupo 17 km):* Opepe was the site of an abandoned Maori village, where the road to Napier intersected a Maori track from the Urewera. In 1869, during the campaigns against Te Kooti, the village was being considered for the site of a military stockade when a detachment of 14 cavalrymen camped there and neglected to post sentries while their companions continued on to Tapuaeharuru (Taupo). Their Maori guides deserted, and when a strange Maori appeared the men emerged from their whare unarmed. Too late they saw and recognised as Hauhau others who were with the stranger. Cut off from their rifles, they fled for the safety of the bush, but only five escaped with their lives. The troops' senior officer, Cornet Angus Smith, was subsequently awarded the New Zealand Cross for his part in the affair; an award which scandalised many, as Smith's carelessness had contributed to the tragedy. *A signposted track leads to the graves of the nine victims. One may then cross the highway and follow a track down the Old Taupo Rd, taking a track to the left (15 mins).* The walk ends at an old water trough, built from a six-metre totara log hauled here by the Armed Constabulary once the stockade had been established. The considerable settlement of Opepe township grew up around the stockade. In the bush, with a post and rail fence around the spring which feeds the trough, it is easy to picture one of the soldiers watering his horse, oblivious of the presence of one of Te Kooti's scouts and of the bloodshed which was shortly to follow.

Opepe means "place of the moth".

Mount Tauhara *(1,099 m):* An extinct volcanic cone which seems to preside over the Kaingaroa Plains. On the plains stand vast tracts of pine forest where the road follows wide firebreaks. *The story of the mountain's participation in the mythical "Battle of the Mountains" is told on p.* **231**. Tauhara means "lonely mountain".

✱✱✱ NEW PLYMOUTH

Taranaki   Map 7   Pop. 48,519

164 km NW of Wanganui. Information Centre, cnr Liardet and Leach Sts; tel. (06) 758-6086; Department of Conservation Field Centre, 220 Devon St West, tel. (06) 758-0433.

NEW PLYMOUTH, pivot of the Taranaki, is dominated by the symmetry of snow-capped Taranaki/Egmont. A dormant volcano which last erupted in *c.* 1636, Taranaki rises to a height of 2,518 metres above the surrounding plains. The mountain's dominance is more than visual, as the province owes its fertile land to Taranaki's volcanic ash and to the mountain's vital climatic role. The city was once totally dependent on surrounding lush farmlands, but since the sixties has developed from a market town to become the focus of oil based industries. Its port is formed principally by a breakwater, begun in 1881. Port Taranaki was once the world's largest exporter of cheese, and Kapuni oil condensate is also shipped out, to the refinery near △ Whangarei.

The city, an ideal base from which to explore the many facets of the Taranaki province, was named after Plymouth in Devon, England, for its first settlers were drawn from Devon and Cornwall by the Plymouth Company.

SOME HISTORY

An heroic defence: The first Europeans to settle here were whalers, in 1828. Four years later, about 4,000 well-armed Waikato invaded the area and besieged Otaka pa *(near the port, now the site of the cool stores).* Eight whalers joined the defenders, who numbered less than 400, and after three weeks' fighting the attackers withdrew for want of food.

A New Zealand Company settlement: The town was laid out in 1841 by the Plymouth Company (a subsidiary of the New Zealand Company—*p.* **27**), and the first Europeans to arrive found only 55 Maori living in the vicinity, despite ample evidence of Maori cultivations and traces of pa which showed that the area had once supported a considerable population. In the early 1800s the traditionally armed Taranaki tribes had suffered so heavily at the hands of Waikato tribesmen, who missed no opportunity to try out their newly acquired guns on their poorly equipped neighbours, that most of the Taranaki Maori had migrated south to join Te Rauparaha at Kapiti Island, hoping to get guns of their own and one day to reclaim their ancestral lands from their traditional enemies.

Land troubles between Maori and Pakeha beset the settlement from the first, and in 1855 apprehensive colonists took the first steps towards forming a militia, which was later augmented by troops from Wellington and Auckland. In 1860 the Taranaki Campaigns began; New Plymouth, virtually under siege, became a military settlement, and many settlers left the district in despair. The conflict was triggered off when a local chief, Wiremu Kingi, disputed a fraudulent sale to the Government of land at △ Waitara *(16 km E)*. Governor Gore Brown arbitrarily proclaimed martial law and used troops to drive Kingi and his followers from their ancestral land. Outnumbered by more than two to one, the Maori fought a ferocious guerrilla war which continued sporadically until 1881, when formal peace was made.

After a poor beginning, New Plymouth and its surrounding area have thrived under peaceful conditions, and now contain some of the country's richest dairy land.

ENERGY

The energy province: Vast reserves of natural gas and condensate, both onshore and offshore, have in recent years recast Taranaki's role from being the country's premier dairying region to becoming as well the cradle of its industrial future.

Oil, found in the New Plymouth suburb of Moturoa as early as in 1865 (the first strike in the British Empire, made only six years after the world's first commercial find in the USA), had always promised much for the region and for many years New Plymouth was unique in having her own brand of petrol, "Peak", refined from local oil at Motoroa. *(The field was abandoned in 1972 but the "walking beam" of one of its pumps may still be seen in Bayly Rd, near the port.)*

However, there were no finds of national significance until the discovery of natural gas at Kapuni in 1962. This is now piped to various points of the North Island, supplies New Plymouth's gas- and oil-fired electric power station, and provides significant quantities of oil condensate for shipment through Port Taranaki to the refinery near △ Whangarei. The Kapuni strike was eclipsed in 1969 when offshore drilling rigs tapped gas resources in the vast Maui field off the Taranaki coast. Subsequent finds include the onshore oil fields of McKee, Waihapa, and Kupe. The bulk of the country's needs are met from the refinery at △Whangarei, with Taranaki condensate and crude oil providing over 40 percent of its feedstocks. Drilling elsewhere in the country has so far failed to produce any finds of commercial significance.

Natural gas: Natural gas requires treatment before it can be piped to users. This is carried out at Oaonui (for the offshore Maui field) and Kapuni (for the onshore deposits). Solid particles and liquids brought up with the gas must be removed, and hydrocarbon liquids and traces of water extracted by dehydration and refrigeration to a temperature of -10⁰C. The mixtures drawn off are highly volatile and contain quantities of waste gases. These are returned to the gas stream leaving a stablised condensate for shipment through New Plymouth to the oil refinery at Marsden Point, near △ Whangarei. Gas treatment yields both propane and butane as by-products. The treated natural gas is then piped to various parts of the North Island and also feeds several North Island thermal power stations, among them the power station at the foot of Paritutu in the city. *Kapuni Natural Gas Plant, Kapuni; 20 km NW of △ Hawera. Oaonui Maui Onshore Production Station, Oaonui, 8 km NW of Opunake. Information centre open daily.*

Ammonia urea: Treated natural gas from Kapuni is also used as feedstock to produce about 155,000 tonnes of urea fertiliser annually, both for domestic use and for export. Urea, the white, water-soluble crystalline compound $CO(NH_2)_2$, is used in fertiliser and animal feeds as well as in the manufacture of plastics and other chemical compounds. Until 1828, when a German scientist successfully made synthetic urea, it had been thought that urea could be produced only by certain life processes. About 90,000 tonnes of ammonia is produced as the feedstock for producing urea, with a small surplus sold for industrial use. The Petrochem plant at Kapuni opened at the end of 1982. *Kapuni Ammonia Urea Plant, Kapuni; 20 km NW of △ Hawera.*

Gas-to-methanol: At Waitara, a gas-to-methanol plant produces about 1,200 tonnes per day of chemical-grade methanol, largely for export. Methanol, also known as wood alcohol, is widely used in industry for the manufacture of adhesives and plastics and as a solvent. It can also be added to engine fuels. The project was undertaken by Petralgas Chemicals Ltd, which is a partnership between Petrocorp and Alberta Gas Chemicals of Canada. *Waitara Valley methanol plant, Mamaku Rd. △ Waitara.*

Gas-to-gasoline: The Methanex gas-to-gasoline plant at Motunui, near Waitara, began as an ambitious joint venture between the government and Mobil Oil, and has since been privatised.

The synthetic gasoline plant involves the conversion of natural gas to methanol which is passed through the Mobil-developed zeolite catalytic process to produce a

---

Consult the Index when looking for a name in this Guide.

high-octane gasoline. Three methanol production units feed into the zeolite process with an output that meets over one-third of the nation's needs. The multi-million dollar plant commenced production in 1986 and was enlarged in 1994. *Motunui synthetic petrol plant, Main Rd North, Waitara; 6 km E of Waitara. Information and display centre open daily; tel. (06) 754-8009.*

McKee oil fields: Onshore oil fields (which contrast with the dominant gas fields), too, have made significant contributions to the country's fuel needs. *Otaraoa Rd, Waitara. An observation platform with explanatory diagram overlooks the production station; open daily.*

The origins of an industry: Deposits of petroleum and natural gas originate in sediments which were formed over millions of years under the prehistoric oceans which covered many parts of the earth. Then, as now, tiny plants and animals lived in the shallower waters and around the coasts, and as they died their remains settled on the sea floor. Sand and mud gradually covered these over, and as sediments accumulated they were compressed by their own enormous weight into sedimentary rock. At the same time, the animal and plant remains were converted by bacteria, pressure, heat and other natural forces into oil and gas. This has been trapped in porous rock layers which often retain the oil and gas as subterranean pools. Later, as the prehistoric oceans drained away, dry land emerged above many of the deposits. In recent years, the search for oil deposits worldwide has switched from the land to the sea bed, a much more costly drilling process but one which has yielded rich returns.

Petroleum products have been used for many centuries. Pitch was used by the ancient Egyptians to coat mummies; from about 1000 B.C. the Chinese made fuel from natural gas, which they had found when digging for salt, and about 600 B.C. Nebuchadnezzar was using asphalt, which had seeped to the surface, to build walls and to pave the streets of Babylon.

The oil industry, however, is of comparatively recent origin, dating from the 1850s and initially based on the technology developed by salt miners to drill for salt. The miners, however, regarded oil as a nuisance when they first encountered it. At first, oil was refined to obtain kerosene for use in lamps. As gas and electric lights began to replace kerosene lanterns about the turn of the century, the motor car emerged and oil rapidly assumed its ascendant place in the economic order.

CHIEF THINGS TO SEE AND DO

Pukekura Park ★★★: Considered the finest park in the country, its Victorian charm makes it difficult to believe that the area was once wasteland and was converted by volunteer labour. One should visit the park both by day, to enjoy its gardens, fernery, Begonia House and grounds, and by night, to see a floodlit waterfall and an elaborate coin-operated illuminated fountain play in the lower of the park's two artificial lakes. From the quaint tea kiosk on the upper lake is a famous view of Taranaki/Egmont. *Liardet St.*

Brooklands Park ★ ★ ★: A splendid reserve adjoining Pukekura Park incorporates the "Bowl of Brooklands" — a soundshell and natural amphitheatre which seats over 16,000. A lake in front of the soundshell mirrors performances of drama, ballet, opera and music.

In the centre of the park stood the home of New Plymouth's first Resident Magistrate, Captain Henry King. The remnants of its fireplace and chimney, built in 1843, may be seen inside the main gates.

Near the park stands **The Gables ★★★**, a quaint cottage hospital built in 1848, at the suggestion of the Governor, Sir George Grey, and the only survivor of four. Perhaps the most important remaining building in Taranaki, it was damned by the first Colonial Surgeon as cold, draughty and inadequate, so that Grey's hopes that Pakeha as well as Maori would use the hospital failed to be realised. Used as a military piquet post during the Taranaki Campaigns and later as an old-age home, it was removed to its present position at the beginning of the century, having originally stood on the site of the Girls' High School. Today the Taranaki Society of Arts stages exhibitions here. *Hours vary.*

Within the reserve is a massive puriri tree, 213 metres high and over 2,000 years old. *Brooklands Park Drive, off Brooklands Rd.*

Taranaki Museum ★★★: One of the finest provincial museums in the country, it includes splendid collections of primitive stone sculpture and vigorous wood-carvings of the Te Atiawa of North Taranaki. Other features are the fabled anchor-stone of the *Tokomaru* canoe, said to have arrived with the Polynesian migration of six centuries ago; a venerated adze said to have come on the same canoe, and an eight-

153

skin hurihuri (dogskin cloak). Displays also cover the history of the province since Pakeha settlement as well as its natural history. Comprehensive manuscript, photograph and art collections are also held. *Ariki St. Open Tuesday - Friday, 10.30 a.m.-4.30 p.m.; Saturday and Sunday, 1-5 p.m. Tel. (06) 758-9583.*

Richmond Cottage ★★: Built in 1853 when the settlement was barely 13 years old by Henry Richmond and Arthur Atkinson, the cottage has for a long time been associated with both families and with the related Hursthouses. Formerly known as Beach Cottage, it was a school for a time (the founder of the Plunket Society, Sir Truby King, was a pupil), and later served as a hotel annexe.

The original stone portion was removed to its present site in 1962 to save it from demolition. Inside is period furniture from the Taranaki Museum with a bearing on the history of the cottage. *Cnr Brougham and Ariki Sts, by the museum. Open weekend and public holidays, 1-4 p.m.; Mon, Wed and Fri, 2-4 p.m. (closed Mon and Wed from June–October).*

Museum of Transport and Aviation and Technology: A large collection of assorted equipment from both air and farm. *Cnr Kent Rd on Highway 3. 7 km S. Open Sundays and public holidays, 10.30 a.m.–4.30 p.m.*

Mount Moturoa ★ ★: From here one enjoys a most spectacular view of the area across the North Taranaki Bight, over the city to Taranaki/Egmont, and inland to the mountains of △ Tongariro National Park. Below rises the 198-metre chimney of the gas-fired thermal power station, to a height of nearly 45 metres above Paritutu.

Around the striking shape of nearby Paritutu (*154 m*) is a reserve which commemorates the first settlers who in 1841 landed in the shadow of the rock from the barque *William Bryan*. The Maori named Paritutu "rising precipice" for the same reason that Captain Cook was prompted to call it "Sugarloaf" — just as the islands at its base, now sanctuaries for gulls, diving petrels and other seabirds, were called the "Sugarloaf Islands". The Maori had fortified pa both here and on the islands, including one on the very tip of Paritutu which was levelled and fortified long before the arrival of the first Europeans. A steep winding track on the landward side leads to the summit.

The area is the relic of an extinct volcano very much older than Taranaki/Egmont. From the carpark a track leads down to a popular surf beach. *Drive towards the port, turn left into Ngamotu Rd and immediately right into Centennial Drive to enter Centennial Park. Continue along Paritutu Rd to Findlay St to reach the lookout on Mt Moturoa.*

St Mary's Church ★★: Established by Bishop Selwyn in 1842, this is the oldest stone church in the country. The foundation stone (unidentified) was hauled from the beach to be laid by the Resident Magistrate in 1845. The original bell, used at the first service, is still in use and hangs outside the church. The organ dates from 1865. The building has been described as "a poem in stone", but one should enter to appreciate the design in full. Along with the early memorials and windows it houses, there are Regimental colours and painted hatchments commemorating the European forces in the Taranaki Campaigns, during which the church was used as a military post and ammunition dump. In the churchyard are the graves of early settlers, including that of George Robinson, builder of the church and of John Sarten, in 1860 the first to die as troops moved against Wiremu Kingi at △ Waitara. Some of the Waikato chiefs killed at Mahoetahi in 1860 were buried surreptitiously in the far corner of the vicarage section.

After seeing the church, one may walk along Cherry Blossom Walk at the rear of the church *(at its best in April and October)*, and walk up Marsland Hill. The track passes the grave of Charles Brown, whose headstone proclaims him to have been "the friend of Keats", the English poet. *Vivian St.*

The remaining section of the stone vicarage (1845) is some distance away *(end of Courtenay St)*. A modern annexe is used by local potters. *Open Sunday and Wednesday, 1-4 p.m.*

Marsland Hill: Now a domain, the hill was once the site of a pa. Later the summit was further levelled and military barracks were built for use in the Taranaki Campaigns. Parts of the barracks were used later in the construction of the North Egmont Mountain House. There is a memorial to the Land Wars and good views of the city. *Robe St; or walk from St Mary's Church.*

Observatory: Situated at the rear of Marsland Hill (*above*), the observatory is open to the public. *Robe St. Open Tuesday evenings, 7.30–9.30 p.m.*

Govett-Brewster Art Gallery ★★★: While mounting travelling and temporary exhibitions, the gallery is building up an exciting permanent collection of contemporary works of art from New Zealand and from other countries around the Pacific, including Australia, Japan, Mexico and the USA. Of special interest is the collection of Len Lye kinetic sculptures, paintings and films. *Open Monday-Friday, 10.30 a.m.-5 p.m.; Saturday and Sunday, 1-5 p.m. Queen St.*

OTHER THINGS TO SEE AND DO

Kawaroa Park: An excellent picnic spot close to the city's centre and near a good beach. A large siege gun here is a relic from World War I. *Weymouth St.*

Fitzroy and East End Beaches: These excellent surf beaches together form a lengthy sweep of sand. *3 km E of city centre.*

Fitzroy Pole ★: In 1844 a nine-metre puriri pole decorated with carvings of "a cowering European beneath a dominating Maori" was erected on what is now the city's eastern boundary to mark the European border beyond which the Pakeha was forbidden to settle. The original pole, burnt in a gorse fire in the 1870s, was replaced by a replica in 1940. *On the road towards Waitara, opp. the fertiliser works.*

Hempton Rose Garden: At its best between October and April. *Hempton St, off Upper Brougham St.*

Whiteley Church: A striking example of modern ecclesiastical architecture and a memorial to the missionary killed at Pukearuhe (*pp.* **157-58**). *Liardet St.* Also of interest is St Joseph's Catholic Church, with its Stations of the Cross executed by local artist Michael Smither. *Powderham and Devon Sts.*

Churchill Heights: Named for Sir Winston, the area offers panoramic views from the port to the coast beyond Waitara, inland to Egmont, and an intimate glimpse of the city. In favourable conditions Mt Ngauruhoe may be seen in the ranges to the east. *Cutfield Rd.*

Rangimarie Maori Arts and Crafts Centre: Here artists may be seen at work and their wares inspected. *Centennial Drive. Visits can be arranged through the Visitor Centre.*

Te Henui walkway: A gentle walk of about three kilometres (one way) winds from the Waiwaka Reserve following the Te Henui Stream up to Welbourne Terrace, through some exquisite natural scenery. En route the **Pukewarangi pa** site is passed, one of the region's most picturesque and readily accessible pre-European sites. With its pronounced earthworks, the pa looks across to three others on the opposite bank, all of which belong to the Te Atiawa sub-tribe of Ngati-tupare-kino. *The site can be visited separately, at the end of Warangi St, off Mangorei Rd just beyond the Girls' High School.*

ENVIRONS

An absorbing all-day drive around the mountain can include many points of interest. See △ Egmont/Taranaki, Road Around and △ Egmont National Park.

Pukeiti Rhododendron Trust ★★★: A world-famous 360-hectare park and bird sanctuary where rhododendrons and azaleas flourish in a native bush setting. The park nestles between the Kaitake (*683 m*) and Pouakai (*1,399 m*) ranges, Pukeiti meaning "little hill". *At its best from September-November. Open all year from dawn to dusk. 29 km from New Plymouth on the Upper Carrington Rd.*

The road to Pukeiti passes the historic farm homestead of Hurworth★ ★ and the Pouakai Zoo Park (*for both, see below*).

Hurworth ★★ (1855-56): This small pioneer cottage is the sole survivor of six houses, all built by a closely knit group which included Sir Harry Atkinson, four times Premier of New Zealand and a bitter political rival of Sir George Grey.

Harry Atkinson (1831-92) was an enigmatic figure on the political scene. Coming to New Zealand at the age of 22, he began clearing bush here, and soon entered local politics. During the Taranaki Campaigns he rose to command the Forest Rangers, showing great skill as a guerilla leader and taking part in a number of major engagements. In 1864 he entered national politics. Although from a then poor and isolated province, he favoured abolition of provincial government and pushed through the Bill which brought this about in 1876. Assuming the Premiership in the same year he attacked the enormous borrowing schemes of the 1870s to rid them of their worst extravagances. At times defeated by those who favoured rapid expansion, he returned to positions of power in periods of depression to provide the sound, prudent financial management for which he is remembered. However, his reputation as a conservative resistant of social change is undeserved: he supported major reforms in education and land tenure; he attempted to introduce a scheme of national insurance

"How much a dunce that has been sent to roam Excels a dunce that has been kept at home!" *William Cowper, The Progress of Error*

more comprehensive and 20 years in advance of that for which Seddon is revered, and he consistently supported the campaign to extend the vote to women. *548 Carrington Rd. Open Wednesday-Sunday, 10 a.m.-noon; 1-4 p.m.*

Pouakai Zoo Park: A four-hectare reserve whose inhabitants include varieties of goat, deer, wallaby and native and exotic birds. A lake is home to waterfowl and there is a walk-through aviary. *Carrington Rd (towards Pukeiti Rhododendron Trust). 14 km. Open daily.*

Sugar Loaf Islands Marine Park ★ ★: The oddly-shaped volcanic upthrusts — islands, rocks and reefs — that spill over into the sea off the coast of Paritutu form an 8 square-kilometre area protected for its unique marine habitats and wildlife.

Early human habitation is revealed in the pits and clearly visible terracing, and quite possibly the islands were then used on a seasonal basis. It is thought by archaeologists that one island, Mataora, which was not inhabited, may have been used as a place to collect gull eggs, a much fancied delicacy. Later, in the 1820s, during the peak of the whaling industry and long after the islands had been given their European name by Captain Cook in 1770, whalers established a base on Moturoa Island.

Today marine mammals are again increasing in numbers, among them fur seals (*seen from June to October*), dolphins (*from October to December*) and in spring, humpback whales pass through the park on their way to breeding grounds (*from August to September*). Numerous species of birds — both sea and land — draw birdwatchers, and beneath the water, intricate volcanic formations supporting seventy odd different species of fish (including an array of reef fish) fascinate divers.

Motouroa, Motumahanga (Saddleback Island), Waikaranga (Seal Rocks) and Wharemu (Lion Rock) are all Wildlife Sanctuaries where landing is prohibited. Regulations (set out in a notice at the breakwater) strictly control fishing. The most popular way to visit the park is by boat. See "Organised excursions", below.

Some beaches: Oakura *(14 km SW)* and △ Waitara *(16 km E)* have popular beaches.

Burgess Park: This area of formal grounds and native bush adjoins the 25-hectare Meeting of the Waters Reserve, a picnic spot where join two good trout rivers, the Mangorei and the Waiwakaiho. The mouth of the Waiwakaiho, a picnic area, adjoins a good beach. *6.5 km on the main south highway. River mouth at end of Clemow Rd.*

Lake Mangamahoe Domain: An ideal picnic spot. From the far end, and in favourable conditions, a spectacular view of Mt Egmont is perfectly mirrored in the lake. Shortly after dawn is the best time to photograph the scene. The lake provides the city's water supply and so boating and swimming are not allowed. There is a small hydro-electric station here. *9.5 k S signposted off S.H.3.*

Taranaki Aviation Transport and Technology Museum: The collection includes a Harvard aircraft, fire engines and a range of agricultural equipment. *Kent Rd, 10 km S, off S.H.3. Open Sun and public holidays, 10.30 a.m.-4.30 p.m.*

Tupare: Attractive gardens landscaped in traditional English style are among the finest in the country. *487 Mangorei Rd off S.H.3 S. Open daily, 9 a.m.-4 p.m. A Queen Elizabeth II Trust property.*

△ **Waitara** *(17 km)*: The Government's attempt in 1860 to enforce the infamous Waitara Land Deal marked the start of the Taranaki Campaigns and 12 years of bloodshed. Today, major energy-based projects are centred here.

ORGANISED EXCURSIONS

Sugar Loaf Islands and Seal Colony ★ ★: Cruises, one in a sturdy old English lifeboat with a lively commentary, give an intimate glimpse of wildlife on the nuggety off-shore islands. *Happy Chaddy's Charters; tel. (06) 758-0228 or (06) 751-1174 (after hrs). Peak Charters; tel. (06) 751-0211. Fishing trips available.*

Horse riding: There are several opportunities to trek through the countryside, both at New Plymouth and at Waitara and Urenui. *Arrange through the Visitor Information Centre.*

Scenic flights: Flights over New Plymouth and the mountain may be arranged. (*Contact the New Plymouth Aero Club; tel. (06) 755-0500.*) There are glider flights and pilot training flights too (*Taranaki Gliding Club Inc. Alfred Rd, Egmont Village, tel. (06) 753-9241*) and helicopter flights around the mountain (*Beck Helicopters Ltd, tel. (06) 764-7073*).

Guided tramps, camps and canoe trips: A four-day guided tramp around the mountain can be organised, as well as canoe and raft trips. Further afield, the 40-odd kilometre **Matemateonga Walkway** follows the Matemateonga Range, eventually to link in with the Whanganui River. Here it is possible to raft, canoe or jet boat down the Whanganui River. *Camp-N-Canoe, tel. (06) 764-6738.*

Duncan & Davies: The internationally known nursery, the largest in the Southern Hemisphere, exports native plants to many parts of the world. *Group tours can be arranged.*

New Plymouth Thermal Power Station: *Conducted tours Wed 10 a.m., Sun 2 p.m.*

★★ NEW PLYMOUTH-TE KUITI ROAD

Taranaki-King Country   Maps 6, 7

169 km Highway 3.

FROM △ NEW PLYMOUTH the road to △ Te Kuiti passes through undulating Taranaki dairyland before climbing Mt Messenger and plunging into the rugged King Country. A number of tiny rivermouth fishing settlements, cluttered with cottages, are passed, and one savours a series of fine seascapes before the road swings inland up the grand Awakino Gorge.

PLACES OF INTEREST ON THE WAY
Listed in the order they are reached, starting from New Plymouth:

△ **Waitara** *(17 km)*: The Government's attempt in 1860 to enforce the infamous Waitara Land Deal here marked the start of the Taranaki Campaigns and 12 years of bloodshed. The town is the centre of major energy-based industries.

Motunui *(23 km)*: The Methanex gas-to-gasoline plant here involves the conversion of natural gas to methanol which is passed through the Mobil-developed zeolite catalytic process to produce a high-octane gasoline. Three methanol production units feed into the zeolite process with an output which meets over one-third of the nation's needs. The multi-million dollar plant commenced production in 1986 and was enlarged in 1994. *Information and display centre with models and video open daily; tel. (06) 754-8009.*

Urenui *(32 km)*: Here, where the summit of nearly every hill was fortified, there once lived a dense Maori population. Urenui Beach *(3 km; turnoff 1.5 km N)* is a favoured picnic and swimming spot. Urenui pa, on the way to the beach, may also be visited.

Urenui was the birthplace of Sir Peter Henry Buck (Te Rangi Hiroa; *c.* 1877-1951), who became an internationally famous authority on Polynesian anthropology. Although honours were showered on him in later life and he became Director of Honolulu's Bishop Museum, his most signal achievement was to fail in 1914 by only a few votes to gain election to Parliament from a European electorate. (He had previously held Cabinet rank as a Maori member.) Buck's life illustrated his own belief that the future New Zealander would derive "physical and cultural superiority from the inter-mixture of two bloods". His ashes lie in a striking memorial at Okoki Pa which symbolises the prow of a Polynesian canoe and reflects the ancient Maori custom of erecting a decorated canoe prow as a memorial. *The memorial may be seen from the main road 4 km N, on a bush-covered knoll. Signposted. The pa site itself may be visited.*

Whitecliffs Brewing Company *(36 km)*: A cheerful boutique brewery produces beer, using solely New Zealand ingredients, and without preservatives.

Pukearuhe *(detour 11.5 km—at 42 km)*: Once a blockhouse settlement, Pukearuhe is today but a name on a map. The blockhouse (1865) was a key point in the Taranaki Campaigns as it commanded the only practical route between Taranaki and the Waikato. Thus Waikato Maori, eager to come south to join the Hauhau movement, found their way cut off.

The inevitable attack came early in 1869. The military settlers at Pukearuhe were out working their holdings when a Ngati Maniapoto war party arrived from the north, and while most hid, a handful went on ahead pretending to have pigs for sale. The few Europeans and their families, disarmed by the friendly gesture, were suddenly struck down—two were tomahawked on the steep path down to the beach. Late the same afternoon the Wesleyan missionary the Rev. John Whiteley was riding towards the redoubt, ignorant of the earlier events of the day, when he was stopped and ordered to return the way he had come. He refused, sensing that all was not well;

his horse was then shot from under him and as Whiteley knelt in prayer he, too, was shot. The unnecessary killings were deplored by Maori leaders and settlers alike. The Maniapoto made no attempt to hold the post, which was from then on garrisoned by the Armed Constabulary as a blockhouse and remained an important position until the field force was demobilised in 1885.

The blockhouse gave its name, Clifton, to the county, but today the only physical traces of the building are concrete steps and a fireplace. The strategic importance of the site was recognised in pre-European times, and a pa stood here from perhaps as early as 1500 A.D. *(Turn left at Mimi turnoff, 7 km beyond Urenui, and continue 10 km down Pukearuhe Rd.)*

Although the "modern" Whiteley Memorial Methodist Church in New Plymouth commemorates the missionary, at Pukearuhe itself a simple cairn marks the place where Whiteley died. From here on the cliff top there is a magnificent view of the Parininihi ("lofty cliffs") which dominate the wild coastline to the north. It was through these inhospitable cliffs that a tunnel was carved to facilitate the driving of stock along the coast, then the only route south. *(The 50-metre tunnel can still be used but in reaching it along the beach extreme care is needed because of the tides. Inquire at Wai-iti Beach for directions.)*

The Whitecliffs walkway links Pukearuhe with Tongaporutu, starting from the Pukearuhe Historic Reserve and following in large part the Kapuni natural gas pipeline whose construction opened up walking access to some of the region's most dramatic forest and coastline. The walk of 9.5 kilometres takes about 5 hours but it can be shortened at various points by cutting through to the beach and returning along the foreshore. *(If this is planned, it is essential to check tide times first as you should be able to reach your destination comfortably within 2 hours either side of low tide.)*

Wai-iti Beach en route to Pukearuhe *(7 km from the main road)* attracts summertime campers. "The Castle" here is a homestead built of rocks from the shore. It was designed by the architect F. Chapman-Taylor.

Pukearuhe means "hill of fern root"; Wai-iti means "little river".

Mount Messenger rest area *(59 km)*: From the carpark at 189 metres there are magnificent views over a well-forested landscape. The prominence (306 m.a.s.l.) is named after Captain Messenger who commanded the defences at Pukearuhe *(see above)*.

Tongaporutu *(72 km)*: The first of a series of superb fishing settlements nestles by the mouth of the river from which it takes its name. The territory hereabouts was keenly disputed in pre-European times and many of the hills bear traces of fortifications.

Behind the ocean beach the sea has carved huge caverns in the sheer sandstone cliffs, and in one of these are some early Maori rock drawings, mostly of a curious foot with six toes. *Park in Clifton Rd by the river and follow the river to the beach. The drawings are near the roof of a cave which faces three enormous wedges of rock on the beach. Allow at least 40 mins. The beach is accessible only at low tide and care must be taken as the tide rises quickly.*

Some distance south is the Drovers' Tunnel, a 50-metre tunnel through the sandstone cliffs down to the beach. *The tunnel may be reached at the end of Clifton Rd, across farmland. Enquire locally for directions. Its exit may also be reached at low tide along the beach from Pukearuhe.*

Tongaporutu means "driving into a southerly at night" and was given by the captain of a passing canoe which struck a southerly gale here at nightfall.

Te Kawau pa *(80 km)*: An island at the mouth of the Kira-tahi Stream, the pa was a key fighting position on the coast. Access was by ladder and a freshwater spring assured drinking supplies. The pa is entrenched in legend as the coastal route was of paramount importance, the trackless interior being virtually impregnable.

Mokau *(88 km)*: The lovely Mokau River, on which the settlement stands, once formed the boundary between Taranaki and Waikato tribal areas and so was the scene of many battles. A Taranaki tribe held the area until in 1815 and again six years later they were defeated in battles on Mokau Beach. They then joined Te Rauparaha *(pp.* **115-16***)* and trekked south to △ Kapiti Island, leaving the gateway to Taranaki open to the Waikato tribes.

During the Land Wars the river was used as a supply route to the King Country, last stronghold of the followers of the Maori King. The final shot of the Taranaki Campaigns (also the last artillery shot of the Land Wars) was fired in 1869, at a Maori settlement on the river mouth.

Painted red and mounted in concrete is a German mine which washed ashore here in 1942. *(By the beach turnoff)*. A number of minefields were laid by the German Navy off Auckland and between Wellington and Lyttelton in 1940-41.

What is said to be the anchor stone of the *Tainui* canoe, one of the canoes in the Polynesian migration of six centuries ago, is set in concrete in Maniaroa pa, which is now an uru pa (a pa now used as a burial ground). *5 km N of the township.* The canoe itself is said to have been buried at △ Kawhia Harbour.

Mokau means "sleeping place".

Awakino *(93 km):* Like the rivers to the south, the Awakino offers good fishing. The road turns inland here to follow the spectacular gorge of the Awakino River through hard-won farmland.

Awakino, inappropriately, means "bad river".

Marokopa turnoff *(95 km):* Those with time in hand and not deterred by a somewhat demanding drive may choose to follow a less direct route which leads through dramatic back country and takes in Marokopa Falls and the "natural bridge" (*p.* **267**). Te Anga Tavern's comprehensive bottle collection may be seen before emerging at △ Waitomo Caves *(approx. 106 km from turnoff).*

Piopio *(146 km):* A small museum features a blacksmith's forge and shop. Nearby a small hydro-electric station perches at the top of the 12-metre Wairere Falls, on the Mokau River. *(Detour 7 km S towards Aria.)*

A piopio is a native thrush.

Madonna Falls *(173 km):* The roadside falls were christened "Our Lady of the Waterfall" in 1975 by the Kohahitanga Church Building Society, a small local religious group which claimed special healing powers for its waters. The falls enjoyed considerable popularity for a time. *173 km. (At 158 km, at Eight Mile Junction, detour right towards Taumarunui on Highway 4 for 15 km; the falls are on the right after crossing the Mapara Stream.)*

△ **Te Kuiti** *(169 km):* Today a farming centre, it was to here that first King Tawhiao and later Te Kooti withdrew, effectively to end the Land Wars. A carved meeting house records local hospitality to Te Kooti. Nearby are the fabled △ Waitomo Caves.

★★ NGARUAWAHIA

Waikato   Maps 5, 6   Pop. 6,181

19 km NW of Hamilton. Information Office, tel. (07) 824-8633.

NGARUAWAHIA, a farming centre, is primarily of importance as the former capital of the Maori King Movement and is still its headquarters.

The Waikato and Waipa Rivers meet here and, as both were once canoe routes of the greatest importance, it was to be expected that a Maori village would grow up on the junction. The first Maori King, Potatau I, was proclaimed at Ngaruawahia in 1858, and the village fortified against the expected attack. But the rivers that spawned the village were to prove its undoing, as once the effectiveness of the British gunboats had been seen at Meremere and Rangiriri in 1863 the position was abandoned, to fall without opposition. The following year a European settlement was laid out and sections sold—quite without justification as the area was Maori-owned—and for a time it seemed destined to enjoy Hamilton's present-day position as the Waikato's principal centre.

Ngaruawahia means "break open the food pits" and refers to an occasion in about 1660 when the local chief saw important invited guests approaching. At his command all the food for the customary ceremonial feast was then displayed on a high triangular framework over 1.5 kilometres in length. The massive food stage was likened to the nearby range of hills, which were bestowed with the name Hakarimata ("the range of cold food"). In early European times it was briefly known as Queenstown, and then as Newcastle (after the Duke of Newcastle who headed a protest against the treatment of the Maori by the British Government).

THE MAORI KING

Before the arrival of the European, the Maori had no concept of being a distinct people: their loyalty was to their family and to their tribe. It was only the arrival of strangers that provoked the word Maori ("usual", or "ordinary") to take on its contemporary meaning, and it was the land question that induced many tribes to settle centuries of grievances in a common cause—to resist the Europeans who sought to buy, and later to confiscate their land. This was the principal reason for Waikato, Taupo and some other tribes in 1858 electing a "King", Te Wherowhero, who took the title of Potatau 1. As King, Potatau was expected to protect their lands from sale and to restore law and order.

Although the election of a king represented a hardening of Maori nationalism, its main purpose was to elect a paramount chief whose authority over the Maori people would be absolute and enable him both to enforce peaceful co-existence and to administer Maori affairs within their own boundaries. It was incorrectly seen as a form of rebellion, and so the blessings the Movement should have brought were never realised.

After the devastating Waikato Campaigns, the king and his followers were forced south of the Puniu River (near Te Awamutu) into what is still known as the King Country, where they remained almost devoid of European contact until King Tawhiao (who succeeded his father in 1860) made formal peace in 1881.

The followers of the Maori king gradually filtered back to the Waikato headquarters, Ngaruawahia, where the Movement's headquarters remain today. The Maori king or queen speaks only for the tribes which support his or her reign, and a number of non-member tribes do not recognise the king or queen as other than a paramount chief of a tribal federation. With no administrative function, the monarch's role is neither constitutional nor political; essentially it is social and cultural, but nevertheless it is becoming progressively more important as the Maori's role in New Zealand society is reassessed. The king or queen is informally recognised by the Government, the headquarters have been officially visited by British Royalty, and the Government is generally represented at major ceremonial occasions.

Election and proclamation: As the king or queen is paramount chief of a confederation of several important tribes, his or her tangi (funeral) is a spectacular occasion. High chiefs assemble to choose a successor and although the monarch's oldest surviving son is preferred, succession remains a matter of discretion. Queen Te Atairangikaahu, the first queen and sixth person to hold the office, was proclaimed in 1966.

The new monarch's proclamation and accession take place on the last day of the tangi, shortly before the late monarch's interment and in the presence of the body. The king or queen elect wears an inherited kaitaka (cloak for those of the highest rank) of great antiquity, and attends an ecumenical service on the marae at Turangawaewae. At the conclusion of the service the senior descendant of the "Kingmaker", Wiremu Tamihana, proclaims the king or queen by laying a Bible (used in every former coronation) on his or her head. As the ceremony is performed, the late monarch's flag is lowered and that of the successor is hoisted to the top of the flagpole. The ceremony concludes with short speeches, prayers, hymns and a Benediction. Some time later the new king or queen accompanies the funeral party to lay the late monarch to rest in the Royal Burial Ground on Taupiri Mountain.

Terminology: The "Maori King Movement" is a term which acquired a derogatory connotation between 1860-80 when the Movement was deliberately ridiculed by the settlers. "Maori Kingship" is perhaps a better expression as it more closely reflects the term Kingitanga and as there is no territorial association. However, the term "Maori King Movement" has gained currency and so has been used throughout the text of this book. The expression "Kingites", followers of the Maori King, is open to the same criticism, and has fallen into disuse.

HEADQUARTERS OF THE MAORI KING MOVEMENT ★ ★ ★

Turangawaewae Pa ★★★: The headquarters of Maori Kingship and the official residence of the present monarch, the Maori Queen, Te Arikinui Dame Te Atairangikaahu, DBE. It was not until 1920 that the first two hectares of land here were purchased from Pakeha owners and work was begun on the pa.

Mahinarangi House (1929) has an exterior carved by Waikato Maori and an interior carved by Arawa. The tekoteko above the maihi apex represents Potatau I, the first Maori King, in the traditional posture of a warrior guardian. Above the window is a relief carving of the *Tainui* canoe, the largest figure representing its captain, Hoturoa. According to tradition, the *Tainui* brought the forebears of the Waikato and Maniapoto tribes to New Zealand in a migration from Polynesia about six centuries ago. The kumara they brought with them is shown by a flax kit. Inside the building is the Maori throne, once kept at Morrinsville. A feature is the royal coat of arms carved on the massive doors. Unusual are the seven stars (it was contrary to etiquette to carve heavenly bodies) which represent Te Matariki or the Pleiades, the first appearance of which (in June) indicated the beginning of the Maori year and foretold calm weather. "Te Paki o Matariki", as the coat of arms is entitled, expressed the determined and prophetic hope of peace and "calm" among the peoples

---

Camping grounds, motels and hotels are listed in the Automobile Association handbooks.

---

of New Zealand. Under the stars the gods Atua Pai (the god of good) and Atua Kino (the god of evil) are shown, wrestling for the world. Between them is Manawa, who has two tongues, one for speaking truth and the other for ill. The design dates from 1870.

Beside Mahinarangi stands **Turongo House** (1938), the Queen's official residence, conspicuous for its quaint pentagonal tower on its northern corner. Two miniature pataka symbolise dual aspects of Maori life: one faces on to the marae, representing traditional Maori culture, the other faces out from the marae, symbolic of the European side to Maori life.

Turongo House, Ngaruawahia.

The tetrahedral roof of the **Kimi-ora Cultural Complex** (1974) is a striking visual feature. An interior wall is decorated with one of the largest murals in the country. *The marae is not open to the public except on Regatta Day (nearest Sat to 17 March), but may be seen in River Rd and also, more distantly, from the main road riverbridge, a little upstream and to the left.*

The Point: A pleasant picnic spot at the junction of the Waikato and Waipa Rivers. Close by (and standing on the site of his 1860 tomb, where his body rested before burial on Taupiri), is a memorial to Potatau I, the first Maori King. Also nearby is a gun turret from the *Pioneer,* which helped take Ngaruawahia on 8 December 1863. *Off the main road, across the railway lines.*

A regatta has been held at The Point each March since 1896 (*on the nearest Saturday to St Patrick's Day*). In a unique carnival the emphasis is on traditional Maori canoe races and hurdle races. The winner of the Maori girls' canoe race becomes the prize for the kawhaki tamahine (chase for the bride) in which the quarry is chased by a number of canoes in an effort to be the craft which carries her across the finishing line. The Parade of the Great War Canoes is the major attraction, and their salute to the Maori Queen and her distinguished guests is a splendid spectacle.

Turangawaewae House ★: When this House opened on 18 March 1920, it was intended to be the Maori Parliament, where Maori policy could be clarified and consolidated before presentation to Government. However, the most important aspect of the building was that it partially fulfilled the 1881 prophecy of Tawhiao, the second Maori King who after 18 years' exile in the King Country expressed his desire that "Ngaruawahia will [once more] be my turangawaewae" (literally, "a place where one puts one's feet").

Turangawaewae house overlooks the area (now in reserve or with housing on it) sloping to the Waikato River where Tawhiao and his ancestors had a great pa. Tawhiao abandoned it just before General Cameron and the militia reached Ngaruawahia on 8 December 1863.

One of the first decisions of the Maori Parliament was to buy the land which is now Turangawaewae marae, the official marae of the Kingitanga. But the desire for a Maori Parliament waned dramatically in the 1920s. In later decades the building became a health clinic and the Maori Land Court. Today it provides offices for the Tainui Trust Board which manages the Tainui confederation's interests.

Apart from the carved gables and ornamented double doors, the building of brick and stucco is of European design. The great hall (the council chamber) is somewhat medieval in style with panelling and great arched beams, but the rafters are richly decorated with an array of Maori waituhi (rafter) patterns. At one end of the hall is a dais (where the royal throne once sat) and rising from it is a giant carved obelisk, "The Needle". This recalls the wisdom of the first Maori King: "The white thread, the red thread and the dark thread, all are threaded on to the one needle" (i.e., all people are equal in the sight of God). *By the main highway S of the river bridge.*

ENVIRONS

Waingaro Hot Springs: Three hot mineral pools (and a long hot-water slide which twirls and winds for 137 metres) are open daily and in the evenings. There is also accommodation, good camping and barbecue facilities scattered through the park. *Waingaro, 42 km NW; tel. (07) 825-4761.*

Taupiri Mountain ★★ (*288 m*): On its slopes, a fortified pa is now the Waikato tribes' most sacred burial ground. *Signposted 6.5 km N on Highway 1.* Taupiri means "closely clinging loved one". It was here that the great Te Putu (*p.* **119**), who consolidated the power of the mid-Waikato tribes and whose direct descendant is the Maori Queen, was assassinated.

Hakarimata walkways: There are several tracks in the bush-clad Hakarimata Range to the west of the town. Perhaps the best is the walk to the Hakarimata trig (*371 m above sea level; 3 hrs return*), with views over the Waikato.

NINETY MILE BEACH ★★★

Northland   Map 1

18.5 km NW of Kaitaia (to Waipapakauri).

TE-ONEROA-O-TOHE, "the long beach of Tohe", arches in a magnificent unbroken stretch of white sand for some 103 kilometres (64 miles), from west of △ Kaitaia almost to Cape Maria Van Diemen. Its European name is a misnomer, and the subject of speculation, but it is possible that its length was originally calculated in kilometres, as the beach is over 90 kilometres long.

The beach features in the enchanting Maori legend of the spirits, which fascinates visitors to △ Cape Reinga.

A surf-casting contest is staged here annually (*about Feb*) and there is good surfing at Ahipara and Wreck Bay. But for all this, Ninety Mile Beach is nationally known mainly for the delicacy of its toheroa (*Paphies ventricosa*). Toheroa are also present on beaches near △ Dargaville and △ Levin and along Foveaux Strait. But at present, the numbers are so low that there is often a total ban on their being taken.

TOHEROA

When available the shellfish are considered the country's finest seafood. A type of clam and not unlike a large pipi, the toheroa grows to 150 mm in length and likes fresh water in lagoons whose seepage promotes the growth of the plankton on which the toheroa feeds. When it is being chased, the toheroa can move through the sand with astonishing speed.

Their relation, the tuatua, which thrives in the same habitat, is plentiful and to the connoisseur nearly as tasty. It is easy for the novice to mistake the tuatua for toheroa, but the former are somewhat smaller and have a sweeter taste. Both are eaten raw, baked in the shell, minced for fritters or made into soup.

SOME NOTES

Aupouri Forest programme: The programme involves the reclamation of 29,000 hectares of drifting sand in an area north of △ Kaitaia and parallel to Ninety Mile Beach. Although these sand-dune forests were originally planned to prevent good land from being engulfed, the scheme has succeeded in establishing profitable timber forests which are only slightly less productive than other forest areas.

The prevailing wind drives sand inland and the dunes are first anchored with grass, *Spinifex hirsutus* (a native grass) on the foredunes and *Ammophila arenaria* (marram) inland. In the second stage, yellow lupin *(Lupin arboreus)* is planted to provide nitrogen for the grass and later for the trees. Initially the young lupin plants are sheltered by the grass and then they in turn are ready to shelter infant trees so that within about five years the area is ready for tree planting. *Pinus radiata* was selected for this purpose as it has proved to be both productive and resilient to coastal conditions. An information office at the Aupouri Forest Headquarters *(just N of Waipapakauri)* is open on weekdays, and a small museum depicts the history of the district.

A world land-speed record: On 26 January 1932 the Australian Norman ("Wizard") Smith set a world land-speed record of 164.08 mph over 10 miles (i.e., 264 km/h over 16 kilometres). He had earlier failed in attempts over the measured mile, reaching speeds of 200 mph, as against the then record of 245 mph (394 km/h). Smith's track was on the beach north of Hukatere *(the highest point on the sandhills backing the beach and distinguishable by its forest fire lookout post).*

Warning: Advice should be obtained locally before vehicles are driven any distance on the beach. Vehicular access points are at Ahipara *(14.5 km SW of Kaitaia),* through Waipapakauri *(18.5 km N of Kaitaia)* and from Pukenui to the beach in front of the forest fire tower at Hukatere. Access down Te Paki Stream is closed to the public because of hazardous quicksands. The safest way to enjoy the beach is on one of the guided tours run from △ Kaitaia.

POINTS OF INTEREST ON THE BEACH
(from S to N)

Wreck Bay: At the southern end of the beach a short walk from the Ahipara access round a rocky headland leads to Wreck Bay, named after the wreck of the *Favourite,* which foundered in 1870. Her paddle-shaft can be seen protruding from the sea like a submarine's periscope, and at low tide her engine casing can be reached.

Matapia Island: The only island off the beach, it is said locally to be the anchor of the canoe from which in mythology Maui dragged up the North Island. A better-known version of the legend suggests that Stewart Island was the anchor-stone, but Matapia, pierced by a hole, certainly looks more like it.

Along the beach, particularly between Hukatere and The Bluff, are midden heaps of shell, testimony to the extent and the size of the Maori population that the beach once supported.

The Bluff: A rocky outcrop severed from the mainland by the beach. Vehicular access is available from Te Kao settlement to The Bluff, known to the Maori as Te Waka-te-haua. *66 km up the beach.*

Twilight Beach: At the northern extremity of the beach the more energetic may climb to Scotts Point to reach Twilight Beach *(1 hr)* and Te Waioraropa Stream, from which the departing spirits of the legend are said to have drunk on their way north.

★ NORSEWOOD

Hawke's Bay   Map 11, 12   Pop. 330

84 km SW of Hastings; 76 km NE of Palmerston North

NORSEWOOD, severed by Highway 2, its two parts linked only by a viaduct, can be passed by travellers unaware of its existence let alone its unique character. For Norsewood, as its name suggests, shares its origins with △ Dannevirke as a Scandinavian bush settlement, but unlike Dannevirke, at Norsewood the Nordic atmosphere persists.

The town was the home of Kirsten Neilson, the originator of New Zealand's Health Stamps (issued annually since 1929).

SOME HISTORY

A "Scandy" settlement: The Scandinavians who settled here (locally, with their descendants, referred to as "Scandies") came mainly on the *Hovding* in 1872, and were assisted by the Government to settle in the bush and complete a road through it, now Highway 2.

However, the railway by-passed the township (which, confidently, had already built its Railway Hotel) and so did not bring to Norsewood the growth and prosperity it brought to Dannevirke.

In 1888 bush fires reduced most of the town to ashes. Some saw the fire as the work of God, for the previous week a popular vote had abolished local Prohibition— "Yet the church was burnt down and the pub was saved," commented the *Daily Telegraph*. A nationwide appeal helped re-establish the community.

Today the settlement has a successful clothing industry, "Norsewear", and is something of a mecca for descendants of the original Scandies. On rare occasions children perform Scandinavian folk-dances in its main street.

POINTS OF INTEREST

Upper Norsewood: Housed in an 1888 cottage built for the Lutheran minister Pastor Ries is the Norsewood Pioneer Museum, a collection of material with an emphasis on articles brought on the *Hovding* or used by the Scandinavian settlers. *Main St, Upper Norsewood. Open daily; 9 a.m.–4.30 p.m.* In contrast is **St Anskar's Church**, opposite the pioneer cottage and symbolising a ship.

Also at the north end of the village, in a glassed boathouse, is the fishing boat *Bindalsfareing*, a centennial gift from the Norwegian Government. At the other end of the main street is an elaborate memorial to H.J. Beck, a Scandinavian settler who died in the Boer War. The memorial is a focal point for Anzac Day observances.

Lower Norsewood: Opposite the Norsewear factory, with its tempting factory shop, is a picnic area with flying foxes, swings and waterwheel.

Anzac Park: A sylvan haven from the hurried highway. *2 km N of the township on Highway 2.*

TOURING NOTE

Alternative route to Waipukurau: Instead of continuing on Highway 2 to Waipukurau, the northbound traveller may branch right along Kopua Road *(turnoff 2 km N of Norsewood)*, passing Seven Star Abbey (a Cistercian monastery) and passing through the village of Takapau. Through Takapau bear right along Orua Wharo road. Three kilometres from this turnoff a short drive leads to a stately Italianate two-storeyed homestead, formerly Orua Wharo Station (1860-97; *in private ownership)*. Continue on to follow signposted route to Waipukurau. *Detour adds 5 km.*

OHAKUNE   *King Country   Map 6   Pop. 1,426*

100 km NE of Wanganui. Ruapehu Visitor Centre, 54 Clyde St, tel. (06) 385-8427; and Ohakune Field Centre, Ohakune Mountain Rd, tel. (06) 385-8578

IN WINTER a bustling ski resort and in summer frequented by visitors to the △ Tongariro National Park, Ohakune was for many years primarily a market-gardening town, with tens of thousands of tonnes of produce being sent out to the cities each year. The Turoa skifield on the western slopes of Mt Ruapehu has generated a rash of ski chalets among the older buildings, and all the trappings of a winter sports centre. In summer the town draws many wilderness walkers, rafters and canoeists, along with mountainbikers who explore the network of tracks in the forests of Rangataua and Erua.

Like other King Country settlements, Ohakune owes its origins to the main trunk railway which was pushed through the dense bush of the hitherto forbidden King Country once peace had been made with the Maori King in 1881. Settlement, in a clearing once the site of a pa, dates from the 1890s. Once the railway opened the town boomed and in 20 years about 370 million feet of timber was railed out.

Today, the township spreads up the hill to Ohakune Junction, a name that lingers despite the demise of the branch line which used to run to the mill at Raetihi. The native forests have largely given way to sheep, cattle raising and market gardening.

Ohakune means "a place to be careful in", but the reason for taking care is lost in antiquity. Now, perhaps it can be construed as advice to winter sports enthusiasts.

THINGS TO SEE AND DO

Turoa skifields ★★★: The skiing season lasts from about June to October, with all equipment available for hire in the town. Chairlifts, ski patrols and ski schools operate in season. The skiing here is more open than at Whakapapa on the northern Ruapehu slopes, with skiers being less restricted to defined runs and with a generally less rocky terrain. *Ohakune Mountain Rd. There is a shuttle service.*

Ohakune Mountain Road ★★★: In all seasons a magnificent 17-kilometre drive, winding from Ohakune Junction *(600 m above sea level)* through splendid bush, to reach the 23-metre drop of Mangawhero Falls on Mt Ruapehu and the Turoa skifields *(1,600 m above sea level).*

Mangawhero Forest walk: One of the easiest walks in the Tongariro National Park, the three-kilometre track leads through luxuriant rain forest past extinct volcanic vents and limestone cliffs containing fossilised shellfish. One may also see rotting sleepers, the remnants of a tramway which in the 1940s and 1950s carried logs to the mill at Ohakune Junction. *Start opposite the DOC ranger station on Ohakune Mountain Rd. Leaflet available. Allow 1 ½ hrs for the round trip.*

Waitonga Falls walk: A walking track leads through progressively more stunted beech forest as it rises to reach boggy wetlands and then descends into a valley to reach the highest falls in the park (*63 m*). *Start from carpark 10 km up the Ohakune Mountain Road. Allow 2 hrs.*

Rotokura Ecological Area: On the lower slopes of Mt. Ruapehu, tracks lead through native bush around two exquisite lakes, stocked with fish. *End of Karioi Station Rd (turn off Highway 49 at 11.5 km E). 2 hrs return.*

Rafting: Raft trips on the Tongariro River can be organised at any time of year.

Makatote viaduct (1907): Lying in dense bush, the spidery steel viaduct *(79-m high, the highest on the main trunk line)* stands as a monument to the ingenuity of early engineers, whose task of linking Auckland and Wellington was a formidable one. *At 22 km N, S.H.4 passes beneath it.* The final spike was driven at Manganuioteao Viaduct in November, 1908 *(19 km N).*

Bay of Plenty   Map 9   Pop. 3,989   **★ OPOTIKI**

59.5 km E of Whakatane. Visitor Information Centre and Department of Conservation Information; tel. (07) 315-8484.

OPOTIKI, "the place of many children", was once the largest of a number of Maori settlements around Opotiki Harbour. Today a farming centre, Opotiki has over 25 kilometres of safe, sandy swimming beaches within easy reach, with good surfing, skindiving and spear-fishing. Inland lies excellent deer, pig and goat-shooting country, in the △ Urewera National Park. Within the town is a martyr's church which stirs poignant memories.

Those not following the intriguing △ East Cape Road to △ Gisborne may choose in fine weather to tackle the tortuous old coach route through virgin bush over the Motu hills, rather than the somewhat slick Waioeka Scenic Highway (*Highway 2*). Mountain bikers also find the Motu a challenge.

CHURCH OF ST STEPHEN THE MARTYR ★★★

The Church of St Stephen the Martyr was built by the Rev. Carl Sylvius Volkner (1819-65), a German Lutheran missionary who came to Opotiki in 1859. In settler mythology Volkner is said to have ministered tirelessly to the local Maori only to be mindlessly slaughtered by a visiting Hauhau prophet, Kereopa Te Rau. He, it is said, then gouged out and swallowed Volkner's eyes before taking his severed head into the church. There he is supposed to have harangued his local converts with the head resting on the rim of the pulpit, and conducted a macabre parody of the Communion service by having them sip Volkner's blood from the Communion chalice.

Kereopa's subsequent execution at Napier is still deeply resented by local Maori, whose account differs sharply and is more in keeping with the historical record. Maori leaders largely blamed the missionaries for their people's then-parlous condition: "(They) showed us this beautiful scabbard all adorned with gold and jewels and we admired it and hung it up in our whare, and then came a man in a red coat and took it down and all of a sudden drew a sword out of it and cut off our heads". More than this, when war flared some missionaries stayed with their flocks, ostensibly to preach but in fact to spy. Little wonder local Whakatohea felt betrayed by Volkner when they discovered that in letters to Governor Grey he was siding with the settlers' cause. Volkner, who had ignored a warning not to return with Rev. T. S. Grace from a trip to Auckland, was "executed according to law . . . fairly tried . . . openly confronted with his own letters giving information to the soldiers, our enemies. He was one of our people; we had adopted him into our tribe . . . He was a traitor and we hanged him according to the law of nations." Had this been a mindless act against the Pakeha, Grace would scarcely have been allowed to return to Auckland unscathed. Indeed, some writers suggest that the settlers embroidered the account in their efforts to keep British troops in New Zealand at Britain's expense.

Over the next three years intermittent skirmishes took placed in the Opotiki district, which was particularly vulnerable to surprise raids by Hauhau sheltering in the

165

nearby Urewera country. The church was surrounded by a redoubt, loopholes cut in its tower (also occasionally used as a gaol), and ammunition stored in the nave. At night the local settlers slept within the safety of its walls. Once the wars in the area were over, some of the soldiers garrisoned here elected to stay, and so Opotiki originated as a military settlement. The church was rededicated in 1875, and renamed after the first Christian martyr, St Stephen.

Photographs of those who took part in the martyrdom are by the font and the chalice, Volkner's Bible and Grace's prayer-book are on display by the pulpit, still apparently stained with Volkner's blood. In 1910 the sanctuary was added to the church bringing Volkner's grave within the church walls, but the original headstone can been seen in the exterior of the east wall. The sand-blasted east windows, a centennial gift from the neighbouring Maori parish of Te Kaha, depict the martyrdom of St Stephen. As a recognition of injustice, the bodies of five Maori executed at Auckland were exhumed and returned to the area in 1989. *Church St.*

Opotiki Heritage and Agricultural Society Museum: A local collection affords an insight into the hardships of settler life. *123 Church St (opp. St. Stephens Church).*

ENVIRONS

Hukutaia Domain ★: A magnificent 4.5-hectare block of bush in which many plants are identified yet remain in an unspoiled environment. The reserve includes one of New Zealand's oldest trees, a puriri named Taketakerau, once used as a burial tree by a local tribe. *7 km W. Signposted. Turnoff at Waioeka Bridge. Walks within the park are signposted.*

On the way to the Domain, at Waioeka Bridge, in a favourable light one may see a furrow marking the course of a 2.4 x 1.2 metre escape trench dug by the Rev. J.A. Wilson, who established the first mission station *(above the site of the golf clubhouse)* in 1840. The trench provided rapid access to the canoe hidden on the river bank. *(Over the Waioeka Bridge, park by the gum trees. The furrow runs straight up the hill to left of the large tree in front of the clubhouse.)*

Waiotahi Beach: A long sandy beach, backed by pohutukawa trees is good for fishing as well as for swimming. *6 km W.*

At its western end *(10 km)* stands a modern carved **"Gateway to the East Cape"**, on which is depicted Tarawa, an ancestor of the local Whakatohea. In tradition he and his brother Tuwharanui sailed in the *Te Arautauta* canoe from "Hawaiki" to rejoin their people here bringing with them two pet fish. These they released into a fresh-water spring on the bluff here, so giving rise to the town's full name of O-Potiki-mai Tawhiti (two pets from afar).

Motu River excursions: A breathtaking white-water rafting adventure can be arranged *(Book through the Information Centre.)* or an exhilarating jet boat trip *(Motu River Jet Boat Tour; tel/fax (07) 315-8107).*

OPUNAKE   *Taranaki   Map 7   Pop. 1,637*

61.5 km S of New Plymouth.

OPUNAKE, the dairy centre where export cheese was first produced in Taranaki, is better known for its beach and for good sea-fishing. Offshore may be seen the production platform for the Maui natural gas field.

Settlement dates from the Taranaki Campaigns when, in 1865, New Plymouth-based British troops landed on the beach at dawn and established a camp on the clifftop. There they built a formidable redoubt with walls three metres thick as part of a series of fortifications which extended along the coast for some 137 kilometres to Pukearuhe.

Opunake means "place of Punake".

Opunake Beach: The iron-blacked sands of the beach are characteristic of this part of the coast. Above the powerhouse surge chamber is the levelled clifftop where the redoubt was sited. The **Opunake Walkway** *(7 km)* follows the coastline.

SOME HISTORY

A lone marksman: In 1833, during the intertribal wars of the early nineteenth century and one of many Waikato raids into Taranaki, 800 invaders laid siege to Te Namu pa, the last stronghold of the Taranaki tribes. The attackers burnt the surrounding whare and, over a period of a month, five times unsuccessfully stormed the pa. Repulsed for the sixth time by boulders and a single musket, the well-armed Waikato prepared to withdraw, only to be routed by a counter-attack by the 150 defenders. The hero of the day was Wiremu Kingi (not the Wiremu Kingi of the Waitara Land Deal), who used the Taranaki's sole musket to such telling effect that he was given the name of Te Matakatea, "the eagle-eye". *The remains of the pa are on private property on the north-west town boundary. Casual visitors are not encouraged.*

Wreck of the "Worsley": At Aitken Bay, just north of Opunake, the SS *Worsley* was wrecked in 1862 with a cargo of gold. Te Matakatea and Te Ua (who later founded Hauhauism) protected the passengers and crew from hostile Maori who were eager to dispose of them and to pillage the cargo. As a reward, Te Matakatea was given a ship's lifeboat by the Government. One of the wrecked ship's masts was the first flagstaff erected by Te Ua when launching the Hauhau cult, whose frenzied followers were to strike fear in the hearts of the bravest of the British troops.

The Hauhau Movement: The impact of early missionaries on Maori culture and indigenous religion was devastating. All too swiftly many Maori abandoned their former beliefs and embraced Christianity. But when land troubles arose, many of the Maori came to see the missionaries as agents of land-hungry settlers, and when war broke out the Maori felt they were fighting not only the British Crown but also the religion the British had brought to New Zealand. Indeed Bishop Selwyn was sufficiently indiscreet as to become chaplain to the armed forces.

Dispirited by defeats in the early stages of the wars and seemingly betrayed by the missionaries and their God, some Maori found in Hauhauism a spiritual basis for united action against the settlers.

Like the Ringatu religion (*p.* **86**) which stemmed from it, Hauhauism was a Maori revivalist movement based on the Old Testament, and the plight of the Israelites under the Egyptians was likened to that of the Maori under the Pakeha. Services took the form of a frenzied dance around a tall niu flagpole while unintelligible chants were intoned to will the Europeans to leave the country. The movement (also called Paimarire) takes its name from the cry "Hapa, hapa, paimarire hau", shouted by Hauhau warriors as they ran into battle with their right arms raised, to give them protection from bullets—those who were shot were considered simply to have lacked faith.

The founder of Hauhauism, Te Ua Haumene (?1825-?) of the Ngati Ruanui tribe, was captured by Waikato tribesmen as a child. Educated by missionaries at Kawhia, he was later freed and returned to Taranaki where in 1862 he was visited by the Angel Gabriel, who charged him to found a new religion. To recruit followers Te Ua organised an attack on a detachment of military settlers in which Captain T.W.J. Lloyd was decapitated, and his head taken on a tour of the North Island. The militant cult "spread like fire in the fern" and by 1865 (the year in which the Hauhau martyred Volkner at △ Opotiki), a tall niu pole stood in nearly every sizable village from Taranaki to the Bay of Plenty (except in Arawa country) and from north of Wellington to the Waikato. However, when Te Ua was captured in 1866 and taken on tour with Sir George Grey, the sight of their leader with the Governor discredited him so completely that within a few months he had faded from history.

Hauhauism provided the most intense fighting of any phase of the Land Wars, during which its followers fought with unparalleled zeal and with a complete disregard for their safety engendered by a belief that bullets could not harm true believers.

Te Kooti later based his Ringatu movement on Hauhauism, and Ratana (*p.* **187**) also borrowed some of its ideas and ceremonies.

★★★ ORAKEI KORAKO

Volcanic Plateau   Map 8

37 km N of Taupo; 68 km S of Rotorua; tel. (07) 378-3131.

THE THERMAL VALLEY of Orakei Korako, reached by jet boat across the Waikato River, is renowned for the constantly changing colours of its silica terraces. The valley's hot springs pour into Lake Ohakuri, on the Waikato River, created behind the Ohakuri Dam. When the lake was filled in 1961, part of the thermal valley was

---

"He gave the impression that very many cities had rubbed him smooth." — Graham Greene (*A Gun for Sale*).

---

flooded and it was thought that its wonders might be destroyed. However, the flooding actually rejuvenated activity higher up the valley and, if anything, increased its attractiveness. *The thermal reserve is open daily, 8.30 a.m. last tour summer, 4.30 p.m., winter 4 p.m.; tel. (07) 378-3131. A floatplane service is available from Taupo and from Rotorua.*

SOME NOTES

Silica: Minerals, among them silica, are brought to the surface dissolved in the waters of the hot springs. Around some vents the silica forms a crust of siliceous sinter, which protects the ground from erosion and occasionally forms terraces. Where the walls of a vent are lined with sinter, hot water may emerge crystal clear, but where the water percolates through rock it may emerge as a mud paste, as in the case of boiling mud pools. These mud pools may build into cones, termed "mud volcanoes".

Algae: The kaleidoscopic colours of the silica terraces are created by algae, unicellular plants which live and feed on minerals in water of up to 76⁰C. As the plants die, silica builds up over them and so the algae accelerate the rate of the terraces' growth.

THINGS TO SEE IN THE VALLEY

Aladdin's Cave ★★★: Ruatapu ("sacred cave"), formed by a volcanic eruption, was reserved for use by Maori women as a place where they might adorn themselves in a "pool of mirrors". Orakei korako, "the place of adorning", takes its name from this custom.
   The entrance is framed by tall tree ferns, which filter the sunlight to lend a glow to the varied colours within. Mosses, fern and climbing plants cling to the cave's walls and roof.
   Waiwhakaata ("pool of mirrors") is the name given to the hot pool at the bottom of the cave, 39 metres below the entrance. It is also a Wishing Pool, and visitors are invited to dip their left hands into the water and make a secret wish. To the left of the pool a narrow entrance leads to Rahurahu Cave. The cave's roof, up to 19.5 metres high, is covered with glow-worms (*p.* **266**), which glow green but may be seen only at night.

Diamond Geyser ★★: The geyser plays intermittently up to 3 metres and at times to 9 metres. It is notable for coral-like silica formations.

The Great Golden Fleece ★★: Like the famous Pink and White Terraces, destroyed in the Tarawera eruption of 1886, the Great Golden Fleece is a fault scarp dating from *c.* 130 A.D., built up with centuries of siliceous growth. No less than 38 metres long, 4.5 metres high, and 102 mm thick, it is believed to be the largest of its kind in the world. The terrace varies in colour with the weather and with the rate at which water is flowing over it from the "Artist's Palette".

The Artist's Palette: A one and a half-hectare level silica terrace, riddled with over 100 hot springs and small geysers, and with the wide range of colours which gives it its name.
   Also worthy of note are the **Emerald Terrace,** the **Hochstetter Cauldron** (named for the eminent geologist-explorer who was an early visitor here) and **Cascade Terrace.**

OREWA ★★   *Auckland   Map 4   Pop. 5,596*

40 km N of Auckland.

IN SUMMER this tranquil seaside town, hub of the "Hibiscus Coast" and one of the North Island's top beach resorts, swells to city proportions. Then sideshows materialise to cater for the influx and to augment the natural attractions of a splendid three-kilometre beach, sheltered estuary and the thermal springs of nearby △ Waiwera (*8 km N*). A loop road leads through Eaves Scenic Reserve, at the northern end of the beach, near where secluded **Orewa House**, a centre for the arts, makes an interesting stop.
   Looking out to sea, the waters are sheltered by the Mahinerangi Peninsula to the north and the Whangaparaoa Peninsula to the south. In the extreme distance may be seen Little and Great Barrier Islands, with the silhouette of Kawau Island imposed upon them. Nearer still is Motuora Island.

Silverdale Pioneer Village: Featured are herb gardens and a cluster of early and reconstructed buildings including a Methodist church (1860), parsonage (1877), primary school (1878), school residence (1903), an early bushman's hut and replicas of gumdiggers' huts. *Silverdale, 5 km S.*

Horowhenua   Map 13   Pop. 6,360   ★★ **OTAKI**

74 km N of Wellington.

OF ALL THE SETTLEMENTS along the coast north of Wellington, Otaki is perhaps the most interesting. Its population today is thinly spread from "Otaki Railway" to the sea, but the district was well-populated in pre-European times and, in the 1800s, was dominated by Te Rauparaha from his △ Kapiti Island stronghold.

The missionary Octavius Hadfield (later Bishop Hadfield) arrived here in 1839 and not only introduced Christianity to the region but also induced local Maori to till the rich alluvial soil and to send the first of an unending stream of produce to Wellington and elsewhere. Today Otaki is the centre of a considerable market-gardening district and wine-making has begun at Te Horo. To the south is an excellent pottery. The town is also home to the country's only Maori Racing Club, which features an excellent horse-racing track.

The district's equitable climate led to the building here, in 1932, of the King George V Health Camp, where many children have benefited from a few weeks' stay. The oldest of the country's health camps, today it helps combat the effects of unemployment and loneliness rather than malnutrition. Health camps are financed from the sale of "health stamps", issued by the Post Office annually since 1929 at a surcharge, and keenly sought by philatelists around the world.

The first Maori university: Te Wananga o Raukawa (the University of Raukawa), situated in a tranquil setting here, is the first Maori university in New Zealand. Students are drawn from all cultures and tribes to work towards such degrees as a Bachelor of Maori Administration, Bachelor of Maori Laws and Philosophy, and the Bachelor of Hapu (sub-tribe) Development. A private university, established in 1981, it also emphasises the teaching of the Maori language. The university is a logical extension of the Kohanga reo ("language nests" for pre-school children) and Kura Kaupapa Maori (total immersion courses in Maori schools) which have emerged in the recent past as a central feature of modern Maoritanga.

SOME HISTORY

Bishop Hadfield (1814-1904): A chronic asthmatic whose formal education was disrupted by illness and who was not expected to live long, Octavius Hadfield came to New Zealand as a deacon to serve as long as his health would allow. Although he thought this would be only for a matter of months, he not only lived to be 90 but also rose to be Primate of New Zealand. As a peacemaker he interceded between Te Rauparaha's warring allies and restrained both Te Rauparaha and Te Rangihaeata from attacking Wellington during the uneasy weeks that followed the Wairau Massacre, (*p.* **284**).

As an authority on Maori custom, he was often consulted by Governors but his defence of Wiremu Kingi when war broke out in Taranaki rendered him for a time one of the most unpopular men in the colony. It was his passion for truth that led him to declare that "great crimes [by the colonists] ought to be called by their proper names", a description with which later generations were to agree.

Hadfield's mission at Otaki was, in about 1850, regarded as a model, but the cumulative effects of the Land Wars in the Taranaki and the rise of the King Movement aggravated by European settlement in the area, largely undermined the work of the mission.

Rangiatea Maori Church: Until its tragic destruction by arson in October 1995, Rangiatea ranked as the finest of the "Maori" churches. Its unpretentious exterior masked the eloquent simplicity of its interior, in striking contrast to the perhaps overly rich embellishments found in the other well-known "Maori" churches, at Rotorua, Tikitiki and Putiki.

Local tradition suggested that the Ngati Raukawa built the church on soil brought from "Hawaiki" on the *Tainui* canoe, and that its name, Rangiatea, referred to the home of Io, the Maori's Supreme God, as well as to the revered island in the Society Islands from which the soil is said to have come. However, both the tradition of tapu soil and the reference to Io are suspect. The early missionaries appear to have known nothing of the "sacred soil", and in its first years the church was known simply as "the Native Church".

Building began in 1849 when giant totara trees were dragged from nearby forests. Three enormous pillars (symbolising the Trinity) supported the 26-metre ridgepole (symbolic of the one God). According to tradition, the missionary Archdeacon Samuel Williams doubted the Maori's ability to build a church as long as 29 metres and so by night stealthily cut three metres from the ridgepole. Even today one must marvel at Williams's confidence in their ability to tackle the project at all, and it is still a matter of speculation as to just how the pillars were erected. Exterior

169

buttresses were added for support in *c.* 1911, when totara shingles were replaced with iron and the wall thatching by weatherboards.

Interior wall decorations featured rough totara slabs painted with red ochre, alternating with tukutuku panels depicting the single purapura whetu (stars in heaven) design. The rafters, too, were decorated with a single pattern, the mangopare (hammerhead shark). Conspicuous was the lack of carved panels. These would have depicted ancestors and ancestral gods and so were considered unsuitable for a church which represented a complete break with tradition.

The carved totara pulpit (1950) with its six mythical Maori demi-gods supporting the Word of the Gospel was a copy of that in the Church of St Faith (Rotorua). The lectern was presented by Bishop Hadfield's descendants and was carved by one of them. The 49 uprights of the semi-circular maire sanctuary rails, originally the only carving in the church, were each carved with a different design. Above the totara altar were the words "Ko ahau te Huarahi te pono me te ora" ("I am the way, the truth and the life"), and four brass memorials commemorate the first two Maori to be ordained into the Anglican mission, Archdeacon Samuel Williams (who lived here from 1847-52; *p.* **97**), Bishop Hadfield, and his son, Henry Hadfield (who in 1909 assisted in renovating the church).

Displayed in the vestry was a framed portion of an altar frontal, an early gift from Queen Victoria, who is reputed personally to have executed its needlework. When the frontal fell into disrepair, its plight was pointed out to King George VI, who reciprocated by providing a new altar frontal. With the frontals was a copy of the first Bible to be printed in Maori, and the first Church Register whose entry 990 would have recorded the funeral of Te Rauparaha.

A local mythology appears to have developed surrounding the circumstances of Te Rauparaha's burial. A monument to the chief stands opposite the church, over the place where he is said to have been buried. Local tradition persists that as soon as the Christian burial service had begun, an argument developed as to whether one who had never been formally received into the Church should be buried in consecrated ground. A second grave was hurriedly prepared here, just outside the churchyard. But, the story continues, an ignominious burial ill-became one of the greatest fighting chiefs of all time, and the same night a group of his followers returned and removed his remains to △ Kapiti Island, where they were reinterred with traditional formality. Accounts of what actually took place vary, but it is most likely that the Ngati Toa chief's bones still lie under the **tombstone** which bears his name (*shaded by twin Norfolk pines to the rear of the churchyard*). Certainly there is nothing in the contemporary accounts to support what appears to be a twentieth-century version of the events. *Te Rauparaha St, Otaki Township. Signposted 2.5 km from Highway 1.* A **monument** to the coming of Christianity to the area stands beside the **memorial** to Te Rauparaha.

THINGS TO SEE AND DO

Otaki Maori Mission: The Roman Catholic mission, established here in 1844, has an early church (*c.* 1857) and buildings dating from the turn of the century. A memorial marks the site of the first church, on the crest of Pukekaraka, the small hill which overlooks the mission. Also on its crest are memorials and graves of early missionaries, and a small flagpole which, according to local tradition, was part of the mast of the *Tainui* canoe.

The spirit of ecumenicalism was alien to the age, and the presence of other creeds in the area propagating "the most damnable heresies" enraged the Anglican Hadfield. "I have now got both Wesleyans and Papists in my neighbourhood to my great sorrow," Hadfield lamented. "I do not know which will do the most harm." *Te Rauparaha St. 800 m beyond Rangiatea Church.*

Te Horo Vineyards: In a cool orchard setting fruit wines (made from forty different varieties), mead and sparkling wines may be sampled in the Parsonage Hill Wine Bar and Cafe. *Highway 1, Te Horo; tel. (06) 364-3284.*

Raukawa (1936): A modern meeting house whose **carvings** principally record ancestors prominent in Ngati Raukawa history. *Mill Rd.*

Otaki Gorge: An interesting drive, with good swimming, fishing, walking and picnicking en route. *9 km SE.* The **Tararua Outdoor Recreation Centre** here offers several adventure activities — rafting, canoeing, kayaking and abseiling among them. *Tel/fax (06) 364-3110.*

Mangaone walkway: Known locally as the Reikorangi Track, the three-hour walk follows an old roadline on the left bank of the Waikanae River in the western foothills of the Tararuas. It links the eight kilometres between Mangaone North Road (*E of Te Horo*) and Mangaone South Road (*E of Waikanae*), and forms part of the New Zealand walkways system. *Several streams must be forded.*

OTOROHANGA

King Country   Map 6   Pop. 2,605

59 km S of Hamilton. Information Centre, 87 Maniapoto St; tel. (07) 873-8951.

OTOROHANGA, home to a major campervan industry, is set on the fertile Waipa River flats. The slopes of Mt Pirongia form a gentle backdrop to the town. The settlement began as a camp of construction workers on the main trunk railway and was a base for the earliest visitors to nearby Waitomo Caves after they had been discovered by Europeans in 1887. An extensive flood-protection scheme was implemented after the disastrous floods of 1958 when the Waipa inundated the town.

The town's imaginative aviary and native bird breeding programme provides an intriguing break for the through traveller.

Otorohanga means "food for a journey" and refers to a chief who went to Taupo carrying with him a small amount of food which he made last the whole journey by means of a magic chant.

THINGS TO SEE AND DO

Kiwi House and Native Bird Centre ★★★: Excellent nocturnal houses guarantee that visitors will be able to see a pair of kiwi. A breeding centre here (necessarily closed to the public) has perfected both the art of incubating kiwi eggs and rearing techniques. Birds have been exported from here to zoos with approved facilities in such countries as Japan, the Netherlands, West Germany and the USA.

The kiwi belongs to the order Apterygiformes and, with the now-extinct moa, is New Zealand's most ancient bird, dating back over 7 million years. About 30 centimetres in height and with a long, tapering beak with nostrils at the end, the tail-less kiwi has a shaggy plumage mottled brown or grey in colour. The female has the longer beak, while the bird's name records the "kee-wee" cry of the male. Their natural habitat is native bush and, though once thought almost extinct, there are now known to be numbers of kiwi throughout New Zealand in the areas of native bush which remain, but because of their semi-nocturnal habits they are seldom seen.

The hen lays an egg of remarkable size, weighing about 500 grams, possibly the largest of any bird in relation to its size. Then, as if exhausted by her gargantuan effort, most species leave it for the male to perform the matronly task of sitting on the egg during the 11-week incubation period. Also successfully bred here is the **tuatara**, a small protected native lizard (*Sphenodon punctatus*), the only survivor of the order of prehistoric reptiles which included the giant dinosaurs.

A large, walk-through **aviary** houses over 300 different birds, many native birds among them. *Alex Telfer Drive, off Kakamutu Rd. Open daily, tel. (07) 873-7391. The Kiwi House is set in spacious grounds in which to picnic, and close by is a* **deer park**, *also with a large picnic area.*

Otorohanga Historical Museum: The collection includes a number of early local photographs. *Kakamutu Rd. Open Sunday, 2–4 p.m.; other times by arrangement; tel. (07) 873-8758.*

Huiputea: A lonely, towering and venerable kahikatea around which, in 1822, after their crushing defeat of the Waikato at Matakitaki (△ Pirongia), a Ngapuhi war party established a base. Here they were taken by surprise at night and were annihilated by the Waikato and Maniapoto. Waikato women taken prisoner at Matakitaki (and who were privy to the pending attack) had successfully distracted them by turning their captors' attention from war to love. A short time afterwards the chastened Ngapuhi returned home to the Bay of Islands. *End of Pine St, off Maniapoto St; across railway line.*

ENVIRONS

△ Waitomo Caves ★★★: A series of limestone caves with a bewildering tracery of stalactites and stalagmites, and a glow-worm grotto where visitors glide in silence on an underground river. *16 km.*

Haurua monument: A roadside monument here commemorates both in Maori and English the gathering nearby in 1857 of Ngati Maniapoto chiefs, at which the selection of Potatau Te Wherowhero as first Maori king was confirmed and the concept of hereditary kingship established. The plaque also records that Potatau had been appointed king by a gathering of many Maori chiefs at Pukawa (*p.* **244**), on the shores of Lake Taupo, in November 1856, but that he desired that the final decision be referred to his elders of Maniapoto.

Haurua was one of several great meetings held by the Maori to appoint a king. It was important because Ngati Maniapoto (the tribe occupying the territory that was later to become known as "The King Country") supported the nomination of Potatau

171

Te Wherowhero, and they stipulated the office should be hereditary. However because Governor Grey and Bishop Selwyn warned Potatau that grievous trouble would befall his peoples should he accept the kingship, this meeting at Haurua was called Te Puna o te Roimata ("the well-spring of tears").

Potatau attended the meeting and after listening to the decision of the Maniapoto chiefs, remained silent for a time and then said simply, "E pai ana" ("It is good").

7.5 km S on S.H.3 (memorial stands in a lay-by).

PAEROA   Waikato   Map 5   Pop. 3,954

76 km NE of Hamilton; 33 km S of Thames. Information Centre, Belmont Rd; tel. (07) 862-8636.

PAEROA grew up as a port on the Ohinemuri River in times when ships regularly traded between Auckland and the upper reaches of the Waihou and Ohinemuri Rivers. The port installations have gone and the river, stocked with trout, is hidden by a large stopbank.

For a time the town benefited from the boom of the Coromandel gold rushes but it was the draining of the extensive Hauraki Plains, today lined with canals, which brought prosperity to the town.

Today a farming and administrative centre, Paeroa is best known for mineral drinking waters, marketed nationally as "Lemon and Paeroa". A giant-size "bottle" greets those approaching from the south, but sadly the town's bottling plant, which turned a local mineral spring to such good account, has since closed and the drink is now manufactured in Auckland. Earlier the spring was used by gold miners, who found it a useful Sunday-morning antidote for the excesses of the night before.

Paeroa takes its name from the old Maori name for the Coromandel Range, Te Paeroa-o-Toi—"the long range of Toi", a very early Polynesian explorer (*pp.* **9-10**).

THINGS TO SEE AND DO

Historical Maritime Park ★ ★: The museum, on the site of the bustling Puke Wharf where European settlers first landed, is restoring a number of venerable small ships, some of which operate to ferry visitors on the river. One vessel, the paddle steamer *Kopu*, had spent nearly half a century under water before being raised and its restoration begun. The museum building (originally the post office for the gold-mining village of Waitekauri) displays items associated with the sea. *4 km NW Highway 2, the Auckland exit from the town. Open daily; tel. (07) 862-7121.*

Paeroa Museum: Exhibits here relate to the history of the town, early shipping on the river and gold mining in the Karangahake Gorge. A special feature is a 500-piece collection of Royal Albert China. *Belmont Rd. Hours vary.*

ENVIRONS

Karangahake Gorge ★ ★: The gorge which links Paeroa with Waihi was the scene of intense gold-mining. There is an interesting walkway through the gorge (*p.* **243**).

Miranda Wildlife Reserve ★ ★: By the edge of the Hauraki Plains on the Firth of Thames, rich mudflats draw a diversity of birds, many of which winter over or live permanently here. (*Miranda Naturalists Trust Visitor Centre offers information and can arrange accommodation: Kaiaua–Miranda Rd; tel. (09) 232-2781.*)

Close by are **Miranda Hot Springs,** a large thermal pool complex, complete with sauna and picnic area (*open daily, 10 a.m.–9 p.m.; tel. (07) 867-3055*). *At Miranda, 47 km NW of Paeroa.*

Gemstones: The Coromandel Peninsula is renowned for its gemstones. Wilderness Gems Ltd at Ngatea process stones for jewellery (*23 km NW; 13 River Rd; tel. (07) 867-7417*).

PAHIATUA   Wairarapa   Map 12   Pop. 2,599

66 km NE of Masterton; 38.5 km SE of Palmerston North. Information Centre, Main St; tel. (06) 376-6619.

THE PRINCIPAL FEATURE of the upper Wairarapa's main centre is its more-than-broad main street. No less than 60 metres across, its width was provided by the town's planners who envisaged a railway running through its very centre. Fortunately when the railway came the line merely touched the town's outskirts, leaving the centre of the expansive main street to be developed into garden, picnic and play areas.

Like other towns in the upper Wairarapa and southern Hawke's Bay, Pahiatua began in the 1880s as a roading settlement in the dense Seventy Mile Bush.

Pahiatua means "resting place of a god", a meaning which gave amusement to the late Sir Keith Holyoake (born at nearby Mangamutu), Member of Parliament for the district, one of the country's longest-serving Prime Ministers (1957; 1960-72) and subsequently its first politician to become Governor-General.

THINGS TO SEE AND DO

Pahiatua and District Museum: A colonial cottage houses items of local interest. *Sedcole St. Open Sundays, 2-4 p.m.*

Carnival Park Reserve: Adjoining the motor camp and picnic area is a pocket of native bush, enlivened by exotics. Close by is good trout fishing in the Mangatainoka River. *800 m. Signposted on the southern exit from town.*

Polish refugees' memorial: During and after World War II, New Zealand was host to 734 Polish children made homeless by the German invasion. With many orphans among them, they spent up to four years in a special camp at Pahiatua. Most remained in New Zealand and in 1975 gathered to unveil a memorial sculpture on the site of the old camp. *3 km S of Pahiatua on State Highway 2.*

Marima Domain: A scenic reserve of hillside bush and riverside trees, and a perfect picnic spot. Swimming and trout fishing possible. *17 km. At Hamua, 14 km S on Highway 2, turn right along Hukanui Rd and follow to river bridge. Enter through gate immediately before bridge.*

TOURING NOTE

Tui Brewery tours ★: DB's Mangatainoka Brewery is famous for its Tui East India Pale Ale, known as "the beer round here" throughout the Wairarapa. There is good picnicking, swimming and fishing by the Mangatainoka bridge. *Mangatainoka. 5 km N on Highway 2. To visit (and perhaps test the magic) tel. (06) 376-7549.*

"Pahiatua Track": The so-called "Pahiatua Track" over the Tararua Range affords a direct route to △ Palmerston North. Magnificent views are obtained over both the Wairarapa Valley and the Manawatu Plains. *38 km. Turnoff signposted in Main St.*

Northland   Maps 2, 3   Pop. 2,928   ★★★ **PAIHIA**

71 km NW of Whangarei. Information Bay of Islands, Marsden Rd, tel. (09) 402-7426; Fullers Northland, Maritime Building; tel. (09) 402-7421; King's Tours and Cruises, Maritime Building; tel. (09) 402-8288.

TRADITION PERSISTS that Paihia acquired its name when the missionary the Rev. Henry Williams was seeking a suitable site for a mission station. When he arrived here, he is said to have seen the golden beaches, looked out across the island-studded arm of the Bay of Islands, and exclaimed to his Maori guides "Pai [good] here!" Although the name may reflect Henry Williams's then inadequate grasp of the Maori tongue, the thousands who visit Paihia each year endorse his sentiments. Today, the town meets the criteria of the most demanding holidaymaker.

There is no known Maori word "Paihia", but some consider it a corruption of "Pahia", meaning "mashed food".

Although by road △ Russell, on the opposite shore, is some considerable distance away, a passenger ferry from Paihia and a car ferry from nearby Opua provide swift links.

SOME HISTORY

Mission settlement: In 1823 the Rev. Henry Williams came to New Zealand with the Rev. Samuel Marsden as a member of the Church Missionary Society to establish the country's third mission station, at Paihia. Missions were already in the area at Rangihoua (1814) and Kerikeri (1819). At once buildings were erected and before the end of the year a house, a store and a raupo church (believed to be the country's first) were in use. Henry Williams was joined by his brother, the Rev. William Williams, in 1826.

As the mission developed Henry Williams realised the need for a small ship to enable the missionaries to travel more easily around the country. With William Hall, in 1824-26 he designed and built a schooner of 50 tons, appropriately named the

173

Herald. A large crowd of Maori gathered for the launching and the ship all but capsized when a triumphant haha was performed on board. The *Herald* sailed to Sydney three times before it was wrecked on the bar at Hokianga Harbour in 1828.

Although some printing had been done at Kerikeri, the arrival at Paihia of William Colenso (*pp.* **144-45**) in 1834 marked an important stage in the mission's growth. Missionary, explorer, botanist, politician, Colenso is best remembered as a printer, and is often credited with being the country's first.

POINTS OF INTEREST

Church of St Paul ★(1926): This church was built as a memorial to the missionary brothers Archdeacon Henry Williams (1782-1867) and Bishop William Williams (1800-78).

Henry Williams arrived in 1823 to found the mission at Paihia. During the War in the North he was in a difficult position. Determined not to align himself with any one faction but to be just towards all, he was at times accused by the settlers of supporting Hone Heke's "rebellion". After the war he again found himself the centre of controversy; this time with the Church Missionary Society, when he refused to give up land he had purchased for his family well in excess of the area allowed by the Church. Henry Williams, by then an Archdeacon, was summarily dismissed. When the injustice of the situation was finally realised, he was reinstated, and died at "The Retreat" at Pakaraka in 1867.

In contrast with his brother, William Williams was a scholar rather than a man of action. He compiled a Maori dictionary (1844) and translated the New Testament into Maori (1837). After eight years' teaching at the Paihia mission, William Williams left his brother in 1834 to establish mission stations in the Poverty Bay-East Cape area. He became the first Bishop of Waiapu and later retired to Napier, where he died in 1878.

The present church is the fourth on the site. The first was built of raupo in 1823, and in 1855 a second was built of lath and plaster. This in turn gave way to a wooden building in 1874 which, to make way for the present stone building, was in 1925 removed to Taumarere, near △ Kawakawa, where it still stands.

The site lays claim to many "firsts": New Zealand's first church (1823), the first address by a Bishop (by Bishop Broughton, first Bishop of Australia, in 1838), the first consecrated ground, the first confirmation, the first ordination (all 1838) and the country's first organ (now in the Wanganui Museum). The memorial in front of the church was erected by a number of Maori tribes to honour Henry Williams. *Marsden Rd.*

The foreshore: Many events of Paihia's early history are recorded on New Zealand Historic Places Trust plaques along the foreshore where runs Marsden Road.

Aquatic World ★ ★: A small but intriguing collection of Bay of Islands marine life, with a "touch tank" for children. Of particular interest is a Toadstool groper, first noted off the Poor Knights Islands in 1969, and a curious albino crayfish.*Waterfront.*

Museum of Shipwrecks★★: Aboard the barque *Tui*, moored at Waitangi Bridge, relics and treasures are displayed. These were recovered from such famous shipwrecks as the *Boyd*, the *Elingamite* and the *Wairarapa (for all, see index).* Included is jewellery salvaged on behalf of the Rothschild family. A film-slide programme depicts salvage operations and the fish and sea bed of the Northland coast. *Open daily.*

Opua–Paihia Walkway: The walk follows the coastline to the wharf at Opua (*3½ hrs one way; Paihia Taxis can collect you from the other end*).

ORGANISED EXCURSIONS

Cream Trip ★★★: This 64-kilometre cruise among the Bay's enchanting islands has for years had the reputation for being the finest launch trip in the country. The excursion grew from a dairy run servicing coastal farms but now takes in the Marsden Cross at Oihi Bay, Moturoa and Roberton Island, and both Oraukawa and Otehei Bays. *The 4½-hour trip runs daily, leaving Paihia at 10 a.m. and Russell at 10.15 a.m. Fullers, tel. (09) 402-7421. (Oct to May daily; June to Sept, Mon, Wed, Thurs, Sat only.)*

Cape Brett (Hole in the Rock) Cruise ★ ★ ★: A half-day cruise runs daily out to and through fascinating Piercy Island at the entrance to the Bay of Islands. *Fullers, tel. (09) 402-7421 or King's Tours and Cruises, tel. 402-8288 freephone 0508-888-282.*

Sailing the *R.Tucker Thompson* ★ ★ ★: On this stately tall ship, a replica of an old schooner, you can take the helm or learn to set the sails in the manner of a century ago. An idyllic way in which to explore the Bay of Islands. *Fullers, tel. (09) 402-7421.*

Swimming with dolphins ★ ★ ★: Perhaps the most engaging of all mammals are present the year round in the Bay of Islands. The trip gives plenty of scope for photography and a chance to swim with the dolphins — and sometimes other forms of marine life! The trip visits exquisite **Urupukapuka Island**, and on the morning excursion (*Oct to May, 8 a.m.*) there is the option of spending a few hours there and being collected later in the day. *Dolphin Encounters, Fullers, tel. (09) 402-7421.*

Otehei Bay (Urupukapuka Island) ★ ★: A stopover on the island — to walk, to swim or to view marine life from the underwater viewing vessel *Nautilus* — combines well with the Cream Trip, the Cape Brett Cruise and Dolphin Encounters. The island was made famous by Zane Grey, who set up a big-game fishing camp here in the 1920s. *Fullers, tel. (09) 402-7421. Cabins are available for longer stays.*

Subsea adventure ★ ★: An underwater viewing vessel on Urupukapuka Island allows passengers to view marine life on the sea-bed. The trip may be combined with the Cream Trip, Cape Brett Cruise or Dolphin Encounters. *Fullers, tel. (09) 402-7421.*

Wildlife Nature Cruise: A cruise with a special commentary makes a stop at Moturua Island, a spot where the Frenchman Marion du Fresne in 1772 claimed New Zealand for France (*see p.* **58**). In the course of a 2½ hour walk on the island the North Island bush robin and the kiwi may be seen. *King's, tel. (09) 402-8288.*

Sea kayaking: A favourite guided trip explores the mangrove forest and visits Haruru Falls (*4 hrs*). The full-day excursion paddles past the Waitangi Treaty House and visits Motumaire Island and on the overnight camp there is snorkelling on Urupukapuka Island. *Coastal Kayakers, tel. (09) 402-8105.*

Cape Reinga coach trip ★ ★ ★: Entertaining coach trips run north to Cape Reinga, the northernmost point accessible by road. A highlight is the journey along △ Ninety Mile Beach. *Fullers, tel. (09) 402-7421 or King's, tel. (09) 402-8288.*

Deep-sea game fishing: Charters may be arranged through the Bay of Islands Swordfish Club *(tel. (09) 402-7773).* Increasingly, big fish are simply tagged and returned to the sea.

Diving: Whether to take fish or to wonder at the exotic colours of the sponges, day trips can be arranged. Certified divers can explore the wreck of the Greenpeace ship, *Rainbow Warrior*, at Matauri Bay. *Paihia Dive Hire and Charter; tel. (09) 402-7551 or Bay Guides, Down 'N' Under Action Shop, tel. (09) 402-8428.* The latter also organises **abseiling** expeditions.

ENVIRONS

Waitangi Treaty House ★★★: The attractive house and gardens where the first signatures were affixed to the Treaty of Waitangi in 1840. *2.5 km. (See △ Waitangi.)*

Haruru Falls (Waitangi Falls)★: Set on the Waitangi River, the falls are particularly spectacular after rain. *3 km. Detour off the Puketona road.*

Opua Forest: On the hills inland from Paihia and Opua, the forest contains one of the few substantial areas of native bush in the region. For the most part the vegetation comprises young regenerating forest, recovering from past logging and burning. At first kauri, then tanekaha and, more recently, rimu and totara were logged. Gumdiggers, too, modified parts of the forest, setting fire to it to make their task easier. *Three roads give ready access, from each of which graded tracks lead to good vantage points—School Rd to the north-east, Opua-Oramahoe Rd through the centre, and Whangae-Oramahoe Rd on the western boundary.*

★ PALLISER (Cape), Road to

Wairarapa   *Maps 12, 13*

Featherston to Cape Palliser 76 km; Martinborough to Cape Palliser 66 km.

THE ROAD to Cape Palliser leads along the level grasslands of Lake Wairarapa's eastern shores to Lake Ferry. Meeting the sea, the road swings left to follow the savage coastline of Palliser Bay to the Cape itself, the most southerly point of the North Island.

Initially one may travel by way of either △ Martinborough or △ Featherston. Two streams must be forded in the latter stages.

POINTS OF INTEREST ON THE WAY

△ **Martinborough:** A farming and world-renowned **wine-producing** township whose streets are laid out in the form of a Union Jack. The site of the country's **first sheep station** is signposted eight kilometres beyond Martinborough on the road to Lake Ferry. A detour may be made to see **glow-worm caves**.

175

PALLISER (CAPE), ROAD TO — *concluded*

Lake Wairarapa: Scene of a large conservation scheme. *(See △ Featherston.)*

Lake Ferry: A fishing settlement on Lake Onoke (place of the earthworm) whose hotel, on the original coastal route to Wellington, is said to have acquired its first licence on condition that its publican maintain a ferry service. Vehicular access across is now provided for in the Lake Wairarapa conservation scheme. The coastal route lost favour when the road from Featherston to Wellington opened across the Rimutakas. Although it offers excellent surfcasting, the ocean beach shelves too sharply for safe bathing.

Putangirua Pinnacles ★: A 50-minute walk up a shingled stream bed leads round a deceptive left bend to an area where the valley closes in and where huge grey pillars, backed by sheer, fluted cliffs, rise vertically on all sides—a phenomenon created by uneven erosion. *Allow 2 hrs. Park at the picnic area, a short distance from the road. Stout shoes are essential. Signposted 17 km from Lake Ferry. Occasionally a bulldozed track enables visitors to drive all but to the pinnacles themsevles.*

Near the turnoff, at Te Kopi, was the site of an early whaling station. This was inundated when the 1855 earthquake devastated the province, lifting the shoreline here by over a metre and causing sea cliffs to collapse.

Prehistoric stone walls: A fascinating archaeological feature is a series of stone walls running at right-angles to the coast, the largest of which is at Whatarangi *(just S of the Whatarangi Stream)*. Other groups are at Te Humanga, on the right bank of the mouth of the Pararaki River, and on the right bank of the Waiwhero Stream. It is believed that these divided kumara plantations. Extensive archaeological work has been carried out in Palliser Bay.

Ngawi: The largest settlement on the Cape is the focal point for commercial fishing. A diversity of fish may be bought (or caught), and crayfish are generally available.

Kupe's sail: By the Mangatoe Stream is an anchor from the *Benavon,* a ship which in 1890 perished on Cape Palliser's rocks. On the rock face above the flat may be seen "Kupe's sail". The legendary Polynesian explorer, Kupe, is said to have camped on the flat here about 1,000 years ago, and to have admired distant Mt Tapuaenuku, in the South Island's Kaikoura Ranges. His inspection of the peak gave the Cape its Maori name of Matakitakiakupe. While here, he is reputed to have indulged in a canoe-sail building competition with his companion, Ngake, in which Kupe was the victor.

Cape Palliser Lighthouse: On this rocky and stormy coast there have been many shipwrecks and many lives lost. So much so that before the light was first exhibited here in 1897, wrecks in Palliser Bay and on the surrounding coast were almost commonplace, as ships were driven ashore in Cook Strait gales. As late as 1924 the steamer *Ripple* is believed to have foundered in Palliser Bay, with the loss of all hands. The 17.7 metre tower stands about 60 metres above sea level and the light, giving two flashes each 30 seconds, is visible for 35 kilometres. The light itself is on a hilltop, with the keeper's dwelling below, the two linked by a long flight of steps which need to be negotiated carefully in stormy weather.

The lighthouse and nearby fishing are popular with visitors, as is a neighbouring seal colony. The colony, the largest in the North Island, does not migrate and so may be seen the year round.

Haurangi Forest Park: Popular with hunter and tramper, the park, which covers much of the Cape, also offers some spectacular vantage points. *Resident ranger at Te Kopi.*

PALMERSTON NORTH ★

Manawatu   Maps 12,13   Pop. 75,200 (urban area)

144.5 km NE of Wellington. Information Centre, Civic Centre, The Square; tel. (06) 358-5003.

THE PLEASING PROSPECT of Palmerston North and the trim, level Manawatu countryside makes it difficult to picture the plains as once clothed in dense bush.

From a humble clearing without any apparent strategic advantage, Palmerston North has blossomed into a major communications centre and the country's eighth largest city. The early settlers indiscriminately axed and burnt the native forests, but the city has made good the loss·with many hectares of splendid parks, and has capitalised on the forethought of the settlers who provided a spacious square in the city's centre.

The city is home to a number of agricultural research centres, including Massey University, and a diversity of industries which include the large Glaxo Laboratories.

Originally called simply "Palmerston" after the British peer and Prime Minister, Lord Palmerston, the name worried local settlers who felt their town lacked identity and was confused with other Palmerstons, notably the town near Dunedin. A public meeting was held to decide on a new name but after a night's discussion all that could be agreed on was that "Palmerston *North*" was an improvement—"and all went home dissatisfied".

SOME HISTORY

A rival vanquished: Although the local Rangitane (who claim descent from Kupe, Whatonga and Turi) had joined in a number of collective but vain attempts to rid the district of the troublesome Te Rauparaha (*pp.* **115-16**), they escaped the savage reprisals inflicted on their allies and remained, in the comparative safety of the bush, to control most of their land and so negotiate sales with the settlers. Also spared the agony of the Land Wars (the Rangitane fought for the Government), the region has a history first of agricultural, and latterly of industrial, growth.

For a time if fell to coastal △ Foxton to serve as the district's hub, as an earlier New Zealand Company scheme to settle the Manawatu had foundered when the Land Commissioners set aside most of its alleged land purchases.

When Palmerston North was founded in the 360-hectare bush clearing of Papaioea in 1866, it was at first isolated by surrounding forests, the Manawatu River serving as its only link with Foxton and the outside world. Yet sawmills were soon shipping timber downriver to the port at △ Foxton, a horse-drawn wooden-railed tramway was built through the bush, and in 1876 a railway replaced the tardy tram to link the two towns and accelerate Palmerston North's progress. Over-anxious to win land, settlers burnt far more timber than they milled, as witnessed the smarting eyes and ash-sprinkled appearance of the traveller of the day. Rivalry between Foxton and Palmerston North was intense, and great was the elation of Palmerstonians when in 1886 the railway from Wellington by-passed Foxton to come to the town and so finally determine its expansive destiny.

Over the next 30 years the bush was steadily cleared, the land developed for farming, and both freezing works and dairy factories established.

The Manawatu and the railway: It is intriguing to note the social and economic effects that railways and their planners had on the development of the Manawatu-Horowhenua district.

The first line linked Palmerston North with the port of Foxton, and though this spurred the growth of Palmerston North, Foxton remained paramount. For financial reasons the Government dropped its plan to build a line from Wellington to Foxton, and in 1880 handed the project over to the Wellington-Manawatu Railway Company, the largest private company in the country, formed by a group of Wellington merchants specifically to build the line. The grateful Government granted the company some 86,000 hectares of land to offset part of the capital cost, and the company not unexpectedly charted the line's course so that it opened up this land. So it was that the railway's course defied logic and followed the Tararua foothills to by-pass Foxton and run all the way to Palmerston North. The line opened in 1886, after such towns as Shannon, Tokomaru and Levin had been founded as railway company settlements, and it spelt the end of Foxton's commercial domination of the district.

In 1908, the year in which the Main Trunk line linking Auckland and Wellington was opened, the company was taken over by the Government and its lines and rolling stock incorporated into the national network. The story ended in 1959 when the original line between Palmerston North and Foxton, relegated to a branch line, finally closed and Foxton, which had once with justification seen itself as a major railway junction, was left without any rail service whatsoever.

A RESEARCH CENTRE

Set in a prospering yet varied agricultural district, Palmerston North is home to a number of research projects.

The **AgResearch Grasslands**, part of the Pastoral Research Institute of New Zealand (one of the ten Crown-owned Research Institutes formed in 1992) breeds new pasture plants to suit the wide range of farming situations, sports turf and amenity needs. These form the basis for a thriving seed export business to over 40 countries.

At Ballantrae, a hill country station near Woodville, and Aorangi, a lowland station near Kairanga, new pasture grazing management systems are developed. *Opp. Massey University on Highway 57. Visits by those involved in grassland industries can be arranged, given adequate notice; tel. (06) 356-8019.*

The **Palmerston North Seed Testing Station** serves some 85,000 farmers and 1.8 million hectares of farmland. Good seed worth over $30 million is harvested annually in New Zealand, about one-third for export. Samples are submitted to the station from all over the country (and some from Australia) for testing and certification, and the station's work ensures not only that export seed complies with overseas requirements but also that seed used locally is up to the prescribed standard of cleanliness and does not contain other crop or weed seeds. *Church St. Visits may be arranged; tel. (06) 356-8019.*

The **NZ Dairy Research Institute** plays a pivotal role in maintaining the efficiency and competitiveness of the country's dairy industry, conducting scientific research and evaluating new products. *Opp. Massey University on Highway 57.*

The New Zealand Dairy Board, at its **Awahuri Artificial Breeding Centre,** maintains a large bull stud, and production and research laboratories on an 80-hectare farm. Under normal conditions a sire may be mated to between 30 and 50 cows in one season, but by artificial breeding the same sire may serve as many as 100,000 cows in a single season. The centre is a link in the board's artificial breeding service, the country's principal organisation for effecting herd improvement. *At Awahuri, 11 km from Palmerston North on the main route to Wanganui. Interested visitors may tel. (06) 353-6264.*

OTHER THINGS TO SEE AND DO

"The Square": The visionaries who planned the original bush settlement set aside a 6.8-hectare square which, although many years were to pass before it was enclosed with buildings, is today both the feature and the commercial heart of the city. The planners had not anticipated the railway's invasion, and the Square was an obvious site for the station; but fortunately the railway has now been removed (1963) in a reversion to the original concept of a spacious garden area sprinkled with fountains and shaded by trees. More recently, the modern Civic Centre has encroached upon the Square.

Within the Square and dominated by a clock tower is an odd collection of memorabilia. Included are a neo-Gothic fountain dedicated to the 1902 coronation of Edward VII and an ornate statue of the Rangitane chief Peeti Te Awe Awe (1820-84). The statue, erected by his sister, Ereni, recalls the chief whose father was one of the few to survive a massacre engineered by Te Rauparaha at a feast to which he had invited a number of Rangitane—the guest who was quick to repay in kind Te Rauparaha's lack of hospitality. Like others of his tribe, Te Awe Awe went on to fight with distinction for the Government in the Land Wars. In recognition of the loyalty of the Rangitane, the Government presented the tribe with a large flag incorporating the Union Jack and the name Tane-nui-a-rangi (the ancestor after whom the tribe is named). A treasured possession, the flag is flown only on occasions of special significance.

Legacies of the railway's removal are the broad Main Street and Pioneer Highway, both of which radiate from the Square.

"Square Edge": Housed in the old Municipal Council Chambers on the edge of the Square is the Manawatu Community Arts Centre. Here artists may be seen at work, crafts are for sale and numerous community activities are based. *The Square. Open weekdays and Saturday morning.*

Theatres: The city has three live theatres of note. Centrepoint Theatre and Restaurant *(cnr Pitt and Church Sts; tel. (06) 358-6983);* Abbey Theatre *(369 Church St; tel. (06) 357-7977);* and The Globe *(cnr Pitt and Main Sts; tel. (06) 358-8699).*

Massey University of Manawatu (1928): From a single-faculty agricultural college, Massey has expanded to full autonomous university status. It is named for one-time farmer William Fergusson Massey (1856-1925), leader of the Reform Party and Prime Minister for 13 years, from 1912 until his death in 1925, just three years before the college was opened.

Expansion brought with it a number of striking buildings and has made the university the national centre for veterinary science, food sciences and biotechnology. Important research is conducted here, particularly within the Faculty of Agricultural and Horticultural Sciences, and the university co-operates closely with other research institutes in the area *(described above). Information leaflets available from the University office. The campus is open to the public. 3 km S on Highway 57, the route to Shannon.*

Overlooking the University is the **Monro Lookout,** a memorial to C.S. Monro, who in 1870 returned to Nelson from school in Britain and organised the first rugby football club. Monro lived on the hill here for most of his life.

The Science Centre and Manawatu Museum ★ ★: Of special interest is historical material of Maori and European origin illustrating the theme "Manawatu and Man". The complex includes **"Totaranui"**, a house built by one of the city's first European settlers (*c.* 1875); Awahou South School, a one-room school house built at the beginning of the century; Callesen Smithy, a reconstruction of a local forge, and

Snelson's Store, a reconstruction of the city's first store, now housing one of the largest collections of printing presses and equipment in New Zealand. Science and technology come alive in the "hands-on" Science Centre, which includes a butterfly house. *396 Main St. Open daily, 10 a.m.–5 p.m.*

Manawatu Art Gallery: A modern gallery houses a collection in which works by New Zealand artists predominate. *Main St West. Open Monday–Friday, 10 a.m.–4.30 p.m.; weekends, 11.30 a.m–4.30 p.m.*

Rugby Museum: The shrine to the country's national sport includes photographs, badges, jerseys, caps and all the ephemera of rugbyphilia. *87 Cuba St. Open daily; Mon–Sat, 10 a.m.–12 noon, 1.30–4 p.m.; Sun 1.30–4 p.m.*

The Esplanade ★★: Here one finds a host of secluded picnic spots shaded by mature trees. Also here are fine rose gardens, a begonia house, aviary, sports grounds, swimming pool, miniature golf course and miniature railway. Just upriver lies Centennial Lake with its many ducks. *By river bridge on Shannon exit from city.*
    A riverside walkway extends for over 10 kilometres from Maxwells Line to Staces Road, and is accessible from a number of points. *The full walk takes about 2½ hrs one way.*

Bledisloe Park: Native bush, picnic spots and safe bathing for children in a woodland stream. *Signposted immediately before Massey University on the Shannon exit from city.*

Anzac Park viewpoint: An ideal spot for a panorama of the city and surrounding countryside to as far away as Taranaki/Egmont and Ruapehu. *End of Cliff Rd, signposted immediately across river bridge on Shannon exit from city. The city's observatory is located here.*

Hoffman kiln (*c.* 1916): A venerable Hoffman oblong continuous-brick kiln is not only a monument to the country's brick-making industry but is also a highly regarded example of industrial architecture at its best. *Brick and Pipes Ltd premises, 615 Featherston St. Seen from the road.*

ENVIRONS

Manawatu Gorge ★★: The road through this magnificent gorge was built in 1871-72 and proved a most difficult piece of construction, workmen at times having to be suspended by ropes from the clifftops.
    Several theories have been advanced to account for the striking geomorphic feature of a young river slicing through the North Island's mountainous "backbone". Defying logic, the Manawatu River rises in the eastern Ruahine Range (north of Norsewood) and instead of flowing east into Hawke Bay, cuts back through the Manawatu Gorge to reach the sea near Foxton. One suggestion is that there was a sag in the ranges before they emerged from the sea through which the Manawatu River subsequently flowed to cut out the gorge as the ranges were slowly uplifted. But if the formation is a puzzle to geographers, it presented no difficulty to the Maori. For in legend a mighty totara tree which once grew on the Puketoi range smashed through the mountains as it journeyed to the sea, carving out the Manawatu River's bed as it went.
    This stretch of river has a fascination for the more intrepid canoeist. **Jet-boat trips** may be arranged (*tel. (06) 357-5469*). *The gorge commences at 16 km on the road to Woodville.*

Tokomaru Steam Engine Museum ★★: Displayed here is a growing assortment of working steam engines dating back over a century. Included is the engine from Wellington's Patent Slip (1869), a Shand Mason steam fire-engine (1887), a Fowler traction engine (1904) and a steam road roller (1914). A steam train runs on regular "live steam days". *Tokomaru. On Highway 57 at 11.5 km N of Shannon and 19.5 km S of Palmerston North. Open daily; tel. (06) 329-8867.*

Some walks and picnic spots: Pohangina Valley Domain is a 280-hectare idyllic bush reserve on the banks of the Pohangina River. It offers safe swimming and attractive bush walks. The Beehive Creek Track (*1½ hrs one way*) starts at the Beehive Creek bridge on the Pohangina Valley Road and loops back to the road 3 km north. *42 km NE; turnoff at Ashhurst.*
    Half-way, the road passes Raumai Reserve, which also has good picnic and swimming spots as well as a number of walks ranging from the ten-minute Fern Walk to the longer Old Coach Road. *19 km.*

Beaches: Good beaches include Foxton Beach (*38.5 km*), Himatangi Beach (*37 km; for both see △ Foxton*) and Hokio Beach (*67 km; see △ Levin*).

TOURING NOTE

"Pahiatua Track": A route to Woodville or to the Wairarapa, other than through the impressive Manawatu Gorge, is the giddy 39-kilometre Aokautere-to-Pahiatua road, which offers wide views of Palmerston North and the Manawatu plains. This road can be incorporated into a half-day round trip by driving through the gorge and returning to Palmerston North by way of the "Pahiatua Track".

Mount Stewart Memorial (*135 m*): The memorial was erected in 1940 to mark the centenary of the colonisation of New Zealand. Mount Stewart was named after John Tiffin Stewart, Chief Surveyor of the Wellington Provincial Government. From the top of the lookout one obtains extensive views over the Manawatu plains. *18.5 km W on the road to Bulls, by the roadside. Some 8 km distant is the homestead and gardens of Mt Lees Reserve (p. 83).*

PAPAKURA

Auckland South   *Map 4*   *Pop. 36,553 (district)*

34 km SE of Auckland.

PAPAKURA, like other outlying settlements around Auckland, has blossomed dramatically since the end of the 1939-45 war from a small country village into a substantial commercial and light-industrial centre. Nearby are the buildings of the former Papakura Military Camp, which until its closure in 1991 was among the Army's largest establishments.

Papakura means "level land of red soil".

SOME HISTORY

A frontier town: The area was first settled in the late 1840s. As it is on the south-eastern arm of Manukau Harbour, the principal access was by sea, until the outbreak of war hastened construction of the Great South Road, south from Auckland. By the time the wooden Selwyn Chapel had opened in 1862, the fear of invasion from the Waikato made Papakura a frontier town, with settlers crowding in to sleep in the comparative safety of the tiny Selwyn Chapel and in the fortified Presbyterian Church.

Once the wars had ended Papakura progressed less rapidly than its founders had expected, and it has really only come into its own in the last three decades.

POINTS OF INTEREST

Christ Church Selwyn Chapel: The original wooden chapel, one of a chain of churches built by Bishop Selwyn to a similar design and one in which settlers huddled for safety, was completed in 1862. The stone sanctuary was added as a war memorial after World War I. Neighbouring Christ Church reflects in modern style the atmosphere and the line of the quaint chapel. *Cnr Great South Rd and Coles Cres.*

First Presbyterian Church (1859): Like some other churches south of Auckland, this was fortified in 1863 as settlers feared attack by the Waikato tribes. Its walls were made bulletproof with sand packed between their weatherboards and linings, and loopholes were cut for rifles. Unlike some others, it was spared attack, but it was actions such as this which reinforced the Maori dissidents' view that the missionaries and the Church were agents of the Government, and so reduced the role the Church could play in bringing about peace.

The original church now serves as a church hall. *Coles Cres, off Great South Rd.*

Papakura Museum: The collection is housed in the old fire station. *Averill St. Open Tues and Thurs, 10 a.m.–4 p.m.; Sun, 1–4 p.m.*

Pukekiwiriki pa site: As well as being a fine example of pre-European fortification, the pa site affords a panorama of the South Auckland area from Manurewa to Pukekohe and out to the Manukau Heads. *Red Hill Rd, off the Hunua exit from the town. A 200-m walk through native bush ends with a short climb up stone steps to reach the summit. A notice board records the pa's history.*

ENVIRONS

Hunua Falls: Here one may picnic in a scenic reserve close to the falls themselves. *16 km E of Papakura. Signposted from Hunua. A short level walk leads to the foot of the falls, and a steep 10-min walk reaches their top.*

Maraetai Beach: One of a splendid series of golden beaches, many backed by pohutukawa, facing north towards Waiheke Island. *27 km NE.*

Tokotoru Tapu Church, Mataitai (1912): A curious little Maori church. *27 km E from Papakura, beyond Clevedon on the road to Kawakawa Bay.*

St John's Anglican Church, Drury (1862): The tiny Selwyn Chapel rests on a knoll, with yew trees and a monument to Land War casualties in its churchyard. *5 km S on Highway 1.*

Taranaki   Maps 7, 13   Pop. 1,938   **PATEA**

101 km SE of New Plymouth; 64 km NW of Wanganui.

PATEA is a market town set in dairying and sheep country. Founded in the 1860s during the Taranaki Campaigns, it was an important military settlement with redoubts on either side of the Patea River which flows through the town. Never the subject of attack, it was the only post in southern Taranaki to be held throughout the Land Wars.

The vista of Taranaki/Egmont, framed by the verandahed shopfronts of the town's main street, is much photographed.

POINTS OF INTEREST

"Aotea" canoe: A concrete model of the *Aotea* canoe, 16.8 metres long and 1.5 metres broad, rests on pillars in the middle of the town, and commemorates Turi, captain of the canoe which is said to have brought Polynesians to the district many generations ago. Those represented in the canoe are Turi, his wife and infant child, his son, his brother Rewa, and five others. The canoe came from "Hawaiki" to Kawhia, from where the travellers trekked overland to Patea, "a place where the earth smells sweet". The model was erected in 1933 by those who claim descent from the voyagers.

South Taranaki Museum *: An extraordinary collection of items from the district's past includes relics of Colonial and Imperial troops and the signal cannon from the *Harriet* (*p.* **129**). *127 Egmont St. Open daily.*

Lake Rotorangi: A 47-kilometre lake in a bush setting, created in 1984 when the Patea River was dammed for hydro-electric power. Cruises, fishing trips and house-boat holidays may be arranged (*details from Information Centre in Hawera and Stratford). Access from Highway 3 at 10 km N of Patea. Also from Hawera and Eltham.* The **Rotorangi Hydro Walk** follows the lakeside. *Ball Rd*).

Waikato   Map 6   Pop. 608   **★ PIRONGIA**

13 km W of Te Awamutu

PIRONGIA, like several other Waikato townships, developed when military settlers took up confiscated land. As it was as a frontier town (its Alexandra Hotel recalls its original name), a redoubt was built near the river.

Behind rises graceful Mt Pirongia (*962 m*), whose slopes are included in a forest park whose headquarters are in the town. Pirongia is a contraction of Pirongia-te-aroaro-o-Kahu, meaning "the health-restoring purification of Kahukeke". Kahukeke, the wife of Rakatawa, accompanied her husband on a journey on which they named a number of features. When she came to the mountain she stopped to crush rangiora leaves and treated her scratches with their oil.

SOME HISTORY

The rifle overwhelms the mere: In 1822, Hongi Hika and his Ngapuhi from Northland, armed with muskets, swept through the Waikato until a large force of Waikato assembled here to resist them. However, stout resistance turned to panic and confusion as Waikato warriors were killed from a distance by a type of weapon they had never before encountered. Te Wherowhero, leading the defence, counter-attacked, showing extraordinary bravery, but with little success. The death toll is said to have numbered some 2,000. The Ngapuhi remained in the district for some time, but withdrew after their surprise reversal at △ Otorohanga.

Heaphy's Victoria Cross: Before the invasion of Rangiaowhia (*p.* **221**), while troops were awaiting orders to assault Paterangi pa—an assault which did not, in the event, take place—a sharp skirmish took place at Waiari, on 11 February 1864. Soldiers bathing in the river had come under fire from a group of warriors who were supposed to be positioning themselves for a surprise attack but who had been unable to resist such tempting targets. The soldiers were quickly reinforced, and the Maori took cover in the overgrown ditches of long-deserted Waiari pa. During the engagement the artist-surveyor Charles Heaphy, of the Auckland Volunteer Rifles, rescued a wounded comrade under fire, an act which eventually earned him the award of the Victoria Cross. The award was improper (Colonial troops were not eligible) and it was made only after he had doggedly claimed recognition over a period of years. Forty Maori were recorded as killed for the loss of six British lives. A redoubt was subsequently built to guard the river crossing. *Waiari pa is in good condition, on private farmland, on a bend in the Mangapiko River. Ask directions and permission locally. Heaphy's sword is in the Te Awamutu Museum.*

The Land Wars end: A remarkable incident occurred in 1881, when King Tawhiao and about 600 followers came into Pirongia and in token of peace laid a large number of rifles at the feet of Major William Mair. Mair accepted the spirit of the gesture but his offer to return the rifles was refused; to compromise, Mair gave his own rifle to Tawhiao as a symbol of friendship. This moving ceremony marked the formal end of the Land Wars and a significant advance in inter-racial relations.

THINGS TO SEE AND DO

Pirongia Forest Park: The park is of interest to walker, tramper, birdwatcher and botanist. The vegetation is a "transition zone", where more northern and more southern vegetation types overlap. Absent, though, are kauri (normally found as far south as Kawhia) and southern beech (found as far north as Mt Te Aroha). *Information from DOC, 18 London St, Hamilton; tel. (07) 838-3363.*

Pukeroa Native Timber Museum: Specimens of New Zealand native timbers are displayed and wood-turned items sold. *12 km NW. Corcoran Rd, Te Pahu; tel. (07) 825-9732.*

Alexandra Redoubt (1872) ★ ★: The earthworks of the redoubt built after the fighting are still in good condition. *Opp. Bellot St, walk to knoll on left.*

Matakitaki pa memorial: The memorial marks the scene of the Waikato's stand against Hongi Hika. *On northern exit from town.*

Puniu River: To the south, the river marked the aukati (confiscation) line—the southern extremity of armed settlement and the boundary with the King Country.

PORIRUA

Wellington   Map 13   Pop. 46,601

20 km N of Wellington. Information Centre, Newall St; tel. (04) 237-4375.

PORIRUA was originally planned as a satellite town for △ Wellington when, after World War II it was realised that the Hutt Valley would be unable to contain the capital's growing population. In recent years it has blossomed as a city with a distinct character of its own, though for some time it was handicapped by a pre-dominance of low-cost housing. Porirua has since attracted a range of industries and emerged as a confident, multi-cultural community.

Prominent on the hillside just north of Porirua city are the Police and Traffic Training Colleges.

The city is named for nearby Porirua Harbour, "Parirua" being the name bestowed by the legendary voyager Kupe, and meaning "the place of two flowings of the tide". The harbour has two arms.

SOME HISTORY

From Tara to Te Rauparaha: According to tradition, the earliest inhabitants were moa hunter of the tribe Tini-o-Maruiwi. They were displaced when, about 900 years ago, the sons of Whatonga (*p.* **9**), Tara and Tautoki, came south from the Mahia Peninsula and established what became the tribes of Ngai Tara and Ngati Ira. The tribes continued in uninterrupted possession until Te Rauparaha migrated south from the Waikato and established himself on △ Kapiti Island.

Whalers were active in the area, and subsequently Sydney merchants were frustrated by the Treaty of Waitangi (*pp.* **24-26**) in their speculative bid to purchase the whole of the Porirua Basin. During the fighting of the 1840s, the troubles spread from the Hutt Valley to envelop the area, stockades were built, and the harbour witnessed the occasional skirmish between naval vessels and the canoes of Te Rangihaeata. On nearby Plimmerton Beach, Te Rauparaha was the subject of a sensational arrest. *(For an account of the war see p.* **262***).*

For a time local settlers hoped that Porirua Harbour might rival that of Wellington, but the possibility was dispelled when the floor of the harbour was raised appreciably in the earthquake of 1855.

POINTS OF INTEREST

Titahi Bay ★★: One of the best of the Wellington beaches, it is sandy and affords good surfing.

Plimmerton Beach: A well-sheltered strip of sand where Te Rauparaha was taken prisoner at dawn. *7 km NE.* Just south of Plimmerton, Highway 1 crosses the mouth of the Pauatahanui Inlet. Near the northern end of the bridge are the remains of the Paremata Barracks (1847; *pp.* **296-97**).

Porirua Museum: A lively collection brings the area's history to life; exhibitions vary from traditional Maori herbal remedies to the origin of nursery rhymes. *Te Hiko St. Open Tues–Fri, 10 a.m.–4.30 p.m.; weekends and public holidays, 1–4.30 p.m.*

Police Centennial Museum: Displays include a history of policing in New Zealand, highlighted by exhibits from specific cases, various weapons used in crime among them. There is also a reference library of books, reports and photographs. *Police College, Memorial Wing. Open by appointment.*

Cultural centre: Page 90 Artspace *Norrie St.* There is a **multi-cultural marae** for use by all Polynesian groups (*at Waitangirua; open Mon–Fri; tel. (04) 235-8202*).

Gear Homestead (*c. 1883*)**:** A stately home built by the Gear Meat Company's founder, and its grounds, are open to the public. *Papakowhai, off Highway 1.*

Mana Island (*3 km offshore from Titahi Bay*)**:** The island, with an area of about 800 hectares, was named by Kupe to commemorate his safe crossing from Rarotonga as Te Mana-o-Kupe-ki-Aotearoa ("the ability of Kupe to cross the ocean to Aotearoa"). Purchased from the Ngati Toa in 1832 and site of the country's first sheep farm, today its lack of rodents renders it a suitable place for the liberation into the wild of endangered species of birds, such as the flightless takahe.

Colonial Knob walkway: One of the best walks in the region. *Description p.295.*

Auckland   *Map 4*   *Pop. 176 (locality)*   **★ PUHOI**

53 km N of Auckland, signposted off Highway 1.

PUHOI, a minute settlement serving a mixed farming area, is one of few localities to have retained something of its national origins. Though known as a "German" settlement, its pioneers actually came from the German-speaking Bohemian district of Staab, about 105 kilometres south-west of Prague.

A local fable tells of a visitor to the town who asked at a public meeting, "Who is the Chairman?" and received the unexpected reply, "We're all Ghermans here."

Puhoi means "slow water", a reference to the slow-moving tidal river. At high tide, canoeists can paddle for about three hours downstream to Wenderholm, a particular delight for birdwatchers.

SOME HISTORY

A Bohemian settlement: A Bohemian, Capt. Martin Krippner, had visited New Zealand and at his prompting the first of three groups left Staab to come to this country in 1863. The courage and determination of the 83 colonists is a source of wonder. Few of them had ever even seen the sea, and they had to travel over 1,600 kilometres to reach it, yet they willingly undertook the hazardous and cramped 106-day voyage to an Auckland they found to be "a poor collection of shanties". Sixteen-hectare lots were granted to the settlers by the Provincial Government, the lure that had drawn them so far from home. After a struggle to clear the dense forest—a struggle made the more desperate by the threat of starvation—the settlement of Puhoi emerged on the banks of the Puhoi River. The river was for many years the town's chief link with the outside world but even then settlers would sometimes carry their produce (including shingles and fence posts) all the way to Auckland.

Puhoi was for a time isolated by geographical and linguistic barriers, so it is not surprising that Bohemian dances and other customs remain a part of local tradition. Puhoi's early isolation is also reputed to be perpetuated in the colloquialism, "up the boohai" (meaning "the back of beyond"). The original German settlers, it is said, had difficulty in pronouncing "Puhoi".

Peaceful Puhoi was suddenly regarded as a threat to the nation's security when anti-German paranoia swept the country on the outbreak of World War I. The startling suggestion was made that its entire population, by then many of them native-born New Zealanders, should be imprisoned for the duration of the war. The idea had to be rejected officially, and the town's own repudiation was shown by its patriotic fund-raising and the number of its men who volunteered for service overseas.

POINTS OF INTEREST

Wayside Calvary: Although common in the Catholic countries of Europe, wayside shrines are seldom seen in New Zealand and this, a memorial to the early settlers, is believed to have been the country's first. *On the exit from Puhoi towards Highway 1.*

The Church of St Peter and St Paul.

Church of St Peter and St Paul (1881): A typical building of its period, it is distinguished by the Bohemian names on its memorial windows. The altar piece is a Bohemian painting (1885) requested by the first settlers and a copy of one they remembered in the parish church of Littiz, near Pilsen. There is a small **museum** in the old Convent School (1923) (*open daily in summer; weekends in winter*).

Puhoi Hotel: A handsome two-storeyed colonial building, the hotel (now relegated to a tavern) houses relics of Puhoi's past. An entertaining collection of photographs shows how the descendants of the first settlers have remained very much in evidence. Also displayed is the district's first liquor licence, issued to the "German Hotel" in 1879.

PUKEKOHE *

Auckland South   Map 4   Pop. 15,009

51 km S of Auckland.

PUKEKOHE has become synonymous with "vegetables", for this flourishing town is set in fertile, closely cropped, rolling land which provides the whole country with vast quantities of the season's earliest onions and potatoes. Vegetable processing complements the town's market-gardening role. As in other such towns, a variety of racial groups till the soil in harmony.

National car-racing interest focuses on Pukekohe each January, when the New Zealand International Grand Prix is staged here.

Pukekohe means "hill where the kohehohe tree grows".

SOME HISTORY

The shadow of tragedy: Pukekohe's first attempted settlement got off to a false start. Local Maori sold the Pukekohe Block to the Government in 1843, but when they saw how it was profiting on land sales to settlers, they protested strongly. The settlers involved were moved away and compensated so lavishly that the Auckland

Provincial Council later investigated why it was that a settler such as John Williamson was granted nearly 800 hectares at Waiuku to make up for a mere 157 hectares at Pukekohe. The Government's purchase at Pukekohe was renegotiated.

Unlike the neighbouring districts of Mauku and Pukekohe East (which were settled before the Waikato Campaigns began), the eventual settlement at Pukekohe proper was spared the agony of war; yet it was nonetheless founded in the shadow of tragedy. Fifty-six of its pioneers died of whooping cough and bronchitis on their journey out aboard the *Ganges*. The sadly depleted band, predominantly Cornish and Irish, arrived at fortified Auckland in 1864 and set off to found a frontier town here in dense bush, where they carved out holdings and planted their first crops.

POINTS OF INTEREST

Pioneer Memorial Cottage: In a cottage believed to date from 1859 and to have been garrisoned by British troops during the Waikato Campaigns is a display of china, silverware and items of the colonial period. The park in which the cottage stands is a shaded picnic spot. *Stadium Drive in Roulston Park. Open on Sundays from 2– 4 p.m.*

Pukekohe Hill ★★ *(213 m)*: The hill affords an unrivalled view of the patchwork quilt of Pukekohe's famed market gardens. The view stretches as far as Auckland City, the Manukau Harbour and the mouth of the Waikato River. A direction table records points of interest. *Anzac Rd via Queen St and Kitchener Rd. 2 km.*

ENVIRONS

Pukekohe East Presbyterian Church ★ (1862): This unpretentious little building still bears scars from the fighting it once saw. It was built just three years after Pukekohe East had been settled by groups from Scotland and Cornwall, but before it had been standing for 12 months it had been stockaded, surrounded by a deep trench and occupied as a garrison-house. For as relations between Maori and Pakeha led inexorably to war, the settlers south of Auckland built, and in cases like this improvised, redoubts and similar fortifications.

It was here in September 1863 that 17 settlers held out for several hours against a Maori war party of about 200, which surrounded them until the sound of British bugles in the bush heralded a story-book rescue. During the furious fighting a dazed kereru (native pigeon) perched on the church roof, and seemed to the defenders to be a symbol of hope. British casualties numbered three killed and eight wounded, and Maori losses totalled about 40 dead. None of the settlers was more than scratched. The next day a detachment of militia arrived from Drury to take over and garrison the church.

Splintered bullet-holes remain in its ceiling and there is one inside the rear wall, above the pulpit. Outside, the line of the trench that surrounded the church is still apparent, and the back of the gravestone of "Betsy, the beloved wife of William Hodge" has been scoured by a bullet. Plaques record the day of the battle, the church's role both as schoolhouse (1863-80) and as the first site of local government in Franklin (1862). A large stone marks the common grave of six of the Maori casualties. *Leave Pukekohe by the exit to Bombay and turn left along Pukekohe Rd beyond the Pukekohe East Hall. 5 km.*

St Bride's Anglican Church, Mauku (1859): Mauku was a settled area when Pukekohe proper was still a dense forest of rimu and puriri, and within three years of settlement had its church. Like other churches in South Auckland, it was in 1863, when the Waikato Wars seemed inevitable, stockaded with heavy logs and its walls loopholed for rifles. The 54 loopholes, though boarded up, are still plainly visible. The church became headquarters for a local group of Forest Rangers who saw action in the district though the building itself never came under fire.

The church is named after St Bride's in Fleet Street, London, once the church of one of its founders. London's St Bride's is pictured in the left light of the east window. The right light depicts Bishop Selwyn, who helped establish St Bride's, Mauku, and also the church itself as it appeared during the Land Wars. The two St Bride's exchange greetings each St Bride's Day *(1 February). Findlay Rd, Mauku. 10 km W.*

Alexandra Redoubt, Tuakau ★★: Built in July 1863 on a bluff 90 metres above the Waikato River, it is the best preserved of all the forts built at this time. The large redoubt is rectangular, with flanking angles protruding from diagonally opposite corners. Its site commands the broad and lazy river, and paved the way for the successful operations of the British river fleet assembled for the Waikato Campaigns.

Near the Waikato Heads stood the army supply depot of Camerontown, attacked and sacked by Ngati Maniapoto in September 1863. Hearing the firing, a detachment of the 65th Regiment hurried from Alexandra Redoubt to engage the attackers. As its commanding officer lay mortally wounded, he handed over command to Colour-Sergeant Edward McKenna whose valour in leading the party under heavy fire won him both a commission and the Victoria Cross. Lance-Corporal John Ryan was also awarded the Empire's highest decoration, but before he received it he was drowned in the Waikato River while trying to save a comrade. In all, two VCs and six DCMs were awarded for gallantry shown during the engagement. *In the redoubt, now surrounded by a cemetery, a memorial records the names of the British troops who died in action in the district in 1863-64. Drive to Tuakau and leave on the Port Waikato exit. The Alexandra Redoubt turnoff is signposted. 14.5 km.*

Port Waikato: A fishing, camping and holiday settlement on the broad mouth of the Waikato River where gunboats operating on the river were outfitted and serviced during the Waikato Campaigns. *42 km via Tuakau.*

PUTARURU   *Waikato   Map 8   Pop. 3, 989*

64.5 km SE of Hamilton; 55 km NW of Rotorua. Visitor Centre, tel. (07) 883-7284.

PUTARURU, centre of the Waikato timber trade, grew up as a timber town and its industries today are based on the vast areas of exotic forest since planted in the area. The town was laid out in 1905 but until the late 1930s surrounding farmland, like much of the volcanic plateau, was usable only for forestry. Cattle died of a mysterious "bush sickness". Once the soil's cobalt deficiency was analysed the way was clear to bring into production much new farmland and the town is now a market centre.

Putaruru, more correctly Putaaruru, means "the nest of a ruru (morepork)".

Putaruru Timber Museum * *: Collections here illustrate the emergence of the country's timber industry. An old mill building houses machinery (including a large number of chainsaws) used in logging and milling and a timber camp cookhouse shows how cooks provided for the exhausted logging gangs. There is also an excellent woodturners' display. *3 km S on Highway 1. Open daily 9 a.m.–4 p.m. (except Saturday); tel. (07) 883-7621.*

RAETIHI   *Wanganui   Map 6   Pop. 1,247*

89 km NE of Wanganui. Information Centre, 9A Seddon St, tel. (06) 385-4805

RAETIHI was founded in 1892 in a densely bushed area. The Whanganui River as far as Pipiriki was then the district's principal means of access and wagoners found the town site to be the nearest area of level ground for a stopping point.

Disaster struck in 1918 when fire devastated vast areas of native forestlands in so great a blaze that as far away as Wellington the smoke forced schools to close. Nine sawmills, over 150 houses and at least three people perished. The townships of △ Ohakune, Raetihi and Rangataua escaped conflagration by the narrowest of margins. It was years before the district could recover and a long time before logging and milling could be reorganised. These activities continue, along with sheep and cattle raising, and some dairying and market gardening.

The distinctive twin towers belong to the town's Ratana church (*pp.* **188–89**). Nearby are the Whakapapa and Turoa skifields of △ Tongariro National Park, the scenic Whanganui River and the trout-stocked waters of the Manganuioteao, Whakapapanui and the Mangawhero.

The small **Waimarino Museum**, complete with police cells(1919), is housed in the former railway station (1917), re-sited in the main street. *Seddon St. Open Sunday 2–4 p.m. or on request.*

Canoe trips on the Whanganui River, some of which visit the Bridge to Nowhere and the magnificent "Drop Scene", are run from the Raetihi Motor Camp; *tel. (06) 385-4176.*

RAGLAN **   *Waikato   Map 6   Pop. 2,278*

48 km W of Hamilton.

RAGLAN, at holiday times a bustling seaside resort, is a peaceful spot with houses generously scattered on the hills around its palm-treed main street. The outstanding features of Hamilton's seaside town are the safe, sheltered reaches of its picturesque and sprawling harbour, and sand dunes blacked with iron. Excellent fishing, both in the harbour and along the open beaches, and good whitebaiting in numerous local streams, attract visitors.

A small museum traces the history of the district. *(Green St. Open weekends and school holidays.)*

SOME HISTORY

A doubtful honour: The first settlers came from Taranaki in 1854, and four years later named the town in honour of Lord Raglan, Commander-in-Chief of the British Army in the Crimea at the time of the disastrous Charge of the Light Brigade. Earlier, in 1835, the missionary James Wallis and his wife, Mary Ann, had arrived to set up the first mission station, at Te Horea, across the harbour *(indicated by a memorial in the main street).*

Though the town was a military outpost during the Land Wars, it saw little fighting. However, for years after, Raglan made little progress, partly because of its isolated position and partly because of the Maori King's ban on land sales to Europeans.

Te Awaitaia (*c.* 1796-1866): This chief of the local Ngati Mahanga used his powerful influence to protect the Wesleyan missionaries and to build the first church in Raglan. Baptised Wiremu Naera (William Naylor) in 1834, he swore allegiance to Queen Victoria, induced Waikato chiefs to release their Taranaki slaves, and led a Christian mission to the Taranaki tribes. His opposition to Maori Kingship nearly prevented the election of the first King, and he later placed the Raglan settlers under his protection from the King's supporters. In his lifetime described as "the most powerful man now living", he is today in some quarters considered to have been an enemy of Maori nationalism. *A memorial erected by the Government in 1868 is signposted off the main street.*

Return of a golf-course: For some years, attempts by Maori to assert claims to ancestral land had a special focus at Raglan. Here a bitter struggle ensued over a golf-course that had been built on burial grounds of the local Tainui Awhiro. The land, originally taken by the Crown under compulsory powers in 1941 for use as a military air strip, was not returned by the Crown until 1988. *A stone carving commemorates the return of the land.*

POINTS OF INTEREST

Ocean Beach and Whale Bay: A drive along the southern shores to Whale Bay(*10 km*) is rewarded by spectacular seascapes which sweep as far north as the Waikato Heads. The bleak northern harbour shore is deceptively distant by road. Beyond Whale Bay, a narrow, winding road leads to the start of the **Te Toto Track** to the summit of Mt Karioi (*see below*).

Towards Whale Bay in the Bryant Scenic Reserve, a 15-minute walk leads to **Ocean Beach**, an exposed stretch of sand, black with iron, but popular in summer. (*6.5 km. Park by the Crusader Bible Camp, the old Bryant homestead.*)

The waves along this stretch of the coast are a mecca for surfers who come to ride "the longest left in the world".

Bridal Veil Falls ★★: A 10-minute walk along an easy path through dense bush leads to the single plume which hurtles from a cleft in a rock wall to plummet a sheer 60 metres to a pool below. *21 km. Signposted on the direct road to Kawhia. A steep track continues down to the foot of the falls and to an even more spectacular vantage point.* Beyond the falls is the oddity of Lake Disappear which in very wet weather extends over a wide area in an elevated valley but which within days vanishes through fissures in the rock.

Pirongia Forest Park: The park, which covers some 13,000 hectares, is centred on Mt Pirongia (*962 m*) some distance to the south-east, but also includes the slopes of Mt Karioi (*756 m*). Two tracks link to traverse the mountain. The **Te Toko Track** on the western side (*start at Whaanga Rd, beyond Whale Bay, see above*) climbs steeply to a lookout point offering wonderful views along the coastline(*2 hrs*) and then more gently to the summit of Karioi (*another 1 hr*). On the southern flank, the shorter, steeper **Wairake Track** also leads to the summit (*2 hrs. Start from Ruapuke Rd*). See △ *Pirongia. 62 km SE. Information on tracks in the forest park is available from the Department of Conservation, 18 London St, Hamilton; tel. (07) 838-3363.*

Rangitikei   Map 13   Pop. 501   **RATANA**

23 km SE of Wanganui.

RATANA is a trim township which grew up on the Ratana family property after one of its members had the vision which led to the founding of the Ratana Church. The town, a religious community, has no economic basis and its inhabitants work in the surrounding towns and district. The population is unique in being multi-tribal and bound only by a common belief. It is well served with public buildings provided by the Ratana Church, including the expansive, 3,000 square-metre conference centre, Te Manuao, whose verandah portrays the seven great ancestral canoes along with Cook's *Endeavour* and Tasman's *Heemskerck.*

THE RATANA MOVEMENT

Messianic movements: Throughout history, suppressed minority groups have awaited those who would lead them from captivity. The Maori were no exception and for years had looked for the messianic deliverer whose coming had been prophesied (among others) by Te Kooti as one "who will arise from the west and will unite the people". The mana of the chiefs had gone, the pakeha had subjugated the entire Maori people and in 1907 it was accepted that "as clover killed the fern, and the European dog the Maori dog, as the Maori rat was destroyed by the pakeha rat, so our [Maori] people also will be gradually supplanted and exterminated by the Europeans".

The Maori population had dwindled to a mere 40,000 and appeared doomed. A rise in the birthrate saw a promising recovery but the world-wide 1918 influenza epidemic killed a disproportionate number of Maori and was a severe setback, popularly believed as a visitation by the Maori gods on those who had adopted Christianity.

Ratana emerges: Tuhupotiki Wiremu (Bill) Ratana (1870-1939), a champion ploughman and wheat-stacker, was sitting on the verandah of his home at Ratana on 18 November 1918 when he experienced a vision. An angel appeared and charged him to cleanse himself and his family—"Ratana, I appoint you as the Mouthpiece of God for the multitude of this land. Unite the Maori people, turning them to Jehovah of the Thousands, for this is his compassion to all of you." Ratana was to turn the Maori away from their superstitions and back to Jehovah, to destroy the tohunga and to cure his people.

In a fit of repentance Ratana threw out his beer and smashed the telephone which, according to legend, he used in his bookmaking activities. Word spread quickly and first his relatives and then Maori from far and wide streamed towards the Ratana homestead. There Ratana performed remarkable acts of faith-healing and is said to have had his followers sign a covenant in which they abandoned Maori superstitions and acknowledged the Trinity. Soon extra buses were running from Marton and Wanganui, and every passing train stopped at tiny Ratana station to disgorge passengers. Soon, too, letters were pouring in from all over the country from Maori and Pakeha alike, for Ratana's signature on a carbon-copied letter could prove sufficient to effect a cure by post.

Ratana met with considerable success in his attempt to unify the Maori people but encountered opposition from the Maori King Movement and ran into increasing suspicion from the established churches. Never intended as a separate church but simply as a means to convert Maori to Christianity generally, the Ratana Movement was forced to break with the other established churches and in 1925 the existence of the Ratana Church was proclaimed. Since then it has worked closely with the Methodists.

When Ratana died in 1939, his funeral was attended by the Prime Minister, Members of Parliament and about 3,000 of his followers. Stooped, moustached and devoted to a pipe, he generated an air of mystery yet shunned publicity. He regarded himself solely as the mouthpiece of God, not as a prophet and not, as some of his followers insisted, as Christ reincarnate. Ill-educated, he yet knew much of herbal remedies and his familiarity with the psychology of the tohunga probably gave him his faith-healing powers, though he used no ancient charms. The movement is understandably sensitive about the more colourful aspects of Ratana's career as these tend to cloud his considerable achievements.

Ratana was impatient for Maori reforms and allied his movement to the Labour Party with reform in view. The Ratana Movement quickly became a powerful political force and for 25 years it held all four Maori seats in Parliament. Perhaps the most extravagant of his prophecies was a claim that his movement would one day actually be "the Government", yet incredibly from 1946-49 and 1957-60 the Ratana group of Members held the Parliamentary balance of power and kept the Labour Party in office. But even with this advantage the Ratana Members could not force a settlement of their traditional complaints (such as ratification of the Treaty of Waitangi) and inevitably lost some prestige.

The movement's numbers were set at 47,202 in the 1991 Census. By comparison there were 47,391 Mormons and 69,858 Baptists.

The symbol △ indicates a place with its own entry elsewhere in this Alphabetical Section.

RATANA TEMPLE ★★

The Ratana Temple and its decor are charged with symbolism. The building's distinctive twin towers are called Arepa and Omeka after two of Ratana's sons, both saints of the Church and named after the Greek letters Alpha and Omega, the beginning and the end.

Most striking is the absence of traditional Maori art inside the temple, barred by Ratana as it would suggest old superstitions. A star and crescent, Te Whetu Marama (the Shining Light), represent Ratana's mission. The star (whetu) relates to the Star of Bethlehem and also to the stars that guided the early Polynesian canoes, and the moon (marama), too, is a powerful symbol often found on old ko (digging sticks) to encourage fertility. The pattern of concentric circles above the main door is Te Kahoi,o Ihoa (the Eye of God). The colours used represent the Father (blue), Son (white), Holy Ghost (red), their Holy Angels (purple) and Ratana himself (gold).

Before the temple are the graves of Ratana and his wife. Some distance away is a museum which contains crutches, wheelchairs and spectacles discarded by those healed by Ratana, and an assortment of ornaments, clothing and weapons kept safely here because they were believed to contain unhealthy atua (spirits).

There are a number of Ratana churches throughout the North Island but the Ratana Temple here is by far the largest.

The temple is generally open to the public and the museum may be seen by arrangement with the Church authorities. The original Ratana homestead, beside the Te Manuao conference centre, is in striking contrast with the newer buildings.

Northland   *Map 1*   ★★★ REINGA (Cape)

116 km NW of Kaitaia. Department of Conservation field base, Cape Reinga Shop, Cape Reinga Lighthouse; tel. (09) 409-7540.

CAPE REINGA is popularly regarded as the country's northernmost point, but in fact Surville Cliffs (formerly named Kerr Point) on North Cape are almost five kilometres farther north. However, Cape Reinga is the more readily accessible and is given added fascination by the Maori legend of the spirits. The small lighthouse settlement on the Cape is accustomed to visitors but has no facilities for them. There is camping nearby, to the east, at Tapotupotu and Spirits Bay (Kapowairua), and en route at Rarawa Beach (*turn-off just N of Ngataki*).

Conducted tours to the Cape are run from △ Kaitaia and △ Paihia and are recommended both for the entertaining commentary they provide and for the leg of the trip along △ Ninety Mile Beach.

SOME HISTORY

A near encounter: The expanse of ocean off the Cape was the scene set for a meeting which, had it taken place, would have gone down in history as one of the most extraordinary coincidences of all time. Captain James Cook, shortly after rediscovering New Zealand in 1769 and only a few days after he had formally claimed the land for Britain, was caught in a hurricane as his ship rounded North Cape on its way west.

At the same time the French explorer de Surville (*see p. 20*), while en route to Tahiti, was forced by his crew's ill-health to look for the land Tasman had discovered over a century before. After sighting land at Hokianga he turned to sail round North Cape when he ran into the same hurricane. So it was that somewhere off Cape Reinga the paths of the two explorers actually crossed, but in the storm neither was aware of the other's presence.

POINTS OF INTEREST AT CAPE REINGA

Cape Reinga Lighthouse: There are spectacular views from here, to the west along the coast to Cape Maria Van Diemen and eastwards to North Cape. Ahead the Pacific Ocean meets the Tasman Sea, and beyond, quite unexpectedly, are the Three Kings Islands.

The familiar light was not built until 1941 when the manned lighthouse at Cape Maria Van Diemen, built 63 years earlier, was made automatic. The light stands in a 10.5-metre tower 165 metres above sea level. One of the most powerful in the country, it flashes once each 26 seconds and is visible for some 50 kilometres.

The venerated pohutukawa: Below the lighthouse juts the Cape itself, broken only by a gnarled pohutukawa. According to tradition, the spirits of the departed Maori journeyed back to their Pacific homeland, "Hawaiki". Travelling up Ninety Mile Beach they carried tokens of their home area, seaweed, fern or manuka, which they left at Te Arai Rock (*3 km S of The Bluff on Ninety Mile Beach*). At Twilight Beach the spirits turned inland towards Cape Reinga and crossed a stream from which they might drink. However, if a person was gravely but not fatally ill, his spirit could choose not to drink but to return to his ailing body. The spirits who drank journeyed on to the tortured pohutukawa tree on the very tip of the Cape where they passed down its exposed roots into the sea bed. The spirits surfaced again on Ohau Island, the largest of the Three Kings, to farewell New Zealand before continuing on to "Hawaiki". The story gives the Cape its name of Reinga, "the underworld".

The pohutukawa is said to be over 800 years old.

Three Kings Islands: In fine weather the islands can be seen on the horizon as something of an anticlimax for those who anticipate a vast void of ocean.

The trans-Tasman steamer *Elingamite* (2,585 tons), in 1902 ran aground in fog on West Island, one of the Kings, with the loss of 45 lives. The master's certificate was suspended for alleged grossly negligent navigation but eight years later he was completely exonerated, as an Australian naval survey showed that the charted position of the islands was grossly in error. Gold bullion carried on the *Elingamite,* then valued at £17,320 is still being salvaged.

The islands were named by Abel Tasman in 1643 as it was there that his ships anchored on the night of the Epiphany.

Pandora Bank: The reef seen beyond Cape Maria Van Diemen when sea conditions allow was where the collier *Kaitawa* was lost with her crew of 29 in May 1966.

ROAD TO CAPE REINGA

The 116-kilometre road from Kaitaia to Cape Reinga leads along a narrow peninsula and includes alternating views of the Pacific Ocean and the Tasman Sea. It passes the Aupouri Forest, waste land once kauri gum-digging fields, and undulating desert-like sandhills, before finally leading through the Te Paki reserves to emerge at the Cape itself.

Aupouri Forest: *Described under △ Ninety Mile Beach.*

Houhora Heads *(S of Houhora, detour 5 km):* An attractive inlet with picnicking and camping places. Across the inlet looms the hump of Mt Camel *(245 m),* named by Cook in 1769 as a "high mountain or hill standing upon a disart [sic] shore". Note the planting to halt sand encroachment.

To the left of the camping area is the old Subritzky Homestead, built in the 1850s by an early Polish settler from local materials and plastered with a paste made from powdered seashells. It has been restored by his descendants. Near the homestead, the Wagener Museum contains extensive displays of Maori artefacts, natural history, firearms, kauri gum, whaling material and Victoriana. Less usual is a collection of early automatic vending machines. *Open daily (except Christmas Day and Good Friday), 9 a.m.–5 p.m.* The country's most northern golf course is situated here and there is also good camping *(tel. (09) 409-8564).*

Houhora: The settlement boasts New Zealand's most northerly tavern but is a pale shadow of the town it once was, when hundreds of gum diggers thronged the area. The old hotel, beside the new tavern, was built by combining a number of buildings, and the bar is actually an old woolshed dragged here by bullocks from △ Ninety Mile Beach in 1902. *52 km.*

Te Kao: Prominent are the distinctive twin towers of the Ratana Church, a Maori revivalist religion dating from the 1920s. *(For notes on the Ratana faith, see △ Ratana.)*

Parengarenga Harbour: The harbour was once linked to Auckland by a regular passenger-boat service, but now, seen from the road, it looks almost deserted. The 1,600-hectare, brilliantly white sandspit at its entrance contains some of the world's purest silica sand, an ingredient in glass making. The sand is shipped by barge to glassworks at Whangarei and Auckland.

Each year, in late February and early March, godwits gather on the sandspit until it is all but black. After days of mounting excitement and as if at a given signal, the birds rise to fill the sky, blot out the sun, circle the harbour and leave on their annual migration to Siberia and Alaska. The bar-tailed godwit *(Limosa lapponica)* is a familiar sight in summer, often seen in flocks of 100 or more feeding on mud and sand flats.

Te Paki Station: The 16,870-hectare station was the scene of an attempt made by a public company to grow tung oil trees. The occasional **tung tree** can be seen, but

A traveller may lie with authority. *Proverb*

the venture (and the company) collapsed as there was inadequate shelter for the seedlings. *101 km.*

CAPE REINGA WALKWAY

Starting from the Cape, one may walk along the coast east to Spirits Bay (*10 ½ hrs*), or walk south along Te Werahi Beach to Cape Maria Van Diemen and then along Twilight Beach to Ninety Mile Beach and so to Ahipara (*7 hrs to Te Paki stream*). There are no huts for overnight stops and adequate equipment is essential. *Full details of the walkway are available at the Information Centre, 6–8 South Rd, Kaitaia and the DOC field base at Cape Reinga lighthouse (tel. (09) 409-7540).*

Wairarapa   Map 12   Pop. 128   **RIVERSDALE**

55 km E of Masterton.

A SANDY SURF beach on an otherwise generally inaccessible stretch of coastline has led a number of Wairarapa families to build holiday homes at Riversdale. Well sheltered by hills and pine plantations from the prevailing north-westerly, the settlement enjoys a micro-climate and when Wellington is being buffeted by the prevailing winds, the Wairarapa coast can be basking in sunshine. There is good bathing, surfing, fishing and golfing and canoe trips on the Whareama River (*Kahutara Canoes; tel. (06) 308-8453 and Seven Oaks Canoeing Adventures; tel. (06) 372-3801*).

★★★ ROTORUA

Volcanic Plateau   Map 8   Pop. 53,702 (urban area)

221 km SE of Auckland; 92 km S of Tauranga; 84 km NE of Taupo. Tourism Rotorua Visitor Information, 67 Fenton St; tel. (07) 348-5179; fax (07) 348-6044. Best of Maori Tourism, 109 Fenton St; tel. 0800-105-205 (toll free); fax (07) 348-7832.

TOWERING GEYSERS, bubbling mud and kaleidoscopic silica terraces draw most of the visitors to the lakeside city of Rotorua. Yet emphasis on its thermal sights, and its role as a centre of the Arawa tribe, tend to obscure the city's beginnings as a spa town—although the Tudoresque architecture of the magnificent old Bath House and other prominent buildings is a legacy of an attempt to capture the atmosphere of the traditional European spa.

"Soir de Rotorua" (Night in Rotorua) is just one of the local names for the ever-present pungent odour of hydrogen sulphide which pervades the city, a natural gas which smells of rotten eggs. Rotorua has been called "Sulphur City"; the Maori name for the Government Gardens area is less charitable—Whangapipiro, "an evil-smelling place". Curiously, after a short time in the city one's consciousness of the smell almost disappears.

As nowhere else, aspects of Maori tradition may be savoured by the visitor, among them carvers at work, regular Maori concerts and hangi (at which food cooked in earth ovens is served).

Rotorua means "second lake".

SOME HISTORY

A successful trick: Once the *Arawa* canoe had come to rest on the Bay of Plenty coast at Maketu in about the fourteenth century, parties are said to have moved inland to explore the interior, led among others by Ngatoroirangi (who is credited with bringing volcanic activity to the region, *see below*) and Tia (who named Lake Taupo). It was some little time later that Ihenga, also from the *Arawa*, set out from the coast. Arriving at Rotorua he saw smoke and realised that others were already established there. Furtively he substituted his own nets and posts for those he found at an old tuahu (sacred shrine) by the lake, and when he met the inhabitants he boldly proclaimed that the land was his as he had been living there longer. When the inhabitants challenged Ihenga's claim, he suggested that they compare tuahu to see whose was the older. Ihenga's ruse succeeded and the inhabitants reluctantly made way. Thus the Rotorua area was claimed for the Arawa tribe.

They used the hot pools for bathing, the boiling pools for cooking, and built whare (houses) naturally heated by the warm earth.

Hongi Hika invades: The adventurous Te Rauparaha, once established on Kapiti

Island near Wellington, travelled to Rotorua to recruit followers. While on the island of Motutawa, in the centre of Rotokakahi (Green Lake), a party of Ngapuhi from the Bay of Islands arrived on the lake shore. As one of his relatives had been killed at Thames during a Ngapuhi raid some time earlier, Te Rauparaha persuaded the local Arawa sub-tribe to ferry some of the Ngapuhi across to the island, there to strike them down in the course of a simulated feast of welcome. Such an insult could not pass unrevenged, compounded as it was by the fact that a nephew of the famed Hongi Hika was among the victims.

So it was that early in 1823 Hongi assembled a war party and left the Bay of Islands, sailing down the coast. By the time he reached Tauranga his forces numbered 1,200, but while there he learned that the Arawa had gathered safely on Mokoia Island in the centre of Lake Rotorua and had prudently taken every canoe in the district with them. Undaunted, Hongi took his own canoes inland, making his way over lakes and through bush towards Lake Rotorua. Of the several portages he used, that between Lake Rotoehu and Rotoiti is the most famous and still bears the name of "Hongi's Track".

For several days Hongi's Ngapuhi, whose plentiful muskets were plainly destined to overwhelm the traditionally armed Arawa, set the defenders' nerves on edge by sailing round and round Mokoia Island before finally attacking. According to Arawa tradition, the attack took place on a misty morning. Arawa sentries could not see the approaching Ngapuhi and so it was left to a flock of tarapunga (gulls) to rise sharply and scream a warning to the Arawa to defend the beaches. Throughout the battle the tarapunga circled, watching the conquest of their beloved Arawa, and it is said that the spirits of the Arawa dead entered the bodies of the gulls which are to this day tapu (sacred). Hongi himself might well have been killed had he not been wearing the helmet given him in Britain some years earlier by George IV.

As battle raged one of the women with the Ngapuhi, an Arawa who had married a Ngapuhi on an earlier expedition, implored Hongi to spare her sub-tribe, which had not been involved in the slaughter on Rotokakahi. Reluctantly Hongi agreed, but only to spare those who "passed between her thighs". The woman, Te Aokapurangi, shrewdly clambered to the gable of the Tamatekapua meeting house (later rebuilt at Ohinemutu, *see below*), where she sat astride the ridge, and the many who crowded into the house "passed between her thighs" as they entered. This event gave rise to the saying: "Ano! ko te whare whawhao a Te Aokapurangi!" ("This is like the crammed-full house of Te Aokapurangi!"). Those in the house were saved, but many of the others perished and many more were taken prisoner.

The battle won, the Ngapuhi withdrew. While returning to the coast, a Ngati Pikiao chief crossed their path in "Hongi's Track" and was promptly slain (*where now stands a memorial*). As a reprisal, a band of Ngati Pikiao crept into the Ngapuhi camp at night to recover the body and to kill and carry off a Ngapuhi chief.

The Ngapuhi eventually made their way back to the Bay of Islands, leaving Maketu and the surrounding area virtually deserted, and it was several years before any Arawa lived there again.

An impromptu defence: The Arawa—motivated by the opportunity to even old scores with the tribes of Waikato and Ngati Haua—were "loyal" to the Government throughout the Land Wars, and this was recognised by the presentation of a bust of Queen Victoria, still standing at Ohinemutu (*see below*).

During the Waikato Campaigns in 1864 it was learned that about 800 Maori in the Bay of Plenty and East Cape planned to pass through Arawa territory so that they could join the Waikato and other followers of the Maori King (*pp.* **159-60**). The Arawa refused them permission to cross, but found themselves without the necessary weapons needed to repel the intruders. The local Civil Commissioner refused an Arawa request for rifles, but the less suspicious William Mair, newly appointed Magistrate at Taupo, persuaded Imperial military officers at Tauranga to give the Arawa their sporting ammunition. Storekeepers even emptied their tea-chests for their lead linings, and the Arawa set to work making cartridges at Mourea.

A party of related Tuwharetoa from Taupo joined the Arawa, and a combined force of 400 crossed Rotoiti in canoes to meet the intruders as they advanced along "Hongi's Track". The groups clashed along the southern shores of the lake, where the main road now runs, an encounter which ended in the defeat of the trespassers, who retreated to the coast. Battle was resumed near △ Maketu and culminated in the total rout of the invaders.

To Kooti attacks: In 1870 Rotorua was again under attack, for Te Kooti (*pp.* **85**), infuriated by the tribe's unswerving loyalty to the Government, had pronounced a curse on the Arawa. Despite his defeat and narrow escape at Te Porere only three months before, in February 1870 Te Kooti planned to subject Ohinemutu (as Rotorua was then known) to the kind of surprise attack that had been successful at Gisborne, Mohaka and Whakatane.

First he moved his men as if Tauranga were his objective. The feint succeeded, and, as Te Kooti had hoped, the Colonial forces left Rotorua unguarded as they hastened to bolster Tauranga's defences. Lieutenant Gilbert Mair, however, appreciated the danger and with a small number of Arawa secretly hurried back, arriving just in time to see an Arawa chief, under a flag of truce, about to accept Te Kooti's offer of "peace".

Running up to the chief, Mair tore the white flag from his hands, jumped on it in disgust, and shouted to his men to attack Te Kooti's advance guard—for although many of Te Kooti's men were related to the Arawa, it seems certain that had they been allowed inside the defences, they would have turned on the unsuspecting defenders in the same way that they had at △ Mohaka.

As it was Te Kooti's men retreated hastily, and all day and into the night Mair and his "Flying Column", although outnumbered by about five to one, harried them relentlessly. Mair's band encountered ambush after ambush as Te Kooti's rearguard fought for time for their women and wounded to escape, but by the day's end the dead included some of Te Kooti's most ruthless lieutenants. For his part in the victory Mair was promoted to Captain and awarded the New Zealand Cross, a decoration which ranked equal with the Victoria Cross. (Mair is buried at St Faith's, Ohinemutu.)

A spa town: When the wars ended, the attractions of local thermal activity began to draw increasing numbers of visitors. The principal settlement on the lake was then the Maori village of Ohinemutu, and to take advantage of the curative properties of the thermal waters, the Government developed "Rotorua" as a spa town and tourist centre.

An agreement was entered into with the owners of the land, the Ngati Whakaue sub-tribe living at Ohinemutu, for the lease of about 800 hectares for the purpose of establishing the government township of Rotorua, and confirmed in law as the Thermal Springs Districts Act of 1881.

However it proved difficult for the Maori landowners to collect rents from absentee leaseholders, and so in 1890 the Government agreed to purchase the town area for £8,250, with the Ngati Whakaue also presenting 400 hectares to the nation as reserves.

The first building in the new township was a government bath-house, which opened in 1882. By 1908 the largest bath-house in the Southern Hemisphere, the present imposing structure had opened under the direction of a balneologist. Uniquely, until 1922 the town had no effective form of local government, being administered from the capital through the Department of Tourist and Health Resorts.

Most of those who come to Rotorua today take the waters simply for enjoyment and a feeling of wellbeing, but Queen Elizabeth Hospital (*beside the Government Gardens*) continues the spa tradition and is the national centre for the treatment of rheumatism. Hydrotherapy plays a major role, along with physiotherapy and occupational therapy. Outpatients are referred to the hospital from all parts of New Zealand, as well as from overseas.

THERMAL ACTIVITY

Thermal activity, although principally associated with Rotorua, is found in New Zealand as far north as Kaikohe and as far south as the Copland River (near Fox Glacier in the South Island). However the most intense activity lies in what is known as the Taupo Volcanic Zone, which includes Rotorua. One theory to account for the phenomenon of hot springs is that the water begins as rainfall and seeps through the earth's crust to be heated by contact with hot rocks. In volcanic districts, however, it is usually the result of molten rock cooling slightly and solidifying to trap steam and other gases, so causing pressures to rise until the steam and the gases force their way out and up to the earth's surface. Investigations reveal that the hot springs in the Government Gardens are fed by water heated under pressure to more than 200ºC.

A geyser erupts when an underground column of water is heated beyond boiling point and flashes into steam, violently expelling the water held above the flash point. Because of the part played by pressures, geysers are generally most active when barometric pressures are low.

Botanists have observed an intriguing link between the thermal areas and tropical ferns. The warm ground can provide habitats similar to those of much hotter countries and the varieties of tropical fern which flourish in locations such as Waimangu and Orakei Korako are not found elsewhere in the country.

Residents at Rotorua have come to terms with the mixed blessings the activity offers. In the past many had bores and used tapped steam for cooking, for heating homes and for private swimming pools. In industry steam has been used in timber kilns, to render fat, to steam-clean vehicles, to heat glasshouses and to ripen fruit. But against this, the upkeep of roads is high, steam frequently wafts from drains and occasionally structural damage occurs. In churchyards at Ohinemutu and Whakarewarewa the graves are raised above the ground, and on Arikikapakapa Golf Course less customary hazards include pools of boiling mud. Periodically the extensive use of the steam gives rise to fears for the future of the geyser valley. Restrictions were imposed in 1986 to reduce the number of bores.

The Arawa legend which tells of the coming of volcanic activity to the country recounts how the tohunga Ngatoroirangi climbed to the summit of Mt Tongariro *(south of Taupo)* and was in danger of freezing to death. He prayed to the gods in his far off "Hawaiki" homeland to send fire to save him, and this they did. The fire travelled underground to emerge first at White Island, and then at various points in the Rotorua and Taupo regions, before finally bursting through the tip of Tongariro in time to save the famed tohunga of the *Arawa* canoe. Wherever the fire had surfaced in the course of the journey, thermal activity was left behind.

LAKE ROTORUA

Lake Rotorua, nearly circular in shape and on whose southern brink the city stands, has the enchanting Mokoia Island almost at its very centre. The largest of the many lakes in the region, Rotorua provides an appropriate setting for the greatest of all Maori love stories, the romance of Hinemoa and Tutanekai *(related in description of Mokoia Island, below).*

Trout fishing enthusiasts troll the waters and fish the mouths of the many streams which flow into the lake. The lake is drained by Ohau Channel, which leads Rotorua's waters into Lake Rotoiti before they plunge over Okere Falls and flow down the Kaituna River. *Boats are for hire, fishing trips may be arranged and excursions to Mokoia Island and scenic flights by float-plane all run from the lakefront. The stately* Lakeland Queen *offers a selection of meals as it cruises the lake (tel. (07) 348-6634 for reservations).*

The lake provides the setting for the annual marathon, when each April thousands' of runners circle the lake.

THERMAL AREAS ★★★

Activity along the Taupo Volcanic Zone extends in a broad belt from △ Tongariro National Park in the south to △ White Island in the Bay of Plenty, but is concentrated around Rotorua at Whakarewarewa, Waimangu, Waiotapu and Tikitere, and near △ Taupo. Each of these areas has its own distinct fascination, and it can never be said that to have seen one is to have seen them all—as is shown by visitors who continually argue as to which is "the best".

Carved gateway
and model pa,
Whakarewarewa.

Whakarewarewa ★★★: Perhaps the best known of the thermal areas, "Whaka" is also closest to the city. The path to Whakarewarewa Maori Village, where the sub-tribe displaced by the Tarawera eruption *(see below)* now lives, leads across a bridge from which children have for generations dived for coins into a river yellowed with sulphur. The villagers use the hot pools for bathing, cooking, washing and heating, and some houses have pipes protruding from their foundations to direct steam away from their floorboards. A carved Maori meeting house may be seen before entering the reserve.

The small Maori reserve which the visitor sees first is where cooking, laundering and bathing take place. The main reserve features a Geyser Flat, a silica terrace of about a hectare pierced by seven active geysers. The two most reliable geysers are the Prince of Wales Feathers, which plays spasmodically up to 12 metres and whose playing heralds the awakening of Pohutu. Pohutu ("splashing") is New Zealand's largest geyser and plays to about 30 metres, occasionally for hours at a time. Near Wairoa geyser is "The Brainpot", a symmetrical silica basin which legend says was used to cook the heads of enemies.

The reserve also includes a number of boiling mud pools which plop an endless series of intriguing patterns. Above stands Rotowhio Model pa, palisaded and including the buildings characteristic of the pre-European pa. The carved entrance-way depicts the lovers Hinemoa and Tutanekai embracing. By the pa is the **Maori Arts and Crafts Institute** (*tel. (07) 348-9147*) where carvers may be seen at work and there is a cultural concert daily (*12.15 p.m.*). Nearby is a **nocturnal house** where the kiwi (*p. 171*) may be seen.

Before milling activity banished fish from the stream which flows through the valley, trout could be caught in its cold waters and swung straight into a boiling pool for cooking. *3 km S. Open daily, 8.30 a.m.–5.30 p.m. Guided tours hourly.*

Waiotapu ★ ★ ★: Here one finds a variety of phenomena noted for their colour. Most remarkable of all is the Lady Knox Geyser, named in 1904 after the daughter of Lord Ranfurly, then Governor-General. At the beginning of the century warders would bring prisoners here from a nearby prison farm to wash their clothes in a hot pool. They found that when the water became soapy the pool would erupt, but to no great height as the pool's surface area was too great. A warder had the prisoners build a rock cairn over the pool to confine its waters and drive the geyser higher, and today silica has coated the cairn to give it the semblance of being natural, but the geyser must still be triggered by the use of soap.

At the reserve itself the main area of activity is pitted with giant craters caused when the ground above collapsed after it was undermined by a subterranean thermal stream. Beyond the craters lies the Artist's Palette, over a hectare of silica terraces delicately tinged with all the colours of the spectrum. At the foot of the terraces are the elegant Bridal Veil Falls, falls which vary in colour from pinkish-white to a rich gold after heavy rain. On the return is a Champagne Pool which effervesces when a scoop of sand is tossed into it.

The road into the area passes one of the largest mud pools in the district. *Turnoff signposted 30.5 km S on the road to Taupo. Detour 2 km. Open daily during daylight hours. Allow 45 mins. Lady Knox Geyser, which is soaped daily at 10.15 a.m., is in a separate private area.* On the way to Waiotapu, by the junction of the roads to Taupo and Waikaremoana, stands candy-striped Rainbow Mountain, topped by a forest-fire lookout. Occasionally vapours may be seen rising from its slopes.

Waimangu ★ ★ ★: The valley has a sullen character and sights of a brooding vastness. Before leaving the office visitors may pause to study some early photographs of the region before it was devastated by the 1886 Tarawera eruption. Until then the wonders of the Pink and White Terraces, two separate and enormous fan-like silica terraces on the shores of Lake Rotomahana, had drawn visitors from all over the world. Without warning in the early hours of 10 June 1886 the northern peak of Mt Tarawera, hitherto believed extinct, erupted violently. The range split in two as a series of eruptions culminated in Lake Rotomahana's exploding with a roar heard as far away as Christchurch. The Maori villages of Te Wairoa, Te Ariki and Moura were inundated, the entire area devastated, roads and bridges shattered, and ash and debris strewn over some 16,000 square kilometres. At least 153 people perished and the unique Pink and White Terraces were obliterated. It is said that the disaster was preceded by the appearance of a phantom canoe on neighbouring Lake Tarawera (*see below*).

The thermal attractions are seen on a walk down to the shores of Lake Rotomahana, really the second lake in the crater as it refilled with water some time after the eruption. The Waimangu Cauldron, a boiling lake of over four hectares and one of the largest in the world, is dominated by the impressive, red-streaked and steaming Cathedral Rocks. The Cauldron fills a crater left by an eruption in 1917 that destroyed a tourist hotel. Nearby is the crater of the now-extinct Waimangu Geyser, once the world's largest, which played up to an incredible 488 metres between 1900 and 1904. Ruamoko's Throat, formed by the 1886 eruption, is a lake of a fantastic turquoise backed by scarlet cliffs. The thermal attractions end at Warbrick Terrace and the track leads on to the shores of Lake Rotomahana to give one a view across the water to Mt Tarawera. Pause by the lake and in tranquillity reflect on the devastation of that June morning in 1886. *19 km on the main road to Taupo.*

Signposted. Open daily during daylight hours. Those on the Waimangu Round Trip (reservations tel. (07) 347-1199) then cross the lake to pass the steaming cliffs, to cross to Lake Tarawera and so reach Te Wairoa Buried Village. Other visitors should allow 2½ hrs for the walk and a boat trip on the lake (tel. (07) 366-6137).

Tikitere ★★: Also known as Hell's Gate, Tikitere is the most active thermal area in the district, with a series of furiously bubbling pools. Highlight of a visit is the picturesque thermal Kakahi Falls where visitors are welcome to splash under its pleasantly warm waters. The Sulphur Bath is a cauldron of water useful for septic cuts, bites and some skin ailments, and bottles may be filled with its most useful lotion. One of the pools, Huritini, is named after a Maori princesss who is said to have thrown herself into its boiling waters after learning of her husband's infidelity. A hot swim may be enjoyed in an uninviting but relaxing thermal bath, grey with obsidian and excellent for rheumatic complaints. *18 km E, signposted on the road to Whakatane. Open daily, 9 a.m.–5 p.m.*

TROUT SPRINGS ★★★

Rainbow Springs: These remarkable springs feature a walk through a stand of bush with hundreds of native ferns filtering the light. Trout pools include rainbow, brown and North American brook trout, with underwater viewing of some of the largest trout to be seen anywhere. From Fairy Springs about 16 million litres gush in an hour, swirling millions of particles of pumice and obsidian to tint the pool a bewitching shade of blue. Also to be seen are a nocturnal kiwi house, a fresh-water aquarium and introduced game including the famed Captain Cooker, a species of pig whose forebears were released by the explorer over 200 years ago. There is a good restaurant for light lunches. A track leads to the **Skyline Skyride** to the summit of Mt Ngongotaha. *5 km on Highway 5 to Hamilton and Auckland. Open daily; tel. (07) 347-9301.*

At the adjoining **Rainbow Farm** (*show times 10.30, 11.45 a.m., 1, 2.30 p.m.*) audiences participate in aspects of farming, from milking cows to "bidding" at sheep auctions. Sheep are shorn and working dogs demonstrated (*tel. (07) 347-9301*).

Paradise Valley Springs: The valley includes such big game as lions (*fed daily, 2 p.m.*) as well as trout and a delightful bush walk. The valley is better visited for half a day than for an hour or so. *11 km NW. Signposted on the Auckland exit to the city. Open daily. The lions are fed at 2.30 p.m.*

Close by is the **Ngongotaha Trout Hatchery** where fish are taken from the Ngongotaha Stream, stripped of their eggs and held in pools while they are fed back to good condition before being released. In a single year over 38,000 fish are taken from the stream. Once the eggs are hatched, some of the fry are held for about six months, until they reach fingerling stage (the size of one's finger), when they are tagged for identification and released throughout the Bay of Plenty. Over 6,000 million eggs from this hatchery have been flown to Colorado, USA, for release there. *Open daily, 9 a.m.–4 p.m. Ngongotaha Valley Rd.*

THINGS TO SEE AND DO IN THE CITY

Whakarewarewa thermal area ★★★: *Described above.*

Government Gardens ★★★: Together with its trim sports greens, the gardens are dominated by the magnificent old Tudor-styled Bath-house. Built in 1906-7 for the Department of Tourist and Health Resorts, the Elizabethan-styled building was a deliberate attempt to capture the elegance of a fashionable European spa. Thermal pools were in its wings and massage cubicles were in what is now a licensed restaurant. The building also contains a musuem and an art gallery.

The formal gardens are spiced with thermal activity and include the Arawa Soldiers' Memorial (1927), which symbolises the history of the local tribes and their contact with the Pakeha. At its base is the *Arawa* canoe from which the Arawa trace their descent, and at its top is Rehua, the star that guided the canoe on its epic voyage. The Maori Regimental Badge incorporates two weapons, taiaha and tewhatewha, and the words Te Hokowhitu a Tu (the name of the war-party of Tu Matauenga, the god of war). Above busts of Queen Victoria and Edward VII are four graphic panels depicting Te Kuraimonoa (a beauty of "Hawaiki", from whose union with her celestial lover, Puhaorangi, the Arawa are descended); Governor Hobson signing the Treaty of Waitangi (and watched by Tupara Tanira, reputed to be the only Arawa chief to sign it); traditional Maori weapons of war, and the Rev. Thomas Chapman preaching. Atop the monument is George V.

Behind the Bath-house is a sports and conference centre. Close by are **Polynesian Pools** and **The Orchid Gardens** (*for both see below*). *At the end of Arawa St, by the lake.*

Rotorua Art and History Museum ★ ★ ★: Housed in the Bath-house, the museum has imaginative displays, including those dramatising the horrors of the

Tarawera eruption. Among the most important of the Maori artefacts are carved barge-boards from the Houmaitawhiti meeting house (1860) at Rotoiti executed by famed Ngati Tarawhai carvers from Okataina; early nineteenth-century palisading from Ohinemutu, and a curious female pumice figure, Pani, a kumara goddess depicted in the act of giving birth (most fertility gods found to date are of Rongo, a male). A large collection of photographs traces the area's development. Many important artefacts have been placed on deposit here by local Maori families.

A gallery of contemporary art shows touring exhibitions, mounts its own special exhibitions and has a New Zealand collection which ranges from early prints through historical photographs to examples of the work of major New Zealand artists. Also held is a collection of sculpture in Italian marble by an Australian, Charles Francis Summers. Originally shown at the 1906 Christchurch Exhibition, the works were brought to the bath-house and for many years added to its elegance. *Government Gardens. Open daily, 10 a.m. – 4.30 p.m; tel. (07) 348-4199.*

Polynesian Pools Thermal Baths ★ ★ ★: There are numerous thermal swimming pools in and around the city, both public and private, of which these are the most important. Three springs are used in the complex; the Old Priest Bath (discovered when Father Mahony came for treatment from Tauranga in 1878) is beneficial for functional nervous diseases, arthritic complaints such as gout and rheumatism, fibrositis and nervous debility — indeed it is said to have cured Father Mahony's rheumatism. The Rachel Spring contains an alkaline sulphuretted water which acts as a skin emollient and as a soothing sedative agent valuable in cases of sunburn, convalescence and spastic ailments. The Radium Spring has stimulating properties for rheumatic ailments and functional diseases. Despite the medicinal benefits, the great majority of visitors go simply to enjoy a good hot swim, an utterly self-indulgent Aix massage (*booking essential*) and the licensed restaurant and bar. *End of Hinemoa St, adjoining the Government Gardens; open daily from 6.30 a.m.–10 p.m.; tel. (07) 348-1328.*

The Orchid Gardens: A special feature of the Gardens is an unusual water organ which plays for 15 mins on the hour. An intriguing **microworld** uses technology to give intimate perspectives of nature. *Hinemaru St. Open daily; tel. (07) 347-6699.*

Ohinemutu Maori village ★★★: This was once the main Maori settlement on Lake Rotorua, and the city grew up around it. A concentration of thermal activity here is used for cooking, washing and heating. The village takes its name from a rock on the lakeside, Ohinemutu ("the girl cut off from the world"), named by a chief who lamented his daughter's death at the hands of his enemies.

St Faith's Anglican Church, the second on the site, was built in Tudor style in 1910. Additions in 1965 widened the nave and added the side chapel, which features a sand-blasted window depicting a Christ dressed in a korowai (chief's cloak) seemingly walking on the waters of Lake Rotorua. The interior is richly embellished with Maori carvings and tukutuku lattice panels. One of the founders of the church at Ohinemutu was the American, Seymour Mills Spencer (1810-98), born in Hartford, Connecticut, who for half a century preached to the Arawa. He invariably travelled with an umbrella, at times using it as a tent, and became known as "the parson with the umbrella". Spencer is depicted in a small window above the organ chancel, preaching to a group of Maori, his characteristic umbrella unfurled. The headstone of his grave is to the left of the church entrance.

Another grave of interest is that of Capt. Gilbert Mair, NZC (1843-1923), one of the most colourful officers in the colonial forces during the latter stages of the Land Wars and accorded the highest respect by the Arawa tribe. Brought up in Northland, Mair befriended Arawa working the kauri gum-fields, and in 1867 anticipated a Kingite-Hauhau attack on Ohinemutu and saved the Arawa from certain massacre by holding the war party at bay until reinforcements could arrive. Three years later he again saved Ohinemutu, this time by thwarting an attack by Te Kooti. The running battle, in which Mair won his New Zealand Cross for gallantry, cost Te Kooti many of his best men and he never again risked a battle in the open. Mair's subsequent relentless harrying of Te Kooti through the Urewera forest hastened the end of the wars.

There was once a pa on the end of this peninsula, but in the 1700s it collapsed into the lake with the loss of many lives.

Standing in front of the church is a bust of Queen Victoria, a gift to the Arawa in 1870 from the country's first royal visitor, Prince Albert, the second son of the Queen. It commemorates Arawa support of the Government throughout the Land Wars. By the monument are small cooking vents.

Tamatekapua (1873), the outstanding carved meeting house opposite the church, is named for an earlier house that stood on Mokoia Island. It was used as a church by early missionaries of all denominations. The present exterior dates from 1941 but inside are some venerated carvings said to date from about 1800. The house is named after the captain of the *Arawa* canoe, and carved figures on the interior

197

poupou represent passengers on the canoe. The tekoteko figure, at the top of the centre post, is Ihenga, who claimed the hot lakes district for the Arawa people, and the tekoteko-aro figure at its base is Ngatoroirangi, the canoe's navigator and tohunga who in legend brought thermal activity to the region. The fifth poupou on the left depicts Tutanekai playing his flute to guide his lover to Mokoia. *800 m from the Post Office, on the lakefront.*

Kuirau Domain: A 20-hectare reserve which contains a number of boiling mud pools, steam vents and small geysers. Included is a miniature railway, a small aquarium with a collection of tropical fish *(open daily)*, a miniature golf course, free thermal foot-pools and picnic areas by a warm lake where ducks swim in comfort. *By Ranolf St.*

Agrodome Leisure Park ★ ★ ★: An entertaining exhibition of the country's sheep industry. Regular demonstrations show shearing and dogs working sheep. Rams of each breed of sheep found in New Zealand are on show. *Riverdale Park, A & P Showgrounds, Ngongotaha. Shows are staged every day at 9.15 a.m., 11 a.m. and 2.30 p.m. (except for the 2.30 p.m. show on Christmas Day). It is advisable to telephone in advance; tel. (07) 357-4350.*

Mt Ngongotaha ★ ★ ★(*778 m*)**:** Towering above the city, Ngongotaha's lookout platform at the summit affords a panorama of city, lakes and surrounding countryside. A ngongotaha is a carved mouthpiece of a calabash, and the mountain is so named because according to legend Ihenga, navigator of the *Arawa* canoe, was given a drink of water here by a patupaiarehe (fairy) when exploring the area. *12 km from Rotorua. Turnoff signposted 2.5 km on the road to Hamilton.* The **Aorangi Peak restaurant** here is especially popular on clear evenings *(Mountain Rd; tel. (07) 347-0046)*.

The **Skyline gondola** lifts visitors well up the hillside to a restaraunt and the start of a popular **luge (toboggan) track**, serviced by a chairlift. Among other hillside attractions are a simulator, a laser exhibition and a shooting-gallery. *Fairy Springs Rd; operates 9 a.m.–4.30 p.m. and later in peak periods.*

R.S.A. Museum: The Returned Services Association Museum includes weapons, war medals, models, plans and photographs. *Haupapa St. Open daily, 10 a.m.-noon; 1-2 p.m. All visitors are requested to check with the front office before admission.*

ENVIRONS

Mokoia Island ★★★: Mokoia is alive with the greatest of Maori love stories, the romance of the maid Hinemoa and the young chief Tutanekai. Hinemoa lived with her family on the shores of Lake Rotorua and much against their wishes fell in love with Tutanekai who lived on Mokoia. The lovers arranged for Hinemoa to take a canoe by night and to sail it to Mokoia while Tutanekai played his flute to guide her. Alas, her people suspected Hinemoa's intentions and beached the heavy canoes. Night after night Hinemoa could hear the sounds of Tutanekai's flute, floating across the water in a tune of hope and despair. Finally she could wait no longer. That night, using six calabashes (dried gourds used to hold water) to support herself, she began her long swim to the island. Tutanekai, unaware that Hinemoa was on her way, grew weary and returned to his where to sleep. Hinemoa arrived exhausted and shivering on the deserted beach but luckily found the hot pool now named after her. As she bathed she saw Tutanekai's slave passing by on his way to fetch his master some water. Disguising her voice, she asked him for a drink and promptly but quite deliberately smashed his calabash. The slave returned to Tutanekai and told him of the insulting behaviour of the stranger in the pool. Enraged, Tutanakei seized a mere, ran to the pool and shouted a challenge. "It is I," whispered Hinemoa, stepping from the shadows into her lover's embrace.

Highlights of a visit are a swim in Hinemoa's Pool and a wish by the Arawa Wishing Rock.

The island was once completely terraced and under cultivation. In 1823 Hongi Hika, the Ngapuhi fighting chief from the △ Bay of Islands, brought canoes across from the coast, through Hongi's Track and attacked the island fortress to avenge a tribal murder. Because of his superior firepower the outcome was never in doubt, and after feasting on the Arawa dead Hongi made his way back home. The gulls which encircle the island are said to represent the spirits of departed Arawa chiefs.

Also on the island is a large and ancient stone sculpture of Matuatonga, an Arawa god. Although it was carved from local stone, the tradition persists that it came to New Zealand on the *Arawa* canoe; but this is taken to mean that the god's mana and the skill with which the carving was executed were brought by the canoe.

Mokoia's name is a pun; a chief was fatally stabbed over the eye in a closely tattooed place with a sharpened ko and so the name combines moko (tattoo) and ko (digging implement). *The island, which is Maori land, is reached by the launch Ngaroto leaving from the Lakefront; tel. (07) 347-9852. There are 4 km of bush walks on the island.*

Lake Rotoiti ★★★: A lovely lake, renowned for trout fishing, it is a well-known holiday resort with facilities for visitors generally concentrated at Okere Falls. The lake was once used regularly as a link in a canoe route to Lake Rotorua, canoes being dragged up from Lake Okataina or across from Lake Rotoehu. Its southern shores saw first the invading Hongi, and 40 years later the Kingites, whose planned crossing of Arawa territory ended in a bloody battle there *(described above)*.

There are several carved meeting houses near the lake which may be visited. *(Permission must be sought locally.)* Rotoiti means "little lake".

Close to Okere township are the falls themselves *(see below)*. *15 km NE of Rotorua on the road to Whakatane, Okere Falls is 21 km on the road to Tauranga. Scenic launch cruises are run from Okere Falls and include views of Moose Lodge, a private home seen only from the lake, where Queen Elizabeth II stayed for five days during her 1953–54 visit.*

Hongi's Track ★★★: Piercing one and a half kilometres of exquisite bush between Lakes Rotoiti and Rotoehu, Hongi's Track was originally called Ko Te Whakamaru-ra o Hinehopu ("the sunshade of Hinehopu"). About four centuries ago the chieftainess Hinehopu is said to have planted a matai to mark the place where she met her husband, Pikiao. The tree is still known as "the sacred tree of Hinehopu" and is tapu. The traveller should pause by the tree, make a speech to honour it, and place a small offering of greenery—usually a fern frond—at its base. One is then protected from evil spirits for the remainder of the journey. The ritual is known as uru-uru whenua. *(The tree is signposted, fenced off, on the northern side of the road.)* Nearby is the Takaarewa Memorial Stone *(on the opp. side, farther west)*, which commemorates Te Amotu Takanawa, a local Ngati Pikiao chief killed here in 1823 by Hongi Hika's Ngapuhi warriors returning from their attack on Mokoia Island (see *p. 192*). In recognition of Hongi's epic journey, in the course of which he sailed his canoes down Lake Rotoehu and carried them through this track to Rotoiti, the track was renamed "Hongi's Track". Hinehopu, at Lake Rotoiti's eastern end, perpetuates the chieftainess. *31 km NE, on the road to Whakatane.*

Lake Okataina ★★★: Bush-girt and totally unspoiled, this is perhaps the most enchanting of Rotorua's màny lakes. The road leads through native bush, at one stage beneath a three-kilometre canopy of kotukutuku (native fuchsia), whose flowers fall in late spring to form a crimson carpet on the roadway. By night, glow-worms along the roadside add a touch of fantasy.

The lake is completely surrounded by dense sub-tropical forest dominated by giant tree ferns and with no apparent sign of its once being a major centre of early Maori culture. The Ngati Tarawhai sub-tribe were among the greatest carvers of the nineteenth century, fashioning canoes and meeting houses for other tribes.

Okataina means "place of laughter" and relates to a rock, submerged some time after the Tarawera eruption when the lake rose 12 metres, where the chief Te Rangi-Takaroro once sat and enjoyed a joke with his followers. However, Okataina has a serenity in sharp contrast with the frivolity its name suggests.

There are many sandy beaches and the bush abounds with native birds (including the occasional kiwi) and deer. Consistently good bags of rainbow trout are taken throughout the season. A bush walk follows a well-defined path around to the heavily wooded Maori Point, site of Te Koutu pa, where many old rua (storage pits) may be seen *(allow 1 hr)*. The Western Okataina Walkway leads from Ruato (on Highway 30) to Miller Road, near Lake Okareka *(22 km; a good 6 hrs one way)*. There are shorter bush walks in the vicinity of the Okataina Education and Recreation Centre.

As there is no road along the lake's shore, one should savour the lake's beauty from a launch. Okataina Tourist Lodge offers facilities and a selection of craft. Fishing gear is for hire and guided fishing trips are run. *31 km east from Rotorua. At 24 km turnoff is signposted on Lake Rotoiti.*

Lake Tarawera ★★★: The lake's present tranquillity is in stark contrast with the devastation of the 1886 eruption. *(For details of eruption, see Waimangu, above.)* At Tarawera Landing are examples of Maori rock drawings, kokowai (red ochre) paintings of canoes, for a time submerged by the lake's waters after the eruption *(follow the path to the left of the jetty)*. Spencer Road follows the lake shore past a number of charming inlets to Kariri Point, where stands the Spencer Family Mausoleum, erected by the family of the early American missionary, the Rev. S.M. Spencer. The mausoleum stands on the site of Spencer's first mission station in the region, established in 1844. *At 2.5 km park by the boatsheds and follow track 100 m up on the point.*

On 31 May 1866 two separate tourist parties on their way across the lake to see the Pink and White Terraces saw a fully dressed and manned war canoe speed past. As there had never been such a canoe on the lake, the event caused widespread excitement and was taken by local Maori to be an omen of disaster. Had it not been documented by independent eye-witnesses, the incident would have simply evoked

199

scepticism, yet only 11 days later came the devasation of Tarawera's eruption to fulfil the gloomiest prophecies and to heighten for all time the mystery of the phantom war canoe. *17 km SE of Rotorua (the approach road passes both the Blue and Green Lakes and the Buried Village, see below). Tarawera Launch Services operate 2 ½ hr cruises at 11 a.m. daily, providing access to Hotwater Beach, Mt Tarawera and Tarawera Falls; tel. (07) 362-8595.*

Te Wairoa Buried Village ★★ (the excavated ruins of a Maori village): Once the starting point for visits to the famous Pink and White Terraces and boasting two hotels, the village was buried under nearly 2.5 metres of mud and debris in the 1886 Tarawera eruption *(described under Waimangu, above)*. Features of a visit are a small museum with photographs taken both before and after the disaster, the ruins of a hotel and flour mill, and a stone pataka (storehouse) unusual in both material and design. The remnants of the tohunga's whare may be seen. The 110-year-old tohunga was widely blamed for the disaster as he had predicted it. Buried in the eruption, he was found alive after four days, only to die later in hospital. The tohunga's prophecy was based on reported sightings of a phantom canoe, a carving of which is displayed in the shop. Also in the grounds is part of a war canoe, said to be a section of a canoe brought by Hongi Hika when he invaded the district in 1823 and which was later used to ferry visitors across Lake Tarawera to the Pink and White Terraces.

   A steep descent follows the course of precipitous **Te Wairoa Falls**. *14 km E. Open daily during daylight hours; tel. (07) 362-8287.*

Blue and Green Lakes ★: The lakes are divided by a narrow isthmus which provides an excellent vantage point from which to compare and contrast their colours, most marked on a fine day. They are properly named Tikitapu and Rotokakahi respectively; the first name·refers to an incident when a chief's daughter lost a venerated tiki while swimming in the lake; the latter was named for its kakahi (freshwater shellfish) wiped out in the Tarawera eruption. *11 km and 16 km E of Rotorua.*

Okere Falls ★: On the outlet from Lake Rotoiti, this is where the waters of the Kaituna River foam through a narrow cleft. Hinemoa Steps, a modern innovation, leads down through the rock to the foot of the falls and to caves where, it is said, Maori women hid in times of war. Above the falls is the site of kopuakina pa, home of the chief Tutea, who in legend had a tame taniwha (water monster) which acted as a watchdog and warned Tutea of approaching enemies. When he died, Tutea was buried in a cave under the falls and for many years they bore his name. *21 km. Detour signposted at Okere on the main road to Tauranga. A 10-min walk ends in a sharp descent to the caves. En route the road passes the two Mazes and Te Amorangi Trust Museum (see below).*

   Below the carpark was a small hydro-electric power station that was the first government (as against private) supply in the country (1901).

Mazes: Two mazes, close neighbours, compete with each other to frustrate the senses. *Te Ngae Park 3-D Maze and Fairbank Maze, both near the airport, 7 km E on Highway 30.*

Te Amorangi Trust Museum: A collection of Maori, missionary and pioneer material, and a plethora of early equipment, housed in and around an old farmhouse in which muskets were discovered hidden in the walls. The old Whakarewarewa Post Office, moved here, contains a collection of telecommunications equipment. Model steam trains run occasionally. *7 km NE. 35 Robinson Ave, Holdens Bay, near airport. Open Thurs and Sun, 10 a.m.–4 p.m.; tel. (07) 345-9525.* It was from **Hinemoa Point** here that Hinemoa set out on her fabled swim to Mokoia Island.

Whakarewarewa Forest Park: The 3,830-hectare park, with its well-known grove of majestic Redwoods, adjoins the Whakarewarewa thermal reserve *(above)*. Various walks offer views of the Blue and Green Lakes. Redwood Memorial Grove, Long Mile and the Blue and Green lakes are picnic areas. *Details of walks available from the Forestry Corporation Visitor Information Centre, Longmile Rd. Open daily; tel. (07) 346-2028.*

DRIVE AROUND LAKE ROTORUA

49 km. Leave Rotorua on Highway 5 to proceed clockwise around the lake. Allow a full day. To assist the traveller, stopping points have been suggested in geographical order but are dealt with individually above.

Mt Ngongotaha ★★★: From here there is an unrivalled panorama of the city and district. *At 2 km detour 10 km to reach the summit. Turnoff signposted. (Described under "Environs", above.)*

Rainbow Springs and Rainbow Farm★★★: A stop to hand-feed trout in a cool bush setting and experience aspects of farm life. *4 km. Described under "Trout Springs", above.*

Okere Falls ★: Here the combined waters of Lakes Rotorua and Rotoiti foam through a narrow cleft. *21 km. Detour to Okere signposted at Okere on the main road to Tauranga. (Described under "Environs", above.)*

Tikitere Thermal Area (Hell's Gate) ★★: A frenzy of thermal activity. *Detour along Highway 30 towards Whakatane. (Described under "Thermal Areas", above.)*

The Mazes: There are two challenging mazes. *Described under "Environs", above.*

Te Amorangi Trust Museum: A collection of Maori, missionary and pioneer material. *Turnoff signposted "Holdens Bay". (Described under "Environs", above.)*

DRIVES TO LAKES ROTOITI, ROTOEHU AND ROTOMA

74 km return. Allow ½ day. Leave Rotorua and follow the signposted route towards Whakatane.

Tikitere Thermal Area (Hell's Gate) ★★: A frenzy of thermal activity. *17 km. (Described under "Thermal Areas", above.)*

Lake Rotoiti ★★★: The main road skirts the southern shores of this lovely lake, and several carved meeting houses are of interest. *(Described under "Environs", above.)*

Hongi's Track ★★★: The one-and-a-half-kilometre track where Hongi's men carried their canoes to launch an attack on Mokoia Island pierces the exquisite bush between Lakes Rotoiti and Rotoehu. *30.5 km. (Described under "Environs", above.)*

Lake Rotoehu: Smaller than Rotoiti but equally picturesque and with good trout fishing. *35 km.*

Lake Rotoma: This lake resembles Rotoehu. The suggested drive ends at the summit of Rotoma Hill at the eastern end of the lake. Returning to Rotorua, and if time permits, a detour may be made to **Lake Okataina.** *(Described under "Environs", above.)*

DRIVE TO TE WAIROA BURIED VILLAGE AND LAKE TARAWERA

32 km return. Allow ½ day. Leave Rotorua on Highway 30, turning SE where signposted.

Blue and Green Lakes ★: In favourable light the contrast in colour between the lakes is most remarkable. *11 km; described under "Environs", above.*

Te Wairoa Buried Village ★★: The partial excavations of a village buried by the 1886 eruption of Mt Tarawera. *14.5 km; described under "Environs", above.*

Lake Tarawera ★★★: A view across to the mountain after which the lake is named, and a brief detour to see some Maori rock drawings. *16 km; described under "Environs", above.* Returning to Rotorua, a detour may be made to the tiny holiday settlement on Lake Okareka.

ORGANISED EXCURSIONS

Most points of interest in the area are reached by coach tours which depart daily from the Travel Centre, Amohau Street. A minimum number of passengers is required for most tours, and it is advisable to book to avoid a tour being cancelled. Details are available from the Visitor Centre and travel agents. Best of Maori Tourism (109 Fenton St; tel. 0800-105-205 (toll free); fax (07) 348-7832) markets tours offered by Maori operators.

Hangi on a marae ★ ★ ★: The major hotels have excellent hangi and cultural shows, but nothing is more atmospheric or as entertaining as an evening on a local marae, with Maori protocol, singing, dancing and a traditional umu earth oven dinner. *Tamaki Tours, tel. (07) 346-2823; Rotoiti Tours, tel. (07) 348-8969; or Ki Te Whai Ao, tel. (07) 332-3446. Overnight stays on a marae can also be arranged.*

Tarawera Crater expeditions ★ ★: 4WD vehicles or helicopters scale the slopes of the mountain for a view inside (and a memorable slide down the scoria into) the colourful craters. There is an astonishing a panorama from 1,097 metres over nine lakes to White Island and to Mt Ngauruhoe. *There are several operators. Book* *through the Visitor Centre. Make sure that the trip you choose actually goes to the summit (some brochures are misleading), and take old shoes for the scoria slide!*

Waimangu round trip * * *: An all-day tour includes Waimangu Thermal Valley and Lake Rotomahana, where launches take visitors past the spectacular steaming cliffs to the narrow isthmus which divides the lake from Lake Tarawera. Te Wairoa Buried Village and the Blue and Green lakes are also visited. *All described above. Careys Sightseeing Ltd, tel. (07) 347-1199.*

Volcanic Wilderness Safari * * *: A remarkable two-day trip into the heart of the forest (and Maori folklore), with horse-trekking, rafting and hot swims in the bush. *Tamaki Tours, tel. (07) 346-2823.* Similar are the one- and two-day expeditions of **Trek Whirinaki** (*Whirinaki Tours, tel. (07) 347-6075*). *From about Nov–March.*

Scenic flights: Flights run from the lakefront jetty and the airport (*11 km NE*) and afford a remarkable variety of views, giving a new dimension to the thermal activity, including a glimpse into the shattered chasms of Mt Tarawera or out to smouldering △ White Island, in the Bay of Plenty.

Adventure activities: White-water rafting over the 7-metre high Okere Falls (Grade 5+ and the world's highest commercially rafted falls) is heart-stopping (but not time consuming). Among other trips available are an all-day trip on the Rangitaiki (Grade 3/4) and 2 to 3 day wilderness expeditions on the Motu (Grade 3/4) (*Several operators; book through the Visitor Centre*). More tranquil is **kayaking** on Lakes Okataina and Tarawera (*tel. (07) 348-9451*). There is **tandem skydiving** (*tel. (07) 345-7520*) from Rotorua Airport and **bungy jumping** at △ Taupo (*tel. (07) 377-1135*). **Jet-boating** is 48-km away on the pretty Kaituna River at Longridge Park (*tel. (07) 533-1515*) and 74 km away at the foot of the thundering Huka Falls at △ Wairakei (*tel. (07) 374-8572*). There is **swimming with dolphins** at △ Whakatane (*92 km; tel. (07) 308-4636*).

RUATORIA   East Coast   Map 10   Pop. 794

132 km N of Gisborne.

RUATORIA is the centre of the Ngati Porou, principal tribe on the East Coast whose marae is nearby at Mangahanea.

Traces of natural gas were found in the vicinity last century, and since then there has been unsuccessful drilling in the area. Perhaps the prospectors should have heeded a local legend which affirms that there is no oil in the district, merely surface traces left when a whale, carried by Rongokako (a legendary giant), dropped to the ground. In recent years a vigorous pine afforestation programme has helped to stabilise erosion-prone land.

The North Island's highest temperature of 39.2°C was recorded here on 7 February 1973. (On the same day, Rangiora recorded the country's highest — 42.4°C.)

Ruatoria means "Toria's kumara pit".

SOME NOTES

Sir Apirana Ngata (1874-1950): The first Maori to graduate from a New Zealand university, he was by the age of 23 both MA and LL.B. After practising law he became travelling secretary for the Young Maori Party and dedicated the remainder of his life to the service of his people. Apirana Ngata toiled to raise the level of Maori education, to consolidate communal land and to bring undeveloped Maori land into production; but perhaps of all his considerable achievements the most apparent today is his rescue of Maori arts and crafts. At the age of 31 Ngata entered Parliament where he served for 38 years and held a number of Cabinet posts. As a fund-raiser for Maori projects he knew no peer but unfortunately Ngata's zeal led him into embarrassing situations which culminated with a Commission reporting in 1934 that as Minister he had misused public funds, though not for personal gain but for the good of the Maori people. He resigned from Parliament and later wrote a number of books. A Ngati Porou, Ngata died at his home at nearby Waiomatatini in 1950.

A national hero: Te Moananuiakiwa Ngarimu, VC (1913-43), born near Waipiro Bay, became the first Maori to win the Victoria Cross, the Armed Services' highest award for valour. He commanded a platoon of "C" Company (Ngati Porou) at Tebaga Gap, Tunisia, on 26 March 1943 when, as his citation reads: "He led his men with great determination and skill straight up the face of the [vital] hill undeterred by the intense mortar and machine-gun fire . . . personally annihilating at least two enemy machine-gun posts." All night, though severely wounded, Ngarimu defended the position but died the next morning in a strong enemy counter attack.

To commemorate his exploits, the Ngarimu VC and 28th Maori Battalion Memorial Scholarship was inaugurated in 1945 to assist with Maori education.

MOUNT HIKURANGI

Mount Hikurangi (*1,839 m*) stands due west of Ruatoria. The highest point on the Raukumara Range, Hikurangi is the first point in New Zealand (and, it is claimed, the world) to see the new day's sun.

When the mythical Maui dragged up the North Island, Mount Hikurangi is said to have been the first part of the island to appear above the water. Local tradition is that Maui's canoe was actually left on the slopes of Hikurangi, where local Maori can still see it with its sails and broken bailer. (A better-known version of the legend has the South Island as the canoe from which Maui was fishing.)

Here, too, an attempt was made to snare Rongokako, the legendary giant who in a single stride once stepped from Cape Kidnappers to Mahia Peninsula. An enormous tree was cut, its trunk planted in Hikurangi's peak and bent over to complete a huge snare. However, the giant saw the trap and when he tripped it with his staff, it sprang back to shatter Hikurangi's peak, and the rope which formed the snare's noose snaked out in a westerly direction to form the Arowhara mountain ridge. Rongokako calmly waded back to "Hawaiki".

Hikurangi means "summit of the sky" and was the name of a well-remembered mountain in "Hawaiki". In 1991 a long-standing grievance was resolved with the government returning the mountain to the Ngati Porou Runanga in trust for the tribe and with a conservation covenant.

POINTS OF INTEREST

Whakarua Memorial Hall ★★: A modern decorative hall, which is in part a memorial to Ngarimu, VC. *The turnoff is signposted in the main street.*

Mangahanea marae ★★: The focal point for the Ngati Porou tribe. The Hinetapora meeting house here dates from 1896, though many of its carvings are older. The "Star of Bethlehem" in the pare (carved lintel) over the door is a reminder that the house is also used for religious meetings. *At Mangahanea, 3 km.*

Ngata homestead ★★: Sir Apirana's former home is a colonial homestead known simply as "The Bungalow". Beside it stand the elegantly carved Porourangi meeting house and a simply decorated hall. The meeting house, dating from 1888 and rebuilt in 1934, is one of the most important houses on the Coast. Of particular interest are the simplicity of the figures, their rounded rather than pointed tongues, their four or five toes and the occasional crossed-feet motif. *The homestead is on private property to Waiomatatini, 13 km from Ruatoria (no exit). Obtain permission before visiting the marae. On the way there are wide views of the mountain ranges and over the Waiapu valley.*

Northland   *Maps 2, 3*   *Pop. 1,051*   ★★★ **RUSSELL**

68 km NW of Whangarei (via Kawakawa and Opua ferry). Information from Fullers Northland, The Strand, tel. (09) 403-7866, and from the Department of Conservation Bay of Islands Maritime and Historic Park Visitor Centre, The Strand, tel. (09) 403-7685.

A PEACEFUL and picturesque township set deep in the △ Bay of Islands, Russell is renowned as a big-game fishing centre and as a holiday town of major historical interest. Its tranquillity belies the frantic activity of its wild early days when, as the centre of the first European settlement, it was known as "the Hell-hole of the Pacific".

The town is linked by ferry to △ Pahia, △ Waitangi and Opua (vehicular), and can also be reached by road from △ Kawakawa and Whakapara. Originally a Maori village, the settlement was first called Kororareka ("sweet blue penguin"), but was renamed Russell after the country's first "capital" (which was close by) and after Lord John Russell, Secretary of State for the Colonies and later Prime Minister of Great Britain.

SOME HISTORY

"Hell-hole of the Pacific": The town began as the native village of Kororareka and acquired its first Europeans—ship deserters and time-expired convicts from New South Wales—after whaling ships began calling here for provisions from the early 1800s.

By 1840 Kororareka was the largest European settlement in the country, by which

203

time it had become an important whaling, sealing and mercantile centre where hundreds of ships called each year.

Despite the efforts of the mission stations nearby it was very much a lawless frontier town, a jumble of Maori and European architecture jammed with gun-toting Maori and Pakeha, crowded with grog-shops and crammed with Maori ship-girls and adventurers of every breed. Its licentiousness was probably exaggerated by the missionaries, but the town certainly included the flotsam and jetsam of the world and well-earned its unsavoury title of "Hell-hole of the Pacific". Felton Mathew (1801-47), the country's first Surveyor-General, arrived with Captain Hobson and reported that Kororareka was "a vile hole, full of impudent, half-drunken people".

The first capital: Soon after his arrival and the signing of the Treaty of Waitangi in 1840, Captain William Hobson *(see pp.* **43-44***)* purchased about 124 hectares at Okiato (near Russell) as a site for the country's capital. An ambitious plan was prepared but only one of its roads was ever built, leading inappropriately from Government House to the gaol.

The infant township was named "Russell" and for nine months was the "capital" of New Zealand. Hobson, his choice opposed by his superiors in New South Wales, looked for yet another site and early in 1841 moved the seat of government to Auckland, where it remained until 1865. "Russell" continued to house the Bond Store, a detachment of troops and the Police Magistrate, but its fate was sealed when Government House and its offices were burned to the ground in 1842. Soon even its name was lost. In an effort to escape its bawdy image, Kororareka, less than eight kilometres away, was renamed Russell.

Today the pleasant point of Okiato is sprinkled with holiday homes, including one which gained notoriety as the dream home of a drug dealer convicted of murder in the sensational 1982 "Mr Asia" trial in Britain. All that remains of New Zealand's first capital is a well, fenced off and on a reserve, near Okiato Lodge. *Okiato. Turn off by NZ Historic Places Trust marker immediately before the descent to the Opua ferry 7 km from Russell and bear right.*

Hone Heke and the flagstaff: Hone Heke Pokai (*c.* 1810-50), a nephew of the famous Ngapuhi fighting chief Hongi Hika and a signatory to the Treaty of Waitangi, is celebrated for his resentment of the symbol of British sovereignty, the flagstaff at Kororareka, which he felled on no less than four occasions. Heke was tall, clever and chivalrous, and only pride and restless ambition marred his greatness.

For years the local Ngapuhi had profited in their trade with the numerous visiting ships, and Heke had collected a £5 due from every ship to enter Kororareka Harbour. This happy state of affairs ended in 1841 when the Government imposed the first customs duties. These made revictualling at Kororareka more expensive and, coupled with a fall in the world price for whale oil, had the effect of discouraging visits from whaling ships. This loss of revenue combined with the widespread belief that the Treaty of Waitangi was only to be observed by Europeans until they were strong enough to seize all the Maori land, led to the celebrated first axing of the shipping-signal flagstaff on Flagstaff Hill in 1844.

The Governor agreed to remove the customs duties; Heke offered to renew the mast. For a time it appeared that the friction had ended but the American consular agent at the Bay of Islands encouraged Heke to go further. He is said to have described to Heke the successful American War of Independence waged against British colonial rule, and to have given him an American ensign to fly from his canoe. On 9 January 1845 the flagstaff fell for the second time.

The flagstaff was renewed once more, a £100 reward was offered for Heke's capture, and "friendly" Maori were posted to guard the new mast. But so great was Heke's mana that only 10 days later he strode alone through the armed guard and for the third time felled the mast.

Foolishly, the Governor chose to replace the flagstaff, to sheath it with iron and encircle it with a blockhouse. Heke accepted the challenge. A diversionary movement drew the troops away, leaving the way clear to land by night, to surprise the blockhouses at dawn and, on 11 March 1845, to fell the flagstaff yet again. (In the 1980s the flagstaff has again become a focus of protest against the continuing alienation of communally owned Maori land.)

The fall of Kororareka: After the flagstaff had fallen for the fourth time, Heke's men attacked the township. The defence was haphazard and unco-ordinated. After a spark from the pipe of a careless defender had exploded the stockade magazine, the European population was evacuated and the day ended with naval ships in the bay lobbing the occasional shot into the town while Heke's men drank grog from the

"All saints can do miracles, but few of them can keep a hotel." *Mark Twain, Notebook*

bars and loaded canoes with loot. The next day they completed their pillaging and set fire to the buildings, one by one, sparing only the churches and mission buildings. The naval ships sailed sorrowfully for Auckland. leaving the town a ruin, never to regain its importance.

So began the War in the North, "Heke's War", which continued until Heke was defeated at Ruapekapeka (*p.* **117**) in 1846. Heke was granted a full and unconditional pardon. He died four years later and was given a Christian burial.

POINTS OF INTEREST

Details of organised excursions, including adventure activities, are listed under △ Paihia. Boat cruises usually call at Russell before setting out.

The waterfront: The Strand today has a serenity it seldom knew in the early days when it was crowded with grog shops overlooking a bay in which whaling ships from the world over lay at anchor. The police station building (*c.* 1870) was originally the customs house, built when the Bay of Islands saw a considerable amount of overseas shipping and when the American whaling industry was still flourishing. The grog shops have long gone but the Duke of Marlborough Hotel claims to hold the oldest liquor licence in the country. Now mounted close to the beach is a cannon used in the defence of the town. At the southern end of The Strand stands the supremely elegant Pompallier House ★★★ *(described below).*

Christ Church ★★★ (1836): Even were it not for the memorable events it has witnessed, Christ Church, as the oldest surviving church in the country, would have a special place in history. Unlike most of the very early churches it was built not as part of a mission station but by local settlers. Against the unpromising background of a bawdy brawling village, an appeal for funds was launched in 1834 and the building was completed two years later. Among the donors were the Rev. Samuel Marsden (*p.* **22**) and the naturalist Charles Darwin who visited New Zealand in the course of his five-year voyage on the *Beagle*, during which he made the observations that formed the basis for his landmark work, *The Origin of Species*, 1859.

As the only building of consequence in the town, the church was used for a variety of purposes. It was in its role as public hall that a meeting was held here in 1840, immediately on Captain Hobson's arrival in New Zealand. The gathering saw Hobson perform the first official act on the shores of the colony as he read the Crown Proclamation which declared New Zealand to be a dependency of New South Wales and his Commission as its first Lieutenant-Governor. Within a week the first copies of the Treaty of Waitangi were signed across the bay.

The same year the church, while serving as a court house, was the centre of a sensational trial in which a local Maori was charged with the murder of a European. Anxious that he be dealt with according to Maori custom, a group of Maori tried to free the prisoner and only the timely intervention of an interpreter from the mission averted bloodshed.

During the 1845 attack on Kororareka (Russell) there was a clash on the southern boundary of the churchyard between seamen from HMS *Hazard* and Heke's men. Two Royal Marines and four seamen, killed before the Maori withdrew, are buried in the churchyard. The original headboard from their grave is inside the church. The church itself was badly damaged, and, despite repairs and later renovations, some scars have survived. On the north-west corner a weatherboard has been chipped by a cannonball from the *Hazard* and holes from musket balls are seen near the south-east and south-west corners.

Originally unlined, the church had a low roof, small windows and old-fashioned box pews. The building was renovated in 1871 when the present high-pitched roof was built, the old pews demolished and their timber used as panelling.

In the churchyard are many interesting graves, the oldest dating from 1836 (*far left*). Among them are those of Tamati Waka Nene (a Ngapuhi chief who was largely responsible for the Maori's acceptance of the Treaty of Waitangi and who fought for the settlers against Hone Heke), Hannah King Lethbridge (now known to be the second European girl to be born in New Zealand), Dr Samuel Ford (the country's first resident surgeon), members of the Clendon family (James R. Clendon was the first honorary United States Consul), the men from the *Hazard* who fell in the fighting, and a number of whalers whose headstones often tell of untimely deaths. *Cnr Church and Robertson Sts.*

Pompallier House ★ ★ ★: A distinctly French colonial two-storeyed building sits near the waterfront, so different from the rest of the country's architecture as to seem out of place. It had its origins not as a home but as a printery, quickly constructed ahead of better living accommodation as the Marist brothers, whose mission was here, had to counter the propaganda that the Protestant presses were putting out, often denigrating the Church of Rome.

The structure, of *pisé de terre* (a mixture of clay, mud and ash commonly used in France), was built in 1841–42 to house the mission's printing presses. These for several years produced booklets of religious instruction printed in Maori.

In charge of the activities was Bishop Jean Baptiste François Pompallier (1801–71), a Frenchman and the first Roman Catholic Bishop of the South-West Pacific, who arrived in 1838 to establish the first Roman Catholic mission in New Zealand at Kororareka (Russell).

After the sacking of Kororareka (Russell) in 1845 and when it became apparent that the town would not regain its former importance, Bishop Pompallier moved the mission to Auckland and, in 1856, sold the building for £375 to James Callaghan, who used it as a tannery. It had been one of few buildings spared in the fighting.

By about 1877 the building had deteriorated to the point of collapse when a new owner, James Greenway, acquired and renovated it, primarily because of a housing shortage in Russell. The *pisé* structure was strengthened and over the next few years the building was remodelled to become an elegant showpiece quite at odds with its origins. Outer walls, verandahs with Union Jack-styled railings, a chimney, door, windows and a lean-to at the rear were all added round the old building, completely enclosing the original structure. The whole exercise weakened the fabric of the building and provoked a decision to restore the building to its state in Pompallier's time, returning it to a more accurate reflection of the early contact period.

Pompallier, after a lifetime of intensive work under conditions of great hardship, finally left New Zealand in 1868. He was appointed Archbishop of Amasie (near Paris) and died there in 1871. *The Strand. Open daily (except Good Friday and Christmas Day), 9.30 a.m.–5 p.m.* At the end of the beach next to Pompallier House stands the Bungalow, built in 1853 by Captain James R. Clendon, the first American Consul, and later used as a school by his daughter.

Nearby, off the southern tip of the bay, is the quaint hump of Mill Island, so named because the settlement's flour mill was built there to be safe from native rats.

Bay of Islands Maritime and Historic Park Visitors' Centre: The Department of Conservation Centre provides details and displays of the Park. *Described on p. 57. Southern end of foreshore.*

Captain Cook Memorial Museum (incorporating Russell Centennial Museum): Displayed here is a scale model of Cook's *Endeavour* and a small collection of items of historical interest. These include the original subscription list for the Christ Church building appeal (1834) and Colenso's own copy of his first printed placard (1836). *York St. Open daily, 10 a.m.–4 p.m.*

Flagstaff Hill ★ ★ (Maiki Hill): The site of the succession of flagstaffs which fell to Hone Heke's axe and led to the sacking of the town. A memorial here records the episodes, but perhaps a greater attraction is a splendid panorama from Paihia through 180 degrees to the natural fortress of Tapeka Point, host to a pa site. In recent years the flagstaff has again been the focal point of protests against the government's handling of land claims under the Waitangi Tribunal. *Signposted at the north of the town. A road leads to the summit.*

Tapeka Point: The point ends in a pa site, now a reserve included in the Maritime Park. Access can be awkward and care should be taken near the precipitous cliffs. *2 km. Signposted. Beyond Flagstaff Hill.*

Long Beach ★ ★ (Oneroa Bay): Situated on the other side of the peninsula from Russell, this is a glorious stretch of sand more suited to swimming than to the town beach. *Signposted. 800 m.*

Shrine of St Peter Chanel: A simple, modern shrine which is unique within New Zealand. Father Chanel, a Marist missionary in the Pacific under Bishop Pompallier, was martyred in 1841 by natives of Futuna (a French possession in the Horne Islands, north of Fiji). Bishop Pompallier recovered his body and brought it to Russell, where it rested from 1842–47. Later the saint's body was shipped back to his native France. The martyr was canonised in 1954. *End of Chapel St.*

Short walks: Two short walks in the **Ngaiotonga Reserve** lead to a spectacular **Kauri Grove** (*20 mins*) and to a **Twin-bole Kauri** (*10 mins*). A number of kauri still bear the scars of their being bled for gum. *16 km. Signposted off Russell Rd.*

Ngaiotonga–Russell Forest Walkway: The 21-kilometre track (*9 hrs*) starts on the Ngaiotonga Saddle (*20 km E on the Russell Road*) and emerges at the southern end to link in with Punaruku Road. There are stands of kauri and other native trees, old logging roads and views from trig stations. *Details from the DOC Visitor Centre.*

Cape Brett Track: A 17.5 km tramp only for the fit and experienced, but with extraordinary seascapes. *8 hrs. Start at Oke Bay (beyond Rawhiti) 36 km E. Rawhiti is easily reached by boat. The old lighthouse keeper's house now accommodates trampers; no cooking facilities. Book through DOC. Access occasionally restricted.*

△ **Bay of Islands** ★ ★ ★: A general description appears under this heading.

EXCURSIONS AND ACTIVITIES

There is much to see and do in and around the Bay. For details, see △ Paihia, "Excursions and activities".

Cream Trip ★★★: This half-day cruise among the enchanting islands of the Bay is perhaps the finest launch trip in the country. *Details p.* **174**.

Cape Brett Trip ★★: A half-day cruise runs out to, and right through, intriguing Piercy Island at the entrance to the Bay of Islands. *Details p.* **175**.

Local Russell Bus Trip: A 1½-hour tour takes in most of the local points of interest. *Book at Fullers Northland.*

Horowhenua Maps 12, 13 Pop. 1,465 **SHANNON**

32 km SW of Palmerston North.

THE SMALL FARMING CENTRE of Shannon was laid out by the Wellington-Manawatu Railway Company as a railway settlement on land granted to the company by the Government to meet part of the capital cost involved in the project (*see p.* **177**). Appropriately enough, the town is named for one of the company's directors and its first building was a signal box (1886).

For many years Shannon's prosperity was based on local flaxmills, for during the early years of the twentieth century several large mills obtained flax from the huge Makerua Swamp, situated between Linton and Shannon. This swamp contained 5,800 hectares of flax at the time of World War I, but the advent of "yellow-leaf" disease and a slump in the overseas market led to the draining of the swamp during the 1920s and its conversion to pasture. Three kilometres north of Shannon there was situated the largest flax mill in New Zealand, the Miranui Mill, owned by A. & L. Seifert's Flaxdressing Co. Ltd. It was operated from 1907 until 1935, and at the peak of its production employed some 300 men in the mill and swamp.

From an economic viewpoint Shannon has been eclipsed by the growth of △ Levin, another company settlement, but the presence of both rich land and the Main Trunk railway line have long suggested a capacity for development.

POINTS OF INTEREST

Flaxville Model Township: A miniature village built on a scale of 1:24 replicates a typical early twentieth-century New Zealand rural town. Although imaginary, over twenty of the models are based on early Shannon buildings. *Stout St.*

Poutu marae: The marae comprises a meeting-house, dining hall and other facilities for tribal gatherings. A feature is **Turongo Church** (1879), a fine example of a Maori church. It was moved here in 1965 and houses one of the country's oldest organs. *To W of the town.* ·

Tokomaru Steam Engine Museum ★★: On display is a growing assortment of working steam engines dating back over a century, including the engine from Wellington's Patent Slip (1869), a Shand Mason steam fire-engine (1887), a Fowler traction engine (1904) and a steam roller (1914). A steam train runs on regular "live steam" days. *Tokomaru. On Highway 57 at 11.5 km N of Shannon and 19.5 km S of Palmerston North; open daily; tel. (06) 329-8867.*

Mangahao Power Scheme: Although a minor station by today's standards, in its time Mangahao was considered an outstanding engineering achievement as the main ranges of the Tararuas were twice tunnelled to feed water across the divide and down a 275-metre drop. The project was completed in 1924 and, with a capacity of 19,200 kW, was then both the country's largest scheme and the first State project to be completed in the North Island.

From the town the pipe-lines to the power station may be seen on the hillside. *The powerhouse may be inspected and is 6.5 km from Shannon (signposted). One may drive on up the tortuous hydro road to No. 3 lake (16 km), No. 2 lake (21 km) and No. 1 lake (24 km) ending at No. 1 dam.* The artificial lakes, unsuited for swimming, fishing or boating, still bear the scars left when the water level was raised half a century ago.

Moutoa floodgates: *8 km W. (See △ Foxton.)*

STRATFORD   *Taranaki   Map 7   Pop. 5,664*

43 km SE of New Plymouth. Visitor Information, Broadway; tel. (06) 765-6708.

STRATFORD, a market centre, is important to the visitor as a departure point for the eastern slopes of △ Egmont National Park for walking, climbing and skiing. Here, too, starts the Stratford to △ Taumarunui Heritage Trail, an historic route through to the central North Island. The network of trout streams in the area make Stratford an ideal base from which to fish. The Patea River runs through the town, originally named "Stratford-on-Patea" in the manner of Shakespeare's birthplace. All of the streets are named from his works. The ancient Maori trail along which General Chute (*p.* **101**) made his famous march in 1866 passed through the area. Eleven years later the town of Stratford, which began as a sawmilling base in dense bush, was surveyed, and in 1878 the first sections were sold.

Set close by and amidst trees and pastures, and designed to minimise intrusion into the skyline, the Stratford Power Station (1976) was the second to be based on natural gas, annually using some 400 million cubic metres of untreated gas piped from the Kapuni field.

On a clear day, the peaks of △ Tongariro National Park may be seen over 100 kilometres to the east, as well as lonely Taranaki/Egmont a short distance west.

THINGS TO SEE AND DO

King Edward Park: A 20-hectare bush reserve on the banks of the Patea River. *One block W of the main road, Broadway.*

Taranaki Pioneer Village ★: The reconstructed village incorporates many salvaged old buildings — the veteran Kaponga gaol and the tiny Mangatoki church among them — and displays a wealth of pioneering memorabilia. *1 km S. Open daily; tel. (06) 765-5399.*

Scenic flights: These may be arranged through the Stratford Aero Club (*tel. (06) 765-6628*) or Beck Helicopters Ltd (*tel. (06) 764-7073*).

ENVIRONS

Stratford Mountain House ★ ★: The main skiing centre on the eastern slopes of Taranaki/Egmont and starting point for a number of walks. *14.5 km W. Pembroke Rd. (See △ Egmont National Park.)*

Dawson Falls ★: *26 km W along Opunake Rd. (See △ Egmont National Park.)*

Hollards Garden ★: An informal 3.8-hectare garden, first developed in the 1920s by a local farmer, displays magnificent rhododendrons (including the unique "Kaponga" rhododendron), camellias and azaleas. A remarkable swamp garden features a host of moisture-loving plants. *3 km N of Kaponga. Upper Manaia Rd. Open daily. Administered by the Queen Elizabeth II National Trust.*

Lake Rotorangi: A 47-kilometre lake in a bush setting, created in 1984 when the Patea River was dammed for hydro-electric power. Cruises, fishing trips and relaxing house-boat holidays may be arranged (*details from Information Centre or Houseboat Holidays; tel. (06) 765-6978). Access to the houseboat base at Glen Nui, in the north, is signposted from Eltham on Highway 3 (10 km S of Stratford). Access also from △ Patea and △ Hawera.* The **Rotorangi Hydro Walk** follows the lakeside *Ball Rd*).

TOURING NOTE

Road around Egmont/Taranaki: Points of interest on the road around the mountain are described under △ Egmont/Taranaki, Road Around.

Road to Taumarunui *(State Highway 43: 155 km: driving time 3 hrs)*: A slow and winding road, not always sealed and threading through scenes of dramatic contrasts, has been developed as a "heritage trail". The road passes through farmland both fertile and marginal, and areas of wilderness, of early Maori trails and of now-derelict townships abandoned by the transient populations who forged the rail link between Stratford and Taumarunui. The "Whanga pub" at **Whangamomona** *(65 km)* has a timeless if antiquated air. Further on, the 85-metre **Mount Dampier Falls** *(a short detour up Moki Rd at 84 km: turn into Mangapapa Rd; there is then a 300-metre walk to the falls)* are well worth a visit. In the region of the **Tangarakau Gorge ★ ★** *(at 94 km)* the route passes through some of the most rugged and picturesque native bush to be seen from the road in the North Island. The grave of Joshua Morgan, the surveyor who laid the line for the road, lies by the roadside. *(A "Heritage Trail" pamphlet is available from Tourism Taranaki, New Plymouth and other Information Centres.)*

Rangitikei   Map 12   Pop. 2,586   TAIHAPE

33 km SE of Waiouru; 88 km NE of Bulls. Department of Conservation Field Centre, Broadway, Mangaweka; tel. (06) 382-5824.

TAIHAPE'S beginnings as a railway settlement are today still evident in its site beside the main trunk line and a proliferation of characteristic railway houses. The town is set in rugged country whose white papa-walled river gorges and changing seasonal colourings have proved irresistible to landscape artists.

Today, while retaining an important role as a railway town, Taihape serves the surrounding farming area and the military camp at △ Waiouru. There is an annual "Gumboot Day" (*Easter Tues*), when the "Gumboot City" lets its hair down.

SOME HISTORY

A railway town: The town site was once an uninhabited clearing known as Otaihape ("the place of Tai the Hunchback"). When peace was made with King Tawhiao in 1881, the way was clear for a railway to be driven through the heart of the North Island— earlier closed to Europeans—and within three years surveyors had cut a track through the area. Settlers arrived in 1894, lured from Canterbury to work as sawmillers and roadmen by the offer of five- to seven-hectare sections. The settlement was consolidated by the coming of the railway in 1904 and the construction workers who later took up neighbouring farmland. Intensive milling cleared the dense bush and yielded good if in places precipitous farmland.

POINTS OF INTEREST

Taihape Museum: The collection has an emphasis on sawmilling and farming. *Huia St. Open Sun 1-4 p.m.; daily in school holidays.*

Mangaweka: Set on a shelf above the white-walled Rangitikei River and dominated by the slender spire of St Patrick's Church, the township was once a railway settlement known for its impressive viaduct, since dismantled. Today the traveller may pause for refreshments inside a venerable DC-3 aircraft. *22 km S.*

River rafting: White water rafting on the wild Grade 5 Rangitikei tempts the intrepid. *River Valley Ventures, tel. (06) 388-1444 (also abseiling); Rangitikei River Adventures, tel/fax (06) 382-5747.*

TOURING NOTE

"Inland Patea" route to △ Napier: Until the arrival of the railway at Taihape, this route was the district's only link with the outside world, and even Karioi Station at the foot of Mt Ruapehu looked on Napier as "its" town. By the 1870s huge sheep runs in the Inland Patea were well stocked, and wool was packhorsed along the tortuous track to Napier. Progress on upgrading it to a road was slow and it was not until 1893 that a stage-coach could successfully tackle the three-day journey from Napier to Taihape through one of the North Island's most sparsely populated areas. The harsh country through which the road threads is taken up by large sheep stations, among them Ngamatea (48,000 hectares), the largest in the North Island. The area was named after Patea, a Waimarama Maori who fled inland to escape his murdered wife's vengeful relations. *169 km.*

TAUMARUNUI

King Country   Map 6   Pop. 6,541

162 km S of Hamilton; 168 km N of Wanganui. Visitor Information Centre, Railway Station, Hakiaha St; tel. (07) 895-7494. Department of Conservation Visitor Centre, Cherry Grove; tel. (07) 895-8201.

IN THE HEART of the once formidable King Country, Taumarunui stands on the upper reaches of the Whanganui River. The town serves surrounding farmland — generally sheep, cattle, deer and dairy — and freshwater sports, fishing and the wilderness of the △ Tongariro National Park challenge the visitor. There is an annual jet-boat race on the river.

Taumarunui means "a large screen", a reference to the sun screen for which the chief Pehi Taroa asked to shade him from the sun as he lay dying.

SOME HISTORY

A river link: Both the △ Whanganui River and the Ongarue which flows into it at this point were part of an intricate network of canoe routes linking the centre of the North Island with the Wanganui district and the sea. It was to be expected that on such an important river junction a Maori settlement would develop.

As in the whole of the King Country, European settlement came late. After their defeats in the Waikato, King Tawhiao and his followers withdrew to the King Country (so giving it its name) and Europeans intruded at their peril. Only after a formal peace was made in 1881 could the Government push its Main Trunk railway south from △ Te Awamutu and open up new farmland.

In the 1890s the riverboat service between Wanganui and Pipiriki was extended upstream to Taumarunui to form the principal route to the town until the railway from △ Te Kuiti opened in 1903. The North Island Main Trunk line was completed five years later. The long river journey down to Wanganui, once a highlight of tourist travel, took three days. Overnight stops were made at an elegant houseboat hotel and at a popular hotel at Pipiriki, both since destroyed by fire. Unfortunately the condition of the river deteriorated and in 1934 passenger services on the upper river ceased.

POINTS OF INTEREST

Trips on the rivers: The grandeur and excitement of the Whanganui River are best savoured from the water. Canoeing, kayaking, motor-canoeing and jet-boat trips are all available, and there are combination expeditions for those who wish to explore some of the North Island's most rugged back country. Some trips visit beautiful **Pipiriki** and others the curious **"Bridge to Nowhere"**. In summer canoe parties leave Cherry Grove to make their way down the Whanganui River, some 232 kilometres to the sea. *Wades Landing Outdoors, tel. (07) 895-5995; Plateau Outdoor Adventure Guides, tel/fax (07) 893-2740; Yeti Tours, tel. (06) 385-8197; Pioneer Jet Boat Tours, tel. (07) 895-8074 and Baldwin Adventure Tours, (tel. (06) 343-6346).*

Walkways: Two 2-to-3 hour forested loop tracks are within easy reach of Taumarunui. The first lies in the **Ohinetonga Reserve** and encompasses a small lagoon *(turn-off Highway 4 at Owhango, 20 km SE and start at Whakapapa Bridge)* and the second, **Te Maire Walkway** offers bush and river valley views. *(Start Te Maire Valley Rd, off River Rd, 15 km SW.)*

More strenuous and further afield is the **Mangapurua Walkway** a 2-to-3 day tramp through remote native forest into the enigmatic **"Bridge to Nowhere"**, an imposing structure on a tributary built in 1936 in an abortive scheme to open up land for farmers. *Accessible either from the Kaiwhakauku Valley, near Whakahoro, 62 km SW of Taumarunui via Owhango and Kaitieke or from the end of Ruatiti Rd, 30 km NW of △ Raetihi. It is also possible to arrange to be picked up by boat. Options can be discussed with DOC.*

TAUPO ★★★

Volcanic Plateau   Map 8   Pop. 30,271   (urban area)

84 km S of Rotorua; 155 km NW of Napier; 381 km NE of Wellington; 287 km SE of Auckland. Visitor Information Centre, Tongariro St; tel. (07) 378-9000. Department of Conservation Field Centre, Centennial Drive; tel. (07) 378-3885.

UNDOUBTEDLY Taupo's most magical approach is from the north. From the roar and steam of △ Wairakei's geothermal power installations and the thunder of Huka Falls, the road crests a hill to unfold the distant huddled peaks of Tongariro, Ruapehu and smoking Ngauruhoe. Lake Taupo opens out in broad panorama, and finally the town sprawls at the traveller's feet—from the water's edge to the foothills of Mt Tauhara. Well down the lake may be seen the green and pumiced hump of Motutaiko Island. The road dips sharply to cross the Waikato River by a bridge which also controls the lake's level, and climbs again to reach the town's main street.

If Taupo's very setting has magnetic appeal, so too has its fabled trout fishing and many thermal pools.

Taupo is an abbreviation of Taupo-nui a-Tia, "the great shoulder mat of Tia". The reason for the name is obscure, but Tia, a passenger on the *Arawa* canoe, is said to have slept here for a long time.

SOME HISTORY

Tuwharetoa: The pattern of allegiances formed by the Tuwharetoa tribe of Lake Taupo is typical of those formed by larger tribes. The tribe traces its origins to

Tuwharetoa, a descendant of Ngatoroirangi, famed tohunga and navigator of the *Arawa* canoe. In legend Ngatoroirangi hurled a tree from the summit of Mt Tauhara which pierced the ground and caused the water to well up and form Lake Taupo. He then travelled on to bring fire to the volcanoes at the southern end of the lake.

Through their illustrious forebear, Tuwharetoa are closely related to the neighbouring Arawa tribe of Rotorua, who claim descent from the same canoe—Tuwharetoa himself is said to have fathered Tutanekai, lover of Hinemoa in the well-known Arawa legend *(p. 198)*.

Originally Tuwharetoa formed part of the large Ngati Awa tribe centred on Whakatane, but was pressured into leaving the Bay of Plenty for new land. On arriving at Lake Taupo in the 1700s, Tuwharetoa allied with (and later absorbed) the local Ngati Kurapoto—also descended from the *Arawa* canoe—to overcome two local fair-skinned tribes of tangata whenua (indigenous people) and to take complete possession of the area. Judicious intermarriage established allegiances with neighbouring tribes (buffers which cushioned intrusions by coastal tribes), leaving the Tuwharetoa to grow more numerous and more powerful in relative security.

European settlement: The Taupo township area was closely peopled in pre-European times and was known as Tapuaeharuru, "resounding footsteps". Missionaries visited the area from 1839, but the settlement dates from 1869, when an Armed Constabulary post was established during the campaign against Te Kooti.

In the same year Te Kooti's followers surprised and overwhelmed an Armed Constabulary detachment at nearby Opepe *(see below)*, after which the road through to Napier, which formed the troops' main supply line, was fortified at strategic intervals.

Thermal activity in the area attracted increasing numbers of visitors, but it was not until after 1950 that Taupo enlarged its role of holiday town; the Wairakei geothermal power project was launched, neighbouring timber plantations were expanded and, with the cobalt deficiency identified, large areas of new farmland were developed.

TROUT FISHING

Splendid trout are hooked from Lake Taupo by the tonne each day, so much so that at the mouth of the Waitahanui River in the evening, the anglers are often lined so close to each other that they form a "picket fence". There is always good fishing somewhere on the lake, either trolling or casting from the shore.

Although fishing settlements are scattered on the lake's eastern shores, many anglers prefer to fish the lake and streams at remote Western Bay, generally accessible only by boat, float plane or helicopter. Trout from Taupo average about 1.5 kilograms and the angler may expect catches of over twice this weight.

Visitor Centres and most hotels and motels in the Taupo and Turangi areas can advise on licences, hire of rods, tackle and boats. There is no closed season. Fishing launches are available for charter on the lake.

Trout were introduced to New Zealand in 1868 when brown trout eggs were brought from Tasmania, obtained from fish originally taken to Tasmania from Britain. It was 16 years later that the first rainbow ova arrived at Auckland, from California. Hatcheries were constructed and gradually trout were established throughout the country. Hatcheries still fulfil an important function as some lakes and rivers, though rich in food, lack adequate spawning grounds. Today eggs are sent from the hatcheries to many parts of the world, including Australia, Britain, Italy, France and Denmark. New Zealand's rainbow trout are descended from the one shipment and are generally considered to be the only pure strain left. Rainbow ova have even been sent from the hatchery at △ Turangi *(on the lake's southern shores)* back to the Californian breeding grounds from which the original shipment came.

THERMAL POOLS ★★★

A number of motels and hotels have hot pools and in some areas of Taupo private homes are situated on a hot-water belt providing their own hot pools.

De Brett Thermal Pools ("The Terraces"): Attractive pools with a thrilling waterslide are found in a valley immediately behind a magnificent colonial hotel building. Private pools are available. *400 m on the Napier–Taupo Road. Open daily; 7.30 a.m.–9.30 p.m.; tel. (07) 378-8559.*

A.C. Baths: The name of the A.C. Baths reflects their genesis, for over a century ago it was here that the soldiers of the Armed Constabulary would bathe. The lido pool is maintained at 37°C and the private pools at 40°C. *Spa Rd, off main street. Open Sunday–Thursday, 8 a.m.–9 p.m.; Friday and Saturday, 8 a.m.–10 p.m. Also included are a sauna, spa pool and solarium. Tel. (07) 378-7321.*

Tokaanu Thermal Pools: At the southern end of Lake Taupo, thermal baths neighbour a small thermal area; *Tokaanu. 58 km S; tel. (07) 386-8575.*

OTHER POINTS OF INTEREST NEAR THE TOWN

Taupo Regional Museum of Art and History: A small collection includes the **Reid Maori carvings** and displays of Taupo's sawmilling days. Prominent, too, is the complete skeleton of a moa found by schoolboys in the Waikaremoana forest in 1970. *Story Place (opposite end of Te Heuheu St near Visitor Information Centre). Open Monday to Saturday, 10.30 a.m.– 4.30 p.m.*

Close by is the **Redoubt and Old Courthouse** where the **earthworks** of the Armed Constabulary redoubt which spawned the township stand above the boat harbour and enclose a small **pumice hut** (*c.* 1874), once its magazine. The old courthouse (1881) nearby was originally built as a hall for the soldiers. *Off Story Place. Walk towards the river, passing the old courthouse to reach the earthworks.*

Spa Thermal Park: An area of parkland, with flying fox and boundless open space. A track leads downriver to Huka Falls. *County Rd, off Spa Rd.*

Cherry Island: Poised like a giant canoe in the middle of the swiftly flowing Waikato River, and complete with tearooms, it cultivates a farmyard atmosphere with numerous animals and fish. *Open daily, 9 a.m.–5 p.m. Signposted off Spa Rd.*

Huka Village: A recreated Victorian village serves as a family leisure park. *Huka Falls Rd. Open daily.*

Wairakei Park ★ ★ ★: A cluster of attractions on the Waikato River includes "Craters of the Moon" and a thermal valley, a prawn farm, the Huka Jet to the foot of the Huka Falls, a honey centre and the Taupo Observatory. *See △ Wairakei.*

LAKE TAUPO ★★★

Lake Taupo, of some 619 square kilometres, lies in a series of volcanic craters. Its serenity masks the scene of the country's most violent volcanic eruptions of the past several thousand years. In one of these, about 135 A.D., pumice was showered over thousands of square kilometres of surrounding countryside, so providing a well-defined ash layer for today's archaeologists.

The largest of the rivers entering the lake is Tongariro, at its southern tip. Strictly this is an extension of the Waikato River, which flows out of the lake by Taupo township to thunder almost at once over the Huka Falls. At the outlet, gates in the road bridge control the level of the lake and the water flow down to the vital Waikato hydro-electric power stations *(see △ Waikato River)*. There are numerous delightful camping and swimming spots around the lake. Large numbers of water skiers come to Taupo and inshore are restricted to specified ski lanes.

Lake viewpoint, Taupo township.

PLACES OF INTEREST AROUND THE LAKE

Presented clockwise in geographical order, starting from Taupo township. Note: the eastern and southern shores are sprinkled with so many holiday settlements, camping grounds and attractive picnic places that only a few have been specifically mentioned. In contrast, the lake's western shoreline is accessible by land only at a very few points. An interesting drive of some 150 km may be made around the lake.

Waitahanui River mouth: When the fishing is good a "picket fence" of anglers forms across the river mouth.

Hatepe: A fishing settlement between the road and the lake and set in tall trees.

Jellicoe Point: A green finger pointing out towards Motutaiko Island, the lake's only island of any size. Fortified by the Tuwharetoa as a refuge in times of danger (an invasion by Waikato tribes was successfully thwarted here), the island was used later as a burial ground. Pohutukawa grow on the island although, inexplicably, are not found elsewhere around the lake.

△ **Turangi ★:** Hydro town for the vast Tongariro power complex. The Tongariro River hereabouts is a mecca for anglers.

△ **Tokaanu ★:** A village with hot springs and a small thermal area.

△ **Waihi ★:** A picturesque hamlet at the lake's edge.

Pukawa: The Rev. Thomas Samuel Grace (1815-79) built his mission house here; it was abandoned to fall into ruin in 1863 when he and his family fled from the Hauhau. The present quaint homestead was built beside the ruins of the old in the 1880s when Grace's son, Lawrence, returned to farm the property. Grace was actively sympathetic to the Maori cause and encouraged the Maori to consider land sales carefully and to insist on their rights when trading with the Pakeha. Forced by war to abandon the Pukawa Mission, Grace was seized along with Volkner at △ Opotiki, when the latter was martyred. Later Grace served at Tauranga where he died in 1879. His association with the Tuwharetoa of Taupo was reinforced when his son Lawrence married a sister of Te Heuheu Tukino V (Tureiti). *1.5 km from the main road. The homestead, still occupied by Grace's descendants, is on high ground to the S of the settlement.*

Omori and Kuratau Spit: A delightful spot complete with jetty and boat ramp. The road leads past Te Rae Point to a scenic reserve by the water's edge. *2.5 km from the main road.*

Kuratau Hydro-Electric Power Station (1962): This station, on the Kuratau River, incorporates a 15-metre rock-fill dam. Two 4,000-hp horizontal Francis turbines drive two 3,000–W Swedish-made ASEA generators. *2.5 km from the main road.*

Karangahape Cliffs: These tall, sheer, fluted cliffs, plainly visible from the other side of the lake, should be seen from a boat in sunlight to appreciate their fantastic colouring—vivid blues, greens, browns, reds and even purples. Here, as elsewhere, are burial caves in the most inaccessible of clefts, and at their feet is water of rare purity. *Not accessible by road.*

Motuwhara Island: A jumble of rocks a short distance off Tangingatahi Point near which the taniwha Horomatangi is said to have lived. This legendary lizard (since transformed into a sometimes-submerged brown rock) is said to have formed the Karapiti Blowhole near Wairakei; until recently the blowhole was an awesome spectacle but it has since been unintentionally tamed by the geothermal power scheme.

Kinloch: A lakeside settlement, with its own marina. For some years it was one-time Prime Minister Sir Keith Holyoake's summer retreat and rejoiced under the suggestion of being the country's "summertime capital". A number of streets are named after the Holyoake family. Popular for water skiing. From here one can walk on to **Kawakawa Bay**, otherwise accessible only by boat (*5 hrs return*).

Acacia Bay: A delightful corner of the lake with a growing number of holiday and permanent homes. *Boats for hire.*
   A short distance beyond is **Jerusalem Bay,** another spot favoured by swimmers and boat-owners.

ARATIATIA-WAIRAKEI ROUND TRIP ★★★

The timing of this 34-km round trip is important if one is to see the Aratiatia Rapids, which only flow at set hours (10–11.30 a.m.; 2.30–4 p.m. and most spectacular when the water first surges down them). Most of the points of interest outlined below are described in greater detail elsewhere in the text.
   Leave Taupo at about 9 a.m. or 1.30 p.m. The trip may be tailored to fill a crowded half day or a leisurely full day. From the lake front drive north up the main street (Tongariro St) and turn right immediately along Spa Rd.

Waikato Lookout Point (Hell's Gate) (*2.5 km*): From here the view is down sheer steaming cliffs to the green waters of the Waikato River. In the distance rises the shroud of Wairakei. Here, too, is the heart-stopping **Taupo Bungy**.

213

Native Plant Nursery *(5 km)*: Native trees and plants are propagated here, primarily to restore areas disfigured by hydro-electric power schemes. *Centennial Dr. Visits may be arranged; tel. (07) 378-5450.*

Turn left into Rakanui and Aratiatia Rds:

Aratiatia Rapids ★★★ *(13.5 km)*: The rapids here would have vanished completely but for public outcry as the result of a hydro-electric power scheme. When "turned on" the waters reappear, to foam down their old bed. The river flows down the rapids at set hours *(above)*, save in exceptional circumstances. *Lookout points are signposted on the river's right bank.* A detour leads to the power station, which may be visited *(see △ Wairakei).*

Cross the river and turn left on rejoining the main road and proceed to:

△ **Wairakei** ★★★: Here the steam and baffled roar of geothermal power installations hint of volcanic fury close to the earth's crust.

Wairakei Power Station *(18.5 km—detour 800 m)*: Here steam led from the bores drives generators.

Return to the main road and continue on to:

Wairakei Thermal Valley ★★ *(21 km—detour 1.5 km)*: Various minerals give intense and contrasting colour to the boiling mudpools of this steaming rainbow valley.

Return to the main road and continue a short distance to:

Geothermal Power Project Information Office *(21 km)*: Here are displays, models, photographs and diagrams of drilling equipment and the techniques employed to harness the underground steamfield. Tours of the neighbouring borefield and the powerhouse may be arranged. *Open daily (except statutory holidays), 9 a.m.–4 p.m.*

Beyond the Wairakei Resort *(25 km)* it is well worth deviating briefly to see the **"Craters of the Moon"** *(continuing on Highway 1 and turning right up Karapiti Rd). Alternatively, turn first left to reach the:*

Taupo Observatory ★★, **Prawn Farm** ★★★ and **Huka Jet** ★★★ on the river, and the **N. Z. Honey Hive** ★★ *(see p. 259).*

Follow Huka Falls Rd to reach the:

Huka Falls ★★★: Here the Waikato River surges over an 11-metre shelf. *Allow 20 mins.*

Huka Village: A recreated historic village set in an orchard with craftspeople at work. *Open daily, 10 a.m.–5 p.m.*

Continue on to rejoin Highway 1 at:

The Lookout *(32 km)*: The lookout offers an unparalleled view of the township of Taupo, the lake and the mountains.

Continue on to return to Taupo township at 34 km.

OTHER ENVIRONS OF TAUPO

Mt Tauhara *(1,099 m)*: An extinct volcanic cone presiding in solitude over the lake and the Kaingaroa Plains, assuring those who climb it of a superb panorama. Tauhara means "lonely mountain", and refers as much to its geographical position as to its unfortunate love affair in mythology when, with other mountains, Tauhara fell for the graceful Pihanga *(see △ Tongariro National Park). 5.5 km along Highway 5 towards Napier, detour 800 m to park by gate. Allow 3 hrs for the return climb.*

Opepe Graves ★: Opepe was the site of an abandoned Maori village, where the road to Napier intersected a Maori track from the Urewera. In 1869, during the campaigns against Te Kooti, the village was being considered for the site of a military stockade when a detachment of 14 cavalrymen camped there and negligently omitted to post sentries while their companions continued on to Tapuaeharuru (Taupo). Their Maori guides deserted and, when a strange Maori appeared, the men emerged from their whare unarmed. Too late they saw and recognised as Hauhau others who were with the stranger. Cut off from their rifles, they fled for the safety of the bush, but only five escaped with their lives. One intrepid soul, who had been drying off his saturated uniform at the time, struggled through bush and bitter cold all the way to

Fort Galatea, 64 kilometres away, quite naked. The troops' senior officer, Cornet Angus Smith, was subsequently awarded the New Zealand Cross for his part in the affair; an award which scandalised many as Smith's carelessness had contributed to the tragedy. *A track leads to the graves of the nine victims. One may then cross the highway and follow a track down the Old Taupo Rd, taking a track to the left (15 mins).* The walk ends at an old water trough, built from a six-metre totara log hauled here by the Armed Constabulary once the stockade had been established. The considerable settlement of Opepe township grew up around the stockade. In the bush, with a post and rail fence around the spring which feeds the trough, it is easy to picture one of the soldiers watering his horse, oblivious of the presence of one of Te Kooti's scouts and of the bloodshed which was shortly to follow.
Opepe means "place of the moth". *17 km on Highway 5, towards Napier.*

△ **Orakei Korako** ★★★: A varied thermal area of individual character set on the banks of Lake Ohakuri, a hydro lake on the Waikato River. *37 km.*

△ **Tongariro National Park** ★★★: A park centred on the volcanic peaks which cluster at the southern end of Lake Taupo. The drive around the mountains can be a rewarding all-day trip.

ORGANISED EXCURSIONS

Lake trips: To savour the vast expanse of fresh water, there are leisurely half-day trips on the replica steamboat **"Ernest Kemp"** to see cliff-side contemporary Maori rock carvings by local artist Jono Randall and, for those who prefer canvas, on the **"Barbary"**, a ketch said to have once been won by Errol Flynn in a card game, or the **"Spirit of Musick"** *(for both, tel. (07) 378-3444).* A jet boat provides quick access to remote crannies, combining this with placid river rafting *(tel. (07) 374-8338).* Boats may also be hired at the boat harbour *(tel. (07) 378-5596).*

River trips: Short trips on the Waikato River may be made on the stately 1908 riverboat, MV *Waireka* (the **"African Queen"**), to visit the awesome Huka Falls and the Aratiatia Rapids as well as the unique, geothermally-heated prawn farm *(tel. (07) 374-8338).* Alternatively, **"Huka Jet"** offers one of the country's most thrilling river trips as it speeds up the Waikato and spins in the froth beneath the Huka Falls *(tel. (07) 374-8572; bookings essential).*

Rafting: Wild whitewater rafting and sedate raft fishing can both be arranged on the Tongariro River, among others *(Rapid Sensations, tel. (07) 378-7902; River Rats, tel. (07) 386-7492;).*

Bungy jumping: Watch, if you cannot bear to participate, as jumpers leap 50 metres *(tel. (07) 377-1135).*

Tandem Skydiving: For those who like to fall further, there is a 30-second free fall from 3,000 metres; *tel. (07) 377-0428.*

Scenic flights: Conventional flights circle the volcanic giants of the Tongariro National Park *(Wonderflights, tel. (07) 378-8559).* Helicopters poise above the torrent of the Huka Falls *(tel. (07) 374-8405).*

Horse trekking: Trekking through volcanic landscapes. *Taupo Horse Treks, tel. (07) 378-0356.*

Mountain biking: Bikes may be hired. Among the best routes is the 2-hour track from Poihipi Rd, via Q Line Rd to Highway 1 adjacent to the "Craters of the Moon". *Details of hire bikes from the Visitor Information Centre.*

★★★ TAURANGA

Bay of Plenty   Maps 5, 8   Pop. 70,803 (urban area)

216 km SE of Auckland; 88 km N of Rotorua; Visitor Information Centre, The Strand; tel. (07) 578-8103. Department of Conservation Field Centre, Cnr McLean and Anson Sts; tel. (07) 578-7677.

TAURANGA sprawls pleasantly on the shores of the harbour that bears its name. Surrounding rich soils blend with a most temperate climate to yield much of the country's citrus fruit, and such sub-tropical varieties as kiwifruit, tamarillos (tree tomatoes) and feijoas. Offshore, in waters teeming with big-game fish, lie △ Mayor and Motiti Islands; to the west the land builds gently to the hills of the Kaimai Range.

The city grew up as a military settlement on confiscated Maori land and for many years was a quiet farming and marketing town—an ideal place for retirement or for holidaying. However, the diagnosis of the cobalt deficiency in nearby pumice lands which had previously rendered idle land capable of supporting livestock, and the maturing of vast neighbouring forest areas, saw Tauranga's population double in a decade and its port at △ Mount Maunganui become the country's largest exporter. The opening of the Kaimai Tunnel (1978), providing a direct link to the Waikato, and the building of the Tauranga Harbour Bridge (1988), bringing Mount Maunganui within minutes of Tauranga *(17.5 km reduced to 5 km)*, have further increased the port's role — Tauranga, after all, means "sheltered anchorage". Today a vigorous commercial centre, the city has lost little of its charm and in summer draws many visitors.

Annual festivals held at Tauranga include the National Jazz Festival *(Easter)* and the Festival of Tauranga *(August)*.

BIG-GAME FISHING

The well-stocked waters around △ Mayor Island and Motiti Island draw big-game fishing enthusiasts from all over the world. The season extends from late December to early May. *Charters can be arranged but advance booking is essential; contact the Visitor Information Centre (tel. (07) 578-8103) or the Tauranga Big Game Fishing Club (Headquarters, Sulphur Point; PO Box 501, Tauranga; tel. (07) 578-6203).*

SOME HISTORY

Ngapuhi invasions: The Ngapuhi of Northland were among the first tribes to obtain a plentiful supply of firearms from early European traders. In 1818, armed with newly acquired weapons, they embarked on a widespread campaign of conquest. The Tauranga district, unlike the Coromandel, Rotorua and the rest of the Bay of Plenty, was spared the initial devastation by the brilliance of its local Ngaiterangi chief, Te Waru. Faced with the annihilation of his tribe, Te Waru succeeded in capturing a Ngapuhi chief before the Ngapuhi could attack his pa at Otumoetai (now a suburb of Tauranga). To the astonishment of the Ngapuhi, Te Waru not only released his prisoner (it would have been customary for Te Waru to have killed and eaten him), but also armed him and insisted on being taken prisoner himself. His desperate gamble enabled him to negotiate a peace that lasted 14 years.

In 1832 the Ngapuhi again came to Tauranga on an expedition designed not for revenge but to atone for the remarkable Girls' War at Kororareka (Russell), an affair which had nothing to do with the Ngaiterangi, arising as it did from girls exchanging insults on the beach there. First Mercury Island and then Mayor Island were devastated, but when the Ngapuhi reached Motiti Island they found it deserted. Before long they saw a large fleet of canoes approaching and ran to welcome expected reinforcements—only to be overwhelmed by a powerful force of Ngaiterangi. Only two Ngapuhi survived.

A missionary settlement: Captain Cook in 1769 had noted that the Tauranga district had a large number of "forts" and concluded "that these people had neighbouring enemies and were always exposed to hostile attacks". His deductions were proved correct in 1828 when the Bay of Islands missionaries Henry Williams, Hamlin and Davis sailed here in the *Herald* and were amazed when they called again just days later to find that in the meantime a pa had been destroyed and nearly a third of the population annihilated by a band of Ngati Maru marauders from Hauraki. This so disconcerted the missionaries that they waited seven years before opening a mission station on Te Papa Peninsula, where the city of Tauranga now stands. In 1837, after only two years, tribal wars threatened and the mission was closed, but it was reopened the following year by the Rev. Alfred Nesbitt Brown.

Brown purchased about seven hectares from the Ngaiterangi and built an elegant mission house *(see below)*. By 1839 he had acquired for the Church Missionary Society the whole of Te Papa Peninsula, as he shrewdly considered the 400 hectares to be a likely place for settlers should the country be colonised. The boundary between the CMS property and the Maori-held land was a ditch, and before settlers could arrive it was to be the setting of a major battle.

The Battle of Gate Pa: To prevent reinforcements and supplies reaching the followers of the Maori King who were fighting in the Waikato, the Government in January 1864 sent troops to the tiny settlement at Tauranga (then little more than a mission station and a handful of traders) to build two redoubts. When the soldiers arrived, most of the local Ngaiterangi were fighting in the Waikato but they hurried back and quickly built a well-fortified pa some distance inland. When it was completed, Rawiri Puhirake sent a letter to the commanding officer at Tauranga advising him of this fact, and added that his followers had thoughtfully also built 16 kilometres of road up from the harbour "so that the soldiers would not be too weary to fight"! The chivalrous offer was ignored and so a second pa was built, closer to Tauranga.

As it stood near an entrance to the mission land, it became known as "Gate Pa".

On 28 April 1864 troops surrounded Gate Pa and at dawn the next day pounded it in one of the fiercest artillery barrages of the New Zealand Wars. By late afternoon a breach had been opened in the palisades but the first assault wave was driven off and later troops, once inside the pa, were confused by its maze of trenches and tunnels, and were forced to withdraw with heavy losses. The British lost 31 killed and 80 wounded (about a third of their entire assault force), and when evening fell the Ngaiterangi divided into small parties and slipped through the British lines to fight again at Te Ranga.

Two Victoria Crosses were won that day, but perhaps even braver were the exploits of Heni te Kirikaramu (Jane Foley), a Maori King supporter who took an active part in the fighting. When she heard the mortally wounded Colonel Booth crying out for water, she filled a can and, under fire, carried it out to four of the wounded soldiers as they lay on the fringe of the pa. Her deed typified the compassion shown to prisoners by the Ngaiterangi that day.

A few weeks later the Maori began to dig themselves in at Te Ranga, but on this occasion were not given time to complete their pa. An artillery barrage was followed by a bayonet charge, and in desperate hand-to-hand fighting the British exacted terrible vengeance—about 120 Maori were killed for the loss of 10 British dead and 39 wounded. Resistance in the district ended with much Ngaiterangi tribal land being confiscated. (*A commemorative plaque 2.5 km from Barkes Corner along Pye's Pa Rd stands behind a hedge. The depression in which it lies marks the site of the Te Ranga pa rifle pits. The pa straddled the rather narrow ridge.*)

In 1981 an Act of Parliament authorised payment of $250,000 to a Trust Board as compensation for land confiscated from the local Maori after the Gate Pa and Te Ranga engagements. It reversed a finding by a Royal Commission in 1928 that the land seizures were justified on the grounds of the Maori's "rebellion" against the Queen. The Act also granted a symbolic "pardon" to all those involved. Subsequently, in 1988, the 4-hectare Te Ranga battle-site where so many Maori died was returned to the Tauranga Moana Trust Board for use as a burial ground.

A WALK AROUND "THE CAMP" ★★★

"The Camp", as its name suggests, was originally the site of a military settlement on a cliff overlooking the harbour. On two bushed knolls stand the Military Cemetery and the earthworks of the Monmouth Redoubt. Today these are linked by Robbins Park, which includes a Begonia House *(open daily)*, rose gardens and picnic area. Close by is the stately old mission house *(conducted tours, Mon-Sat, 2 p.m.)*. Park at the end of The Strand and follow the path up to the redoubt.

The Monmouth Redoubt: The redoubt was built in January 1864 by British troops sent to cut the supply route from the East Coast to the Waikato used by supporters of the Maori King. The troops included the 43rd Monmouth Light Infantry, after whom the redoubt is named. The redoubt's earthworks, including a deep moat-like trench, are well preserved, and a number of guns used in the campaigns are in the enclosure.

When the Kingites threatened to attack Tauranga township, the European women and children were first moved to the mission house nearby, and when the situation worsened they shifted to the redoubt itself. The troops were on a permanent full alert and even slept in full battle dress, with emergency rations close by. After six weeks the women and children were shipped out to Auckland. In April 1864 troops from here took part in the disastrous attack on Gate Pa *(described above)*. *Walk along Cliff Rd and turn into Mission St.*

Tauranga Mission House ★★★: Better known as 'The Elms", this is one of the country's oldest homes, built over the period 1838-47 by Archdeacon A. N. Brown (1803-84), one of New Zealand's early missionaries. Despite Brown's energy— he had to walk some 1,100 kilometres to reach all of his 800 communicants—the mission was not a success and was closed when military settlers took over confiscated land in the district. During the battles of Gate Pa and Te Ranga, Brown tended the wounded and buried the dead of both sides. In 1873 he purchased the property from his employers, the Church Missionary Society.

As only the unbecoming rear of an otherwise elegant building can be seen from the street, visitors should walk round the gardens to see the house to its best advantage.

Perhaps the oldest in the country, the **garden** includes an English oak planted by Brown in 1838 and two towering Norfolk pines which flank the old entrance. Norfolk pines were favoured by missionaries as their top branches form a cross, and this particular pair was used as a navigation aid by early sailors into Tauranga Harbour who called them "The Archdeacon's Sentinels". Also in the garden stands a quaint one-roomed **library ★★** (1842), built by Brown to house his extensive

217

collection. Close by is a reconstruction of the original 1843 chapel, and beside it the old mission bell (1835). The chapel contains items of historical interest, none more so than the folding dining table at which Brown entertained a number of officers on the eve of the Battle of Gate Pa — little knowing that over the next two days he was to bury all but one of his guests.

The garden is open to the public during daylight hours. Return to Cliff Rd, turn left and continue to Mirrielees Rd and walk up the drive across the railway overpass:

Otemataha Pa Military Cemetery: On an old pa site lie many of the dead from the Gate Pa and Te Ranga engagements and the graves of Archdeacon Brown and Col. H. J. P. Booth, who died at Gate Pa to earn the unenviable distinction of being the most senior officer to be killed in the entire Land Wars. A monument to Rawiri Puhirake, the Ngaiterangi chief killed at Te Ranga, contains a frieze depicting Heni te Kirikaramu carrying water to the enemy wounded—it incorrectly depicts Heni as a man (for a time her gallantry was attributed to Rawiri) and using a traditional calabash instead of an old iron can. It is of course possible that more than she were involved. Also of interest is the grave of Captain John Faine Charles Hamilton (commander of HMS *Esk*), after whom Hamilton city is named. He was a casualty at Gate Pa, and his heroism that day was still very much in mind when the Hamilton military settlement was established in the Waikato. *Return along Cliff Rd, turn right into Monmouth St and left into Willow St.*

A huge aspen tree (*on a grassed reserve on the corner of Willow and McLean Sts opp. the clock tower*) is said to have grown from an aspen stake used by a soldier to tether a horse in the 1860s. The stake took root and is now one of the city's largest trees. *Follow McLean St back to The Strand.*

Te Awanui war canoe (1973): Carved from kauri, the canoe rests in its Te Urungu ("pillow") except when in use on the harbour on ceremonial occasions. The boulder by the canoe was brought from the slopes of Mauao (Mt Maunganui) and placed here to symbolise the joining of the tribes across the waters of the harbour.

OTHER POINTS OF INTEREST

Gate Pa ★: The scene of the famous battle described above. The pa site is cut by a main highway, with St George's Church (1900) and a memorial on the one side and a reserve on the other. A plan of the engagement is in the church foyer, together with a piece of shell exploded in the fighting and a plaque and picture which commemorate Heni te Kirikaramu with the text: "If thine enemy hunger, feed him; If he thirst, give him to drink" (Romans, 12:20). The text reflects a unique "Order of the Day" which is said to have framed a code for the fighting and some say was found on one of the Kingite casualties at Te Ranga. *Cameron Rd, on the way to Greerton. 5 km from city centre.*

Tauranga Historic Village ★★★: A bustling recreation of Victorian colonial life, complete with steam train, wharf, saw mill, gold battery and shops. Working displays capture the smell as well as the appearance of the original. Military cottages moved here date from the Land Wars, as do headstones in the cemetery for soldiers who fell at Gate Pa, Te Ranga, Te Papa, Pukehina and elsewhere in the locality (*removed here for safekeeping*). The flagpole once adorned the Monmouth Redoubt. The church is an amalgam of a number of old buildings, even incorporating parts of a hotel. Special, too, is the collection of early valve radios, dating back to the 1920s. On live days the old machinery glints as the wheels turn and the village bustles with energy. The 1877 "L" Class steam train operates, there are rides on a replica 1910 double-decker and the blacksmith's shop springs to life. *155, 17th Avenue West; Open daily, 9 a.m.–6 p.m. (5 p.m. in winter); tel. (07) 578-1302.*

Waikareao Estuary Walkway: Two easy walkways link to follow the shores of the sheltered estuary, where the eye inevitably drifts to the sacred burial ground of Motu-o-pae Island. **Daisy Hardwick Walk** starts at the end of Maxwells Rd, Otumoetai (end of causeway), and joins with the **McCardles Bush Boardwalk,** through mangroves and rushes. *2 hrs for complete circuit.*

Harbour markets: *Thurs–Sun, from 10 a.m.*

ENVIRONS

Beaches: Magnificent Ocean Beach ★★★, which stretches for several kilometres, is reached at either △ Mount Maunganui *(5 km)* or at Papamoa *(16 km)*. Within the sheltered reaches of Tauranga's near-landlocked harbour are numerous tidal beaches, the most pleasant of which are the resort of Omokoroa★ (*21 km W; turnoff signposted at 16 km*) and the willowed cove of Pahoia (*22 km W; turnoff signposted at 18 km*).

△ **Mount Maunganui ★★★:** A summer resort and major port just across the harbour. *5 km.*

World of Horses: At an equestrian theme park there is trail riding for riders of all ages, working stables and appropriate displays. *14 km N, off S.H.2 at Station Road, Whakamarama; tel. (07) 548-0404.*

Hot pools: As well as the hot pools at △ Maketu and △ Katikati, and the hot salt-water pool at △ Mount Maunganui, there are three thermal pool complexes nearby. **Fernland Spa Hot Pools** *Cambridge Rd, open daily, 10 a.m.-10 p.m.)* are set in native bush, and **Welcome Bay Hot Pools** *(Welcome Bay Rd, open weekends and school holidays)* have a lengthy water slide. The hot pools at **Plummers Point** are among the most pleasant in the district, with a large pool cool enough for reasonably strenuous swimming and a hotter pool for soaking in *(Plummers Point Caravan Park and Hot Thermal Pools, Omokoroa; 19 km; tel. (07) 548-0669.).*

Rerekawau (Kaiate) Falls*: The road to the falls affords unusual glimpses of the Mount Maunganui isthmus, and at the falls a path follows a stream to descend the same rock face as the tumbling water. *19 km. On the old road to Mt Maunganui, take the Welcome Bay turnoff and at 14.5 km turn right along Waitoa Rd for 5 km.*

Ohauiti Walkway: A pleasant circular one-hour walk, with sweeping views of the city, the harbour and the coast from Motiti Island to the Aldermen Islands. *12 km up the Ohauiti Rd. Turn off Highway 29 at Hairini.*

McLaren Falls Park* *: Nestled in the upper Wairoa River valley, the park offers walks through picturesque native bush spiced with thousands of exotics. In summer, as well as swimming in the natural river pools here, there is canoeing and white-water rafting. Adjoining the park is **Marshalls Animal Park.** *(Open daily, December–February,10 a.m.–5 p.m. At other times of year, open weekends and public holidays or by arrangement; tel. (07) 543-1029.) 11 km on Highway 29 towards Hamilton; turn off along McLaren Falls Rd.*

Puketoki Scenic Reserve (Whakamarama)*: Since the 1920s the 32-hectare reserve, with its splendid stand of bush, has been popular with locals. Walking along the tracks here is particularly refreshing on a summer's day. *22.5 km. Leyland Rd. Turn off the main road 14.5 km W of Tauranga at Te Puna Stream; continue 8 km.*

Kiwifruit Country **: Every aspect of the country's best known fruit, from vine to packing case, and ancillary products, is displayed at an extensive export orchard. *365 km SE on S.H.2. Tel. (07) 573-6340.*

Longridge Park **: Kiwifruit, native bush, a variety of animals and unforgettable jet-boat rides and rafting trips on the Kaituna River, await the visitor. *40 km SE on Highway 33. Tel. (07) 533-1515.*

△**Maketu*:** Final resting place of the *Arawa* canoe and for generations an Arawa stronghold. *44 km E.*

△ **Katikati:** Both the Katikati Bird Gardens and the Sapphire Hot Springs near Katikati may be visited in a day. *39 km NW.*

ORGANISED EXCURSIONS

Launch trips: Several launch and fishing excursions are run from Tauranga Wharf, including trips to △ Mayor Island and Motiti Island.

Outdoor expeditions: Canoeing and rafting expeditions are mounted on the white waters of the Wairoa River. Hunting and trout fishing expeditions may be arranged. *Details from the Information Office.*

Waikato   Maps 5, 8   Pop. 3,473   **★ TE AROHA**

53 km NE of Hamilton. Information Office, 102 Whitaker St; tel. (07) 884-8052. Department of Conservation, Old Gardener's Cottage, Domain; tel. (07) 884-9303.

A FARMING TOWN nestling at the foot of Mt Te Aroha (at 953 metres the highest peak in the Kaimai-Coromandel Ranges), Te Aroha's early role as a fashionable spa is recalled by the fanciful Victoriana of its quaint Tourist Gardens — an image revived with their refurbishment.

SOME HISTORY

The power of love: The traditional explanation of the town's name is that Kahumata Mamoe once lost his way in the dense bush. To regain his bearings he climbed the highest peak, and great was his joy when he saw his beloved village below. In a surge of relief he stamped on the ground and cried out his great love (te aroha), whereupon from the mountain there surged a healing power which impregnated the springs which rise in the Te Aroha Domain. The clear pool in one cleft of rock became known as "The Mirror of Te Mamoe" and served as a wishing well for newly married couples. When the curative properties of the spring were discovered by the Pakeha, a bore was sunk on the site of the pool and this inadvertently gave rise to a geyser of hot soda water — which still plays half-hourly and is regarded as the only known hot soda-water fountain in the world.

A golden spa: The town was founded in 1880, the year in which the Waihou River was freed from snags and rendered navigable, and gold was discovered close by. Gold mining was carried on until 1921, without spectacular results, and in the early 1900s the Government developed the Tourist Domain in Te Aroha as a spa.

TE AROHA DOMAIN ★★

Hot spa pools: Elegant bathhouses and quaint kiosks over Vichy-type drinking fountains, dating from the late 1880s, are surrounded by trim greens, but the ageing No. 1 Bathhouse has given way to a new complex of spa pools. These comprise five private pools and the original No. 2 hot pools. *Open daily (except Christmas Day) from noon to 9 p.m. Te Aroha Soda Spa Baths; for bookings tel. (07) 884-8717.*

Mokena Soda Geyser: This curious hot water soda geyser, some 200 feet deep, marks the site of "The Mirror of Te Mamoe" *(see "Some History", above). Behind the soda baths complex. It plays modestly every 30 minutes.*

Te Aroha and District Museum: The Cadman Building, now stripped of its baths, houses a local collection of relics relating to the town. Note china with the Te Aroha motif and an early spa poster (also reproduced!). *Open Sat, Sun and public holidays, 1–4 p.m. (1–3 p.m., April to Sept); tel. (07) 884-8527.*

OTHER THINGS TO SEE AND DO

St Marks Church (1926): The country's oldest organ (reputed to have been built in 1712 by Renatus Harris and for nearly 137 years in All Saints Church, Baschurch, Shropshire) was sent here in 1927. Unusual are its stops, which are arranged horizontally. *13 Kenrick St.*

Scaling Mt Te Aroha (952 m.a.s.l.): From the Domain marked tracks lead through the bush to Bald Spur (*323 m*), an easy climb. It continues on to the summit of Mt Te Aroha, a 3-hour walk, from which on an exceptionally clear day one may see Little Barrier Island (*161 km*), Cape Runaway (*280 km*) and south-west across the island as far as Taranaki/Egmont (*245 km*). Those who would savour the breathtaking view without the exertion may take the bus which operates along a 7-km private road to the summit. *Closed to private traffic. Book through the Information Centre.*

Wairere Falls ★ ★: The Falls View Track (*45 mins one way*) links in with the Wairere, an old Maori trail east over the Kaimais, after offering a splendid view of the towering 150-metre Wairere Falls. Walks here in the Wairere Scenic Reserve provide an attractive half-day outing. *26 km SE. Goodwin Rd, off Old Te Aroha Rd. Information on this and other walks in the Kaimai Ranges is available from the Department of Conservation.*

TE AWAMUTU ★

Waikato   Map 6   Pop. 8,466

29 km S of Hamilton. Information Office, cnr Arawata St and Gorst Ave; tel. (07) 871-3259.

TE AWAMUTU, a pleasant South Waikato farming centre famous for its rose gardens, lies in lush dairyland ribboned with hedgerows.

The town originated as a Maori settlement, and a mission station was established in 1839 by the Rev. B. Y. Ashwell. During the Waikato Campaigns Charles Heaphy (1820-81), eminent explorer, surveyor and early artist, won the Victoria Cross nearby, and when the campaigns ended military settlers were allocated land here. The Puniu

River (*south of Kihikihi*) marked the Government's confiscation line and with justly embittered supporters of the Maori King in the "King Country" close by, the settlers' existence was tenuous. However, once the railway from Auckland reached the town in 1880 and King Tawhiao made peace the following year, the rate of development quickened.

Te Awamutu means "the end of the channel", as the river above this point was snagged and unsuitable for canoes.

Sale day is Thursday when stock passing through the sale yards attracts considerable interest (*Selwyn Lane/Mahoe St*). A rose show is held each November, usually on the first Sunday.

SOME HISTORY

The invasion of Rangiaowhia (Hairini): The late summer of 1864 saw the final strategic moves in the Waikato Campaign to secure the fertile Waikato plains for British occupation. The events are still the subject of intense controversy.

On 21 February 1864, in a surprise move by night, cavalry with bridle chains muffled skirted Paterangi pa to the west of Te Awamutu and moved on to the unprotected village of Rangiaowhia — a thriving settlement with fields of maize and potatoes which the troops were anxious to keep from Kingite forces at Paterangi.

There were about 100 men in the village, and numerous women and children. A number sought refuge in the two missionary churches (*St Paul's still stands*), but others elected to fight it out from inside a large whare. Ferocious exchanges of fire took place, despite the Maori's being greatly outnumbered, and neighbouring huts were set alight by the troops. Finally the thatch of the whare caught fire. One of the occupants, an old man, emerged with his hands held high. Officers shouted to hold fire but, unarmed and defenceless, he was gunned down in a massive volley. The officers were enraged, and one tried without success to have a soldier of the 65th Regiment arrested. "He was not the only one who fired," his commander protested.

Worse was to follow. Even with the whare ablaze none within dared emulate the old man, though two dashed out, firing their final shots, and fell to waiting rifles. Finally the burning house collapsed and those remaining within perished in the flames.

Accounts of the incident vary. The British version was that the whare was ignited accidentally, when both sides were shooting through the raupo walls, and that there were only armed warriors within. (The defenders were provided with cover by reason of the floor's being excavated, as was usual, about half a metre below the level of the ground outside.) Locally the belief persists that the whare was fired deliberately and with the full knowledge of there being women and children inside. The killing of the old man, however, is not disputed but is attributed to the anger of cavalrymen whose commander, Colonel Marmaduke Nixon, had been killed early on in the encounter.

Within a matter of hours the Kingites poured eastwards into the invaded village and hastily threw up defences for their supply headquarters. Trenches were built to cut the road from Te Awamutu to Hairini, and when an outlying British picket came under fire from Ngati Maniapoto the following day, troops were moved up from Te Awamutu to give the Kingites little time in which to strengthen their defences. Three six-pounder guns were brought up, and one British veteran recalled, "It was as pretty a bit of hot firing as I have ever seen. The Armstrongs were sending their shells screeching over us, and the Maori bullets were cutting near the fern near me in as even a swathe almost as you could cut it with a slash-hook." A bayonet charge saw the Maori lines break in confusion, providing an opportunity for the cavalry (on one of the few occasions they could be used in the duration of the entire wars) to ride, with sabres swinging, into the retreating Maori. The fortunate escaped across the swamp or down the south side of Hairini hill; those who could not were cut down. Afterwards the village of Rangiaowhia was looted by the troops, who returned to Te Awamutu laden with food and Maori artefacts.

In the event the ploy succeeded. Paterangi pa had been outflanked and isolated from essential supplies. Subsequent events might have been very different had the Kingites succeeded in regaining control of the route. Instead, the final reckoning, at Orakau, became inevitable.

"Peace shall never be made, never! never!": A month later came the Battle of Orakau, fought eight kilometres from here and one of the epics of the Land Wars. As *Rewi's Last Stand*, it was the basis for one of the first feature films to be made in New Zealand.

Rewi Maniapoto (1815-94), war chief of the local Ngati Maniapoto, was a prominent member of the Maori King Movement (*pp.* **159-60**) and leader of its more militant faction. The year before, Rewi had expelled the Government Magistrate, Sir John Gorst, from Te Awamutu because Gorst was publishing a newspaper, *Pihoihoi* ("the lark which sits on the housetop") to counter the Kingites' *Te Hokioi* (a mythical bird). When war broke out, Rewi commanded the Kingite forces, and despite a series of defeats the counsel of others prevailed and against his better judgement Rewi built a pa at Orakau.

On 31 March 1864 the position was attacked by over 2,000 soldiers (under General Cameron) who for three days were held at bay by Rewi's force of only 300, including some women and children.

On the third and final day, General Cameron sent a messenger to propose terms of peace, but although the pa's supplies of food and ammunition were all but exhausted, the reply of the Maori was: "Kaore e mau te rongo, ake, ake!" ("Peace shall never be made, never!, never!") An offer of safe passage for the women and children was rejected out of hand: "Ki te mata nga tane, me mate ano nga wahine, me nga tamariki." ("If the men die, the women and children must die also.") The battle was renewed and in an heroic rush from the pa about half the defenders, Rewi among them, burst through the British lines to the safety of the King Country.

In later years Rewi mellowed to play a key role in fostering Maori-Pakeha relations. *A memorial to Rewi stands in Kihikihi's main street, 3 km S, and a descriptive monument marks the site of Orakau pa, 4 km on the Kihikihi-Arapuni road.*

POINTS OF INTEREST

St John's Anglican Church ★★ (1854): One of the country's oldest, the church was built by the Church Missionary Society, Maori converts contributed timber and funds to assist the European carpenters, and on the north roof are the footprints of children who walked on the planks during building operations.

The East window, among the country's oldest stained glass windows, is probably the work of William Wailes, a leading exponent of the art. Depicted are St Peter's ship, the Last Supper (Judas lacks a halo) and the Supper at Emmaus. The remaining old windows are of welded hoop iron and the bell is believed to have been brought from an earlier mission church near Δ Raglan. Also of interest are memorial tablets erected by British regiments, and a number of graves, including those of British and Maori casualties in the battles at Rangiaowhia, and three of the children of the Rev. John Morgan, one of the first missionaries.

Beside the old church, and in striking contrast, is the New Parish Church of St John (1965) designed by Professor R. Toy and F. O. Jones. One must enter the building to appreciate fully the use made of Belgian slab glass and raw textures.

Opposite the church is Selwyn Park, a good picnic spot where *(beside the Public Relations Office)* a plaque marks the site of the Otawhao Mission (1839-63). The mission closed when war threatened, although Sir John Gorst *(see above)* continued living in the now-vanished mission house. *Arawata St.*

Te Awamutu and District Museum ★★: A small but comprehensive collection featuring the Waikato Campaigns and Maori and pioneer relics. A prize exhibit is a famous carving called Uenuku, a sacred relic of Tainui, said to have been brought to New Zealand in the Polynesian migration of about six centuries ago. Capt. Charles Heaphy's sword is also held here, as are two mere belonging to Tamihana Te Waharoa (1802–66), "The Kingmaker". *Roche St, next to library. Open Tues–Fri, 10 a.m.–4 p.m.; weekends, 2–4 p.m. Tel. (07) 871-4326.*

Aotearoa Institute ★: Established to provide training in such areas as carpentry, mechanics and computers, the centre also preserves the traditional skills of Maori craftspeople. The visitor may watch carvers and weavers at work, or browse among the many finished products. The centre also restores Maori artefacts. *Factory Rd. Open Mon–Fri 8.30 a.m.–5 p.m.; tel. (07) 871-4257.*

Te Awamutu Rose Gardens: Over 2,000 bushes represent over 80 varieties. Local residents, too, lose few opportunities to plant roses in their own gardens. *Gorst Ave/ Arawata St.* One may walk through Pioneer Walk to **War Memorial Park** with its attractive garden displays and picnic spots.

Waikato Rail Museum ★: A large static display of steam locomotives includes a Fa which was built in 1892. *Signposted off Racecourse Rd. Open by arrangement, tel. (07) 856-6694.*

Equine Pool ★: Here racehorses swim as part of their exercise programme. *Waipa Racing Club, Racecourse Rd. Best viewing time, 6–9 a.m. Tel. (07) 871-7047.*

ENVIRONS

Ngaroto Lake: An open stretch of water in lush farmland, the lake is favoured by boat owners and picnickers, but is unsuitable for swimming. A pleasant drive. *11 km. Turnoff signposed at 4 km on the road to Hamilton.*

Kihikihi: In the main street is the grave of Rewi Maniapoto, hero of the nearby Battle of Orakau. A memorial on the site of Orakau pa, including a bronze relief map showing the disposition of forces and the Kingites' line of retreat, is on the Arapuni road. *(4 km E. Picnic area.)*

Hairini: The locality here was of importance in pre-European times. The mission stations have proved highly successful, but the village's prolific farming operations (encouraged by the missionaries and, for a time, the Government) carried with them the eventual cause of the village's destruction as a food bowl for the Kingite forces.

The Anglican mission church, **St Paul's** (1856), in which Maori villagers huddled for safety during the Battle of Rangiaowhia, still stands, much admired for its sanctuary window (*c.* 1854-55). It is among the country's earliest stained glass, depicting St Paul (in centre light) flanked by the blinded Elymas and St Paul in Malta shaking a viper from his hand. The rival Catholic mission founded in 1844 by Bishop Pompallier is marked only by its cemetery, for the second of the mission churches in which the Maori sheltered (and which came under fire from the troops during the fighting) has not survived. The fighting over, the land here was surveyed and allotted to men of the First Company, Forest Rangers, who had taken part in the battles. The soldiers' town sections were at Kihikihi.

There was, understandably, intense rivalry between the Anglican and the Catholic missions, and the inevitable debate took place between the missionaries, the Rev. John Morgan and Father John Pezant as to the respective merits of their creeds. Rev. Morgan may, however, have been less than accurate in his summation when he reported that the Catholics had admitted defeat. *5 km E.*

△ **Pirongia ★:** An historic township nestling at the foot of a softly bushed prominence. *13 km W.*

△ **Kawhia ★★:** Its qualities of isolation and tranquillity impel one to linger rather than to visit fleetingly. *69 km W.*

△ **Waitomo Caves ★★★:** A fantasy of glow-worms and delicate limestone statuary. *45 km SW.*

Waikato Map 5 Pop. 842 **TE KAUWHATA**

53 km N of Hamilton.

TE KAUWHATA is a small farming town well known in early days of the wine industry for the successful governmental research into vine-growing and winemaking carried out here. Its name means "the storehouse in the lake".

POINTS OF INTEREST

Te Kauwhata Winery: Cook's winery here keeps alive the township's long-established tradition in winemaking. For many years a Government research station here serviced the country's burgeoning wine industry, but in 1991 its work was moved to Hawke's Bay, where other horticultural research is also carried out. *Paddys Rd.*

Rangiriri battle site: Scene of a major clash during the Waikato Campaigns. *On Highway 1, 2 km S of Te Kauwhata turnoff. (See △ Huntly.)*

King Country Map 6 Pop. 4,624 **TE KUITI**

80 km S of Hamilton. Visitor Information Centre, Rora St; tel. (07) 878-8077. Department of Conservation, Field Centre, 78 Taupiri St; tel. (07) 878-7297. Pureora Forest Park Field Centre, (20 km E of Benneydale); tel. (07) 878-4773.

TE KUITI began as a railway construction camp in 1887 and today combines the role of farming centre with that of mining (coal, limestone and serpentine), timber milling and related industries. For the visitor its importance lies in its proximity to the fabled △ Waitomo Caves.

Te Kuiti is an abbreviation of Te Kuititanga, "the narrowing in", which may be taken as a reference either to the constriction of the Mangakewa Valley at this point, or to the Maori land confiscations after the Waikato Campaigns.

Today the town styles itself the Shearing Capital. The New Zealand Shearing Championships are held in April each year during the "Te Kuiti Muster", when the town celebrates its farming heritage.

SOME HISTORY

A tense beginning: After the Battle of Orakau, fought near △ Te Awamutu in 1864, followers of the Maori King Movement (*pp.* **159-60**) fled to the safety of the Maori village of Te Kuititanga near here. King Tawhiao and his followers lived here for 17 years during which time Europeans intruded into the King Country at their peril. In 1872, after unsuccessful campaigns in the wild Urewera Country, Te Kooti joined Tawhiao at Te Kuititanga and enjoyed the King's protection until he was pardoned. European settlement could begin only once a formal peace was made in 1881.

But with the railway came further trouble. Te Mahuki Manukura (*b. 1848-?*), a local chief, emerged as a prophet who, influenced by Te Whiti, founded a new religion based on the Old Testament and turned Te Kumi (*N of the town*) into a second Parihaka (*see index*) . He preached that the Pakeha could not be forced out, but that by observance of scriptural signs and divine commands his followers would triumph. He called his sect Tekaumarua, "the twelve apostles". In 1883 Mahuki obstructed a railway survey party and spent a year in gaol after trying to take Pirongia by force. He then preached that the Maori millennium would dawn on 2 November 1890, and in anticipation his followers "occupied" Te Kuiti. The failure of this prophecy combined with his arrest and subsequent imprisonment saw his movement collapse.

TE TOKANGANUI-A-NOHO MEETING HOUSE ★★

Of considerable historical interest is the carved meeting house Te Tokanganui-a-Noho, built in 1878 by followers of Te Kooti. After use by Te Kooti, it was presented (when he was pardoned) to the local Ngati Maniapoto as a gesture of thanks for their hospitality and protection during his refuge here.

The porch carvings are particularly splendid. Among them are two fine portrayals of Marakihau, an ocean taniwha which could suck food or whole canoeloads of men and cargo through his long, tubular tongue. Marakihau is shown as a human with a fish's tail, his tongue held by a five-fingered hand. Hands in the other carvings all have three fingers and a thumb, but the significance of his having five fingers is not known.

The house's name ("the large army of stay-at-home") comes from a legend in which too small a war party sought revenge and was decimated. *The meeting house is on the main route through the town, by the railway crossing. Permission must be sought before entering.*

ENVIRONS

△ **Waitomo Caves** ★★★**:** A series of limestone caves with fantastic formations whose crowning glory is a glow-worm cavern. *19 km NW.*

Mangaokewa Scenic Reserve ★★**:** An area of native bush dominated by limestone cliffs. A popular picnic place. *4 km S, signposted off the Mangakino road.*

Pureora Forest Park: The 83,000-hectare forest contains one of the finest stands of virgin podocarp forest in the North Island, though the vegetation varies with the depth of the pumice soil distributed by the volcanic eruptions of over 2,000 years ago. The youngest forests near Lake Taupo are dominated by the podocarps—rimu, matai and totara—whereas to the west, where the pumice soils decrease, the older forests are characterised by hardwoods such as tawa.

The forest is home to the rare North Island kokako, or blue-wattled crow *(Callaeas cinerea wilsoni)*. The kokako, a little bigger than a blackbird, has dark, blue-grey plumage tinged with brown, a black face and a short, black bill. Its small wings make the bird poorly equipped for flight, and it moves in a series of bounds. Its call is similar to, but deeper than, that of the tui, and it also has a characteristic cat-like mew. *Details of walks in the forest are available from the Department of Conservation Field Centre at Pureora Forest Park, tel. (07) 878-4773; 57 km SE of Te Kuiti (20 km E of Benneydale). One walk traces the line of an old bush railway.*

TOURING NOTE

Te Kuiti-New Plymouth road *(Highway 3; 169 km)***:** For points of interest en route see △ New Plymouth-Te Kuiti Road.

Road to △ Mangakino *(Highway 30; 86 km)***:** The route passes through Benneydale *(38 km)*, a tiny country hamlet whose residents were unsettled when, in 1978, protests by conservationists sharply reduced the milling of native timbers in nearby Pureora Forest *(see above)*.

Some 12 kilometres east of the Pureora Forest Park Field Centre *(see above)*, at Pouakani, the road passes near a massive **totara**, thought to be the largest specimen in the country and between 1,750 and 1,850 years old.

TE KUITI-NEW PLYMOUTH ROAD

See △ New Plymouth-Te Kuiti Rd.

Bay of Plenty   Maps 5, 8   Pop. 5,960   TE PUKE

31 km SE of Tauranga. Information Centre, 72 Jellicoe St; tel. (07) 573-9172.

TE PUKE, like △ Katikati, began as a settlement of Ulstermen organised by George Vesey Stewart (1842-1920). Although Te Puke was a more successful venture than Katikati, it was not until the soil's cobalt deficiency was diagnosed in the late 1930s that Stewart's catchcry of "Tickle the soil with a hoe and it will laugh a harvest" came true.

Today Te Puke is a flourishing fruitgrowing and dairying centre, exporting huge quantities of kiwifruit and earning the sobriquet "Kiwifruit Capital of the World". An annual Kiwifruit Harvest Festival (*May*) coincides with the picking season. A quarter of the country's citrus fruit is also grown here. Te Puke means "the hill".

Tribute to a chieftainess: A granite archway dating from 1920 marks the entrance to Jubilee Park. Now on its third site, it recalls Hera Mita, a high-born local chieftainess who worked strenuously to raise funds for the 1914-18 War effort. Such was her enthusiasm that, although ill with the influenza then sweeping the country, she left her sickbed to attend a major fund-raising carnival ball, but died the following day. *By carpark fronting Commerce Lane.*

KIWIFRUIT

In the 1960s the fuzzy kiwifruit was at the forefront of the country's boom in horticulture, which led to land being turned into small, intensively farmed units. Until its name was changed to assist with export promotion the fruit, *Actinidia chinesis*, was known as the "Chinese gooseberry", reflecting its origins in the Yangtse Valley in China. Vines exported from the Bay of Plenty have assisted the establishment of orchards in many parts of the world, including California, the Mediterranean, Japan and Kenya. The vines, which take about five years to reach maturity, are costly to establish as they require sturdy trellises to bear their weight.

The fruit, harvested in the autumn, is a valuable source of vitamin C, containing in one single fruit more than one's daily requirement. Low in calories, the fruit is also a source of proleolytic acid, which serves to remove cholesterol. Its unusual green and succulent flesh is sought after, for its flavour and its decorative qualities. *Farm and orchard tours can be arranged through the Visitor Information Centre.*

ENVIRONS

Mount Otanewainuku (640 metres)**:** A looped track climbs through unspoilt native bush to reach the summit, the highest point between Tauranga and Rotorua *(1½ hrs return)*. A short loop walk leads through rimu trees *(20 mins)*.

△ **Maketu:** Final resting place of the *Arawa* canoe and for generations an Arawa stronghold. *(16 km NE.)* Nearby **Pukehina**, a beach settlement on a long sand spit, has the advantages of both surf and sheltered inner harbour beaches. *(21 km NE.)*

Kiwifruit Country ★★: Every aspect of the country's best known fruit, from vine to packing case, and ancillary products, is displayed at an extensive export orchard. *6 km E on S.H.2 Tel. (07) 573-6340.*

Longridge Park ★★: Kiwifruit, native bush, a variety of animals and unforgettable jet-boat rides and rafting trips on the Kaituna River, await the visitor. *17 km SE on S.H.33. Tel. (07) 533-1515.*

★ THAMES

Coromandel Peninsula   Map 5   Pop. 6,456

119 km SE of Auckland. Visitor Information Centre, 405 Queen St; tel/fax (07) 868-7284. DOC Field Centre, Kauaeranga Valley; tel. (07) 868-6381.

THAMES, at the foot of the Coromandel Range, looks out across the Firth of Thames as it broods on the fantastic gold-rush days it once knew and contemplates the portents of proposed new mining ventures in its rugged hills.

The principal town on the peninsula, Thames is a blend of old and new as it busies itself with servicing surrounding farmland and an increasing population around the coast. Among its industries are those which owe their origins to foundries established well over a century ago to serve the gold mines. There are vineyards just south of the town, where local wines may be sampled.

The town is a base from which to explore the peninsula and has many intriguing gold-mining relics, not easily found without the aid of local knowledge.

SOME HISTORY

Captain Cook's visit: When Captain Cook called here in 1769 he wrote: "We saw a number of natives and landed at one of their Villages the Inhabitants of which received us with open arms." He took a longboat up the Waihou River where he was most impressed by the splendid kahikatea (white pine) for which the district was later renowned but which was cut out by sawmillers in the first two decades of this century for use as butter boxes.

It was Cook who gave Thames its name, albeit indirectly. Originally Cook named the Waihou River "Thames", "on account of it bearing some resemblence to that river in england". Today that resemblance seems most unlikely, but a combination of impressions contributed to Cook's name. The Thames in its lower reaches had tidal mud banks and here "the tide of flood runs as strong as it doth in the River Thams below bridge".

Having sailed on, Cook pondered: "Should it ever become an object of settleing [sic] this country the best place for the first fixing of a Colony would be either in the River Thames or the Bay of Islands." *Cook's landing, on 21 November 1769, is commemorated by a simple stone cairn at Kopu (6.5 km S) and by a stone cairn and anchor at Netherton, near his actual landing place (25 km).*

Gold: Gold was found at Coromandel in 1852 but it was not until after the Waikato Campaigns had ended 11 years later that delicate negotiations with local Maori (who had fought against the Government) opened the way for prospecting in the Thames area. A number of miners staked out claims and on 10 August 1867 came the discovery of the fabulous "Shotover" on the Kuranui Stream. The find electrified the world and the stampede to the Thames area began.

Within a year a town of 18,000 had sprung up—half as large again as Auckland, then suffering from the post-war withdrawal of Imperial troops and the transfer of the capital to Wellington. To Auckland, the gold rush and the commerce it generated came as a godsend.

Amazing finds came quickly—the Golden Crown, the Manukau, the Caledonian. The last in a single year yielded over 361,000 ounces of a then-value of nearly £1 million. Alluvial gold was scarce and 1868-69 saw the expense of working quartz claims force most of the small bands of miners to give way to larger companies, many backed by Auckland financiers. Mining companies paid enormous dividends and the trading in gold shares both in the Auckland Stock Exchange and on Thames's "Scrip Corner" (*Albert and Brown Sts*) was so furious that shares were subdivided into half and then into quarter units.

At its peak in 1871, when gold worth £1.19 million was produced, over 70 mines were operating and both by day and by night the 693 stamps in 40 batteries smashed the quartz to powder, their rhythmic thumping a constant background to life in the town. Visitors could not sleep for the noise, residents could not sleep without it. But output declined steadily and by 1924 it had all but ceased.

Today some residents have their "claims", although most are worked only sufficiently to enable them to be renewed or simply as a hobby, but the universal assumption is that there is still gold to be won.

Two towns: Thames actually comprised two separate settlements, "Shortland", which had port facilities on the Waihou, and "Grahamstown" farther north. In 1873 the two towns merged and became known as Thames, the name Cook had originally given to the Waihou River.

For years the town was virtually inaccessible by land. Ships traded across the gulf from Auckland and up the Waihou, and it was not until the 1880s that land problems with neighbouring Maori were overcome and a road for wheeled traffic opened to Te Aroha. About the time of World War I, the decline in gold production saw Thames's role change from a gold town to a market centre for surrounding farmland. In the 1920s the vast Hauraki Plains drainage scheme was completed and the town's future assured.

GOLD-MINING RELICS

Thames Mineralogical Museum and School of Mines★: In the Museum and the adjacent School of Mines, where mine managers were trained from 1885 to 1954, one may inspect the specialised and extensive collection of over 5,000 mineral samples, from both local and overseas sources. There is also a collection of historic photographs. *Cnr Cochrane and Brown Sts. Open daily, Oct–April, 11 a.m.–4 p.m; May–Sept, 11 a.m–3 p.m.; closed Mon. Details of conducted tours over the School of Mines section, from the Information Centre.*

Thames Historical Museum: The collection portrays the history of the district. *Pollen St. Open daily; 1 p.m.–4 p.m.*

Goldmine and stamper battery: Guided tours are conducted over the old Golden Crown mine and of an operational stamper battery. *Check opening hours with Information Centre.*

Queen of Beauty Pump: The deeper the mineshafts went, the greater the problem of flooding became. A pumping association was formed to provide common drainage and in 1898 an overseas concern built a huge pump in the old Queen of Beauty mineshaft. The first few metres of the shaft (the remainder now filled in for safety) can be seen along with the remains of the pump, which once raised 13,600 litres of water per minute from a depth of 305 metres and was the largest in the hemisphere. For a time the pump drained the area but eventually the deeper levels flooded and water slowly forced the closure of the whole goldfield. A pair of mine cages, used to lower men down the shafts, is nearby. *Behind the Power House, once the pump's engine-house. Cnr Bella and Campbell Sts.*

OTHER POINTS OF INTEREST

Totara Pa Cemetery ★: From here one obtains outstanding views of the town, the coast and the Firth of Thames. The cemetery is on the site of the old Totara pa, a Ngati Maru stronghold which fell in 1821 to Hongi Hika (*p. 122*) and his invading Ngapuhi from Northland. Hundreds of defenders were killed or taken prisoner.

It is said that for three days Hongi launched a series of unsuccessful frontal assaults on the pa. He then feigned peace as a kohuru (act of treachery), and withdrew. As the unsuspecting Ngati Maru prematurely celebrated his withdrawal, Hongi returned by night to surprise and overwhelm them. Some of the earthworks remain, behind the Historic Places Trust Board. *Turnoff signposted 2.5 km S.*

World War I Memorial: A good view of the town is obtained from here. To the west is a reclaimed area originally started with tailings from the mineshafts. *Signposted to the N of the town. Waiotahi Creek Rd.*

Karaka Bird Hide: A board walk leads through mangroves to a suitable view of the Firth of Thames. *Brown St.*

Jet boating on the Waihou River: Trips with an informative commentary are run up the river to the Historical Maritime Park near △ Paeroa, where venerable small ships are restored. *Hauraki Jet Tours; tel. (07) 868-9459.*

ENVIRONS

Kauaeranga Valley: The well-bushed and rugged valley affords a welter of river swimming holes, bush walks and tramps, as well as sources of gemstones and good trout fishing. The valley was a major source of timber up to about 1929, and there are many remains of dams, trestle bridges and river booms used by the timber-workers to flush the logs down tributaries and into the main Kauaeranga River. A Department of Conservation office *(at 13 km E)* exhibits old photographs and the early history of kauri logging, and has details of walks and tramps into the exceptionally rugged hinterland. The road continues a further 10 km beyond. *Turn inland on the southern exit from town. Bank St. There are camp sites in the valley.*

Miranda Wildlife Reserve ★ ★: By the edge of the Hauraki Plains on the Firth of Thames, rich mudflats draw a diversity of birds, many of which winter over or live here permanently. *The Miranda Naturalists Trust Visitor Centre offers information and can arrange accommodation (Kaiaua–Miranda Rd; tel. (09) 232-2781).*

Close by are **Miranda Hot Springs,** a large thermal pool complex, complete with sauna and picnic area *(open daily, 10 a.m.–9 p.m.; tel. (07) 867-3055).*
At Miranda 30.5 km W.

TIRAU   *Waikato   Map 8   Pop. 679*

55 km SE of Hamilton; 54 km NW of Rotorua.

TIRAU, a small farming centre, stands on a major road junction. Its name means "many cabbage trees". Travellers often browse in its several antique shops.

OKOROIRE HOT SPRINGS ★

In a delightful setting, shaded by plane trees, stands the Okoroire Hot Springs Hotel. The nearby Waihou River and a small golf course supplement the appeal of the hot springs, whose mineral waters contain predominantly sodium chloride, although their most noticeable ingredient is sodium silicate. *The hot springs are a series of private pools. Open daily; tel. (07) 883-4876. Signposted 6.5 km NE of Tirau.* Adjacent is an excellent 9-hole golf course.

Tui Apiaries and Museum: The honey shop here is irresistible. *4 km. Highway 5 to Rotorua. Open daily.*

TOKAANU ★   *Volcanic Plateau   Map 8 Pop. 128*

5 km W of Turangi; 58 km SW of Taupo township.

THE VENERABLE VILLAGE of Tokaanu, caught between the volcanoes of the △ Tongariro National Park and the trout-filled waters of △ Lake Taupo, contrasts with the modernity of neighbouring △ Turangi.

The village has a varied history. At one stage Te Kooti had his headquarters here; later it served as an Armed Constabulary post, and later still as a lakeside port, when steamers ran the length of the lake to link Tokaanu with Taupo township.

Above the settlement can be seen the four huge penstocks installed to feed the generators of the Tokaanu Power Station (1974), an integral part of the Tongariro hydro-electric power scheme.

Tokaanu means "a cold stone".

POINTS OF INTEREST

St Paul's Anglican Church: Decorated with tukutuku (woven panels) and rafter patterns, St Paul's is a memorial to the Rev. Thomas Samuel Grace (1815-79) and his wife Agnes, Church Missionary Society missionaries who in 1855 became the first Pakeha to live in the Taupo area.

The shattered bell in the porch was a gift to the Rev. Thomas Grace from the women of a Scottish parish and was first hung at Pukawa (*on Lake Taupo just N of Waihi*) "to welcome, with its sound, the poor savage to the house of God". The bell was cracked by over-enthusiastic parishioners anxious that settlements across the lake might hear it, and then broken when a group of Hauhau unsuccessfully tried to convert it into bullets.

A bronze plaque in the church commemorates the Maori martyrs Manihera and Kereopa, two Christian converts sent to the Taupo area from Wanganui by the Rev. Richard Taylor. The converts were chiefs of a Taranaki tribe, Ngati Ruanui, which a few years earlier had inflicted a humiliating defeat on the Tuwharetoa when that Taupo tribe had attacked them. Tuwharetoa took revenge by killing the two Ngati Ruanui missionaries, near Tokaanu, on 12 March 1847. The martyrs' remains were reburied in the churchyard after they were found in the path of the Tokaanu power station's tailrace tunnel. The Kereopa buried here should not be confused with the Hauhau prophet of the same name who was involved in the martyrdom of the Rev. Carl Volkner at Opotiki (*pp.* **165-66**).

The small church vestry takes the form of a separate, whare-style building. Nearby is the **Catholic Church of St Mary,** also decorated with tukutuku, beside the Puhaorangi meeting house (1931).

Tokaanu Thermal Pools ★: The area includes boiling mudpools, silica formations and hot springs of varying colours. An unspoiled spot where mud belches from the least expected places. There is a 20-minute loop track. Adjacent are the relaxing natural mineral pools, for generations recognised by the local Ngati Tuwharetoa people for their therapeutic qualities. *Mangaroa St. Administered by the Department of Conservation; tel. (07) 386-8575. Open daily, 10 a.m.–9 p.m.; private pools available.*

Tokaanu Power Station: Tours over the hydro-electric power station are run from the ECNZ visitor centre, where there are informative displays and models. The station here is part of the ingenious Tongariro Hydro-electric Power scheme conceived in the 1970s. *Described under △ Turangi. The centre (signposted off Highway 47) is open Monday to Saturday, 10 a.m.–4 p.m.; tel. (07) 386-8615.*

Mt Maunganamu: A curious solitary hill, Maunganamu is locally regarded as being the "child" of nearby Mt Pihanga. Its name means "sandfly mountain". *The 30-min walk to the summit gives a panorama of the lake.*

ENVIRONS

△ **Waihi *:** A picturesque lakeside hamlet. *3 km.*

Waikato   Map 8   Pop. 16,636   **TOKOROA**

61 km SW of Rotorua; 67 km N of Taupo. Visitor Information Centre, Highway 1; tel. (07) 886-8872.

TOKOROA exploded to its present size from little more than a hamlet in two decades with the establishment of a timber utilisation industry at Kinleith. Like other company settlements, such as △ Kawerau, it has enjoyed the advantages of detailed town planning.

    The meaning of Tokoroa is obscure, but it may refer to a chief who was killed during a siege of Mt Pohaturoa (*p. 41*), 27 kilometres to the south.

KINLEITH PULP AND PAPER MILL

New Zealand's largest pulp and paper mill complex, now employing about 1,000 people, was designed in 1953 by NZ Forest Products Ltd as an integrated forest–factory industry. Wood for the mill here is drawn from the company's surrounding 64,000 hectares of forest. (NZFP Forest Ltd, with some 146,000 hectares in the central North Island, is the largest private forest owner in the country.) A wide range of pulp and packaging papers are manufactured on the site, the mill producing 200,000 tonnes of market pulp and 235,000 tonnes of kraft paper per annum. A large proportion of these products is exported to Asian markets A substantial proportion of the plant's energy requirements are generated within the process and by the burning of wood waste; *6.5 km S of Tokoroa. The mill is not open to the general public.*

★★★ **TOLAGA BAY**

East Cape   Map 10   Pop. 462

55.5 km N of Gisborne.

"THE COUNTRY is agreeable beyond description, and, with proper cultivation, might be rendered a kind of second Paradise." So wrote Sydney Parkinson, an official artist on Cook's first voyage when the *Endeavour* called here in 1769, and his prediction has been fulfilled. An excellent swimming beach, lent distinction by a very long jetty, is the scene of occasional race meetings. Trout and sea fishing, an intriguing walk to Cooks Cove and an English-style pub give the bay a singular charm. The town, by the mouth of the Uawa River, is a small sheep-farming centre set in fertile river flats which include vineyards and kiwifruit orchards.

    The name Tolaga is a corruption thought to be the result of misunderstanding. The Maori at Anaura Bay either told Captain Cook that the bay was a turanga (landing place) or else misunderstood him as asking the direction the wind was blowing, and replied "Teraki" ("north-east"). Cook took the bay's name to be Tolaga, a name most Maori of the time could not even pronounce.

COOKS COVE ★★★

Tolaga Bay was the third bay Captain Cook visited on his first voyage to New Zealand. From Gisborne he had gone to Anaura Bay (*north*) and was directed back to Tolaga Bay, as it was a more suitable place to take on water. During a six-day stay, wood, water and wild celery were collected from Cooks Cove, and brooms made from manuka. Cook found the local Maori "not only very friendly but ready to traffic with us for what little they had". Cook's naturalists collected many specimens to take back for study in England and the ti or "cabbage tree" was renamed here, as Cook found the taste of its leaves when boiled resembled that vegetable. The islands in the mouth of the cove he described as "two high rocks; one is high and round like a corn stack, but the other is long with holes through it like the arches of a bridge''. The description is still valid. The "Hole in the Wall" at the Cove (*to the left as one approaches*) fascinated Cook's naturalist, Banks, who praised it as "certainly the most magnificent surprise I have ever met with. So much is pure nature superior to art in these cases!" Fifty-six years later the early trader-turned-author Joel Polack noticed rock drawings of canoes, men, women, dogs, pigs and "some obscenities drawn with tolerable accuracy" inside the arch. But by 1878 these had worn away and disappeared

Cooks Cove,
Tolaga Bay.

without trace, as had the well from which Cook drew his water. *The cove is on private property immediately S of the bay but is reached along the Cooks Cove Walkway, an easy 5-km return trip of about 2 ½ hrs. Take the Wharf Rd turnoff from the highway, 2 km S of Tolaga Bay township, and park opposite entrance to walkway. The track is closed for the lambing season each year, from 1 August to 30 September.*

TONGARIRO NATIONAL PARK ★★★

Volcanic Plateau   Maps 6, 8   75,227 hectares

Auckland to Whakapapa Village 345 km; Wellington to Whakapapa Village 341 km; Turangi to Whakapapa Village 48 km. Department of Conservation Visitor Centre, Whakapapa Field Centre, Mount Ruapehu (tel. (07) 892-3729); Ohakune Field Centre, Ohakune Mountain Rd (tel. (06) 385-8578); Turangi Field Centre, Turangi Place, Turangi (tel. (07) 386-8607).

IN A COUNTRY of contrasts, perhaps nothing is more striking than the peaks of the Tongariro National Park rising starkly from a surrounding plateau of tussock and near-desert. Yet viewed from the south-west, the aspect is that of another range, for snow and ice contrast with dense forest and fern. The area well merits its recognition by UNESCO, who in 1991 accorded it World Heritage status.

Smouldering Ngauruhoe (*2,291 m*) periodically belches steam and gas into the sky but, unlike Ruapehu, since 1975 has been relatively subdued. In winter the volcano is a combination of steam and snow, a paradox rare in temperate climes.

Neighbouring Ruapehu (*2,797 m*) perpetually snow-capped and the North Island's highest peak, also provides its principal skiing grounds. Yet the mountain's apparent tranquillity is misleading, for Ruapehu, too, is an active volcano and is presently in eruption.

Tongariro (*1,968 m*), northernmost of the three volcanoes, its truncated peaks a maze of craters, is the lowest of the three yet has given its name to the park.

As a National Park the area offers more than winter sport and exhilarating scenery. A variety of walks and tramps pass through constantly changing surroundings, and a challenge to experienced climbers is the conquest of all three main peaks in a single day. Activities within the park centre on the Chateau Tongariro (known simply as "the Chateau") at Whakapapa Village, close to the Park Visitor Centre and one of Ruapehu's principal skiing grounds. (The North Island's lowest officially-recorded temperature was registered here in 1937, with -13.6°.)

The park has a splendid network of tracks and huts for use by trampers at nominal cost. The ranger stations keep books in which trampers' intentions are recorded as a safety precaution.

SOME GEOLOGY

The volcanoes of Tongariro National Park lie at the extremity of a volcanic chain which extends through White Island and the Kermadecs to the islands of Tonga, 1,900 kilometres to the north-east.

In geological terms the volcanoes are of recent origin, dating back about two million years. During the last Ice Age these volcanic heaps of scoria and lava would have reached their greatest heights, and have been modified subsequently by erosion and eruption. At this time, too, glaciers extended down Ruapehu to about 1,220 metres.

Ruapehu has erupted many times over the past few thousand years, both from its summit and from a cone 1,525 metres up its northern slopes, its present series of eruptions dating from September 1995. Previously the most recent major eruptions were in 1945 (when fine ash fell as far away as Wellington), in 1969, 1971, 1974 and 1975. An "early warning" system has been installed.

Tongariro is somewhat more complex and contains a maze of craters, some mildly active. On its slopes, at Ketetahi, are furious hot springs, fumeroles and boiling mudpools, whose drifting steam may be seen many kilometres away.

The country's most continuously active volcano, Ngauruhoe, as recently as 1954 began a series of ash explosions which culminated in a massive eruption of lava pouring down its western face to build up in the saddle between the volcano and Pukekaikore. All the while, molten lava was hurled more than 300 metres into the air, and by the time the fury had subsided the volcano's silhouette had been altered drastically, with about 3.8 million cubic metres of fresh lava deposited on its slopes.

SOME MYTHS AND LEGENDS

This wild, at times desolate, region has predictably given rise to a number of Maori myths and legends. The tales recounted here served as oral maps of much of central North Island.

Battle of the Mountains: In mythological times, when mountains lived and loved, many mountains dwelt in the centre of the North Island—Taranaki (Mt Egmont), Tauhara and Putauaki (Mt Edgecumbe) among them. Alas, all the mountains here were male, with the exception of lovely Pihanga, whose bush-robed slopes sweep gently above Turangi. All loved Pihanga, and each wanted her for his wife. But Pihanga loved only Tongariro, who in battle defeated the other suitors, leaving them no choice but to cry their farewells and depart.

Taranaki went west, carving out the course of the Whanganui River as he went, and came to rest near New Plymouth, where he became the sacred peak of the Taranaki tribes. Putauaki chose to travel to the warm Bay of Plenty, and reached Kawerau where he became the Ngati Awa's sacred mountain and is now called Mt Edgecumbe. But the tardy Tauhara moved with reluctance, continually pausing to gaze back at lovely Pihanga, and when dawn came — ending the hours of darkness, the only time when mountains and fairies could move — he had reached only the north-eastern shore of Lake Taupo where he still stands today. Tauhara means "the lonely mountain" (but this has come to be translated as "the lonely lover").

The Taranaki tribes dispute the version of the myth given here and have their own (*see △ Egmont National Park*).

The coming of fire: In legend, Ngatoroirangi (navigator and tohunga of the *Arawa* canoe and forebear of both the Tuwharetoa tribe of Lake Taupo and the Arawa of Rotorua) journeyed inland from the Bay of Plenty to claim the land in the centre of the island. On seeing the mountain of Tongariro he decided to kindle a fire on its peak and so make plain his claim to the surrounding land. After declaring the mountain tapu and bidding his followers to fast until his return, he began his climb, taking with him his female slave, Auruhoe.

His followers, however, broke the fast and the mountain gods in their anger sent snow and blizzards so that Ngatoroirangi all but perished. He prayed to his gods in far-off "Hawaiki" to send fire to warm him, and to lend strength to his plea

Ngatoroirangi sacrificed the hapless Auruhoe. The gods heard him and sent fire underground, which burst to the surface at Whakaari (White Island), Rotorua, Tarawera, Paeroa, Orakei Korako and Taupo. Finally it blazed forth from the craters of Ngauruhoe and Tongariro, in time to revive the frozen climber. His strength regained, Ngatoroirangi, as a gesture of gratitude, hurled the body of Auruhoe into the freshly kindled crater of the volcano now named after her—"Ngauruhoe" (but called simply "Auruhoe" by the Maori of South Taupo until comparatively recent times).

For a long time the peaks were collectively known as "Tongariro" ("carried away on the south wind"), as the wind had carried Ngatoroirangi's prayers north to his tropical "Hawaiki". In time the name has come to refer only to a section of the chain, Ngauruhoe being named for the unfortunate slave and Ruapehu ("exploding crater") for its volcanic activity.

EARLY CLIMBS

Many of the would-be early climbers were turned back by local Maori to whom the peaks were tapu. The first recorded ascent of Ngauruhoe was made in 1839 by the botanist-explorer John Carne Bidwill (1815-53), whose brother Charles pioneered the Wairarapa sheep country a short time later. The volcano was then active, and Bidwill returned to encounter a displeased Te Heuheu Tukino II (Mananui) and it was 12 years before the second ascent was made.

Sir George Grey claimed to have scaled Ruapehu in 1853, but it seems that he climbed not the main peak but Te Heuheu Ridge, and it was left for George Beetham and J. P. Maxwell to be the first to see the crater lake, as late as 1879.

BOTANICAL FEATURES

Within the park are more than 500 different species of native plants, among them 12 types of native conifer, 36 varieties of orchid, and more than 60 species of fern. The most widespread tree is the hardy mountain beech. Red beech is found on Tongariro's north-eastern slopes, and stands of rimu are found near Erua and Ohakune. These rimu are magnificent trees of up to 30 metres high and well over 600 years old. South of the Ohakune Mountain Road, below 915 metres, are towering red and silver beech, frequented by parakeets, robins and kaka.

Below 1,220 metres are areas of native inaka scrubland (*Dracophyllum subulatum*) which give a heath-like appearance to the red tussock grasslands. Through the summer months there are flowers to be seen—ourisia in December and January, then gentian and mountain daisies in February and March. Even in winter, creeping coprosmas with red fruit, and creeping mapou with deep mauve fruit, dash the grasslands with colour.

The alpine gravelfields above 1,370 metres are scattered with plants such as the mountain inaka, the white- or mauve-flowered parahebes, two species of mountain buttercup, the everlasting daisy and the mountain anisotome.

Alien plants have made their way into the park, as early management tended to be haphazard and directionless. One plan was to introduce grouse and partridge for game shooters, and to that end large areas of heather and heath were established. Both are now widespread in northern and western areas of the park up to 1,220 metres yet may in the long term be eliminated as their growth is retarded by surrounding native plants.

Another alien plant, one which could change the whole character of the park, is *Pinus contorta*, a menace whose windblown seed has become established within the park and threatened to convert its open spaces into a continuous pine forest. A systematic eradication programme is now under way.

A NATIONAL PARK

For many generations the peaks of the park were sacred mountains of the Lake Taupo tribe of Tuwharetoa, who buried their chiefs in caves on the mountainsides and to whom the slopes were strictly tapu. In 1887 the tribe gave the mountaintops to the Government "for the purposes of a National Park" — the country's first, created only 15 years after the world's first had been established at Yellowstone, USA. Today, Tongariro National Park has the added distinction of being listed as a World Heritage site. Initially the land within a radius of a mile (1.6 km) from the volcanic peaks — an area of 2,600 hectares — was gifted by deed (*a facsimile is displayed in the Whakapapa Visitor Centre*). Later the Government added further areas, expanding the park to its present size.

Once the North Island Main Trunk rail route was completed in 1908, more visitors were attracted to the area, and in 1919 the decision was taken to develop the western slopes of Ruapehu as a winter sports resort. With relief workers, prison labour and a bequest from a conservation-minded Scot, R.C. Bruce, the "Bruce Road" (Highway 48) was formed. This now ends at the Iwikau Mountain Village, at the "Top o' the Bruce", where a host of ski clubs have their lodges. Below, at Whakapapa Village, is the Grand Chateau (a first-class hotel), Skotel, motor camp, restaurant, golf course, tennis courts and bowling greens.

Inevitably development has brought modification within the park, but certain parts are designated "wilderness areas" and are unaffected but for some slight tracking. These include the Hauhungatahi Wilderness Area (8,400 ha.) on Ruapehu's western slopes, and the Te Tatau-Pounamu Wilderness Area (6,400 ha.) to the north of Tongariro.

Whakapapa Visitor Centre: A short distance from the Grand Chateau is the Visitor Centre for the Park, with a memorial to Te Heuheu Tukino IV (Horonuku), the donor of the nucleus of the Park. Displayed is a bust of Horonuku, a facsimile of the deed of 1887 which created the Park, and exhibits of the Park's geology, flora and fauna. A **skiing museum** portrays the history of skiing on the mountain from early in the century and an audio-visual presentation highlights points of interest in the Park. A seismograph keeps a permanent record of Ruapehu's volcanic activity. Over the Christmas holiday period, a special programme of guided walks and nature talks is arranged.

Information on all aspects of the park, including maps and pamphlets giving details of a number of walks, is available. Hunting permits are also available. Red deer have been joined by Japanese sika deer, which have made their way into the park from the Kaimanawa Ranges to the east. *Whakapapa Village, behind the Chateau.*

Beyond, the road winds up to 1,622 metres to the varied collection of ski-club lodges which comprise Iwikau Mountain Village. The lodges are available only for members and their guests. The only other accommodation inside the park is at the Grand Chateau, the Ruapehu Skotel, and the motor camp. There is a ranger station on the Ohakune Mountain Road where information and advice are also available.

The Grand Chateau: At 1,127 metres, this is a deluxe hotel which offers first class accommodation within the confines of the park. In summer, those still in need of exercise after tackling the many delightful walks in the area may choose between tennis, golf and bowls. *Whakapapa. At the end of Highway 48.*

SKIING ON RUAPEHU

Despite the park's varied appeal at all times of year, skiing continues to draw the majority of visitors. Although the Grand Chateau dates from 1929, Whakapapa Skifield was first developed commercially only in the 1950s. It now has the largest commercial ski area in New Zealand with a range of modern lifts to suit every skiing ability. Many clubs have lodges for their members on the mountain, at Iwikau Village and, away from the mountain, at △ Ohakune.

Away from the Chateau on Ruapehu's south-western slopes is the more recently developed Turoa Skifield which has chairlifts, T-bar lifts and a range of facilities for beginners. This skifield is reached by Ohakune Mountain Road, a magnificent scenic drive. A club skifield with rope tows is found at Tukino on the upper eastern slopes of Ruapehu (approached by four-wheel-drive vehicles from the Desert Road).

In general, the skiing season extends from June to October. All equipment may be hired at △ Ohakune, the Whakapapa or Turoa Skifields and National Park township.

SOME SHORT WALKS

Listed below are some of the shorter walks, generally in the vicinity of Whakapapa Village, but fuller details and explanatory leaflets on these, and others, are available at the Visitor Centre. Note: The weather can change rapidly on the mountain, so adequate clothing should always be taken. Mist, too, can move swiftly down the slopes, so prudence should prevail whenever it is seen approaching.

Whakapapa Nature Walk: About 1.5 kilometres of tracks lead through an area cultivated with a variety of native plants that can be grown at 945 metres. *Start 300 m above the Whakapapa Visitor Centre.*

Ridge Track: A gently graded track leading through bush to scrub and open countryside to afford views over Whakapapa Village and farmlands to the west. *Start 100 m up from the Visitor Centre. Allow 30 mins.*

Mounds Walk: A short interpretative walk with interesting views leads through mounds created by volcanic activity. *Start below the Visitor Centre. 20 mins return.*

Tawhai Falls: The short walk in to Tawhai Falls is of interest in itself but heightened by the tale of the "haunted whare". By the road, near the start of the track, a whare had been built in 1880 for use by shepherds. It was then a desolate spot where, according to tradition, a Maori woman had once been murdered. Shortly after the hut had been completed a Maori shepherd occupant, too, was found inexplicably slain. The whare was burned to the ground and another (since demolished) built nearby. But even then a supernatural presence persisted, and several people in the hut claimed to have seen the ghost of a young Maori woman staring in at them through the windows. *Signposted 3 km below the Grand Chateau on Highway 48. 10-min walk.*

Taranaki Falls: A circular walk of some 6.5 km through tussock and mountain beech. The falls are passed at mid-way point, where a stream spills 25 metres down an old lava flow. *Start from the road immediately below the Visitor Centre. Allow 2 hrs.*

Silica Rapids: A round trip of about 7 kilometres through beech and fern forest leads to the creamy-white terraces of the Silica Rapids. In contrast is a creek bed browned with iron oxide. Farther on, the track follows a swiftly flowing stream which, as the Punaruku Falls, tumbles over the edge of an old lava flow. *Start from the motorcamp in Whakapapa Village. The track eventually joins the Bruce Rd, which forms the return leg. Allow 2½ hrs.*

Whakapapanui Track: Because the track parallels the road down from the Chateau, those with little time to spare may take the walk on leaving the area and be collected by their driver some 3 kilometres along Highway 48. The track leads through dense bush with occasional clearings frequented by almost tail-less riflemen, New Zealand's smallest bird. The Golden Rapids are passed where stream waters have coated rocks with golden iron oxide derived from volcanic ash. *Start at the motorcamp. Allow 2 hrs (return) for the 6-km trip.*

OTHER WALKS AND TRAMPS

Ketetahi Hot Springs: The track leads uphill through bush, then across tussock and sub-alpine scrub to reach the fumeroles, boiling springs and multi-coloured scoria of a fascinating thermal valley. *It is essential to keep to the track and to exercise care. Should steam obscure the track, wait until it clears before moving.* This comparatively small area, completely surrounded by the park, is still in Maori ownership. Although Tongariro was considered most tapu, these springs were used in the past for their curative properties and today a bathe in the warm stream below the thermal area makes a pleasant break. *The start is signposted on Highway 47A, 6.5 km E of the junction with the Pihanga Saddle route to Turangi. Allow 5 hrs.*

Tama Lakes: On the saddle between Mts Ruapehu and Ngauruhoe are two lakes with sandy shores where, in summer, it is possible to swim. *The track starts below the Whakapapa Visitor Centre. 6 hrs return.*

Round the Mountain Track: Several days may be spent in the wilderness walking a complete circuit of all three mountains. Huts are basic and a degree of fitness is necessary. A detour may be made to the summit of Mt Ngauruhoe.

Tongariro Crossing: One of the most exhilarating day walks in the country starts at the end of Mangatepopo Rd and climbs up the valley to make its way over the saddle between Mts Ngauruhoe and Tongariro. The volcanic landscape of craters, steaming valleys, lakes and hot springs leaves a haunting memory and is in stark contrast with the green forest into which the track descends on the northern side of Tongariro. *7 to 8 hrs. Best walked from the Mangatepopo Rd end (off Highway 47). The track links in with the Ketetahi Hot Springs Track (see above), and ends at Highway 47A. Before setting out it is advisable to arrange pick up transport through the Visitor Centre. Sections of the route are poled, and in winter the inexperienced should not attempt the crossing without a guide.*

Ruapehu Crater Lake: The lake's waters, surrounded by ice and snow, are strongly acid and are warmed from beneath by volcanic steam. Sulphur occasionally forms a yellowish scum on the surface.

The temperature of the Crater Later has varied enormously over the years. Twice it has frozen over (in 1886 and 1926), and at various times its waters have chilled sufficiently to allow bathing in the most unusual of settings. (A publicity picture once depicted bikini-clad teenagers by the lakeside, their skis standing upright in the snow!) At present the usual temperature is between 20° and 40°C and as the waters now have a pH of about 1.0 and are akin to battery acid, swimming is definitely not recommended. In more belligerent mood, the lake has boiled, thrown mud and rock down the mountainside, and even disgorged its entire contents to earn from James Cowan the description of "intermittent geyser".

The lake's outlet is through a tunnel in the ice to the foot of the Whangaehu Glacier. Occasionally the lake's level has dropped rapidly to transform the innocent Whangaehu River into a raging torrent. It was one such occasion that caused the country's worst rail disaster, at Tangiwai in 1953 (*see △ Waiouru*). *The return climb can be made in a day by the relatively fit. Proper equipment, clothing and footwear is essential. Details from the Visitor Centre. The route is unmarked.*

OTHER POINTS OF INTEREST

Te Porere Pa site ★★: Just beyond the park boundary is the tussock fort where, in 1869, Te Kooti was defeated in the last major engagement of the Land Wars.

Te Kooti (*c.* 1830-93; *p.* **85**), a one-time Government soldier, was imprisoned on suspicion of treachery, but escaped to spearhead a remarkable guerrilla campaign against his former masters. After a series of surprise raids from his Urewera retreat, Te Kooti moved his headquarters to Tokaanu (on Lake Taupo), where he had won the reluctant support of Te Heuheu Tukino IV (Horonuku) and most Tuwharetoa. He then constructed this fort at Te Porere, designed to counter Pakeha firearms. Trenches, parapets, flanking angles and loopholes were all incorporated in this "gunfighters" pa; the outpost below seems to have been designed with at least one eye on an escape route up the valley behind.

Here, on 4 October 1869, about 300 of Te Kooti's followers were attacked by a force of 500 under Col. Thomas McDonnell, which included Maori from Wanganui under their chief, "Major Kemp", and the Hawke's Bay tribe of Ngati Kahungunu, traditional enemies of Tuwharetoa. His men outnumbered by two to one, Te Kooti hoisted two flags of obscure symbolism, each white with a half-moon, a cross and the letters "W.J." But undeterred, Government troops rushed the fort from three sides to overwhelm the defenders, some of whom barely managed to escape, Te Kooti and Horonuku among them.

Te Kooti's artistry lay in his bushcraft, and his inexperience in a "set piece" such as that at Te Porere has led historians to question his reasons for experimenting with such tactics—the more so as his strategy in other situations had been, and continued to be, outstandingly successful. Indeed it was noted that only the women, who usually did not take part in raids, "fought like furies and refused to run away".

The bush into which Te Kooti and Horonuku made good their escape lies to the north-west. In the engagement the Government lost four killed and as many wounded, and Te Kooti lost at least 37 dead (buried inside the fort). Te Kooti was himself wounded in the side and hand by a shot which severed one finger, and had he been pursued he would undoubtedly have been captured.

Today the fortifications, though quite apparent, are neither as high as they were a century ago nor as distinctive, for grasses have camouflaged what would then have been fresh walls of volcanic soil. *Signposted off Highway 47. Park by the footbridge, cross the bridge and walk 15 min to reach first the outpost and then, over a second footbridge, the main fort.*

Lake Rotopounamu: A track leads from the Pihanga Saddle road, through bush to reach a virgin lake entirely surrounded by low, bush-covered slopes, with sandy beaches from which to swim. Many species of bird life can be seen. There is a large population of native trout in the lake which, as it has no outlet, are thought to have been introduced by the Maori. *Signposted on the Pihanga Saddle road. 1.5 km walk. Allow 20 mins for the walk in to the lake and a further 1½ hrs to walk around it.*

Tongariro Hydro-electric Power Scheme: A complex scheme of water control and diversion boosts the power output of the chain of stations on the Waikato River by diverting the headwaters of rivers through Lake Taupo. An ECNZ Visitor Centre at the Tokaanu Power Station has excellent displays and models of the scheme and also offers tours over the station. *See △ Turangi and △Tokaanu.*

Raurimu Spiral: Beyond the boundaries of the park, near Raurimu, but not visible from Highway 4, is the Raurimu Spiral, of world renown. An abrupt rise of 213 metres presented the ultimate obstacle to the builders of the North Island Main Trunk railway, and when the engineer R. W. Holmes came up with his masterly design for a spiral, a costly alternative route was under consideration. But Holmes, with an ascending spiral which incorporates a complete circle, three horseshoe curves and two tunnels, artificially increased the distance over which the climb had to be made from some 5.5 to over 11 kilometres, and so reduced the overall gradient to a tolerable 1 in 50. Locomotives of the "Dc" class (78-tonne and 1,425 h.p.) and "Dx" class (96-tonne and 2,570 h.p.) are used to pull most trains over this section. *Just E of Raurimu. Best viewed from the air.*

A DRIVE AROUND THE MOUNTAINS

Approx. 183 km. Allow a full day. The drive provides a spectrum of mountain scenery which ranges from views across desert wastes to vistas framed with rain forest. Starting from the Chateau and travelling anti-clockwise, the points of interest in order are:

Tawhai Falls: *Signposted, see above. On reaching Highway 4, turn left to pass the:*

Makatote Viaduct: The last to be built and the most impressive of the main trunk viaducts. Shortly beyond is an obelisk which marks the driving of the last spike in the North Island Main Trunk railway, on 6 November 1908.

Turning left at the road junction, the route lies along Highway 49A to:

△ **Ohakune:** Here a detour may be made up the scenic Ohakune Mountain Road.

Return to Highway 49; the route runs beside the State forests of Rangataua and Karioi, to the:

Whangaehu River Bridge: Scene of the country's worst rail disaster when, on Christmas Eve 1953, the north-bound Wellington-Auckland express plunged in to the Whangaehu River, suddenly swollen by a surge of water, mud and boulders from Ruapehu's crater lake (*see* △ *Waiouru*).

Continue on to reach:

△ **Waiouru:** A stop may be made to see the intriguing Army Museum.

The route then bears north along the:

Desert Road: A splendid drive which passes through Rangipo Desert.

At Turangi, turn left:

△ **Turangi:** An Information Centre here provides details of the Tongariro hydro-electric power scheme.

Continue west to reach:

△ **Tokaanu:** One may pause for a hot swim, inspect a small thermal area, or detour to see the picturesque lakeside village of △ Waihi.

Turn back towards Turangi, but bear right to follow the road over the:

Pihanga Saddle: During the climb one should pause to take in the dazzling panorama of Lake Taupo. Farther on the road passes the starting point for the 1.5-kilometre walk in to Lake Rotopounamu (*details above*).

The road then skirts Lake Rotoaira before reaching the turnoff to:

Te Porere Tussock Fort (*details above*): Here, in 1869, Te Kooti fought the last major battle of the Land Wars.

Return to the main road to continue south along Highway 47. Steam may be seen billowing from the lower slopes of Tongariro and a signposted 5-min walk may be made to see the 25-m plunge of Matariki Falls. Then turn left, along Highway 48, to return to the Chateau.

To shorten the trip to about 160 km, after driving north along the Desert Road turn left along Highway 47 at Rangipo, before reaching Turangi. This is to omit the Turangi, Tokaanu, Waihi and Pihanga Saddle sections.

TURANGI *

Volcanic Plateau   Map 8   Pop. 4,238

64 km N of Waiouru; 51 km SW of Taupo. Turangi Information Office, Ngawaka Pl.; tel. (07) 386-8999. DOC, Taupo/Tongariro Conservancy, Turangi Place, tel. (07) 386-8607.

TURANGI mushroomed almost overnight from a tiny fishing retreat on the southern tip of Lake Taupo to a town for 10,000. The town was planned in 1964 to meet the temporary needs of the Tongariro Hydro-electric Power Scheme, but was also designed to fulfil a role as the base for a forestry industry and the centre for newly developed farmland in the South Taupo region. Above the town rise the verdant skirts of graceful Pihanga *(1,325 m)*, whose charm, in mythology, led mountains to battle for her love (*see* △ *Tongariro National Park*).

The neighbouring Tongariro River is one of the most famed stretches of trout-fishing water in the world, luring anglers from many countries. At its delta stood a fighting pa of the Tuwharetoa tribe of Taupo. Other good trout rivers include the Tauranga–Taupo, the Waimarino and the Waiotaka.

Nearby are hot springs at △ Tokaanu and the picturesque village of △ Waihi as well as the vast wilderness of △ Tongariro National Park that includes the North Island's finest ski fields. Turangi, named for a chief, means "to stand in the sky".

POINTS OF INTEREST

Tongariro Hydro-electric Power Scheme: This imaginative scheme taps a catchment area of over 2,600 square kilometres of the volcanic uplands, drawing on the headwaters of a number of rivers (among them the Whanganui, Tongariro and Rangitikei) to channel the combined flow through Lakes Rotoaira and Taupo and so down the Waikato River. The added water boosts the output of the eight existing hydro stations on the Waikato by about 16 per cent. The first new station with a capacity of 200 mW and a head of 207 metres was completed at Tokaanu in 1973. The total power increase exceeds half the previous combined output of the entire Waikato chain. Maximum flood levels on the Waikato have not been increased, as under flood conditions water is directed from the headwaters only when it can be stored in Lake Taupo. The average water level in the Waikato in its lower reaches has been increased only slightly.

A second station, Rangipo, has been constructed underground, near the Poutu Intake. With a capacity of 120 mW, it makes use of the 260-metre head between the Moawhango tunnel outfall and the Poutou Intake. *Details of the scheme from the Turangi Information Office.*

Tongariro National Trout Centre★★: The Department of Conservation operates three hatcheries. Here at Tongariro the hatchery is an "ova-collecting", "eyeing" and rearing station for rainbow trout only. The second at Ngongotaha (near △ Rotorua) is basically a rearing station for rainbows, with a smaller production of brook and brown trout. The third, at Wanaka in the South Island, is used primarily for research on uncommon salmonid species within New Zealand.

At the "eyeing" stations, eggs are milked from female trout, fertilised and developed in incubators for about 18 days, to the stage where the eyes are visible. After a "killing-off" process to eliminate weaker eggs, the surviving eggs are retained and in the course of about a month hatch out. The young fish, or fry, are reared at the departmental stations or at others managed by local acclimatisation societies and released after a year when they reach the fingerling stage. The Centre also sends ova overseas.

As well as viewing the operational side of the complex, visitors may see trout in their natural habitat from an underwater viewing chamber and picnic in pleasant surroundings. *3.5 km S on Highway 1. Open daily, 9 a.m.–4 p.m.; tel. (07) 386-8607. The "breeding season" extends from May to October.*

Pihanga Saddle Road Viewpoint: It is worth driving up the Pihanga Saddle road (*Highway 47*) for a dazzling panorama of Lake Taupo. Over the saddle is the start of a 20-minute bush walk in to virgin Lake Rotopounamu. *Turn off Highway 41.*

Walks: Beyond the △ Tongariro National Park boundary, too, there are excellent walks. The small bushclad mound of **Maunganamu** offers great views of the region (*see p.* **229**). A different mood is offered by the cool reflections of forested **Lake Rotopounamu** (*see p.* **235**).

The **Tongariro River Walkway**, follows along a terrace above the river. The track was originally cut to give fishing enthusiasts easier access to the renowned trout river (*signposted off Highway 1, 5.5 km S. or start at the Koura St. swingbridge by the town. 1 ½ hrs one way. A drop-off and pick-up service can be arranged*).

Kaimanawa Forest Park: There is good hunting, particularly for Japanese sika deer, in the Kaimanawa Ranges, a forested area southeast of Turangi. *Hunting permits are obtainable from the Department of Conservation and the Visitor Information Centre.* Wild horses, descendants of those released into the area over a century ago and subsequently crossed with other breeds, may occasionally be seen roaming through the park. Several points of interest, among them the **Pillars of Hercules** and **Tree Trunk Gorge**, are accessible from Highway 1 south of Turangi. *Waipakihi Rd, Rangipo Intake Rd, Tree Trunk Gorge Rd and Kaimanawa Rd.*

ORGANISED EXCURSIONS

Details of the numerous fishing trips, white-water rafting expeditions and scenic flights are available from the Visitor Information Centre. The region is also popular with mountain bikers, and bikes may be hired locally. Experienced guides are available to take parties on such longer walks as the Tongariro Crossing and the Round the Mountain Track.

UPPER HUTT

Wellington region   Map 13   Pop. 37,290 (urban area)

32 km NE of Wellington. For information, tel. (04) 527-6041.

UPPER HUTT has grown more recently but just as rapidly as its larger neighbour, △ Lower Hutt. That over half the city's work force is engaged in its manufacturing industries is a statistic which refutes any impression that the upper valley is little more than a dormitory suburb for Wellington and Lower Hutt.

The city has a significant educational role housing the Central Institute of Technology, near the Trentham Military Camp.

Yearling sales at the fashionable Trentham Racecourse (now held in Auckland) for decades drew buyers from many parts of the world seeking a bargain such as Phar Lap, the fabled Australasian champion which sold here in 1928 for a mere £168. The national rifle championships are staged annually at the Trentham range.

Upper Hutt is named for its position on the Hutt River. The river is named for Sir William Hutt, sometime chairman of the New Zealand Company.

THINGS TO SEE AND DO

Trentham Memorial Park: Included in the park are Barton and Dominion Bush, the last surviving fragments of the luxuriant bush which once covered the whole of the valley floor. *Fergusson Drive, Trentham.*

Maidstone Park: A shaded picnicking and sporting area much frequented by summertime Sunday cricketers and strollers. Alongside is the Maidstone Memorial Pool. *Park St. Signposted from city centre.*

Harcourt Park: An area with pleasant picnic places and an adventure playground. *Akatarawa Rd.*

Wallaceville Blockhouse ★: Built in 1860 as part of Wellington's outlying defences when war flared, the unbecoming blockhouse never came under attack. Similar forts were built in various parts of the North Island, but this is one of the few to have survived. *Blockhouse Lane, off McHardy St, off Fergusson Drive immediately S of Quinn's Post Hotel.*

A further relic of the fighting is an old cannon used at Pauatahanui in the campaigns against Te Rangihaeata. Now painted bright red, it is mounted in Trentham Military Camp, where thousands of soldiers trained for two world wars. *Camp Rd, off Fergusson Drive.*

Silverstream Railway Museum: Here veteran rollingstock for use on a small track is restored and maintained. Aircraft are also displayed and what is reputed to be the oldest cottage in the valley, Waiora Cottage (*c.* 1868) has been moved here to serve as a period museum. *Reynolds Bach Drive, Silverstream. Operates Sundays and public holidays, 11 a.m.–4.30 p.m.; tel. (04) 563-7348.*

Orongomai marae: A Maori club welcomes Sunday evening visitors to the modern Mawaihakona house. *Park St (nr railway station); tel. (04) 528-6693.*

ENVIRONS

See also points of interest listed under △ Lower Hutt and △ Wellington.

Kaitoke Reservoir ★★: A number of delightful picnicking and swimming spots are set in a bushy gorge. *Signposted off Highway 2 at 13 km N.*

Staglands: A wildlife park in the Akatarawa Valley where animals and birds such as deer, goats, parrots and peacocks can be seen in natural surroundings. *16 km. Open daily 10 a.m. to 5 p.m.*

Akatarawa road to Waikanae (*37 km*): Just north of the city the Akatarawa road branches off Highway 2 to pass the confluence of the Akatarawa and Hutt Rivers (popular with picnickers and swimmers) and to wind through splendid bush. The road passes several swimming holes before crossing the Akatarawa Range to emerge at △ Waikanae. (*The route is described under △ Wellington, "Suggested Drives".*)

Tararua Forest Park: The rugged Tararua Ranges offer fine tramping and hunting. From the Upper Hutt access point the well-known and aptly named "Puffer Track" begins. *Access road signposted off Highway 2 at 14 km N.*

Cannon Point Walkway: *See p. 295.*

UREWERA NATIONAL PARK ★★★

Map 9   211,062 hectares

Department of Conservation, Aniwaniwa Field Centre (Te Urewera National Park Visitor Centre), Highway 38, Aniwaniwa (Lake Waikaremoana); tel. (06) 837-3803. Ruatahuna Field Base, Main Rd, Ruatahuna; tel. (07) 366-5392).Te Ikawhenua Field Centre, Highway 38, △ Murupara; tel. (07) 366-5641).

TE UREWERA NATIONAL PARK is set in the rugged Urewera Ranges, which form part of the North Island's 650-kilometre mountain backbone extending from

Wellington to East Cape. The majestic primeval forest, almost overwhelming in its intensity, offers unequalled hunting and tramping, and is complemented by the many attractions of △ Lake Waikaremoana. With neighbouring Whirinaki Forest Park, it comprises the largest remaining area of native forest in the North Island.

Parts of the park were designated for settlement by servicemen returned from World War I and were again threatened during the Depression, when the Government was urged to mill the timber and clear for farmland. It was not until 1954 that an initial area (around Waikaremoana) was declared a National Park, and it is now the country's third largest.

Even today the visitor can sense the remoteness of the Tuhoe, who as late as 1891 rebuffed Vice-regal visitors and three years later allowed Prime Minister Richard Seddon to enter the meeting house Te Whai-a-te-Motu at Mataatua only after his party had surrendered their knives, pipes and tobacco.

SOME HISTORY

Children of the Mist: The Tuhoe people of the Urewera led a spartan existence. They were too far from the sea to have a reliable source of food, their local rivers were poorly stocked with fish and there was a scarcity of flax for clothing, so the population was never great and always far from well fed. Their name "Children of the Mist" (bestowed by Elsdon Best) recalls their mythical ancestress Hine-Pukohu-Rangi, the "Maid of the Mist", and her marriage with a mountain, and perhaps explains why the Tuhoe were prepared to lead a life of such isolation and hardship. Tradition has it that the indigenous tangata whenua (people of the land), intermarried with descendants of the *Mataatua* (one of the canoes of the Polynesian "migration" to New Zealand), and it is from this later union that the Tuhoe are descended.

Because of their isolation, the Tuhoe were for a long time suspicious of the European. The coast where they might have traded was occupied by traditional enemies, and in any event they had little with which to barter. In 1830 their first musket cost the Tuhoe as many as 10 slaves, though the price later dropped to one for one. The wilderness in which they lived deterred missionaries, the other common form of early European contact, and so meetings between the Tuhoe and the Pakeha were few and far between. So it was that Te Kooti found a ready following in the Tuhoe during the final stages of the Land Wars.

Te Kooti and the Urewera Campaigns: After Te Kooti (*p.* 85) had escaped from the Chatham Islands, he used the Urewera country as a base for lightning raids on the surrounding districts. In an attempt to flush Te Kooti and his followers out of the bush, Colonel Whitmore, Commander of Colonial troops in the field, briefly invaded the Urewera country in May 1869. His columns forced their way through the unmapped forests and suffered tremendous deprivations, but, though they made no contact with their quarry, destroyed the food supplies of all but two of the major Tuhoe settlements.

The chase moved out of the bush when Te Kooti attacked Rotorua but he returned to the Urewera for the last campaigns of the war. For nearly two more years troops under such leaders as Gilbert Mair (*pp.* **197-98**) relentlessly hunted Te Kooti through the forests and several times he barely escaped capture—at Te Hapua a premature gunshot gave him warning, and in the final skirmish of the wars (14 February 1872) he was saved only because the troops' ammunition was damp. The morale of the Tuhoe, who had sheltered Te Kooti, finally collapsed under the combined pressures of war and famine, and Te Kooti lost their active support. Finally, he slipped through to the safety of the King Country where he remained until pardoned in 1883.

A charismatic spiritual leader: The settlement of Maungapohatu (*in isolated bush some 24 kilometres north of Lake Waikaremoana as the crow flies*), was once a thriving settlement and the home of the self-styled latter-day Christ and "younger brother of Jesus", Rua Kenana (1869–1937) who offered his followers seven wives and everlasting life. The settlement was headquarters for his Te Wairau Tapu religion, a Maori revivalist movement which was founded here in 1905 when Rua returned from shearing on the East Coast and set himself up as a New Testament prophet, styling himself as Te Kooti's spiritual heir. A fabled Round Temple was built while the colourful Rua brought a communal form of prosperity to the Tuhoe — a prosperity they had never known before. But Rua, as he built a nation within a nation, defied the licensing laws of the "occupying power" and in 1916 his zealous followers shot it out with the police who had come here to arrest him for liquor offences. A year's imprisonment resulted. Although for a time his following dissipated after his death in 1937, after he had failed to fulfil his promise to rise from the dead, he is possibly more revered today than at any time during his life. While perhaps Rua's most memorable performance was his "attempt" to walk across the waters of Whakatane Heads (*see* △ *Whakatane*), in recent years Rua has been reassessed by historians and credited with playing an important role in maintaining Maori cultural identity during a most difficult era.

Little remains of the settlement's former glory. Survivors of the first mission here, founded in 1918 by the Presbyterian J.G. Laughton, are the **mission house** of pit-sawn timber, and the old **school room** built from the timber salvaged from Rua's dance hall. Rua's Round Temple stood just above the present meeting house. *19 km along a logging road E of Ruatahuna. Private property. Visitors are not encouraged.*

FLORA

There is a wide variety of flora in the forests, from luxuriant kohekohe in the mild climate of the Bay of Plenty to caps of mountain beech on the mountain tops. Soil, rainfall and site help govern the composition of the forests, but the dominant factor is altitude. As height increases species appear, assume abundance and then disappear as more hardy species take their place. The general pattern of change is at about 760 metres from rimu/northern rata/tawa forests to beech/rimu forests. At about 900 metres the rimu disappears and mountain beech covers the highest ranges. A striking feature of the Urewera forests is, with a single exception, the absence of uncovered or "open" peaks—a view from any prominence shows forest stretching unbroken to the boundaries of the park and beyond. The rimu/northern rata/tawa forest which surrounds Lake Waikaremoana includes miro (on which the Maori would set snares for pigeons attracted by its large red berries) and the ngutu-kaka, now only found in its wild state here and on Great Barrier Island. Native to New Zealand, it resembles the kowhai and has a scarlet flower rather like the beak of a kaka, after which it is named.

HUNTING AND TRAMPING

Hunting: Te Urewera National Park maintains huts and provides information on tracks, accommodation and areas in which to hunt. *Shooting permits are issued at the Visitor centre at Aniwaniwa (Lake Waikaremoana) and Department of Conservation offices at Rotorua, Murupara, Ruatahuna, Gisborne and Opotiki.* Red deer are found throughout forests and Javan rusa deer within the Whakatane and Ohane catchment areas, the lower Waikare River and the Galatea foothills. Pigs and possums are found throughout the park and goats about the eastern forest margins from the Upper Waioeka River south to the Mohaka River.

Tramping: Full details of the tracks and hut locations are available from the Visitor Centre at Aniwaniwa. Overnight trips should not be attempted without first advising the Visitor Centre. The more popular tracks include:

Lake Waikaremoana Track: The 51-kilometre track around the lake, which encompasses striking cliffs, dense native bush and picturesque shorelines, takes 3–4 days to complete. From Onepoto(*near where Highway 38, from the south, first falls in with the lake*), the track first passes the site of the old Armed Constabulary Redoubt. It then climbs up to the Panekiri Range and follows this westwards, towards Panekiri Bluff, while affording the most fabulous views. The route continues clockwise around the lake to reach Hopuruahine Landing (*by Highway 38 on the northern side of the lake*). *Hut tickets must be purchased from the Visitor Centre at Aniwaniwa or any Department of Conservation Office before setting out. There are five huts and many camping spots along the way but there are no facilities for cooking in the huts. A gas cooker should be carried.*

Ruatahuna–Ruatoki–Taneatua, via Whakatane River (*79 km; 4 days*): A route through varied scenery which offers good trout fishing and deer stalking. *See Whakatane River Walk Track Guide.*

Maungapohatu-Tawhana-Waimana (*64 km; 4-5 days*): The track follows an ancient Tuhoe trail down to the Bay of Plenty. *See relevant park booklet for details.*

Taupeupe Saddle-Mt Whakataka (*1 day return*): Magnificent views are obtained from the 1262-metre summit and one can return along the track to Hopuruahine Landing on Lake Waikaremoana.

Mt Manuoha track (*2 days return*): Starting by the Waiotukupuna Stream Bridge (*signposted on the main road near Hopuruahine Landing*), the track leads to the highest point in the park (1,402 m), from where the panorama extends over Poverty Bay and inland as far as Lake Taupo and Mt Ruapehu. *Slatted track only back to Lake Waikareiti from Trig Point (3 days).*

Ruatahuna-Waiau-Manganuiohou-Lake Waikaremoana (*80 km; 5-6 days*): A splendid tramp, along half the park's length, which ends by skirting the lake.

Rua's track (*full 3 days from Maungapohatu*): The track is not particularly difficult and crosses two divides before it meets the Hangaroa road, 64 kilometres from Gisborne.

PLACES OF INTEREST IN AND NEAR THE PARK

△ **Lake Waikaremoana** ★★★: A bush-girt gem, with excellent fishing and a host of rewarding bush walks.

Ruatahuna: The traditional centre of the Tuhoe people, the settlement was under siege during the Urewera Campaigns, and in 1870 alone over 200 Tuhoe died here from starvation.

At nearby Mataatua (*detour 4 km*) is magnificent Te Whai-a-te-Motu ★★★ (1870-88), one of the truly great meeting houses. Of particular interest are the two carvings at the base of the pou-tokomanawa (inside centre poles) which depict the Tuhoe ancestors Paenoa and Whitiawa, dressed in collar and tie to emphasise the impact of European culture. *The house is usually locked. Permission should be sought locally before entering the marae.*

On the side road to Mataatua, about 800 metres beyond the bridge and on the right-hand side, there is a little cemetery containing the graves of Government troops killed near here in the 1869 Campaign.

Whirinaki Forest Park ★ ★ ★: *For details, see p.144.*

WAIHEKE ISLAND

Auckland   See △ Hauraki Gulf (Islands of the)

Bay of Plenty   Map 5   Pop. 4,273   ★★ WAIHI

63 km NW of Tauranga. Information Centre, Seddon St; tel. (07) 863-6715. Waikino Visitor Centre, Old Railway Station, Waikino.

WAIHI lies gently on the wooded lower slopes of the Coromandel Range. The town first blossomed in the gold-rush days of the last century, from when many of its buildings date, for it was here, in the Martha Mine, that the greatest gold strike in New Zealand's history was made.

Forecasters had predicted that Waihi would die when the mine closed, but productive farmland and an electronics industry helped to sustain the town until the opening of the new Martha Mine in 1988, when Waihi once more began to benefit from a gold boom.

Visitors come to follow the Karangahake Gorge Walkway and to ride on the Goldfields Steam Train.

SOME HISTORY

The original Martha Mine: Goldfields in the area were being exploited before John McCombie and his American partner Robert Lee in 1878 found what was to become one of the world's richest mines. Although they overcame strenuous Maori opposition (the area was a tapu burial ground), McCombie and Lee were unable to raise the necessary capital and were forced to abandon their workings. Those who followed struck richer patches of quartz, but the character of mining had changed. High production costs and the sophisticated machinery required to extract gold and silver from the quartz forced the miner without capital to work for wages, leaving the big returns to be won by investors. Eventually a number of claims were combined to form the Martha Extended Company and, helped by both the new cyanide process of gold and silver extraction and an influx of first Auckland and then British investment, the great venture was under way. Under the control of the London-based Waihi Company, the Martha project never looked back and by 1908 nearly £1 million in bullion was being recovered annually and the mine was ranked the world's eleventh richest. Both open-cast and underground mining techniques were used.

Several smaller companies still operated in the area, but none with the success of the Waihi Company whose dividends at times reached 80 per cent annually. As Martha's riches were won, Waihi became the largest town in South Auckland and in 1905 was nearly three times the size of Hamilton.

Despite intensive prospecting the output of gold slowly dwindled. Waihi escaped the worst rigours of the Depression, as precious metals were then one of the few commodities with a ready market, but in 1952 after a number of false alarms Martha finally closed. In all its 66 years it had never failed to show a profit and had produced 8 million ounces of gold and 60 million ounces of silver worth some $360 million. Critics suggest that had the company pursued better staff relations and shown more enterprise in techniques, the old Martha Mine need not have closed and its 550-metre-deep labyrinth of shafts become flooded.

The Waihi Strike: Industrial action at Waihi was a milestone in the emergence of the Labour Movement in New Zealand. In 1911 the Waihi Miners' Union, to which all local mine workers belonged, cancelled its registration under the Industrial Conciliation and Arbitration Act (which compelled those registered to refer disputes to arbitration) and joined the militant "Red" Federation of Labour.

The "Red Feds" aim was to keep one union for all the Waihi mine workers and so, when the engine-drivers and winders withdrew to form and register their own union in May 1912, the remainder were called out on strike.

Gold production was then at its peak, but for months the mines were idle. In an attempt to break the strike, the Government ordered police protection for workers who defied the strike call and inevitably this led to violence. Many strikers were imprisoned and before the strike was called off in November 1912 a police raid on the Miners' Hall had ended with a constable being shot and wounded and a striker being bludgeoned to death. The Federation's supporters were branded as Communists and hundreds were driven from the town, one being forced first to sell his house and furniture for a mere £14.

It was a major setback for the infant Federation of Labour and for the Labour Movement in its first trial of strength. Workers and their families were without wages for over six months as financial support expected from Australian unions, whom the Waihi Union had helped generously in their times of trouble, failed to materialise. Although both the Government and the employers shared most of the blame, the strike appeared to many to be politically orientated rather than an attempt to better the workers' conditions.

The Federation again suffered defeat in the nationwide waterfront strike of October 1913 and finally gave way to the New Zealand Alliance of Labour which in turn was superseded in 1936 by the present Federation of Labour, today representing about 450,000 trade unionists. A number of the original "Red Fed" leaders gained high office—Michael Joseph Savage and Peter Fraser became Labour Prime Ministers, Australian-born Harry Holland became party leader and Robert Semple, "Paddy" Webb and William Parry became Cabinet Ministers.

POINTS OF INTEREST

"New" Martha Mine: After lying dormant for thirty-six years, in 1988, Waihi's gold-producing Martha Hill sprang back to life. Unlike the original miners, who usually dug tunnels to follow the veins of gold and silver bearing quartz, the Waihi Gold Mining Company employs open pit methods Approximately 3,500,000 tonnes of ore and waste rock are mine annually from the open pit to produces 74,000 oz of gold and 520,000 oz of silver annually.

Although the old lake which resulted from the flooding of the earlier workings has disappeared, the new Gilmour Reserve lake is replacing it in the more recent 200-metre-deep pit. The lean shell of the pumphouse (1901), which once raised tonnes of water from the underground labyrinth, still stands. *Waihi Gold Mining Co. conducts tours over the mine and the mill site on weekdays. Book in advance during holidays; tel. (07) 863-8192. A lookout point over the pit may be reached by a walking track.*

Waihi Arts Centre and Museum: The museum's mining collection recalls the immense workings of the Martha Mine and of others in the area. Some idea of the length and extent of the labyrinth of shafts which extends under the town is given by a large plan of the mine. Rock samples, models of equipment and early photographs are also of interest. The adjoining art gallery mounts exhibitions. *Kenny St. Closed winter Saturdays.*

Water Lily Gardens: Tranquil gardens feature a variety of water lilies. Teas and camping. *"Pukekauri", Pukekauri Rd. 8 km. Leave Waihi via Victoria St; at 4 km turn right into Pukekauri Rd and continue 2.5 km. Open November–April; tel. (07) 863-8267.*

Goldfields Steam Train: A vintage train runs between Waihi and Waikino, along a 7-kilometre section of the old track to Paeroa which was phased out when the Kaimai Tunnel opened in 1978. *Runs every fourth Sunday of the month, on public holidays and daily from Boxing Day to the end of January; tel. (07) 863-8251.*

WAIHI BEACH-ATHENREE ROUND TRIP

48 km. Leave Waihi and follow the signposted route to Waihi Beach. Then drive SE along the beach road to Bowentown Heads. Return to Waihi via Athenree Gorge. Athenree Ford is a short detour. The drive takes in:

Waihi Beach ★ ★ ★: A 10-kilometre stretch of ocean beach with many baches. Originally planned as a township for retired miners, it is in the holiday season a major beach and surfing resort. There is a private "Museum of Technology" (*Beach Rd; tel. (07) 863-8081.*).

From Pohutukawa Park at the beach's north end a track leads over the headland to the otherwise inaccessible Orokawa Bay, a delightful beach fringed with pohutukawa but unsafe for swimming. *Allow 1 ½ hrs for the return walk to Orokawa Bay. There is a steep descent to the bay itself.*

Bowentown Heads: Drive to the summit for excellent views of the upper reaches of Tauranga Harbour and pine-clad Matakana Island immediately across the entrance. A scramble down the hillside leads to Cave Bay. There is camping at the Heads, and good sea fishing and abundant shellfish in the inner harbour.

The pa at Bowentown Heads, Te Kura a Maia "a training ground for young warriors", first occupied some 300 to 400 years ago, is a excellent example of a headland pa. The evening light can highlight its terraces in a most spectacular way.

Athenree Ford: A peaceful haven where at low tide delivery vehicles once forded the estuary to reach Bowentown.

KARANGAHAKE GORGE

Note: The **Karangahake Gorge Historic Walkway ★ ★**, *which follows part of the disused railway formation between Paeroa and Waihi, takes in many early mining relics. (Along the Karangahake–Owharoa Falls section (4.5 km) one may walk through a 1-km brick-lined rail tunnel.) Details of tracks from the information centre at Waikino, at the eastern end of the track. A shuttle bus operates at both ends of the track.*

The Karangahake Gorge, which links Waihi with Paeroa, saw intense gold-mining activity with settlements such as Karangahake, Owharoa, Waitekauri and Mackaytown springing up along the gorge. Between 1875 and 1918 nearly £4 million was won here. Now, as at Waihi itself, with superior technology and the resurgence in gold exploration, some of the ground is being reworked. At Waitekauri in 1992, the Golden Cross Mine, largely owned by an American Company, started to produce some 100,000 ounces of gold and 370,00 ounces of silver annually. Karangahake means "meeting of the hunchbacks", a reference to the surrounding hills. The gorge encompasses:

Karangahake: Little is left of the gold town whose battery saw the world's first field test of the revolutionary cyanide process. The foundations of Crown Battery, which crushed quartz from the nearby Waitawheta Gorge, are known locally as the "concrete monastery". The historic walkway starts here, crossing the Ohinemuri River along the top of what was once a combined road and rail bridge. Walking tracks also lead up Mt Karangahake *(953 m; allow 4 hrs for the return climb).*

Owharoa Falls: A broad but delicate fall readily viewed from the road. Owharoa means "food for a journey". *800 m detour up Waitekauri Rd, immediately west of Waikino.*

From here a detour may be made to visit the Water Lily Gardens (*see above*).

Waikino: The remains of the huge Victoria Battery of 200 stamps, which crushed millions of tonnes of ore from the Martha Mine, may be seen here. In the early 1900s the battery was well known around the world for its advanced techniques, but by the time it closed in 1952 the treatment plant was completely obsolete. *The battery remains are across the river. A photograph is in the minuscule dairy.*

TOURING NOTE

Road to Tauranga: The route runs through Athenree Gorge, a pleasing picnic spot. Before dipping in to the gorge (*about 8 km*), in the distance to the right is the site of Puketoki pa. Puketoki pa, a steeply sloped hilltop on a tribal boundary, is reputed to have been the scene of many attacks by would-be invaders, all of whom were beaten off by the local Ngai Tauwhao. Its name ("hill of the axe") is attributed to the practice of beheading captives.

Volcanic Plateau   **Map 8**   ★ WAIHI

On the shores of Lake Taupo, 8 km NW of Turangi; 60 km SW of Taupo.

THE TINY HAMLET of Waihi is in a classic lakeside setting. Its houses, dominated by the simple open spire of St Werenfried's, huddle close by Lake Taupo's sandy shores, and behind loom bush-clad cliffs which seemingly threaten to overwhelm the villagers — a threat twice realised when landslides swept all before them. The village is privately owned.

SOME HISTORY

Ordeal by fire: Christianity came late to the centre of the North Island, by which time the missionaries had to the Maori assumed the appearance of agents for land-hungry Pakeha. Alternately amazed and amused by the open bickering between Anglican, Wesleyan and Roman Catholic missionaries, the Maori were left with but one way in which to determine whose was the superior atua (god). So it was that, according to local tradition, Te Heuheu Tukino III (Iwikau) decided to put two local missionaries to the test, and promised his family's and his tribe's allegiance to whoever won. The trial was simple—each was to bare his posterior and sit on a bed of red-hot coals. Whoever had the more powerful atua would last the longer. Prudently the Anglican missionary, the Rev. Richard Taylor, declined to participate, leaving the way clear for his rival, Father Lampila, merely to make the gesture of lowering his trousers to be declared the winner.

In this unlikely way Catholicism is said to have come to Waihi and to have been embraced by the Te Heuheu family.

Choosing a king: In 1856, at a time when a group of influential Otaki Maori were seeking a chief who might, as "Maori King", unify the divided tribes into a single nation, Te Heuheu Tukino III (Iwikau) (c. 1790-1862) convened a hui (celebration) at nearby Pukawa to mark the opening of his splendid new pataka (foodstore). The hui developed into a full-scale meeting of prominent chiefs which debated the vexed questions of land tenure, laws which seemed to favour the settler, and the need to preserve the identity of the Maori people. Chiefs from all over the North Island were present, and eventually chose the reluctant Potatau as the first "Maori King".

The local missionary, the Rev. T. S. Grace was present and used his influence to dissuade Iwikau from aligning his Tuwharetoa with the King Movement (so sparing the Taupo tribe the land confiscations other member tribes suffered), but this did not prevent Iwikau from travelling to Ngaruawahia to assist in the investiture of his relative, Potatau. It was not until 1864, two years after Iwikau died, that Tuwharetoa eventually joined in the fighting against the Government, at the epic Battle of Orakau (*p. 221*). *(For notes on the Maori King Movement, see △ Ngaruawahia.)*

Landslides: Looking up near the turnoff to Waihi one may see the steaming slopes of Hipaua, a ridge honeycombed with steam vents. In 1846, after heavy rain, a slip blocked the Waimataii Stream. Water backed up until the slip burst and an avalanche of mud and water crashed down to overwhelm Te Rapa pa (*400 m from the present site of Waihi*). All but three of the pa's 57 inhabitants perished, among them the Tuwharetoa paramount chief, Te Heuheu Tukino II (Mananui) and his eight wives. The tragedy earned for his son, Te Heuheu Tukino IV, absent from the pa at the time, the name of Horonuku, literally "landslide". It was Horonuku who gave the nucleus of △ Tongariro National Park to the nation.

The promontory just before Waihi was formed in 1910 when for the second time part of the ridge collapsed into the lake, reclaiming about seven hectares. Miraculously, only one person was killed.

POINTS OF INTEREST

The village is privately owned and appropriate permission should be sought before any building is visited.

Catholic Church of St Werenfried: The charming church is decorated in traditional Maori style. A feature is two old stained-glass windows which depict both Christ and the Virgin as Maori. The church was built about 1889 by the Rev. Father J. W. Swiers in honour of his patron saint, St Werenfried.

Te Heuheu Mausoleum: Back from the road, near the church, is the Te Heuheu Mausoleum, carved in the tradition of the Lake Okataina school of carving with, at its apex, the koruru from the old Te Heuheu family pataka (at whose opening Potatau was elected first "Maori King"). Foundation posts from the pataka have been placed at the entrance to the tomb, and behind, the fence posts have been fashioned into figures in the manner of the traditional palisade to express defiance to interlopers.

In the tomb are the remains of Te Heuheu Tukino II (Mananui) (1780-1846), Te Heuheu the Great, the famed fighting chief who with a number of his family was killed in a landslide close by. Said to have been over 2.1 metres tall, Mananui was in advance of his time in forbidding the practice of cannabalism and, as befitted perhaps the most influential chief of his era, refused to subject his very great mana to a "mere woman" (Queen Victoria), as he would have done had he signed the Treaty of Waitangi.

Also entombed here is Mananui's grandson, Te Heuheu Tukino V (Tureiti) (1865-1921), also paramount chief of the Tuwharetoa, who gave 14,000 hectares of land to Maori servicemen returned from World War I and, at his death, was a Member of the Legislative Council.

Carved meeting houses: The Tapeka meeting house, by the mausoleum, was rebuilt in 1959 and has fine old carvings from earlier meeting houses on the same site. Its tekoteko depicts Te Heuheu I looking out over his domain. Also of interest is Te Mahau meeting house, by the village entrance.

Waihi Falls. These are formed where the Waihi Stream ends spectacularly by plummetting a sheer 91 metres into Lake Taupo. For many years the waterfall was harnessed to provide the community with electricity, and the remains of a powerhouse (which has also served as dairy factory and as sawmill) are by the beach. *Seen from the road's end.*

WAIKANAE

Horowhenua   Map 13   Pop. 7,776

58 km NE of Wellington.

THE ATTRACTIVE and rapidly expanding township of Waikanae spreads from the lower foothills of the Tararuas to the sea. Its blend of pleasant climate, fertile soil, and proximity to Wellington has made Waikanae particularly popular as a place to which to retire. There are trout in the Waikanae River.

A fine beach attracts many holidaymakers. Offshore lies alluring △ Kapiti Island, whose gentle face seems so very much closer when rain is imminent.

Waikanae means "mullet water" and was one of a number of place names said to have been bestowed by the legendary tohunga Haunui-a-Nanaia in the course of an epic journey which took him from Mahia to Pukerua Bay in search of his wife. At Waikanae Hau looked for her out of the corner of his eye, and compared his fish-like glance to that of the mullet. Hau, an ancestor of the Rangitane tribe, named other nearby places such as the Manawatu River, where his "heart stood still with apprehension" at the river's size and depth; Ohau ("the place of Hau"); Otaki ("to stick in place"), where he dug a staff into the ground, and Hokio ("whistling"), where the wind whistled in his ears.

MAORI LEGEND

A telling karakia: In legend Manaia, captain of the *Tokomaru* canoe (one of those in the Polynesian migrations to New Zealand), was pursued from "Hawaiki" by Nuku Tamaroro, seeking revenge for the slaying of his brother. It was off Pukerua that Nuku sighted *Tokomaru*; his three canoes quickly closed on their quarry and through two days and two nights a fierce sea battle raged. Many were killed before Manaia shouted to Nuku, suggesting that precious lives would be saved if the two of them could settle their differences in single combat on the beach. To this Nuku agreed and the canoes went to the shore. But that night, before the fight could take place, the tohunga of the *Tokomaru* canoe recited a powerful karakia (incantation) to such telling effect that a great gale arose to destroy the canoes of Nuku, and those of his men who had survived the sea battle "perished in the teeth of the wind". It was this gale that is said to have covered the plains of Waimea, Waikanae and Te Horo with gravel and sand dunes driven ashore by the force of the wind.

SOME HISTORY

A final tribal battle: The boundary between Te Ati Awa and Ngati Raukawa, both allies of Te Rauparaha, lay some short distance north of the township and it was near the mouth of the Waikanae River that in 1839 the last tribal battle in the area was fought. Both tribes had attended the tangi (funeral) for Te Rangihaeata's (*p. 284*) mother, Waitohi, where old grievances were rekindled. Shortly afterwards, Ngati Raukawa killed some Ngati Ruanui to stop them from building a house, and took others prisoner. The tribes of Te Atiawa, Taranaki and Ngati Ruanui assembled at Waikanae and demanded the return of the prisoners, but the Ngati Raukawa, seemingly bent on war, refused. A series of incidents erupted into a full-scale attack being launched against the combined tribes despite the apparent endeavours of Te Rauparaha, who though he seemed anxious to avoid conflict between his allies, may in fact have been assisting his related Ngati Raukawa.

The combined tribes were triumphant, taking captive many Ngati Raukawa whom they marched back to the main Waikanae settlement and summarily if savagely put to death.

Archdeacon Henry Williams visited the scene a short time later and was able to feel encouraged by the aftermath of the slaughter as he found the Ngati Raukawa dead had been properly buried by the victors: "This is a new feeling," he wrote, "arising from the great change which the introduction of the Gospel has effected among them."

245

THINGS TO SEE AND DO

Southward Car Museum ★★★: A splendid collection of motor cars dating back to a 1895 Benz, and including vintage motorcycles, cycles and fire engines. *Otaihanga Rd, 3 km S. Open daily, 9 a.m.-5 p.m.; tel. (04) 297-1221.*

Waikanae beach: A fine, sandy beach backed by lupin-covered dunes which is visited by summertime trippers from Wellington. A plantation of pines affords shade.

Nga Manu Sanctuary★★: A 15-hectare reserve of bush and wetlands includes walkways, an aviary, a nocturnal kiwi house (where kiwi are bred), picnic places and an information centre. *4 km. Ngarara Rd, off road to Waikanae Beach. Open daily from 10 a.m.*

Waikanae museum: Items of local interest are augmented by an unusual telecommunications collection. *Elizabeth St; open Sat. a.m.*

Reikorangi Pottery: Pottery is displayed outdoors in a pleasant riverside setting. *5 km. Ngatiawa Rd, off Akatarawa Rd. Open daily.*

Hemi Matenga Memorial Park: Tracks in the hills behind Waikanae lead through a fragment of the kohekohe forest that once clothed a wide area. *Access from Tui Cres, Kakariki Grove or Huia St.*

Mangaone walkway: A 3-hour track through regenerating forest. *See △ Otaki.*

WAIKAREMOANA (Lake) ★★★

Te Urewera National Park   *Map 9*

64 km NW of Wairoa. Te Urewera National Park Visitor Centre, Department of Conservation, Aniwaniwa Field Centre, Highway 38, Aniwaniwa; tel. (06) 837-3803.

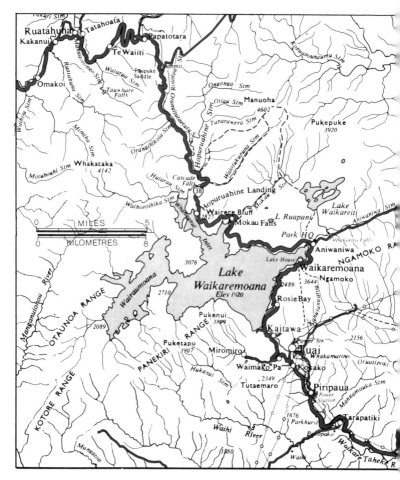

SET IN THE FOREBODING FORESTS of △ Te Urewera National Park, Lake Waikaremoana's "sea of rippling waters" weave an irresistible spell. To the Urewera's legends of the "Children of the Mist", and its drama of the hunt for Te Kooti, Waikaremoana adds its own mystique with the tale of Maahu and his daughter Hau-Mapuhia. The superb trout fishing for which the lake's 55 square kilometres are famed, hunting, swimming, boating and a variety of walks, provide limitless possibilities. The Te Urewera National Park Visitor Centre at Aniwaniwa organises field trips and lectures during the summer holidays.

MYTHOLOGY

A taniwha forms the lake: According to mythology Mahu asked his daughter Hau-Mapuhia to fetch him water from a well, only to be told by her to fetch it for himself. Angry, Mahu went to the well where he waited until his daughter came to look for him, and in a frenzy he drowned her. She transformed into a taniwha (water monster) and her desperate efforts to reach the sea formed the bed of the lake. First she thrust northwards to form the Whanganui arm of the lake, but was barred by the Huiarau Range; she then turned eastwards and gouged the Whanganui-o-Parua arm, but again she was blocked. One by one the arms of the lake were formed until finally Hau-Mapuhia attempted to escape at the lake's outlet near Onepoto. She crashed through the hill, but as she emerged she was caught by the sunlight, fatal to taniwha, and was turned into stone. Today Hau-Mapuhia still lies in the outlet of the lake and from time to time the lake's waters ripple without reason as they recall her titanic struggle.

Later Mahu threw his other children into the Wairau Moana arm of the lake, and they, too, turned into stone and can be seen as the islands named Te Whanau-a-Mahu ("the offspring of Mahu"). Mahu then moved to the coast and showed surprising affection for his murdered daughter by sending her back gifts of shellfish, which account for the shell conglomerate to be found in the district today.

SOME GEOLOGY

Geologists suggest that Lake Waikaremoana was formed when the Waikare-Taheke River undercut soft papa beds at Onepoto at the southern end of the lake until, perhaps helped by an earth tremor, the upper rocks crashed down to dam the original gorge. Water banked up behind this barrier to flood side valleys and form the many arms of the lake. However, the flow of water was not completely stopped—water still seeped out between the huge blocks of sandstone to emerge on the slopes above Kaitawa; but when the lake flooded it overflowed at the outlet. This has now been checked by a hydro-electric power scheme which, when it lowered the lake's level, revealed a standing forest on the lake bed.

A feature of the lake is the looming Panekiri Bluff (*1,158 m*) near Onepoto, which dominates its southern aspects.

SOME HISTORY

Forty years of war: Lake Waikaremoana, held by the Ngati Ruapuni (descendants of Paoa of the *Horouta* canoe), was envied by the Tuhoe people. Despite the Tuhoe's prowess in war, the Ngati Ruapuni, in *c.* 1823, rashly killed two Tuhoe at Hopuruahine, and desecrated their bodies. Inevitably the Tuhoe sought utu (revenge), attacking and defeating the Ngati Ruapuni and starting a war which was to last for 40 years, during which the Ngati Ruapuni were gradually driven from the lake. Since peace was made in 1863 there has been much intermarriage.

WAIKAREMOANA POWER SCHEME

The Waikaremoana Power Scheme consists of three generating stations on the Waikare-Taheke River which drains Lake Waikaremoana and drops 335 metres in less than two kilometres. This natural location was first developed because the supply of coal to Wairoa was being continually interrupted by the ever-changing bar at its harbour entrance. To overcome the power shortage, in 1923 two small generators were installed at Tuai but were quickly replaced by larger units. The Piripaua extension was completed in 1944 and involved the diversion and damming of the river to form Lake Whakamarino.

For the Kaitawa addition, the upper scheme, two intake tunnels were driven through the slip barrier about 18 metres below the lake's water level. The natural leaks were located by divers and sealed with rock fill and grouting, and siphons installed in the original outlet to control the water flow. Lake Kaitawa was raised and enlarged with an earth dam.

Although in its beginnings the scheme supplied power for the Wairoa district only, the extensions combined with larger water-storage capacity and the fact that

Waikaremoana is in a different watershed from the Waikato stations have made the scheme an important part of the North Island power complex.

WALKS AND PLACES OF INTEREST NEAR THE LAKE

△ Te Urewera National Park ★ ★ ★ incorporates the vast stand of ancient forest that surrounds Lake Waikaremoana. There are many splendid walks in the park, ranging from a few minutes' stroll to a five-day tramp around the lake's edge. Even the most transitory visitor should leave the road for at least a short walk in the bush. Information on walks and tramps, including those listed here, may be obtained from the Visitor Centre at Aniwaniwa.

Lake Waikaremoana Track: The 51-kilometre track around the lake, takes 3–4 days to complete. *See p.* **240**.

The following are listed in the order they are reached, driving from south to north.

Onepoto: Here at the southern end of the lake one can detour to see the outlet bay where the lake's waters enter the pipelines to the Kaitawa power station. A short walk leads up to the site of the Armed Constabulary redoubt, built in 1870 to counter Te Kooti. The remains of a stone wall stand by what was once the Parade Ground, and a short walk leads down to military graves beside a lakelet. From the car park a track leads up Panekiri Bluff to Pukenui trig (*4½ hrs return*). From the trig there is a breathtaking panorama of the lake over 600 metres below. The track continues on round the lake to Hopuruahine Landing (*4 days*). From the park entrance at Onepoto, the Onepoto Caves Track winds through a series of caves and overhangs created in the upheaval which blocked the valley and formed Lake Waikaremoana. The track ends at the "Lake Lookout" on the main highway. Care should be taken, and so should a torch. *Allow 2 hrs.*
   Onepoto means "short sandy bay".

Lou's Lookout: A short walk to a wonderful view over the lake. *1 hr return.*

Rosie Bay: Named not after the flower but after a surveyor's daughter, the bay is a popular camping and picnicking spot. Geologically it is a "fault bay" created when a landslide broke away from the Ngamoko Range to form the lake. Evidence of the cleavage can be seen both in the huge jutting rocks above the road and in the jumbled nature of the giant rocks which line the lake shore.

Lake House site: Named for the hotel which once stood here and which dated from the days when the lake was accessible only on horseback. A short distance below is the Waikaremoana Motor Camp where boats may be hired and provisions, fishing tackle and licences obtained.

Ngamoko Track: The steep but rewarding Ngamoko Track (*4 hrs return*), leading to the summit of the Ngamoko Range, starts opposite the Lake House site. An early feature is an exceptionally large rata tree. From the trig station (*1,201 m*) there are wide views over the lakes and out to the coast. In clear conditions Mt Hikurangi can be seen to the north-east.

Te Urewera National Park Visitor Centre, Aniwaniwa: Information about the park and its many tracks, shooting permits and other details are all available at the Visitor Centre. There is also a small but intriguing display of artefacts and photographs. Mementoes of Rua Kenana include his red ensign flag, one of seven flags he used, emblazoned with "Rua tupua" ("Rua, spiritual leader").
   Over the Christmas period a variety of free illustrated lectures and outings of an educational nature are conducted, ranging from botany to bug-hunting.

Hinerau Track ★ ★ ★: An easy path begins outside the Visitor Centre at Aniwaniwa and follows Aniwaniwa Stream through the bush to twin falls in a perfect setting (*30 mins round trip*). The track first passes the delicate Bridal Veil Fall.

Papakorito Falls ★ ★: These 15-metre falls are the grandest of the three falls on the Aniwaniwa Stream, despite a lack of trees. Last century, before the present road was built from Wairoa, organised coach and horseback tours from Gisborne came through this valley. Although designated a "road", it was never much more than a track through the bush. *Detour 1 km along the Old Gisborne Rd which joins the main road opposite the Visitor Centre, Aniwaniwa.*

Walk to Lake Waikareiti ★ ★ ★ (*3 hrs return. Start 200 m beyond the Visitor Centre at Aniwaniwa*): An easy path leads through beech forest, fern and fuchsia gullies to lovely Lake Waikareiti studded with bush-clad islands (one enclosing its own lake) 275 metres above the level of Waikaremoana. From the shelter the track continues to Tawari Bay (*an extra 40 mins return*) and from there a good track leads on round the western and northern shores to Sandy Bay (*a further 6 hrs return*). Boats for Lake Waikareiti may be hired through the Visitor Centre.

248

"Travellers, like poets, are mostly an angry race." *Sir Richard Burton*

Walk to Lake Waikareiti via Waipai Swamp and Lake Ruapani ★ ★ ★ (*6 hrs round trip; start at same place as the Waikareiti walk*): An easy graded track which gives a glimpse of Lake Waikaremoana and passes Waipai Swamp (*2 hrs return*), noted for sundews and orchids in season and for carnivorous plants. Finally Lake Ruapani is reached, a small lake whose grassed verge is surrounded by beech forests. From here the track continues on to link with the Waikareiti Track at Lake Waikareiti.

Mokau Falls ★ ★: Best seen from the road. *500 m beyond Mokau River Bridge.*

Mokau Landing: A large lakeside camping area here is also an ideal spot for fishing, boating and swimming.

Hopuruahine Landing: A branch road leads about 800 metres down to Hopuruahine Inlet, northern terminal of the track round the lake from Onepoto.

Mt Manuoha Track: Starting from the Waiotukupuna Stream bridge (*signposted*), the track leads to the highest point in the park (*1,402 m*) where the panorama extends over Poverty Bay and inland as far as Lake Taupo and Mt Ruapehu (*2 days return*). One can continue on to Pukepuke, Kaipo Lagoon and either Waikareiti or the Ruakuturi River.

Maungapohatu: Former home of the prophet Rua Kenana. (*See* △ *Urewera National Park.*)

Ruatahuna: Centre of the Tuhoe people. (*See* △ *Urewera National Park.*)

Waikato   Map 8   WAIKATO RIVER

THE WAIKATO RIVER, at 354 kilometres the country's longest, grows from no small streams but flows impressively from Lake Taupo to plunge at once over the awesome Huka Falls—though from a geographical viewpoint it is an extension of the Tongariro River which flows into the southern end of the lake. The river gives its name ("flowing water") to a large area south of Auckland and meets the sea not far south of Manukau Harbour. This was not always so, as before the Taupo eruption of *c.* 135 A.D. diverted its course, the Waikato flowed out on the other coast into the Firth of Thames.

The river was an important trade and access route for both Maori and European, and near Hamilton barges are still used to carry sand and shingle. Today the river is the chief source in the North Island of hydro-electric power—indeed from Orakei Korako to Karapiro the river is virtually a series of artificial lakes—popular venues for water skiing and rowing. Its flow from Lake Taupo is carefully managed so that only occasionally, as in times of heavy rain, does water run to waste over the spillways. The dams are built in narrow gorges cut by the river into the comparatively hard volcanic rock overlying the region. The Tongariro Power Scheme (see △ Turangi) diverts water into Lake Taupo from other catchments, so swelling the Waikato River and substantially increasing the output of the existing stations. Revised forecasts of maximum 500-year flood levels made it necessary to lower the hydro lakes permanently in 1974.

In addition to the eight hydro-electric power stations on the river, there are thermal stations at △ Wairakei and △ Huntly. Unlike the hydro stations which use the water to drive their turbines, these use it to condense steam after it has passed through the turbines.

The river is famous for its English brown and Californian rainbow trout.

WAIKATO RIVER HYDRO-ELECTRIC POWER STATIONS

Aratiatia Power Station (commissioned 1964): Thirteen kilometres downriver, the station was built in a storm of controversy on "at once the most beautiful and most valuable location on the river", but at set hours each day the spillway gates are opened so that visitors can still enjoy the foaming Aratiatia Rapids. (*See* △ *Wairakei.*)

Ohakuri Power Station (commissioned 1961): Eighty kilometres downriver is the North Island's largest artificial lake, of 13 square kilometres. When the project was started, fears were held that the partial flooding of the scenic △ Orakei Korako thermal valley would destroy its remaining attractions but, contrary to general expectation, it seems to have improved them. The lake contains trout and is popular with anglers and boat owners.

An earth dam was chosen as the rock foundations were too variable to support a concrete dam. A feature of its spillway is a fantail-shaped outlet which hurls flood water in a high, wide arc to dissipate its energy.

Four Canadian-made turbines develop 40,000 hp at 125 rpm to drive four 28,000 kW ASEA generators. Annually, 400 million units are fed into the transmission system.

Atiamuri Power Station (1958): Some 88 kilometres downstream, this station features a concrete gravity dam founded on a dome-like formation of extremely hard volcanic rock. An earth wing merges into the left bank, and the powerhouse stands in the former river gorge immediately downstream. Its lake extends about five kilometres upstream, to the Ohakuri Station.

Four 30,000 hp verticle-shaft Francis turbines drive ASEA generators each of 21,000 kW capacity.

Whakamaru Power Station (1956): Some 112 kilometres downstream, the Whakamaru station has a concrete and earth dam with the diversion cut, necessary for construction, preserved as an outlet channel for the spillway. Its lake extends 22.5 kilometres, almost back to Atiamuri.

Four steel penstocks, 5.5 metres in diameter and 66 metres long, convey water from the intakes in the dam to the turbines. Each of four vertical Francis-type turbines is of 35,000 hp capacity and drives a 25,000 kW generator to give the project a rated generating capacity of 100,000 kW.

Maraetai Power Station (1952): About 123 kilometres downstream and with a capacity of 180,000 kW, this was the third in the Waikato chain to be completed. The lake covers only 440 hectares but is 76 metres deep, with precipitous banks. Five vertical Francis-type turbines drive the 36,000 kW generators. The dam's lift down to the powerhouse saves nearly two kilometres' travel by road. As there is insufficient room in the gorge for an orthodox spillway, a tunnel has been built to enable excess water to bypass the station.

Maraetai II: A supplementary station commissioned in 1970, and with its powerhouse on the left bank, it does not generate additional energy but by sharing in the waters of Maraetai Lake enables twice as much water to be drawn off and used to generate power for short periods of peak demand.

Waipapa Power Station (1961): Situated 134 kilometres downstream. Because of doubts about the riverbed rock, a rolled-earth dam of sand, gravel and ignimbrite was built. Three Kaplan-type turbines with movable blades and each of 24,000 hp drive three ASEA generators, each producing 17,000 kW. An unusual feature of this comparatively low head station is that the three penstocks leading water to the turbines are included in the dam structure and so are hidden from view.

Arapuni Power Station (1929): Some 161 kilometres downriver, this the oldest surviving station in the Waikato chain is exceeded in capacity only by Maraetai. Eight vertical Francis-type turbines with a total capacity of 220,000 hp drive vertical generators—four of 17,850 kW and four of 21,600 kW capacity.

Karapiro Power Station (commissioned 1947): Situated 188 kilometres downriver, it has three 42,000 hp Kaplan-type turbines which drive generators of 30,000 kW capacity. Horahora, the first hydro station to be built on the river (in 1910-13 by the Waihi Goldmining Company) operated until 1947, when it was submerged in the creation of Lake Karapiro. There is a small ECNZ Museum here. *For Lake Karapiro description see △ Cambridge.*

WAIMATE NORTH ★★★ *Northland* Map 2, 3

21 km W of Paihia; 19 km NE of Kaikohe.

THE WAIMATE MISSION HOUSE at Waimate North was once the hub of a thriving village. A delightful colonial building, it houses an intriguing collection of missionary items.

SOME HISTORY

"**An enchanter's wand**": The Rev. Samuel Marsden (*p.* **56**), believing that spiritual and practical instruction should where possible be combined, established New Zealand's first inland mission station at Waimate North in 1830. His object was to train the Maori in efficient farming methods while they were given religious instruction and, at the same time, to provide other mission stations with flour, which previously had been imported from Sydney. Marsden authorised the purchase of about 400 hectares of land and moved there Richard Davis (who was to establish the country's first proper farm, modelled on the English mixed farm), together with his fellow-catechists, George Clarke and James Hamlin.

For a time the community thrived. By 1832 three houses and a church had been built, schools for Maori were in operation and when three years later the naturalist Charles Darwin visited Waimate North he could write that "after having passed over so many miles of uninhabited useless country, the sudden appearance of an English farmhouse and its well dressed fields, placed there as if by an enchanter's wand, was exceedingly pleasing". Yet within a few years the farm had failed. The land was not really suitable for the crops grown and once the novelty had worn off, the Maori labourers, soon affluent as they started to cultivate their own plots, required more substantial payment.

With the arrival of Bishop Selwyn in the early 1840s the community's role changed from that of mission farm to theological centre, and in its heyday could boast Bishop Selwyn's "Palace", a "Cathedral" (as the church became with a bishop's presence) and St John's College, which was among other things a training place for clergy, and as such survives in Auckland today.

When Bishop Selwyn left Waimate North at the end of 1844 the centre assumed its final role of mission station. Soon came the War in the North, Heke's War, which effectively ended the missionaries' influence in the area. For over three months British troops camped at the mission, to the disgust of missionary and Maori alike, wrecking a number of the buildings and flattening the carefully manicured gardens.

One by one the mission buildings disappeared and today only the one original building remains.

Waimate North was known to the missionaries as Te Waimate ("stagnant water") and was given its present variation to distinguish it from Waimate in South Canterbury.

WAIMATE MISSION HOUSE ★★★

The charming Waimate Mission House (1831-32) is the second oldest surviving building in New Zealand (only the mission house at △ Kerikeri is older) and the sole survivor of three similar houses built by the missionaries in the early 1830s. For a time George Clarke, who had lived in the older mission house at Kerikeri and who probably designed the three houses here, lived in the house with his family, and after he left to take up a Government post it became in 1842 Bishop Selwyn's "Palace". Selwyn left in 1844 and only the Rev. Robert Burrows, living here during Heke's War, saved the house from the destruction wrought by the British troops.

The house evokes memories of many stirring events—an outraged Hone Heke calling in 1840 to investigate the accidental death of a Maori schoolgirl; Mrs Selwyn insisting on evening dress for the evening meal; Hobson and Maori chiefs gathering on the lawn to add signatures to the Treaty of Waitangi; Heke's wife meeting Tamati Waka Nene to discuss terms of peace; Governor Grey and Heke sitting down to breakfast together once the War in the North was over.

An adaptation of the late Georgian style and an excellent example of early colonial architecture, the house comprises a timber construction planned symmetrically round a central stairhall. Unusual for the period is the inclusion of the kitchen inside the main building rather than in a separate outhouse close behind.

The building has been restored and refurbished with period furniture and items relating to the mission and the missionary families. *Open daily (except Good Friday and Christmas Day), 10 a.m.–5 p.m. Closed Thursday and Friday, June–August; tel. (09) 405-9734.*

OTHER POINTS OF INTEREST

Church of St John the Baptist ★★★: In a picturesque setting near the mission house, the present church, the third on the site, was built in 1871 of timber from an earlier and larger church built in 1839. Bishop Selwyn's description of the earlier church is still appropriate: "It is built entirely of wood painted white, and gives a very English look to the village." In the oak-shaded churchyard are graves with unusual carved wooden headboards found only in Northland. A memorial lychgate records the endeavours of the first missionaries.

The New Zealand Historic Places Trust has marked many sites of importance and has salvaged and restored a number of historic buildings. The Trust relies on individual members for support. For details of membership write to the Trust's Secretary, Private Bag, Wellington.

It was in the first church on the site that the first European marriage in New Zealand took place when, on 11 October 1831, William Gilbert Puckey married Matilda Davis, daughter of the Rev. Richard Davis. *The church is by the mission house and is open daily.*

Church of St John the Baptist, Waimate North.

Oldest oak ★: What is believed to be New Zealand's oldest oak, and also its oldest exotic tree, was first grown at Paihia from an acorn brought from England by the Rev. Richard Davis in August 1824. When Davis was transferred here he brought the young tree with him and replanted it in 1831. *Signposted 100 m on the road to Ohaeawai.*

First road (1830): With the first inland mission came the real need for the first road to be built, from Waimate North to Kerikeri. The road, since vanished, was designed by George Clarke and included a remarkable 19.5-metre bridge. It was along this road that Bishop Selwyn would walk to consult the books he kept in the Stone Store at Kerikeri. *Site signposted on the main road.*

Okuratope Pa: One of Hongi Hika's pa, the well-wooded reserve is presently accessible only across private land. Hongi, with Ruatara, guaranteed the safety of Marsden's missionaries at Waimate, and their mission station at Kerikeri was similarly close to another of his pa. *Te Ahuahu Rd.*

There are numerous other pa in the vicinity, including one on the saddle-shaped crest of **Mt Te Ahuahu** (*373 m; opp. junction of Te Ahuahu Rd and Highway 1*). A curious depression runs vertically down the north face, and a variety of stories tell of this being dug as an escape route and disguised with a ceiling of fern, as the whole hill would then have been covered in scrub. It is, however, a natural watercourse and while historians accept that the pa must have been the subject of attack, they discount suggestions of this being an escape tunnel. It may, however, have been used during a siege to fetch water. The bones of one of Hongi Hika's generals, Te Wera Hauraki, lie under a stone cairn on the summit.

WAIOURU

Volcanic Plateau   Map 8   Pop. 3,145

29 km N of Taihape; 63 km S of Turangi.

SITUATED ON the edge of the Volcanic Plateau, with a spectacular view of the mountains of the △ Tongariro National Park, Waiouru is home to the country's principal Army training camp. For a generation dogged by its wartime reputation for being bleak, barren and bitterly cold (it is 813 metres above sea level), the town has considerable recreational assets which are now being realised. Recent growth renders Waiouru today very much more than the staging post for fuel and food it once was. Even the most transitory visitor may wish to pause at the excellent Army Museum (*described below*).

Surrounding tussock land is used occasionally for artillery practice, and is frequently freckled with the tents of soldiers on manoeuvres. Motorists on the inhospitable Desert Road (the 63 kilometres of Highway 1 that link with △ Turangi) may be surprised to see armoured vehicles moving at speed across the open country, or combat aircraft streaking low overhead on simulated strike missions.

Waiouru means "river of the west", as the Waiouru Stream is the most westerly branch of the Hautapu River.

RANGIPO DESERT

Rangipo Desert lies about 10 kilometres due north of Waiouru, to the west of that section of Highway 1 known as the Desert Road.

In legend, Ngatoroirangi (navigator of the *Arawa* canoe) climbed to the summit of Tongariro and would have perished had the gods not heard his prayers and sent fire to save him (*see* △ *Tongariro National Park*). As the revived Ngatoroirangi stood on the summit of Tongariro and surveyed the land around him, he saw a group of strangers, apparently from the *Takitimu* canoe, approaching across the plains to the east. To protect his newly claimed land Ngatoroirangi appealed to his gods once more, and Ruaumoko (god of volcanoes) answered him again. Smoke and ash poured from the crater of Ngauruhoe, blacking out the sun. Dense fog billowed down the mountain slopes, enveloping the strangers who eventually perished in a great storm of sleet and snow. The place where they died became known as Rangipo, "the place where the sky is dark".

The area, with an annual rainfall of over 1,000 mm, is not a true desert, but the combination of strong drying winds and loose sand and gravel make plant survival almost impossible. But for odd bristle tussocks, large areas would be completely bare. In other places are patches of dwarf broom.

POINTS OF INTEREST

Queen Elizabeth II Army Memorial Museum ★ ★ ★: The New Zealand Army has, since the time of the Land Wars, been involved in a succession of campaigns — from the South African War, through two World Wars, Korea, Malaya, Malaysia and Vietnam to UN peace-keeping duties. The museum houses uniforms and equipment used by participants in these many campaigns, along with medals, insignia and a most extensive collection of weapons. Realistic displays depict scenes of Army life over the years — even including that of the prisoner-of-war. Tanks and guns of varying vintages are also on view. *On the main Highway at Waiouru. Open daily (except Christmas Day), 9 a.m.–4.30 p.m. A "Tears on Greenstone" memorial remembers each of the country's fallen soldiers individually, and an audio-visual presentation is screened regularly. The complex includes tearooms.*

ENVIRONS

△ **Tongariro National Park ★★★:** A wilderness area of desert and mountain which includes the North Island's finest skifields.

Kaimanawa Forest Park: There is good hunting, particularly for Japanese sika deer, in the Kaimanawa Ranges, an area open to the public as a forest park. *Details and hunting permits are available from the Department of Conservation at Turangi.*

TOURING NOTE

Tangiwai Rail disaster: On Christmas Eve 1953 Tangiwai, on the Waiouru-Ohakune road, was the scene of the country's worst rail disaster. Only minutes before the north-bound Wellington-Auckland express thundered towards the Whangaehu River crossing, a wall of water carried mud, ice and rock down from the slopes of Mt Ruapehu and, with a roar that was heard for miles, swept the rail bridge away. A passing motorist saw the rail bridge totter but with only a torchlight was unable to warn the engine driver in time. The engine and the first six carriages hurtled into the raging torrent, there to be smashed to matchwood. One 75-tonne concrete bridge pier came to rest a full 100 metres downriver, and the deck of one carriage was recovered no less than four kilometres away.

About 151 people died in the darkness, and four of those who rescued passengers from carriages that were teetering on the brink of the rushing waters were rewarded for their gallantry. Many on board were travelling to Auckland to see the Queen, then in the course of a Royal Visit, and a number of Maori elders, who could point to other disasters, saw the tragedy as an inevitable consequence of the New Zealand Government's continued failure to ratify the Treaty of Waitangi.

A subsequent inquiry found that the tragedy was caused by a lahar—a sudden release of water from Mt Ruapehu's crater lake. The torrent thundered down the mountainside and along Whangaehu River, carrying with it huge chunks of ice, volcanic ash and mud and enormous boulders. Similar floods had occurred before, and geologists explain that the rounded hills near the Chateau turnoff are actually boulders swept down by massive lahars. Devices have been installed to give warning of any repetition.

Today all that remains of the tragedy are the bankside foundations of the old rail bridge, just on the downriver side of the new rail bridge. The road bridge, too, has been replaced.

Tangiwai, appropriately, means "weeping waters". *9 km W, along Highway 49 towards Ohakune. A granite monument (1989) marks the scene of the tragedy.*

WAIPAWA   Hawke's Bay ' Map 11   Pop. 1,732

43 km SW of Hastings. Visitor Information Centre, District Council, Ruataniwha St; tel. (06) 857-8060.

WAIPAWA is separated from △ Waipukurau by only seven kilometres and two river crossings. Both farming centres, they were founded in 1860 as private towns by station owners, Waipawa by F. S. Abbot (who named it Abbotsford) and Waipukurau by H. R. Russell.

In Tapairu Rd, just south of the Waipawa bridge and 400 metres from the main road, is a signpost reading Etu Kia Mataari Ki Te Tima ("Stop! Look out for the steam engine!"), believed to be the only road sign in Maori still surviving. The crossing is now only for pedestrians.

The meaning of Waipawa is obscure, but is taken to mean "smoky (or steaming) water" as there may once have been thermal springs nearby.

SOME HISTORY

A river port: The town was laid out close to a ford across the Waipawa River. With the destruction of the forests the river became but a shingled shadow of the narrow, deep river it once was, as witness the fact that a wharf originally stood near the site of the road bridge and provisions were shipped in from Napier. Wool and grain were shipped downriver together, and during floods logs would be floated down, to be recovered near Napier.

In 1866, after an abortive attack on △ Napier, a Hauhau (*see index*) war party came south to recruit local Maori to the cause. Settlers here took refuge in a stockade nearby, but the war party withdrew, after a show of strength, when local Maori refused them support.

Central Hawke's Bay Settlers Museum: A local museum portrays the history of the district. *High St. Hours vary.*

ENVIRONS

Te Aute College★: An Anglican school with a predominantly Maori roll. *12 km N on Highway 2. (See p. 97.)*

Ongaonga museum buildings: An early one-roomed, kauri-shingled schoolroom (1874) displaying a collection that includes articles used in the school is the centrepiece of a growing collection of venerable buildings (*open Sunday afternoons or on request*). These include a pioneer bush cottage (of the type built in the 1870s), the old lock-up, a butcher's shop and a turn-of-the-century joinery factory which still houses original tools and machinery. *Ongaonga. 18 km W. (An alternative route to Hastings through Ongaonga by way of State Highway 50.)*

To the west of Ongaonga, in Makaretu Road, is **A'Deane's Bush**, containing perhaps the finest surviving fragment of the bush that once covered the Ruataniwha Plains. Matai and kahikatea predominate, but a feature is a massive totara.

Pourerere Beach: This fine open beach saw the genesis of the province's vast sheep industry as it was to here in 1849 that Fred Tiffen and Edward Davis drove 3,000 merinos up the coast from the Wairarapa. The sheep were then moved further inland to an area illegally leased by the partnership from local Maori, much to the anger of Sir Donald McLean, who shortly afterwards was engaged in negotiating Government land purchases in Hawke's Bay.

Earlier, Captain Cook hove-to off Pourerere in 1773, on his second voyage, and gave the Maori chief Tuanui some seed, two hens, two cocks, two boars and two sows, which he promised not to kill. The number of "Captain Cookers" (as the strain of wild pig is known) in later years suggests that the promise was kept.

The holiday settlement at the beach is some distance south along the foreshore. *40 km SE of Waipawa.*

Kairakau Beach: A good, open beach. *39 km E.*

★★★ WAIPOUA KAURI FOREST

Northland   Map 3

64 km NW of Dargaville. Information from Department of Conservation, Waipoua Forest Field Centre; tel. (09) 439-0605; Trounson Kauri Park; tel. (09) 439-0615.

IN WAIPOUA KAURI FOREST is preserved the last extensive stand of kauri. The forest covers an area of 9,105 hectares of which about 2,500 hectares bear mature kauri. Originally purchased by the Government in 1876 for settlement, the area was proclaimed a forest sanctuary in 1952 after widespread public agitation.

The massive kauri tree grows here in its primitive environment, towering in scattered groups to dwarf surrounding trees such as tawa, towai, rimu, northern rata and kahikatea. The giant trees are easily seen from the main road which leads for about 16 kilometres through the forest.

Waipoua means "water from the evening rain".

THE KAURI

The kauri (*Agathis australis*), native giant of the New Zealand forest, is world-known for its huge size and excellent timber. Similar species grow in Australia, New Guinea, Malaysia, Indonesia, New Caledonia and Fiji. The kauri grows very slowly up to a little over 50 metres with a girth of over 15 metres and a timber content of up to 240 cubic metres. The largest trees are well over 1,000 years old.

A feature of the tree is the way in which when grown under forest conditions it prunes its own lower branches, finally to yield a long uninterrupted trunk, at times the first branches appearing over 12 metres above the ground. Because of this natural pruning, knots are rare and so the large trees yield wide clear boards, straight-grained and easily worked.

The trees once grew as far south as southernmost South Island, but in more recent times covered an area of about 1,200,000 hectares that stretched from Northland to south of Auckland. The enormous amount of milling carried out by early settlers quickly cut out the timber and today only a few pockets of kauri are left, of which the stands of Waipoua Kauri Forest and Trounson Kauri Park are the best known. Kauri regenerates vigorously and is being encouraged in a number of areas, with very little being milled.

The tree slowly sheds its bark and assists soil leaching, making it poor for agriculture. Its effect on the Northland landscape is often apparent, and mounds of bark up to 4.5 metres high can be seen around the oldest trees.

A young kauri is known as a "ricker", a term of nautical origin.

Kauri industries: The kauri is romantically interwoven with the beginnings of Northland settlement. In the early 1800s it was the country's chief export, sought the world over for use as ships' masts, and later became Northland's standard building material. As its slow growth rate could not meet the fantastic pace at which the trees were being cut, the kauri timber boom could not last for long.

The decline in the timber trade, however, was countered by the gum diggers who came in their hundreds, many of them from Dalmatia (now part of Yugoslavia). The gum (a resin exuded by the kauri which hardens on contact with the air) was bled from the trees, collected from around their bases and dug out (often petrified) from the beds of buried prehistoric forests. Potential farmland, already leached by former kauri forests, was dug up, making the land totally unsuitable for farming.

The gum trade reached its peak about 1900, with diggers camped out all over Northland and the Coromandel Peninsula, the gum being exported for use as a base for slow-drying hard varnishes (since largely superseded by quick-drying synthetics) and in the making of linoleum. It was first used by the Maori as fuel, as chewing gum and in tattooing.

The gum is still found, but the trade has gradually dwindled away. So it was that the kauri first attracted commercial interest in New Zealand and then drew large numbers of people from all over Europe who eventually settled in the country.

POINTS OF INTEREST IN THE FOREST

Te Matua Ngahere (Father of the Forest)★★ : By volume the second biggest known tree in New Zealand, its height is 30 metres; mid-girth 16.4 metres; estimated timber content 208 cubic metres; height to its first branch 7 metres. Its age is unknown but it may approach 2,000 years. *Signposted. Detour 800 m return. Track leads 400 m through the bush to the tree. Allow 20 mins.*

Tane Mahuta (God of the Forest)★★ : The largest known kauri in the country, its height is 51.5 metres; mid-girth 13.77 metres; estimated timber content 244.5 cubic metres; height to its first branch 9.4 metres. Estimated age 1,200 years. *Signposted. A short track leads from the main road over a bridge to the tree. Allow 10 mins.*

Kauri Ricker Track ★: A pleasant 15-minute walk through a stand of "ricker" (young kauri). *Signposted N of the Field Centre.*

Maxwell Cottage: A display depicting the life and tools of the kauri bushman is exhibited in the one-roomed cottage where James Maxwell, the forest's first supervisor from 1890–1920, once lived with his wife. *At the Waipoua Department of Conservation Field Centre, detour 2 km from Highway 12. Open daily. Close by, an arboretum contains displays relating to the kauri forest.*

Toatoa Stand: A short crescent track leads to a stand of toatoa (*Phyllocladus glaucus*). One of three species occurring in New Zealand, it is unusual in that it has no leaves but phylloclades (or flattened branchlets) instead. The species here, which is found in the northern half of the North Island, has the largest phylloclades. *Signposted. 5-min walk.*

Lookout: The view from here extends over the forest area and across to the Tasman *Sea. Signposted. Detour 3 km return, S of the forestry office.*

TROUNSON KAURI PARK

The park (566 hectares) had its genesis in a gift to the nation of 30 hectares of fine kauri forest made by James Trounson in 1919. The kauri here are more concentrated if somewhat smaller, and a number of walking tracks lead through the forest. *Camping. Leave the main road on a 5 km detour S of Waipoua Kauri Forest.*

WAIPU   Northland   Map 4   Pop. 1,654

41 km SE of Whangarei. Information Centre, 14 The Centre, tel. (09) 432-0773.

WAIPU, a farming centre which began as a "special settlement", was founded by a group of about 120 Scottish Highlanders who, after disappointment in Nova Scotia and Australia, came to New Zealand in 1853. Land was purchased on the Waipu River and when news of the settlement reached Nova Scotia a further 850 Scots set out to join the band.

Approached from the south, there is a breathtaking spectacle as Pilbrows Hill is crested and the expanse of Bream Bay suddenly unfurls. Below lie the Hen and Chickens Islands and the curve of coast around to Whangarei and Bream Head.

Highland Games each New Year's Day perpetuate the town's concern with things Scottish, as does the Lion of Scotland atop a tall column, the locality's memorial to its founders. Locally made ornamental tiles are sought after nationwide.

SOME HISTORY

The Rev. Norman McLeod (1780-1866): Leader of the Waipu settlers, he was one of the many small farmers who left Scotland in the early 1800s. In 1851, after some years in Nova Scotia and a series of crop failures, McLeod (by then over 70) led a party to Adelaide. They found land difficult to obtain near the coast and so moved to Melbourne. A number then left for the Victorian goldfields and the rest finally came on to New Zealand and settled at Waipu as a self-contained community of 883. McLeod, a strict but inspiring leader of deep Calvinistic faith, had a devoted following and earned a unique place in the story of New Zealand's colonisation.

If McLeod inspired adulation and unquestioning obedience from many, to some he was a despot who, it is alleged, once in Nova Scotia caused a boy's ear to be removed in punishment for petty theft. He was either loved or loathed: there was no room for supervening emotion. It is also recorded, in witness to his powers of oratory, that on Christmas Day 1862 he preached a sermon in an open boat to such telling effect that the oarsmen forgot the breakers; the boat capsized and half the passengers were drowned.

When he died it was felt that no minister could replace him. His pulpit was dismantled and, it is said, pieces shared out among his followers.

The wreck of the "Niagara": Offshore lie the Hen and Chicken Islands where in June 1940 the *Niagara* (13,415 tons) struck a German mine and sank with its cargo of over $5 million in gold bars. No lives were lost and in remarkable salvage operations in deep water most of the gold was recovered by two brilliant Australian deep-sea divers, the brothers W. and J. Johnstone. There is still gold in the wreck.

POINTS OF INTEREST

Waipu House of Memories ★: The house greets its visitors with a cool stare from a life-size portrait of McLeod and preserves not just a chip from a window from his church on Cape Breton (Nova Scotia) but even "a turf from the ground actually trodden" when McLeod carried peat in his native Scotland. More predictable are collections of McLeod's letters, and of portraits and relics which accent the town's Scottish origins. The museum maintains family trees, charting the descendants of those aboard the six ships that journeyed from Nova Scotia. *Main St, by the monument to the early pioneers. Open Monday–Saturday, 9.30 a.m.–noon, 1–4 p.m. (except Good Friday and Christmas Day). Tel. (07) 432-0746.* The nearby church contains stained-glass windows dedicated to McLeod's memory.

Waipu Tile Studio ★: Attractive ceramic tiles depict native birds, plants and other hand painted images. *The Old Waipu Firehouse Art Gallery, West End. Open daily, 10 a.m.–4.30 p.m.; tel. (09) 432-0797.*

Beaches: Waipu Cove (*9 km*) and Langs Beach (*12 km*) offer swimming, surfing and rock fishing which attract visitors from Whangarei.

Waipu Caves: Despite its inviting large entrance, the labyrinth of limestone caves should not be explored alone. Whenever possible, local caving club members are happy to accompany visitors. One of the longest stalagmites in the country, some 2.6 metres high, is to be found in the main cave. *12 km N on Waipu Caves Rd. Details from museum.*

Marsden Point Oil Refinery Visitor Centre: Among the exhibits is a model of the original refinery and its later expansion. *See p.* **305.**

Pony trekking: Two hour rides lead through pretty farming country. *Arrange through the Information Centre.*

WAIPUKURAU

Hawke's Bay   Map 11   Pop. 3,648

50 km SW of Hastings. Visitor Information Centre, District Council; tel. (06) 858-8195.

WAIPUKURAU, a bustling farming centre, is considerly larger than its "twin", △ Waipawa, a bare seven kilometres north across the Waipawa and Tukituki Rivers. Both farming centres, they were founded in 1860 as private towns by station owners, Waipukurau by H. R. Russell and Waipawa by F. S. Abbot. In earlier years the towns' rivalry showed in a number of ways, including (in 1867) a dispute over which should have a telegraph office. A lengthy newspaper debate included the assertion that while Waipawa might have the larger population (as it then did), it was only a town of "rabbit-hutches".

Approaching from the south one crests Pukeora Hill to look down suddenly on the town in its appealing riverside setting. Waipukurau ("stream where mushrooms grow") is locally abbreviated to an unpretentious "Ypuk".

POINTS OF INTEREST NEARBY

Reservoir Hill: Here once stood the Maori pa below which the town was laid out. It gives a view over the town and its vast stockyards, whose sheep pens alone can accommodate upwards of 50,000 head and present a hectic scene on sale day (*Tuesdays*). *On Porangahau exit turn right up St Mary's Rd and follow "Kindergarten" signs. Entry is from Nelson St, off Reservoir Rd.*

Porangahau (*45 kmS*): The township stands on the Porangahau River three kilometres inland from a sandy but somewhat exposed beach.

The locality is best known for an otherwise humble ridge bestowed with the world's longest place name, although the official version, somewhat shorter, ranks in only second place. Taumatawhakatangihangakoauauotamatea (turipukakapimaungahoronuku) pokaiwhenuakitanatahu (the unofficial section is shown in parenthesis) seems to have escaped the abbreviation applied to most other Maori place names and, like others, records an event—it is "the place where Tamatea, the man with big knees, who slid, climbed and swallowed mountains, known as 'landeater', played his flute to his loved one". But the story is not of romance, as the "loved one" was Tamatea's twin brother, killed in a skirmish nearby. (*The hill is 44 km from Waipukurau; 5 km before Porangahau turn right along Mangaorapa Rd and follow this road for 9 km, where a sign indicates the ridge.*)

The Poho-o-Kahungunu carved meeting house (1910–12) at Porangahau replaces an older house and incorporates some of its carvings. The amo are heavily carved, the upper figure depicting a warrior with patu in hand. The maihi are covered with large spirals and realistic human figures at intervals, and end in a curious manaia form which appears at widely separated points throughout the North Island. (*Leaving Porangahau for Waipukurau, immediately over the river bridge turn left for 200 m.*)

North, near Blackhead, may be seen the wreck of the scow *Maroro* (230 tons), which in 1927 was forced by weather to shelter inside Blackhead Reef and was driven ashore to become a total wreck. All hands were saved. Built at Whangaroa in 1904, she had had a remarkable career in which she was posted as "missing" on no fewer than three occasions. (*Drive to Blackhead. The wreck may be reached at low tide some distance down the beach.*)

To the south lies **Cape Turnagain**, a promontory named by Cook in 1769. After landing at △ Gisborne, he had sailed south, hugging the coastline, until reaching the Cape. Here, "Seeing no likelyhood of meeting with a harbour, and the face of the Country Visibly altering for the worse", he shrewdly elected to retrace his route back to the East Cape. Cook's instinct was sound. As he was to observe when he completed his anti-clockwise circumnavigation of the North Island four months later, the coast to the south is indeed wild and inhospitable. Ever since he had discovered Cook Strait, Cook had been sure that he was sailing around an island. However, "being resolved to clear up every doubt that might arise on so important an object", he decided to leave nothing to chance and to see through his circumnavigation until he was actually back at Cape Turnagain. When for the second time Cook turned again here, this time to sail south to explore the South Island, he had for all time laid to rest the speculation in Europe that there existed here *terra australis incognita*, the great unknown continent. (*The Cape is not accessible by road.*)

WAIRAKEI ★★★

Volcanic Plateau   Map 8   Pop. 750

10 km N of Taupo township; 74 km S of Rotorua. Power Project Information Office, Highway 1.

WAIRAKEI is the centre of the country's geothermal power installations which rumble with muted thunder and billow steam clouds to create an unforgettable impression of tamed fury.

To North Islanders, Wairakei is also synonymous with luxury (it actually means "adorning waters", as pools here were used as mirrors), for the comfortable Wairakei Resort offers a choice holiday spot with excellent golf courses and swimming pools along with fine conference facilities.

GEOTHERMAL POWER

Wairakei geothermal power stations: Situated in the centre of the North Island's volcanic belt, Wairakei houses the world's second large-scale geothermal power scheme (the first is at Larderello in Italy). At Wairakei, modified oil-drilling techniques produce a unique technology which, under overseas development programmes, New Zealand has made available to other countries, in particular South America, Indonesia and the Philippines.

To tap the geothermal power a drilling rig first sinks a shaft, which is cased with steel tubes. Control valves are then attached to the wellhead, where hot water (¾ths by weight of the total discharge) is separated, and "dry" steam is led away to generators. The inverted "U" loops in the steam pipes contain stainless steel bellows which allow the loops to flex and so compensate for expansion and contraction. The pipes appear to be leaking where steam traps remove condensed water which, were it to reach the power-house, would damage the turbine blades.

Two power stations stand side by side by the Waikato River as vast quantities of cold water are used to condense the steam as it leaves low-pressure turbines. Condensation of the steam creates a vacuum and so makes the turbines generate almost twice as much electricity as they would if the steam were simply discharged directly into the atmosphere. Power Station A has three groups of turbo-alternators—high-pressure, intermediate- and low-pressure—and Power Station B has three 30,000 kW mixed pressure sets. The total generating capacity is 146 mW.

The characteristic twin towers at the wellheads are "cyclone" silencers, designed to reduce to a tolerable level what would otherwise be a deafening roar. Low-pressure steam and steam surplus to generating requirements go to waste from the silencers.

Drilling at Wairakei has tapped only the fringe of geothermal resources, and exploratory drilling has taken place at a number of different points within the main thermal district. *Further details available from the Information Centre, where a video is screened continuously. The centre is open daily, 9 a.m.–4 p.m.*

Geothermal power, Wairakei.

Ohaaki geothermal power station: The station, with its formidable cooling tower, taps the Broadlands steamfield of some 1,000 hectares in the Reporoa Basin. With a capacity of 116 mW, the station is smaller than Wairakei (140 mW) and differs from it in that temperatures are higher, the gas content of the waters discharged greater, and the field itself much drier.

The station is named for the nearby Ngati-Tahu marae, and is built on ancestral land leased from Maori owners. *23 km N. (40 km S of Rotorua.)*

THE ATTRACTIONS OF WAIRAKEI PARK ★ ★ ★

The cluster of sights and attractions here are promoted collectively as "Wairakei Park".

Wairakei Thermal Valley ★: With an array of exotic thermal colourings, the field is at its best after heavy rain. Wipapa, a geyser, spouts from the hole in the crest of a rock to create, every 12 minutes, a thermal waterfall. *Detour 1.5 km immediately N of the borefield. Camping.*

Craters of the Moon★ ★: A wide, desolate valley pitted with steaming craters, some furiously active. Both the Karapiti Blowhole and the Rogue Bore were near here, but neither site is accessible. *4 km. Karapiti Rd. (signposted at 2 km S on Highway 1). Admission free. Picnic area.*

Nearby, **horse treks** through the volcanic landscape for one or two hours are suitable for all ages (*Taupo Horse Treks, tel. (07) 378-0356*).

Wairakei Prawn Farm★ ★: Giant freshwater prawns are raised in large ponds using waste geothermal heat to warm water drawn from the Waikato River. Succulent prawns are barbecued on the spot. *Off Huka Falls Loop Rd. Guided tours: tel. (07) 374-8474.*

Huka Jet and the "African Queen": Boat trips, wild and sedate, visit the foot of the thunderous Huka Falls (*see p.* **215**).

Taupo Observatory Visitors Centre ★ ★: Displays and audio-visuals by the Institute of Geological and Nuclear Sciences interpret the volcanic landscape. *Off Huka Falls Loop Rd. Open daily; tel. (07) 377-3861.*

NZ Honey Hive ★ ★: An apiary produces a tempting range of honeys, and bees can be seen at work through the walls of a glass apiary. *Huka Falls Loop Rd; Open daily.*

Huka Village: A recreated colonial village, with animals, arts and crafts and souvenirs. *Huka Falls Rd. Open daily.*

Huka Falls ★ ★ ★: Here the Waikato River suddenly narrows to a chasm less than 15 metres across and heaves its vast bulk over an 11-metre ledge to boil furiously in a deep, semi-circular basin. The ledge is a band of silicafied conglomerate created by ancient thermal activity. A bridge crosses the falls to a number of vantage points and marks the start of a 7-kilometre walk down the river's right bank as far as the Aratiatia Rapids. Huka means "foam". *On loop road, 2.5 km S on Highway 1.*

Superb **helicopter rides** hover over the foam (*Helistar Helicopters, tel. (07) 374-8405*).

Upstream is secluded **Huka Lodge**, luxurious haunt of those who place comfort above cost (*tel. (07) 378-5791*).

Aratiatia Rapids ★ ★ ★: But for public outcry these superlative rapids on the Waikato River would have vanished completely as the result of a hydro-electric scheme. Most of the time the river bed is dry, but when the waters are "turned on" the rapids reappear to crash and foam down their old course. For 50 years the site had been officially recognised as "at once the most beautiful and most valuable location on the river", but it was not until 1957 that the Government braved the inevitable controversy and authorised construction. *The river flows down the rapids from 10–11.30 a.m. and from 2.30–4 p.m. except in exceptional circumstances. Lookout points are signposted on the river's right bank. A short detour leads to the powerhouse.*

Aratiatia means "pathway of stakes", a series of pegs stuck in the ground to assist climbers making a steep ascent. The name has been applied to the rapids as the river zig-zags here. *5 km E of Wairakei. Signposted.*

WAIROA   *Hawke's Bay   Map 11   Pop. 5,030*

119 km NE of Napier; 93 km SW of Gisborne. Information Centre, Marine Parade; tel/fax (06) 838-7440. Department of Conservation Field Centre, 272 Marine Parade; tel/fax (06) 838-8252.

FOR THE TRAVELLER it is surprising to find a lighthouse not only inland but also by Wairoa's main street. The lighthouse, which once stood on Portland Island off the tip of △ Mahia Peninsula, is the main feature of the town's "Marine Parade", where the banks of the Wairoa River have been enlivened with Phoenix palms and relics of local historical interest.

The only town of substance in northern Hawke's Bay, Wairoa is set in a dairying, sheep- and cattle-raising district. In summer the town caters for a number of visitors, as △ Lake Waikaremoana, △ Te Urewera National Park, △ Morere Hot Springs and the △ Mahia Peninsula are all relatively close by. The town suffered grievously and lost its road bridge when Cyclone Bola devastated the region in 1988.

SOME HISTORY

From Clyde to Wairoa: As with other settlements on this stretch of coast, the first Europeans to arrive were flax traders in the 1820s, and in 1839 Captain W. B. Rhodes established a trading post and whaling station nearby. Settlement was delayed as the local Maori would not sell land, but when coastal shipping trade with Napier grew, areas were leased for farming.

In 1865 the Government purchased the site for a town originally named "Clyde" but changed to Wairoa as it was confused with the Central Otago town of the same name. The original name is retained in North Clyde, a suburban area on the northern bank of the river. In the year the site was purchased the advent of Hauhauism (*p.* **167**) brought change to the attitude of some local Maori and led to a series of skirmishes between Hauhau converts and the settlers. These culminated in a decisive battle near the Waikare-Taheke River in which Ngati Porou, fighting for the Government, set fire to dry fern and so forced the Hauhau to flee inland to the Urewera country.

The building of a temple: In the late 1890s Te Matenga Tamati claimed to be Te Kooti's spiritual successor and directed his followers to build "Kowhiti Temple" from 12 enormous posts, each to be named after one of Jacob's 12 children. Totara logs, 12 metres long, were hauled down from Waikaremoana, and when various sub-tribes argued as to which pa was to be honoured with the temple, Tamati declared expansively that the log "Joseph" would lead them to the ordained place. But when in a flash flood the logs were all washed out to sea and "Joseph" ended up on Mahia Peninsula (well outside Tamati's territory) a steamer was hastily chartered to tow the errant log back to his brethren on Iwitea Beach. Because of this, Tamati proclaimed that the temple would not be built by his generation, and the logs (strictly tapu) still lie buried in the sand dunes. Tamati died in 1914 but the rama (guiding light) has yet to shine to direct the start of building. *The site lies between Ohuia and Wairau Lagoons; access by way of Iwitea Pa (9 km E of Wairoa) is difficult.* Nearby **Whakaki Lagoon** is a haven for wildlife.

POINTS OF INTEREST

Portland Island Lighthouse ★: With its tower of solid kauri, the lighthouse stood on Portland Island from 1877 to 1958. But when the lighthouse was replaced it was moved to its present site. Originally the light, visible for 39 kilometres, was provided by a kerosene burner, but in 1920 its wick gave way to an incandescent filament. *Marine Parade, by main river bridge. The light is operated each evening from about 7.30-11 p.m.*

A few hundred metres away is a **memorial** to Pitiera Kopu, a chief of the Ngati Kahungunu who died at Wairoa in 1867. The monument was erected by the Government in recognition of his whole-hearted support of the Pakeha during their campaign of the 1860s, against adherents of the Hauhau Movement. (*p.* **167**)

Wairoa Museum: On display are photographs of early Wairoa, Maori artefacts and articles used by early settlers. *Marine Parade. Access through Public Library. Open weekdays, 10 a.m.-5 p.m.*

Takitimu carved meeting house (1935): Seen upriver from the bridge, the meeting house contains some fine modern carvings, which generally conform to the Gisborne school—the figures have wheku (slanted eyes) and interlocking spirals on shoulders and hips. The pare over both door and window feature takarangi spirals and the tukutuku in the porch are in the poutama design, colloquially known as "steps to heaven"—the diagonal ascent of the panel symbolising growth from childhood to old age, and the horizontal lines symbolising periods of learning.

The house, named for the canoe from which local Maori trace their descent, is a memorial to Sir James Carroll (1853-1926), KCMG, MLC, a notable Maori Parliamentarian. Son of a local chieftainess and one of Wairoa's first European farmers, Carroll fought against Te Kooti in the Waikaremoana expedition and went on to become Member of Parliament, first for Eastern Maori, and then for the European electorate of Waiapu. In 1896 he became the first Maori to hold Ministerial rank and twice was Acting Prime Minister. Though responsible for much sound legislation, Carroll is best remembered as one of the finest speakers ever to sit in Parliament. One speech began, "Standing by this memorial . . . my mind is a hive to which are homing a hundred honeyed memories . . ." *3 km. Waihirere Rd, North Clyde. Arrangements to see the interior may be made through the Information Centre.*

ENVIRONS

△ **Lake Waikaremoana ★ ★ ★:** Set in the dense bush of Te Urewera National Park, it is a much favoured fishing and camping spot. Easily reached are a superb series of waterfalls on the lake's tributaries. *64 km NW.*

△ **Te Urewera National Park ★ ★ ★:** The finest native bush in the North Island affords deer stalking, pig and goat shooting, and magnificent walks and tramps.

△ **Mahia Peninsula:** A somewhat barren promontory separating Hawke from Poverty Bay has isolated beaches and a number of holiday homes. *43 km E.*

△ **Morere ★:** There are hot springs here in a pleasant setting. *40 km E.*

△ **Mohaka:** A tiny settlement high above the Mohaka River which in 1869 was the scene of a surprise attack by Te Kooti. *32 km W, off Highway 2.*

TOURING NOTES

Mohaka detour: Travelling to Napier, a loop road to △ Mohaka makes possible a detour without an appreciable increase in mileage.

Routes to Gisborne: The coastal road to △ Gisborne (Highway 2) passes both △ Morere Hot Springs and △ Mahia Peninsula and affords a spectacular view of Poverty Bay from the crest of the Whareratas. The more demanding inland route is generally considered inferior; however, the 18-metre drop of Te Reinga Falls, and Doneraille Park (a secluded area of native bush with good river swimming and fly fishing) both make pleasant stops. There is also an outstanding view of Poverty Bay, from the 354-metre summit of Gentle Annie.

Northland   Maps 2, 3 ★ ★ ★ **WAITANGI**

2 km N of Paihia.

WAITANGI, an historical reserve close to △ Paihia, in the △ Bay of Islands, is symbolic of New Zealand's nationhood for it was here, on 6 February 1840, that the Treaty of Waitangi was first signed, by which New Zealand became part of the British Empire. The treaty is still in some circles controversial and to some it is appropriate that Waitangi should mean "weeping waters".

The Treaty lies at the heart of the country's social realignment and its embrace of biculturalism. If it is a source of aggravation to Pakeha (fearful of shifts in resources), it is also the major instrument for Maori to achieve equality.

SOME HISTORY

Treaty of Waitangi: The British Government, disillusioned by the successful revolt of its American colonies and already overburdened with administrative difficulties, had no wish to add New Zealand to its extensive Empire and had been careful to exclude the country from its list of territories despite the fact that Captain Cook, acting on orders, had proclaimed British sovereignty by discovery in 1769.

However, the British Government could not prevent haphazard settlement by whalers, sealers, traders, escaped convicts and assorted adventurers, and by 1832 found it necessary to appoint James Busby (1801–71) as "British Resident" but supplied him with no force whatever by which he might impose his authority. Even had a man better fitted for the post been sent, it would still have been impossible for him to enforce any form of law and order.

Meanwhile, in Britain, the New Zealand Company (*p.* **27**) had been formed and was planning large-scale colonisation despite official opposition. In New Zealand many of the missionaries, previously fearful of settlement, now saw advantages in British rule as it promised to prevent exploitation of the Maori. In both countries there was an unjustified fear that France might annex the country and establish a "foreign" colony comparatively close to the British settlements in New South Wales and Tasmania.

Somewhat reluctantly Captain William Hobson RN (1793–1842) (*pp.* **43-44**) was appointed to negotiate with the chiefs for the transfer of sovereignty to the British Crown with "the free and intelligent consent of the natives [to be] expressed according to their established usages". Once this was achieved, Hobson was to be Lieutenant-Governor subject to the over-riding authority of the Governor of New South Wales, and New Zealand was to be a dependency of the colony there.

Hobson arrived at the Bay of Islands on 29 January 1840 and immediately undertook to establish a settled form of government and to investigate land titles. On 5 February the northern chiefs gathered in front of Busby's home at Waitangi (now the "Treaty House") where, with the help of Busby and the missionaries, Hobson explained the terms of the proposed treaty. A debate lasted all day in which many of the chiefs opposed the treaty, and the outcome was in doubt until Tamati Waka Nene, a prominent Ngapuhi chief from Hokianga, spoke eloquently in its favour. The next day the treaty was again read to the assembly and, after much explanation and discussion, was signed by 45 chiefs, the first to sign being Hone Heke. Those who could signed their names, others drew a mark or their distinctive moko (tattoo). Copies of the text were given to officials and missionaires to obtain the signatures of chiefs in southern districts, and within five months most of the influential chiefs in the country had signed.

The treaty was probably misunderstood by a large number of those who signed it. The Maori had no concept of "sovereignty" and this compounded already grave difficulties in comprehension. Also, at times dubious methods were used to obtain the later signatures. One chief believed that his Queen had sent him a blanket and he signed only to acknowledge receipt. On 2 October 1840 the proclamation of British sovereignty was published in the **London Gazette** and so was established in law as in fact. *(The original treaty documents are on public display in Wellington, at the National Archives: see p.* **288**.*)*

On 6 February each year an impressive ceremony has been held on the lawn in front of the Treaty House in which both Maori and Pakeha have commemorated the treaty. In recent years, though, the ceremony has become a focus of controversy, with those who see the treaty as symbolising not nationhood but an unknowing alienation of Maori land, and after events in 1995 the future form of the commemoration is in doubt.

TREATY HOUSE ★★★

The Georgian-styled "Treaty House" was built as his home in 1833 by the newly appointed British Resident, James Busby. The house was designed by the New South Wales Government architect, John Verge, and much of the timber used was shipped from Sydney. Only part of the original plan was built, the wings being added later.

The house was in poor repair when, in 1932, it was purchased by Lord Bledisloe, then Governor-General, and presented to the nation together with 500 hectares of surrounding forest and farmland. The house was restored for public displays and today contains Hongi Hika's flintlock rifle, a rifle presented to the Chief Waikato by George IV, a model of Ruapekapeka pa and an inkstand made from one of the flagstaffs at Russell felled by Hone Heke in 1845. Other displays feature Busby and members of his family, and furnishings of their period.

In the front of the house a kauri flagstaff marks the place where the treaty was signed. To the left is a Norfolk pine, planted by Busby's wife in 1836.

In the grounds is the Maori Centennial Memorial (1940) meeting house, a whare runanga unusual in that it contains carvings from many different tribes throughout the North Island. A meeting house usually has carvings only from its own tribe, but this is a house for all of Aotearoa. A 36.5-metre canoe stands in a canoe house, Te Ana o Maikuku, at Hobson Beach. Other memorials are to Captain Hobson, James and Agnes Busby, and to Sir Joseph Nias (captain of the ship which brought Hobson to New Zealand). *Open daily, 9 a.m.-5 p.m.*

Visitor Centre: The Centre has portraits of the principle people in the Treaty negotiations and such items as Waka Nene's mere, topuni (dogskin cloak) and carved store-house door as well as objects from Ruapekapeka pa. An outstanding audio-visual describes events leading up to the Treaty.

OTHER POINTS OF INTEREST

Haruru Falls walk: The easy walk to the falls crosses a boardwalk through the Hutia Creek Mangrove Forest. *Allow 2 hrs (½ hr to the mangroves). Signposted.* The mangrove (*Avicennia resinifera*) is a remarkable tropical tree which grows as high as 15 metres in tidal, salty, sheltered mudflats. A feature is its "breathing roots" which at times poke above the waterline to give the tree vital oxygen which its roots cannot get from the sour soil. The roots also trap mud and debris around the tree, slowly building up the level of the mudflat until it is above the level of the tide. While the reclaimed land can then sustain plants less tolerant of salt water, the mangrove can no longer survive. Once the reclaimed land becomes dry the mangrove stands must advance seaward or perish, as their roots must be washed by salt water, at least during high tide.

In New Zealand the mangrove is found only in the north of the country and only as far south as Kawhia and Ohiwa Harbours.

Mt Bledisloe (*115 m*): Three kilometres beyond the Treaty House, the mountain affords an unequalled view of the Bay of Islands and has a direction table to identify points of interest. *The summit is a short walk from the car park at the end of the road. The return to Paihia may be made by way of Haruru Falls (floodlit by night) to make a pleasant round trip.*

Waitangi National Marae: On the Paihia side of the river bridge is the country's "national marae", a marae which to each Maori ranks beneath his or her own.

Taranaki   Map 7   Pop. 6,012   ★ **WAITARA**

16 km NE of New Plymouth. Information Service, 62 McLean St; tel. (06) 754-4405.

WAITARA, once a Maori stronghold on the banks of the Waitara River, still has a large Maori population, for years principally dependent on its large freezing works. The town's river port once handled the output from the works, but this is now shipped out through New Plymouth.

In recent times the town has benefited greatly from energy development projects, with the gas-to-gasoline plant at Motunui and the methanol plant in Waitara valley. Nearby, too, are several oil and gas wells. *For notes on the province's energy projects, see pp.* **152–3.**

Waitara means "mountain stream".

SOME HISTORY

Waitara Land Deal: Waitara has its own niche in history, as it was here that the Land Wars began in earnest, in 1860.

In the 1820s Te Ati Awa trekked south from Taranaki to escape the invading Waikato tribes and later helped the Government to put down an uprising. Soon after they sold the land they held near Wellington, and in 1848 returned to their ancestral lands here by the Waitara River. They cultivated the fertile ground and it was soon the envy of a growing body of New Plymouth settlers, who felt hemmed in by Maori land to east and west, and by sea and mountain to north and south.

In the 1850s there crystallised strong feelings among some Maori against land alienation, and they formed a loose resolve (sometimes called the Maori Land League, although no such "league" ever in fact existed outside the propaganda of some Pakeha) to resist further sales of ancestral land to settlers.

Differences between adherents to this resolution and would-be land-sellers developed into a series of feuds throughout Taranaki, but European settlers were never molested. Indeed one settler was warned by each side that a fight would take place on his farm the following day and was asked to remain indoors until it was over.

Governor Gore Browne visited Taranaki in 1859, and in an appeal for peace undertook not to purchase land without the consent of all its owners. But he warned that no one was to interfere with a land sale unless he had an interest in the land involved.

Notwithstanding, the Government immediately agreed to purchase from the chief Teira a block of land on the left bank of the Waitara River which included the site of the present town. Teira, only a minor chief, had some undefined interest in the land, but the concept of communal ownership required the consent of the whole tribe, and the majority, led by the chief Wiremu Kingi, opposed the sale.

It seems that Teira had quarrelled with Wiremu Kingi and may have proposed the sale out of vindictiveness, for when a chief considered he had been insulted by others of his tribe it was common practice for him to act in a way calculated to embroil the whole tribe. The ploy was known as whakahe—putting the other in the wrong.

Despite Wiremu Kingi's protests, the fraudulent deal between Teira and the Government proceeded, and as the Government prepared to take the land by force the outlying settlers moved back to the greater safety of New Plymouth (pop. 2,500).

After Te Ati Awa had been given 24 hours to quit the area, troops moved in to occupy the Waitara block. Neighbouring tribes, even traditional enemies, came to the aid of the dispossessed Te Ati Awa and in June 1860, after a setback at Waireka, inflicted a major defeat on the British Regulars just south of Waitara, at Puketakauere, where many of the troops engaged in attacking two Maori pa were trapped in a swamp and tomahawked. The Government had its revenge a few months later at Mahoetahi, when a combined force of Regulars and Volunteers inflicted a crushing defeat on Te Ati Awa's newly found Waikato allies. (*The road to New Plymouth intersects the battle site immediately beyond the turnoff to Inglewood.*)

In a long drawn-out attack on Pukerangiora pa (*see below*), eight redoubts and "Pratt's Long Sap" were constructed before hostilities ended in 1861 with an agreement between the Government and Hapurona (in place of Wiremu Kingi, who had moved to the Waikato). Terms included Government investigation of the Waitara Block and acceptance of the Queen's sovereignty by Te Ati Awa; but it was not until 1926 that the Government recognised its responsibility for the unhappy affair and granted the Taranaki tribes an annual sum of £5,000 as compensation.

The Waitara Land Deal was proof to the Maori that the Pakeha was not to be trusted, and marked the start of hostilities which were to continue for 21 years.
The Waitara Campaign Trail (19 km) is a signposted route which takes in some of the visible historic sites associated with the First Taranaki Campaign. Start in Waitara Rd. Pamphlet available locally.

POINTS OF INTEREST

Manukorihi pa ★★★: The magnificently carved meeting house (1936) is a memorial to Sir Maui Wiremu Pita Naera Pomare, KBE, CMG, MD (1876–1930). Named Te Ikaroa a Maui ("the long fish of Maui"), it has as its tekoteko the mythical Maui-tikitiki gripping a fishing line whose hook is embedded under the roof of Tonganui, the undersea house Maui hooked when he dragged the North Island up from the ocean. The koruru below Maui-tikitiki represents Maui Pomare, who fished compensation out of the sea of sorrow which surrounded the Waitara Land Deal. Wiremu Kingi is depicted at the base of the pou-koukou-aro, to the right of the porch steps.

Of the figures inside the house, noteworthy are three on the front poutahu to the right of the doorway—Uenuku (said to be high priest in "Hawaiki" at the time of the fabled Polynesian migration to New Zealand), above him Turi (captain of the *Aotea* canoe) and above him, Manaia (captain of the *Tokomaru* canoe). The tukutuku was carried out under the supervision of Sir Apirana Ngata.

Beside the house is a marble statue of Pomare, above the crypt which contains his ashes.

Pomare, whose grandmother was one of the few women who signed the Treaty of Waitangi, led a distinguished Parliamentary career and, with Sir Apirana Ngata and Sir Peter Buck, as one of the Young Maori Party did much to better the lot of the Maori and to encourage pride in Maori culture. In his lifetime the Maori increased both in numbers and social standing, owing in no small measure to Pomare's work in the field of public health. His Parliamentary career spanned two decades during which he held a number of Ministerial posts. As a child Pomare was at Parihaka when the troops marched in and, as one of those who skipped in their path, claimed to have lost a toe when trodden on by a horse.
Visits to the marae are by appointment only; tel. (06) 754-4405 or through the Information Centre.

Viewpoint: From the headland near the pa, high above the river, is a wide view over the town and away to the peak of Taranaki/Egmont. *Off North St, across the bridge.*

Waitara West Walkway: An easy circuit of West Waitara extends for 7 kilometres, taking in the left bank of the Waitara River and a segment of the foreshore. *Follow the orange discs from the river bank.*

ENVIRONS

Pukerangiora (Te Arei) pa ★★★: A heavily bushed pa site in a most dramatic setting high above the Waitara River. Despite its superb site, the pa was the scene of frequent and bitter fighting.

Over the period 1821–22, the local Te Ati Awa gave sanctuary to a Waikato war party and were for seven months besieged in the pa by North Taranaki tribesmen before a large Waikato relief force under Te Wherowhero raised the siege. But in one of those shifts characteristic of Maori allegiances, within a decade Te Wherowhero had returned, this time to annihilate the defending Te Ati Awa and force many of them to leap to their deaths over the precipice.

During that Taranaki Campaigns an attack on the pa saw the construction of the remarkable "Pratt's Long Sap", the most extensive earthworks ever undertaken by British troops in New Zealand. Like other early commanders of British Regulars in the Land Wars, General Sir Thomas Simon Pratt (1797–1879) had a horror of bush warfare, and his preference for frontal advances quickly earned him the settlers' scorn. As was his practice, to assault Pukerangiora General Pratt had a long sap (trench) built which slowly crept towards the palisades of the pa—and which the defenders occasionally filled in again at night. The weeks it took to construct the mile-long (1.6-km) sap and accompaning redoubts were marked by periods of intense fighting, and intervals of humorous exchanges—tobacco was swapped for kits of fruit and troops were occasionally urged to "Lie down, we're going to shoot". But if General Pratt's "mile-a-month" technique led newspapers to comment that "the war at Taranaki maintains its peaceful course", once artillery had been established in the sap a heavy battering soon convinced the defenders that their pa was untenable and their surrender in March 1861 marked the end of the First Taranaki Campaign. *7 km from Waitara, signposted inland just west of the borough boundary. A 5-min walk through the bush leads to the edge of the precipice and an almost aerial view of the river and its plains. The sap was constructed from the north up to within 100 m of the pa.*

★★★ WAITOMO CAVES

King Country   *Map 6*

19 km NW of Te Kuiti; 75 km of Hamilton. Information from the Museum of Caves Information Centre, Main St; tel. (07) 878-7640

BENEATH the rugged King Country hillside, studded by weather-worn limestone outcrops, are a vast and largely uncharted series of caves — and from the unparalleled magnificence of those open to the public, one can but muse as to what further wonders await discovery, and understand the area's lure for speleologists.

Waitomo Caves settlement evolved to serve the large number of visitors who come from all parts of the world to visit one of New Zealand's premier attractions. Augmenting the magic of the caves are a unique specialist cave museum and a traditional weaving centre as well as trout fishing, golf and bush walks.

SOME NOTES

Formation of limestone caves: While this area lay on the sea bed, over a period of about 4 million years it was encrusted by vast numbers of shells and skeletons of marine animals. With the water's movement these ground to dust, cemented to form limestone and were then covered by layers of mudstone and sandstone.

Limestone can be dissolved only by water which contains carbon dioxide, and this was provided by the decaying vegetation on the floor of the forests which covered the deposits soon after they emerged from the sea about 12 million years ago. So it was that caves were slowly formed in the limestone layer by the dissolving action of rainwater, and it was a reversal of that which formed the stalactites (from cave roof) and stalagmites (on the cave floor) inside the cave themselves. As each drip of rainwater seeps through the cave roof it dissolves limestone, and as it lingers before dropping each drip evaporates slightly to leave an infinitesimal ring of limestone behind. In this way endless millions of drips over countless centuries build a tube down from the roof. The stalagmite on the floor below the stalactite is also formed by evaporation but is a solid projection — unlike the generally hollow tube of the stalactite. When the two finally join to form a pillar a film of evaporating water may continue to run down it, thus imperceptibly but steadily increasing its thickness.

The New Zealand glow-worm: The species *Arachnocampa luminosa* is rarely found outside New Zealand, and certainly not in shimmering thousands, as in Waitomo's Glow-worm Grotto. Unrelated to the European glow-worm (a beetle which uses its light to attract its mate), the New Zealand glow-worm belongs to the gnat family. Hatched from an egg, the larva (or glow-worm) grows to 2.5-3.5 centimetres in length. It prepares long sticky threads which it drapes down like fishing lines to snare the insects on which it feeds. The prey is lured to the lines by the glow-worm's light, which can be turned on and off at will, and which is probably produced by a chemical oxidation process.

The life cycle appears to be about 12 months, with the insect in the larva stage for up to nine months, finally hatching into a seldom seen and short-lived fly of about 1 centimetre not unlike a small daddy-long-legs.

THE CAVES ★★★

Waitomo Cave ★★★: This cave takes its name from the Maori words for "water" and "cave" — a reference to the Waitomo River which vanishes into the hillside here. In 1887 Fred Mace and Tane Tinorau, having floated into the cave on a raft, made the first documented exploration. It is world-renowned for its Glow-worm Grotto ★★★ where visitors glide silently by boat beneath a canopy of glow-worms. *Guided tours (45 mins) leave the entrance to the cave regularly between 9 a.m. and 4.30 p.m. (Oct to Feb, 5.30 p.m.) Tickets from Glow-worm Cave ticket office tel. (07) 878-8227).*

Aranui Cave ★ ★: Named for the Maori who discovered it in 1911, here, too, coloured lighting is used to accent limestone formations to remarkable effect. *Guided tours leave daily at 10 a.m., 11 a.m., 1 p.m., 2 p.m. and 3 p.m. More frequently in holiday periods.*

Abseiling and blackwater rafting: On the **"Lost World"** adventure accompanied visitors abseil down a 100-metre hole into the Mapunga cave system (*about 10 km S*). An exhilarating experience, it is nonetheless neither dangerous nor particularly difficult. Alternatively, the **Haggas Honking Holes** caving adventure explores a number of underground waterfalls by abseiling and ladder climbing. *(For both, tel. (07) 878-7788.)*

A second truly memorable experience is "black water rafting" in the Ruakuri Cave, on a journey guided at times by glow-worms. There is also a combined abseiling and rafting trip in the Ruakuri Cave. *Booking essential. Details from the Caves Information Centre.*

Note: In holiday times, when the Waitomo Caves are extremely busy, the best time to visit is early morning or late afternoon.

OTHER THINGS TO SEE AND DO

Waitomo Museum of Caves ★ ★ ★: Complementing the cave systems is a specialist museum which focuses on various aspects of the caves from their formation to their exploration and lighting. Detailed displays illustrate life within the caves, including insects such as the cave weta as well as the glow-worm, and give an appreciation of the ecosystem of which the caves are a part. Fossils found locally and reconstructed skeletons of various birds (including the moa) found in the caves round out the collection. An audio-visual presentation highlights the underground world of the cave explorer. *Open daily.*

Ohaki Maori Cultural Centre ★ ★: First established as a Maori weaving centre to preserve the skills of two venerable weavers, it provides a rare opportunity to admire the dexterity of traditional weavers.

The centre is now augmented by a reconstructed Maori village, complete with wharepuni (sleeping houses), wharetohutohu (learning house) and pataka (food storage house), where the traditional Maori lifestyle is explained. Concert parties often perform in the evening.*On exit towards Te Kuiti; tel. (07) 878-6610.*

Waitomo walkway ★: An interesting walk through picturesque limestone country leads past the steep-sided gorge of the Upper Waitomo Valley where lies a spectacular natural bridge. *Start by museum. Allow half a day (if return journey is not made by car). The walk to the gorge alone takes 1 hr (return).*

Horse trekking: Back country riding can be an invigorating experience. Expeditions range from a one hour gentle ride to three-day expeditions for the more hardy. *Waitomo Horse Trekking; tel. (07) 878-7649.*

ENVIRONS

Marokopa Falls ★★: The Marokopa River bounds over three 6 to 12-metre falls before plummeting a spectacular 36 metres over the falls proper, where a fault has formed on a contact zone of limestone and igneous rocks. *Signposted 32 km on the road to Marokopa. 10-min walk. A track leads to the base of the falls.*

Mangapohue (Te Koipu) Natural Bridge ★: A remarkable 15-metre limestone arch which bridges the Mangapohue Stream and is the remnant of an underground river channel, the rest of the cave having collapsed and eroded away many thousands of years ago. *Signposted 26 km on the road to Marokopa. Cross the paddocks and the footbridge and continue 100 m upstream. 10-min walk.*

△ **Kawhia Harbour** ★★: An isolated area of enigmatic charm. *79 km.*

Auckland South   Map 4   Pop. 4,442   WAIUKU

65 km S of Auckland. Information Centre, 2 Queen St; tel. (09) 235-8924.

THE FARMING CENTRE of Waiuku assumed national prominence with the establishment at neighbouring Glenbrook of a steel industry based on local ironsands. These sand dunes, now anchored by forests, had earlier wandered, moving inland 20 metres or so each year, encroaching on good farmland and engulfing at least one homestead. Horticulture is now assuming greater importance in the locality, with glasshouses becoming more numerous.

Waiuku ("wai"—water; "uku"—wash) was the name given the area after Tamakea, a local but grubby warrior, was washed clean by his friends to enable him to win the heart of a visiting chieftainess. Pronunciation is corrupted locally to "Wai-uk" (to rhyme with "Why-hook").

SOME HISTORY

An adaptable town: The story of Waiuku is one of tenacity. Among the oldest of South Auckland settlements, it grew and prospered on the trade route between Auckland and Waikato. There was a portage here, between the Manukau Harbour and a Waikato tributary, but although a short canal was often mooted, it was never cut. During the Waikato Campaigns many of Waiuku's settlers were evacuated to Onehunga. By the time the Campaigns ended, the once-flourishing Maori farms and orchards in the Waikato had been destroyed, and the trade, once Waiuku's lifeblood, ceased to flow. Local residents switched to clearing the dense puriri forest and draining vast areas of flax swamp, but as the town developed in its new role as a farming centre, it was again threatened, this time by the rapid growth of nearby △Pukekohe. Waiuku's need was industry, and this came in the shape of the New Zealand Steel Mill to realise at last a remark first made in 1874 that there were here "immense dunes of ironsand which will doubtless one day be utilised".

Fortuitous bonfires: It is said that in 1863 local settlers celebrated the marriage of the Prince of Wales (later King Edward VII) with Princess Alexandra of Denmark by lighting bonfires on a number of hilltops. At this time a number of supporters of the Maori King planned to attack outlying settlers, but they mistook the bonfires for military signals and fled. Since then fire has treated Waiuku less kindly, three times in a decade wiping out blocks of shops in the town's centre.

STEEL-MAKING

The Glenbrook Steel Mill: On an arm of the Manukau Harbour, the steel mill draws ironsand from deposits at Waikato North Head, 16 kilometres away, which it converts into reduced primary condensate by the Stelso-Lurgi-NZ Steel direct reduction process. This is then converted into steel in electric furnaces, using a proportion of scrap. Founded in 1965, the company produces steel billets, pipe and galvanised flat products, and its development plans provide for the production of cold-rolled and hot-rolled strip.

A $700 million development programme envisages an increase in iron- and steel-making capacity, from 150,000 tonnes a year to about 775,000 tonnes. Under the plan iron- and steel-making will be based exclusively on the two main local raw materials, ironsand and coal. The existing iron-making process would be unchanged and steel-making, while differing noticeably from the present process, would be based on well-practised, conventional techniques. Four additional multiple hearth/reduction kiln combinations would provide the required iron-making capacity. The new kilns, similar to those used at present, would incorporate new features giving improved performance. Hot sponge iron from these units would be melted continuously in two electric melting furnaces, each with an output of 50 tonnes per hour. The molten pig iron produced in this operation would be fed to an oxygen steel-making furnace capable of producing steel in batches of up to 60 tonnes about every 45 minutes. This steel would be cast in a continuous slab-casting machine similar to the existing billet-casting machine. Slabs of either 165 mm or 210 mm thick, and varying between 650 mm and 1550 mm wide, would be produced.

Following the commissioning of the expanded iron- and steel-making plants, two rolling mills are planned. A hot mill would reduce the thickness of slabs to produce strip in coiled form for subsequent cold rolling or for feed to the pipe-making plant. The cold mill would produce thinner strip from the hot-rolled coil to provide strip with a surface finish suitable for a wide range of coated and uncoated applications, *7 km E. An observation road runs to the left of the plant. Conducted tours are usually run twice daily, Monday-Friday; for information and bookings tel. (09) 235-8089.*

Mill Mine site: From a lookout point, carryalls may be seen hauling loads of iron-bearing sand from open-cast mines to the preliminary treatment plant. *On the north head of the Waikato River. 13 km S. Signposted.* The site is within the Waiuku Forest, originally established by Depression-era relief workers. The forest includes picnic spots along the Waikato river bank.

OTHER POINTS OF INTEREST IN THE AREA

Sailing on the "Jane Gifford" *: The country's oldest sailing scow, the *Jane Gifford* (1908), for over 70 years saw service around the coast. Its flat-bottomed design was ideal for transporting timber, livestock, road metal and sand in the Bay of Plenty and the Hauraki Gulf. The scow was retrieved from the bed of the Waitemata Harbour and lovingly restored. *Adventure excursions depart Waiuku Wharf. For details of sailings and bookings, tel. (09) 235-8924 in advance.*

Glenbrook Vintage Railway and Farm Park *: A nostalgic journey on a steam train takes visitors along the old Waiuku branch line. *Access Rd, Glenbrook, 7 km E. Operates Sundays and public holidays between October and June, and daily over the Christmas holiday period from 11 a.m.–4 p.m. departing on the hour; tel. (09) 636-9361 or (on operating days) (09) 236-3546.*

Waiuku Museum: On display is a collection of Maori artefacts, firearms used in the Land Wars and photographs of local interest. *King St. Open afternoons on Sundays and public holidays; other times by arrangement: tel. (09) 235-8698.* Close by is Hartmann House, a renovated pioneer cottage where handicrafts are for sale.

Towards the town, a short distance from the museum, a small memorial marks the portage which gave rise to the original trading centre.

Sandspit: A pleasant boating and picnic spot with views of Manukau Harbour. *Sandspit Rd. Signposted 2 km.*

St Bride's Anglican Church, Mauku (1859): An historic church, its walls were once loop-holed for rifle slits during the Land Wars. *Described under △ Pukekohe.*

Kariotahi surf beach: A west coast beach excellent for surfing and surfcasting. Patrolled at summer weekends, the beach can be dangerous at low tide. *65 km.*

WAIWERA ★★★ *Auckland Map 4*

48 km N of Auckland.

WAIWERA, on a beach contained by twin towering headlands, for a time enjoyed vogue as a health resort, and its hot springs today make the picturesque settlement a seaside holiday place with a difference. The many inlets of the Mahurangi Harbour lend themselves to kayaking.

HOT SPRINGS

Called Te Rata ("the doctor") by the Maori, the hot springs here were considered sacred, and were defended with fortified pa on four prominent positions.

Glasgow-born Robert Graham arrived in Auckland in 1842 and was sailing north when storms forced his ship to shelter here. Looking ashore he was amazed to see numbers of Maori on the beach scooping out holes and lying in them. Two years later Graham returned and managed to acquire an area of land on the foreshore where he built bath-houses and an hotel. The hot springs quickly gained a therapeutic reputation and soon steamers sailed regularly from Auckland to ferry day-visitors to and fro. Local mineral water was even taken to baths built at Ellerslie about 1877.

One of those who tripped here constantly for treatment was Sir Julius Vogel (1835-99), a free-spending Colonial Treasurer and later Premier whose severe gout rendered necessary a lift-chair to convey him to the upstairs dining room.

POINTS OF INTEREST

Waiwera mineral pools: The waters range in temperature from 28°C to 43°C and are set in a garden of lawns and hibiscus. *Open Sun–Thurs, 9 a.m.–10 p.m. Fri, Sat 9 a.m.–11 p.m. Costumes, etc., for hire.*

Waiwera Beach: A sheltered family bathing beach.

Wenderholm Reserve: Wenderholm (Swedish for "winter home") is a beach and riverside picnic park of 134 hectares in the bay north of Waiwera. The park extends along the cost from the Waiwera to the Puhoi Rivers and offers a combination of surf beach and river estuary, fishing, boating, swimming, and walks along tracks up a bush-covered hill for excellent views of the islands of the Hauraki Gulf. Pohutukawa back the beach with a blaze of crimson in early December, and a profusion of kowhai throughout the park tint it gold in spring. Species of birds include tui, parakeet and kookaburra.

During the latter half of last century, when the usual means of transport in the area was by sea, Wenderholm was a port of call on the local shipping route. The original homestead (1850s), **Couldrey House**, may be visited (*open weekends and public holidays from 1–4 p.m.* It was frequently visited by Sir George Grey and was made available in 1957 to the former British Prime Minister, Sir Anthony Eden, who recuperated here after the double ordeal of surgery and the Suez crisis, which put him out of office. *Signposted off Highway 1, just N of Waiwera.*

★★★ WANGANUI

Wanganui   Map 13   Pop. 41,213

195 km N of Wellington; 164 km SE of New Plymouth; Information Centre next to District Council Chambers, cnr Guyton and St Hills Sts; tel. (06) 345-3286. Department of Conservation Offices, Whanganui Field Centre, 68 Ingestre St; tel. (06) 345-2402 and Pipiriki Field Base: tel. (06) 385-4631.

WANGANUI, one of the country's oldest cities, is given mellow charm by both mature gardens and the impressive Whanganui River that seeps through the valley over which the city spreads.

It was the river that spawned the settlement—it provided ready access to the interior as well as a coastal port to link with Wellington and New Plymouth. Today the port at Castlecliff is experiencing the nationwide decline in coastal shipping. Local secondary industries include woollen mills and meat processing works. Today the city is also known as the home of the country's law enforcement computer.

For over a century the name Wanganui (a corruption of Whanganui) was thought to mean "big harbour" and to refer to a time when the river extended right across the valley from Durie Hill to the foot of St John's Hill. Traditionally it was said to be the name given the area by the Polynesian explorer Kupe.

Recent investigations, however, suggest that Whanganui means "long waiting" (whanga—"to wait"; nui—"long", "big" or "large"). A great chief of Ngati Ruanui of Taranaki is said to have taken a long trip down the coast and, when he reached the Whanganui River, had to wait a considerable time before transport was available to ferry him and his party to the other side. Hence the name, "long waiting".

Originally the New Zealand Company named its settlement "Petre" after one of its directors, Lord Petre. But "Petre" never found common usage, and, after a petition from the settlers, the name was officially changed back to Wanganui.

Annual events: The New Zealand Masters Games are held in February each alternate year (including 1993). More than 40 sports are represented and 3,000 medals won, but the main aim is simply to participate and have fun. The Wanganui Festival is held each year in October or November, in conjunction with the A & P Show, and the Mountains to the Sea Triathlon is held each October.

SOME HISTORY

A river route: From the earliest times of Maori settlement the river was an important canoe and supply route to the interior, the artery in a network of tracks and smaller canoe routes. Its easily fortified cliffs and plentiful food marked it as a certain place for inter-tribal clashes, and in one of these during the early 1800s, the neighbouring Ngati-Apa, in a surprise attack on the Whanganui Maori, are said to have heaped their enemy's dead in a pile four high and nearly a mile (1.6 km) long. The growth of Te Rauparaha's power, based on △ Kapiti Island, caused coastal tribes to sink their differences and in 1829 combine in a united assault on Kapiti. Whanganui contributed to the force, and the canoe *Te Mata-o-Hoturoa*, now in the Wanganui Regional Museum, was said to have taken part.

The enraged Te Rauparaha sent a force of 1,500 to exact utu (revenge) from the Whanganui Maori and for two months Putiki pa was under siege. Finally an offer was sent to the pa that if the defenders would agree to peace, Te Rauparaha's men would send in food. The starving defenders accepted, and opened the gates. But as soon as the Whanganui Maori were busy distributing food, Te Rauparaha's men rushed in and slaughtered them. A cannibal feast of immense proportions followed, and when the missionary the Rev. Richard Taylor arrived in 1843, 13 years later, he found the bones of the victims still strewn around the pa.

First Europeans: Four Europeans and a Negro landed at the river mouth in 1831 led by one Joe Rowe, a Kapiti-based trader in preserved Maori heads. A fight began when Rowe manhandled a Maori who was examining his whaleboat and in the scuffle three of the Europeans were killed and later eaten. The Negro was unharmed, presumably because of his colour, and the surviving European was ransomed for about 11 kilograms of tobacco. Poetically, Rowe's head was dried and preserved by visiting Taupo Maori who, on a trip to Kapiti, had been shocked to recognise the heads of members of their own tribe among Rowe's stock-in-trade. The incident gave Wanganui an undeserved but grisly reputation which for some time caused traders to give the area a wide berth.

In 1840 the missionaries Williams and Hadfield came to collect signatures for the Treaty of Waitangi and promised chiefs a present from the Queen if they signed. Later asked if he knew what he had signed, a local chief replied that his Queen had sent him a blanket and he had been told to make a mark to show that he had got it.

Purchase of town site: The same lack of understanding prevailed two months later when representatives of the New Zealand Company "negotiated" the land purchase of Wanganui. With an assortment of pipes, looking glasses, blankets and jews' harps worth about £700, the company "bought" no less than 16,000 hectares. The goods were put ashore and piled on the site of Moutoa Gardens. From the safety of his ship Colonel William Wakefield described the scene: "Seven hundred naked savages were twisted and entangled in the mass, like a swarm of bees, over the line of goods . . ."

Two days later, when the Maori had recovered, Wakefield went ashore to find 30 pigs and about 10 tonnes of potatoes piled where the goods had been. This was homai o homai ("a gift for a gift") and showed that the Maori had completely mistaken the nature of the transaction. Wakefield did not accept the presents outright but insisted on paying a blanket for each pig, and pipes and tobacco for the potatoes. Later he argued that he had accepted and paid for the return gifts as "a private speculation", and that the second transaction had nothing to do with the land "purchase".

Early settlement: Predictably, the Maori disputed the "land sale" but, notwithstanding, the town of Wanganui was established by the New Zealand Company in the same year. Land purchases at Wellington had been disallowed and the Company was left with settlers but with little arable land. Wanganui was an attractive supplement to Wellington—its rich flat land was easy to clear and simple to cultivate, and the broad river saved expensive roading.

By late 1840 the first settlers had arrived. The following year they had already begun to export pigs and potatoes to Wellington and Nelson, even if they were at the same time "giving themselves over to drunkenness and the lowest debauchery".

Gilfillan massacre (1847): After an incident in which a midshipman had accidentally injured a Maori, utu was exacted with the massacre of four members of the Gilfillan family. (Some suspect that the young Maori who took part in the killings were acting under orders from their chief, who was trying to use the accident as a pretext to provoke a wider conflict.) The Gilfillans had no connection with the earlier incident, but the Maori generally had a strong tribal sense of collective responsibility and so the perpetrators thought little of the atrocity. Other Maori took a different view; they captured those involved and handed them over to the settlers. Four were hanged by the thoroughly alarmed colonists; outlying settlers moved back to the town, newly built stockades were strengthened and the women and children were shipped to Wellington. There was even talk of abandoning the settlement.

A number of skirmishes culminated in the "Battle of St John's Wood" when about 400 Maori occupied the level ridge on St John's Hill which overlooks the town and clashed indecisively with an equal force of British Regulars. The British lost three dead and 11 wounded and the Maori three dead and 10 wounded before both sides withdrew, the Maori explaining that they were leaving because it was time to tend their kumara plantations.

The next year land problems were resolved when £1,000 was paid for some 32,000 hectares. This time a document of sale clearly defined the land involved and concluded, "Now all the land contained within these boundaries . . . we have wept and sighed over, bidden farewell to, and delivered up forever to the Europeans. . . ."

Recovering from its inauspicious start, the town progressed rapidly. Local Maori were unaffected by the later Land Wars and actually saved the settlement from attack when they headed off a Hauhau war party at Moutoa Island. *See Whanganui River, below. An outlying protective* **blockhouse** *(1868) is near Highway 1 on Marangai Coopworth Stud, at 10 km S.*

QUEEN'S PARK

Queen's Park, a block from the main street, is the cultural centre of the city. During the Land Wars the Rutland Stockade was built here, looking across to a second stockade built above Cook's Gardens. The symmetry of the park should also be viewed from the entrance to Cook's Gardens. By the park stand the Regional Museum, Sarjeant (Art) Gallery and Wanganui's War Memorial Hall and Davis Public Library.

Queen's Park, Wanganui.

Wanganui Regional Museum ★★★: The museum houses one of the finest Maori collections in the country. Included are splendid displays of whalebone and greenstone mere and hei-tiki, and no fewer than seven extremely rare "god-sticks". The artefacts are prized by local tribes and the extension of the museum has been declared to be their "common marae".

A feature of the Maori collection is *Te Mata-o-Hoturoa* ("the face of Hoturoa"), a 23-metre war canoe built in 1810 and named after the captain of the *Tainui* canoe. The canoe held 70 men and saw action on the Whanganui River, including fights in 1865 at Puketapu and Ohautahi from which bullets remain embedded in its hull. Also of interest are one of Te Kooti's battle-flags and Major Kemp's sword— one of Queen Victoria's Swords of Honour and said to have been a gift from the Queen after Kemp had declined a knighthood and allegedly asked for "just a sword with which to fight for her". A realistic replica portrays part of the upper storey of one of the Rutland Stockade blockhouses, built in 1847 for the 58th Regiment. New Zealand's first organ, a gift from an uncle in 1829 to the missionary brothers Henry and William Williams, is displayed. The organ has no manual and is operated on the pianola principle by a rotating cylinder. The country's fifth largest museum also exhibits a fine collection of 25 original Lindauer paintings of leading Maori of his day. *Entrance from Watt St. Open Monday–Saturday, 10 a.m.–4.30 p.m. and some evenings; Sundays and public holidays 1–4.30 p.m. Extended hours in summer; closed Christmas Day and Good Friday.*

The Sarjeant Gallery: Housed in a 1919 neo-classical domed building above the Veterans' Steps, is an extraordinarily dynamic gallery whose holdings (especially of contemporary works and photographs) have been shown in Australia. Of particular interest is the country's largest collection of works by Philip Trusttum, images of local photographer Anne Noble and local artist Edith Collier, a 1917 watercolour by Frances Hodgkins, and works by Wanganui-born John Hutton, including his designs for the engraved windows in Coventry Cathedral. *Queen's Park. Open daily.*

Tiny **Tylee cottage** (*c.* 1854), one of the city's oldest buildings, was moved to its present site in 1982 and is now used by the Gallery's "Artists-in-Residence" (*cnr Bell and Cameron Sts*).

OTHER POINTS OF INTEREST

Putiki Church (St Paul's Memorial Church) ★★★: Among the finest of the country's Maori churches, it was built in 1937 as the latest in a series of churches built here, and is an outstanding example of modern carving. Many of the interior fittings are memorials to those who played parts in the mission work at Putiki—the carved altar rails commemorate the Rev. John Mason, the first resident missionary, who drowned in the Turakina River in 1842; the pulpit commemorates the Rev. Richard Taylor, and the carved prayer desk is a gift from Lord and Lady Bledisloe in memory of the Rev. Arona Te Hana, the first Maori clergyman to take charge of the mission. The tukutuku work was carried out locally under the direction of Sir Apirana Ngata. *Anaua St, on the left off the main road south after the City Bridge.*

Putiki pa★: The pa stands on the banks of the river and includes a carved meeting house, Te Paku-o-te-Rangi, which replaced an earlier house washed away in the great flood of 1891. The river rose to levels never before known, inundated the pa and washed many canoes out to sea. Sympathetic tribes made gifts to help build a new house.

The tekoteko (carved figure on the gable) depicts Aokehu, an early Whanganui hero. A giant taniwha (water monster), Tutaeporoporo, once lived in the river near the city bridge and terrified the local population as he devoured those who passed, literally by the canoe-load. Aokehu concealed himself in a hollow log and floated downstream towards the taniwha's lair. The monster rushed out and swallowed the intruder, but once inside Aokehu climbed out of the log and killed the creature from within with saws edged with sharks' teeth. The body of the taniwha drifted ashore, where the grateful people freed their hero. The monster is today depicted on the Wanganui City's coat of arms.

The low doorway is thought to be much older than the rest of the house, and may have been saved from the earlier house of 1865.

Beside the meeting house is a carved pataka (storehouse) which dates from 1891.

The pa was heavily populated and well fortified and withstood an East Coast raid in 1821, but in 1829 Te Rauparaha captured and massacred the defenders. *Kemp St, off the main road south. The pa is on private property and permission must be obtained from the house within the Memorial Gates.*

Virginia Lake★★: A garden showpiece and popular picnic spot, with ducks, swans, splendid winter gardens, shady walks and a walk-through aviary. Near the road is a bronze statue of Peter Pan. A Victorian octagonal band rotunda is still in use.

The lake is on St John's Hill, in the heart of a most attractive residential area. Its Maori name is Rotokawau ("lake of black shags"). A legend tells of a nature-loving chief, Turere, who was killed here by a rival for the maiden Tainui. Furious at his death, the gods visited the area with a thunderstorm of gigantic proportions. The rival was struck dead by lightning and rain poured down until both of the bodies were covered with water. Tainui, arriving late upon the scene, added her own tears to those of the heavens and together they formed the lake. Tainui's statue is by the lake (*a short distance from the winter gardens*). The lake was renamed by settlers who considered it resembled Virginia Water in Surrey, England. *Great North Rd, by the main road 1.5 km N of the city. Winter gardens are open daily, Monday-Friday; Saturday and public holidays in the mornings; Sunday afternoons.*

Durie Hill: An elevator to the top of the hill is reached through a 205-metre tunnel and, in one minute, rises 66 metres through the hill itself. For the more energetic an even better view of the city and surrounds as far as Taranaki/Egmont, Mt Ruapehu and down the coast to Kapiti Island is obtained from the top of the 31.7-metre Durie Hill War Memorial Tower, a short distance from the lift. *There is a distinctive carved Maori gateway entrance to the elevator tunnel which is practically opp. the Wanganui City Bridge. The elevator operates daily, Monday–Saturday; Sunday afternoons. The War Memorial Tower is closed at dusk, and at 6 p.m. at weekends.*

Other good views are obtained from the Bastia Hill Tower (*Mt View Rd*), the St John's Hill lookout (*signposted cnr Parsons St and Great North Rd*), and from the top of Roberts Avenue (*off Somme Parade, Aramoho*).

Moutoa Gardens: A small historic reserve by the river, this was where the purchase of the town site was transacted in 1840. It was designated as the town's market square on the original town plan. The area was a traditional pa site, the Paakatoire marae, and its ownership has been the subject of disputes with local Maori, who deny that it was ever included in the sale. In 1995 the Gardens attracted national attention when about 150 Maori claimed and occupied the site in a peaceful demonstration modelled on the Te Whiti and Parihaka lines of non-violent civil disobedience.

There are a number of memorials here, including one erected by a grateful province to the heroes of the Battle of Moutoa (*see Whanganui River, below*). They are described as having fallen against "fanaticism and barbarism", a phrase which saddened Mark Twain when he visited Wanganui in 1895 and moved him to note that "Patriotism is patriotism — calling it fanaticism cannot degrade it." A war memorial commemorates the Maori dead of World War I (where Whanganui Maori hold their own memorial service each Anzac Day) and a statue of "Major Kemp" (Te Rangihiwinui Kepa, a Putiki chief) incorporates plaques depicting the battles of Moutoa, Pungarehu, Maraetahi and Te Porere. Kemp's sword and portrait are in the Wanganui Regional Museum. Another memorial is to the Maori Pioneer Battalion, to those who fell in the 1914–18 War. The statue of premier John Ballance has periodically lost its head. *Watt St, off Victoria Ave.*

A short distance away is Wairere House where, behind protective pylons of floodlights and television cameras, is housed the **Wanganui Computer Centre**, used by the Police, State Services Commission, Ministry of Transport and Department of Justice to store a variety of information. Included is a national register of motor vehicles and drivers' licences and detailed court records. Established amidst public controversy, the Centre is governed by its own legislation which includes provision for a Privacy Commissioner, appointed for five years to act as the system's watchdog and to investigate complaints that information may be being misused. People have the right to apply to the Privacy Commissioner to obtain a copy of information recorded about them on the computer system. The legislation which authorises operations on the computer and closely controls data in the computer provides for heavy penalties for people who attempt to obtain information from the computer by unlawful means. (Somewhat incongruously, Wairere means "diarrhoea"!)

On the river bank opposite is the sheer drop of **Shakespeare Cliff,** for many years known as McGregor's Leap. In 1847 an early settler, Captain Jock McGregor, crossed the river to look for cattle. He claimed that he was fired upon by a party of Maori—though some suggest he may have been chased for his interest in Maori girls—but for whatever reason, to save his skin McGregor fled downhill and leapt off the cliff to land in the mud at the water's edge. From there he was rescued by a boat sent across the river from the Rutland Stockade. Earlier the cliff top had served as a strong fighting pa, but erosion and repeated earth falls have destroyed much of the earthworks.

Cook's Gardens: The city's sporting centre, where Peter Snell set a world record time of 3 min. 54.4 sec. for the one-mile race on 27 January 1962. The record came as a complete surprise as Snell had never before broken four minutes. A week later, at Christchurch, he set new world marks for the 880 yards and 800 metres. The Athletic Pavilion has been named after Snell to commemorate the ground's evening of glory.

During the wars a military stockade was built overlooking the gardens which are named because they were where the Army cook grew his vegetables.

Above the gardens is the venerable Victorian wooden **Fireball and Watch Tower** (*c.* 1880), whose position presiding over the skyline afforded the night-time fire lookout the best of vantage points. In one celebrated fire, in 1879, the equipment of a visiting circus went up in flames and for a bizarre few hours citizens were treated to the spectacle of zebra and llama fleeing through their streets. The tower now houses the chimes for the city's town clock.

Also above the gardens is the **Ward Observatory** which houses the country's largest refracting telescope. *(Open Monday evenings, weather permitting.)*

The view looking down Maria Place towards Queen's Park is unusual for its symmetry. *St Hill Street.*

Whanganui Riverboat Centre ★: A riverboat museum houses the recently salvaged paddlesteamer, *Waimarie*, built in 1899. From the following year she faithfully plied the Whanganui River until 1952, when she sank at her moorings. The restoration project and photographs and memorabilia convey a sense of life on the river in the earlier part of the century. The steamer was recovered in 1993. *1A Taupo Quay; tel. (06) 347-1863.*

Kowhai Park★: Included in the park is a children's playground with a boating pool, miniature railway and imaginative slides. There is also a pleasant picnic area. *Anzac Parade. From the city, cross Dublin St Bridge and turn right.*

Holly Lodge Winery: Once the only winery on a river thought likely to become a major wine-making region because of the valley's similarity to some major French wine-producing areas. There is a swimming pool and children's playground. The paddle wheeler *Otunui* provides access by river from the city *(tel. (06) 343-9344). From Somme Pde through Aramoho. 8 km. Open daily except Sunday.*

Close by is **Waireka Estate** with a stately old homestead and small museum. *Open to family groups by prior arrangement; tel. (06) 342-5729.*

Wanganui Collegiate School: Founded in 1854, and built on land given by Sir George Grey (after whom a boarding house is named), the school is one of the country's best known private secondary schools. Prince Edward, youngest son of Queen Elizabeth II, spent a short time here as a house tutor in 1982-83. *Liverpool St.*

ENVIRONS

Beaches: The most popular beaches are Castlecliff Beach, on the river mouth *(8 km; follow Taupo Quay and Heads Rd along the right river bank)* and Mowhanau (Kai-iwi) Beach *(16 km; turnoff signposted on the main road N).* Beyond Mowhanau Beach is Ototoka Beach *(24 km; difficult access)* and to the south of the city lies Turakina Beach *(30 km; turn off at Turakina on the main road S).* The township of Turakina is of interest as it was here that the first Health Camp was held, before the movement became established; the town was also the first home of Turakina Maori Girls College (now at Marton), which has been a major influence in Maori education.

Bushy Park Scenic Reserve★: The reserve land was given to the Royal Forest & Bird Protection Society by Mr Frank Moore, son of an original settler, who wished to preserve an area of 85 hectares as an example of the magnificent bush that once covered the area. A 20-minute bush walk leads through the finest bush in the district which includes rata with girths of up to 13.7 metres. The rata is an unusual tree as it originates as a seed which germinates not on the ground but in the fork of another tree, usually a rimu. The seedling puts down roots which grow to the ground, strangling the tree on which it is growing and ultimately incorporating it in its own trunk. The Edwardian homestead (1906) provides bed and breakfast accommodation. *24 km. Drive N to Kai-iwi and detour 8 km inland. Signposted.*

This trip may be combined with a visit to Mowhanau Beach *(6 km from Kai-iwi)* and to the Maori rock drawings at Kohi *(see △ Waverley).*

Bason Botanical Reserve: This reserve is being developed as a combined public park and scientific institution for research and education. Over 4,000 native and exotic trees have been planted, and the Homestead Garden includes more than 100 named camellias. A conservatory includes a tropical house, begonia house and display centre. *10.5km. Rapanui Rd., off Highway 3 N. Open daily.*

Kemp's Pole: Over six metres high and carved from totara, the pole was erected on 30 November 1880. This is the survivor of four poles, erected by Major Kemp to define an area of land to be reserved in trust for local Maori. Before the trust was properly established individual land sales were made and the project failed.

The pole stands near the river on the earthworks of Mataikai, an old fighting pa. As with a number of other deserted pa, the area was later used as a burial ground.

The road rises high above the river and looks across and down to Kaiwhaiki pa on the opposite bank, where old canoes can occasionally be seen. The drive is particularly attractive in autumn. *Follow the road to Raorikia up the right bank of the river. At 21 km the road crosses a bridge. Inquire at the first farmhouse on the right beyond the bridge for permission and for directions. An easy 5-min walk leads to the pole and the pa site. The pole is easily seen from the river.*

Other walks: In addition to those described above, there are several walks that start on Whanganui River Road *(as opposed to Highway 4 which follows the true left bank of the river)* The most notable are the **Aramoana Walk** *(2½ hrs return; start 3 km along the road)* and the longer **Atene Skyline Walk** *(7–8 hrs; start 36 km along the road).* The remote but much-photographed **"Bridge to Nowhere"**, which lies in the regenerating bush of the Mangapurua Valley, is best reached by boat *(see Organised Excursions, below, and △ Taumarunui, at p. 210. The 3 km-walk in to the Bridge begins at Mangapurua Landing, on the Whanganui River).*

WHANGANUI RIVER ★ ★ ★

The Whanganui River winds some 290 kilometres through varied country as it flows from the western slopes of the central mountains to meet the sea at Wanganui. Much of its spectacular scenery is preserved in the Whanganui National Park *(74,231 hectares).* At times the river cascades over rapids and at times is confined to narrow gorges, but below Pipiriki the river is generally docile. Some of its headwaters have been diverted down the Waikato River by the imaginative Tongariro Power Scheme (*see pp.* **236–37**).

In mythology, the Whanganui river bed was gouged out by Taranaki (Mt Egmont) as he fled from the Volcanic Plateau after his fight with Tongariro. *For the myth see △ Egmont National Park.*

The road from Wanganui to Pipiriki is a favoured scenic drive, and launch trips are a great attraction. In summer canoeists paddle downstream from Taumarunui.

The legendary Kupe sails the river: The river was sailed by Kupe, in legend the first Polynesian to discover New Zealand. He is said to have explored the lower reaches of the Whanganui River and was thought to have named it Whanganui ("big harbour") as the river then extended right across the valley where Wanganui lies, from Durie Hill to St John's Hill. Recent investigations, however, suggest that Whanganui means "long waiting" (whanga — "to wait"; nui — "long", "big" or "large"). A great chief of Ngati Ruanui of Taranaki is said to have taken a long trip down the coast and, when he reached the Whanganui River, had to wait a considerable time before transport was available to ferry him and his party to the other side. Hence the name, "long waiting".

Traffic on the river: In pre-European times the river was an important canoe route inland, linking the interior of the North Island with its west coast, and was the main artery in a network of tracks and tributaries.

With the arrival of settlers the river became even more important and a regular steamer service was soon established between Wanganui and △ Taumarunui. The journey between the two settlements took three days, with overnight stops at Pipiriki and at a magnificent houseboat moored on the river. The scenery, particularly grand above Pipiriki, quickly attracted sightseers and the journey soon became an essential part of any overseas visitor's itinerary. Both the houseboat and Pipiriki's elegant hotel have been destroyed by fire, and the Maori settlements along the river banks, once alive with activity, are now but evocative shadows of their former selves.

At the turn of the century settlers began developing the river valley for farming. They met with success in the upper and lower reaches, but were beset with problems of access, bush regeneration, decreasing soil fertility and erosion in the rugged "wilderness" above Pipiriki. In one example, the rehabilitation settlements in the Mangapurua Valley (*32 km above Pipiriki*), were cleared of their virgin forest, developed pastorally and then abandoned by their pioneering "soldier-settlers", all between 1917 and 1942.

Rising costs, road development and the abandonment of farms and river settlements eventually lead to the end of the steamer service in 1958. Since then, however, recreational interests have gradually revived, and now each year many hundreds of visitors travel to the Whanganui River to enjoy the same scenic features as did their riverboat predecessors.

A number of settlements began as mission stations and were given biblical names suggested by the Rev. Richard Taylor (1805-73), an early missionary. His names have been transliterated into Maori equivalents, e.g. Corinth became Koriniti, Jerusalem became Hiruharama and Athens became Atene.

POINTS OF INTEREST ON THE RIVER

The following points of interest are listed in the order they are reached when driving from Wanganui up the true left (i.e. eastern) bank of the river:

Waitaha pa (*7.5 km*): A stile leads to a heavily-defended ridge-top pa whose history vanished with the unknown iwi that occupied it. Erosion has modified the ramparts but these are still impressive (*access permitted*).

Henson brick works (1869) (*8.5 km*): The ruins of an early brick kiln that supplied the infant Wanganui with bricks by barge down the river.

Upokongaro★ *(11 km)*: St Mary's Anglican Church here was built in 1877 at a cost of £268. The east window (1879) is a memorial to a parishioner, Archibald Montgomery, drowned in a shipwreck in the English Channel two years earlier. It depicts the storm in the Sea of Galilee, with Christ walking on the waves and with St Peter later attempting unsuccessfully to emulate his Master.

The church gives the settlement a picturesque air, particularly when viewed from the river. The steeple is most unusual as it has a four-sided base which rises in a three-sided column to give a tortured appearance which varies as one's viewpoint changes.

On the hill just upriver from the church and overlooking the settlement are the earthworks of Buckthorpe's Redoubt, built in 1868 on the site of Opui pa so that a watch could be kept for "hostile" Maori coming downriver to attack Wanganui. The climb to the earthworks affords a pleasant view. *A track leads from the roadside. Allow 20 mins.*

Aramoana *(14 km):* Farther north the road reaches the summit of Aramoana *(500 m),* with its well known and glorious view of the river, seen at its best in autumn when poplars fire the valley with a blaze of colour. Aramoana means "path to the sea".

Parikino *(23 km):* North of the settlement, high in the cliffs above the road, are huge deposits of oyster shells.

Atene (Athens; 37 km): A small meeting house is all that remains of the former village. An old river meander here shows where the Whanganui once flowed in a near circle, around a large hill known as Puketapu, before eroding its way through a narrow isthmus to force a more direct route to the sea. Road signs mark the two ends of the Atene Skyline Walk, which follows the skyline ridge which leads behind the old river bed. Superb views and a wide diversity of native forest types are a feature of this route. A small shelter, with a water supply, is located at the half way point of the walk, which takes about 6-8 hours.

Koriniti (Corinth; 48 km): This was once one of the largest Maori settlements on the river, but its population has dwindled sadly. On the marae are two carved meeting houses—Te Waiherehere, Koriniti's own house, and Poutama, which was transported across the river from its original site in the former village of Karatia. Carvings from an earlier meeting house are now in the Wanganui Regional Museum. Close by is Pepara Church (1920). *Respectful visitors are welcomed on the marae.*

Operiki pa★★ *(49 km):* This was the finest pa site on the river, with earthworks up to 3.5 metres high. It was never successfully attacked and only once did an enemy succeed in entering when, on a cold, wild night, a Waikato war party crept inside through driving rain. Half-frozen, they crouched around a deserted fire trying to restore their numbed circulations before attacking the sleeping defenders. But a woman heard their whispers, quietly alerted her kinsmen and the war party was slaughtered.

On another occasion some Waikato came downriver by canoe and camped on the sloping bank opposite, a short distance upriver. One night they hid and in the morning the defenders looked across to find that the Waikato had apparently fled, leaving their belongings behind and their food still cooking in the ovens. The Operiki Maori were nearly deceived and a number were captured when they crossed the river to investigate. The Waikato then built a large shield and, under its shelter, tried to undermine and collapse the pa walls from the riverside—a Roman and early European siege technique known as "The Sow". The defenders were too alert; they collapsed the mine prematurely, entombing the attackers. *Signposted about 800 m N of Koriniti. A stile gives access to the pa site from the roadside.*

Kawana Flour Mill★ *(56 km):* The mill, which ground flour from 1854 for over 50 years, has been completely rebuilt and restored by the NZ Historic Places Trust. The sole survivor of more than 50 on the river, the mill serves as a fascinating reminder of the wheat-growing era in the Whanganui River Valley. The millstones were a present to local Maori from the then Governor, Sir George Grey, and Kawana is a Maori transliteration of "Governor". The miller's cottage has also been restored, and was shifted from its former site on a hill across the road, to stand alongside the mill. *Open continuously. Signposted 1.5 km N of Matahiwi.*

Ranana (London; 61 km): One of the larger settlements along the river road. A Roman Catholic mission was founded here in the late 1890s and the church built then is still used today. Farming, in particular dairying, was extensive in the area in the early 1900s, the produce being transported to Wanganui by riverboat. Today much of the land is farmed by the Morikaunui Incorporation. A cairn here marks the centenary of the battle of nearby Moutoa Island.

Moutoa Island *(62 km):* The slender, diamond-shaped island is said to be a piece of Taranaki (Mt Egmont) which snapped off as he fled from Tongariro.

The island was a famous pa and, as it was of vital strategic importance, many fights took place here. The most celebrated battle was also the last when, on 14 May 1864, lower Whanganui tribes routed a war party of upriver Hauhau (*p.* **167**) who were pledged to drive the occupants of the infant settlement at Wanganui into the sea. Fifty were killed and the tiny township of Wanganui was saved from attack. "Loyal" Maori held the island and dènied the war party passage downriver, though they were possibly more anxious to protect the mana of their river than to save the settlement. A monument at Moutoa Gardens, Wanganui, records the victors' 16 casualties, among them Lay-Brother Euloge, a member of the nearby Catholic mission, who was trying to prevent the clash. The earthworks on the island are largely overgrown. *Just north of Ranana, a NZ Historic Places Trust marker indicates the only viewpoint from the road. A walking track leads over private land to the river from the first rise north of Ranana, and when the river is low one can cross to the island and inspect the battleground.*

Hiruharama (Jerusalem; *67 km*): A picturesque village set on a bend on the river, the steeple of its slim church silhouetted against the bush. The area was once well populated and the scene of much intertribal fighting both here and on the river bank opposite. The village is known for Mother Mary Joseph Aubert (1835-1926) who, in 1884, came to re-establish the Catholic Mission here. She founded a home to care for destitute Maori children, the aged and the infirm, and made use of ancient Maori herbal remedies. To support the school and the dispensary, the community farmed nearby land and prepared medicines for sale in Wanganui. This was the start of what became the Daughters of Our Lady of the Compassion, a nursing Order which now extends to Australia and Fiji. Mother Aubert was born near Lyon, France, and came to New Zealand in 1861 with Bishop Pompallier. Her work is still carried on at the mission, near the church, but the convent is now for backpackers. There are today homes run by the Order elsewhere in New Zealand.

The settlement is also known for the commune where the poet James K. Baxter (1926-72) spent the last years of his life. Up to 200 people congregated in the commune, which dissolved soon after Baxter's death in 1972. Nothing of it remains today, but it is enshrined in his later writings.

Pipiriki *(79 km)*: The settlement once had an elegant hotel, Pipiriki House, the remnants of which are still in evidence. The hotel, burnt down in 1959, was an overnight stopping place when river travel between Wanganui and Taumarunui was at its zenith. A camping area is now on the hotel's site, and from here a short track leads to the remains of a waterwheel. This once powered the Kaukore flour mill (1854), which ground the wheat then grown on the slopes across the river.

The period house of a former riverboat captain has been restored and now houses a small museum collection of local interest. *(Open daily in holiday periods; at other times on request at the ranger station.)* A short walk follows an easily graded path through native forest to the summit of Pukehinau Hill, overlooking the settlement. Jet boats sweep up and down the river *(tel. (06) 385-4128).*

The 32 kilometres of water above Pipiriki make up perhaps the most beautiful stretch on the whole river. A feature is the "Drop Scene", where a mountain seems to drop into the ground as one approaches and where, in certain light, the river appears to be flowing uphill. Sadly, the spectacle, which once drew tourists from the world over, is not now as evident since slips have modified the landforms. Also of interest is a walk inside Puraroto Cave to visit an underground waterfall. *The only access is from the river.*

During the Land Wars, Pipiriki was an early Hauhau stronghold. After the Battle of Moutoa Island *(above)*, a military force was sent from Wanganui to build three earth redoubts on the right bank *(opp. the present landing beach)*. The force was surrounded by Hauhau and during a 12 days' siege supplies ran low. Their commander wrote messages in Latin and French so that the Hauhau could not understand them, placed them in corked bottles and floated them downriver. As luck would have it, two bottles were found at Wanganui and a relief force was promptly dispatched to raise the siege. In 1982 the scene of the siege, a long-deserted Maori kainga, was designated the **Rangiahua National Marae** and restoration work was carried out on its previously neglected meeting house. The lines of the three redoubts constructed by the troops are clearly visible nearby.

Pipiriki means "little pipi". When a local chief on his deathbed had a craving for pipi (shellfish), a canoe was sent to the river mouth but failed to return before the old man died.

About 6 kilometres beyond Pipiriki on the road to Raetihi is the "Dress Circle", renowned in coaching days as a place where coaches would curl around the inside of a cliff while their passengers gazed down in awe to the stream far below. Today the scene is safer and so less spectacular.

A SUGGESTED DRIVE

Pipiriki and return via △ Raetihi *(180 km return; see Whanganui River, above)*: The road follows the left bank of the Whanganui River and the return is made down Highway 4 ("The Parapara") from Raetihi, past Raukawa Falls. Many picnic spots. The river has been sailed for centuries and the settlements are full of interest.

ORGANISED EXCURSIONS

Trips on the river: The real beauty of the Whanganui River lies above Pipiriki, which can only be fully appreciated when seen from the water. The Visitor Information Centre at Wanganui provides details of tour operators and hire outlets (*tel. (06) 345-3286*). Jet boat tours and canoe hire can be arranged at Wanganui, Pipiriki and △ Taumarunui.

Some trips include a stop at Mangapurua for a 45-minute walk through native forest to the "Bridge to Nowhere" — an imposing structure completed in 1936, but by then would-be farmers were already abandoning the valley and today the bush is reclaiming the land. Guided canoe or kayak trips are run in summer. *River City Tours, tel. (06) 344-2554; Bridge to Nowhere Jet Boat Tours, tel. (06) 385-4128; Whanganui River Experience, tel. 0800-808-686. Baldwin Adventures (tel. (06) 343-6346) also run 5-day motor-canoe trips.*

Scenic flights: Helicopter and Tiger Moth flights may be arranged. *Details from the Visitor Information Centre.*

River road tours: These run up to Pipiriki and back. *Arrange through the Information Centre, or River City Tours, tel. (06) 344-2554.*

WARKWORTH   *Auckland   Map 4   Pop. 1,734*

69 km N of Auckland. Visitor Information Centre, Rodney District Council Bldg, Baxter St.; tel. (09) 425-9081.

THE FARMING TOWN of Warkworth rests by the gently winding Mahurangi River, which in summer is choked by pleasure boats moored alongside wharves in the town's commercial heart. Nearby Sandspit is a springboard for visits to exquisite Kawau Island (*see p. 98*).

The township was named for the Northumberland (UK) town of the same name, possibly because a relative of the settlement's "founder", sawmiller John Anderson Brown (1810–67), had been in charge of a school there for over 50 years.

The annual **Kowhai Festival** each spring celebrates the profusion of the golden native which shines in the town and through the surrounding bush (*Oct*).

SOME HISTORY

Competing companies: Euopean settlement dates from before 1829 when timber traders, seamen among them, cut and dressed kauri spars for the Royal Navy. As shoreside timber was cut out, the parties moved upriver and a small community grew up on the site of Warkworth.

For many years the only communication between Warkworth and Auckland was by ship. Agitation for a regular service saw two companies enter the run, and in the price war that followed residents were divided into rival camps—"Settlers" (supporters of the local company) and "McGregors" (those of the McGregor Steamship Company). Feelings ran high, culminating in 1905 with Alec McGregor's *Claymore* running down and sinking the Settlers' *Kapanui* in Waitemata Harbour, the second time such a collision had occurred.

The area's deposits of high-grade limestone saw the founding in 1865 of the Wilson Portland Cement Co., a venture which grew into one of the country's larger public companies but is no longer based here. The ghostly, battlement-like shell of the cement works (closed 1929) loom by the river (*Wilsons Rd*).

MAHURANGI PENINSULA★★

The Mahurangi Peninsula, a curiously shaped appendage south of Warkworth, points fingerlike towards Auckland.

Spared the clutter of suburbia which has overwhelmed Whangaparaoa Peninsula to the south, Mahurangi has fine beaches, among them Snell's Beach and Algies Bay. Martins Bay (*19 km*) is a splendid camping and swimming spot facing out to Kawau, and Sandspit (*8 km; with a launch service to Kawau Island*), named after an odd protruding finger of sand, is a boating venue.

A road leads through sea-girt farmland to Mahurangi Heads (*19 km*), following the crests of the hills.

SATELLITE EARTH STATION

A 16.5-hectare bowl-shaped site here, sheltered from external radio interference, was chosen to accommodate the first of the large dish antennae necessary to link New Zealand to the world-wide satellite communications system.

New Zealand was first linked to Australia by an undersea telegraph cable laid in 1876, and from there connected to other international circuits. In the early 1900s telegraph cables were laid across the Pacific, and in 1963 a lightweight coaxial cable to Canada joined New Zealand to the COMPAC and CANTAT circuits. These cables were being used to full capacity, and satellite communication (a joint venture by over 100 nations) marked a new phase in the country's communications with the outside world. There are now three giant dishes on the site. *Signposted 5 km S on Highway 1. Public observation gallery with an audio-visual display open daily, 9 a.m.–4 p.m.*

OTHER POINTS OF INTEREST

Kowhai Park: A picnic area and motor camp in the town. A short signposted bush walk leads to kilns used in cement making at the turn of the century. *State Highway 1.*

Parry Kauri Park and Warkworth Museum★: Hard by the carpark and the museum are two huge kauri trees, the larger being the 800-year-old McKinney kauri, 12 metres to its lowest limb and with a girth of 7.6 metres. The park was created by local residents who bought the block to prevent the milling of the trees. Among other displays are kauri gum specimens and native timbers polished to an extraordinary radiance. *2 km. Signposted on the Auckland exit to the town.* Nearby, in Hepburn Creek Road, a woolshed has been turned into a handicrafts gallery. *Redbluff Gallery. Open Mon–Sat, 9 a.m.–5 p.m.*

Sheep World ★★: Here every aspect of sheep farming, a mainstay of the country's economy, can be experienced. Shows include sheep dog mustering and shearing exhibitions, and visitors may try their hand at feeding lambs or spinning yarn. Appropriately, a restaurant serves lamb specialities. *4 km N on Highway 1. All weather shows at 11 a.m., 1 p.m. and 3 p.m.; tel. (09) 425-7444.*

Mahinerangi Honey Centre ★ ★: Here bees work incessantly behind glass-walled hives, and in summer and autumn visitors watch through a viewing window to see the honey being extracted. A shop stocks a bewildering range of honey- and health-based products. *4 km S off Highway 1 in Perry Rd. Open daily from 9 a.m.–5 p.m.; tel. (09) 425-8003.*

Fall's Road: An eight-kilometre round trip leads to a scenic river ford and a waterfall set in a grove of native trees. *Leave town via Woodcocks Rd and return via Falls Rd and Hill St.*

Moirs Hill Walkway: A six-kilometre walk leads through native bush and exotic plantations, and includes views of the Hauraki Gulf. There is an alternative return by way of a loop track through the Pohuehue Scenic Reserve. *Signposted 6 km S on Highway 1, near Redwoods, the forestry headquarters of NZ Forest Products. Allow 3½ hrs.*

Tawharanui Regional Park: Hereford cattle and Romney sheep graze a park with pa sites and white sandy swimming beaches which strides the Tokatu peninsula. Fascination for skindivers lies in an off-shore marine park and reefs incorporating overhangs, tunnels and caves. The rare New Zealand dotterel nests here in sand dunes. Several walks include the energetic **South Coast Walk** (*3 hrs*), with sweeping views, and the shorter **Ecology Trail** (*1½ hrs*), which starts from Anchor Bay. *21 km E of Warkworth, via Matakana.*

Horse trekking: Exhilarating day and overnight treks over farmland and along deserted beaches can be combined with a farm stay. *Pakiri Beach Horse Riding, Rahuikiri Rd; tel. (09) 422-6275.*

Dome Forest Walk: *See p. 300. Signposted 8 km N on Highway 1.*

Goat Island Marine Reserve ★ ★: Since the marine reserve was declared in 1978, fish have been encouraged to return here in large numbers — including some prodigious crayfish. There is absorbing snorkelling and diving (*facilties available*), and for those who would stay dry there are sea aquariums and trips in small boats out to Goat Island itself (*for bookings and information tel. (09) 422-6212*).

WAVERLEY   Wanganui   Maps 7, 13   Pop. 1,55

46 km NW of Wanganui.

WAVERLEY, a small farming centre, is known for the important Maori rock drawings at Kohi and for the exploitation of nearby ironsands.

The town had its share of trouble during the Land Wars, and at the base of the clock tower beside the Post Office are traces of the earthworks of the Wairoa Redoubt. The redoubt was used in 1868 as a base from which Colonel Whitmore launched an attack on a nearby Hauhau pa—an attack which ended in the worst reverse the Government suffered on the west coast. Nineteen of Whitmore's men were killed and 20 wounded, for the loss of a solitary Hauhau. To the amazement of younger Maori, the day ended in a cannibal feast with one of the dead soldiers being cooked in a hangi.

On the coast nearby, at Waipipi, ore-rich ironsands were for some years up to 1987 dredged by a floating plant and shipped to Japan.

KOHI MAORI ROCK DRAWINGS

The Maori rock drawings at Kohi, possibly carved by a tohunga, are perhaps the most important in the North Island. The lizard shapes symbolise Whiro, the god of death and decay, and the bird-like motifs resemble drawings found on the Chatham Islands. *Turn off 3 km W of Waverley and follow Kohi Rd. After a further 3 km a bridge is crossed. Inquire for permission and directions to the rock shelter at the first farmhouse on the right beyond the bridge. The drawings are on private property.*

TOURING NOTE

Ventifacts: Rocks up to the size of oranges with facets highly polished by windblown sand can be found on the surface of the sandhills. *Waitotara Beach, turn off at Waitotara at 11 km SE.*

WELLINGTON ★★★

Wellington   Map 13   Pop. 325,682 (combined urban areas)

655 km S of Auckland. City Information Centre, Civic Sq, 101 Wakefield St; tel. (04) 801-4000. Ferry information centres, tel. (04) 498-2130 and 498-2805; freephone 0800-658-999.

THE CAPITAL CITY of New Zealand stands on the south-west tip of the North Island, on "the very nostrils" of the Fish of Maui. Wellingtonians, who to a great extent comprise public servants and "head office" staff born elsewhere, display an aloofness to the parochial jealousies of other centres. While outsiders scorn the "Windy City" residents admire its picturesque harbour of ever-changing mood, encircled by houses spilling down precipitous slopes. Reclamation has added to the lip of level land where on which the city centre is rising to ever greater heights as much of its Victorian architecture gives way to contemporary buildings that meet higher earthquake standards. The clever blend of old and new, with nooks and crannies and unexpected vistas, gives the city's heart a style and vibrance.

Wellington has been "capital" since 1865, the year the New Zealand Company settlement (established here in 1840) finally realised a destiny it had actively pursued for a quarter of a century. Paradoxically it is now Auckland, the former "capital", which advances the Wellingtonians' complaint of over a century ago—of being the country's metropolis yet being ruled by a city of civil servants nearly 700 kilometres distant.

The city is renowned for its wind. A concentrated flow of air is channelled through Cook Strait to render a still day the exception rather than the rule. This can be exacerbated by high-rise buildings creating a "wind funnel" effect in some downtown streets. Critics elsewhere condemn the city for its climate, but some local observers (with a bias the city generally shuns) see the gales which not infrequently sweep the city as developing in its citizens qualities of resourcefulness and independence! Gusts of 248 km/h were recorded on Hawkins Hill in 1959 and 1962, the North Island's strongest ever.

Wellington is named for the first Duke of Wellington in recognition of the Duke's support for the "Wakefield" scheme *(p. 27)* of colonisation. The harbour is officially named Port Nicholson, a name conferred by Captain Herd in 1825 after the then-Harbour Master at Sydney. Used today only in a maritime context, and enshrined in the title of the capital's yacht club, the name was abbreviated by local Maori to "Poneke", now that of a major rugby club.

Annual Events: The formal Opening of Parliament, usually by the Governor-General, takes place as each year's session of Parliament commences *(date varies)*. There is an annual Wine Festival *(Oct/Nov)*, Summer Festival *(Jan–Mar)*, Marine Festival and Boat Show *(March)*, and Dragon Boat Festival *(at Chinese New Year)*. Farther afield is the acclaimed △ Martinborough Festival of Food and Wine *(March)*.

SOME PHYSIOGRAPHY

Wellington's harbour, a major port for container shipping, was formed by a local downwarping of the earth's crust which allowed the sea to invade and "drown" the lower valley of the Hutt River. When first formed, the harbour extended up the Hutt Valley proper as far as Taita Gorge but since then the delta plains, where stands the city of △Lower Hutt, have been naturally built up by river deposits. The harbour is bounded to the north-west by a strip of "fault coast" (along which the Hutt Road now runs) and elsewhere by warped surfaces which have produced shorelines of submergence.

The Miramar peninsula which encloses the harbour was an island until comparatively recently. Maori tradition states that centuries ago a big earthquake raised the land between the island and the mainland, but some geographers prefer to believe that the peninsula is a tombolo—like the Otago Peninsula and Banks Peninsula, an island "tied" to the mainland by a bar gradually formed of deposited material. According to this theory a strait of calm water lay between the island and the mainland which checked coastal currents carrying suspended material such as sand, so causing the waters to deposit their material and form a bar which eventually grew to link the two land areas. Others aver that the process was a combination of both explanations; that a bar formed and was raised in an earthquake.

In the earthquake of 1855 coastal land rose by up to 1.5 metres and a sea shelf—a platform cut by the sea into the cliffs—was lifted out of the water. The harbour bed, too, was raised, so facilitating eventual land reclamation. Up to that time the Basin Reserve (today the capital's principal cricket and soccer ground) had been "reserved" as a sheltered anchorage to be linked to the harbour by a canal (where the broad expanse of Kent and Cambridge Terraces now runs). The upheaval so raised the land that draining, not dredging, became its fate.

SOME HISTORY

The coming of Kupe: When Kupe *(p. 9)*, the legendary explorer credited with the discovery of New Zealand, visited Wellington, he is said to have camped for some time on the island of Motu-kairangi (now Miramar peninsula). Kupe named the other two main harbour islands Matiu (now Somes) and Makaro (now Ward) after his nieces (or possibly his daughters), who accompanied him on his journey.

Ngai-Tara: Although there is evidence that earlier tribes inhabited the Wellington area, most accounts of occupation begin with Whatonga, who, from a pa near the Mahia Peninsula, in Hawke's Bay, is said to have sent his sons Tara and Tautoki to find new land to settle.

Whatonga *(p. 9)* is one of the few Polynesian explorers credited with coming to New Zealand and returning to "Hawaiki". It is popularly said that he first came here by chance, when, while competing in a canoe race, a sudden storm blew his canoe out to sea. His grandfather, Toi, followed in search of him, but in the meantime Whatonga had made his way back home again. On discovering that his grandfather had left to find him, Whatonga returned to New Zealand, to find Toi at Whakatane. Pressure of population there is said to have led Whatonga and his followers first to Mahia and then to Wellington, where his sons, Tara and Tautoki, constructed a pa first on Matiu (Somes Island) and then on Motu-kairangi (Miramar "island"). Wellington's harbour they named Whanganui-a-Tara ("Great Harbour of Tara") in honour of the elder son.

The Ngai-Tara, as Tara's descendants came to be known, increased in number, and gradually pa were constructed round the harbour. Over the years many battles were fought. One raid on the Horowhenua Maori brought a ferocious reprisal, but Wellington's infamous "three-day southerly" rescued the struggling defenders with a storm that deprived the attackers of the sea foods on which they depended. When the storm abated, they were tired, hungry and no match for the local tribe.

In the course of time other tribes migrated south, settled round the harbour and intermarried. The last of these migrations took place in the 1820s after a Waikato invasion of Taranaki prompted Te Ati Awa to migrate south for a time. Although not numerous, Te Ati Awa could still show aggression, and in 1835 a taua under Pomare Ngatata seized a visiting ship, the *Lord Rodney*, and forced its captain to sail them to the Chatham Islands where they settled and decimated the local population.

Although Wellington had enjoyed a share in the whaling and flax trades, when Colonel William Wakefield arrived in the *Tory* in 1839 there was but a single Pakeha on the harbour—one Robinson, who was living in the Hutt Valley with the family of his Maori wife. The tribes holding the harbour were relatively weak, and feared attack from the Ngati Kahungunu of Hawke's Bay and the Wairarapa. For this reason Te Ati Awa, who were in the ascendancy locally, welcomed the arrival of Europeans who, they thought, would offer them security from their neighbouring and more powerful enemies. Indeed Te Ati Awa later helped the settlers to put down the Ngati Toa chief Te Rangihaeata, and it is ironical that subsequently when they returned to their tribal territory in Taranaki, Te Ati Awa were themselves attacked by the Europeans and forcibly dispossessed of their lands (*see* △ *Waitara*).

Edward Gibbon Wakefield (1796-1862): The figure of Wakefield occupies a prominent place in any record of New Zealand settlement. His craving for power first led him to prison as, in an attempt to gain influence by marrying an heiress, he abducted a schoolgirl and married her at Gretna Green. Public scandal and a three-year prison term put paid to Wakefield's hopes of a career in the British Parliament, but while in Newgate Prison he met a number of prisoners who had served terms of transportation in the Australian penal colonies and who gave him material for a book, *A Letter from Sydney* (1829). Publication aroused considerable interest as the *Letter*, believed by many to be genuine, argued that indiscriminate land grants had retarded the progress of New South Wales by creating a labour shortage. Wakefield suggested that future land be sold, not given, at a price calculated to prevent labourers from too quickly becoming landowners, and the proceeds used to finance passages for young labouring migrants. "New people," he deplored, had emerged who "delight in a forced equality ... against nature and truth," a "people who become rotten before they are ripe."

On his release, Wakefield founded the Colonisation Society and within two years had helped bring about a change in the New South Wales land policy. Negotiations with the British Government for a settlement in Western Australia failed, but in 1834 the British Parliament authorised the establishment of a "Wakefield-style" colony by the South Australia Association, however Wakefield promptly left the Association when it fixed a selling price of 12 shillings an acre, a price he thought too low.

From Australia, Wakefield's thoughts turned to New Zealand, and first he formed the New Zealand Association, and then organised the preliminary expedition of the New Zealand Company, led by his brother William. After an incursion into Canadian politics, Wakefield immersed himself in the settlement of this country. In London he unsuccessfully argued that local self-government be granted and that the New Zealand Company exclusively control all future colonisation. Subsequently he fell out with the Company, resigned his directorship in 1849, and busied himself in London with the Church of England settlement for Christchurch and with campaigning for self-government for New Zealand as a whole—an aim realised in 1852. As soon as the necessary Constitution Act was passed by the British Parliament, Wakefield left London and for the first time came to New Zealand, settling in Wellington where he was immediately elected to both the House of Representatives and the Wellington Provincial Council. It was he who successfully moved at the first meeting of the General Assembly that the British system of Ministerial responsibility be adopted, but Wakefield himself was passed over when the first Ministers were chosen. Chilled by icy winds after a crowded election meeting, Wakefield contracted rheumatic fever and never fully recovered.

Wakefield's role in the settlement of New Zealand is greater than that of any other individual. A fascinating man with compelling personality, he was an innovator rather than an administrator. His standing as a theorist is shown by the fact that both John Stuart Mill (with respect) and Karl Marx (with scorn) took note of him. His theory of a "sufficient price" was never completely followed through in practice, and he certainly never envisaged the pastoral society New Zealand was to develop. (*Wakefield lies buried in the evocative Bolton Street Memorial Park, along with many of Wellington's pioneer settlers.*)

The first New Zealand Company settlement: Wellington was the first and most successful of the London-based New Zealand Company settlements, others being at △Wanganui, △New Plymouth and across Cook Strait, at Nelson. *For a description of the NZ Company's operations and the reasons for the eventual failure, see pp.* **27-28.**

The driving force behind the Company was Edward Gibbon Wakefield but all five Wakefield brothers, sons of an English silk merchant, made a contribution to the settlement of New Zealand.

The eldest, Lieutenant-Colonel William Wakefield, was in 1839 hurriedly dispatched from London in the *Tory* to buy land for settlement at Wellington and elsewhere, in anticipation of the British Government's acquiring sovereignty over New Zealand. Knowing that the Government would soon have the sole right to purchase land from the Maori, the New Zealand Company hastily recruited settlers in London, "sold" land and dispatched its first passenger ships; all this before their agent, Lieut-Col. William Wakefield (1803-48) had even arrived at Wellington, let alone purchased any land. The Company had foreseen the future commercial importance of Wellington and had expected its "settlement" there to be chosen as the country's capital—a hope that was not realised until 1865, as Governor Hobson with good reason preferred the hitherto deserted site of Auckland.

About the time that the Company's first settlers were reaching Wellington, Governor Hobson and his entourage of civil servants were moving from Sydney to the Bay of Islands to conclude the Treaty of Waitangi, so setting the scene for a 30-year struggle between the two groups, of which today's rivalry between Wellington and Auckland may be seen as a legacy.

Enter Richard Barrett: When the *Tory* arrived in New Zealand late in 1839, Colonel William Wakefield first inspected a possible site for settlement in the Marlborough Sounds, where he met the irrepressible whaler Richard ("Dicky") Barrett (1807-47). Barrett volunteered to pilot the *Tory* into Port Nicholson, past the treacherous reef now named after him, and assisted as "interpreter" in the subsequent land negotiations. But as Barrett's knowledge of Maori was confined to the occasional colloquial phrase, it was not to be wondered at that some of the 16 chiefs who initially agreed to the land sales later claimed to have misunderstood the nature of the transactions—misunderstandings that led to war.

Some place names were bestowed at this stage—"Lowry Bay" was called after the mate of the *Tory* and, it is said, "Wellington Harbour" was so named by the *Tory*'s crew as their ship's figurehead depicted the Duke of Wellington.

It was barely four months before the first shiploads of settlers arrived to camp along the beaches at Petone or to sleep with only umbrellas for shelter. As one of them, John Plimmer, recalled, "It had been represented to us as a veritable Eden. But, alas, how grievously were we disappointed . . . The wild and stern reality lay before us . . . Our bright prospects vanished into thin air."

If there were sad hearts there was also resolution. Soon raupo huts began to appear, but once the settlers had experienced a Hutt River flood, the infant township of "Britannia" was promptly moved round the harbour to Thorndon. On the beach front (now Lambton Quay) Barrett opened an hotel which for 15 years was the settlement's most important building. A prefabricated two-storeyed structure, shipped from England and originally destined for use as a school, it served not only social and recreational purposes but also as a centre of culture, as courthouse, as ballroom, and even as the Provincial Council chambers. Here were held protest meetings to discuss the burning issues of the moment—such as a proposal to petition Queen Victoria for the removal of Governor Hobson, and to consider what steps could be taken to protect the public from the police (who in 1841 provided the lawlessness they were appointed to combat).

But Barrett quickly tired of Wellington and moved back to his wife's home at New Plymouth. His hotel, however, retained his name and passed through a number of hands before it was taken over for Government offices by 1852. The licence had in 1849 been moved a short distance along Lambton Quay, where Barrett's Hotel traded until 1982. A "new" Barrett's (the fifth) opened in 1990 *(Allen St, nr Courtenay Pl).*

Settlers' Committee: To Colonel Wakefield fell the lot of leading the first New Zealand Company settlement, at Wellington. As Principal Agent for the Company in New Zealand, he was obliged to implement directives from London-based directors, yet at the same time he was *ex officio* president of a "settlers' committee" charged with the administration of law and order, and so was its political head. Colonel Wakefield was caught between a Government tardy in investigating and approving land titles, and settlers anxious to take possession of their land purchases; his lot was not a happy one, and in the ensuing land difficulties he came first to differ and then to duel with Dr Isaac Featherston.

It was the same "settlers' committee" which hastened the arrival at Wellington of the Government's first representatives. The 1,200 colonists here, with no police and no courts, had before leaving Britain agreed that British law should be implemented by a "Council of Colonists". But when the council "imprisoned" the indignant captain of a visiting ship, complaint was made to Governor Hobson at the Bay of Islands.

You cannot drive straight on a twisting lane. *Russian proverb*

The outraged Governor considered that the settlers were guilty of high treason, and immediately dispatched the Colonial Secretary (Lieutenant Willoughby Shortland) with a party of soldiers and constables, ordering him to suppress the council and to enforce the authority of the Crown. So it was that the future capital's first essay into the field of government proved shortlived.

War: Richard Barrett's haphazard knowledge of Maori predictably led to misunderstandings as to the nature and extent of the land "purchases" Colonel Wakefield claimed to have made for the New Zealand Company. Trouble came first to the Company's settlement at Nelson, in 1843. There, despite a willingness on the part of the chiefs to accept the decision once made of the Land Commissioner, the Company provocatively sent surveyors out on to the disputed Wairau Plains. The Ngati Toa chiefs Te Rauparaha and Te Rangihaeata protested in vain and were driven to obstruct the surveyors and burn down their huts. A skirmish when the Nelson settlers tried to arrest them ended with the deaths of 22 settlers, including William's brother, Captain Arthur Wakefield. Success in the Wairau Affray (as it became known) encouraged Maori elsewhere to adopt a stronger line.

Two years later the Land Commissioner, William Spain, investigated the alleged purchases at Wellington and awarded the Company 28,760 hectares, excluding Maori villages, Maori-occupied land and 39 native reserves. But uncertainty remained as to the precise location of the excluded areas and this blazed into hostilities in the Hutt Valley, at the Battle of Boulcott's Farm (*see △Lower Hutt*).

Only then did the Government bow to popular demand and accept the chief Te Puni's generous offer to arm his Te Ati Awa for the forthcoming campaign. After a clash on Pauatahanui Inlet between a naval patrol and a war party led by Te Rangihaeata (for the first time personally taking part in the fighting), the "duplicity" of Te Rauparaha was discovered. The settlers he purported to befriend found that in fact he was recruiting Maori from the Upper Whanganui to fight for his nephew, the more openly rebellious Te Rangihaeata, as well as supplying him with arms obtained from the Government.

Governor Grey reacted swiftly to the revelation and at dawn one morning the unsuspecting Te Rauparaha was kidnapped at his kainga at the entrance to Porirua Harbour (where Plimmerton is today). Troops moved against Te Rangihaeata's pa on the Pauatahanui Inlet, but the capture of one of his scouts was seen and by the time the troops reached the pa, it had been evacuated. Te Rangihaeata, retreating northwards, fortified a ridge above the Horokiri Valley. After it, too, was successfully attacked, he continued north along the ranges and emerged to entrench himself on an island in the centre of a flax swamp north of Levin. There, as he had vowed, the soldiers never got him. On a somewhat indecisive note, hostilities ended with the trial for rebellion of six of Te Rangihaeata's followers. Te Rauparaha was held in captivity until 1848, by which time his thirst for strife had dulled. Throughout his captivity, though treated as guest rather than prisoner, the Ngati Toa chief impressed all who met him—an attitude summed up in a message to his son: "Let not men think that I abide in grief as I now remain in slavery aboard my warship *Calliope*; no it is not so. I know not any grief, though I so remain a prisoner—In my mind I am abiding here as a chief, and my abode is an abode of a chief."

Land reclamation begins: Much of Wellington's commercial area stands on reclaimed land, for originally, as their names suggest, Lambton and Thorndon Quays were lapped by waves and small private jetties jutted out to serve shipping. Land reclamation has continued up to the present (to the dismay of some Wellingtonians who see the city's harmony with its harbour being lost), but the first land came to be reclaimed for the most unlikely of reasons. When the ship *Inconstant* (460 tons) struck rocks near Pencarrow in 1850 and was condemned, the enterprising John Plimmer (1812-1905) purchased the hulk and beached it on the then-foreshore (*on cnr Lambton Quay and Willis St where stands the Bank of New Zealand*). There for 32 years it enjoyed the title of "Noah's Ark" as Plimmer converted it into a busy warehouse, bondstore and auction rooms. To shelter his unusual premises, Plimmer built a breakwater and reclaimed two sections in its lee; yet it was only after a dispute as to ownership was resolved in Plimmer's favour that he was allowed title to the land he had won.

To reach the "Ark", "Plimmer's Steps" led down from Boulcott Street (as new steps still do) from Plimmer's home at their head. Chairs made from the timber of the "Ark" are in the possession of the Alexander Turnbull Library and the Bank of New Zealand.

The capital comes to Wellington: In the final analysis, the directors of the New Zealand Company had shown greater foresight half a world away than had Hobson on the spot when it came to selecting a site for the country's capital. From the outset the settlement at Wellington was bedevilled by erratic communication with the "capital" at Auckland—even in 1842 it took 127 days for news to pass between the centres, and occasionally mail between the two was most quickly sent by way of Sydney.

As population increased and the South Island's settlements expanded, so grew the clamour for a more central capital. Indeed, when Arthur Domett successfully moved in the House of Representatives that the "seat of Government . . . be transferred to some more suitable locality in Cook Strait", he suggested that unless this was done the inhabitants of the South Island (then called "Middle Island", hence its claim to be the "mainland"), might well try to form a separate colony. An "independent commission" (a device by now only too familiar to the New Zealand electorate) was chosen to make the final decision and three commissioners (one appointed by each of the Governors of New South Wales, Victoria and Tasmania!) in 1864 considered sites from Wanganui to Nelson before reporting that Wellington "presented the greatest advantage". So it was that after a quarter of a century of propaganda, frustration and ill-will, the settlement of Wellington finally became "capital". With the title came the administrators of Government, diplomats and then the headquarters of commercial and cultural organisations to change indelibly the character of the settlement. Fate all but intervened. As the move was being made the steamer *White Swan*, on its way to Wellington with a cargo of Governmental records and a contingent of officials, struck a rock off Castlepoint and sank. Most of the documents were lost, as they were cast overboard in the forlorn hope that they might be washed ashore. However, the crew and passengers survived and eventually reached Wellington on the aptly named SS *Stormbird*.

A WALK AROUND THE GOVERNMENT CENTRE ★★★

Allow 1½ hrs (excluding any tour of Parliament Buildings; tel. (04) 471-9457 for times). Start at the Citizens' War Memorial (the "cenotaph") on the corner of Bowen Street and Lambton Quay. Standing on land reclaimed from the sea are the imposing:

Government Buildings ★★★(1876): Of all the wooden buildings in the world only the Japanese Todaiji Temple is larger. Plainly seen is the successful translation into timber of the traditional stone architecture of nineteenth-century "official" buildings. Today housing the university law faculty, the building is a source of pride for Wellingtonians even if their forebears of a century ago condemned the choice of wood as lacking in permanence.

The Italianate 9,411-square-metre building, complete with clock and royal arms, was built on reclaimed land. The framework is of rimu and Tasmanian hardwood, the flooring matai and weatherboards kauri. In all, over 1,100,000 super feet of timber was used. During construction building costs soared to such an extent that an embarrassed Government (the architect was Sir Julius Vogel's talented son-in-law, W. H. Clayton) held no official opening ceremony in order to avoid unwanted publicity.

The building now lacks 22 chimney stacks demolished as an earthquake risk and whose unfortunate absence gives the building a "lightheaded" appearance. *Lambton Quay, opp. Citizens' War Memorial.* In front stands the stooping figure of **Peter Fraser** (1884-1950), the Labour leader and Prime Minister from 1940-49.

Walk up into the pohutukawa-treed grounds of Parliament Buildings, passing the dominating dome of the "Beehive" and:

Richard John Seddon's statue: Seddon (1845-1906), Prime Minister from 1893 until his death in 1906, captured popular imagination as has no other leader. His essential humanity and aggressive platform style endeared him to the hustings, while his Liberal Government introduced the first Old Age Pension (1898) and (rather reluctantly) saw New Zealand become the first country to give women the vote (1893).

Behind the imperious Seddon stands the:

Parliament Buildings complex ★ ★ ★: Tradition has it that the **"Beehive"** (1981), built as the executive wing of Parliament Buildings, was the result of a design sketched on a napkin by the British architect Sir Basil Spence while lunching with then-Prime Minister Sir Keith Holyoake — and said to have been inspired by the motif on a box of "Beehive" matches which was on the table. In the basement are the headquarters of the national Civil Defence system. Also in the wing is **Bellamys**, the Members' catering service whose name recalls the London street vendor who, before the "Mother of Parliaments" at Westminster acquired a dining room, fed hungry MPs. The name lives on here though not at Westminster.

The setting of Parliament Buildings has links with administration which go back to the very founding of Wellington. Initially the home of Colonel William Wakefield stood here and in the course of time gave way to the Governor's residence. The first Parliamentary assembly to meet in Wellington, once the "capital" had been moved, met here and a succession of buildings housed first the Provincial Council's and then Parliament's proceedings. In 1922, the present ponderous block of Takaka marble was completed to contrast with the effervescent Gothic of the adjoining **General Assembly Library Building** (1897). In the original plan the entrance was balanced by a similar wing to the left, but in time this was abandoned and the "Beehive" dome

285

rises in its stead.

Within the central marble block are lofty chambers for both the House of Representatives and the now-abolished Legislative Council, once the Upper House. The latter chamber is still used to receive the "Speech from the Throne" which outlines proposed legislation, and is delivered when a new session of Parliament is formally "opened" by the Governor-General or, occasionally, the British monarch in person. The layout of the chambers is a model of the "Mother of Parliaments" at Westminster, down to the Speaker's mace and the traditional despatch boxes.

Procedures are explained to visitors in the course of conducted tours of the buildings. A simple majority vote is sufficient to enact legislation (a "Bill") which becomes law (an "Act") once the Governor-General, on behalf of the Queen, has fulfilled the formality of "assenting" to it. Three years is the maximum term of any one Parliament.

The buildings are not open to casual sightseers, but conducted tours are organised on weekdays; tel. (04) 471-9457 for times. A gallery accommodates visitors to the debating chamber. The central block is presently being renovated, and a temporary underground chamber has been created nearby. *Notes on the Constitution and party politics appear on pp.* **32–34**.

In front of the General Assembly Library building stands:

John Ballance's statue: Ballance (1839-93), Liberal Prime Minister, was succeeded on his death by Seddon. A sympathetic and courteous journalist, Ballance in Opposition unified the Liberals and in power forged a link with Labour to form the basis for Seddon's subsequent enduring reign. The statue at its unveiling was described as "hideous beyond words" and as adding "a new terror to death".

Continue through the grounds to reach the corner of Molesworth St and Hill St. To the left looking up Hill St is the imposing Sacred Heart Cathedral (1901). Walk up Molesworth St to pass in turn the:

Court of Appeal: The country's highest court *(corner Molesworth and Aitken Sts)*.

National Library (1987) *(see p.* **290***)*: The exhibition galleries are always worth a visit, as is the impressive Reading Room mural by the Maori artist Cliff Whiting portraying the myth of the separation of Rangi and Papa.

St Paul's Anglican Cathedral (1972): A somewhat unprepossessing successor to the enchanting "Old St Paul's" *(see below)*.

State Services Commission: Here stands a statue of Sir Keith Holyoake (1904-1983) who served as Prime Minister in 1957 and from 1960-72. For many years he lived at 41 Pipitea St and would chat to members of the public as he walked to and from his office. *(cnr Molesworth St and Pipitea St)*.

Turn right along Pipitea St and turn left up Murphy St. At the end turn right immediately after passing the United States Embassy into Fitzherbert Tce and the:

Katherine Mansfield Memorial: A shaded garden area on the brink of the motorway. Katherine Mansfield, pen-name of Kathleen Beauchamp (1888-1923), in her short lifetime achieved world renown as a writer of short stories and more recently has gained respect as a letter writer with the publication of her correspondence. As befits the "one peacock in [New Zealand's] literary garden" (although most of her adult life was spent in Europe) her enduring stories *Prelude*, *At the Bay* (Day's Bay), *The Doll's House* and *The Garden Party* are all set in Wellington. A plaque here was given by her father, a successful merchant who established the original garden memorial.

At this point a detour may be made, walking up Tinakori Rd to No. 260 which is the:

Prime Ministerial Residence: Designed by William Clayton and first used, in 1875, by his father-in-law, Premier Julius Vogel, the expansive house and its extensive grounds served as the Prime Ministerial residence until 1937, when the First Labour Government transformed it into a school dental clinic. It was restored to its former splendour by the Fourth Labour Government as a 1990 commemorative project.

From the adjacent Garden for the Blind, cross the motorway bridge and turn right to reach:

Katherine Mansfield's birthplace (1888): The simple wooden house built by her father was the writer's first family home. The family move from here when she was aged five is described in her short story "Prelude". The house has been restored and furnished in period. *25 Tinakori Rd. Open daily (except Mon); tel. (04) 473-7268.*

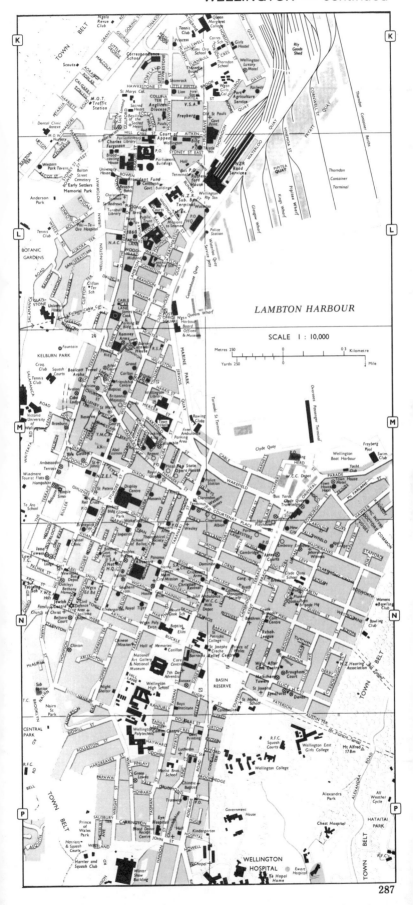

LAMBTON HARBOUR

SCALE 1 : 10,000

Metres 250   0   0.3 Kilometre

Yards 250   0   1 Mile

Return across the motorway bridge, to walk down Hobson St, passing on the left the **Embassy of the Federal Republic of Germany** *(No 90-92) and the* **Australian High Commission** *(No 72-78) and on the right the imposing wooden buildings of* **Queen Margaret's College** *(No 53), a private girls' school. Turn right into Moturoa and Pipitea Sts, and left along Murphy St to visit:*

Old St Paul's (1866) ★★★: A "Selwyn" church designed by the Rev. Frederick Thatcher. It is the interior which gives it immeasurable appeal and captures "at once the quietude and exaltation of the human spirit". Here Thatcher has followed to telling effect an exhortation to have "every beam and rafter seen". Thatcher's design, Gothic of the Early English period, is aligned west-to-east and so takes the full brunt of Wellington's southerlies. Within a year it was necessary to strengthen the building, and the first of a series of alterations was carried out. Originally the tower was in the extreme north-west corner of the church, and there were no ancillary rooms, apart from the quaint octagonal vestry.

Although "Old St Paul's" was built as a temporary cathedral church pending the building of a cathedral proper, few could have foreseen that its role was to last a century. In 1909 the church was first imperilled, but Bishop Wallis refused to allow it to be demolished to make way for a cathedral on the site, and in 1932 a rebuilding scheme would have replaced the timber exterior with concrete walls. But as the new cathedral grew to completion on another site, a 12-year and often acrimonious battle to save the building was won. In 1966 the Government finally accepted the building for preservation and for use as a tranquil setting for music and drama.

Just inside the entrance a plaque honours John Beaglehole, who lead the campaign to save the building and who, as the world authority on Captain Cook, was one of only two New Zealanders ever to be accorded membership of the prestigious Order of the Merit. The other was the physicist Lord Rutherford, who pioneered the nuclear age.

Within the church are the memorabilia acquired from parishioners through a century of worship, of which but a few can be mentioned. The hexagonal oak pulpit (1908) was a gift from the widow of Richard John Seddon in memory of her husband. The great west window, seen from the centre of the aisle, was designed by the eminent artist Charles Decimus Barraud (1822-97), himself a parishioner, but the parish was short of money and only a memorial fund opened on the deaths of Wellingtonians at the Battle of Te Ngutu-o-te-manu (1868) turned the design into reality. The baptistry contains two brasses; one the consecration brass, the other in memory of four sailors "drowned in the service of Mr Josh Rhodes". This latter brass has obscure origins and may have been erected elsewhere before being retrieved from a pile of old timber and placed here. *Mulgrave St. Open Monday-Saturday, 10 a.m.-4.30 p.m.; Sunday, 1-4.30 p.m. Administered by the NZ Historic Places Trust.*

Immediately beyond St Paul's, hard by the road is:

Bishopscourt (1879): Built as the Diocesan Office and Bishop's residence and replacing an earlier Bishopscourt (1860), this imposing two-storey Victorian building in recent years housed the Family Court. The link with justice is a long one: the stocks of the infant settlement, used more often to punish Maori than settler, were sited about here. The eminent Bishop Hadfield lived in the building for its first 15 years.

Continue along Mulgrave St. On the left at no.10 are the:

National Archives ★★★: Exhibited here are priceless items recording the country's social and constitutional evolution. Of paramount importance is the original Treaty of Waitangi, together with eight sheets taken to different parts of the country to obtain additional signatures. Other significant documents include a letter of instructions written by Captain James Cook in 1776, the 1835 Declaration of Independence made by the northern tribes, papers about the Maori Parliament Movement, a 1909 petition complaining of broken Treaty promises, and some of the 25,000 signatures on a **petition** that led to New Zealand becoming the first country to give women the vote. Modern art works include a striking **mural** by Cliff Whiting commemorating the Maori Battalion. *Open weekdays 9 a.m.–5 p.m.; exhibition galleries and Constitution Room also Sat 9 a.m.–1 p.m.* The building also houses the **National Portrait Gallery**.

Continue along Mulgrave St. Straight ahead is the neo-Georgian building of the **Wellington Railway Station** *(1937). On the corner of Mulgrave and Kate Sheppard Place is the venerable:*

Thistle Inn (1866): The country's oldest hotel on its original site.

Turn right to return to the cenotaph. If time permits, walk up Bowen St, passing on the left:

Turnbull House (1916): The original home of Alexander Horsburgh Turnbull, now a community centre with a cheerful lunchtime restaurant and coffee shop. *Open Mon–Fri, 10 a.m.–4 p.m. See p.* **290**. *Opposite is:*

Broadcasting House: Nerve centre of Radio New Zealand.

Turn left along The Terrace and turn up Bolton St to reach, on the right, the:

Sexton's cottage (1857): Here lived the sexton for the historic Bolton St Cemetery whose tranquillity has been disrupted by a motorway. Many of Wellington's earliest citizens are buried here, including Edward Gibbon Wakefield *(see index). The entrance to the cemetery is just beyond the cottage.*

Return to The Terrace, where the walk ends.

SOME VIEWPOINTS ★★★

Mt Victoria *(196 m)*: Best known of the viewpoints and seldom free of Wellington's winds, Mt Victoria affords a superb panorama of city, harbour and strait. From the viewpoint one looks across the water, past Somes Island (an animal quarantine station from 1872 to 1995) to the Hutt Valley, on whose shore the first settlers built their earliest homes. Sweeping left is the Hutt Road, at the feet of sheer hills uplifted along the line of the "Wellington Fault", linking the Valley with the commercial heart of the city. On the hillside above the city a splash of emerald marks Kelburn Park, with the buildings of Victoria University close by. At the foot of Mt Victoria one can see between the buildings the twin thoroughfares of Kent and Cambridge Terraces (in space originally reserved for a canal), which lead to the Basin Reserve (planned as an inner harbour but now the capital's main cricket and soccer ground).

Beyond and to the right of the Basin, the Carillon tower of the National War Memorial rises above the old National Museum and Art Gallery. To the left lie the playing fields of Wellington College, beyond which, among trees, one may see the tower and roofs of Government House, official residence of the Governor-General, the Queen's representative in New Zealand. Farther left, looking along the line of the ridge, is the massive Millard Stand at Athletic Park (spiritual home of New Zealand rugby). The level land around Wellington Airport shows clearly how "Miramar island" has been linked to the mainland. The peninsula across Evans Bay is tipped with the marble of the Massey Memorial.

Near the viewpoints, depicting the Aurora Australis (southern lights), is a ceramic **memorial** to Rear-Admiral Byrd (1887–1957), an American explorer of the Antarctic who pioneered the use of aircraft there and made the first flight over the South Pole. Byrd used New Zealand as a base for his expeditions. The tragic Mt Erebus flight in 1979 was intended to mark the fiftieth anniversary of Byrd's first flight to Antarctica.

The oldest known Maori name for Mt Victoria was Matai-rangi ("to watch the sky"), indicating that it was used as a lookout. Later it became known as Tangi-te-keo ("the sound of a bird's screech"), as in legend two taniwha lived in a lake where now rests Wellington's harbour. One escaped to the sea, so forming the harbour's entrance to Cook Strait. The other became stuck and turned into the isthmus where the airport now stands. Thus cast adrift, the taniwha perished. Its spirit flew to the top of Mt Victoria to mourn over the taniwha's body far below, and its plaintive wailing may still be heard — presumably an explanation for the howling wind hereabouts. *From Oriental Bay follow "Lookout" signposts, turn sharp left up Roseneath Tce, to enter the northern entrance at 2.5 km and park by the Byrd Memorial. Walk up steps to the more advantageous of the lookouts. (The steps pass a cannon for many years fired at noon as a "time gun".) The southern entrance is along Alexandra Rd, off Constable St.*

Cablecar summit: From Lambton Quay, a cablecar winches passengers up 122 metres passing Kelburn Park and the University, to the mellow suburb of Kelburn. Kelburn's developers in 1902 constructed the cablecar line to open up their land. The quaint original cars were in use until 1979, when they were replaced by the present modern Swiss-made cars. From the imaginative Athfield-designed shelter at the summit, rather than returning by cable car, one can walk past the **New Zealand Astronomy Centre** (Carter Observatory) and through the **Botanic Gardens** to Glenmore Street, there to link with a bus service. *Cable Car Lane (off Lambton Quay, opp. Grey St).*

Tinakori Hill *(300 m)*: The summit, bedecked by radio transmission masts, provides perhaps the most exciting view of Wellington. High above the city one looks down on the southern harbour arms to see the suburbs as if on a map. Wellington Radio (established here in 1912) incorporates steel aerial towers which range from about 36 to 47 metres and are arranged so that their tops are at a height of 304 metres above sea level. It exchanges traffic with vessels around the New Zealand coast and is the transmitting station for the South Pacific area of the Long Range Area communications scheme for Commonwealth ships. *Follow Northland bus route to terminus and continue straight ahead to follow road to end. A short walk leads to the summit.*

Massey Memorial: *See "City Marine Drive" (below).*

MUSEUMS, LIBRARIES AND ART GALLERIES

Museum of New Zealand Te Papa Tongarewa ★ ★ ★: The country's national museum of art, history, Maori culture and the natural environment will move in 1998 to new premises on the waterfront. The museum's geology and palaeontology section contains collections dating from 1865, and its botany section has **herbarium collections** assembled by Cook's naturalists, Banks and Solander, and by the missionary Colenso. Outstanding is the "Voices He Putahitanga" audio-visual narrative of the country's history, from the first footfall to the present day.

Relics of **Cook** himself include the original figurehead from his ship *Resolution*, used on his second and third voyages to this country and the Hawaiian feather cloak and helmet he was given in 1779. The **ethnology section** covers Oceania and New Zealand from 1769 onwards.

The fascinating Maori collection, predominantly from the Taranaki and central districts, may be compared with the Auckland Museum's mainly northern material. Pre-eminent is the carved Maori meeting house Te Hau-ki-Turanga (*c.* 1842; "The spirit of Turanga"). From Manutuke (near Gisborne, whose original name was Turanga), the house was purchased in 1867 when the Government agreed to waive some arbitrary land confiscation, and in the euphoria of goodwill the announcement generated, J. C. Richmond took the opportunity to buy for the State what is widely recognised as the finest surviving example of its kind. *(A booklet is available which identifies particular points of interest.)*

The colonial history section records European life in New Zealand up to 1900, and includes an "Early Wellington House" furnished in the style of the 1840s.

The **art collection** includes New Zealand, Australian, British and European nineteenth- and twentieth-century paintings, drawings, graphic art and sculpture. A wide range of etchings and engravings has a particularly strong Rembrandt section. An extensive collection of eighteenth- and nineteenth-century British water-colours is displayed, as well as a selection of early New Zealand water-colours, oils and drawings. The **NZ Academy of Fine Arts**, also housed here, stages stimulating exhibitions.

In front of the main building is the **Carillon**, whose 49 bells are played regularly, and whose tower rises above the Hall of Memories, the nation's memorial to its war dead. *Buckle St. The complex is open daily, 9 a.m.–5 p.m. Guided tours 12.30 p.m. daily (also 1.30 p.m. weekends).*

Shed 11: The National Art Gallery mounts changing exhibitions of contemporary art in an old wharf building. *Customhouse Quay. Open daily (except Mon).*

National Library (Te Puna Matauranga o Aotearoa) ★★★: The library (whose Maori name means "the spring of knowledge") found its first permanent home in 1987, in a purpose-designed building employing sophisticated retrieval and cataloguing systems. Its origins lie in a world-famous collection bequeathed to the country by Alexander Horsburgh Turnbull (1868-1918) and now housed as the **Alexander Turnbull Library ★★★** as a library within the National Library.

An avid bibliophile, Turnbull, who in his later years became a recluse suffering intense pain from cancer, devoted a lifetime and a considerable inheritance to create a library which since his death has more than trebled in size. A critic once noted, "I told him I had the first edition of the second part of *Robinson Crusoe*. He told me he had the first five . . ."

Foremost is the Pacific section, with accounts of nearly every voyage of note since Magellan in 1523, and including Cook's manuscript log from HMS *Eagle* (1755-56). The art collection contains a number of historical works by early visitors to New Zealand, many of them surveyors, who recorded the contemporary scene with sketchbook and pencil much as today's travellers use a camera. The non-Pacific section includes a strong collection of English literature, with many rare first editions and a Milton collection which ranks with the world's finest. Exhibition galleries feature changing displays of material. *70 Molesworth St. Open Mon–Fri 9 a.m.–5 p.m.; Sat 9 a.m.–1 p.m.*

The library was first housed in Turnbull's former home a short distance away. Now, as **Turnbull House** *(Bowen St, opp. the "Beehive")*, this is a meeting place for community groups and has a convivial lunchtime restaurant.

Civic centre complex: The Civic Centre combines the old with the new: a venerable, neo-classical town hall (1902-04) adjoins the Michael Fowler Centre (1983), the latter designed by Warren and Mahoney (also responsible for the Christchurch Town Hall), a feature of whose striking auditorium are **wall hangings** by Gordon Crook.

The stylish **Wellington Public Library (1991)** is designed by the acclaimed local architect, Ian Athfield. A delightful touch to the exterior of the library is a colonnade of metallic **"nikau palms"**, recalling the use for building purposes made of such palms by the first Maori to live by the harbour.

Nearby **Discovery Place (Te Aho a Maui)** (the fishing line of Maui) (1992), is another Athfield building, where children explore the sciences (*hours vary*).

The **City Gallery** occupies the expansive art deco building of the old public library and mounts major exhibitions, usually of contemporary works. *Civic Centre, Victoria, Wakefield Sts.*

A footway links the complex with **Frank Kitts Park**, on the waterfront. The park includes an arresting **albatross water sculpture** by local artist Tanya Ashken. More subdued is the **mast** from the ill-fated inter-island passenger ferry *Wahine*, a memorial to the 51 who perished when it sank in the harbour in 1968, during a freak storm.

National archives★ ★ ★: Displays of the country's evolution include an historic letter of instructions written by Captain Cook in 1776 and the Treaty of Waitangi. *10 Mulgrave St. For description, see page* **288**.

Antrim House ★★: An imposing kauri mansion (1904), reflecting the prosperity of Robert Hannah (1845-1930) whose footwear firm still flourishes, now serves as the national headquarters for the New Zealand Historic Places Trust. Trust publications are on sale and inquiries for membership are welcome. *63 Boulcott St. Open Mon–Fri, noon–3 p.m.*

Otari Museum of Native Plants ★★: An open-air museum, Otari contains a collection of all possible New Zealand species and is used to illustrate ways of using native plants in home gardens. Plants are individually identified, and include shrubs, trees, ferns and grasses from throughout New Zealand and the Chatham Islands. Paths lead through more formal areas to descend into a sheltered, bush-enclosed valley where one may picnic oblivious of nearby suburbia. Otari means "place of the snare", as the suburb of Wilton was noted for its birds. *Wilton Rd. Turn right off the route to Karori 400 m after passing through the tunnel.*

Maritime Museum: This museum is divided into two parts. The upper floor has a large-scale model of Wellington Harbour as its centrepiece, surrounded by paintings, prints, photographs, plans and illuminated addresses. Table cases display nautical instruments, shipping registers and memorabilia relating to ships and companies. The ground floor features displays that complement the character of the building. *Old Harbour Board buildings, Queens Wharf, Jervois Quay. Open daily Mon–Fri; Sat, Sun and public holidays, from 1–4.30 p.m. Tel. (04) 472-8904.*

Bank of New Zealand Archives Museum: Displayed in a replica of an old banking chamber are rare coins, bank notes and other items relating to banking in New Zealand. *Level 2, Grand Annex. 16 Willis St; open weekdays.*

New Zealand Film Archive's Museum of Cinema: Reflecting the recent resurgence of domestic film-making, the museum houses a permanent collection which includes a film book reference library, over 7,000 film posters, stills and early projection and camera equipment. The earliest projector, a pre-1915 model, is in perfect working order. Changing exhibitions are mounted. The Art Cinema, Rialto, shows classic films. *Jervois Quay; tel. (04) 384-7647.*

Cricket Museum: A collection of memorabilia old and new is housed beneath the old grandstand at the city's premier cricket ground. *Sussex St. Open daily in summer; weekends in winter.*

Colonial Cottage Museum (*c.* 1858): An early cottage set in an inviting garden evokes a pioneering atmosphere. *68 Nairn St. Open daily, Mon–Fri, 10 a.m.–4 p.m.; weekends, 1–4.30 p.m.*

Dowse Art Museum ★★★: An excellent collection of New Zealand art with interesting changing exhibitions well displayed. *Laings Rd, Lower Hutt. Open daily (see p. 126).*

Tramway Museum ★ ★: This museum was founded to preserve a fragment of Wellington's tramway system, which closed in 1964. Tramcars that once clanged their way along Lambton Quay now clatter along a track in Queen Elizabeth Park from the Memorial Gates at McKays Crossing to the sea. Trolley buses and ex-Brisbane trams are also on view.

The Memorial Gates recall the 17 months spent here by the US Second Marine Division, which left McKays Crossing in November 1943 to take part with distinction but with considerable losses in the campaigns in the Pacific Islands. Parties of former Marines periodically pilgrimage here from the USA.

The park is an area popular with seaside picnickers and family groups. *44 km N on Highway 1, 4 km beyond Paekakariki. Queen Elizabeth Park (northern end). Enter by the Memorial Gates at McKays Crossing. The tramcars operate at weekends and on public holidays; tel. (04) 292-8361.*

Steam Incorporated: This Paekakariki collection aims to recreate the atmosphere of an NZR locomotive department as the zenith of steam power. Big locomotives (classes 'J' and 'Ka') are being restored to original condition. Locomotives in steam operate occasionally. There is also a collection of restored vintage carriages, used on mainline excursions. *Open Saturday, 9 a.m.–5 p.m. By Highway 1 at Paekakariki.*

Southward Car Museum ★★★: A splendid collection of motor cars dating back to an 1895 Benz, and including vintage motorcycles, cycles and fire engines. *Otaihanga Rd, 3 km S of Waikanae. Open daily; tel. (04) 297-1221.*

PRIVATE GALLERIES

A number of dealer galleries welcome visitors, including:

The Taj (*cnr Kent and Cambridge Tces*); Bowen Gallery (*136 The Terrace*); Brooker Gallery (*128–132 The Terrace*); Christopher Moore Gallery (*136 The Terrace*); Millwood Gallery (*291 Tinakori Rd*); Ferner Gallery (*190 Glenmore St*); New Moon Gallery (*21 Gresham Plaza, Lambton Quay*); Peter McLeavey Gallery (*147 Cuba St*); New Work Studio (*147 Cuba St*); Janne Land Gallery (*170 Cuba St*); Tinakori Gallery (*330 Tinakori Rd*); Merilyn Savill Gallery (*Tinakori Rd*); The Vault (*6 Willis St*); Hamish McKay Gallery (*50 Willis St*); Jensen Gallery (*Furness Lane, off Ghuznee St*); and Page 90 Artspace (*Norrie St, Porirua*).

Information on current exhibitions is published in local newspapers and is also available from the Visitor Information Centre.

CITY MARINE DRIVE ★★★

A 39-km drive round the suburban beaches, principally of the Miramar peninsula. Allow 2½ hrs. Start from Courtenay Pl. towards Oriental Bay. Pass the boat harbour to reach:

Oriental Bay *(800 m):* A summertime lunching and swimming spot with a cosmopolitan flavour on sunny weekends. Views across the harbour and all-day sun lend prestige to the many high-rise apartment buildings hereabouts. The beach, whose alien sand arrived as ballast in sailing vessels, was named not from fancy but for one of the New Zealand Company's first ships. Above presides the former monastery of St Gerard (1905), the first church to be dedicated to the new saint.

Close by, the **Freyberg Tepid Pool** caters for those unwilling to chance the sea. The pool is named for Lord Freyberg, a notable swimmer who was coached on the site as a boy and who went on to win immortality on World War I battlefields, winning the VC, the DSO and two bars and CMG, being mentioned in despatches six times and wounded nine. He commanded the Second New Zealand Expeditionary Force in World War II, winning a third bar to his DSO, and became the country's seventh Governor-General.

Continue to pass the turnoff to Mount Victoria (see "Viewpoints", above). Turn into Evans Bay to look across to the Miramar peninsula tipped with the marble of the Massey Memorial and pass the old:

Patent Slip *(4.5 km):* A popular place for boat repairs. Shortly beyond are facilities for a host of small craft. The Greta Point Tavern here has a popular family restaurant by the water's edge.

At the traffic lights bear left along Cobham Dr to pass end of:

Wellington International Airport *(7 km):* By far the country's busiest airport, its traffic is largely domestic but trans-Tasman flights link with Sydney, Melbourne and Brisbane. The airport is on the "bar" which "ties" Miramar peninsula to the mainland.

Passing the end of the airport, bear left into Shelly Bay to look across to the huddled houses of Hataitai and Roseneath, and reach the:

Massey Memorial *(11 km):* A short flight of steps and a gently sloping path lead up to the marble of the Massey Memorial on the tip of Point Halswell. The Memorial stands on a one-time pa site which on three sides drips sharply to the sea and affords a magnificent view. William Fergusson Massey (1856-1925), an Irish-Scot who when 14 came to New Zealand with his father, rose from being a small farmer to arguing their interests in Parliament through 18 frustrating years of Opposition. Facing the rampant Liberal Seddon, the conservative Opposition was in disarray. But on Seddon's death Massey emerged as the most effective platform politician in the country and led a "Reform" party which ultimately ended the Liberal-Labour reign of 20 years. A conservative by nature, even if self-described as a "true Liberal", Massey checked the "drift to the Left", and proved an astute leader in his 13 years as Prime Minister. World War I overshadowed his administration whose reputation was, in any event, shattered by the Great Depression, but Massey still ranks as second only to Seddon and shares his predecessor's tradition of "pragmatic humanitarianism". Massey University (△ Palmerston North) is named for him.

Steps lead farther up the spur to picnic and barbecue places. Beyond are the remnants of harbour defences built during World War II. Above are the precincts of Mt Crawford prison. *Allow 20 mins. Signposted.*

Round Pt Halswell to pass Mahanga Bay, below:

Point Gordon (*13 km*): Fort Ballance was built here during the "Russian Scare" of the 1880s, when near-hysteria gripped Australia and New Zealand after Czarist Russia opened her Pacific port of Vladivostok. In over a century the mainstay of the capital's coastal defences fired just one shell in earnest — across the bows of an American vessel which attempted to leave port without getting clearance during the Second World War. The Point looks across to Eastbourne.

Continue to reach:

Scorching Bay *(13.5 km)*: Habitation resumes at a pleasant beach scattered with boatsheds and with good rock-fishing perches nearby.

Through Karaka Bay lies:

Worser Bay *(15 km)*: Another appealing beach, named after "Old Worser", James Heberley, the original pilot of the Pilot Station that operated from outside the Heads for many years from 1840. He is said to have acquired the nickname when Mr Justice Chapman one day asked him the weather prospects. Heberley gloomily predicted "Worser". In 1865 the Pilot Station was relocated here. The Pilot's Cottage (1866; in use as such until 1894) stands back from the road. *(229 Marine Pde, at junction with Awa Rd.)* A Ngati Ira pa stood on the narrow spur at the bay's northern head. It was named Kakariki-hutia ("plucked parakeets") after a Ngati Ira chief had hastened to do battle with invaders, having hurriedly eaten several plucked but uncooked birds which were given the credit for his fine performance during the fight.

*Reaching the suburb of Seatoun (where a huge **anchor** from the Wahine forms part of a seaside memorial to the 51 who died in the 1968 sinking of an inter-island ferry: more than 400 of the survivors landed on the beach here), follow Inglis St to cut through the Pass of Branda (17.5 km) to view the Heads and descend to:*

Breaker Bay: Across the water lie the bleak Orongorongos and the inhospitable coast around which the earliest stock was driven to the Wairarapa. Offshore is notorious **Barretts Reef**, where the *Wahine* foundered and capsized in a freak storm as the latest in a series of victims there.

*Continue along a bleak shoreline to pass **Ataturk Park** (with its memorial to the fallen at Gallipoli) and pass the southern extremity of the airport runway (22.5 km) to reach:*

Lyall Bay *(23.5 km)*: A popular swimming beach, with a "corner" much ridden by surfboard riders. From hereabouts the Kaikoura Ranges of the South Island come into view.

The road continues to pass a number of rocky points suitable for picnicking and:

Houghton Bay *(26.5 km)*: An inviting cove but dangerous for swimming.

The road then sweeps round:

Island Bay *(27.5 km)*: Home of a small fishing fleet. The island for which the bay is named is Tapu-te-ranga ("sacred island"), a refuge for Ngati Ira displaced by the Te Ati Awa migration. The island's name may have come from the site of a famed tapu meeting house in "Hawaiki".

Continue on to:

Owhiro Bay *(30 km)*: A walk along the coastline from here leads to a seal colony. (*See "Some Short Walks", below.*)

The coastal run concludes here. Turn up Happy Valley Rd and bear right down Brooklyn Rd after cresting the hill to enjoy a pleasant view of the harbour and Hutt Valley.
  Off Brooklyn Rd (opp. Central Park), turn right into Nairn St. and bear left. At No. 68 Nairn St is the:

Colonial Cottage Museum *(c. 1858)*: A colonial cottage in a style highly popular at the time of its construction has been restored as a cottage museum. *Open weekdays, 10 a.m.–4 p.m.; weekends and public holidays, 1–4.30 p.m.*

Continue to the bottom of Nairn St and bear right into Willis St. Return to city centre.

OTHER THINGS TO SEE AND DO

Botanic Gardens ★★: Twenty-five hectares of native bush and exotic plants spreads from Tinakori Road up to the top terminus of the cable car. On fine afternoons the gardens draw many Wellingtonians, particularly on "Tulip Sunday" (*early October*) when the tulips bloom in colourful array. The Begonia House (*open daily, 10 a.m. 4 p.m.*) and the extensive Lady Norwood Rose Gardens with over 500 different species, are approached from a little farther down Glenmore Street. Alternatively, a somewhat steeper path leads to them, passing a herb garden that includes a section for plants used by early Maori for medicinal purposes. The Education and Environment Centre *(open 9 a.m.-4 p.m.)* explains the role of plant-life in sustaining the environment.

Cable car: A favourite short (downhill) walk through the Botanic Gardens begins with a trip on the country's only cable car, originally installed in 1902 by developers to open up the desirable suburb of Kelburn and still serving commuters. Passengers are winched up 122 vertical metres, passing Kelburn Park and the University, and with stunning views of the city and harbour en route, both by day and by night. *The cable car runs continuously all day and into the evenings; start from Kelburn Ave (off Lambton Quay, opp. Grey St). The best views are to the left of the cars.*

New Zealand Astronomy Centre (Carter Observatory): *Open daily weekdays. Public viewing each Tues and Sat from 7.30 p.m. from March–October. Planetarium sessions 10.15 a.m. to 4.15 p.m. Sat., Sun., and school holidays; tel. (04) 472-5053 (recorded message) or (04) 472-8167. Top of cable car, Botanic Gardens.*

Wellington Zoo★★: The zoo features a wide variety of animals, both native and exotic (including big game) and has as its focus the breeding of rare and endangered species. The kiwi may be seen (the zoo has an excellent breeding record) as may that fearsome-looking but endangered insect, the native giant weta. A miniature train skirts the edge of a large pond *(weekends and school holidays)*, the home of waterfowl. *Newtown Park; tel. (04) 389-8130.*

Wrights Hill gun battery: A maze of underground tunnels, gun emplacements and a replica cannon make up a World War II fortress designed to protect Cook Strait from a feared Japanese invasion. *Wrights Hill Rd, off Campbell St, Karori.*

Markets: Lively **Wakefield market** offers items from colourful clothes and jewellery to craft and posters (*Cnr Jervois Quay and Taranaki St. Operates Fri, Sat, Sun and public holidays*). **Petone Settlers Market** is a huge, indoor market (*weekends*).

BEACHES

Some city beaches: The pick of the capital's inner-harbour beaches are Oriental (crowded at weekends), Worser and Scorching Bays. The outer harbour beaches of Lyall and Island Bays, and also at Titahi Bay, past Δ Porirua, attract surfers the year round. The "City Marine drive" (*above*) passes the first five.

Eastern Bays: Facing the city across the harbour are the sun-drenched beaches of Day's Bay and Eastbourne. *See "Eastern Bays Drive"* (*below*).

West coast beaches: The west coast, north from Paekakariki, is one long continuous beach, sprinkled with a number of settlements progressively less dependent on the capital. These include Paekakariki, Raumati South, Raumati Beach, Paraparaumu (*see "Environs", below*) and Δ Waikanae. Offshore lies enticing Δ Kapiti Island.

SOME WALKS

Waterfront walk: As in the city warehouses, storage depots and wharves give way to boutiques, waterside apartments and restaurants, the once unappealing city shoreline throbs with new vitality. *Start by the railway station and walk along the old wharves to Courtenay Place. Allow 1 hr.*

Butterfly Creek ★★★: The walk begins at Eastbourne and follows a well-defined track which rises to cross a fairly steep ridge and descends through native bush and beech forest. In the valley is the Butterfly Creek swimming hole. It is said that an illicit whisky still in nearby Still Gully provided spirits for Wellingtonians during the 1920s. The whisky was furtively shipped by scow in milk-cans, until the scow rammed the wharf and sank. *Drive to Eastbourne (24 km) and turn up Kowhai St. Signposted. For the walk allow up to half a day. The walk is best undertaken in dry weather. A climb simply to the crest of the ridge affords an unusual aspect of Wellington's harbour and of both Ward Island (left) and Somes Island (right).*

Johnston's Hill: A walk above the suburb of Karori where one enjoys a panorama of city, harbour, Cook Strait and South Island. *Drive to Karori and follow Hatton St and Hatton St Extension to the lookout. Allow 1 hr for the return walk.* Below the lookout rises the tower of the British High Commissioner's residence, part of which was the home of New Zealand's first puisne judge, Mr Justice Chapman (1803-81), who stoutly refused to leave for the greater safety of Wellington township during the turbulence that marred Wellington's first years of settlement.

Owhiro Bay to Red Rocks: An interesting coastal walk of about 8 kilometres return (from the quarry at the end of Owhiro Bay Parade) leads to Red Rocks, a curious volcanic upthrust between track and sea. Three kilometres beyond, at Sinclair Head, a seal colony may be found during winter months. *Walking time: Red Rocks 2 hrs return from quarry; Sinclair Head 3½ hrs return from quarry.*

Pencarrow Light: From the end of the main Eastbourne road, a road closed to public motor traffic leads on towards Pencarrow Head and affords good views of the entrance to Wellington Harbour.

As early as 1842 there was an attempt of sorts to guide ships into Wellington Harbour, and in 1849 a shed was built with a window facing seawards and an ordinary lamp placed in its window. Though there were representations for a proper light, it was not until 1859 that Pencarrow Light began operating as the first lighthouse erected in New Zealand. Many shipwrecks have occurred in the vicinity, the largest being SS *Devon* (3,934 tons), which was stranded below Pencarrow Light in 1913 and became a total loss. The 39-tonne wreck of the coastal trader *Paiaka*, which ran aground during a storm in 1906, has been preserved. By Burdan's Gate there is a **memorial** to the victims of the *Wahine* disaster of 1968.

Use of Pencarrow Light was discontinued when Baring Head Lighthouse (*9.5 km S*) became operational in 1935. Today the tower remains a day marker for shipping and aircraft, and in 1959 was declared an Historic Place by the New Zealand Historic Places Trust. *16 km return. Allow 3 hrs. Alternatively, walk the 15 km one-way through to the Wainuiomata coast road near Baring Head.*

Northern Walkway: From Kelburn's Botanic Gardens the Northern Walkway winds above the suburbs through several parks, including Tinakori Hill, Trelissick Park, Khandallah Park and Johnsonville. *16 km; allow 4 hrs. Leaflet available.*

Eastern Walkway: This rather exposed path, steep in places, follows the southern end of the Miramar Peninsula. En route are wonderful seascapes, pa sites and a memorial to those who fell at Anzac Cove (Gallipoli). *Start at Pass of Branda (Breaker Bay) and end at Tarakena Bay. 4.5 km. Allow 1½ hrs. Leaflet available.*

Southern Walkway: Contained within the city itself, the walkway runs from Oriental Parade to ramble along the town belt before descending to Island Bay where buses can return you to your starting point. There are superb views of the city en route. *11 km; allow 4 hrs. Leaflet available.*

Colonial Knob Walkway: This walk takes in the hills to the west of Porirua. On a clear day the view from Colonial Knob is an amazing one, encompassing Mana and △ Kapiti Islands, the distant peak of Taranaki, the Inland Kaikouras of the South Island, the Marlborough Sounds and the city and harbour of Wellington itself. *7.5 km; allow 3–4 hours round trip. Start from Elsdon Youth Camp, Rahia St, Porirua.*

Makara Walkway: A coastal route, with swimming as well as picnicking possibilities. A Maori pa and the remains of World War II gun emplacements are seen en route. *6 km return; allow 3-4 hours. Start from Makara Beach, beyond Karori, 16 km from the city centre.*

Cannon Point Walkway: The route traverses the hills to the west of Upper Hutt, an area which was milled before being farmed, and some of which is covered with regenerating bush. Cannon Point's name was derived from a fallen tree, which when viewed from below resembled a cannon. Subsequently the area was used for training manoeuvres by US Army personnel during World War II. *Allow 3 hrs for the initial 5-km circular route. Start from Tulsa Grove; in Totara Park, Upper Hutt.*

Other walkways are described under △ Waikanae, △ Lower Hutt, △ Palliser (Cape) Road to △ Masterton and △ Carterton.

SOME OTHER SUGGESTED DRIVES

AKATARAWA-WAIKANAE ROUND TRIP: Ideally this 130-kilometre, all-day round trip should conclude in the late afternoon, with the sun setting behind the distant South Island as one drives south along the coast. One may picnic in the Akatarawa valley or on one of the several beaches. There are several restaurants between △Waikanae and Paremata. For notes on △Lower Hutt and △Upper Hutt, see their respective entries.

Leave Wellington by the Hutt motorway and follow Highway 2, pausing at:

Percy's Scenic Reserve *(12 km)*: A pleasant bush reserve, excellent for picnicking and strolling.

Continue up the valley to cross the river at Silverstream and pass through Heretaunga and Trentham; detour along Blockhouse Lane off McHardy St to see:

Wallaceville Blockhouse: Built in 1860 as part of Wellington's outlying defences when land war flared, the unbecoming blockhouse never came under attack. Similar forts were built in various parts of the North Island, but this is one of very few to have survived.

Return to Highway 2 and continue N passing:

Quinn's Post Hotel: The hotel takes its name from the Anzac landing at Gallipoli and reflects the nearby presence of Trentham military camp.

Continue through △Upper Hutt's commercial centre; turn left along Akatarawa Rd towards △Waikanae at 36 km. There are several picnic and river-swimming spots by the roadside, including **Clouston Park** *(at 50.5 km)*, after which the road runs past **Staglands** *(51.5 km)*, a popular wildlife park and picnic place before winding through bush up the Akatarawa valley to the:

Summit *(59.5 km)*: From a height of some 450 metres one may, on an exceptionally clear day, see Mt Egmont as a blue triangle resting on the sea.

Descend to reach:

△Waikanae *(72 km)*: Centre of a market-gardening district and a popular seaside settlement favoured by the more affluent retired. The Southward Car Museum is in Otaihanga Road *(3 km S)*.

Cross the railway, turn left to follow Highway 1 back to Wellington, passing:

Kapiti Lookout *(76.5 km)*: A vantage point from which to view the green and gentle face which △Kapiti Island turns towards the land. From here the road leads towards a knoll on which stands a massive statue erected in 1958 to mark the centenary of the visitation to St Bernadette Soubirous at Lourdes. It presides over the township of:

Paraparaumu *(78 km)*: A vigorous commuter settlement where many Wellingtonians have beach cottages. Here one may turn off to Paraparaumu Beach *(detour 9 km)* to pass the airport (from which scenic flights operate in classic aircraft) and reach the coast, where a bustling shopping centre and outdoor amusements centre complement a safe, sandy beach and an equable climate. From the coast depart trips to △ Kapiti Island's nature and marine reserves. Paraparaumu means "scraps of food in an earth oven". Just north is **Lindale**, a tourist complex where visitors can see sheep and sheepdog demonstrations and sample delicious "Kapiti Cheese". *(Main Rd North; see below)*. South, at Raumati, tours through the delectable **Nyco Chocolates** factory are irresistible to many.

Continue S to cross the railway line at:

McKays Crossing *(85.5 km)*: An area well known to the US Second Marine Corps, who camped here from June 1942 to November 1943, when they left to fight in the Pacific. The Memorial Gates record their stay. Beyond the gates, in **Queen Elizabeth Park,** is the Tramway Museum *(see "Museums, Libraries and Art Galleries", above)*. A road leads through the gates down to the sea.

Continue S to reach:

Paekakariki *(89 km)*: Another settlement on the same stretch of sandy beach. Queen Elizabeth Park extends south to here and incorporates a number of amusements as well as seaside picnic spots *(signposted)*. At Paekakariki, by the main highway, is **Steam Incorporated** where "J" and "Ka" locomotives are being restored *(see "Museums, Libraries and Art Galleries", above)*. (The Hill Road to Pauatahanui from Paekakariki affords an unparalleled, almost aerial, view of the coast and of △ Kapiti Island.)
From here the road south is trapped between the sheer hill face and sea-swept rocks with the contours of the South Island often visible in the distance. Paekakariki means "perch of the kakariki [parakeets]".

Continue S through Pukerua Bay to:

Plimmerton *(103 km)*: It was by the beach here (across the railway line) that Te Rauparaha was quietly captured at dawn *(see "War", above)*.

Continue S to enter Paremata and at 105 km detour 400 m right down Pascoe Ave to reach the Ngati Toa Domain and what little remains of the:

Paremata Barracks (1847): When Te Rangihaeata threatened the township of Wellington from his Pauatahanui stronghold, Governor Sir George Grey decided to establish a military post here to deter war parties from launching a northern attack on Wellington. In 1846 a temporary stockade was established, where 200 soldiers spent a wet and miserable winter, muttering of mutiny. Work then began on a grandiose two-storeyed stone barracks, with towers to house small cannon. A high tender was preferred as the contractor was officially thought "more likely to complete his Contract efficiently and satisfactorily", but neither hope was realised. Tardiness was aggravated by foundation problems; the mortar used (of beach sand and crushed seashell) proved so inferior that the first fires burnt through the fireplaces, and one tower was so badly cracked by the one and only cannon shot ever fired from it that it had to be abandoned. Within a year a series of earthquakes forced the total abandonment of the barracks, and in the great earthquake of 1855 they crumbled finally to ruin. But in any event delays in building had meant that by the time the renowned 65th Regiment had moved into the barracks, war in the area was over. *The ruins are fenced off beside the Mana Cruising Club's clubhouse.*

Rejoin the main road and continue S to cross the:

Paremata Bridge (*105 km*): Built for the Centennial Exhibition of 1940, prior to which road access to Wellington was by way of the Paekakariki Hill Road and Pauatahanui, the bridge spans the entrance to the Pauatahanui Inlet, an arm of Porirua Harbour which saw much activity and the occasional skirmish between naval boat and Maori war canoe during the campaign against Te Rangihaeata. Today a host of boats ride gently at their moorings and in summer many families picnic around the inlet's sheltered shore while watching yachts on the harbour. A "paremata" is a return feast for one previously given.

The main road continues S to pass:

△**Porirua** (*110 km*): A satellite city for Wellington which has burgeoned in recent years.

Continue S along the motorway to descend to Ngauranga Gorge and return to Wellington City.

HAYWARDS-PAEKAKARIKI ROUND TRIP (*106 km*): This half-day trip to some extent repeats sections of the Akatarawa-Waikanae Round Trip (*above*) but is quite different in character.

Leave Wellington by the Hutt motorway and follow Highway 2 towards △Upper Hutt, pausing at:

Percy's Scenic Reserve (*12 km*). *Continue up the Hutt Valley, turning left over Haywards (signposted) at 22.5 km to pass the:*

Haywards Substation (*23 km*): Southernmost station in the North Island Grid and one of the major installations of the inter-island power transmission system.

Continue on to descend into the pleasant valleys of Judgeford and Pauatahanui, and emerge at:

Pauatahanui Inlet (*32 km*): An arm of Porirua Harbour which saw much activity during the campaign against Te Rangihaeata in the 1840s. Over the bridge is Taylor-Stace cottage (1847), now a crafts shop. Pauatahanui means "big shellfish".

Opp. the bridge here turn up the driveway of:

St Alban's Anglican Church, Pauatahanui: This church stands on the site of the pa from which Te Rangihaeata menaced the infant settlement of Wellington in the 1840s. It was captured in 1846 and a military redoubt was established overlooking the waters of the inlet, which then lapped the foot of the ridge. The harbour bed rose in the 1855 earthquake. The occasional indentation in the paddock behind the church is sufficient to fire the imagination.

Bear right to follow the:

Paekakariki Hill Road: This enters a bushed gorge with an appealing picnic place, **Battle Hill Farm Park**, below the point where, in 1846, the rearguard of the retreating Te Rangihaeata made a brief stand (known as the Battle of Horokiri) to gain time for the women and the wounded. *The road climbs to pass quite suddenly through a cutting and emerge abruptly at an expansive view of the coast. Pause at the:*

Summit viewpoint (*45 km*)**:** The summit affords a breathtaking view down to the coast, where the sea laps the sand of a beach which arcs north to point towards △ Kapiti Island. To the west the South Island may often be seen, and to the north Taranaki/Egmont occasionally appears as a solitary blue triangle on the horizon.

Descend steeply to reach:

Paekakariki (*50 km*). From this point, follow the route back to Wellington as for the Akatarawa-Waikanae Round Trip (above). If time allows, one may drive 4 km N to the Tramway Museum in Queen Elizabeth Park (McKays Crossing entrance); open weekends and public holidays.

EASTERN BAYS DRIVE (*51.5 km return*): This drive skirts Wellington Harbour to pass through the sought-after residential suburbs of the Eastern Bays.

Leave Wellington by the Hutt motorway to Petone, passing the foot of:

Ngauranga Gorge (*5 km*): It was here that the Te Atiawa chief Wharepouri (*see index*) had his kainga when the first settlers arrived. Ngauranga means "people who came by canoe".

The route then follows the:

Hutt Road: A ledge caught between sea and the sheer uplift of the "Wellington Fault", itself uplifted in the earthquake of 1855.

At 10 km bear left to cross the Petone overbridge and follow The Esplanade passing:

Te Puni Street (*11 km*): A street named for the "friendly" Te Atiawa chief Te Puni (?-1870) whose followers were settled along the Petone foreshore when the first settlers arrived. With Te Wharepouri of Ngauranga he welcomed the arrival of the Pakeha and helped defend them against Te Rangihaeata of Pauatahanui. Among the toasts at the opening of Barrett's Hotel was "Te Puni and the chiefs", and in recognition of his helpfulness, in 1848 the New Zealand Company presented him with an engraved silver cup (*now in the Museum of New Zealand, Wellington*). His name is commemorated in Epuni, an area of Lower Hutt. The chief is buried in a small private **cemetery** in Te Puni Street.

Continue along The Esplanade to pass first the:

Petone Settlers' Museum ★★ *(12 km)*: An interesting collection traces the history of the area. *Open weekdays (not Tues) 12 noon-4 p.m.; weekends 1-5 p.m.* The building is itself the Provincial Memorial (1940), commemorating Wellington's first settlers who landed on the beach here. The memorial records the names of the first N.Z. Company passenger ships and the settlers they carried.

Continue on to skirt the roundabout by the:

Hutt Park Raceway (*14 km*): Home of Wellington trotting.

Follow signposts "Eastern Bays" to pass Port Rd and a succession of sheltered bays, among them:

Lowry Bay (*18 km*), **York Bay** (*19 km*), **Mahina Bay** (*20 km*), and:

Days Bay (*28.5 km*): Here the road passes in front of the spacious grounds of Wellesley College, an Anglican boys' preparatory school, and Williams Park, a favoured tree-shaded picnic park with tennis courts.

Continue on to pass through:

Eastbourne (*22 km*): Largest of the settlements. Houses spill down steep, well-bushed hillsides and here, as elsewhere, a number of residents have private "cable cars" to winch them between street and home. A walk to Butterfly Creek (*allow ½ day; see "Some Walks", above*) gives access to a sheltered valley behind the ridge. Little blue penguins come ashore hereabouts each evening (*details of penguin spotting tours, best from September to February, from the City Information Centre*).

Continue on to the road's end at 26 km.

Pencarrow Light: The walk to the old Pencarrow Light starts here (*see "Some Walks", above*).

Return to Wellington by the same route. A detour may be made at the Hutt Park Roundabout to drive up Wainui Hill (signposted "Wainuiomata") for a spectacular and quite different view of the harbour across the clustered buildings of the lower Hutt Valley.

WAINUIOMATA: From the growing settlement at Wainuiomata, Wainuiomata Valley Road leads to the coast and to the Cape Turakirae marine terraces. (*See △Lower Hutt, "Environs".*)

WAIRARAPA: Because of a growing volume of traffic on west coast roads, Wellingtonians are increasingly looking to the Wairarapa as a recreational area, driving to such points as △ Cape Palliser (*140 km*), △ Riversdale (*147 km*), △ Castlepoint (*169 km*) and the wine-growing district of △ Martinborough.

OTHER ENVIRONS

△ **Kapiti Island** ★ ★**:** An enticing island offshore from △ Waikanae, with a bird sanctuary which may be visited.

Lindale Agriculture and Tourist Centre ★**:** A farm park and home to an innovative cheese factory producing "Kapiti Cheeses", speciality cheeses many of which are unique. Visitors may see the cheeses being made, and sample and purchase them. There is also the temptation of gourmet ice-cream. A farm and horse park stages farm shows and horse-riding. *42 km NE on Highway 1, north of Paekakariki. Open daily.*

Makara: Makara Beach (Ohariu Bay; *17 km*) is a shingled beach which links rocky points that offer good fishing in a wild and somewhat desolate corner of the island. A cluster of baches hugs the shore that witnessed one of the last cannibal feasts of consequence, when at the close of Te Rauparaha's exploits 150 Muaupoko were accounted for. Makara means "head".

On Quartz Hill, a short distance inland, stand the buildings of Makara Radio, which once received radio signals from the world over. Until new technology diminished its importance it was one of the country's major receiving stations.

The **Makara Walkway** (*see p. 295*) starts from Makara Beach.

Tararua Forest Park: The rugged Tararua Ranges form part of the southern vertebrae of the North Island's mountain backbone and sever the Wairarapa from the west coast. Indeed there is no road across between the Akatarawa road and the "Pahiatua Track", a distance of some 131 kilometres. The park has a number of imposing peaks of which the highest is Mitre (at 1,571 metres almost as high as its better-known namesake at Milford Sound). Many impressive tracks thread through the bush and there are a large number of huts. Tararua means "twin peaks". *Details and hunting permits from DOC. There are a number of access points to the park both from the west coast, the upper Hutt Valley and the Wairarapa.*

ORGANISED EXCURSIONS

Sightseeing tours: Regular coach tours run daily. The city is magical viewed from the heights by night. *Wally Hammond's Wellington City Scenic Tours (tel. (04) 472-0869); Harbour Capital Tours (tel. (04) 499-1282) and Wellington Heritage Highlights Tours (tel. (04) 478-8315.*

Tour of Parliament: Tour times vary according to whether the House is in session. *Tel. (04) 471-9457; Parliament Buildings, Molesworth and Bowen Sts.*

Picton ferry: A pleasant day may be spent on the inter-island ferries, sailing out of Wellington Harbour, across Cook Strait and through the languid Marlborough Sounds. A short time is spent at Picton (the South Island's northern rail terminal) before the ferry returns to Wellington. *Bookings, tel. (04) 498-3999.* A "Wine Trail Weekender" package trip includes the cruise, accommodation and a visit to several of Marlborough's outstanding wineries.

Harbour cruise: Several companies run trips on the harbour, occasionally with lunch or dinner *(details from Information Centre).* The East by West Ferry also runs a regular commuter service across the harbour to Days Bay, a popular picnicking and swimming spot *(departs Queens Wharf; tel. (04) 499-1273).*

Helicopter sightseeing: Trips leave from the city waterfront. *Helipro, Queens Wharf; tel. (09) 472-1550.*

Whale watching: Day trips operate to Kaikoura to join whale-watching expeditions *(see South Island volume). Details from Visitor Information Centre.*

Auckland   Map 4   Pop. 1,621   **WELLSFORD**

89 km NW of Auckland; 85 km SE of Whangarei.

THE FARMING CENTRE of Wellsford, on the neck of land which links Northland with the Auckland region, stands close by the shores of △Kaipara Harbour and the historic settlement of Port Albert.

Wellsford grew on the fringe of Albertland, on a "gum ridge" that divided native bush from bleak gumfield. At the turn of the century the kauri gum had virtually gone, the local population numbered less than 30 and the district as a whole was sparsely settled. But as the Albertland settlement declined, emphasis shifted to the more strategically situated settlement at Wellsford, and the town's steady growth began.

The name "Wellsford" is said to have been formed from the first letters of the surnames of some of the earliest settlers.

ENVIRONS

Mangawhai Forest: The forest, originally established to check the inland drift of sand, spreads over 10 kilometres of coastline. The trees are predominantly pine, with some eucalyptus. Hard by the shore, despite their stunted, wind- and sand-blasted appearance, the trees hold the seaward dunes from drifting and create an essential protective barrier for the rest of the forest. Entry to most of the area is restricted, but there is access to one of the finest beaches on the east coast along Pacific Road, Te Arai Point Road and Lake Road, where there is good surfcasting and swimming, but no camping. **Lake Tomarata,** which adjoins the forest and is reached along Tomarata Lake Road, has a boat ramp and offers the alternative of freshwater swimming. *18 km NE.*

Dome Forest Walkway: A 4.3-kilometre walk of about 2 hours leads through native bush to a flat-topped hill (*336 m*) providing views of the Hauraki Gulf. Those who continue some 800 metres past the summit see the Waiwhiu Kauri Grove, with about 20 mature kauri trees. *Signposted 12 km S on Highway 1, opp. Kraacks Rd.*

WHAKATANE ★★

Bay of Plenty   Map 9   Pop. 32,112 (urban area)

92 km NE of Rotorua; 100 km SE of Tauranga. Visitor Information Centre, Boon St; tel. (07) 308-6058. Department of Conservation Field Centre, National Bank Building, 236 The Strand; tel. (07) 308-7213.

WHAKATANE, distribution centre for surrounding dairy and fat-lamb farms, is from an industrial viewpoint dominated by the vast board mills which employ over a third of the town's workforce. In summer Whakatane's Ohope Beach draws many visitors.

Inland lie vast areas of exotic forest. The now-fertile Rangitaiki Plains to the west were swampy wastelands before a Government drainage scheme was implemented. Recent years have seen a substantial increase in horticulture and the establishment of a number of deer farms.

SOME HISTORY

Toi: A millennium ago Toi te Huatahi ("Toi the first-born"), one of the best-known early Polynesian explorers and the original ancestor of a number of tribes, is said to have landed here in his unsuccessful and exhausting search for his lost grandson, Whatonga (*p. 9*). Abandoning his quest and electing to settle here, Toi built a pa on the highest point of Whakatane Heads, where earthworks traditionally believed to be the pa site may be seen today. There are actually two contiguous pa, one of the Classic and the other of the Archaic period, and both have been the subject of archaeological investigation. Ash-shower studies may establish the approximate age of the earlier site.

After Toi arrived he became known as Toi Kairakau ("Toi the wood-eater"), presumably because he was forced to change his diet and to rely on forest foods. This suggests that Toi brought no plants with him and arrived before horticulture was practised.

Tradition records that it was at Whakatane that Toi and his grandson were finally reunited, as Whatonga in turn had come from "Hawaiki" in search of his grandfather.

A manly deed: About two centuries after Toi, the *Mataatua* canoe arrived here from "Hawaiki", as one of the canoes of the Polynesian migration of the fourteenth century. According to tradition, the males went ashore to explore the new land, leaving the women in the canoe. But the canoe began to drift out to sea and as the paddles of large canoes were tapu to women, they were helpless until in desperation the captain's daughter, Wairaka, seized a paddle and cried, "Kia Whakatane au i ahau" ("I will act as a man"). Other women followed her example, and they brought the canoe safely back to shore. In recognition of Wairaka's defiance the area was named Whakatane ("to be manly"). A modern statue of Wairaka stands on the rocks at Whakatane Heads.

The "Kate" and the birth of settlement: In July 1865 James Falloon, a half-caste interpreter and native agent, arrived at Whakatane to investigate the murder of the Rev. Carl Volkner at nearby △Opotiki. He found the local Ngati Awa under the sway of a visiting Taranaki Hauhau who urged them to attack Falloon's 28-ton cutter, *Kate*, to kill those aboard and to loot and burn the vessel.

Martial law was proclaimed two months later, and by the end of the year a large area of the eastern Bay of Plenty had been confiscated by the Government. Whakatane township, surveyed in 1867, was peopled with military settlers, who were allotted their town acre (0.4 ha.) and their country section here. Such a settlement was to prove an irresistible challenge for Te Kooti.

Te Kooti's Whakatane raid: After the Poverty Bay massacre near Gisborne and his subsequent defeat at Ngatapa, Te Kooti *(p.* **85***)* reorganised his followers and in March 1869 chose Whakatane for his first attack on the Bay of Plenty settlements. His men marched out of the bush and as they approached the small military settlement at Whakatane, came to a modest redoubt close to a flour mill, managed by a Frenchman, Jean Guerren. There were about seven in the redoubt, and Guerren was by himself in the mill.

A war party of 100 attacked the mill, and the Frenchman, a brilliant marksman, fought superbly to protect it. For two days Te Kooti's men were held at bay, but when they learned how few defenders there were they rushed both the mill and the redoubt. Guerren was forced to run to the greater safety of the redoubt, where he helped defend its narrow gateway until shot dead. The attackers swarmed over the redoubt's earth walls to tomahawk the remaining defenders, with the exception of two women. Te Kooti's men marched on to nearby Rauporoa pa, carrying a white flag of truce—Te Kooti's favourite ploy for lulling the suspicions of Maori who were fighting for the Government.

The ruse all but succeeded, for a credulous defender shouting, "It is peace, peace; there's the white flag!" had to be restrained from opening a heavy sliding gate. Eventually the pa was abandoned and the way left clear for Te Kooti to march on to Whakatane, which by then had been evacuated. His men burned most of the buildings and became very drunk on rum from the store. When the news reached Tauranga, Captain Gilbert Mair *(pp.* **197-98***)* rode through the night along the coast, raising a force of "friendly" Maori as he went.

The next day a Government steamer landed European reinforcements at Whakatane and the combined forces compelled Te Kooti to retreat to the dense Urewera country. Whakatane was left a smoking ruin. *The scene of the Frenchman's battle with Te Kooti is marked by a memorial, whose mill-stone is actually from his mill, 5.5 km S of Whakatane on the main road to Opotoki.*

After his pardon in 1883, Te Kooti was granted land at Wainui, at the head of Ohiwa Harbour near Ohiwa, where he died 10 years later. His burial place was a closely guarded secret, but some believe it to be near the Ohiwa Heads.

POINTS OF INTEREST

Pohaturoa Rock: In the centre of the town, and now an imposing rock arch, this was once a tapu cave where tohunga performed tattooing and other sacred rites. In 1927 it was dedicated as a memorial to the fallen of World War I. Beside the rock is a model of a canoe and a memorial to Te Hurinui Apanui, a noted local Maori chief. *The Strand.*

Nga Tapuwae O Toi Walkway * * *: The circular walk*(round trip 7 hrs)*, which takes in Toi's pa, Kohi Point and Ohope Beach, can easily be joined at several points.

Most walkers start by climbing up to Kapu te Rangi ("Ridge of Heaven"), traditionally known as Toi's pa, which comprises some of the oldest known earthworks in the country. From the **Kohi Point Lookout** the track continues on around Kohi Point to Otarawairere Bay and Ohope Beach, on the eastern side of the point. There are spectacular views in every direction and some magnificent stands of pohutukawa. The return route lies via the Ohope Scenic Reserve, Burma Rd, White Horse Drive and Mokorua Gorge. *Maps and details are available from the Visitor Information Centre and the DOC Office. The walkway officially begins and ends at the bottom of Mokorua Gorge, just south of Whakatane.*

Kohi Point Lookout *(by road)*: The traditional site of Kapu-te-Rangi ("Ridge of the Heaven"), Toi's pa, comprises some of the oldest known earthworks in the country. *1.5 km. Kohi Point Lookout Rd, off Otarawairere Rd (off the road to Ohope). It is also possible to drive down to Otarawairere Bay.*

Whakatane Heads * *(1.5 km)*: An interesting short drive or walk leads to the Heads. The road passes Wairaka marae, named after the legendary saviour of the *Mataatua* canoe.

Farther on is Ana-a-Muriwai ("The Cave of Muriwai"), a cave which according to tradition was "given" to Muriwai by Irekawa, her grandfather. Muriwai, who came on the *Mataatua* canoe and was believed to have supernatural powers, lived for many years the life of a hermit in this cave, and from time to time was consulted on matters of importance.

On a rock at the Heads is a plaque which marks the traditional landing place of the *Mataatua* canoe, and on another prominent rock stands a slender modern statue of Wairaka.

The Heads witnessed a bizarre event in the extraordinary career of Rua Kenana (*pp.* **240-41**), who in 1905 styled himself the "younger brother" of Christ and offered eternal life (and seven wives) to his followers. In his heyday, about 1910, he announced his intention to "walk upon the water" in the manner of Christ. A large crowd gathered at Whakatane Heads to watch; Rua poised to take his first step, then suddenly turned to the hushed and expectant throng and asked if they genuinely believed he could perform the feat. When the crowd gave a loud cheer of support, Rua declared that in such circumstances a demonstration was unnecessary and he directed that they all go home.

Wairere waterfall: Few townships have a waterfall such as this in their centre. It is said to have been used by Whatonga as a landmark in his quest for his grandfather, as he had been told that Toi was settled in a pa near the waterfall. *Mataatua St. Behind Commercial Hotel.*

Whakatane Museum: On display are Maori artefacts, largely of local origin, and outstanding collections of New Zealand books. *Boon St. Open weekdays 10 a.m.-4.30 p.m.; weekends, 1.30-4 p.m.*

ENVIRONS

Ohope Beach ★★★: One of the most desirable of the Bay of Plenty seaside settlements, it has a safe ocean beach, backed by pohutukawa, and is favoured by both surfers and fishing enthusiasts. Open sea and sheltered harbour are separated by slim Ohiwa peninsula, virtually an extension of Ohope. In particular Ohiwa harbour is good for shellfish, flounder and for water-skiing. Above Ohope firestation, the remains of Tauwhare Pa, a pre-European pa, may be seen on the hillside.

The road to Ohope passes Puketapu Lookout and the road to Kohi Point Lookout, Toi's pa *(see above). 6.5 km E of Whakatane.*

Matata Wildlife Refuge: A coastal sanctuary provides a wintering over area for the rare white heron and is home to large numbers of various species of waterfowl. A track leads around the lagoon here and there is an observation platform. Occasionally the fernbird is seen. *Arawa St (coastal end of Mair St). Park at the Matata Domain. There is camping nearby.*

Awakeri Hot Springs: Here are soda thermal pools alongside a picnic area and camping ground. *14 km SW on Highway 30, the road to Rotorua. Open daily to 9.30 p.m. Motel accommodation, camping and caravan sites; tel. (07) 304-9117.*

△ **Te Urewera National Park ★ ★ ★:** A Maori craft training centre displays old photographs and drawings associated with the Park and offers a 20-minute audio-visual presentation. *14 Morrison St, Taneatua, 13 km S of Whakatane.* Trampers can reach the Park by following either the Whakatane River valley through Ruatoki or the Waimana valley through Matahi.

Waimana Valley: A popular area for picnics and casual camping. There is an outdoor education hut at Ngutuoha. Grassy clearings with poplars and old fruit trees are reminders that this tranquil spot was well populated and prosperous in the days of Rua Kenana. *Road access from Whakatane via Waimana and Matahi. 50 km.*

ORGANISED EXCURSIONS

Dolphin watching ★ ★ ★: Swim with the dolphins in their natural environment or simply watch their captivating antics along with other marine life, from the comfort of a boat. The fortunate see whales as they migrate through the Bay of Plenty. *Dolphins Down Under, 92 The Strand; tel/fax (07) 308-4636. All wet suits, snorkels and masks supplied — as well as hot showers after the trip. No experience needed.*

Visits to △ White Island ★ ★ ★: A thrilling experience awaits those who fly over this active island volcano to peer down into its crater in the certain knowledge that sooner rather than later it will erupt once more. Eruptions in 1992 temporarily coated the island in a thin blanket of red ash. To walk on the island and savour its fury, visit by boat or helicopter. *Vulcan Helicopters (tel. (07) 308-4636 or freephone 0800-804-354) land on the island to make an awesome 1½ hr guided walk. The boat trip with Pee Jay Charters (tel. (07) 312-9075) also includes a guided walk. Aspects of the island and marine life may also be seen on White Island Day Cruises (tel. (07) 312-4236). Details of other operators from the Visitor Information Centre.*

Visits to Motuhora (Whale Island): Once occupied and exploited by the Ngatiawa the 143-hectare volcanic island, six kilometres north off the coast of Whakatane, is now a wildlife refuge. Only excursions organised by the Department of Conservation are permitted to land. *Over the summer months DOC runs guided trips to inspect the birdlife and visit archaeological sites. Advance booking essential; tel. (07) 308-7213.*

Jet-boating: The waters of the spectacular Rangitaiki River, with rapids and narrow, densely bushed gorges, afford a magnificent setting for jet-boating. *Kiwi Jet Boat Tours (tel. (07) 307-0663).*

White-water rafting: Quiet one-day scenic trips or one to four-day exhilarating expeditions on the narrow, twisting Motu River set in rugged country. (*Motu River Expeditions; tel. (07) 308-7213. Whakatane Raft Tours; tel. (07) 308-7760.) Combination raft, helicopter and jet boat trips are also possible.*

Big-game fishing: Charters may be arranged locally for those who would fish the famed waters of the Bay of Plenty. *Details from the Visitor Information Centre.*

★★★ WHANGAMATA

Coromandel Peninsula   Map 5   Pop. 3,564

30 km N of Waihi. Information Centre, Port Rd; tel. (07) 865-8340.

WHANGAMATA, once a quiet retreat but now a top surfing resort, is in summer transformed into a boisterous holiday town. The renowned surf of Ocean Beach contrasts with the sheltered ski-lanes of Whangamata Harbour and, as nearest port to △ Mayor Island, its harbour is also a haven for deep-sea fishing enthusiasts. *Chartered skin-diving and fishing trips are run.*

Like other settlements of the △ Coromandel Peninsula, Whangamata has a history of kauri bushmen and gold prospectors. To the north lies Tairua Forest, first established during the Depression. In addition to walking in the forests there is mountain biking, abseiling, windsurfing, and sea kayaking.(*Arrange through the Information Centre.*)

Whangamata means "obsidian harbour", a reference to obsidian washed ashore here from Mayor Island and prized by the Maori who came to collect it for use in tool-making.

ENVIRONS

Wentworth Valley: The valley has bushed picnic spots and swimming holes and is favoured by rock hunters. From the road's end a walk leads in to Wentworth Falls (*about 2 hrs return*) and continues either to reach the top of the falls or down to the bottom, where old gold workings extend under the waterfall. (*Care is needed as some vertical shafts are not covered in. A torch is advisable.*) The Wires Track (so called as it follows the route of the first telephone line into the locality) continues on to afford a three-hour trek over the ranges to Hikutaia (mid-way between Paeroa and Thames). *Turn off inland at 2.5 km S.*

Parakowhai Valley: A good walk (*3 hrs return*) leads in to the deserted Royal Sovereign Mine. On the way an old quarry is passed, features of which are curious hexagonal rock rods, poking out from the rock face. There is good river swimming. *Turn off inland 6.5 km S along Quarry Rd.*

Onemana: A particularly appealing bay. *13.5 km. Turn off 6.5 km N.*

Opoutere: The ocean beach here is good for surf-casting. At its southern end **Wharekawa Wildlife Refuge** provides protection for the endangered New Zealand dotterel and variable oyster catcher. *19 km N.*

Otahu river mouth: A delightful pohutukawa-shaded picnic place beside a swimming area. *800 m S.*

Whiritoa: A pleasant beach, good for surf-casting but unsuitable for swimming. *Short detour at 16 km S.*

WHANGANUI NATIONAL PARK★★★

Wanganui   Map 13   74,000 hectares

The Park stretches along parts of the Whanganui River's banks, between △ Wanganui and △ Taumarunui. See description of Whanganui River, p. 274.

WHANGAREI ★★

Northland   Maps 2,4   Pop. 62,644 (urban area)

174 km N of Auckland. Whangarei Visitors Bureau, Tarewa Park, 93 Otaika Rd; tel. (09) 438-1079. Department of Conservation, 149–151 Bank St; tel. (09) 438-0299.

WHANGAREI, the regional centre and only city of Northland, has a thriving port which came late into the country's commercial pattern but quickly assumed a commanding role. Nursed by a sheltered harbour (the name Whangarei may mean "cherished harbour"), the city owes its prosperity to the proximity of some of the deepest harbour waters in New Zealand. The draught offered by Marsden Point brought the country's major oil refinery, then its first oil-fired power station.

Settlement at Whangarei dates from 1839, but when war broke out in the Bay of Islands six years later there were only 48 Europeans living here, all of whom fled to the safety of Auckland. From this hesitant start the area was slow to recover.

The rugged magnificence of the city's harbour hills is crowned by Mt Manaia (*404 m*) whose five jagged peaks are the natural curiosities from which myths grow.

Offshore lie the Poor Knights Islands, one of the diving world's favourite locations, described below.

MAORI MYTHOLOGY

Manaia and Hautatu: On top of Mt Manaia stood the pa of Manaia, paramount chief of Whangarei. Opposite, on Marsden Point, lived the minor chief Hautatu, married to Pito, the most beautiful girl in the district. The jealous Manaia sent Hautatu to lead a war party to the Bay of Plenty and while he was gone built a causeway right across the harbour to Marsden Point. By night Manaia led a war party over the causeway to slaughter those left in Hautatu's pa and to carry the lovely Pito back to his mountain home.

With justified rage Hautatu returned successfully to attack Manaia's pa. Manaia, his two children and Pito fled along the mountain top, chased by Hautatu who was about to strike Pito down when all five were struck by lightning and turned into stone.

So it is that today the five figures, with an eerie sense of urgency, form a timeless tableau on Mt Manaia's summit. Below them, from Taurikura, the "remains" of Manaia's causeway run jetty-like out into the harbour. *There is a marvellous climb to the summit from McLeods Bay (2 hrs return).*

SOME NOTES ON NORTHLAND

Though the first European settlements in the country were in Northland, drawn by the region's early kauri timber and gum trades, the area remained exploited rather than developed with the result that even in the 1920s it was known as "The Roadless North", a reflection of the primitive transport facilities which were retarding progress. Not until the 1930s did an all-weather road first link Whangarei with Auckland.

Since then the transformation has been impressive, particularly around Whangarei, and a slick roadway system has now contracted Northland into a compact region. But on the east coast pockets of lush pasture are surrounded by large areas of scrub on land depleted by kauri bark.

Today Northland's economy is based on dairying, sheep and cattle farming, citrus orchards and horticulture. Whangarei, by far the largest centre, dominates the area commercially and, in addition to an oil refinery and oil-fired power station, houses the nationally important cement works at Portland. Port Whangarei handles the region's produce.

"The city has a face, the country a soul." *Jacques de Lacretelle, Idée dans un chapeau*

MARSDEN POINT

Marsden Oil-fired Power Stations: Built in 1965-67 at a cost of $27 million, when the country's power needs had been underestimated and an oil-fired power station was the only feasible way in which to avoid a serious winter power shortage, Marsden A had by 1992 become not only too costly to run but also surplus to requirements. The filling of Lake Dunstan to drive the huge Clyde Dam in Central Otago has meant that other, cheaper stand-by stations can meet temporary shortfalls from the hydro-electric dams, and both Marsden A and its later companion, Marsden B, were finally closed in 1992.

Dominating the complex is a 121-metre zebra-striped concrete chimney which generated sufficient draught to ensure that the waste gases dissipated harmlessly, high in the atmosphere.

Fuel oil was piped from the adjoining oil refinery and stored in huge tanks, each with a capacity of 19 million litres.

NZ Refining Company Ltd's Oil Refinery: This is the second refinery built in New Zealand. The first was in New Plymouth where until May 1975, small quantities (approx. 600 tonnes a year) of locally produced crude oil were processed. However, the Marsden Point refinery has the capacity to supply much of New Zealand's gasoline and diesel-oil requirements, and all of its fuel oil and bitumen needs. The plant renders New Zealand self-sufficient in refined products. Over 40 per cent of the feedstocks come from the country's own oil and gas fields.

Until 1964 the country's fuel, its largest single import, had to be shipped here in a refined state. Now crude oil, considerably cheaper than refined oil products, can be imported. Also indigenous condensates from Taranaki are processed here.

Crude oil yields a variety of useful products. It is refined here by first partially vaporising it, then by separating the various streams in a "fractionating tower" or "distiller". The product withdrawn at the top of the tower (the "overheads") is further processed to make gasolines, while further down, in order, diesel oils and residue are obtained. The residue is then either blended to make fuel oils or refined further to make bitumen. The most volatile product, gas, is obtained mainly from the gasoline process, and is used to fuel the refinery furnaces. The combustion gases from the furnaces are vented to the atmosphere from the top of the 100-metre-high chimney, whence they dissipate harmlessly. Surplus gas is disposed of safely by burning in the 60-metre-high flare stack.

The nearby harbour facilities are able to handle tankers of 130,000 tonnes.

Marsden Point Visitor Centre: Visitors are introduced to the technology of oil refining and the history of the district through exhibits and an informative audio-visual display. *8 km off Highway 1, 31 km S of Whangarei. Open daily, 10 a.m–5 p.m.*

OTHER THINGS TO SEE AND DO

Claphams Clock Museum ★ ★ ★: The collection contains about 1300 clocks of every shape and size, whose chorus of ticks and chimes alone merits a visit. The oldest clock dates from 1636. *Rose Gardens, Water St. Open daily 10 a.m.–4 p.m.*

Reyburn House: The city's oldest residence displays arts, crafts, early photographs and regular exhibitions of local art. One may picnic here on the waterfront. *Lower Quay St. Open weekdays, 10 a.m.–4 p.m.; weekends, 1–4 p.m..*

Museum of Fishes: A collection of mounted fish, including some of New Zealand's great record catches as well as rare and some protected species. A giant bass head serves as a curious letter-box! *Town Basin, Quay St; tel. (09) 438-5681.*

Fernery and Snow Conservatory: An unusual fernery in natural surroundings displays some 85 varieties of native ferns, among them New Zealand's celebrated "silver fern". A hot-house provides colourful exotic plants. *Entry from First Avenue or Cafler Park, off Water St. Open 10 a.m.–4 p.m. daily.*

Craft Quarry: A co-operative venture in a delightful bush setting offers local arts and crafts for sale. *Selwyn Ave. Open daily, 10 a.m.–4 p.m. (longer in summer). A short walk leads to a pa site above the quarry.*

Parahaki Scenic Reserve ★ ★: In pre-European times the volcanic prominence of Parahaki provided Maori with an ideal defensive position. Settlements extended for about three kilometres along the ridge, making it one of the largest pa complexes in the country. In the 1700s a bloody battle took place here which the local defenders lost.

Today a war memorial stands on Mt Parahaki (*241 m*) and affords a magnificent panorama of the city and harbour. The flare of the oil refinery on distant Marsden Point is visible by night and day. *Memorial Drive off Riverside Drive.*

Mair Park: A grassed and well-bushed area at the foot of Mt Parahaki is named after the Mair family, the second to settle in Whangarei. The park is popular with picnickers and includes bush walks and a natural swimming pool. A walking track from the river footbridge leads up Mt Parahaki to the war memorial (*see above*).

From Mair Park, it is possible to link in with the **Hatea River Walk** which leads through bush along the eastern side of the Hatea River. (*The complete track starts at the end of Vale Rd and finishes at Whareora Rd.*) The return walk can be made on the western side of the river, finishing at Mair Park. *Signposted off Hatea Drive.*

A.H. Reed Memorial Kauri Park ★: Attractive walks through stands of kauri, some 500 years old, lead to a waterfall. *2 km. Signposted off the road to Ngunguru. Allow 45 mins.*

SOME BEACHES

Along with much of Northland's east coast, Whangarei boasts some beautiful beaches. The harbour's northern coastline offers particularly good bathing, with spectacular beaches on the open coast, at Ocean Beach (*36 km SE*) and Pataua (*31 km E*), and on the Tutukaka coast, between Sandy Bay and Ngunguru (*41 km and 24 km NE respectively*). South east lie Ruakaka (*32 km*) with its racecourse set next to the surf, and Waipu Cove (*50 km*).

THE POOR KNIGHTS ISLANDS MARINE RESERVE ★ ★ ★

Administered by the Department of Conservation, 149–151 Bank St; tel. (09) 438-0299. Those intending to fish in the general area should consult with the Department as to the current fishing regulations and the location of the closed fishing areas. Landing on the islands is not permitted.

Poor Knights Islands ★ ★ ★: A haven for skindivers. Volcanic in origin, the islands provide a labyrinth of caves, tunnels and arches housing a bewildering variety of highly coloured sponges and spectacular fish swept here by a subtropical current significantly warmer than surrounding coastal waters. The two main islands (Tawhiti Rahi and Aorangi) were well cultivated by the Maori but are now nature reserves, with landing permits restricted to *bona fide* scientific parties. Both sustain healthy populations of tuatara, gecko and skink, and the brightly coloured Poor Knights lily (raupo-taranga) is endemic. The islands are the only known nesting-place of the Buller's shearwater.

24 km NE of Tutukaka. Whangarei Deep Sea Anglers' Club, Tutukaka (tel. (09) 434-3818) can arrange fishing, diving and sightseeing trips around the islands. A number other operators based in Tutukaka and Whangarei can organise guided diving excursions. Aqua Action, Marina Rd, Tutukaka; tel. (09) 434-3867; Knight Diver Tours, 30 Whangarei Heads Rd, Whangarei; tel. (09) 436-2584; The Dive Connection, 140 Lower Cameron St, Whangarei; tel. (09) 430-0818; The Dive Shop, water St; tel/fax (09) 438-3521. Most companies also offer dive courses.

OTHER ENVIRONS

Northland Regional Museum and Whangarei Kiwi House ★ ★: An ambitious museum project grew up around the **Clarke homestead** (1885) — a home built for the early doctor, Dr Alexander Clarke. Largely in its original condition, the rooms (*open to the public*) are sensitively furnished in period and include, among other typical family items, Dr Clarke's set of surgical instruments and medical textbooks. These remain in the room that served as his surgery-study.

Close by are the **Oruaiti Chapel** (1861), moved here and used for weddings and christenings; the old **Riponui Pah schoolhouse**, and a curious **hexagonal tower** in which the Whangarei author Jane Mander (1877–1949) used to write. Mander, who spent her childhood as a sawmiller's daughter, moving from one isolated region to another, published *The Story of a New Zealand River* in 1920, after working on it for 20 years. Her subsequent novels did not match the success of her first which, set on the Otamatea River, is one of the first by a New Zealand author to use a local setting and is of considerable historical interest.

A specially-designed nocturnal **Kiwi House** exhibits the flightless bird in as natural environment as possible.

A short distance away is a spacious **Exhibition Centre** which houses displays of local historical interest. Most conspicuous is the Fraser Collection, a significant regional collection of Maori artefacts, which includes an unusual beaked bird-headed waka tupapaku (bone burial chest). *4 km on Highway 14 towards Dargaville. Signposted. Open daily; tel. (09) 438-9630. Attractive walks thread through the native bush that backs on to the homestead. "Live" days, when a team of bullocks is among a number of working exhibits, are staged periodically during the summer.*

Whangarei Falls★★: A much-photographed waterfall of some 24 metres, and a pleasant picnic place. *Signposted on the road to Ngunguru. 6 km. A track leads down to the bridge below the falls.*

Wairau Falls: Locally regarded as a "miniature Niagara", the 13.7-metre falls have an even and crescent-shaped spread of water that is the more remarkable after rain. *Turnoff 26 km W of Whangarei on the road to Kaikohe via Maungatapere. Detour 4 km return. Signposted. Allow 1 hr for the return trip. A rough track leads from the railing down to the foot of the falls.*

ORGANISED EXCURSIONS

Abbey Caves: Two hours may be spent exploring a completely natural glow-worm cave. *Off Abbey Caves Rd. Book through the Visitors Bureau.*

Horse trekking: From a Trail Ride Centre on the east coast, rides range from two-hour sessions to two-to-five day treks. *Whananaki Trail Rides, Hailes Rd, off Whananaki North Rd (off Highway 1 N); tel. (09) 433-8299).*

Chartered launch and fishing trips: These run on Whangarei Harbour and from Tutukaka. *Details from the Visitors Bureau.*

Scenic flights: Operate by arrangement with the Northland Districts Aero Club. *Tel. (09) 436-0890, Onerahi Aerodrome.*

Local tours: Tours of sights, fishing trips, farm stays and farm visits can be arranged through the Visitors Bureau.

SUGGESTED DRIVES

A DRIVE TO THE HEADS★★: A 35-kilometre drive along the harbour's northern shore to exposed Ocean Beach passes a number of beaches and picnic places. At Taurikura, by the foot of Mt Manaia, a curious rock shelf leads out into the harbour, the remains of the "causeway" built by Manaia in the myth recounted above. From here are good views of the oil refinery on Marsden Point. From Parua Bay a branch road leads 13 kilometres to the twin beaches of Pataua; Pataua South, a favourite seaside settlement, is linked with Pataua North by a footbridge across the estuary. *71 km return, plus 26 km for the detour to Pataua.*

TUTUKAKA ROUND TRIP (*80 km*)**:** A leisurely day may be spent driving through the countryside to explore a chain of splendid coves and beaches. *Follow Ngunguru Rd in a north-easterly direction. Places of interest are listed in the order in which they are reached:*

Ngunguru (*24 km*)**:** A domain here is shaded by pohutukawa trees and there is safe bathing in the sheltered harbour.

Tutukaka (*29 km*)**:** A major deep-sea fishing base in an idyllic setting, this is an increasingly popular holiday spot. The Whangarei Deep Sea Anglers' Club has its headquarters here and charter boats are available for big-game or line fishing and for sightseeing trips around the Poor Knights and Dome Cave, a vast natural amphitheatre. Safe sandy beaches, rock fishing and favoured skindiving haunts complete the settlement's appeal.

Matapouri (*35 km*)**:** Another grand beach. Two kilometres to the north lies Whale Bay, an idyllic cove reached by a short walking track from the main road or a 20-minute coastal walk from Matapouri.

Woolley Bay (*39 km*)**:** A sheltered stretch of sandy beach favoured by picnickers.

Sandy Bay (*41 km*)**:** A popular surf beach.

From here the road runs inland to:

Hikurangi (*64 km*)**:** A small farming and one-time coalmining town 16 kilometres north of Whangarei.

TOURING NOTE

An alternative and more scenic, if somewhat slower, route to △Russell and the △Bay of Islands lies along the Whakapara-Russell Road. Short detours lead to Helena and Oakura Bays. *Leave Highway 1 at Whakapara, 22 km N of Whangarei.*

WHANGAROA HARBOUR ★★

Northland   Map 2

77 km E of Kaitaia; 58 km NW of Paihia.

DEEP, slender and near-landlocked, Whangaroa Harbour has an enigmatic charm. In its picturesque qualities it eclipses the seascapes of the nearby △Bay of Islands, for there is brooding savagery in surrounding sheer and jagged breccia pinnacles in some way symbolic of the slaughter the harbour once saw.

The puzzle is compounded from an economic viewpoint as the harbour is sparsely populated, perhaps as a legacy of times a century and a half ago when few trading ships dared enter its sheltered waters. Yet this relative absence of settlement only accents the harbour's great appeal. As a base for big-game fishing, with a number of superior beaches, and with several walkways in reserves incorporated somewhat curiously in the Bay of Islands Maritime Park, the area has unlimited scope for the holidaymaker.

A combination of two different types of eroded rock, volcanic breccia and tuffaceous rock of miocene age, explain the pinnacles known as the "Twelve Apostles", the most conspicuous of which are "St Paul" (*rising behind Whangaroa township*) and "St Peter" (*on the opposite shore*). Accounts vary as to precisely which pinnacles comprise the remaining 10.

Whangaroa means "long harbour".

SOME HISTORY

The burning of the "Boyd": The ship *Boyd* (about 600 tons), which had taken convicts from England to New South Wales, called at Whangaroa Harbour in 1809 to take on a load of kauri spars for its return voyage. Its complement of about 70 included a number of Maori, among them Tara, a chief from Whangaroa. For some reason, possibly for laziness or for theft, Tara had been flogged as the ship crossed the Tasman Sea. Precisely what took place at Whangaroa to avenge Tara's maltreatment is uncertain, but it seems that when a party of sailors when ashore to cut spars, they were suddenly struck down. The Maori then donned their victims' uniforms and returned by night to surprise those left aboard the *Boyd*. While it was being ransacked, an accidental explosion of gunpowder set fire to the ship; it burned to the waterline and only four of its company survived.

The "massacre" received world-wide publicity which discouraged Europeans from visiting the area and actually delayed the start of missionary work in New Zealand.

The *Boyd* still lies on the harbour floor, off Red Island. An attempt to raise the hulk several years ago was unsuccessful, largely because of its size and condition.

Settlement: Ships had visited the harbour from at least 1805 and possibly from 1790, but after the *Boyd* massacre no ship dared call for 10 years. The Wesleyan Mission came and went, and it was not until 1840 that the first permanent settlers arrived there, remarkably late for the district. Shipbuilding began at Totara North, where over 80 ships of up to 320 tons were constructed. Much kauri was milled locally, whalers operated out of bases near the heads in the early 1900s, and for a time copper was mined by the Pupuke River. Today there is mainly sheep and cattle farming in the area with some dairying, fishing and sawmilling. To a lesser extent there is crayfishing, scalloping and oyster farming.

HARBOUR CRUISES ★★★

The only way truly to appreciate the magnificence of the harbour is by launch. Trips are run daily in summer (less frequently in winter) from Whangaroa to pass over the wreck of the *Boyd* and cruise past Totara North, along the western coastline through the harbour entrance and back by the eastern side. Guided sea kayaking trips also operate in the area. *Information Boyd Gallery.*

POINTS OF INTEREST IN THE AREA

Whangaroa: The township of Whangaroa is dominated by the fantastic formation of St Paul's Rock. The view from its summit, an energetic one-hour climb return, is well worth the effort. Across the water rises fellow Apostle, St Peter. The popular two-hour harbour cruise runs from here. Fishing trips and big-game fishing charters may also be arranged. *Enquiries about the climb, and launch bookings, at Boyd Gallery, on the Waterfront.*

Kaeo: Today the township serves a farming community. In 1823 the country's first Methodist Mission, "Wesleydale", was established here. Both the place and the time were unfortunate as the area was then frequently the scene of tribal war which served to compound the already grave difficulties faced by the missionaries. The ailing Ngati Huruhuru chief, Te Ara, found it increasingly difficult to provide the protection he had guaranteed the mission, and when he died in 1827, hostile Maori took the opportunity to ransack the station and destroy the buildings. The missionaries fled to the △Bay of Islands. Six months later their endeavours were resumed in the more favourable atmosphere of △Hokianga Harbour. A district museum displays local history in a venerable Post Office building.

Totara North: The old Gumstore Hostel (1890) now provides inexpensive accommodation for backpackers (*tel. (09) 405-1838*). Nearby, Lane Cove Cottage in a perfect setting, sleeps sixteen (*accessible by boat or via Campbell Rd, a 2 hr walk*). (*Book through DOC, Kerikeri Field Centre tel. (09) 407-8474.*)

Matauri Bay and "Rainbow Warrior" memorial: The memorial overlooks the Cavalli Islands, the last resting place of the *Rainbow Warrior*, the Greenpeace ship bombed in Auckland Harbour in 1985 by French agents to prevent Greenpeace from demonstrating against French nuclear testing in the Pacific. The incident, in which a crew member died, severely strained relations with France. The wreck, which was scuttled here, has developed a marine life attractive to skin divers. The Cavalli Islands were named by Cook after he had been given some fish, possibly trevally.

The Maori-styled Samuel Marsden Memorial Church recalls Marsden's first landing in New Zealand (1814) at Matauri Bay, when he averted a clash between local Maori and those from the Bay of Islands. *24 km via coast road.*

Ocean Beaches ★ ★ ★: Matauri, Tauranga, Mahinepua and Wainui Bays are splendid beaches reached by the "million-dollar-view" coast road.

WHITE ISLAND

Off the Bay of Plenty Coast   Map 9

51 km N of Whakatane.

WHITE ISLAND, a smouldering volcano at the northern end of the Taupo-Rotorua Volcanic Zone, is in a volcanic belt which extends from Ruapehu across the Pacific to Samoa. There is intense thermal activity on the island—with steam and natural gas vents, holes of sulphuric acid and boiling pools. The island was named by Captain Cook in 1769 "because as such it always appeared to us". Its Maori name, Whakaari, means "to make visible".

Visits to △ White Island ★ ★ ★: A thrilling experience awaits those who fly over this active island volcano to peer down into its crater. To walk on the island and savour its fury, visit by boat or helicopter. *Vulcan Helicopters (tel. (07) 308-4636 or freephone 0800-804-354) land on the island to make an awesome 1½ hr guided walk. The boat trip with Pee Jay Charters (tel. (07) 312-9075) also includes a guided walk. Aspects of the island and marine life may also be seen on White Island Day Cruises (tel. (07) 312-4236). Details of other operators from the Visitor Information Centre.*

MAORI MYTHOLOGY

A blazing row: In times when mountains walked, talked, loved and fought, two sister mountains, Whakaari (White Island) and Motuhora (Whale Island) lived on the Huiarau Range. One night they broke away and pushed down to the sea they had always wanted to visit. As they went Whakaari gouged the bed of the Whakatane River, and Motuhora, being tall and slim, formed the narrow gorges of the Waimana River. Feeling hungry, the plump Whakaari sent her sister to find food while she kindled a fire. Suddenly Whakaari saw the first flush of dawn and, knowing that when the sun's rays touched her they would transfix her to the spot forever, she fled out to sea. Motuhora returned to find her sister gone. Furious, she picked up a blazing log and chased after her. The sun's rays caught the pair before Motuhora could reach her sister, and with all her remaining strength she hurled the blazing log at Whakaari. So it was that fire came to the volcano and so it is that Motuhora (Whale Island) is closer to the shore.

MINING DISASTER

For a number of years sulphur deposits were mined on the island. In 1913 there was a sharp increase in volcanic activity and on 10 September 1914 an unexpected explosion precipitated a landslide that swept the entire mining settlement out to sea, leaving no trace of all 12 people on the island.

Further unsuccessful attempts were made to mine the sulphur deposits but the island is now simply a private scenic reserve, regularly visited by muttonbirders from the Bay of Plenty.

WHITIANGA ★★★

Coromandel Peninsula   Map 5   Pop. 2,949

68 km NE of Thames; 116 km N of Waihi. Whitianga Information Centre, Albert St; tel. (07) 866-5555.

WHITIANGA, on Mercury Bay and in the heart of the △Coromandel Peninsula, overlooks a placid estuary where boats lie at anchor. The absence of a harbour bar renders this the most accessible anchorage on the coast. Each summer thousands of visitors shatter the settlement's peace and replace it with a carnival air.

The minuscule Mercury Bay Boating Club passed into the annals of sporting history when the Auckland financier Michael Fay used it to launch a celebrated challenge for the America's Cup against the San Diego Yacht Club. The sporting world witnessed a shocking mismatch of boats in 1988 before the issue was settled, off water, by the New York Law Courts. A more conventional challenge failed in 1992 but the country was well-rewarded when it won the America's Cup in 1995.

The fishing fleet supplies a local processing plant, and many tonnes of crayfish, scallops and other fish are taken for both domestic consumption and export. From here, too, big-game fishing charters may be arranged to fish the well-stocked waters of Mercury Bay. Several restaurants feature local seafood on their menus.

The early Polynesian explorer Kupe (*p. 9*) is said to have called here, the town's full name being Whitianga-a-Kupe, "Kupe's crossing place". Later, in *c.* 1150 A.D., a chief associated with the Toi migration is said to have established Wharetaewa Pa, north of Buffalo Beach.

SOME HISTORY

The transit of Mercury: The chief purpose of Captain Cook's first voyage to the Pacific was to take a party of scientists to Tahiti to observe the transit of Venus in June 1769. These observations, added to those from other areas, enabled the distance between the earth and the sun to be calculated and there was not to be another opportunity until 1874. The observations made, Cook opened his "secret additional instructions" and sailed south-west to rediscover New Zealand. It was while the *Endeavour* was anchored in Mercury Bay that Cook carried out his direction "to take possession of Convenient Situations in the Country in the Name of the King of Great Britain" and the British flag was formally hoisted on 15 November 1769 when the place was claimed for George III. During their stay at Mercury Bay, Cook and his party made observations of the transit of Mercury, and Cook named the bay after the planet.

After Cook came traders who in a period of frantic exploitation exported over 600 million board feet of kauri timber and 100,000 tonnes of gum from the Whitianga area alone.

BIG-GAME FISHING

The big-game fishing season extends from November to the end of April. In February and March the fishing is at its best — tuna, black and striped marlin, mako and thresher sharks, and kingfish all being plentiful. *Charters may be arranged through the Whitianga Information Centre. Advance booking advisable.*

DIVING

The coastline and offshore islands provide wide variety for the diver. Colourful sponges, underwater vegetation and fish can be seen and ensure that snorkelling along the coastline is both fascinating and exciting. Spearfishing for kingfish is possible around the reefs of Neverfail and Richards Rocks. The sheltered waters of the Mercury Islands make diving possible the year round. *Charter boats are available.*

OTHER THINGS TO SEE AND DO

Mercury Bay District Museum: Housed in the old dairy factory, the museum's displays include tools used by kauri millers, kauri-gum specimens and items salvaged from shipwrecks. *The Esplanade. Open daily, 10 a.m.–4 p.m.; in winter Tues., Thurs and Sun, 11 a.m.–2 p.m.*

An old stone storehouse, at one time the only store on the west side of the harbour, may be seen by the boat-launching ramp (*Robinson Rd*).

Buffalo Beach★★: A popular 4-kilometre stretch of particularly safe and sandy beach adjacent to the town is at the same time testimony to the easterly gales experienced in the area, for it was in one such gale that HMS *Buffalo* was wrecked in 1840. The *Buffalo* had taken convicts to Australia and had come here to load kauri spars for her return journey. Though anchored off Cooks Beach, the ship was driven by the wind across the bay to perish on Buffalo Beach with the loss of two lives. Convict leg-irons and other relics have at times been washed up (*in the museum*). A cannon and roundshot from the wreck are mounted in the RSA Memorial Park (*Albert St, by the Information Centre*).

Ferry Landing ★ ★: A short ferry trip across the Narrows from Whitianga Wharf is Ferry Landing. The stone wharf here was built for the timber trade in 1837 and is reputedly the oldest wharf in the country. The original township was on this side of the estuary. From here short walks lead to interesting spots. Just up harbour and near the stone wharf juts **Whitianga Rock ★ ★**, the Ngati Hei pa site which fascinated Cook during his stay in the area, and which subsequently provided the stones with which the wharf was built. Cook wrote: 'The Situation is such that the best Engineer in Europe could not have choose'd a better for a small number of men to hold against a greater, it is strong by nature and made more so by Art. It is only accessible on the land side, and there have been cut a Ditch and a bank raised on the inside . . . ' Most of its earthworks have disappeared but traces of the ditch Cook mentioned and some post holes may still be seen. The view from the rock's summit is by itself worth a short walk, and to walk on over Whitianga Rock is to see a boom built of stone taken from the pa fortifications and designed to trap kauri logs as they were floated downriver.

A passenger ferry runs continuously from 7.30 a.m.–6.30 p.m. (except for an hour at lunchtime) and at other times by arrangement with the ferryman. The service is extended to 10 p.m. over the summer period. By road Ferry Landing is reached via Coroglen and Purangi Road, a distance of 42 kilometres, yet the ferry trip takes but four minutes. To summon the ferry, raise the white arm attached to the Ferry Building. There is a minibus service on the other side, and a good coastal walk.

Shakespeare Cliffs: The Cook Memorial on Shakespeare Cliffs looks down on the three-kilometre arc of Cooks Beach and, at its foot, the cove of lovely Lonely Bay (*reached down steps cut in the cliff face*). It was at the eastern end of Cooks Beach, about 300 metres west of the Purangi River mouth, that Cook's party made their observations, but the monument was built here before this had been established. The view is over Mercury Bay, sprinkled with quaintly shaped islands, and to the west to Buffalo Beach and beyond. At the western foot of the cliffs, on Flaxmill (or Homestead) Bay, the rocks have been undercut to form a natural soundshell. *A roadway leads up to the memorial, 1.5 km on road from Ferry Landing.* There is a later, 1969 bicentenary memorial at the Purangi end of Cooks Beach. Contrary to local tradition, Cook had several times made contact with the Maori before his arrival here.

ORGANISED EXCURSIONS

The peninsula is essentially a place for those who would sample the outdoors and there is a wide range of organised activities for them close at hand. These include scuba diving off the Mercury Islands, deep-sea fishing, sea kayaking, dolphin watching, glass-bottomed boat trips, river cruises to the Purangi Winery, river-rafting, mountain biking, horse trekking over historic trails with stunning views en route, and conducted walks through well-bushed ranges. *A number of operators are active locally. Arrange through the Information Centre.*

ENVIRONS

Wharekaho Bay (Simpsons Beach)★★: An excellent beach, favoured by surfers and surf-casters, which can be good for shell collecting. It is separated from Buffalo Beach by a promontory on which, in pre-European times, stood the principal residential pa in the locality. Cook visited the "Fortified Village" in November 1769 and noted that: "These seem'd to be prepared against a siege having laid up in store an immence quantity of fernroots and a good many dry'd fish. . . ." (*The site is on private property.*) On the beach itself stands a clump of venerable and massive pohutukawa, hard by the sand. Local folklore has it that Cook described these in his journals, but in fact the tree in question was a kahikatea on the Waihou River. *7 km N.*

Hahei ★: A charming holiday spot. See △ *Coromandel Peninsula.*

Hotwater Beach: Here thermal springs heat sea water. See △ *Coromandel Peninsula.*

Kuaotunu: Magnificent seascapes are obtained from Black Jack Road. *18 km. See* △ *Coromandel Peninsula.* Just before the settlement, along Waitaia Rd, is the **Otama Forest Park Access Walkway** across farmland, with the possibility of a side-track to an abandoned goldmine.

WOODVILLE

Hawke's Bay   Map 12   Pop. 1,647

27 km E of Palmerston North; 82 km NE of Masterton. Information Centre, Vogel St; tel/fax (06) 376-5742.

WOODVILLE remains today as it began, very much a junction town busy with transit traffic. Here both the road and railway from Wellington by way of the Wairarapa link with systems from the Manawatu and from Hawke's Bay, so giving the town its original name—simply "The Junction".

The town's present name is probably a reference to its site, originally in the dense Seventy Mile Bush. Today, the bush gone, there is a tree-shaded park where travellers may picnic. (*Ormond St, Ross St.*) The town's major industry is the training of racehorses.

MANAWATU GORGE★★

The road through this magnificent gorge was built in 1871-72 and proved a most difficult piece of construction, workmen at times having to be suspended by ropes from the cliff tops.

The gorge is the more remarkable as it was formed by a river, the Manawatu, which actually rises in the eastern Ruahine Range and apparently defies logic by cutting back through the North Island's mountainous "backbone" to reach the sea on the "wrong" coast. *5 km W on the road to Palmerston North. For geological notes and a fuller description, see p. 179.*

POINTS OF INTEREST

Pioneer Museum: A small museum of local interest. *Ormond St. Open Friday evening and Sunday, 2–4 p.m. Key available locally.*

Coppermine Creek: Ever since copper-bearing rock was first discovered on the south-eastern edge of the Ruahine Ranges in 1888, optimistic companies have come and gone but payable copper has remained elusive. The most recent group, in the early 1930s, took in an engine and with wires stretched over the ground, tried to trace the copper by generating electricity. As with earlier attempts, shafts were driven but even with 1000 metres of rails laid and German expertise, they still failed to find the mother lode.

A steep **track** leads from the carpark up the stream to Coppermine Hut (*30 mins*). Beyond, the track follows through bush to the main ridge. A loop walk may be made by returning via the steep Mangaatua Stream. *13 km N. Coppermine Rd, off Pinfold Rd.*

TOURING NOTE

Alternative routes to △Palmerston North: As alternatives to travelling through the gorge, one may detour north to follow the saddle route to Ashhurst or turn south to Pahiatua and then cross the "Pahiatua Track". Both offer good views of the countryside.

GLOSSARY OF MAORI WORDS

In this glossary the meaning is given of Maori words used in the text. Most have more than one meaning, and that given here is the meaning appropriate to the context in which the words appear. Readers are referred to the "Brief Maori Vocabulary" on pp. 39-40 and to A Dictionary of the Maori Language (7th edition, 1971) by Herbert W. Williams (Government Printer), the dictionary originally compiled by Bishop William Williams and first published at Paihia in 1844.

Translations of place names, which appear throughout the text, are not repeated here.

amo upright supports of lower end of **maihi** on front gable of house (diagram *p.* **15**)
ariki chief, priest, leader (see *p.* **12**)
atua god, demon, supernatural being
aukati line which one may not pass
haka dance (see *pp.* **17-18**)
hangi oven comprising a hole in the ground in which food is cooked by heated stones
hapu section of tribe (see *p.* **12**)
harakeke flax—a general name covering all varieties
heke tipi rafter (diagram *p.* **15**)
heru comb for the hair
hiki charm—for raising things from the sea, for causing people to migrate, or for freeing hands from **tapu**
homai o homai a gift for a gift
hongi greeting by pressing noses together (see *p.* **16**)
hue calabash gourd
hui assembly
hurukuri dogskin cloak
inanga *Dracophyllum longifolium*—native grass tree
iwi nation, people (= tribe)
kahikatea *Podocarpus (Dacrycarpus) dacrydioides*—white pine
kainga unfortified place of residence
kaitaka cloak of finest flax with ornamental border
kaka *Nestor meridionalis*—native parrot (**ka** = screech)
kakahi *Hydridella menziesi*—freshwater bivalve mollusc
kakapo *Strigops habroptilus*—ground parrot
kamahi *Weinmannia racemosa*—lowland forest tree
karaka *Corynocarpus laevigatus*—forest tree
karakia charm, spell, incantation
karanga call, summon
kaumatu old men
kauri *Agathis australis*—forest tree (see *p.* **255**)
kawhaki tamahine chase for the bride
kereru *Hemiphaga novaeseelandiae*—wood pigeon
kingitanga pertaining to the Maori King Movement
kiore *Rattus exulans*—native rat
kiwi *Apteryx*—wingless bird (see *p.* **171**)
ko digging stick
koaro *Galaxias huttoni*—freshwater fish
kohekohe *Dysoxylum spectabile*—native tree
kohuru deal treacherously
kokako *Callaeas cinerea wilsoni*—North Island blue-wattled crow
kokowai red ochre
korowai cloak ornamented with black twisted thrums
koruru gable figure (diagram *p.* **15**)
kotukutuku *Fuchsia excorticata*—a native fuchsia
kowhai *Sophora* spp.—native tree species
kumara *Ipomoea batatas*—sweet potato
maihi facing boards on gable of house (diagram *p.* **15**)
maire *Nestegis* spp.—native tree species
mako *Isurus oxyrinchus*—mako shark
mana authority, prestige, psychic force (see *p.* **13**)
manaia grotesque beaked figure
mangeao *Litsea calicaris*—native tree
mangopare *Sphyrna zygaena*—hammerhead shark
manuka *Leptospermum scoparium*—shrub, so-called "tea tree" as early settlers used its leaves for brewing tea; occasionally confused with the **ti** tree
marai enclosed space in front of house, courtyard
marakihau fabulous sea monster with tubular tongue
marama moon
matai *Podocarpus spicatus*—black pine
mere short flat stone weapon for hand-to-hand fighting

miro *Podocarpus ferrugineus*—brown pine
moa *Dinornis gigantea* and other species—extinct bird of order Dinornithiformes (see *p.* **11**)
moko tattooing
morehu survivors
ngutukaka pattern or ornamental painting for internal house decoration; also the name of an epiphytic plant
nikau *Rhopalostylis sapida*—New Zealand palm
niu literally a small stick used for purposes of divination, but here used to refer to a tall pole erected by Hauhau for ceremonial purposes
noa free from tapu or any other restriction (see *pp.* **12-13**)
pa stockade, fortified place
pahu gong of stone or wood
pai good, excellent
pakeha foreign, a person of predominantly European descent
pakipaki dried human head
papa earth
parakehe *Gastrodia cunninghamii* or *Orthoceras strictum*—species of large orchid
pare carved slab over door (diagram *p.* **15**)
pataka storehouse raised upon posts
patu club, weapon
patupaiarehe sprite, fairy
patu pounamu greenstone club
paua *Haliotis* spp.—univalve mollusc
peruperu dance
pipi *Paphies australis*—common edible bivalve
pohutukawa *Metrosideros excelsa*—red-flowered native tree
poi ball, lump—e.g., light raupo ball with string attached twirled to the accompaniment of a song
poitoito skirting board at base of walls of house
ponga *Cyathea spp.*—tree fern
pou-koukou-aro post directly under front gable of house (diagram *p.* **15**)
pounamu greenstone, jade
poupou upright slab forming solid framework of walls of house (diagram *p.* **15**)
pou-tahuhu second front post supporting ridgepole of house
poutama stepped pattern on **tukutuku** ornament of walls of house or mat
pou-tokomanawa third post supporting ridgepole from front of house
powhiri formal welcome (see *p.* **16**)
pukatea *Laurelia novae-zelandiae*—native tree
pukeko *Porphyrio porphyrio*—swamp hen
purapura-whetu pattern of carving or ornamental lattice-work—"stars in heaven"
puriri *Vitex lucens*—native tree
rahui a mark to warn against trespassing
rama torch or other artificial light
rangiora *Brachyglottis repanda*—native shrub
raparapa projecting portion of **maihi** on house (diagram *p.* **15**)
rata *Metrosideros robusta* and *M. umbellata*—species of forest tree
raupo *Typha augustifolia*—a bulrush
rewarewa *Knightia excelsa*—native forest tree
rimu *Dacrydium cupressinum*—red pine
rua pit for storing food
ruru *Ninox novaeseelandiae*—owl or morepork
taiaha weapon of hard wood about 1.6 metres long with one end carved and decorated, the other a flat smooth blade
takahe *Notornis mantelli*—a large and rare flightless bird closely related to the **pukeko**
takarangi spiral design
tanekaha *Phyllocladus trichomanoides*—celery pine
tangata whenua people of the land (see *p.* **11**)
tangi lamentation, mourning (i.e., funeral)
tangiwai transparent variety of greenstone, jade
taniwha water monster
tapu under strict religious or superstitious restrictions (see *pp.* **12-13**)
tara punga *Larus novaehollandiae*—red-billed gull
taro plant of the arum family cultivated for food
taua war party
tawa *Beilschmiedia tawa*—native tree
tekoteko carved gable figure (diagram *p.* **15**)
tewhatewha axe-like weapon carved from a single piece of wood or bone
ti *Cordyline* spp.—cabbage tree (see note for **manuka**, above)

tiki greenstone figure worn on string around the neck

tiwakawaka *Rhipidura fuliginosa* and *R. flabellifera*—fantail bird

toatoa *Phyllocladus glaucus*—native tree

toheroa *Paphies ventricosa*—edible bivalve mollusc (see *p.* **162**)

tohunga skilled person, wizard, priest

totara *Podocarpus totara*—native forest tree

towai *Paratrophis banksii*—native tree

tuahu (or **tuaahu**) a sacred place consisting of an enclosure containing a mound used for mystic rites

tuatara *Sphenodon punctatus*—a reptile resembling a large lizard

tuatua *Paphies subtriangulata*—a bivalve mollusc similar to the **toheroa**

tui *Prosthemadera novaeseelandiae*—parson bird

tukutuku ornamental lattice-work between upright slabs of the walls of a house

uhi chisel for puncturing skin in tattooing

uku white clay used as soap

uru-uruwhenua perform rites whereby an object is placed on a **wahi tapu** (sacred place) with appropriate **karakia**

utu return (for anything), satisfaction, ransom, reward, price, make response (see *p.* **13**)

wai water

waiata song

waiata aroha love song

waiata tangi song of sorrow

wero challenge by throwing a spear

weta *Pachyrhamna acanthocera*—an insect, a cave weta

whakahe ploy of deliberately putting another person in the wrong

whakapapa genealogical table

whanau family (note: it is questionable whether the Maori had any real concept of the family as a nuclear unit)

whare house, hut, shed

whare runanga meeting house (diagram *p.* **15**)

whare wananga house for instruction in occult lore

wheke squid, octopus

wheku distorted figure in carving

whetu star

INDEX

Place names and natural features appear in bold type.
Names of ships and canoes appear in italics.
For subjects of a more general nature, refer to the Table of Contents on p. 6.

INDEX

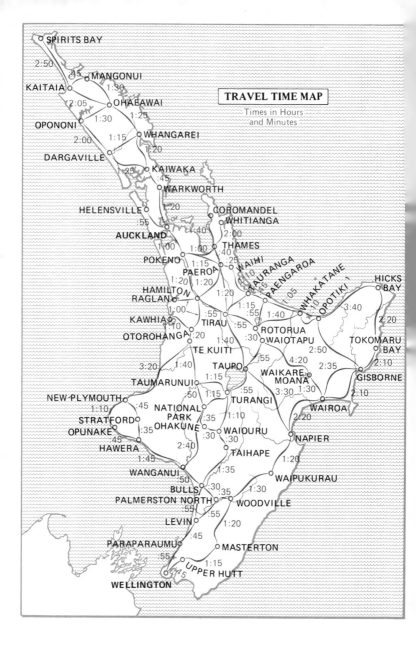

TRAVEL TIME GUIDE
(supplied by the Ministry of Transport)

The times, in hours and minutes, represent:
(a) Driving time for a driver who travels at about 80 km/h on open stretches of road plus a safety factor of 5-10 minutes per hour for traffic delays (and short stops for petrol, refreshments, etc.)
(b) Driving time *only* for a driver who travels at about 70 km/h on open stretches of road or who is using a low-powered car. These drivers should allow another 5-10 minutes per hour for safety.

Holiday time: In heavy traffic during public holidays or on Sundays, allow an extra 15-20 minutes on roads approaching main centres or important holiday centres.

Long trips: Share the driving if you have another driver as a passenger. Normally, don't plan a trip of more than 8 hours' driving in one day if you do it all yourself.

Meals and rests: During trips of over 4-5 hours, allow an extra hour for a rest or a meal. Make a practice of stopping for a short rest every couple of hours, at least on long trips. This will reduce fatigue and inattention.

Tired drivers have accidents – avoid rushing – plan your trip and enjoy a safe holiday.